THE MAKARS

J. A Tasioulas is a fellow in English at Newnham College, Cambridge. She was born in Glasgow and received her M.A. from Glasgow University before becoming a Snell Exhibitioner to Balliol College, Oxford. At Oxford she obtained a doctorate in medieval literature and was a junior fellow at New College before becoming a lecturer in English Studies at the University of Stirling. She has published on the literature and culture of the Old English period and of the later Middle Ages.

The Makars

THE POEMS OF HENRYSON, DUNBAR AND DOUGLAS

Edited, introduced and annotated by

J. A. TASIOULAS

CANONGATE
CLASSICS
88

This edition first published as a Canongate Classic
in 1999 by Canongate Books Ltd, 14 High Street,
Edinburgh EH1 1TE. Introduction, glossary and
notes © 1999 J. A. Tasioulas. All rights reserved.
The publishers gratefully acknowledge general sub-
sidy from the Scottish Arts Council towards the
Canongate Classics series and a specific grant to-
wards the publication of this volume.
Set in Plantin by Hewer Text Ltd, Edinburgh.
Printed and bound by WSOY, Porvoo, Finland.

British Library Cataloguing-in-Publication Data
A catalogue record for this book is available
on request from the British Library.
ISBN 0 86241 820 8

In Memory of

ANNA MORGAN
(1934–1996)

CONTENTS

The Poems of William Dunbar

CONTENTS

Gavin Douglas

EDITOR'S NOTE

The aim of this edition is to bring together the works of the three most famous poets of late fifteenth and early sixteenth-century Scotland: Robert Henryson, William Dunbar and Gavin Douglas. The complete poems of Henryson and Dunbar are collected in this volume, including those poems which have recently fallen out of favour with critics as being of doubtful attribution, the intention being to give as complete a picture of the authors and the times as possible. As for Douglas, the complete text of his *Palis of Honoure* is presented here, though not the *Enead* as no collection could include it in its entirety and it has been the policy of this edition not to reduce poems to extracts.

The edition has been designed for the non-specialist reader: the spelling of the texts has been slightly modernised, very detailed glosses are provided, and difficult lines have been translated in full. Each poem is introduced in the endnotes in order to place it in its historical and literary context, and each is provided with explanatory notes on obscure or difficult points. The edition does not discuss the various manuscripts of the poems. In each case a copy-text has been selected and is emended only where necessary. Readers requiring to know about the sources and alternative readings are referred to the editions of Priscilla Bawcutt, Denton Fox and James Kinsley. I am greatly indebted to the work of these scholars, and indeed to all the previous editors of the poems contained in this volume. In the preparation of this edition I have made extensive use of their work and wish to acknowledge this debt.

I am also grateful to a number of people and institutions who made the editing of this book not only possible but enjoyable. The University of Stirling provided me with a semester's sabbatical leave in order to complete the volume, and also provided a friendly and stimulating environment in which to work. My colleagues, particularly Brian Murdoch, Fiona Watson, Robin Sowerby, Neil Keeble and Alasdair Macrae, were a source of advice and support, and without the initiative and forbearance of Rory Watson, also my editor at Canongate, the edition would never have come into being. I wish also to thank Laura and Jim Cleary, Diane Watt, Michelle Morgan, Martin Davies, and, especially, Adrian Murdoch for all their assistance of various kinds, and Douglas Gray for his help and kindness when I embarked on this project. Many of my medieval literature students at the University of Stirling saw this volume through and for their enthusiasm, questions and insights I wish also to express my thanks. The edition would not have been possible without the help of many libraries and their staff: the National Library of Scotland; the Bodleian Library, Oxford; the British Library; Stirling University Library; and Glasgow University Library. Finally, I wish to thank my husband, John Tasioulas, for everything, but particularly his intellectual stimulus and his reassuring presence.

INTRODUCTION

Medieval maps of Scotland are usually poorly drawn, its islands disappearing into land masses or into the sea, with warnings in various regions about wolves, wild men or even monsters. To many it seemed like a mysterious and terrible land, its people as fierce as its weather, wild and dangerous like the country itself. As the Middle Ages ended, the ferocious reputation still remained. It was Scots who formed the bodyguard of the kings of France and who were known throughout Europe as the fiercest of soldiers. Four successive Scottish kings died violently: James II and James IV in battle, James I and III murdered; and if the danger was not enemies without then it was enemies within as the noble families vied for power. But such violence is only one side of the story. It was also a period of growth and activity in which the great Scottish burghs emerged, magnificent churches and abbeys were built and palaces were erected. As the Middle Ages came to a close in Scotland and the Renaissance dawned, Scots became known abroad as merchants, students, scholars and also poets. Indeed, Scotland at the close of the fifteenth century and beginning of the sixteenth was home to a thriving poetic tradition ranging from ballad to epic and from romance to fable. The list of his 'brether' poets provided by William Dunbar in his 'Lament for the Makars' ('I that in Heill wes and Gladnes') is a lengthy one. The works of some of them have been lost to us, while the identity of others is not clear, but in the midst of the catalogue we find the name of Robert Henryson, one of the country's greatest early poets. Add to this the name of Dunbar himself, and of his near contemporary Gavin Douglas, and the result is three of Scotland's finest ever poets.

Robert Henryson

Not much is known about the life of Robert Henryson. Indeed, much of what is generally believed about him is derived from two lines in Dunbar's 'I that in heill wes and gladnes'. It is said of Death that:

> In Dunfermelyne he has done roune
> With Maister Robert Henrisoune (11.81–2)

These lines, though brief, are valuable in providing a setting for the poet's life, a suggestion of his social status, and a likely date of death. The poem is usually dated to 1505 or 1506 and it can therefore be assumed that Henryson had heard Death's 'whisper' before this point. As for Henryson's association with Dunfermline, this is also attested to in the early printed editions of his poetry which describe him as a Dunfermline schoolmaster. The title of 'maister', given to him by Dunbar, was reserved for those with a university degree, a qualification which would be compatible with employment as a teacher. In so far as there are believed to be any facts about the life of Robert Henryson, these end here.

However, there are a number of other possible references to the poet in fifteenth-century Scottish documents. The records of the University of Glasgow (founded 1451) indicate that a Robert Henryson was admitted as a graduate member in 1462, already being both a master of arts and a bachelor in canon law. As these degrees were evidently not obtained from the University of Glasgow, and as there is no mention of a Robert Henryson in the only other Scottish university in existence at this point, St Andrews, these degrees must have been obtained abroad. The name Robert Henryson appears again, this time with a legal connection in the town records of Dunfermline, acting as a notary public on behalf of the Abbot of Dunfermline throughout the 1470s. Though there is no firm evidence to connect these figures with the poet, it would not have been unheard of for a schoolmaster to act also as a notary public, and the dates, the place and the qualifications are all compatible with the picture of Henryson presented by Dunbar.

If the Robert Henryson registered at Glasgow University, the public notary in Dunfermline, and Robert Henryson the poet are all the same man then he can be assumed to have been well travelled, well educated and an experienced figure in medieval public life. For a Scot wishing to study canon law in the fifteenth century there were various options available. The most likely choice would have been Paris but other universities such as that at Orleans would have been a possibility. As for the life of a public notary, it would have involved property deals, financial transactions, wills and cases in court.

However, even if none of these conjectures can be established with certainty, the idea of Henryson as a rural schoolmaster quietly removed from the world should not be accepted too readily. Dunfermline was very far from being a village in the fifteenth century. In fact, it was a prestigious and important royal burgh, the birthplace, home and final resting place of numerous Scottish monarchs since at least the eleventh century In the magnificent abbey were buried David I, Robert Bruce, David II, and also Malcolm Canmore and his queen, Saint Margaret. It was, therefore, a place of pilgrimage but its influence was not derived solely from the past. Dunfermline's abbot was one of the most powerful churchmen in Scotland and both James III and James IV were frequent visitors to the palace there. The town also benefited from its central position, close to both Edinburgh and Stirling and consequently close to the political and cultural heart of Scotland. Such a town would have needed civil servants, lawyers, church officials and clerics, but it also depended upon farmers, craftsmen, merchants, bakers, fishermen, brewers, weavers, builders and a host of other trades and professions.

Henryson's poetry reflects both the greatness and the day-to-day bustle of medieval Dunfermline. His *Fables* show an awareness of legal practice, the workings of the ecclesiastical courts, and a vision of a bestial parliament gathering at the command of a 'wyld lyoun'. They also present a world of cadgers with their wicker baskets of fish dreaming of fox-fur mittens, and of mice running for their lives across straw-covered floors. The king of the ancient gods and the shorn sheep 'quaking for cauld' both have their place in Henryson's poetry. The lofty and the homely, the learned and the colloquial, the humorous and the ponderous are all found within his work, often blended together in a way that brings the great within the comprehension and judgement of ordinary men, and takes ordinary Scottish lives and reveals the heroism inherent in them.

The same poet can produce both a humorously obscene invective against quack doctors in '*Sum Practysis of Medecyne*' and a skilful reworking of classical legend in *Orpheus and Eurydice*. But there is erudition even in the obscenity and touching humanity in the portrayal of classical figures who remain static and distant in so much medieval poetry. Henryson's underworld is a desolate Scottish moor in which the mud makes it difficult for Orpheus to stay on his feet; the Furies are three sisters on a 'brig'. And yet this is also one of the most learned of all Henryson's poems, drawing upon medieval philosophical commentaries, theological works, musical treatises and classical tales, to present the story of Orpheus' attempt to bring his wife back from the dead.

The formal *moralitas*, the explicit moral found at the end of *Orpheus and Eurydice*, is a feature of the *Fables* too, but there is a moral purpose behind most of Henryson's poetry. Religion is crucial to most medieval authors, and although only 'The Annunciation' is overtly a religious poem, the idea of an ordered universe watched over by a just God is fundamental to all of Henryson's work. Harmony is a key theme, but in many of Henryson's poems, from *Orpheus* to the *Fables*, order and harmony are threatened to the point where the anguished sheep can cry 'Lord God, why do you sleep so long?'. Concern for the soul of mankind is mixed in Henryson with a very real concern for the body, and religious sentiment and social satire co-exist in much of his work.

While it is not possible to say when, exactly, the poems were written or even in what order they were written, they can be dated to the latter part of the fifteenth century, a period of trouble and unrest in Scotland. James III was an unpopular king, his reign characterised by withdrawal and apparent in-difference towards his people, disinterest that led ultimately to a lack of well-enforced justice and corruption in the traditional areas of power, both religious and secular. The Church and the law courts are both satirised in Henryson's poetry, and the duties of a king are laid down more than once, for he is not one of those poets who will settle for the world to come. The importance of the next world is never forgotten but he is still concerned with those who suffer in this one: the oppressed, the defenceless, and the poor. Occasionally the victims are wholly innocent but the majority are struggling not just with the world's faults but to some extent with their own. In the end, this is perhaps Henryson's particular gift, that the world he presents is not one of easy opposition between good and evil but that he demands compassion for its victims nevertheless.

William Dunbar

A vision of flawed humanity is also a feature of Dunbar's verse. Compassion, however, is not for the most part the aim of his poetry which is more inclined to offer a stinging invective against the greed, back-biting and selfishness of court society than a sympathetic portrayal of the plight of the poor sinner. If Henryson's world combines high and low, nobleman and peasant, Dunbar's is concerned with a far narrower social milieu. Occasionally, he deals with country matters, even contrasting the sinful practices of the town with the honest practices of country folk, but 'Ane murlandis man' does not have the enthusiasm for the simple life, the cosy nest 'warme as wolle' stuffed full with 'beinis and nuttis' of Henryson's 'The Twa Mice'. It is satire directed at the law courts and the burgh but the way of life of the astonished countrymen is not presented as a viable alternative.

We do not know a great deal about Dunbar but what we do know places him at the court of James IV. Like Henryson, he is usually referred to as 'maister' and is likely to be the William Dunbar who graduated from St Andrews University in 1479. There is then, however, a silence of twenty years until he appears in the records once more, this time in the royal accounts which note the payment of his salary for the year 1500–1501. Thereafter, his name appears at regular intervals in the court accounts, at first as the recipient of a small pension, equivalent to what would have been received by a mason or falconer, but from 1510 receiving a very substantial £80 per year. In spite of the regularity of these payments his role in the court is not clear. It is unlikely that he was a professional poet, though he may have earned his living from his pen as a scribe or secretary. He was ordained as a priest in 1504 and was perhaps a chaplain in the royal household in the last years of his life, though his death too is a mystery. The last mention of him in the treasurer's accounts is dated 14 May, 1513, a few months before James IV made his disastrous march upon England and died with a large part of his army at Flodden. The silence after this event may be due to the fragmentary state of the records but there is no mention of Dunbar in the accounts of James V. It could be imagined that he had simply left the court, but the silence is so complete that most critics assume that he was dead by 1515 at the latest.

His biographers' concern with payments made in the royal accounts is matched only by the zeal with which Dunbar himself pressed court officials on the matter of money. His gentle and not-so-gentle compositions on the subject show him complaining of neglect, haggling with wardrobe masters over promised new clothes, and reminding the king himself of his loyal – and insufficiently rewarded – service. For the most part the subject is handled with humour, and occasionally with pathos, the poet presenting himself as a neglected old horse, left out in the cold, or as a 'terrified' victim of the queen's 'dog', and keeper of the wardrobe, James. Similar in theme, though less humorous and light-hearted are those poems in which Dunbar complains of his lack of a benefice or church living. As a priest, his desire was for a parish of his own but it appears that he never received one, in spite of his complaints that many churchmen had so many parishes that they could not attend to them all and merely collected the income.

Dunbar's satire on the Church can be biting, and his depictions of court life no doubt stung many, his attacks tending to be more specific and personal than those of Henryson. Named persons in the court are held up to ridicule and accepted court practice is shown to be merely self-serving, but the scope and helpless despair of Henryson's social satire is not matched by anything in Dunbar. A difference in personal style is no doubt a large part of this but the differing reigns of James III and James IV may also be a factor. Unlike his father, James IV was a popular king, creating unity where James III had sown dissent. The noble families united behind him and he in turn was in contact not just with the noblemen but with the people, travelling throughout his realm, attending the local courts, and building and expanding palaces throughout Scotland. There was still corruption, and corruption at the highest level, the king himself appointing his own illegitimate son at the age of eleven to the archbishopric of St Andrews, for example, but Dunbar's vitriol is saved for specific examples. John Damien, James IV's alchemist, who attempted to fly from the battlements of Stirling Castle, is a case in point and is the subject of a number of Dunbar's poems. His virtuosity in personal attack reaches its height, however, in a type of poetry known as flyting, and *The Flyting of Dumbar and Kennedie* establishes Dunbar as a master of this genre of outrageous verbal abuse.

But the poet who could dismiss the unfortunate Kennedy as a 'cuntbittin' coward is also capable of poems of dignified praise and noble eulogy. Visiting knights, the new queen and even the town of Aberdeen are exalted in verse by Dunbar and a significant number of his poems are related to formal state occasions. Most notable is *The Thrissill and the Rois*, written to celebrate the marriage of James IV to Margaret Tudor, one of the grandest and most significant events in the history of sixteenth-century Scotland, and presented by Dunbar as the wedding of the Scottish thistle and English rose. In this poem and in *The Goldyn Targe* Dunbar reveals his skills in allegory, a complex metaphorical genre but rendered as skilfully as the fifteen-line poem on his headache.

The Goldyn Targe reveals yet another side to Dunbar: the moral poet. Like Henryson and Gavin Douglas, there is a profoundly religious side to Dunbar's work and many of his poems are concerned with death, mutability and the sinful state of humanity. This can take the form of a poetic instruction on how to prepare for confession such as 'O synfull man, thir ar the fourty dayis', or a brief comment on the world being as changeable as the Scottish weather as in 'I seik aboute this warld onstable'. Other poems celebrate the nativity of Christ, his death and resurrection, or the superlative beauty and goodness of the Virgin Mary. Here, Dunbar reaches the height of the style known as 'aureate diction', the elaborate and heavily Latinate language that was a feature of sixteenth-century verse. In doing so, he completes almost a full range of styles and genres.

This range is one of Dunbar's most impressive achievements, for he is a poet at once capable of the loftiest religious lyric and the bawdiest sexual pun. Complaints on the 'sickness' of his purse and allegories on the painful and irrational nature of love stand side by side. He is a witty poet, as many of his contemporaries learned to their cost, and yet also the author of many moving and melancholy pieces dealing with neglect, transience and loss.

Gavin Douglas

Gavin Douglas was also in holy orders but his fortunes were very different from those of his contemporary, Dunbar. He was a younger son of Archibald 'Bell-the-Cat' Douglas, the fifth earl of Angus, and was probably born around 1475 in Tantallon Castle, East Lothian, the stronghold of the Douglas family. They were a powerful clan and were to become even more so in the poet's lifetime. As a younger son, Gavin Douglas was bound for a career in the Church but the Church in the early sixteenth century was as much a place of politics as religion, and he was involved in power struggles throughout his life.

The first definite reference we have to Gavin Douglas is once again found in the records of Scotland's ancient universities. Like Dunbar, he was a graduate of St Andrews, completing his masters degree in 1494, and from there it seems that he went to his first church position, being recorded as dean of Dunkeld as early as January 1497. His first important benefice, however, was the provostry of the collegiate church of St Giles in the heart of Edinburgh. This is the first real sign of royal favour, the position being in the gift of the king, and Douglas held it from at least 1503. He must have been in Edinburgh when Margaret Tudor and her retinue arrived for her marriage to James IV, a group of which William Dunbar formed a part, composing poems of welcome to the new queen. No such verse appears to have been composed by Douglas. Though he was part of the same court circle as Dunbar and concerned with many of the same things, not least of which was the securement of a church benefice, the poetry which survives is not of an occasional or personal nature.

The Palis of Honoure belongs to this early period of Douglas' life, being written possibly just before he was granted the position at St Giles. Indeed, it may have been this poem that brought him to the attention of the king. Unlike Dunbar's verse, this is not a direct plea for preferment, but its subject matter would have been of likely interest to the monarch. Within the framework of an allegorical dream-vision, the poet presents a typically obtuse dreamer who must learn what it is to be a true courtier. The poet examines duty, tradition, emotion, loyalty, indeed all of the concerns which make up true honour. It is a deeply learned poem, almost encyclopaedic in places, with an interest in music, astrology and the classical gods, for example, which is reminiscent of Henryson, though even wider in scope. References to classical history, myth and geography combine with Christian theology and references to the Bible. The poem draws upon a vast number of texts but notably upon the works of the Roman writers Ovid and Virgil, and it is this preoccupation with the classics which would be the inspiration for Douglas' other great literary work, the translation into Scots of Virgil's epic poem the *Aeneid*. Douglas' *Enead* is once again concerned with the theme of honour, the problems of love and duty, loyalty and piety, as we see the fall of a great civilisation and the rise of another. It was completed on 22 July 1513, around six weeks before James IV was killed at Flodden.

This disastrous event for Scotland which coincided with Dunbar's disappearance from the records had, however, the opposite effect in the life of Douglas. Many noblemen and churchmen had died with their king and the country was in political turmoil, the heir to the throne being the eighteen-month old James V. It is not surprising that a family as powerful as the Douglases should have played a prominent role in the new order, but the marriage of Gavin's nephew, now the sixth earl of Angus, brought them to the centre of power. Less than a year after the death of James IV, Angus married the widowed queen,

Margaret Tudor. Gavin Douglas now found himself as an adviser to the queen and his own fortunes changed accordingly. He was put forward for several of the most prominent church positions in the country, finally being successful in his bid to become bishop of Dunkeld. Like everything else in Scotland at this point, however, this position too was surrounded by intrigue and dissent, and Douglas had to endure brief imprisonment in Edinburgh Castle and St Andrews before he could take office. The charge against him was that he had broken the laws concerning the purchase of benefices, but the real reason seems likely to have been the desire of other noble families to prevent the Douglases from gaining too much power. This was accomplished for a while but, with the help of the queen and even the pope himself, Douglas was installed in the bishopric by 1516.

The years which immediately followed were comparatively peaceful. Douglas appears not to have written during this period of his life but became instead a patron in his own right, with numerous works dedicated to him. However, the peace did not last and as problems grew in the marriage of Margaret Tudor and the earl of Angus, so the queen's enmity towards Gavin Douglas increased. Angus tried to appeal to his wife's brother, Henry VIII, sending Douglas on a mission to London. However, amidst the plots and counter-plots, Douglas found himself accused of high treason. He spent the last few months of his life in exile, dying, apparently from the plague, in September 1522. The poet who had so eloquently revealed the fickle and transitory nature of the world in his *Palis of Honoure* being defeated by earthly treachery in the end.

The Poems of
ROBERT HENRYSON

The Fables
THE PROLOGUE

1

Thocht feinyeit fabils of ald poetré
Be not al grunded upon truth, yit than,
Thair polite termes of sweit rhetoré
Richt plesand ar unto the eir of man;
And als the caus that thay first began   5
Wes to repreif the haill misleving
Of man be figure of ane uther thing.

2

In lyke maner as throw the bustious eird,
Swa it be laubourit with grit diligence,
Springis the flouris and the corne abreird,   10
Hailsum and gude to mannis sustenence,
Sa dois spring ane morall sweit sentence
Oute of the subtell dyte of poetry,
To gude purpois, quha culd it weill apply.

3

The nuttis schell, thocht it be hard and teuch,   15
Haldis the kirnell, sweit and delectabill;
Sa lyis thair ane doctrine wyse aneuch
And full of frute, under ane fenyeit fabill.

---

1. thocht *although* feinyeit
   fabils *fictitious stories*
2. grunded upon *based on* yit
   than *nevertheless*
3. polite termes *polished language*
   rhetoré *rhetoric*
4. richt *very* plesand *pleasing*
   eir *ear*
6. repreif *rebuke* haill *whole*
   misleving *wicked lifestyle*
7. be figure *by example*
8. lyke maner *the same way*
   throw *through* bustious
   eird *rough earth*
9. swa *providing* laubourit *tended*

10. flouris *flowers* corne *corn*
    abreird *in first shoots*
11. hailsum *wholesome* gude *good*
    mannis *man's*
12. sentence *meaning*
13. subtell *subtle* dyte *writing*
14. purpois *purpose*
    quha *whoever* culd *could*
15. nuttis *nut's* schell *shell*
    teuch *tough*
16. haldis *holds* kirnell *kernel*
    sweit *sweet*
    delectabill *delicious*
17. lyis *lies* aneuch *enough*
18. frute *fruit*

12–14. 'So out of the subtle writing of poetry there grows a nice, moral
meaning, with good results, for anyone who can apply it well'.

And clerkis sayis, it is richt profitabill
Amangis ernist to ming ane merie sport,   20
To light the spreit and gar the tyme be schort.

4

Forther mair, ane bow that is ay bent
Worthis unsmart and dullis on the string;
Sa dois the mynd that is ay diligent
In ernistfull thochtis and in studying.   25
With sad materis sum merines to ming
Accordis weill; thus Esope said, iwis:
Dulcius arrident seria picta iocis.

5

Of this authour, my maisteris, with your leif
Submitting me to your correctioun,   30
In mother toung, of Latyng, I wald preif
To mak ane maner of translatioun;
Nocht of my self, for vane presumptioun,
Bot be requeist and precept of ane lord,
Of quhome the name it neidis not record.   35

6

In hamelie language and in termes rude
Me neidis wryte, for quhy of eloquence

19. clerkis *clerks* sayis *say*
    richt *very*
20. amangis *amongst* ernist *serious*
    matters ming *mingle* merie
    sport *entertainment*
21. light *relieve* spreit *spirit*
    gar *make*
22. forther mair *furthermore*
    ay *always*
23. worthis *becomes*
    unsmart *weak* dullis *slackens*
25. ernistfull *serious*
    thochtis *thoughts*
27. accordis weill *is appropriate*
    Esope *Aesop* iwis *truly*
28. Dulcius arrident seria picta
    iocis *serious issues please us more*

when they are adorned with
pleasant things
29. maisteris *masters*
    leif *permission*
31. in *into* mother toung *mother*
    tongue i.e. Scots of
    Latyng *from Latin* preif *attempt*
32. ane maner *some kind*
33. of my self *at my own*
    instigation vane *vain*
34. precept *command*
35. quhome *whom* it neidis not *it*
    is not necessary to
36. hamelie *homely* rude *plain*
37. me neidis *I must* for
    quhy *because*

19–20. 'And clerks say that it is very profitable to mingle some
entertainment amongst serious matters'.

Nor rethorike I never understude.
Thairfoir meiklie I pray your reverence,
Gif ye find ocht that throw my negligence, 40
Be deminute or yit superfluous,
Correct it at your willis gratious.

7

My author in his fabillis tellis how
That brutal beistis spak and understude,
And to gude purpois dispute and argow, 45
Ane sillogisme propone and eik conclude,
Putting exempill and similitude
How mony men in operatioun
Ar like to beistis in conditioun.

8

Na mervell is ane man be lyke ane beist, 50
Quhilk lufis ay carnall and foull delyte,
That schame can not him renye nor arreist,
Bot takis all the lust and appetyte,
Quhilk throw custum and the daylie ryte
Syne in the mynd sa fast is radicate 55
That he in brutal beist is transformate.

9

This nobill clerk, Esope, as I haif tauld,
In gay metir, facound and purperat,

39. meiklie *meekly*   pray *beg*
40. gif *if*   ocht *anything*
41. deminute *defective*   yit *even*
42. at your willis gratious *as you graciously please*
44. brutal beistis *brute beasts*
45. argow *argue*
46. sillogisme *argument*   propone *put forward*   eik *also*
47. putting *showing by means of*   exempill *example*   similitude *likeness*
48. operatioun *behaviour*
49. conditioun *character*
50. na meruel is *it is no wonder*
51. lufis *loves*   carnall *fleshly*   delyte *pleasure*
52. schame *shame*   renye *rein in*   arreist *stop*
53. bot takis all *but he entirely accepts*
54. ryte *habit*
55. syne *then*   radicate *rooted*
56. in *into*   transformate *transformed*

50–6. 'It is no wonder that a man is likened to a beast, who always loves fleshly and foul pleasure, to the extent that shame cannot rein him in nor stop him, but he indulges entirely in lust and appetite, which through custom and daily habit then becomes so firmly rooted in the mind that he is transformed into a brute beast'.

Be figure wrait his buke, for he nocht wald
Tak the disdane of hie nor low estate.   60
And to begin, first of ane cok he wrate,
Seikand his meit, quhilk fand ane jolie stone,
Of quhome the fabill ye sall heir anone.

THE COCK AND THE JASP

10

Ane cok sum tyme with feddram fresch and gay,
Richt cant and crous, albeit he was bot pure,   65
Flew furth upon ane dunghill sone be day;
To get his dennar set was al his cure.
Scraipand amang the as, be aventure
He fand ane jolie jasp, richt precious,
Wes castin furth in sweeping of the hous.   70

11

As damisellis wantoun and insolent,
That fane wald play and on the streit be sene,
To swoping of the hous thay tak na tent
Quhat be thairin, swa that the flure be clene;
Jowellis ar tint, as oftymis hes bene sene,   75

58. metir *verse* facound *eloquent*
purperat *splendid*
59. be figure *using metaphors*
wrait *wrote* nocht wald *did not
want*
60. tak *receive* hie *high*
estate *rank*
61. cok *cock*
62. seikand *seeking* meit *food*
fand *found* jolie *pretty*
63. heir *hear* anone *at once*
64. feddram *feathers*
65. richt *very* cant *lively*
crous *bold* albeit *even though*
pure *poor*
66. sone be day *at dawn*

67. dennar *dinner* set *directed*
cure *effort*
68. scraipand *scraping* as *ash* be
aventure *by chance*
69. fand *found* jolie *pretty*
jasp *jasper; jewel*
70. wes castin furth *which had been
thrown out*
71. damisellis *girls*
wantoun *thoughtless*
72. fane wald play *want to enjoy
themselves* sene *seen*
73. swoping *sweeping* tak na
tent *do not pay attention*
74. swa that *so long as* flure *floor*
75. jowellis *jewels* tint *lost*
oftymis *often*

71-4. 'Thoughtless and insolent serving girls, who want to enjoy
themselves and be seen out on the street, don't pay attention to what
might be caught up in the sweeping of the house, so long as the floor
is clean'.

Upon the flure, and swopit furth anone.
Peradventure sa wes the samin stone.

12
Sa marvelland upon the stane, quod he:
'O gentill jasp, o riche and nobill thing,
Thocht I the find thow ganis not for me;   80
Thow art ane jowell for ane lord or king.
Pietie it wer thow suld ly in this mydding,
Be buryit thus amang this muke and mold,
And thow so fair and worth sa mekill gold.

13
'It is pietie I suld the find, for quhy   85
Thy grit vertew, nor yit thy cullour cleir
I may nouther extoll nor magnify,
And thow to me may mak bot lyttill cheir.
To grit lordis thocht thow be leif and deir,
I lufe fer better thing of les availl,   90
As draf or corne, to fill my tume intraill.

14
'I had lever ga skraip heir with my naillis
Amangis this mow, and luke my lifys fude,
As draf or corne, small wormis or snaillis,
Or ony meit wald do my stomok gude,   95
Than of jaspis ane mekill multitude;

76. swopit *swept* anone *at once*
77. peradventure *perhaps*
samin *same*
78. quod *said*
79. gentill *fine*
80. ganis not *are not suitable*
82. pietie *pity* suld *should*
mydding *dung heap*
83. muke *muck* mold *dirt*
84. sa mekill *so much*
85. the *you* for quhy *because*
86. vertew *power* cullour *colour*
87. nouther *neither* extoll *praise*
magnify *glorify*
88. mak *provide* lyttil cheir *small comfort*
89. grit *great* leif *beloved*
90. lufe *love* availl *value*
91. as *such as* draf *draff; brewer's malt dregs* tume intraill *empty belly*
92. had lever *would rather* skraip *scrape*
93. mow *earth* luke *look for* lifys *life's*
95. meit *food*

And thow agane, upon the samin wyis,
For les availl may me as now dispyis.

15

'Thow hes na corne and thairof haif I neid;
Thy cullour dois bot confort to the sicht,   100
And that is not aneuch my wame to feid,
For wyfis sayis lukand werkis ar licht.
I wald sum meit have, get it geve I micht,
For houngrie men may not leve on lukis,
Had I dry breid, I compt not for na cukis.   105

16

'Quhar suld thow mak thy habitatioun?
Quhar suld thow dwell, bot in ane royall tour?
Quhar suld thow sit, bot on ane kingis croun,
Exaltit in worschip and in grit honour?
Rise, gentill jasp, of all stanis the flour,   110
Out of this midding and pas quhar thow suld be.
Thow ganis not for me, nor I for the.'

17

Levand this jowell law upon the ground,
To seik his meit this cok his wayis went.
Bot quhen, or how, or quhome be it wes found,   115
As now I set to hald na argument.
Bot of the inward sentence and intent
Of this fabill, as myne author dois write,
I sall reheirs in rude and hamelie dite.

97. agane *in return* upon the
  samin wyis *in the same way*
98. availl *worth* dispyis *despise*
99. neid *need*
100. dois bot confort *only brings
  comfort* sicht *sight*
101. aneuch *enough* wame *belly*
102. wyfis *women* lukand *looking*
  werkis *works* licht *light*
103. geve *if*
104. leve *live* lukis *looks*
105. compt *care* cukis *cooks*

106. quhar *where*
107. tour *tower*
109. worschip *esteem*
110. stanis *stones* flour *flower*
111. pas *go*
113. levand *leaving* law *low*
115. quhome be *by whom*
116. set *intend*
117. sentence *meaning*
118. reheirs *relate* rude *rough*
  hamelie *homely* dite *style*

97–8. 'And you in return, in the same way, can now despise me for being
  less worthy'.
102. 'For women say that looking at work is light work'.
112. 'You are not suitable for me, nor I for you'.

Moralitas

18

This jolie jasp had properteis sevin: 120
The first, of cullour it was mervelous,
Part lyke the fyre and part lyke to the hevin;
It makis ane man stark and victorious,
Preservis als fra cacis perrillous.
Quha hes this stane sall have gude hap to speid;   125
Of fyre nor water' him neidis not to dreid.

19

This gentill jasp, richt different of hew,
Betakinnis perfite prudence and cunning,
Ornate with mony deidis of vertew,
Mair excellent than ony eirthly thing,   130
Quhilk makis men in honour for to ring,
Happie and stark to wyn the victorie
Of all vicis and spirituall enemie.

20

Quha may be hardie, riche and gratious?
Quha can eschew perrell and aventure?   135
Quha can governe ane realme, cietie or hous
Without science? No man, I yow assure.
It is riches that ever sall indure,
Quhilk maith, nor moist, nor uther rust can freit;
To mannis saull it is eternall meit.   140

21

This cok, desyrand mair the sempill corne
Than ony jasp, may till ane fule be peir,

123. stark *strong*
124. preservis *preserves* als *also*
    cacis *events*
125. hap *fortune* speid *succeed*
126. dreid *fear*
127. different *varied* hew *colour*
128. betakinnis *signifies*
    perfite *perfect* prudence *wisdom*
    cunning *knowledge*
129. ornate *adorned* deidis *deeds*
131. ring *reign*

132. happie *fortunate*
133. of *against*
134. quha *who* hardie *brave*
135. eschew *overcome*
    aventure *risk*
137. science *knowledge*
138. indure *endure*
139. maith *moth* moist *damp*
    freit *destroy*
140. saull *soul*
142. fule *fool* peir *equal*

Quhilk at science makis bot ane moik and scorne
And na gude can; als lytill will he leir:
His hart wammillis wyse argument to heir,   145
As dois ane sow to quhome men for the nanis
In hir draf-troich wald saw the precious stanis.

22

Quha is enemie to science and cunning
Bot ignorants, that understandis nocht?
Quhilk is sa nobill, sa precious, and sa ding,   150
That it may not with eirdlie thing be bocht?
Weill wer that man, over all uther, that mocht
All his lyfe dayis in perfite studie wair
To get science, for him neidis na mair.

23

Bot now, allace, this jasp is tynt and hid;   155
We seik it nocht nor preis it for to find.
Haif we richis, na better lyfe we bid
Of science thocht the saull be bair and blind.
Of this mater to speik it wer bot wind,
Thairfore I ceis and will na forther say.   160
Ga seik the jasp, quha will, for thair it lay.

THE TWO MICE

24

Esope, myne authour, makis mentioun
Of twa myis, and thay were sisteris deir,
Of quham the eldest dwelt in ane borous toun;
The uther wynnit uponland weill neir,   165

143. moik *mockery*
144. can *knows* leir *learn*
145. wammillis *is sickened*
146. for the nanis *on purpose*
147. draf-troich *trough* saw *sow*
149. ignorants *ignorance*
150. ding *worthy*
151. eirdlie *earthly* bocht *bought*
152. weill *happy* mocht *could*
153. wair *spend*

155. tynt *destroyed*
156. preis *endeavour*
157. haif we *as long as we have*
   bid *ask*
160. ceis *cease*
163. twa *two* myis *mice*
164. borous *burgh*
165. wynnit *dwelled* uponland *in the country*

144. 'And knows nothing good; and will learn just as little'.
156–7. 'We do not seek it nor endeavour to find it. As long as we have riches we ask for no better life'.

Soliter, quhyle under busk, quhyle under breir,
Quhilis in the corne, in uther mennis skaith,
As owtlawis dois, and levit on hir waith.

25

This rurall mous into the wynter tyde
Had hunger, cauld, and tholit grit distres;   170
The uther mous, that in the burgh can byde,
Was gild brother and made ane fre burges,
Toll-fre als, but custum mair or les,
And fredome had to ga quhairever scho list,
Amang the cheis in ark, and meill in kist.   175

26

Ane tyme quhen scho wes full and unfutesair,
Scho tuke in mynd hir sister uponland,
And langit for to heir of hir welfair,
To se quhat lyfe scho had under the wand.
Bairfute, allone, with pykestaf in hir hand,   180
As pure pylgryme scho passit owt of town
To seik hir sister, baith oure daill and down.

27

Furth mony wilsum wayis can scho walk:
Throw mosse and mure, throw bankis, busk and breir,
Fra fur to fur, cryand fra balk to balk: 185
'Cum furth to me, my awin sister deir.
Cry peip anis!' With that the mous culd heir,
And knew hir voce, as kinnisman will do,
Be verray kynd, and furth scho come hir to.

166. soliter *alone*
  quhyle *sometimes*   busk *bush*
  breir *briar*
167. in *to*   skaith *detriment*
168. levit *lived*   waith *plunder*
169. tyde *time*
170. tholit *suffered*
171. can byde *lived*
172. gild *guild*   fre burges *free citizen*
173. toll-fre *tax-free*   but *without* custum *customs duty*
174. list *pleased*
175. cheis *cheese*   ark *bin* meill *meal*   kist *chest*

176. unfutesair *not footsore*
178. langit *longed*   heir *hear*
179. under the wand *in the greenwood*
180. pykestaf *stick*
181. pure *poor*
182. oure *over*   daill *dale* down *hill*
183. furth *over*   wilsum *wild*
184. mosse *bog*   mure *moor* busk *bush*
185. fur *furrow*   balk *plough ridge*
187. peip *peep!*   anis *once*
188. voce *voice*
189. be *by*   kynd *nature*

28

The hartlie joy, God geve ye had sene   190
Beis kithit quhen that thir sisteris met.
And grit kyndnes wes schawin thame betwene,
For quhylis thay leuch, and quhylis for joy thay gret,
Quhyle kissit sweit, quhylis in armis plet;
And thus thay fure quhill soberit wes thair mude,   195
Syne fute for fute unto the chalmer yude.

29

As I hard say, it was ane sober wane,
Of fog and farne full misterlyk wes maid,
Ane sillie scheill under ane erdfast stane,
Of quhilk the entres wes not hie nor braid;   200
And in the samin thay went, but mair abaid,
Withoutin fyre or candill birnand bricht,
For comonly sic pykeris luffis not lycht.

30

Quhen thay wer lugit thus, thir sely myse,
The youngest sister into hir butterie glyde,   205
And brocht furth nuttis and peis insteid of spyce;
Giff this wes gude fair, I do it on thame besyde.
The burges mous prompit forth in pryde,
And said: 'Sister, is this your dayly fude?'
'Quhy not?' quod scho. 'Is not this meit rycht
    gude?'   210

190. hartlie *heartfelt* geve *grant*
191. beis kithit *is shown* thir *these*
192. kyndnes *affection*
    schawin *shown*
193. leuch *laughed* gret *wept*
194. plet *embraced*
195. fure *behaved* quhill *until*
    mude *mood*
196. syne *then* fute for
    fute *keeping pace together*
    chalmer *chamber* yude *went*
197. hard say *heard tell*
    sober *humble* wane *dwelling*
198. fog *wintergrass* farne *fern*

misterlyk *skilfully*
199. sillie *humble* scheill *hut*
    erdfast stane *embedded rock*
200. entres *doorway* braid *broad*
201. but *without* abaid *delay*
202. birnand *burning*
203. pykeris *pilferers* lycht *light*
204. lugit *lodged* sely *simple*
205. butterie *larder* glyde *glided*
206. peis *peas*
207. giff *whether* fair *fare; food*
    do *leave* besyde *present*
208. burges *burgess; town*
    prompit *burst forth*

207. 'I leave it to those who were there to decide whether or not it was
    good food'.

31

'Na, be my saull, I think it bot ane scorne.'
'Madame,' quod scho, 'ye be the mair to blame.
My mother sayd, sister, quhen we wer borne,
That I and ye lay baith within ane wame:
I keip the rate and custome of my dame,   215
And of my syre, leving in povertie,
For landis have we nane in propertie.'

32

'My fair sister,' quod scho, 'have me excusit;
This rude dyat and I can not accord.
To tender meit my stomok is ay usit,   220
For quhy I fair als weill as ony lord.
Thir wydderit peis and nuttis, or thay be bord,
Will brek my teith and mak my wame ful sklender,
Quhilk wes before usit to meitis tender.'

33

'Weil, weil, sister,' quod the rurall mous,   225
'Geve it pleis yow, sic thing as ye se heir,
Baith meit and dreink, harberie and hous,
Sal be your awin, will ye remane al yeir.
Ye sall it have wyth blyith and mery cheir,
And that suld mak the maissis that ar rude,   230
Amang freindis, richt tender and wonder gude.

34

'Quhat plesure is in the feistis delicate,
The quhilkis ar gevin with ane glowmand brow?
Ane gentill hart is better recreate

211. saull *soul* scorne *insult*	226. geve *if*
214. wame *womb*	227. harberie *lodging*
215. rate *habit* dame *mother*	228. will ye *even if you*
216. syre *father* leving *living*	229. blyith *happy* cheir *expression*
218. have me excusit *excuse me*	230. maissis *dishes* rude *plain*
219. dyat *diet*	231. wonder *extremely*
220. tender meit *delicate food*	232. feistis *feasts*
usit *accustomed*	233. the quhilkis *which*
221. for quhy *because*	gevin *given* glowmand
222. thir *these* wydderit *dried up*	brow *frowning face*
or *before* bord *pierced*	234. gentill *noble*
223. wame *belly* sklender *lean*	recreate *refreshed*

With blyith visage, than seith to him ane kow.   235
Ane modicum is mair for till allow,
Swa that gude will be kerver at the dais,
Than thrawin vult and mony spycit mais.'

35

For all hir mery exhortatioun,
This burges mous had littill will to sing,   240
Bot hevilie scho kest hir browis doun
For all the daynteis that scho culd hir bring.
Yit at the last scho said, half in hething:
'Sister, this victuall and your royall feist
May weill suffice unto ane rurall beist.   245

36

'Lat be this hole and cum into my place;
I sall to yow schaw be experience
My Gude Friday is better nor your Pace,
My dische likingis is worth your haill expence.
I have housis anew of grit defence;   250
Of cat, na fall, na trap I have na dreid.'
'I grant,' quod scho, and on togidder thay yeid.

37

In skugry ay, throw rankest gers and corne,
And under buskis prevelie couth thay creip.
The eldest wes the gyde and went beforne,   255
The younger to hir wayis tuke gude keip.
On nicht thay ran, and on the day can sleip,
Quhill in the morning, or the laverok sang,
Thay fand the town, and in blythlie couth gang.

235. visage *face* seith *boil*
   kow *cow*
236. modicum *small amount* for
   till allow *to be commended*
237. swa that *providing that*
   gude *goodness* kerver *carver*
   dais *high table*
238. thrawin *bad-tempered*
   vult *face* mais *dish*
239. exhortatioun *argument*
241. hevilie *sorrowfully*
243. hething *mockery*
244. victuall *food*
247. schaw *show*

248. nor *than* Pace *Easter*
249. dische likingis *dish lickings i.e.*
   leftovers expence *expenditure*
250. anew *in plenty*
   defence *security*
251. fall *box trap*
252. yeid *went*
253. skugry *secrecy*
   rankest *thickest* gers *grass*
254. buskis *bushes*
   prevelie *stealthily*
256. tuke gude keip *paid attention*
258. or *before* laverok *skylark*
259. fand *found* couth gang *went*

38
Not fer fra thyne unto ane worthie wane,   260
This burges brocht thame sone quhare thay suld be.
Withowt 'God speid!' thair herberie wes tane,
Into ane spence with vittell grit plentie;
Baith cheis and butter upon thair skelfis hie,
And flesche and fische aneuch, baith fresche and
        salt,   265
And sekkis full of grotis, meill, and malt.

39
Eftir, quhen thay disposit wer to dyne,
Withowtin grace thay wesche and went to meit,
With all coursis that cukis culd devyne,
Muttoun and beif, strikin in tailyeis greit.   270
Ane lordis fair thus couth thay counterfeit
Except ane thing: thay drank the watter cleir
Insteid of wyne; bot yit thay maid gude cheir.

40
With blyith upcast and merie countenance,
The eldest sister sperit at hir gest   275
Gif that scho be ressone fand difference
Betwix that chalmer and hir sarie nest.
'Ye, dame,' quod scho, 'bot how lang will this lest?'
'For evermair, I wait, and langer to.'
'Gif it be swa, ye ar at eis,' quod scho.   280

41
Till eik thair cheir ane subcharge furth scho brocht –
Ane plait of grottis, and ane dische full of meill;

260. thyne *there* wane *dwelling*
262. God speid *'God speed'; a
    greeting* herberie *lodging*
    tane *entered*
263. spence *larder* vittell *food*
264. skelfis *shelves*
265. flesche *meat* aneuch *in
    plenty* salt *cured*
266. sekkis *sacks* grotis *groats;
    huskless oats*
268. withowtin grace *without
    saying grace* wesche *wash*
269. cukis *cooks* devyne *invent*

270. strikin *carved* tailyeis *slices*
271. counterfeit *imitate*
274. upcast *teasing*
275. sperit at *asked* gest *guest*
276. be ressone *by use of reason*
277. chalmer *chamber*
    sarie *wretched*
278. ye *yes* lest *last*
279. wait *expect*
280. eis *ease*
281. till eik *to increase*
    cheir *enjoyment* subcharge *extra
    course*

Thraf caikkis als, I trow, scho spairit nocht
Aboundantlie about hir for to deill;
And mane full fyne scho brocht insteid of geill,   285
And ane quhyte candill owt of ane coffer stall,
Insteid of spyce to gust thair mouth withall.

42

This maid thay merie quhill thay micht na mair,
And 'Haill, Yule! Haill!' cryit upon hie.
Yit efter joy oftymes cummis cair,   290
And troubill efter grit prosperitie.
Thus as thay sat in all thair jolitie,
The spenser come with keyis in his hand,
Oppinnit the dure and thame at denner fand.

43

Thay taryit not to wesche, as I suppose,   295
Bot on to ga, quha that micht formest win.
The burges had ane hole, and in scho gois;
Hir sister had na hole to hyde hir in.
To se that selie mous it wes grit sin,
So desolate and will of ane gude reid;   300
For verray dreid she fell in swoun neir deid.

44

Bot as God wald, it fell ane happie cace:
The spenser had na laser for to byde,
Nowther to seik nor serche, to sker nor chace,

283. thraf caikkis *oatcakes*
   trow *believe*
284. aboundantlie *abundantly*
   deill *distribute*
285. mane *white bread*   geill *jelly*
286. quhyte *white*   coffer *box*
   stall *stole*
287. gust *give relish to*
288. this *thus*   quhill *until*
   micht *could*
289. Yule *Christmas*   upon
   hie *loudly*
290. cair *sorrow*

293. spenser *steward*
294. dure *door*   fand *found*
295. taryit not *did not stop*
   wesche *wash*
296. ga *go*   formest *foremost*
299. sin *pity*
300. will of *at a loss for*   reid *plan*
301. in swoun *in a faint*
302. wald *wished*   it fell *there
   befell*   cace *chance*
303. laser *leisure*   byde *wait*
304. sker *scare*

295–6. 'I don't suppose that they stopped to wash, but instead they
   rushed off, racing against each other'.

Bot on he went, and left the dure up wydc.   305
The bald burges his passing weill hes spyde;
Out of hir hole scho come and cryit on hie:
'How fair ye, sister? Cry peip, quhairever ye be!'

45

This rurall mous lay flatling on the ground,
And for the deith scho was full sair dredand,   310
For till hir hart straik mony wofull stound;
As in ane fever scho trimbillit, fute and hand.
And quhan hir sister in sic ply hir fand,
For verray pietie scho began to greit,
Syne confort hir with wordis hunny sweit.   315

46

'Quhy ly ye thus? Ryse up, my sister deir!
Cum to your meit; this perrell is overpast.'
The uther answerit hir with hevie cheir:
'I may not eit, sa sair I am agast!
I had lever thir fourty dayis fast   320
With watter caill, and to gnaw benis or peis,
Than all your feist in this dreid and diseis.'

47

With fair tretie yit scho gart hir upryse,
And to the burde thay went and togidder sat,
And scantlie had thay drunkin anis or twyse,   325
Quhen in come Gib Hunter, our jolie cat,
And bad 'God speid!' The burges up with that,
And till hir hole scho went as fyre of flint;
Bawdronis the uther be the bak hes hint.

305. up *open*	319. agast *terrified*
306. bald *bold* passing *leaving*	320. lever *rather*
spyde *spied*	321. watter caill *cabbage broth*
309. flatling *prostrate*	benis *beans*
310. sair *greatly* dredand *dreading*	322. feist *feast* diseis *distress*
311. straik *struck* stound *beat*	323. tretie *pleading* gart *caused*
312. trimbillit *trembled*	324. burde *table*
313. ply *state*	325. scantlie *scarcely* anis *once*
314. greit *weep*	326. up *got up*
315. syne *then* hunny *honey*	327. hint *seized*
318. hevie *sad* cheir *expression*	

310. 'And she was very much afraid of dying'.
320. 'I would rather fast for the next forty days'.

48

Fra fute to fute he kest hir to and fra,   330
Quhylis up, quhylis doun, als cant as ony kid;
Quhylis wald he lat hir rin under the stra,
Quhylis wald he wink, and play with hir buk heid.
Thus to the selie mous grit pane he did,
Quhill at the last, throw fortune and gude hap,   335
Betwix ane dosor and the wall scho crap.

49

And up in haist behind ane parraling
Scho clam so hie that Gilbert micht not get hir,
Syne be the cluke thair craftelie can hing
Till he wes gane; hir cheir wes all the better.   340
Syne doun scho lap quhen thair wes nane to let hir,
And to the burges mous loud can scho cry,
'Fairweill, sister, thy feist heir I defy!

50

'Thy mangerie is mingit all with cair,
Thy guse is gude, thy gansell sour as gall;   345
The subcharge of thy service is bot sair;
Sa sall thow find heir efterwart ma fall.
I thank yone courtyne and yone perpall wall
Of my defence now fra yone crewell beist.
Almichtie God keip me fra sic ane feist!   350

51

'Wer I into the kith that I come fra,
For weill nor wo suld I never cum agane.'
With that scho tuke hir leif and furth can ga,

330. kest *tossed*
331. quhylis *sometimes* als *as*
    cant *lively* kid *kid; baby goat*
332. rin *run* stra *straw*
333. buk heid *blind man's buff*
335. hap *luck*
336. dosor *wall-hanging* crap *crept*
337. parraling *tapestry*
338. clam *climbed*
339. syne *then* cluke *claw*
    craftelie *skilfully* can hing *hung*
341. lap *leapt* let *prevent*
343. defy *decline*

344. mangerie *feast*
    mingit *mingled* cair *sorrow*
345. guse *goose* gansell *sauce*
    gall *bile*
346. subcharge *extra course*
    service *dinner* sair *sorrow*
347. heir *here* ma fall *it may*
    happen
348. courtyne *curtain* perpall
    wall *partition*
349. of *for*
350. keip me *protect me*
351. into *in* kith *country*

Quhylis throw the corne, and quhylis throw the plane.
Quhen scho wes furth and fre, scho wes full fane,   355
And merilie markit unto the mure.
I can not tell how weill thairefter scho fure.

52

Bot I hard say scho passit to hir den,
Als warme as woll, suppose it wes not greit,
Full beinly stuffit, baith but and ben,   360
Of beinis and nuttis, peis, ry and quheit.
Quhenever scho list, scho had aneuch to eit,
In quyet and eis, withoutin ony dreid;
Bot to hir sisteris feist na mair scho yeid.

Moralitas
53

Freindis, ye may find, and ye will tak heid,   365
Into this fabill ane gude moralitie:
As fitchis myngit ar with nobill seid,
Swa intermellit is adversitie
With eirdlie joy, swa that na estate is frie,
Without trubill and sum vexatioun,   370
And namelie thay quhilk clymmis up maist hie,
That ar not content with small possessioun.

54

Blissed be sempill lyfe withoutin dreid;
Blissed be sober feist in quietie.
Quha hes aneuch, of na mair hes he neid,   375
Thocht it be littill into quantatie.
Grit aboundance and blind prosperitie
Oftymes makis ane evill conclusioun;

354. plane *valley*
355. fane *glad*
356. markit *went*   mure *moor*
357. fure *fared*
358. hard *heard*
359. woll *wool*   suppose *even if*
  greit *grand*
360. beinly *well*   but and ben *outer and inner rooms*
361. ry *rye*   quheit *wheat*
362. list *pleased*   aneuch *enough*

363. quyet *quiet*   eis *ease*
364. yeid *went*
365. and *if*
367. fitches *vetches; worthless plants*   myngit *mingled*   seid *seed*
368. intermellit *intermixed*
369. eirdlie *earthly*   estate *class of person*   frie *free*
370. namelie *especially*   clymmis *climb*
374. sober *moderate*   quietie *peace*

378. 'Often leads to a bad end'.

The sweitest lyfe, thairfor, in this cuntrie,
Is sickernes with small possessioun.   380

55

O wantoun man, that usis for to feid
Thy wambe, and makis it a god to be,
Luke to thy self! I warne the weill, but dreid,
The cat cummis, and to the mous hes ee.
Quhat vaillis than thy feist and royaltie,   385
With dreidfull hart and tribulatioun?
Best thing in eird, thairfor, I say for me,
Is blyithnes in hart with small possessioun.

56

Thy awin fyre, my freind, sa it be bot ane gleid,
It warmis weill, and is worth gold to the;   390
And Solomon sayis, gif that thow will reid:
'Under the hevin thair can not better be
Than ay be blyith and leif in honestie.'
Quhairfor I may conclude be this ressoun:
Of eirthly joy it beiris maist degre,   395
Blyithnes in hart, with small possessioun.

THE COCK AND THE FOX

57

Thocht brutall beistis be irrationall,
That is to say, wantand discretioun,
Yet ilk ane in thair kynd naturall
Hes mony divers inclinatioun: 400
The bair busteous, the wolf, the wylde lyoun,
The fox fenyeit, craftie and cawtelows,
The dog to bark on nicht and keip the hows.

380. sikerness *security*
381. usis *is accustomed*
383. but dreid *without doubt*
384. ee *eye*
385. vaillis than *use is then*
387. eird *earth*
389. gleid *ember*
390. the *you*
392. not *nothing*
393. leif in honestie *live virtuously*
394. ressoun *statement*
395. beiris maist degre *holds the*
    highest place
397. brutall beistis *brute beasts*
398. wantand *lacking in*
399. ilk *each* in *according to*
    kynd *species*
400. divers *different*
    inclinatioun *characteristics*
401. bair *boar* busteous *strong*
402. fenyeit *deceitful*
    cawtelows *cunning*
403. on *at* keip *guard*

58

Sa different thay ar in properteis,
Unknawin to man, and sa infinite, 405
In kynd havand sa fell diversiteis,
My cunning it excedis for to dyte.
For thy as now I purpose for to wryte
Ane cais I fand, quhilk fell this ather yeir
Betwix ane foxe and ane gentill Chantecleir. 410

59

Ane wedow dwelt in till ane drop thay dayis
Quhilk wan hir fude of spinning on hir rok,
And na mair had, forsuth, as the fabill sayis,
Except of hennis scho had ane lyttill flok,
And thame to keip scho had ane jolie cok, 415
Richt curageous, that to this wedow ay
Devydit nicht and crew befoir the day.

60

Ane lyttill fra this foirsaid wedowis hows,
Ane thornie schaw thair wes of grit defencc,
Quhairin ane foxe, craftie and cautelous, 420
Maid his repair and daylie residence,
Quhilk to this wedow did grit violence
In pyking of pultrie baith day and nicht,
And na way be revengit on him scho micht.

404. properteis *dispositions*
406. havand *having* fell *many*
diversiteis *differences*
407. cunning *ability* dyte *write*
408. for thy *therefore*
purpose *intend*
409. cais *example* fand *came*
upon fell *occurred* this ather
yeir *a year or so ago*
410. gentill *noble*
411. wedow *widow* in till *in*
drop *small village* thay *those*
412. wan *earned* fude *food*

413. forsuth *truly*
415. keip *protect* jolie *handsome*
416. to *for* ay *always*
417. devydit *divided*
418. lyttil fra *short distance from*
419. schaw *thicket* grit
defence *great security*
420. cautelous *cunning*
421. repair *abode*
422. violence *harm*
423. pyking *stealing*
pultrie *poultry*

407. 'It exceeds my ability to write about it'.
424. 'And she could not be revenged upon him in any way'.

61

This wylie tod, quhen that the lark couth sing,   425
Full sair hungrie unto the toun him drest,
Quhair Chantecleir, in to the gray dawing
Werie for nicht, wes flowen fra his nest.
Lowrence this saw and in his mind he kest
The jeperdie, the wayis and the wyle,   430
Be quhat menis he micht this cok begyle.

62

Dissimuland in to countenance and cheir,
On kneis fell and simuland thus he said:
'Gude morne, my maister, gentill Chantecleir.'
With that the cok start bakwart in ane braid: 435
'Schir, be my saull, ye neid not be effraid
Nor yit for me to start nor fle abak.
I come bot heir service to yow to mak.

63

'Wald I not serve to yow it wer bot blame,
As I have done to your progenitouris.   440
Your father full oft fillit hes my wame,
And send me meit fra midding to the muris,
And at his end I did my besie curis
To hald his heid and gif him drinkis warme;
Syne, at the last, the sweit swelt in my arme.'   445

425. wylie *wily* tod *fox* couth
    sing *sang*
426. sair *bitterly* toun *village*
    him drest *took himself*
427. dawing *dawn*
428. werie *weary* for nicht *because
    of the night*
429. kest *considered*
430. jeperdie *scheme*
    wayis *devices* wyle *trick*
431. menis *means* begyle *deceive*
432. dissimuland *dissembling*
    cheir *expression*
433. simuland *pretending*

435. in ane braid *with a jump*
436. be *by* saull *soul*
    effraid *afraid*
437. for *from* fle abak *run away*
439. blame *disgrace*
440. progenitouris *ancestors*
441. fillit *filled* wame *belly*
442. send *sent* meit *food*
    midding *midden* muris *moors*
443. end *death* besie curis *very
    best*
444. hald *hold* heid *head* gif *give*
445. syne *until* sweit *dear one*
    swelt *died*

432. 'Putting on a false look and expression'.
438. 'I only come here to do you a service'.

64

'Knew ye my father?' quod the cok and leuch.
'Yea, my fair sone, I held up his heid
Quhen that he deit under ane birkin beuch,
Syne said the dirigie quhen that he wes deid.
Betwix us twa how suld thair be ane feid?   450
Quhame suld ye traist bot me, your servitour,
That to your father did sa grit honour?

65

'Quhen I behald your fedderis fair and gent,
Your beik, your breist, your hekill and your kame,
Schir, be my saull and the blissit sacrament,   455
My hart is warme, me think I am at hame.
To mak yow blyith, I wald creip on my wame,
In froist and snaw, in wedder wan and weit,
And lay my lyart loikkis under your feit.'

66

This fenyeit foxe, fals and dissimulate,   460
Maid to this cok ane cavillatioun:
'Ye ar, me think, changit and degenerate
Fra your father of his conditioun,
Of craftie crawing he micht beir the croun,
For he wald on his tais stand and craw—   465
This wes na le; I stude beside and saw.'

67

With that the cok, upon his tais hie,
Kest up his beik and sang with all his micht.
Quod schir Lowrence: 'Weill said, sa mot I the,

446. leuch *laughed*
448. deit *died* birkin beuch *birch tree*
449. syne *then* dirigie *dirge*
450. feid *feud*
451. quhame *whom* traist *trust* servitour *servant*
453. fedderis *feathers* gent *fine*
454. beik *beak* hekill *hackle* kame *comb*
455. schir *sir* blissit *blessed*
457. blyith *happy*
458. wedder *weather* wan *dull* weit *wet*
459. lyart loikkis *grey locks* feit *feet*
460. dissimulate *dissembling*
461. cavillatioun *cavil; false charge*
462. degenerate *grown worse*
464. craftie *skilful* croun *crown*
465. tais *toes*
466. le *lie*
469. sa mot I the *so may I prosper* i.e. *I do not tell a lie*

Ye ar your fatheris sone and air upricht.   470
Bot of his cunning yit ye want ane slicht,
For,' quod the tod, 'he wald, and haif na dout,
Baith wink and craw and turne him thryis about.'

68

The cok, inflate with wind and fals vanegloir,
That mony puttis unto confusioun,   475
Traisting to win ane grit worschip thairfor,
Unwarlie winkand, walkit up and doun,
And syne to chant and craw he maid him boun.
And suddandlie, be he had crawin ane note,
The foxe wes war and hint him be the throte.   480

69

Syne to the woid but tarie with him hyit,
Of that cryme haifand bot lytill dout.
With that Pertok, Sprutok and Toppok cryit;
The wedow hard and with ane cry come out.
Seand the cace, scho sichit and gaif ane schout: 485
'How, murther, hay!' with ane hiddeous beir.
'Allace, now lost is gentill Chantecleir!'

70

As scho wer woid, with mony yell and cry,
Ryvand hir hair, upon hir breist can beit;
Syne paill of hew, half in ane extasy,   490
Fell doun for cair in swoning and in sweit.

470. air *heir* upricht *rightful*
471. cunning *skill* want *lack*
    slicht *little*
473. wink *close his eyes*
    thryis *three times*
474. inflate *inflated*
    vanegloir *vainglory; pride*
476. traisting *hoping*
    worschip *honour*
477. unwarlie *heedlessly*
478. maid him boun *made himself
    ready*
479. be *by the time*

480. war *ready* hint *seized*
481. woid *wood* but tarie *without
    delay* hyit *hastened*
482. haifand *having* dout *doubt*
484. hard *heard*
485. seand *seeing* cace *situation*
    sichit *sighed*
486. murther *murder* beir *noise*
488. woid *mad*
489. ryvand *tearing* can beit *beat*
490. of hew *in colour*
    extasy *frenzy*
491. cair *sorrow* sweit *sweat*

475. 'Which places many in confusion'.
482. 'Having little doubt about his crime'.

With that the selie hennis left thair meit,
And quhill this wyfe wes lyand thus in swoun,
Fell of that cace in disputatioun.

71
'Allace,' quod Pertok, makand sair murning,   495
With teiris grit that our hir cheikis fell,
'Yone wes our drowrie and our dayis darling,
Our nichtingall, and als our orloge bell,
Our walkryfe watche, us for to warne and tell
Quhen that Aurora with hir curcheis gray   500
Put up hir heid betwix the nicht and day.

72
'Quha sall our lemman be? Quha sall us leid?
Quhen we ar sad quha sall unto us sing?
With his sweit bill he wald brek us the breid;
In all this warld wes thair ane kynder thing?   505
In paramouris he wald do us plesing,
At his power, as nature did him geif.
Now efter him, allace, how shall we leif?'

73
Quod Sprutok than: 'Ceis, sister, of your sorrow,
Ye be to mad, for him sic murning mais.   510
We sall fair weill, I find Sanct Johne to borrow;
The proverb sayis, 'als gude lufe cummis as gais'.
I will put on my haly dais clayis

492. selie *poor*   meit *food*
494. disputatioun *debate*
495. sair murning *bitter lamentation*
496. grit *great*   our *over*
497. drowrie *love*   dayis *day's*
498. nichtingall *nightingale* orloge *clock*
499. walkryfe watche *careful watchman*
500. curcheis *headress*
501. heid *head*
502. lemman *lover*   leid *lead*

504. brek us *break for us*
506. paramouris *sexual love* plesing *pleasure*
507. at *to the extent of*
508. leif *live*
509. ceis *cease*
510. to mad *too emotional* sic *such*   mais *make*
511. to borrow *as a pledge*
512. als *as*   lufe *love*   gais *goes*
513. haly dais clayis *holy day's clothes; Sunday best*

494. 'Fell into a debate about the situation'.
510–11. 'You are too emotional, you show such grief for him. As St John is my witness, we'll get on fine'.

And mak me fresch agane this jolie May,
Syne chant this sang: 'Wes never wedow sa gay!'   515

74

'He wes angry and held us ay in aw,
And woundit with the speir of jelowsy.
Of chalmerglew, Pertok, full weill ye knaw,
Waistit he was, of nature cauld and dry.
Sen he is gone, thairfor, sister, say I,   520
Be blyith in baill, for that is best remeid.
Let quik to quik, and deid ga to the deid.'

75

Than Pertok spak, that feinyeit faith befoir:
'In lust but lufe he set all his delyte.
Sister, ye wait, of sic as him ane scoir   525
Wald not suffice to slaik our appetyte.
I hecht yow be my hand, sen he is quyte,
Within ane oulk, for schame and I durst speik,
To get ane berne suld better claw oure breik.'

76

Than Toppok lyke ane curate spak full crous: 530
'Yone wes ane verray vengeance from the hevin.
He wes sa lous and sa lecherous.
Seis could he nocht with kittokis ma than sevin.
Bot rychteous God, haldand the balandis evin,

515. chant *sing*
516. held *kept*   aw *fear*
518. chalmerglew *bedroom-sport*
519. waistit *worn out*
520. sen *since*
521. blyith in baill *cheerful in sorrow*   remeid *remedy*
522. quik *living*   deid *dead*
523. feinyeit *feigned*   faith *fidelity*
524. but lufe *without love*
525. wait *know*   scoir *score; large number*
526. slaik *satisfy*

527. hecht *promise* is quyte *has got what he deserves*
528. oulk *week*   schame *modesty* and *if*   durst speik *dare speak*
529. berne *man*   breik *rump*
530. curate *clergyman* crous *confidently*
531. verray *true*
532. lous *immoral*
533. kittokis *lovers*   ma *more*
534. rychteous *righteous* haldand *holding*   balandis *scales*

527–9. 'I promise you by this hand, if modesty allowed me to speak of such things, that since he has got what he deserves, we could get a man within one week who would claw our rumps better'.
534–6. 'But righteous God, holding the scales of justice evenly, though He is patient, smites very severely adulterers who will not repent'.

Smytis rycht sair, thocht He be patient,   535
Adulteraris that will thame not repent.

77
'Prydefull he wes, and joyit of his sin,
And comptit not for Goddis favour nor feid,
Bot traistit ay to rax and sa to rin,
Quhill at the last his sinnis can him leid   540
To schamefull end and to yone suddand deid.
Thairfor it is the verray hand of God
That causit him be werryit with the tod.'

78
Quhen this wes said, this wedow fra hir swoun
Start up on fute, and on hir kennettis cryde: 545
'How! Berkye, Berrie, Bell, Bawsie Broun,
rype schaw, rin weil, Curtes, Nuttieclyde,
Togidder all, but grunching, furth ye glyde!
Reskew my nobill cok or he be slane,
Or ellis to me se ye cum never agane.'   550

79
With that, but baid, thay braidet over the bent;
As fyre of flint thay over the feildis flaw.
Full wichtlie thay throw wood and wateris went
And ceissit not schir Lourence quhill thay saw.
Bot quhen he saw the kennettis cum on raw,   555
Unto the cok in mynd he said: 'God sen
That I and thow wer fairlie in my den.'

535. smytis *smites* sair *severely*
537. joyit of *rejoiced in*
538. comptit not for *did not care about* feid *anger*
539. traistit *trusted* rax *have his way* rin *go his own way*
540. quhill *until* can him leid *led him*
541. suddand *sudden* deid *death*
543. werryit with *killed by* tod *fox*
545. kennettis *small hounds*
548. but grunching *without grumbling* glyde *go*
549. reskew *rescue* or *before*
550. se ye *see that you*
551. but baid *without delay* braidet *darted* bent *field*
552. fyre of flint *fire from a flint* flaw *flew*
553. wichtlie *swiftly*
555. on raw *in a line*
556. in mynd *in his mind* sen *grant*
557. fairlie *safely*

554. 'And did not stop until they saw sir Laurence'.

80

Then said the cok, with sum gude spirit inspyrit:
'Do my counsall and I sall warrand the:
Hungrie thow art and for grit travell tyrit,   560
Richt faint of force and may not ferther fle.
Swyith turne agane and say that I and ye
Freindis ar maid and fellowis for ane yeir,
Than will thay stint, I stand for it, and not steir.'

81

This tod, thocht he wes fals and frivolus,   565
And had frawdis his querrell to defend,
Desavit wes be menis richt mervelous,
For falset failyeis ay at the latter end.
He start about and cryit as he wes kend;
With that the cok he braid out to a bewch.   570
Now juge ye all quhairat schir Lowrence lewch.

82

Begylit thus, the tod under the tre
On kneis fell and said: 'Gude Chantecleir,
Cum doun agane and I, but meit or fe,
Sal be your man and servand for ane yeir.'   575
'Na, fals theif and revar, stand not me neir.
My bludy hekill and my nek sa bla
Hes partit freindschip for ever betwene us twa.

83

'I wes unwyse that winkit at thy will,
Quhairthrow almaist I loissit had my heid.'   580

558. inspyrit *inspired*
559. do my counsall *follow my advice*   warrand the *protect you*
560. travell *effort*   tyrit *tired*
561. faint *weak*   force *strength*   fle *flee*
562. swyith *quickly*
564. fellowis *companions*
565. stint *stop*   I stand for it *I guarantee it*   steir *move*
566. frawdis *tricks*
567. desavit wes *was deceived*   menis *means*
568. falset *falsehood*   failyeis ay *always fails*   at the latter end *in the end*
569. start *turned*   kend *told*
570. braid *leapt*   bewch *branch*
571. juge *judge*   lewch *laughed*
572. begylit *tricked*
574. but meit or fe *without board or wages*
575. servand *servant*
576. revar *robber*
577. hekill *hackle*   bla *bruised*
580. loissit *lost*

571. 'Now you can all judge what sir Laurence had to laugh about'.

'I was mair fule,' quod he, 'coud nocht be still,
Bot spake to put my pray in to pleid.'
'Fair on, fals theif, God keip me fra thy feid.'
With that the cok over the feildis tuke his flicht,
And in at the wedowis lewer couth he licht.   585

Moralitas

84

Now worthie folk, suppose this be ane fabill
And overheillit wyth typis figurall,
Yit may ye find ane sentence richt agreabill
Under thir fenyeit termis textuall:
To our purpose this cok weill may we call   590
Nyse proud men, woid and vaneglorious
Of kin and blude, quhilk ar presumpteous.

85

Fy, puft up pryde, thow is full poysonabill.
Quha favoris the on force man haif ane fall.
Thy strenth is nocht, thy stule standis unstabill,   595
Tak witnes of the feyndis infernall
Quhilk houndit doun wes fra that hevinlie hall
To hellis hole and to that hiddeous hous,
Because in pryde thay wer presumpteous.

86

This fenyeit foxe may weill be figurate   600
To flatteraris with plesand wordis quhyte,

581. mair fule *more foolish* still *quiet*
582. to put *and made* in to pleid *a matter for debate*
583. fair on *go on* feid *hatred*
585. lewer *louver; chimney* couth he licht *he alighted*
586. suppose *even if*
587. overheillit *covered* typis figurall *symbolic emblems*
588. sentence *meaning*
589. thir *these* fenyeit *fictional* textuall *literal*
591. nyse *foolish* woid *arrogant*
592. kin *ancestry* presumpteous *foolhardy*
593. fy *fie* poysonabill *poisonous*
594. favoris the *trusts in you* on force *of necessity* man *must*
595. nocht *nothing* stule *throne*
596. tak witnes *take note* feyndis infernall *hellish fiends*
597. houndit *driven*
600. figurate *used as a figure*
601. to *for* flatteraris *flatterers* quhyte *fair*

589. 'Beneath these literal words of the fiction'.

With fals mening and mynd maist toxicate,
To loif and le that settes thair haill delyte.
All worthie folk at sic suld haif despyte,
For quhair is thair mair perrellous pestilence   605
Nor gif to learis haistelie credence?

87
The wickit mynd and adullatioun
Of sucker sweit haifand the similitude,
Bitter as gall and full of poysoun
To taist it is, quha cleirlie understude.   610
For thy, as now schortlie to conclude,
Thir twa sinnis, flatterie and vaneglore,
Ar vennomous: gude folk, fle thame thairfoir.

THE FOX AND THE WOLF
88
Leif we this wedow glaid, I yow assure,
Of Chantecleir, mair blyith than I can tell,   615
And speik we of the fatal aventure
And destenie that to this foxe befell,
Quhilk durst na mair with miching intermell
Als lang as leme or licht wes of the day,
Bot bydand nicht full styll lurkand he lay,   620

602. mynd *intention*
  toxicate *poisonous*
603. loif *flatter* le *lie* haill *whole*
604. at sic *for such as those*
  despyte *contempt*
606. nor *than* gif *give*
  learis *liars* haistelie *readily*
607. adullatioun *false flattery*
608. sucker sweit *sugar sweet*
  haifand *having*
  similitude *likeness*
610. cleirlie *clearly*

611. for thy *therefore*
612. vaneglore *pride*
613. fle *flee*
614. wedow *widow* glaid *happy*
615. of *about* blyith *joyful*
616. aventure *adventure*
618. quhilk *who*
  miching *pilfering*
  intermell *concern himself*
619. als *as* leme *ray*
620. bydand *awaiting*
  lurkand *lurking*

606. 'Than readily to believe liars'.
607–10. 'The wicked intention and flattering behaviour seems like sweet
  sugar, but for anyone who clearly understands it, it is as bitter as gall
  to taste and full of poison'.

89

Quhill that Thetes, the goddes of the flude,
Phebus had callit to the harbery,
And Hesperous put of his cluddie hude,
Schawand his lustie visage in the sky.
Than Lourence luikit up quhair he couth ly,   625
And kest his hand upon his ee on hicht,
Merie and glade that cummit wes the nicht.

90

Out of the wod unto ane hill he went,
Quhair he micht se the tuinkling sternis cleir,
And all the planetis of the firmament,   630
Thair cours and eik thair moving in thair spheir,
Sum retrograde and sum stationeir,
And of the zodiak in quhat degre
Thay wer ilk ane, as Lowrence leirnit me.

91

Than Saturne auld wes enterit in Capricorne,   635
And Juppiter movit in Sagittarie,
And Mars up in the Rammis heid wes borne,
And Phebus in the Lyoun furth can carie;
Venus the Crab, the Mone wes in Aquarie;
Mercurius, the god of eloquence,   640
Into the Virgyn maid his residence.

621. quhill *until*   Thetes *Thetis*
   flude *sea*
622. Phebus *Phoebus*
   harbery *shelter*
623. Hesperous *Hesperus* of *off*
   cluddie hude *cloudy hood*
624. schawand *showing*
   lustie *bright*   visage *face*
625. Lowrence *the fox*
   luikit *looked*   couth ly *lay*
626. ee *eye*   on hicht *above*
629. sternis *stars*
630. planetis *planets*
631. spheir *sphere*

632. retrograde *moving backwards*
   stationeir *stationary*
633. degre *degree*
634. ilk *each*   leirnit *taught*
635. auld *old*
636. Sagittarie *Sagittarius*
637. Rammis heid *Ram's head;*
   Aries
638. Lyoun *Lion; Leo*   can
   carie *took his way*
639. Mone *Moon*
   Aquarie *Aquarius*
640. Mercurius *Mercury*
641. the Virgyn *Virgo*

621-2. 'Until Thetis, the goddess of the sea, had called Phoebus to his
   night's shelter'.
626. 'And shaded his eyes with his hand'.

92

But astrolab, quadrant, or almanak,
Teichit of nature be instructioun,
The moving of the hevin this tod can tak,
Quhat influence and constellatioun   645
Wes lyke to fall upon the eirth adoun;
And to him self he said, withoutin mair,
'Weill worth the, father, that send me to the lair.

93

'My destenie and eik my weird I watt,
My aventure is cleirlie to me kend,   650
With mischeif myngit is my mortall fait
My misleving the soner bot gif I mend;
Deid is reward of sin and schamefull end.
Thairfoir I will ga seik sum confessour
And schryiff me clene of my sinnis to this hour.   655

94

'Allace,' quod he, 'richt waryit ar we thevis:
Our lyifis set ilk nicht in aventure,
Our cursit craft full mony man mischevis,
For ever we steill and ever alyk ar pure.
In dreid and schame our dayis we indure,   660
Syne 'Widdinek' and 'Crakraip' callit als,
And till our hyre ar hangit be the hals.'

642. but *without* astrolab *astrolabe*
  almanak *almanac*
643. teichit of *taught by* be *by*
644. tod *fox* tak *ascertain*
646. lyke *likely* eirth *earth*
  adoun *down*
647. withoutin mair *without more*
  ado
648. weill worth the *God bless you*
  lair *knowledge*
649. eik *also* weird *fate*
  watt *know*
650. aventure *fate* kend *taught*
651. mischeif *harm*
  myngit *mingled* fait *fate*

652. misleving *bad living*
  soner *sooner* bot gif *unless*
653. deid *death*
654. ga *go* confessour *confessor*
655. schryiff *confess* clene *entirely*
656. richt *very* waryit *cursed*
  thevis *thieves*
657. lyifis *lives* aventure *danger*
658. mischevis *harms*
659. steill *steal* alyk *still*
  pure *poor*
660. indure *endure*
661. syne *until* widdinek *withy-
  neck* crakraip *crack-rope*
662. till *for* hyre *reward* hals *neck*

643. 'Taught by the instruction of nature'.
648. 'God bless you, father, who gave to me the knowledge'.
652. 'Unless I mend my wicked ways soon'.
662. 'And also have to endure being called "withy-neck" and "crack-rope" '.

95

Accusand thus his cankerit conscience,
In to ane craig he kest about his ee,
So saw he cummand, ane lyttill than frome thence,   665
Ane worthie doctour of divinitie,
Freir Wolf Waitskaith, in science wonder sle,
To preiche and pray was new cummit fra the closter,
With beidis in hand, sayand his Pater Noster.

96

Seand this wolf, this wylie tratour tod   670
On kneis fell, with hude in to his nek:
'Welcome, my gostlie father under God',
Quod he, with mony binge and mony bek.
'Ha,' quod the wolf, 'schir Tod, for quhat effek
Mak ye sic feir? Ryse up, put on your hude!'   675
'Father,' quod he, 'I haif grit cause to dude:

97

'Ye ar the lanterne and the sicker way
Suld gyde sic sempill folk as me to grace.
Your bair feit and your russet coull of gray,
Your lene cheik, your paill and pietious face,   680
Schawis to me your perfite halines,
For weill wer him that anis in his lyve
Had hap to yow his sinnis for to schryve.'

663. accusand *accusing*
cankerit *rotten*
664. in to *from* craig *crag* ee *eye*
665. cummand *coming* than frome
thence *way off*
666. divinitie *divinity*
667. freir *friar* Waitskaith *Do-
Harm* science *learning*
sle *accomplished*
668. preiche *preach* new *recently*
cummit *come*
669. beidis *rosary-beads* Pater
Noster *'Our Father'; the Lord's
Prayer*
670. seand *seeing* tod *fox*
671. hude *hood* in to *down around*

672. gostlie *spiritual*
673. binge *bend* bek *bow*
674. for quhat effek *to what
purpose*
675. mak . . . feir *behave*
676. dude *do it*
677. sicker *sure*
679. feit *feet* russet cowll *coarse
cowl*
680. pieteous *pious*
681. halines *holiness*
682. weill wer him *he would be
well off* anis *once*
683. had hap *had the good fortune*
schryve *confess*

98

'A, selie Lowrence,' quod the wolf, and leuch,
'It plesis me that ye ar penitent.'   685
'Of reif and stouth, schir, I can tell aneuch,
That causis me full sair for to repent.
Bot father, byde still heir upon the bent,
I yow beseik, and heir me to declair
My conscience, that prikkis me sa sair.'   690

99

'Weill,' quod the wolf, 'sit doun upon thy kne.'
And he doun bair heid sat full humilly,
And syne began with 'Benedicitie'.
Quhen I this saw, I drew ane lytill by,
For it effeiris nouther to heir nor spy,   695
Nor to reveill thing said under that seill.
Bot unto the tod this gait the wolf couth mele:

100

'Art thow contrite and sorie in thy spreit
For thy trespas?' 'Na, schir, I can not duid.
Me think that hennis ar sa honie sweit,   700
And lambes flesche that new ar lettin bluid.
For to repent my mynd can not concluid,
Bot of this thing, that I haif slane sa few.'
'Weill,' quod the wolf, 'in faith thow art ane schrew.

101

'Sen thow can not forthink thy wickitnes,   705
Will thow forbeir in tyme to cum, and mend?'

684. selie *foolish*   leuch *laughed*
686. reif *theft*   stouth *robbery*
    aneuch *a good deal*
688. byde *wait*   bent *field*
689. beseik *beg*   declair *reveal*
691. sit doun upon thy kne *kneel down*
692. bair heid *bare-headed*
    humilly *humbly*
694. drew *moved*   by *way off*
695. effeiris *is proper*
    nouther *neither*   spy *look*
696. seill *sealed confession*
697. this gait *in this way*   couth
    mele *spoke*
698. spreit *heart*
699. duid *do it*
700. honie *honey*
701. lettin bluid *bled*
702. concluid *decide*
703. bot of *except for*
704. schrew *villain*
705. forthink *repent*
706. forbeir *refrain from sinning*
    mend *mend your ways*

702–3. 'The only thing I can make up my mind to repent about is that I
have slain so few'.

'And I forbeir, how sall I leif, allace,
Haifand nane uther craft me to defend?
Neid causis me to steill quhair ever I wend:
I eschame to thig, I can not wirk, ye wait,   710
Yit wald I fane pretend to gentill stait.'

102

'Weill,' quod the wolf, 'thow wantis pointis twa
Belangand to perfyte confessioun;
To the thrid part of penitence let us ga:
Will thow tak pane for thy transgressioun?'   715
'A, schir, considder my complexioun,
Selie and waik, and of my nature tender;
Lo, will ye se, I am baith lene and sklender.

103

'Yit neuertheles I wald, swa it wer licht,
Schort, and not grevand to my tendernes,   720
Tak part of pane, fulfill it gif I micht,
To set my selie saull in way of grace.'
'Thow sall', quod he, 'forbeir flesch untill Pasche
To tame this corps, that cursit carioun,
And heir I reik the full remissioun.'   725

104

'I grant thairto, swa ye will gif me leif
To eit puddingis, or laip ane lyttill blude,
Or heid, or feit, or paynchis let me preif,
In cace I falt of flesch in to my fude.'

707. and *if* leif *live*
708. haifand *having* me to defend *to support myself*
709. wend *go*
710. eschame *am ashamed* thig *beg* wait *know*
711. fane *happily* pretend to *aspire to* gentill stait *noble way of life*
712. wantis *are deficient in*
713. belangand *pertaining*
715. tak pane *perform penance*
716. complexioun *constitution*
717. selie *poor* waik *weak*
718. lene *lean* sklender *slender*
719. wald *would be willing*

swa *providing* licht *light*
720. grevand *harmful* tendernes *delicate nature*
721. tak part of pane *to do some penance* gif *if*
722. selie saull *wretched soul*
723. forbeir flesche *give up meat* Pasche *Easter*
724. corps *body* carioun *flesh*
725. reik *grant* remissioun *pardon*
726. swa *providing* leif *permission*
727. puddingis *sausages* laip *lap*
728. paynchis *tripe* preif *taste*
729. falt of *feel the lack of* fude *diet*

'For grit mister I gif the leif to dude　　　　　730
Twyse in the oulk, for neid may haif na law.'
'God yeild yow, schir, for that text weill I knaw.'

105

Quhen this wes said, the wolf his wayis went.
The foxe on fute he fuir unto the flude;
To fang him fisch haillelie wes his intent.　　　　　735
Bot quhen he saw the watter and wallis wod,
Astonist all in to ane stair he stude,
And said, 'Better that I had biddin at hame
Nor bene ane fischar, in the Devillis name.

106

'Now man I scraip my meit out of the sand,　　　　　740
For I haif nouther boittis, net, nor bait.'
As he wes thus for falt of meit murnand,
Lukand about, his leving for to lait,
Under ane tre he saw ane trip of gait.
Than wes he blyith, and in ane hewch him hid,　　　　　745
And fra the gait he stall ane lytill kid.

107

Syne over the heuch unto the see he hyis,
And tuke the kid be the hornis twane,
And in the watter outher twyis or thryis
He dowkit him, and till him can he sayne,　　　　　750
'Ga doun, schir Kid, cum up, schir Salmond, agane',
Quhill he wes deid, syne to the land him dreuch,
And of that new-maid salmond eit aneuch.

730. for *in*　mister *necessity*
　　　dude *do it*
731. oulk *week*　neid *necessity*
732. yeild *protect*
734. fuir *went*　flude *sea*
735. fang *catch*　haillelie *entirely*
736. wallis *waves*　wod *wild*
737. in to ane stair *staring*
738. biddin *stayed*
739. nor bene *than been*
　　　fischar *fisherman*
740. man *must*
741. boittis *boats*
742. falt *lack*
　　　murnand *complaining*

743. leving *sustenance*
744. trip *flock*　gait *goats*
745. blyith *happy*　heweh *crag*
746. stall *stole*
747. hyis *hastens*
749. outher *either*　twyis or
　　　thryis *twice or three times*
750. dowkit *plunged*　till *to*　can
　　　he sayne *he said*
751. ga *go*　salmond *salmon*
752. quhill *until*　deid *dead*
　　　dreuch *dragged*
753. new-maid *newly created*
　　　aneuch *enough*

108

Thus fynelie fillit with young tender meit,
Unto ane derne for dreid he him addrest,   755
Under ane busk, quhair that the sone can beit,
To beik his breist and bellie he thocht best,
And rekleslie he said, quhair he did rest,
Straikand his wame aganis the sonis heit,
'Upon this wame set wer ane bolt full meit.'   760

109

Quhen this wes said, the keipar of the gait,
Cairfull in hart his kid wes stollen away,
On everilk syde full warlie couth he wait,
Quhill at the last he saw quhair Lowrence lay.
Ane bow he bent, ane flane with fedderis gray   765
He haillit to the heid, and or he steird
The foxe he prikkit fast unto the eird.

110

'Now,' quod the foxe, 'allace and wellaway!
Gorrit I am, and may na forther gang.
Me think na man may speik ane word in play   770
Bot now on dayis in ernist it is tane.'
The hird him hynt, and out he drew his flane,
And for his kid and uther violence,
He tuke his skyn and maid ane recompence.

---

754. fynelie *finally*
755. derne *hiding place*
     dreid *fear* addrest *went*
756. busk *bush* can beit *beat down*
757. beik *warm* breist *chest*
759. straikand *stroking*
     wame *belly* aganis *in*
760. bolt *arrow* meit *fittingly*
761. keipar of the gait *goatherd*
762. cairfull in hart *sorrowful*
763. everilk *every*
     warlie *carefully* wait *look*
765. flane *arrow* fedderis *feathers*
766. haillit to the heid *lined up*

with his eye or *before*
     steird *stirred*
767. prikkit fast *impaled*
     eird *earth*
768. wellaway *woe is me*
769. gorrit *gored* gang *go*
770. play *jest*
771. now on dayis *nowadays* in
     ernist *seriously* tane *taken*
772. hird *herdsman* hynt *took*
773. violence *damage*
774. maid ane recompence *received
     compensation*

760. 'An arrow could be shot at my belly very fittingly'.

Moralitas

111

This suddand deith and unprovysit end   775
Of this fals tod, without contritioun,
Exempill is exhortand folk to mend,
For dreid of sic ane lyke conclusioun.
For mony gois now to confessioun
Can not repent, nor for thair sinnis greit,   780
Because thay think thair lustie lyfe sa sweit.

112

Sum bene also, throw consuetude and ryte,
Vincust with carnall sensualitie:
Suppose thay be as for the tyme contreyte,
Can not forbeir, nor fra thair sinnis fle.   785
Use drawis nature swa in propertie
Of beist and man that neidlingis thay man do
As thay of lang tyme hes bene hantit to.

113

Be war, gude folke, and feir this suddane schoit
Quhilk smytis sair withoutin resistence.   790
Attend wyislie, and in your hartis noit,
Aganis deith may na man mak defence.
Ceis of your sin; remord your conscience;
Do wilfull pennance here; and ye sall wend,
Efter your deith, to blis withouttin end.   795

---

775. suddand *sudden*
  unprovysit *unforeseen*
777. exhortand *urging*
778. lyke conclusioun *similar end*
779. gois *go*
780. greit *weep*
781. lustie *happy*
782. bene *are* consuetude *habit*
  ryte *custom*
783. vincust with *vanquished
  by*
784. suppose *even if*

  contreyte *contrite*
785. forbeir *stop*
786. use *custom* drawis *guides*
  propertie *character*
787. neidlingis *of necessity*
788. hantit *accustomed*
789. schoit *shot*
790. resistence *defence*
791. attend *consider*
  wyislie *wisely* noit *note*
793. remord *examine*
794. wend *go*

786–8. 'Custom guides nature in the characters of both beast and man to
  the extent that they are forced to do what they've been accustomed to
  doing for so long'.

THE TRIAL OF THE FOX

114

This foirsaid foxe that deit for his misdeid,
Had not ane barne wes gottin richteouslie
That to his airschip micht of law succeid,
Except ane sone, the quhilk in lemanrye
He gottin had in purches privelie,   800
And till his name wes callit Fatherwar,
That luifit weill with pultrie to tig and tar.

115

It followis weill be ressoun naturall,
And gre be gre of richt comparisoun,
Of euill cummis war, of war cummis werst of all;   805
Of wrangus get cummis wrang successioun.
This foxe, bastard of generatioun,
Of verray kynde behuifit to be fals;
Swa wes his father, and his grandschir als.

116

As nature will, seikand his meit be sent,   810
Of cace he fand his fatheris carioun,
Nakit, new slane, and till him is he went,
Tuke up his heid, and on his kne fell doun,
Thankand grit God of that conclusioun,
And said, 'Now sall I bruke, sen I am air,   815
The boundis quhair thow wes wont for to repair.'

796. foirsaid *aforementioned*
  dcit *died* misdeid *wickedness*
797. barne *child* gottin *conceived*
  richteouslie *legitimately*
798. airschip *heirdom* of *by*
799. sone *son* lemanrye *illicit love*
800. in purches *with a concubine*
  privelie *secretly*
801. Fatherwar *Worse than his father*
802. luifit *loved* pultrie *poultry*
  tig *paw* tar *provoke*
804. gre *step* richt *careful*
805. war *worse* werst *worst*
806. wrangus *wrongful*
  get *begetting*

807. of generatioun *in his birth*
808. kynde *nature* behuifit *was
  bound*
809. swa *as*
  grandschir *grandfather*
810. will *intends* seikand *seeking*
  sent *scent*
811. of cace *by chance*
  fand *found* carioun *corpse*
812. till *to* went *gone*
813. tuke *lifted*
815. bruke *have possession*
  sen *since* air *heir*
816. boundis *lands*
  wont *accustomed* repair *go*

797–8. 'Did not have a legitimate child who could lawfully be put
  forward as his heir'.

117

Fy, covetice, unkynd and venemous!
The sone wes fane he fand his father deid,
Be suddand schot for deidis odious,
That he micht ringe and raxe in till his steid,   820
Dreidand na thing the samin lyfe to leid
In thift and reif as did his father befoir,
Bot to the end, attent he tuke no moir.

118

Yit nevertheles, throw naturall pietie,
The carioun upon his bak he tais.   825
'Now find I weill this proverb trew,' quod he,
' "Ay rinnis the foxe, als lang as he fute hais." '
Syne with the corps unto ane peitpoit gais
Of watter full, and kest him in the deip,
And to the Devill he gaif his banis to keip.   830

119

O fulische man! Plungit in wardlynes
To conqueis wrangwis guidis, gold and rent,
To put thy saull in pane or hevines,
To riche thy air, quhilk efter thow art went,
Have he thy gude, he takis bot small tent   835
To sing or say for thy salvatioun.
Fra thow be dede, done is thy devotioun.

817. fy *fie* covetice *greed*
818. fane *glad* fand *found*
819. be suddand *suddenly* for *on account of*
820. ringe *reign* raxe *rule* in till *in* steid *place*
821. dreidand *fearing* na thing *not at all* samin *same* leid *lead*
822. thift *theft* reif *robbery*
823. attent he tuke *he thought*
824. pietie *pity*
825. tais *takes*
827. ay *always* rinnis *runs*
fute *feet*
828. peitpoit *peat hole* gais *goes*
830. banis *bones*
831. fulische *foolish* wardlynes *worldly things*
832. conqueis *obtain* wrangwis *ill-gotten* guidis *goods* rent *possessions*
833. saull *soul* hevines *sorrow*
834. riche *enrich* air *heir* quhilk *who* went *gone*
835. tent *care*
837. fra *from the moment*

823. 'But he thought no more about the end of it all'.
835–7. 'Once he has your goods, he takes little care to sing psalms or say prayers for your salvation. From the moment you are dead, his devotion to you is finished'.

120

This tod to rest him he passit to ane craig,
And thair he hard ane buisteous bugill blaw
Quhilk, as he thocht, maid all the warld to waig.   840
Than start he up quhen he this hard, and saw
Ane unicorne come lansand over ane law,
With horne in hand: ane buste in breist he bure;
Ane pursephant semelie, I yow assure.

121

Unto ane bank quhair he micht se about   845
On everilk syde, in haist he culd him hy,
Schot out his voce full schyll, and gaif ane schout,
And 'Oyas! Oyas!' twyse or thryse did cry.
With that the beistis in the feild thairby,
All mervelland quhat sic ane thing suld mene,   850
Gritlie agast, thay gaderit on ane grene.

122

Out of his buste ane bill sone can he braid
And red the text withoutin tarying.
Commandand silence, sadlie thus he said,
'We, nobill Lyoun, of all beistis the king,   855
Greting to God, ay lestand but ending,
To brutall beistis and irrationall
I send, as to my subjectis grit and small.

123

'My celsitude and hie magnificence
Lattis yow to wit, that evin incontinent,   860

838. passit *went*
839. hard *heard* buisteous *harsh*
  bugill *trumpet*
840. waig *shake*
842. lansand *springing* law *hill*
843. buste *box* in breist *round his
  neck* bure *carried*
844. pursephant *herald* semelie *fair*
846. culd him hy *hurried*
847. schyll *resonantly*
848. oyas *oyez*
850. mervelland *wondering*

mene *mean*
851. agast *in surprise*
  gaderit *gathered*
852. bill *document* braid *pull out*
854. sadlie *solemnly*
856. greting to God *glory be to
  God* ay lestand *everlasting*
  but *without*
857. brutall beistis *brute beasts*
859. celsitude *kingliness* hie *high*
860. lattis yow to wit *informs you*
  evin incontinent *without delay*

857. 'To brute and non-human creatures'.

Thinkis the morne with royall deligence
Upon this hill to hald ane parliament.
Straitlie thairfoir I gif commandement
For to compeir befoir my tribunall,
Under all pane and perrell that may fall.'   865

124

The morrow come, and Phebus with his bemis
Consumit had the mistie cluddis gray;
The ground wes grene, and as the gold it glemis,
With gers growand gudelie, grit, and gay,
The spyce thay spred to spring on everilk spray;   870
The lark, the maveis, and the merll full hie
Sweitlie can sing, trippand fra tre to tre.

125

The leopardis come, a croun of massie gold
Beirand thay brocht unto that hillis hicht,
With jaspis jonit, and royall rubeis rold,   875
And mony diveris dyamontis dicht.
With pollis proud ane palyeoun doun thay picht,
And in that throne thair sat ane wild lyoun,
In rob royall, with sceptour, swerd, and croun.

126

Efter the tennour of the cry befoir,   880
That gais on fut, all beistis in the eird,

861. thinkis *he intends* the
  morne *tomorrow* deligence *care*
863. straitlie *strictly*
864. compeir *appear*
  tribunall *court*
865. under *under threat of*
866. Phebus *Phoebus* bemis *beams*
867. consumit *absorbed,*
  cluddis *clouds*
868. glemis *gleams*
869. gers *plants*
870. spyce *spices* spring *grow*
  everilk spray *every shoot*
871. maveis *song thrush*
  merll *blackbird*

872. trippand *hopping*
873. leopardis *leopards*
  croun *crown* massie *solid*
874. beirand *carrying* hicht *crest*
875. jaspis *jaspers* jonit *attached*
  rold *adorned with*
876. diveris *different*
  dyamontis *diamonds* dicht *set*
877. pollis *poles*
  palyeoun *pavilion* picht *pitched*
879. rob *robe* sceptour *sceptre*
880. efter the tennour *in
  accordance with the message*
881. that *everything that*
  gais *goes* eird *earth*

875–6. 'With jaspers attached to it, and adorned with royal rubies, and
  set with many different diamonds'.

As thay commandit wer, withoutin moir,
Befoir thair lord the lyoun thay appeird.
And quhat thay wer, to me as Lowrence leird,
I sall reheirs ane part of everilk kynd,   885
Als fer as now occurris to my mynd.

127
The Minotaur, ane monster mervelous,
Bellerophont, that beist of bastardrie,
The warwolf, and the Pegase perillous,
Transformit be assent of sorcerie,   890
The linx, the tiger full of tiranie,
The elephant, and eik the dromedarie,
The cameill with his cran-nek furth can carie.

128
The leopard, as I haif tauld beforne,
The anteloip, the sparth furth couth speid,   895
The peyntit pantheir, and the unicorne,
The rayndeir ran throw reveir, rone, and reid,
The jolie jonet, and the gentill steid,
The asse, the mule, the hors of everilk kynd,
The da, the ra, the hornit hart, the hynd.   900

129
The bull, the beir, the bugill, and the bair,
The wodwys, wildcat, and the wild wolfyne,
The hardbakkit hurcheoun, and the hirpland hair;
Baith ottcr, and aip, and pennit porcupyne;
The gukit gait, the selie scheip, the swyne,   905

882. withoutin moir *without delay*
884. leird *taught*
885. reheirs *name*
888. Bellerophont *Bellerophon*
  beist of bastardrie *hybrid beast*
889. warwolf *werwolf*
  pegase *pegasus*
890. assent *help*
891. tiranie *violence*
893. cameill *camel* cran-nek *neck
  like a crane* can carie *goes*
895. sparth *pard*
896. peyntit *painted*
897. rayndeir *reindeer*

reveir *river* rone *thicket*
reid *reeds*
898. jolie jonet *pretty jennet*
  gentill steid *noble horse*
900. da *doe* ra *roe-deer*
  hynd *hind*
901. bugill *wild ox* bair *boar*
902. wodwys *wild man*
  wolfyne *wolverine*
903. hurcheoun *hedgehog* hirpland
  hair *limping hare*
904. aip *ape* pennit *quilled*
905. gukit gait *stupid goat* selie
  scheip *foolish sheep*

The baver, bakon, and the balterand brok;
The fowmart with the fyber furth can flok.

130
The gray grewhound, the slewthound, furth can slyde,
With doggis all divers and different;
The rattoun ran, the globard furth can glyde,　　　910
The quhrynand quhitret with the quhasill went;
The feitho that hes furrit mony fent,
The mertrik, with the cunning and the con,
The bowranbane, and eik the lerion.

131
The marmisset the mowdewart couth leid,　　　915
Because that nature denyit had hir sicht.
Thus dressit thay all furth for dreid of deid;
The musk, the lytill mous with all hir micht
In haist haikit unto that hillis hicht,
And mony kynd of beistis I couth not knaw,　　　920
Befoir thair lord the lyoun thay loutit law.

132
Seing thir beistis all at his bidding boun,
He gaif ane braid and blenkit him about,
Than flatlingis to his feit thay fell all doun,
For dreid of deith, thay droupit all in dout.　　　925
The lyoun lukit quhen he saw thame lout,

906. baver *beaver*　bakon *bison*
　　balterand brok *waddling badger*
907. fowmart *polecat*
　　fyber *beaver*　can flok *flocked*
908. grewhound *greyhound*
　　slewthound *sleuth-hound; blood-*
　　hound　can slyde *moved*
910. rattoun *rat*
　　globard *dormouse*　can
　　glyde *moved stealthily*
911. quhrynand quhitret *whining*
　　white rat: stoat　quhasill *weasel*
912. feitho *polecat*　furrit *provided*
　　fur for　fent *vent; garment*
　　trimming
913. mertrik *marten*

cunning *rabbit*　con *squirrel*
914. bowranbane *otter*　lerion *dormouse*
915. marmisset *marmoset; small*
　　monkey　mowdewart *mole,*
　　couth leid *led*
917. dressit *proceeded*　deid *death*
918. musk *civet cat*
919. haikit *hiked*　hicht *top*
921. loutit *bowed down*　law *low*
922. boun *ready*
923. gaif ane braid *made a sudden*
　　movement　blenkit *looked*
924. flatlingis to *prostrate at*
925. droupit *dropped down*
　　dout *fear*
926. lout *bow down*

And bad thame, with ane countcnancc full sweit,
'Be not efferit, bot stand up on your feit.

133

'I lat yow wit, my micht is merciabill
And steiris nane that ar to me prostrait;   930
Angrie, austerne, and als unamyabill
To all that standfray ar to myne estait.
I rug, I reif all beistys that makis debait
Aganis the micht of my magnyficence:
Se nane pretend to pryde in my presence.   935

134

'My celsitude and my hie majestie
With micht and mercie myngit sall be ay.
The lawest heir I can full sone up hie,
And mak him maister over yow all I may;
The dromedarie, gif he will mak deray,   940
The grit camell, thocht he wer neuer sa crous,
I can him law als lytill as ane mous.

135

'Se neir be twentie mylis quhair I am
The kid ga saiflie be the gaittis syde,
The tod Lowrie luke not to the lam,   945
Na revand beistis nouther ryn nor ryde.'
Thay couchit all efter that this wes cryde.

---

927. countenance *expression*
sweit *kind*
928. efferit *afraid*
929. wit *know* micht *power*
merciabill *merciful*
930. steiris *molests*
prostrait *humble*
931. austerne *stern*
unamyabill *hostile*
932. standfray *rebellious*
estait *position*
933. rug *pull apart* reif *tear in
pieces* makis debait *argue*
936. celsitude *kingliness*

937. myngit *combined*
938. lawest *lowest* heir *here*
up *put up*
940. gif *if* mak deray *cause a
disturbance*
941. crous *bold*
942. law *bring low*
943. se neir be *see that within*
quhair *of where*
944. saiflie *safely* gaittis *goat's*
946. revand *plundering* ryn *run*
ryde *raid*
947. couchit *lay down*

The justice bad the court for to gar fence,
The sutis call, and foirfalt all absence.

136
The panther, with his payntit coit-armour,   950
Fensit the court, as of the law effeird,
Than Tod Lowrie luikit quhair he couth lour,
And start on fute, all stonist and all steird,
Ryifand his hair, he cryit with ane reird,
Quaikand for dreid and sichand couth he say,   955
'Allace, this hour, allace, this dulefull day!

137
'I wait this suddand semblie that I se,
Haifand the pointis of ane parliament,
Is maid to mar sic misdoars as me.
Thairfoir geve I me schaw, I will be schent;   960
I will be socht, and I be red absent.
To byde or fle, it makis no remeid;
All is alyke, thair followis not bot deid.'

138
Perplexit thus in his hart can he mene
Throw falset how he micht him self defend.   965
His hude he drew laich attoure his ene,
And winkand with the ane eye furth he wend.

948. justice *court officer* gar
  fence *open the proceedings*
949. sutis *legal suits*
  foirfalt *forfeit*
950. coit-armour *herald's coat*
951. of the law effeird *required by law*
952. lour *lurk*
953. start on fute *jumped to his feet* stonist *astonished*
  steird *perturbed*
954. ryifand *tearing* reird *loud voice*
955. sichand *sighing*
956. duleful *sorrowful*

957. wait *know* suddand *impromptu*
  semblie *assembly*
958. haifand *having*
  pointis *attributes*
959. mar *harm* misdoars *wrong-doers*
960. geve *if* me schaw *show myself* schent *punished*
961. socht *sought* and if red *marked as*
962. byde *stay* remeid *difference*
964. mene *consider*
965. falset *trickery*
966. laich *low* attour *over* ene *eyes*
967. winkand *peering*

949. 'Call those involved in legal suits and cause those absent to forfeit their estates'.

Clinscheand he come, that he micht not be kend,
And for dreddour that he suld bene arreist,
He playit bukhude behind, fra beist to beist.   970

139

O fylit spreit, and cankerit conscience!
Befoir ane roy renyeit with richteousnes,
Blakinnit cheikis and schamefull countenance!
Fairweill thy fame; now gone is all thy grace!
The phisnomie, the favour of thy face,   975
For thy defence is foull and disfigurate,
Brocht to the licht basit, blunt, and blait.

140

Be thow atteichit with thift, or with tressoun,
For thy misdeid wrangous, and wickit fay,
Thy cheir changis, Lowrence, thow man luke doun,   980
Thy worschip of this warld is went away.
Luke to this tod, how he wes in effray,
And fle the filth of falset, I the reid,
Quhairthrow thair fallowis syn and schamefull deid.

141

Compeirand thus befoir thair lord and king,   985
In ordour set, as to thair estait effeird,

968. clinscheand *limping*
kend *recognised*
969. dreddour *fear*
970. bukhude *hide-and-seek*
971. fylit spreit *defiled soul*
cankerit *rotten*
972. roy *king* renyeit *arraigned*
973. blakinnit *pale*
974. fame *reputation*
975. phisnomie *physiognomy*
favour *appearance*
976. disfigurate *deformed*
977. basit *dejected* blunt *dull*
blait *stupid*
978. atteichit with *accused of*

thift *theft* tressoun *treason*
979. wrangous *evil* wickit
fay *faithlessness*
980. cheir *expression* man *may*
981. worschip *honour* of *in*
went *gone*
982. effray *fear*
983. falset *falsehood* I the reid *I
advise you*
984. quhairthrow *through which*
fallowis *follows* deid *death*
985. compeirand *appearing*
986. ordour *order* estait *rank*
effeird *was fitting*

975–7. 'Your physiognomy, the appearance of your face, is too foul and
deformed to be used in your defence, it shows you to be base, dull and
stupid'.

Of everilk kynd he gart ane part furth bring,
And awfullie he spak, and at thame speird
Geve there wes ony beist in to this eird
Absent, and thairto gart thame deiplie sweir,   990
And thay said nane, except ane gray stude meir.

142

'Ga, make ane message sone unto that stude.'
The court than cryit, 'My lord, quha sall it be?'
'Cum furth, Lowrie, lurkand under thy hude.'
'Aa, schir, mercie! Lo, I have bot ane ee,   995
Hurt in the hoche, and cruikit as ye may se.
The wolf is better in ambassatry,
And mair cunning in clergie fer than I.'

143

Rampand he said, 'Ga furth, ye brybouris baith!'
And thay to ga withowtin tarying.   1000
Over ron and rute thay ran togidder raith,
And fand the meir at hir meit in the morning.
'Now,' quod the tod, 'madame, cum to the king.
The court is callit, and ye ar *contumax*.'
'Let be, Lowrence,' quod scho, 'your cowrtlie
    knax.'   1005

144

'Maistres,' quod he, 'cum to the court ye mon;
The lyoun hes commandit so in deid.'
'Schir Tod, tak ye the flyrdome and the fon.

987. gart *caused* furth bring *to be brought forward*
988. awfullie *majestically* speird *asked*
989. geve *if*
990. deiplie *solemnly*
991. stude meir *brood-mare*
992. make ane message *send a messanger*
993. quha *who*
995. ane *one*
996. hoche *hock; ankle*

998. cunning *knowledgeable* clergie *clerkly matters*
999. rampand *raging* brybouris *wretches* baith *both*
1000. to *two*
1001. ron *undergrowth* raith *quickly*
1002. meit *food*
1004. contumax *in contempt of court*
1005. cowrtlie knax *legal nonsense*
1006. maistres *madam* mon *must*

1008-9. 'Sir Fox, the joke is on you; I have a year's exemption from service, if you care to read'.

I hauc rcspitc anc ycir, and ye will reid.'
'I can not spell,' quod he, 'sa God me speid.   1010
Heir is the wolf, ane nobill clerk at all,
And of this message is maid principall.

145

'He is autentik, and ane man of age,
And hes grit practik of the chanceliary.
Let him ga luke, and reid your privilage,   1015
And I sall stand and beir witnes yow by.'
'Quhair is thy respite?' quod the wolf in hy.
'Schir, it is heir under my hufe, weill hid.'
'Hald up thy heill,' quod he, and so scho did.

146

Thocht he wes blindit with pryde, yit he presumis 1020
To luke doun law, quhair that hir letter lay.
With that the meir gird him upon the gumis
And straik the hattrell of his heid away.
Half out of lyif thair lenand doun he lay.
'Allace,' quod Lowrence, 'Lupus, thow art loist.'   1025
'His cunning', quod the meir, 'wes worth sum
    coist.

147

'Lowrence,' quod scho, 'will thow luke on my letter,
Sen that the wolf na thing thairof can wyn?'
'Na, be Sanct Bryde!' quod he. 'Me think it better
To sleip in haill nor in ane hurt skyn.   1030
Ane skrow I fand, and this wes writtin in—

1008. flyrdome *humbug*   fon *folly*
1009. respite *exemption from
    service*   and *if*
1010. spell *read*   speid *save*
1012. principall *chief perpetrator*
1013. autentik *reliable*
1014. practik *experience*
    chanceliary *chancellery; courts*
1015. privilage *letter of exemption*
1017. in hy *quickly*
1020. presumis *condescends*

1022. gird *hit*
1023. straik *struck*   hattrell *top*
1024. lenand *lying*
1025. *Lupus Wolf*
1026. wes worth *deserved*
    coist *payment*
1028. wyn *learn*
1029. Sanct Bryde *St Bride
    (Brigid)*
1030. haill *whole*   nor *than*
1031. skrow *scroll*

1023. 'And took the top of his head off.

For fyve schillingis I wald not anis forfaut him—
Felix quem faciunt aliena pericula cautum.'

148
With brokin skap and bludie cheikis reid,
This wretched wolf weipand thus on he went,   1035
Of his menye markand to get remeid;
To tell the king the cace wes his intent.
'Schir,' quod the tod, 'byde still upon this bent,
And fra your browis wesche away the blude,
And tak ane drink, for it will do yow gude.'   1040

149
To fetche watter this fraudfull foxe furth fure;
Sydelingis a bank he socht unto ane syke.
On cace, he meittis, cummand fra the mure,
Ane trip of lambis dansand on ane dyke.
This tratour tod, this tirrant, and this tyke,   1045
The fattest of this flock he fellit hais,
And eit his fill, syne to the wolf he gais.

150
Thay drank togidder, and syne thair journey takis
Befoir the king, syne kneillit on thair kne.
'Quhair is yone meir, schir Tod, wes *contumax*?'   1050
Than Lowrence said, 'My lord, speir not at me,
This new maid doctour of divinitie,
With his reid cap can tell yow weill aneuch.'
With that the lyoun and all the laif thay leuch.

1032. anis *once* forfaut him *go
    against it*
1033. felix quem faciunt aliena
    pericula cautum *happy is he who
    learns from the misfortunes of
    others*
1034. skap *scalp*
1036. menye *injuries*
    markand *intending*
    remeid *treatment*
1038. bent *grass*
1041. fure *went*

1042. sydelingis *sidling along*
    socht unto *came upon*
    syke *stream*
1043. on cace *by chance*
    mure *moor*
1044. trip *flock* dansand
    on *skipping over* dyke *low wall*
1045. tirrant *tyrant* tyke *tyke; cur*
1046. fellit *killed*
1051. speir *ask*
1053. reid *red*
1054. laif *rest* leuch *laughed*

1037. 'His intention was to tell the king the whole story'.

151

'Tell on the cais, now Lowrence, let us heir.'   1055
'This wittie wolf,' quod he, 'this clerk of age,
On your behalf he bad the meir compeir,
And scho allegit to ane privilage—
'Cum neir, and se, and ye sall haif your wage.'
Because he red hir rispite plane and weill,   1060
Yone reid bonat scho raucht him with hir heill.'

152

The lyoun said, 'Be yone reid cap I ken
This taill is trew, quha tent unto it takis.
The greitest clerkis ar not the wysest men;
The hurt of ane happie the uther makis.'   1065
As thay wer carpand in this cais, with knakis,
And all the court in merines and in gam,
Swa come the yow, the mother of the lam.

153

Befoir the justice on hir kneis fell,
Put out hir playnt on this wyis wofully: 1070
'This harlet huresone and this hound of hell,
He devorit hes my lamb full doggitly,
Within ane myle, in contrair to your cry.
For Goddis lufe, my lord, gif me the law
Of this lurker!' With that Lowrence let draw.   1075

1055. cais *case*
1056. wittie *learned* of
 age *venerable*
1057. bad *asked* compeir *to
 appear*
1058. allegit to *claimed to have*
1060. red *read* rispite *exemption*
1061. bonat *bonnet; hat*
 raucht *gave*
1063. tent unto it takis *takes heed
 of it*
1066. carpand *talking* knakis *jests*
1067. gam *play*

1068. yow *ewe*
1070. put out *made*
 playnt *complaint* wyis *way*
1071. harlet *harlot* huresone *son
 of a whore*
1072. devorit hes *has devoured*
 doggitly *cruelly*
1073. in contrair to *in violation of*
 cry *edict*
1074. the law *justice*
1075. of *upon* let draw *began to
 withdraw*

1065. 'One man's loss is another man's gain'.

154

'Byde!' quod the lyoun. 'Lymmer, let us se
Gif it be suthe the selie yow hes said.'
'Aa, soverane lord, saif your mercie!' quod he.
'My purpois wes with him for to haif plaid.
Causles he fled as he had bene effraid;   1080
For dreid of deith, he duschit over ane dyke
And brak his nek.' 'Thow leis,' quod scho, 'fals tyke!

155

'His deith be practik may be previt eith:
Thy gorrie gumis and thy bludie snout;
The woll, the flesche, yit stikkis on thy teith;   1085
And that is evidence aneuch, but dout.'
The justice bad ga cheis ane assyis about,
And so thay did, and fand that he wes fals
Of murther, thift, and party tressoun als.

156

Thay band him fast, the justice bad belyif   1090
To gif the dome, and tak off all his clais.
The wolf, that new maid doctour, couth him schrif,
Syne furth him led and to the gallous gais,
And at the ledder fute his leif he tais.
The aip wes basare and bad him sone ascend,   1095
And hangit him, and thus he maid his end.

Moralitas

157

Richt as the mynour in his minorall
Fair gold with fyre may fra the leid weill wyn,

1076. lymmer *wretch*
1077. suthe *true* selie *simple*
1078. saif *grant*
1079. purpois *intention*
    plaid *played*
1080. causles *without provocation*
    effraid *afraid*
1081. duschit *dashed*
1082. leis *lie*
1083. be practik *by evidence*
    eith *easily*
1086. but *without*
1087. assyis *judical inquiry*
1088. fals *guilty*

1089. party tressoun *sedition;*
    offence against the state
1090. band *bound* bad *asked*
    belyif *at once*
1091. dome *judgement* clais *clothes*
1092. couth him schrif *gave him*
    confession
1093. gallous *gallows*
1094. ledder *ladder* leif *leave*
    tais *takes*
1095. aip *ape* basare *executioner*
1097. mynour *miner*
    minorall *work with metals*
1098. leid *lead* wyn *separate*

Richt so under ane fabill figurall
Sad sentence men may seik, and efter fyne,   1100
As daylie dois the doctouris of devyne,
That to our leving full weill can apply,
And paynt thair mater furth be poetry.

158

The lyoun is the warld be liklynace,
To quhome loutis baith empriour and king,   1105
And thinkis of this warld to get mincresce,
Thinkand daylie to get mair leving;
Sum for to reull, and sum to raxe and ring,
Sum gadderis geir, sum gold, sum uther gude;
To wyn this warld, sum wirkis as thay wer wod.   1110

159

The meir is men of contemplatioun,
Of pennance walkand in this wildernes,
As monkis and othir men of religioun
That presis God to pleis in everilk place,
Abstractit from this warldis wretchitnes,   1115
In wilfull povertee, fra pomp and pryde,
And fra this warld in mynd ar mortyfyde.

160

This wolf I likkin to sensualitie,
As quhen lyke brutall beistis we accord
Our mynd all to this warldis vanitie,   1120
Lyking to tak and loif him as our lord.
Fle fast thairfra, gif thow will richt remord,

1099. figurall *symbolic*
1100. sad *solemn*
    sentence *message* fyne *find*
1101. devyne *divinity*
1102. leving *way of life*
    apply *interpret*
1104. warld *world* be liklynace *in likeness*
1105. loutis *bows*
1107. leving *property*
1108. reull *rule* raxe *have power* ring *reign*
1109. gadderis *gather*
    geir *possessions* gude *goods*
1110. wod *mad*
1114. presis *endeavour* pleis *please*
1115. abstractit *removed*
1117. mortyfyde *dead*
1119. accord *give*
1121. lyking *desiring* loif *love*
1122. thairfra *from it* remord *feel remorse*

1117. 'And in their minds are dead to the things of this world'.

Than sall ressoun ryse, rax, and ring,
And for thy saull thair is na better thing.

161
Hir hufe I likkin to the thocht of deid: 1125
Will thow remember, man, that thow man de?
Thow may brek sensualiteis heid,
And fleschlie lust away fra the sall fle.
Fra thow begin thy mynd to mortifie,
Salomonis saying thow may persaif heirin: 1130
'Think on thy end; thow sall not glaidlie sin.'

162
This tod I likkin to temptationis,
Beirand to mynd mony thochtis vane
That daylie sagis men of religiounis,
Ay reddie for to trap thame in a trayne.   1135
Yit gif thay se sensualitie neir slane,
And suddand deith draw neir with panis sore,
Thay go abak, and temptis thame no moir.

163
O Mary myld, mediatour of mercy meik,
Sitt doun before thy sone celestiall,   1140
For us synnaris his celsitude beseik
Us to defend fra pane and perrellis all,
And help us up unto that hevinlie hall,
In gloir quhair we may se the face of God.
And thus endis the talking of the tod.   1145

THE SHEEP AND THE DOG
164
Esope ane taill puttis in memorie
How that ane doig, because that he wes pure,

1123. ressoun *reason*
1125. hir *her*   deid *death*
1126. man *must*
1128. sall *shall*
1129. fra *from the time*
1130. Salomonis *Solomon's*
      persaif *perceive*
1132. temptationis *temptation*
1134. sagis *beseiges*
1136. se *see*   neir *nearly*

1137. panis *pains*
1138. temptis *tempt*
1139. mediatour *mediator*   meik *meek*
1140. sone *son*
1141. celsitude *majesty*
      beseik *beseech*
1144. gloir *glory*
1146. Esope *Aesop*   taill *tale*
      puttis in memorie *records*
1147. doig *dog*   pure *poor*

Callit ane scheip to the consistorie,
Ane certane breid fra him for to recure.
Ane fraudfull wolf wes juge that tyme and bure   1150
Authoritie and jurisdictioun,
And on the scheip send furth ane strait summoun.

165

For by the use and cours and commoun style,
On this maner maid his citatioun:
'I, maister wolf, partles of fraud and gyle,   1155
Under the panis of hie suspensioun,
Of grit cursing, and interdictioun,
Schir Scheip, I charge the straitly to compeir,
And answer to ane doig befoir me heir.'

166

Schir Corbie Ravin wes maid apparitour,   1160
Quha pykit had full mony scheipis ee.
The charge hes tane, and on the letteris bure;
Summonit the scheip befoir the wolf, that he
'Peremptourlie within the dayis thre,
Compeir under the panis in this bill,   1165
To heir quhat Perrie Doig will say the till.'

167

This summondis maid befoir witnes anew,
The ravin, as to his office weill effeird,
Indorsat hes the write, and on he flew.

1148. scheip *sheep*
consistorie *ecclesiastical court*
1149. breid *loaf of bread*
recure *recover*
1150. fraudfull *dishonest* bure *bore*
1152. strait *immediate*
summoun *summons*
1153. by *in accordance with*
use *usual practice* cours *legal*
custom commoun style *standard form of legal documentation*
1154. citatioun *citation*
1155. partles of *having no part of*
gyle *guile*
1156. panis *pains* hie *total*
suspensioun *suspension*

1157. grit cursing *excommunication*
interdictioun *exclusion*
1158. schir *sir* compeir *appear*
1160. Corbie Ravin *Corbie, the raven* apparitour *summoner*
1161. pykit *pecked*
scheipis *sheep's* ee *eyes*
1162. tane *taken* bure *carried*
1164. peremptourlie *peremptory*
1165. panis *penalties*
1166. the till *to you*
1167. anew *many*
1168. weill effeird *was entirely proper*
1169. indorsat *endorsed*
write *summons*

The selie scheip durst lay na mouth on eird   1170
Till he befoir the awfull juge appeird.
The oure of cause quhilk that the juge usit than,
Quhen Hesperus to schaw his face began.

168
The foxe wes clerk and noter in the cause.
The gled, the graip up at the bar couth stand,   1175
As advocatis expert in to the lawis,
The doggis pley togidder tuke on hand,
Quhilk wer confidderit straitlie in ane band
Aganis the scheip to procure the sentence;
Thocht it wes fals, thay had na conscience.   1180

169
The clerk callit the scheip, and he wes thair.
The advocatis on this wyse couth propone:
'Ane certane breid, worth fyve schilling or mair,
Thow aw the doig, of quhilk the terme is gone.'
Of his awin heid, but advocate, allone,   1185
The scheip avysitlie gaif answer in the cace:
'Heir I'declyne the juge, the tyme, the place.

170
'This is my cause, in motive and effect:
The law sayis it is richt perrillous
Till enter pley befoir ane juge suspect,   1190

1170. selie *poor* durst *dared* eird *earth*
1171. awfull *stern*
1172. oure *time* cause *case* usit *customarily used*
1174. noter *notary*
1175. gled *kite* graip *vulture* couth stand *stood*
1176. advocatis *advocates; barristers*
1177. doggis pley *dog's suit*
1178. confidderit *united* straitlie *intimately* band *alliance*
1179. aganis *against* procure *win*

sentence *judgement*
1180. thocht *although*
1182. wyse *way* couth propone *stated the case*
1184. aw *owe* terme *time for* repayment
1185. of *following* heid *counsel* but *without*
1186. avysitlie *advisedly*
1187. declyne *reject*
1188. motive *reasoning* effect *intent*
1190. enter pley *enter a plea*

1170. 'The poor sheep didn't dare take the time to nibble the grass'.
1172–3. 'It was the judge's custom to call the case when the evening star appeared in the sky'.

And ye, schir Wolf, hes bene richt odious
To me, for with your tuskis ravenous
Hes slane full mony kinnismen of myne.
Thairfoir as juge suspect I yow declyne.

171

'And schortlie, of this court ye memberis all,   1195
Baith assessouris, clerk, and advocate,
To me and myne ar ennemies mortall
And ay hes bene, as mony scheipheird wate.
The place is fer, the tyme is feriate,
Quhairfoir na juge suld sit in consistory   1200
Sa lait at evin: I yow accuse for thy.'

172

Quhen that the juge in this wyse wes accusit,
He bad the parteis cheis with ane assent
Twa arbeteris, as in the law is usit,
For to declair and gif arbitriment   1205
Quhidder the scheip suld answer in jugement
Befoir the wolf; and so thay did, but weir,
Of quhome the namis efterwart ye sall heir.

173

The beir, the brok, the mater tuke on hand,
For to discyde gif this exceptioun   1210
Wes of na strenth, or lauchfully mycht stand;
And thairupon as jugis thay sat doun
And held ane lang quhyle disputatioun,

1192. tuskis *fangs*
1195. schortlie *in short*
1196. assessouris *advisers to the judge*
1198. scheipheird *shepherd* wate *knows*
1199. feriate *out of term*
1200. consistory *ecclesiastical court*
1201. at evin *in the evening* accuse *challenge* for thy *therefore*
1203. bad *told* cheis *choose* ane assent *agreement*

1204. twa *two* arbeteris *arbitrators* usit *customary*
1205. declair *judge* arbitriment *decision*
1206. in jugement *in a court of law*
1207. but weir *without doubt*
1209. beir *bear* brok *badger*
1210. discyde *decide* exceptioun *plea*
1211. na strenth *any merit* lauchfully *lawfully*

Seikand full mony decretalis of the law,
And glosis als, the veritie to knaw.   1215

174

Of civile mony volum thay revolve,
The codies and digestis new and ald,
Contra et pro, strait argumentis thay resolve,
Sum a doctryne and sum a nothir hald;
For prayer nor price, trow ye, thay wald fald?   1220
Bot held the glose and text of the decreis
As trew jugis, I schrew thame ay that leis.

175

Schortlie to mak ane end of this debait,
The arbiteris than summar and plane
The sentence gave, and proces fulminait: 1225
The scheip suld pas befoir the wolf agane
And end his pley. Than wes he nathing fane,
For fra thair sentence couth he not appeill.
On clerkis I do it, gif this sentence wes leill.

176

The scheip agane befoir the wolf derenyeit,   1230
But advocate, abasitlie couth stand.
Up rais the doig and on the scheip thus plenyeit:
'Ane soume I payit have befoir the hand
For certane breid.' Thairto ane borrow he fand,

1214. seikand *seeking*
decretalis *papal decrees*
1215. glosis *explanations*
veritie *truth*
1216. civile *Roman law*
revolve *consult*
1217. codies *legal codes*
digestis *digests*
1218. *contra et pro against and for*
strait *rigorous* resolve *analyse*
1219. a *one*
1220. prayer *petition* price *bribe*
trow *believe* fald *turn from truth*
1222. schrew *curse* leis *lie*
1224. summar *summarily*

plane *clearly*
1225. proces fulminait *process of judgement*
1227. pley *plea* nathing fane *not at all happy*
1229. on *to* do *refer* leill *legal*
1230. derenyeit *appeared*
1231. but *without*
abasitlie *dejectedly*
1232. on *against*
plenyeit *complained*
1233. soume *sum of money* befoir the hand *in advance*
1234. borrow *pledge*
fand *produced*

1229. 'I refer the matter to the clerks to consider whether or not this judgement was legal'.

That wrangouslie the scheip did hald the breid;   1235
Quhilk he denyit, and thair began the pleid.

177
And quhen the scheip this stryif had contestait,
The justice in the cause furth can proceid.
Lowrence the actis and the proces wrait,
And thus the pley unto the end thay speid.   1240
This cursit court, corruptit all for meid,
Aganis faith, gude law, and eik conscience,
For this fals doig pronuncit the sentence.

178
And it till put to executioun,
The wolf chargit the scheip, without delay,   1245
Under the panis of interdictioun,
The soume of silver or the breid to pay.
Of this sentence, allace, quhat sall I say,
Quhilk dampnit hes the selie innocent,
And justifyit the wrangous jugement?   1250

179
The scheip, dreidand mair persecutioun,
Obeyit to the sentence, and couth tak
His way unto ane merchand of the toun,
And sauld the woll that he bure on his bak,
Syne bocht the breid, and to the doig couth mak   1255
Reddie payment, as it commandit was;
Naikit and bair syne to the feild couth pas.

1235. wrangouslie *wrongfully*
1236. pleid *debate*
1237. stryif *dispute*
  contestait *contested*
1239. actis *actions*
  proces *proceedings*   wrait *wrote down*
1240. pley *suit*
1241. meid *money*
1243. for *in favour of*
  pronuncit *pronounced*
1244. till *to*   to execution *into effect*

1245. chargit *ordered*
1246. panis *threat*
  interdictioun *exclusion*
1249. dampnit *condemned*
1250. justifyit *upheld*
1253. merchand *merchant*
1254. sauld *sold*   woll *wool*
  bure *bore*
1255. bocht *bought*
1256. reddie *prompt*

Moralitas

180

This selie scheip may present the figure
Of pure commounis, that daylie ar opprest
Be tirrane men, quhilkis settis all thair cure   1260
Be fals meinis to mak ane wrang conquest,
In hope this present lyfe suld ever lest.
Bot all begylit, thay will in schort tyme end,
And efter deith to lestand panis wend.

181

This wolf I likkin to ane schiref stout   1265
Quhilk byis ane forfalt at the kingis hand,
And hes with him ane cursit assyis about,
And dytis all the pure men up on land;
Fra the crownar haif laid on him his wand—
Thocht he wer trew as ever wes Sanct Johne—   1270
Slane sall he be, or with the juge compone.

182

This ravin I likkin to ane fals crownair,
Quhilk hes ane porteous of the inditement,
And passis furth befoir the justice air,
All misdoaris to bring to jugement.   1275
Bot luke gif he be of ane trew intent,
To scraip out Johne, and wryte in Will or Wat,
And swa ane bud at boith the parteis skat.

1259. pure *poor*
  commounis *common people*
1260. tirrane *villainous*
  settis *devote*   cure *attention*
1261. meinis *means* conquest *gain*
1262. ever last *last forever*
1263. begylit *is false*
1264. lestand *everlasting*   wend *go*
1265. schiref stout *powerful sheriff*
1266. byis *buys*   forfalt *forfeit*
1267. assyis *assize; travelling court*
1268. dytis *charges*

1269. fra *as soon as*
  crownar *coroner*
1270. trew *honest*   Sanct Johne *St John*
1271. or *unless* compone *in financial agreement*
1273. porteous *list*
1274. justice air *circuit court*
1276. luke gif *decide whether*
1277. scraip out *erase*
1278. bud *bribe*   skat *exacts*

1260–1. 'By villainous men who spend all their time trying to make unlawful gains by false means'.

183
Of this fals tod, of quhilk I spak befoir,
And of this gled, quhat thay micht signify,   1280
Of thair nature, as now I speik no moir.
Bot of this scheip and of his cairfull cry
I sall reheirs, for as I passit by
Quhair that he lay, on cais I lukit doun,
And hard him mak sair lamentatioun.   1285

184
'Allace,' quod he, 'this cursit consistorie
In middis of the winter now is maid,
Quhen Boreas with blastis bitterlie
And hard froistes thir flouris doun can faid.
On bankis bair now may I mak na baid.'   1290
And with that word in to ane coif he crap,
Fra hair wedder and froistis him to hap.

185
Quaikand for cauld, sair murnand ay amang,
Kest up his ee unto the hevinnis hicht,
And said, 'Lord God, quhy sleipis thow sa lang?   1295
Walk, and discerne my cause groundit on richt.
Se how I am be fraud, maistrie, and slicht
Peillit full bair, and so is mony one
Now in this warld richt wonder wo begone.

186
'Se how this cursit syn of covetice   1300
Exylit hes baith lufe, lawtie, and law.
Now few or nane will execute justice,
In falt of quhome, the pure man is overthraw.

1280. gled *kite*
1282. cairfull *sorrowfull*
1283. reheirs *relate*
1284. on cais *by chance* lukit *looked*
1286. consistorie *ecclesiastical court*
1288. Boreas *the north wind*
1289. flouris *flowers* doun can
faid *cause to wither*
1290. baid *abode*
1291. coif *cave* crap *crept*
1292. hair wedder *freezing
weather* hap *cover up*

1293. murnand *lamenting* ay
amang *continually*
1294. hicht *height*
1296. walk *awake* discerne *judge*
groundit *based*
1297. maistrie *force* slicht *deceit*
1298. peillit *stripped*
1300. covetice *greed*
1301. exylit *driven out*
lawtie *loyalty*
1303. in falt of quhome *in the absence
of which* overthraw *destroyed*

The veritie, suppois the jugis knaw,
Thay ar so blindit with affectioun,   1305
But dreid, for meid, thay thoill the richt go doun.

187
'Seis thow not, lord, this warld overturnit is,
As quha wald change gude gold in leid or tyn?
The pure is peillit, the lord may do na mis,
And simonie is haldin for na syn.   1310
Now is he blyith with okker maist may wyn.
Gentrice is slane, and pietie is ago.
Allace, gude lord, quhy tholis thow it so?

188
'Thow tholis this evin for our grit offence;
Thow sendis us troubill and plaigis soir,   1315
As hunger, derth, grit weir, or pestilence
Bot few amendis now thair lyfe thairfoir.
We pure pepill as now may do no moir
Bot pray to the: sen that we ar opprest
In to this eirth, grant us in hevin gude rest.'   1320

1304. veritie *truth* suppois *even if*
1305. affectioun *bias*
1306. meid *wealth* thoill *allow*
1307. seis *see* overturnit *turned upside down*
1308. as quha wald *as if someone were to* leid *lead* tyn *tin*
1309. lord *wealthy man* na mis *nothing wrong*
1310. simonie *simony* haldin *considered*
1311. blyith *happy* okker *money-lending*
1312. gentrice *kindness* pietie *pity* ago *gone*
1313. tholis *allow*
1314. evin *in return*
1315. plaigis *plagues*
1316. derth *deprivation* weir *war*
1317. amendis *changes* thairfoir *because of it*
1319. sen that *since*
1320. in to *on*

1304–6. 'Even if the judges know the truth, they are so blinded by their bias that without fear they accept bribes and allow justice to be defeated'.
1311. 'Now the man is happy who can make the most from exorbitant money-lending'.

THE LION AND THE MOUSE
Prologue

189

In middis of June, that joly sweit seasoun,
Quhen that fair Phebus with his bemis bricht
Had dryit up the dew fra daill and doun,
And all the land maid with his lemis licht,
In ane mornyng, betwix midday and nicht,   1325
I rais and put all sleuth and sleip asyde,
And to ane wod I went allone but gyde.

190

Sweit wes the smell of flouris quhyte and reid,
The noyes of birdis richt delitious,
The bewis braid blomit abone my heid,   1330
The ground growand with gers gratious.
Of all plesance that place wes plenteous,
With sweit odouris and birdis harmony.
The morning myld – my mirth wes mair forthy.

191

The rosis reid arrayit on rone and ryce,   1335
The prymeros and the purpour viola.
To heir it wes ane poynt of paradice,
Sic mirth the mavis and the merle couth ma.
The blossummis blythe brak upon bank and bra.

1321. middis *middle* joly *joyful*
1322. quhen *when*
   Phebus *Phoebus; the sun*
   bemis *beams*
1323. dryit *dried* daill *dale*
   doun *hillside*
1324. lemis *rays*
1326. rais *arose* sleuth *sloth*
1327. wod *wood* but gyde *without a guide*
1328. flouris *flowers*
   quhyte *white* reid *red*
1329. noyes *noise* richt *very*
   delitious *delightful*
1330. bewis *boughs* braid *broad*
   blomit *bloomed* abone *above*

1331. growand *growing*
   gers *plants* gratious *beautiful*
1332. plesance *pleasure*
   plenteous *abundant*
1334. mirth *happiness*
   mair *greater* forthy *therefore*
1335. rosis *roses* arrayit *scattered*
   rone *hedgerows* ryce *branches*
1336. prymeros *primrose*
   purpour *purple* viola *violet*
1337. poynt *part*
1338. sic *such* mavis *thrush*
   merle *blackbird* couth ma *made*
1339. blythe *blissful* brak
   upon *burst forth* bra *brae; hillside*

1324. 'And made all the land light with his rays'.
1325. 'One morning, between night and noon'.

The smell of herbis and the fowlis cry,   1340
Contending quha suld have the victory.

192
Me to conserve than fra the sonis heit,
Under the schaddow of ane hawthorne grene
I lenit doun amang the flouris sweit,
Syne maid a cors and closit baith my ene.   1345
On sleip I fell amang thir bewis bene,
And in my dreme me thocht come throw the schaw
The fairest man that ever befoir I saw.

193
His gowne wes of ane claith als quhyte as milk,
His chymmeris wes of chambelate purpour broun,   1350
His hude of scarlet, bordowrit weill with silk,
On hekillit wyis untill his girdill doun,
His bonat round and of the auld fassoun,
His beird wes quhyte, his ene wes grit and gray,
With lokker hair quhilk over his schulderis lay.   1355

194
Ane roll of paper in his hand he bair,
Ane swannis pen stikand under his eir,
Ane inkhorne with ane prettie gilt pennair,
Ane bag of silk, all at his belt can beir:
Thus wes he gudelie grathit in his geir,   1360

1340. herbis *plants*
1341. contending *competing*
    quha *who*
1342. conserve *protect* sonis *sun's*
1344. lenit doun *lay down*
1345. syne *then* maid a cors *made
    the sign of the cross* ene *eyes*
1346. on sleip *asleep*
    bewis *boughs* bene *pleasant*
1347. schaw *wood*
1349. claith *cloth*
1350. chymmeris *robe*
    chambelate *fine wool* purpour
    broun *dark purple*

1351. hude *hood*
    bordowrit *trimmed*
1352. on hekillit wyis *like a cock's
    hackle* girdill *belt*
1353. bonat *hat* fassoun *fashion*
1354. beird *beard* grit *large*
1355. lokker *curly*
1356. roll *scroll*
1357. swannis pen *swan's feather*
    stikand *sticking* under *behind*
1358. gilt *gilded* pennair *pen-case*
1360. gudelie *well*
    grathit *equipped* geir *attire*

1340–1. 'The scent of the plants and the song of the birds, competing as
to who should be victorious'.

Of stature large and with ane feirfull face.
Evin quhair I lay he come ane sturdie pace,

195
And said, 'God speid, my sone', and I wes fane
Of that couth word and of his cumpany.
With reverence I salusit him agane: 1365
'Welcome, father', and he sat doun me by.
'Displeis yow not, my gude maister, thocht I
Demand your birth, your facultye and name,
Quhy ye come heir or quhair ye dwell at hame.'

196
'My sone,' said he, 'I am of gentill blude. 1370
My native land is Rome, withoutin nay,
And in that towne first to the sculis I yude,
In civile law studyit full mony ane day,
And now my winning is in hevin for ay.
Esope I hecht; my writing and my werk 1375
Is couth and kend to mony cunning clerk.'

197
'O maister Esope, poet lawriate,
God wait, ye ar full deir welcum to me!
Ar ye not he that all thir fabillis wrate,
Quhilk in effect, suppois thay fenyeit be, 1380
Ar full of prudence and moralitie?'
'Fair sone,' said he, 'I am the samin man.'
God wait gif that my hert wes merie than.

1361. feirfull *inspiring respect*
1362. evin *right up to* ane sturdie pace *with a strong step*
1363. God speid *greetings* sone *son* fane *glad*
1364. couth *kind*
1365. salusit *greeted* agane *in return*
1367. displeis yow not *do not be displeased* thocht *if*
1368. demand *ask* birth *birthplace* facultye *profession*
1369. quhy *why*
1370. gentill *noble*
1371. withoutin nay *without doubt*
1372. sculis *university* yude *went*
1374. winning *dwelling* for ay *forever*
1375. Esope *Aesop* I hecht *I am called*
1376. couth *familar* kend *known* cunning *learned*
1377. lawriate *laureate*
1378. wait *knows* full deir *very much*
1379. thir *those*
1380. in effect *in fact* suppois *even if* fenyeit *fictitious*
1381. prudence *wisdom*
1382. samin *same*
1383. wait *knows* than *then*

198

I said, 'Esope, my maister venerabill,
I yow beseik hartlie for cheritie   1385
Ye wald dedene to tell ane prettie fabill
Concludand with ane gude moralitie'
Schaikand his heid he said, 'My sone, lat be,
For quhat is it worth to tell ane fenyeit taill
Quhen haly preiching may nathing availl?   1390

199

'Now in this warld, me think, richt few or nane
To Goddis word that hes devotioun.
The eir is deif, the hart is hard as stane;
Now oppin sin without correctioun,
The hart inclynand to the eirth ay doun.   1395
Sa roustit is the warld with canker blak
That now my taillis may lytill succour mak.'

200

'Yit gentill schir,' said I, 'for my requeist,
Not to displeis your fatherheid, I pray,
Under the figure of ane brutall beist,   1400
Ane morall fabill ye wald denye to say.
Quha wait nor I may leir and beir away

1385. beseik *beseech*
    hartlie *sincerely*
1386. dedene *consent*
    prettie *skilfull*
1388. schaikand *shaking* lat
    be *cease your requests*
1390. haly preiching *holy*
    preaching availl *accomplish*
1391. richt few *there are very few*
1392. devotioun *respect*
1393. deif *deaf* hart *heart*
    stane *stone*

1394. oppin *open*
1395. inclynand *inclining*
1396. roustit *corrupted* canker *sin*
1397. taillis *tales* succour
    mak *help*
1398. yit *yet* schir *sir*
1399. fatherheid *honour*
1400. figure *appearance* brutall
    beist *brute beast*
1401. denye *consent*
1402. quha wait nor *who knows*
    but leir *learn*

1391–2. 'It seems to me that there are now very few or none in this
    world who have respect for God's word'.
1394–5. 'Now people sin openly, without correction, with the heart
    always inclining downwards towards earthly things'.
1402–3. 'Who knows, I might learn and take away something from it
    which might afterwards be of use.

Sum thing thairby heirefter may availl?'
'I grant,' quod he, and thus begouth ane taill:

The Fable
201
Ane lyoun at his pray verray foirrun,   1405
To recreat his limmis and to rest,
Beikand his breist and belly at the sun,
Under ane tre lay in the fair forest.
Swa come ane trip of myis out of thair nest,
Richt tait and trig, all dansand in ane gyis,   1410
And over the lyoun lansit twyis or thryis.

202
He lay so still, the myis wes not effeird,
Bot to and fro out over him tuke thair trace,
Sum tirlit at the campis of his beird,
Sum spairit not to claw him on the face.   1415
Merie and glaid thus dansit thay ane space,
Till at last the nobill lyoun woke,
And with his pow the maister mous he tuke.

203
Scho gave ane cry, and all the laif, agast,
Their dansing left and hid thame sone alquhair. 1420
Scho that wes tane cryit and weipit fast,
And said 'Allace' oftymes that scho come thair:
'Now am I tane ane wofull presonair,

1403. thairby *from it* availl *be of use*
1404. begouth *began*
1405. lyoun *lion* at his pray *from hunting his prey* verray *rightful* foirrun *exhausted*
1406. recreat *refresh* limmis *limbs*
1407. beikand *warming*
1409. trip *troop* myis *mice*
1410. tait *lively* trig *nimble* dansand *dancing* gyis *jig*

1411. lansit *hopped*
1412. effeird *frightened*
1413. tuke *took* trace *way*
1414. tirlit *tugged* campis *whiskers*
1415. spairit not *did not refrain*
1416. ane space *a while*
1418. pow *paw* maister *chief*
1419. laif *rest* agast *terrified*
1420. sone *immediately* alquhair *elsewhere*
1421. tane *captured*

1405. 'A lion, exhausted from hunting his rightful prey'.

And for my gilt traistis incontinent
Of lyfe and deith to thoill the jugement.'   1425

204

Than spak the lyoun to that cairfull mous:
'Thow cative wretche and vile unworthie thing,
Over malapart and eik presumpteous
Thow wes to mak out over me thy tripping.
Knew thow not weill I wes baith lord and king   1430
Of beistis all?' 'Yes,' quod the mous, 'I knaw,
Bot I misknew because ye lay so law.

205

'Lord, I beseik thy kingly royaltie,
Heir quhat I say, and tak in patience.
Considder first my simple povertie   1435
And syne thy mychtie hie magnyfycence;
Se als how thingis done of neglygence,
Nouther of malice nor of presumptioun,
The rather suld have grace and remissioun.

206

'We wer repleit and had grit aboundance   1440
Of alkin thingis, sic as to us effeird;
The sweit sesoun provokit us to dance
And mak sic mirth as nature to us leird.
Ye lay so still and law upon the eird
That, be my sawll, we weind ye had bene deid –   1445
Elles wald we not have dancit over your heid.'

1424. gilt *guilt* traistis *expect*
    incontinent *immediately*
1425. thoill *undergo*
1426. cairfull *sorrowful*
1427. cative *miserable*
1428. over *overly*
    malapart *impertinent* eik *also*
1429. tripping *dancing*
1432. misknew *made a mistake*
    law *low*
1434. heir *hear*

1436. syne *then*
1438. nouther *neither*
1439. rather *sooner*
    remissioun *pardon*
1440. repleit *full up*
1441. alkin *all kinds of* sic *such*
    effeird *was fitting*
1443. leird *taught*
1445. sawll *soul* weind *thought*
1446. elles *otherwise*

1424–5. 'And on account of my guilt I expect immediately to undergo trial for my life'.
1428–9. 'You were overly impertinent and also presumptuous to perform your dancing over my body'.

207
'Thy fals excuse,' the lyoun said agane,
'Sall not availl ane myte, I underta.
I put the cace I had bene deid or slane,
And syne my skyn bene stoppit ful of stra;   1450
Thocht thow had found my figure lyand swa,
Because it bare the prent of my persoun
Thow suld for feir on kneis have fallin doun.

208
'For thy trespas thow can mak na defence,
My nobill persoun thus to vilipend;   1455
Of thy feiris nor thy awin negligence
For to excuse thow can na cause pretend;
Thairfoir thow suffer sall ane schamefull end
And deith, sic as to tressoun is decreit –
Onto the gallous harlit be the feit.'   1460

209
'Na! Mercie, lord, at thy gentrice I ase!
As thow art king of beistis coronate,
Sober thy wraith and let it overpas
And mak thy mynd to mercy inclynate;

1448. availl *help* myte *bit* I
    underta *I promise you*
1449. I put the cace *let us suppose*
1450. stoppit *stuffed* stra *straw*
1451. thocht *even if* figure *likeness*
1452. bare *bore* prent *appearance*
1454. trespas *wrongdoing*
1455. vilipend *dishonour*
1456. feiris *companions* awin *own*
1457. pretend *produce*

1459. tressoun *treason*
    decreit *decreed*
1460. gallous *gallows*
    harlit *dragged* be *by*
1461. at *to* gentrice *generosity*
    ase *appeal*
1462. coronate *crowned*
1463. sober *moderate*
    wraith *anger* overpas *pass away*
1464. inclynate *inclined*

1449–52. 'Let us suppose that I was in fact dead or slain, and then my
    skin had been stuffed full of straw; even if you had found my likeness
    lying like this, you should have fallen down on your knees in fear,
    because it bore the appearance of my person'.
1456–7. 'You can produce no reason which will excuse your companions
    or your own negligence'.
1459–60. 'And death, which is the punishment decreed for treason: you
    shall be dragged by the feet onto the gallows'.
1462. 'As you are crowned the king of beasts'.
1472–4. 'When strict adherence to the law sits in the judgement seat who

I grant offence is done to thyne estate   1465
Quhairfoir I worthie am to suffer deid,
Bot gif thy kinglie mercie reik remeid.

210
'In everie juge mercie and reuth suld be
As assessouris and collaterall;
Without mercie justice is crueltie,   1470
As said is in the lawis spirituall.
Quhen rigour sittis in the tribunall
The equitie of law quha may sustene?
Richt few or nane but mercie gang betwene.

211
'Alswa ye knaw the honour triumphall   1475
Of all victour upon the strenth dependis
Of his conqueist, quhilk manlie in battell
Throw jeopardie of weir lang defendis.
Quhat pryce or loving, quhen the battell endis,
Is said of him that overcummis ane man   1480
Him to defend quhilk nouther may nor can?

212
'Ane thowsand myis to kill and eik devoir
Is lytill manheid to ane strang lyoun;

1465. grant *admit* is done *has*
  been done estate *high rank*
1466. I worthie am *I deserve*
  deid *death*
1467. bot gif *unless* reik
  remeid *grant pardon*
1468. juge *judge* reuth *pity*
1469. assessouris *advisers*
  collaterall *colleagues*
1471. lawis spirituall *canon law*
1472. rigour *strictness*
  tribunall *seat of judgement*
1473. equitie of law *spirit of*

justice sustene *endure*
1474. but *unless* gang
  betwene *intercedes*
1476. all *every* victour *victor*
1477. manlie *bravely*
1478. jeopardie of weir *daring feats*
  of arms defendis *resists*
1479. pryce *honourable words*
  loving *praise*
1480. ane *one*
1482. myis *mice*
1483. manheid *sign of courage*
  strang *strong*

can endure the spirit of justice? Very few or none unless mercy
intercedes'.
1475–8. 'Also, you know that the triumphant honour of every victor
  depends upon the strength of the enemy he conquers, who must bravely
  defend himself in battle again and again by daring feats of arms'.
1481. 'Who is neither able to nor capable of defending himself'.

Full lytill worschip have ye wyn thairfoir,
To qwhais strenth is na comparisoun.   1485
It will degraid sum part of your renoun
To sla ane mous quhilk may mak na defence,
Bot askand mercie at your excellence.

213
'Also it semis not your celsitude,
Quhilk usis daylie meittis delitious,   1490
To fyle your teith or lippis with my blude,
Quhilk to your stomok is contagious.
Unhailsum meit is of ane sarie mous,
And that namelie untill ane strang lyoun,
Wont till be fed with gentill vennesoun.   1495

214
'My lyfe is lytill worth, my deith is les,
Yit and I leif, I may peradventure
Supple your hienes beand in distres:
For oft is sene ane man of small stature
Reskewit hes ane lord of hie honour,   1500
Keipit that wes, in poynt to be overthrawin
Throw misfortoun: sic cace may be your awin.'

1484. worschip *honour* wyn *won*
1486. degraid *diminish*
1487. sla *slay*
1488. bot *except for* at *from*
1489. it semis not *it does not befit*
  celsitude *majesty*
1490. usis *is accustomed to*
  meittis *food*
1491. fyle *defile* blude *blood*
1492. stomok *stomach*
  contagious *harmful*
1493. unhailsum *unhealthy*
  sarie *wretched*
1494. namelie untill *especially to*

strang *strong*
1495. wont till *accustomed to*
  gentill *noble* vennesoun *venison*
1496. les *less*
1497. and I leif *if I live*
  peradventure *perhaps*
1498. supple *assist*
  hienes *highness* beand *being*
1499. sene *seen* small stature *low
  rank*
1500. reskewit *rescued*
1501. keipit *captured* in
  poynt *about*
1502. awin *own*

1493. 'The meat of a wretched mouse is unhealthy'.
1496. 'My life is worth little, my death even less'.
1501. 'Who was captured, and about to be brought down'.

215

Quhen this wes said, the lyoun his language
Paissit, and thocht according to ressoun,
And gart mercie his cruell ire asswage,　　　　　1505
And to the mous grantit remissioun;
Oppinnit his pow, and scho on kneis fell doun,
And baith hir handis unto the hevin upheild,
Cryand, 'Almichty God mot yow foryeild!'

216

Quhen scho wes gone the lyoun held to hunt,　　　1510
For he had nocht, bot levit on his pray,
And slew baith tayme and wyld, as he wes wont,
And in the cuntrie maid ane grit deray;
Till at the last the pepill fand the way
This cruell lyoun how that thay mycht tak:　　　1515
Of hempyn cordis strang nettis couth thay mak,

217

And in ane rod, quhair he wes wont to ryn,
With raipis rude fra tre to tre it band;
Syne kest ane range on raw the wod within,
With hornis blast and kennettis fast calland.　　1520
The lyoun fled, and throw the ron rynnand,
Fell in the net and hankit fute and heid;
For all his strenth he couth mak na remeid,

1503. paissit *moderated*
1504. gart . . . asswage *calmed*
　　ire *anger*
1506. remissioun *pardon*
1507. pow *paw*
1508. upheild *raised*
1509. mot *may* foryeild *reward*
1510. held *proceeded*
1511. nocht *nothing* levit *lived*
　　pray *hunting*
1512. tayme *tame*
　　wont *accustomed*
1513. cuntrie *country*
　　deray *disturbance*

1514. pepill *people* fand *found*
1515. tak *capture*
1516. hempyn cordis *hemp ropes*
1517. rod *path* ryn *run*
1518. raipis *ropes* rude *strong*
　　band *bound*
1519. kest *arranged* range on
　　raw *line of hunters*
1520. kennettis *hunting dogs*
1521. ron *undergrowth*
　　rynnand *running*
1522. hankit *entangled*
1523. couth mak na remeid *could
　　not help himself*

1505. 'And mercy calmed his cruel anger'.

218

Welterand about with hiddeous rummissing.
Quhyle to, quhyle fra, quhill he mycht succour
   get.   1525
Bot all in vane – it vailyeit him nathing –
The mair he flang the faster wes the net.
The raipis rude wes sa about him plet
On everilk syde that succour saw he nane;
Bot styll lyand, thus murnand maid his mane.   1530

219

'O lamit lyoun, liggand heir sa law,
Quhair is the mycht of thy magnyfycence,
Of quhome all brutall beist in eird stude aw,
And dred to luke upon thy excellence?
But hoip or help, but succour or defence,   1535
In bandis strang heir man I ly, allace,
Till I be slane; I se nane uther grace.

220

'Thair is na wy that will my harmis wreik,
Nor creature do confort to my croun.
Quha sall me bute? Quha sall my bandis breik?   1540
Quha sall me put fra pane of this presoun?'
Be he had maid this lamentatioun,
Throw aventure, the lytill mous come neir,
And of the lyoun hard the pietuous beir.

221

And suddanlic it come intill hir mynd   1545
That it suld be the lyoun did hir grace,

1524. welterand *thrashing*
    rummissing *roaring*
1525. quhyle *sometimes*
    succour *help*
1526. vailyeit *availed; helped*
1527. flang *flung about*
    faster *tighter*
1528. plet *entwined*
1530. styll lyand *lying still*
    murnand *mourning* mane *lament*
1531. lamit *crippled*
    liggand *lying* law *low*
1532. mycht *power*
1533. stude aw *stood in awe*

1534. dred *feared*
1535. but *without* hoip *hope*
1536. man *must* allace *allas*
1537. grace *outcome*
1538. wy *creature* wreik *avenge*
1539. confort *comfort*
1540. bute *help* breik *break*
1541. put *rescue*
1542. be *when*
1543. throw aventure *by chance*
1544. hard *heard* beir *lament*
1545. intill *into*
1546. did hir grace *showed her
    mercy*

And said: 'Now wer I fals and richt unkynd
Bot gif I quit sum part of thy gentrace
Thow did to me.' And on this way scho gais
To hir fellowis and on thame fast can cry: 1550
'Cum help! Cum help!' And thay come all in hy.

222

'Lo,' quod the mous, 'this is the samin lyoun
That grantit grace to me quhen I wes tane,
And now is fast heir bundin in presoun,
Brekand his hart with sair murning and mane.   1555
Bot we him help, of souccour wait he nane;
Cum help to quyte ane gude turne for ane uther.
Go, lous him sone!' And thay said, 'Ye, gude brother!'

223

Thay tuke na knyfe, thair teith wes scharpe anewch;
To se that sicht forsuith it wes grit wounder,   1560
How that thay ran amang the rapis tewch,
Befoir, behind, sum yeid abone, sum under,
And schuir the raipis of the net in schunder;
Syne bad him ryse, and he start up anone
And thankit thame, syne on his way is gone.   1565

224

Now is the lyoun fre of all danger,
Lows and delyverit to his libertie
Be lytill beistis of ane small power,
As ye have hard, because he had pietie.
Quod I, 'Maister, is thair ane moralitie   1570
In this fabill?' 'Yea, sone,' he said, 'richt gude.'
'I pray yow, schir,' quod I, 'ye wald conclude.'

1548. bot gif *unless*   quit *repay*
  gentrace *kindness*
1549. gais *goes*
1550. fellowis *companions*
  fast *quickly*
1551. in hy *in haste*
1553. tane *captured*
1554. bundin *tied up*
1555. mane *lamentation*
1556. bot *unless*   wait *knows*
1558. lous *loosen*   sone *at once*
1559. anewch *enough*

1560. forsuith *indeed*
1561. rapis tewch *strong ropes*
1562. yeid *went*   abone *above*
1563. schuir *cut*   in schunder *in
  pieces*
1564. bad *asked*   start *leapt*
1567. lows *free*
1569. hard *heard*   pietie *pity*
1570. quod *said*   moralitie *moral*
1572. conclude *draw a moral
  conclusion*

Moralitas

225

As I suppois, this mychtie gay lyoun
May signifie ane prince or empriour,
Ane potestate or yit ane king with croun –   1575
Quhilk suld be walkrife gyde and governour
Of his pepill – that takis na labour
To reule and steir the land and justice keip,
Bot lyis still in lustis, sleuth, and sleip.

226

The fair forest with levis, lowne and le,   1580
With foulis sang and flouris ferlie sweit,
Is bot the warld and his prosperitie,
As fals plesance myngit with cair repleit.
Richt as the rois with froist and wynter weit
Faidis, swa dois the warld, and thame desavis   1585
Quhilk in thair lustis maist confidence havis.

227

Thir lytill myis ar bot the commountie,
Wantoun, unwyse, without correctioun:
Thair lordis and princis quhen that thay se
Of justice mak nane executioun,   1590
Thay dreid nathing to mak rebellioun

1573. suppois *interpret it*
  gay *handsome*
1575. potestate *potentate; ruler*
1576. walkrife *vigilant*
1577. labour *care*
1578. reule *rule* steir *guide*
1579. lustis *pleasure* sleuth *sloth*
1580. levis *leaves*
  lowne *unruffled* le *sheltered*
1581. foulis sang *birds' song*
  flouris *flowers* ferlie *wondrously*
1582. bot *only* warld *world*
1583. plesance *pleasure*
  myngit *mingled* cair *sorrow*

repleit *abundant*
1584. richt *just* rois *rose*
  weit *rain*
1585. faidis *fades* swa *so*
  desavis *deceives*
1586. confidence *trust* havis *have*
1587. thir *these*
  commountie *common people*
1588. wantoun *wilful*
  unwyse *foolish*
  correctioun *discipline*
1591. dreid *fear* nathing *not at
  all* mak rebellioun *rebel*

1584–6. 'Just as the rose fades on account of frost and winter rain, so
  does the world, and deceives those who place most trust in earthly
  pleasures'.
1589–90. 'When they see their lords and princes fail to execute justice'.

And disobey, forquhy thay stand nane aw,
That garris thame thair soveranis misknaw.

228

Be this fabill ye lordis of prudence
May considder the vertew of pietie,   1595
And to remit sumtyme ane grit offence,
And mitigate with mercy crueltie.
Oftymis is sene ane man of small degre
Hes quit ane kinbute, baith of gude and ill,
As lord hes done rigour or grace him till.   1600

229

Quha wait how sone ane lord of grit renoun,
Rolland in wardlie lust and vane plesance,
May be overthrawin, destroyit and put doun
Throw fals fortoun, quhilk of all variance
Is haill maistres, and leidar of the dance   1605
Till injust men, and blindis thame so soir
That thay na perrell can provyde befoir?

230

Thir rurall men, that stentit hes the net
In quhilk the lyoun suddandlie wes tane,
Waittit alway amendis for to get,   1610
For hurt men wrytis in the marbill stane.

1592. forquhy *because*   stand nane
    aw *feel no respect*
1593. soveranis *sovereigns*
    misknaw *fail to know*
1594. be *by*   prudence *wisdom*
1595. pietie *pity*
1596. remit *pardon*
1597. mitigate *soften*
1598. small degre *low rank*
1599. quit *paid back*   kinbute *debt*
1601. quha *who*   wait *knows*
1602. rolland *wallowing*
    wardlie *worldly*

1604. fortoun *fortune*
    variance *changeableness*
1605. haill *completely*
    maistres *mistress*   leidar *leader*
1606. injust *sinful*   blindis *blinds*
    soir *grievously*
1607. perrell *danger*
    provyde *foresee*
1608. rurall *country*
    stentit *stretched out*
1610. waittit *waited*
    amendis *compensation*
1611. marbill *marble*

1597. 'And soften cruelty with mercy'.
1598–1600. 'It is often seen that a man of low rank has paid back a debt,
    either for good or ill, depending on whether the lord has been severe
    or merciful towards him'.
1611. 'For men set their injuries in stone' i.e. they never forget the
    wrong done to them.

Mair till expound as now I lett allane,
Bot king and lord may weill wit quhat I mene:
Figure heirof oftymis hes bene sene.

231

Quhen this wes said, quod Esope: 'My fair child,   1615
Perswaid the kirkmen ythandly to pray
That tressoun of this cuntrie be exyld,
And justice regne, and lordis keip thair fay
Unto thair soverane king baith nycht and day.'
And with that word he vanist and I woke;   1620
Syne throw the schaw my journey hamewart tuke.

THE PREACHING OF THE SWALLOW

232

The hie prudence and wirking mervelous,
The profound wit of God omnipotent,
Is sa perfyte and sa ingenious,
Excelland far all mannis jugement,   1625
For quhy to him all thing is ay present
Rycht as it is or ony tyme sall be,
Befoir the sicht of his divinitie.

233

Thairfoir our saull with sensualitie
So fetterit is in presoun corporall   1630

1612. expound *explain* as now *for now*
1613. wit *know*
1614. figure *illustration* heirof *of this*
1616. perswaid *persuade* kirkmen *churchmen* ythandly *constantly*
1617. tressoun *treason* of *from* exyld *driven out*
1618. fay *faith*
1620. vanist *vanished*
1621. syne *then* schaw *wood* hamewart *homewards*

1622. hie *great* prudence *wisdom* wirking *works*
1623. wit *wisdom*
1624. sa *so* perfyte *perfect* ingenious *skilful*
1625. excelland *excelling* far *by far*
1626. for quhy *because* ay *always*
1627. rycht *just*
1628. sicht *sight*
1629. saull *soul* with *by*
1630. fetterit *fettered* presoun *prison* corporall *corporeal*

1629–32. 'Therefore indulgence in sensual pleasure shackles our soul to the body's prison so that we cannot clearly understand or see God as he is, nor anything belonging to heaven'.

We may not cleirlie understand nor se
God as he is, nor thingis celestiall.
Our mirk and deidlie corps materiale
Blindis the spirituall operatioun,
Lyke as ane man wer bundin in presoun.   1635

234

In *Metaphisik* Aristotell sayis
That mannis saull is lyke ane bakkis ee,
Quhilk lurkis still als lang as licht of day is,
And in the gloming cummis furth to fle;
Hir ene ar waik, the sone scho may not se: 1640
Sa is our saull with fantasie opprest
To knaw the thingis in nature manifest.

235

For God is in his power infinite,
And mannis saull is febill and over small,
Of understanding waik and unperfite   1645
To comprehend him that contenis all.
Nane suld presume, be ressoun naturall,
To seirche the secreitis of the Trinitie,
Bot trow fermelie and lat all ressoun be.

236

Yit nevertheles we may haif knawlegeing   1650
Of God almychtie be his creatouris,

1633. mirk *dark* deidlie *mortal*
    corps materiale *physical body*
1634. blindis *blinds*
    operatioun *capacity*
1635. lyke as *just as if*
    bundin *confined*
1636. Metaphysik *Metaphysics*
    Aristotell *Aristotle*
1637. bakkis ee *bat's eye*
1638. lurkis *hides* licht *light*
1639. gloming *gloaming; twilight*
    fle *fly*
1640. ene *eyes* waik *weak*
    sone *sun* scho *she*

1641. fantasie *illusion*
    opprest *weighed down*
1642. manifest *obvious*
1644. over *too*
1645. unperfite *imperfect*
1646. contenis *contains*
1647. nane *none* ressoun *reason*
1648. seirche *explore*
    secreitis *mysteries* Trinitie *Holy
    Trinity*
1649. trow *believe* fermlie *firmly*
    lat *let* ressoun *argument*
1650. knawlegeing *knowledge*
1651. be *by* creatouris *creatures*

1641–2. 'In the same way, our soul is weighed down with illusions as it
attempts to discover things that are naturally obvious'.

That he is gude, fair, wyis and bening.
Exempill tak be thir jolie flouris,
Rycht sweit of smell and plesant of colouris,
Sum grene, sum blew, sum purpour, quhyte, and
    reid,   1655
Thus distribute be gift of his godheid.

237

The firmament payntit with sternis cleir
From eist to west rolland in cirkill round,
And everilk planet in his proper spheir
In moving makand harmonie and sound;   1660
The fyre, the air, the watter and the ground –
Till understand it is aneuch, iwis,
That God in all his werkis wittie is.

238

Luke weill the fische that swimmis in the se;
Luke weill in eirth all kynd of bestyall;   1665
The foulis fair, sa forcelie thay fle,
Scheddand the air with pennis grit and small;
Syne luke to man that he maid last of all,
Lyke to his image and his similitude:
Be thir we knaw that God is fair and gude.   1670

1652. wyis *wise* bening *benign*
1653. exempill tak be *take the example of* thir *these* jolie *pretty* flouris *flowers*
1655. purpour *purple* quhyte *white*
1656. distribute *distributed* be *by*
1657. payntit *painted* sternis *stars* cleir *bright*
1658. rolland *revolving* cirkill *circle*
1659. everilk *every* spheir *sphere*
1660. makand *making*
1661. ground *earth*

1662. till *to* aneuch *enough* iwis *truly*
1663. werkis *works* wittie is *is wise*
1664. luke weill *consider well*
1665. in *on* bestyall *animals*
1666. foulis *birds* forcelie *powerfully* fle *flie*
1667. scheddand *cutting through* pennis *wings*
1668. syne *then*
1669. lyke to his image *in his own image* similitude *likeness*
1670. be thir *by these*

1662–3. 'Truly, it is enough to understand that God is wise in all his works'.

239
All creature he maid for the behufe
Of man and to his supportatioun
In to this eirth, baith under and abufe,
In number, wecht and dew proportioun,
The difference of tyme and ilk seasoun   1675
Concorddand till our opurtunitie,
As daylie by experience we may se.

240
The somer with his jolie mantill grene,
With flouris fair furrit on everilk fent,
Quhilk Flora goddes, of the flouris quene,   1680
Hes to that lord as for his seasoun lent,
And Phebus with his goldin bemis gent
Hes purfellit and payntit plesandly,
With heit and moysture stilland from the sky.

241
Syne harvest hait, quhen Ceres that goddes   1685
His barnis benit hes with abundance,
And Bachus, god of wyne, renewit hes
The tume pyipis in Italie and France
With wynis wicht and liquour of plesance,

1671. behufe *benefit*
1672. supportatioun *support*
1673. in to *in* under and
abufe *below and above*
1674. wecht *weight* dew *due*
1675. ilk *each*
1676. concorddand till *in
accordance with* opurtunitie *need*
1678. somer *summer*
jolie *splendid* mantill *cloak*
1679. furrit *as trimming*
fent *opening*
1680. quene *queen*
1682. Phebus *Phoebus; the sun*

bemis *beams* gent *beautiful*
1683. purfellit *adorned*
payntit *painted*
plesandly *pleasingly*
1684. heit *heat* stilland *distilling;
flowing gently*
1685. harvest hait *hot autumn*
1686. barnis *barns* benit hes *has
filled*
1687. Bachus *Bacchus* wyne *wine*
renewit *refilled*
1688. tume pyipis *empty casks*
1689. wicht *strong* of
plesance *pleasing*

1685–90. 'Then comes hot autumn, when the goddess Ceres has filled
men's barns with abundance, and Bacchus, god of wine, has refilled the
empty casks in Italy and France with strong wines and pleasing liquor,
and the season's plenty fills her cornucopia, so infinite in its bounty
that neither wheat nor corn could ever fill it'.

And *copia temporis* to fill hir horne, 1690
That never wes full of quheit nor uther corne.

242

Syne wynter wan, quhen austerne Eolus,
God of the wynd, with blastis boreall
The grene garment of somer glorious
Hes all to-rent and revin in pecis small. 1695
Than flouris fair faidit with froist man fall,
And birdis blyith changeis thair noitis sweit
In styll murning, neir slane with snaw and sleit.

243

Thir dalis deip with dubbis drounit is,
Baith hill and holt heillit with frostis hair, 1700
And bewis bene are bethit bair of blis,
Be wickit windis of the winter wair.
All wyld beistis than from the bentis bair
Drawis for dreid unto thair dennis deip,
Coucheand for cauld in coifis thamc to kcip. 1705

244

Syne cummis ver quhen winter is away,
The secretar of somer with his sell,

1690. copia temporis *the season's*
  abundance horne *cornucopia;*
  horn of plenty
1691. quheit *wheat*
1692. wan *gloomy* austerne *severe*
  Eolus *Aeolus*
1693. boreall *northern*
1695. to-rent *torn apart*
  revin *ripped*
1696. than *then* faidit *withered*
  man *must*
1697. blyith *happy*
  changeis *change* noitis *notes*
1698. in *into* styll murning *silent*
  mourning neir *nearly* sleit *sleet*
1699. dalis deip *deep hollows*

dubbis *puddles* drounit
is *overflow*
1700. holt *wood* heillit *covered*
  frostis hair *hoar-frost*
1701. bewis bene *fine boughs*
  bethit bair *stripped bare*
  blis *delight*
1702. be *by* wair *stormy*
1703. than *then* bentis *countryside*
1704. drawis *go* dreid *fear*
  dennis *dens*
1705. coucheand *cowering*
  coifis *caves* keip *protect*
1706. ver *spring*
1707. secretar *secretary*
  somer *summer* sell *seal*

1699. 'The deep hollows overflow with puddles'.
1701–2. 'And fine boughs are stripped bare of all nature's delights by the
  stormy winter's wicked winds'.
1705. 'Cowering in caves to protect themselves against the cold'.

Quhen columbie up keikis throw the clay,
Quhilk fleit wes befoir with froistes fell.
The mavis and the merle beginnis to mell;   1710
The lark on loft with uthir birdis smale
Than drawis furth fra derne, over doun and daill.

245

That samin seasoun, in to ane soft morning,
Rycht blyth that bitter blastis wer ago,
Unto the wod, to se the flouris spring   1715
And heir the mavis sing and birdis mo,
I passit furth, syne lukit to and fro
To se the soill that wes richt sessonabill:
Sappie, and to resave all seidis abill.

240

Moving thusgait, grit myrth I tuke in mynd   1720
Of lauboraris to se the besines,
Sum makand dyke, and sum the pleuch can wynd,
Sum sawand seidis fast frome place to place,
The harrowis hoppand in the saweris trace.
It wes grit joy to him that luifit corne   1725
To se thame laubour, baith at evin and morne.

1708. columbie *columbine*
keikis *peeps*
1709. fleit *chased away*   fell *many*
1710. mavis *thrush*
merle *blackbird*   mell *sing*
1711. on loft *on high*
1712. drawis furth *comes forth*
derne *hiding*   doun *hill*
1713. samin *same*   in to *upon*
1714. ago *gone*   blyth *happy*
1715. wod *wood*   spring *grow*
1716. heir *hear*   mo *more*
1717. lukit *looked*
1718. richt sessonabill *very
seasonable*

1719. sappie *moist*   resave *receive*
seidis *seeds*   abill *ready*
1720. thusgait *in this way*
grit *great*   myrth *delight*
1721. lauboraris *labourers*
besines *activity*
1722. makand *making*   dyke *walls*
pleuch *plough*   can wynd *drove*
1723. sawand *sowing*
1724. harrowis *harrows; spiked
tools*   hoppand *hopping*   saweris
trace *sowers' tracks*
1725. luifit *loved*
1726. baith *both*   evin *evening*

1708–9. 'When columbine, which was earlier chased away by many
frosts, peeps up again through the earth'.
1718–19. 'To see the soil that was just as it should have been in that
season: moist and ready to receive all the seeds. Moving in this way, I
took great delight in seeing the activity of the labourers'. .

241
And as I baid under ane bank full bene,
In hart gritlie rejosit of that sicht,
Unto ane hedge, under ane hawthorne grene,
Of small birdis thair come ane ferlie flicht,   1730
And doun belyif can on the leifis licht
On everilk syde about me quhair I stude,
Rycht mervellous, ane mekill multitude.

248
Amang the quhilks ane swallow loud couth cry,
On that hawthorne hie in the croip sittand: 1735
'O ye birdis on bewis heir me by,
Ye sall weill knaw and wyislie understand:
Quhair danger is or perrell appeirand,
It is grit wisedome to provyde befoir
It to devoyd, for dreid it hurt yow moir.'   1740

249
'Schir Swallow,' quod the lark agane and leuch,
'Quhat have ye sene that causis yow to dreid?'
'Se ye yone churll,' quod scho, 'beyond yone pleuch,
Fast sawand hemp and – lo, see! – linget seid?
Yone lint will grow in lytill tyme in deid,   1745
And thairof will yone churll his nettis mak,
Under the quhilk he thinkis us to tak.

250
'Thairfoir I reid we pas quhen he is gone
At evin, and with our naillis scharp and small
Out of the eirth scraip we yone seid anone   1750

1727. baid *paused* bene *pleasant*
1728. hart *heart* rejosit *gladdened*
   of *at*
1730. ferlie flicht *sudden flight*
1731. belyif *at once* can . . .
   licht *alighted*
1732. everilk *every* stude *stood*
1733. mekill *great*
1734. the quhilks *which* couth
   cry *cried*
1735. croip *treetop*
1736. bewis *branches*
1738. appeirand *likely*

1739. provyde *make provision*
   befoir *in advance*
1740. devoyd *remove* dreid *fear*
1741. schir *sir* quod *said*
   agane *in reply* leuch *laughed*
1743. yone *that* churll *peasant*
1744. linget seid *flax seed*
1745. lint *flax* in deid *indeed*
1746. nettis *nets* mak *make*
1747. thinkis *intends* tak *capture*
1748. reid *advise* pas *go*
1749. naillis *claws*
1750. anone *directly*

And eit it up, for gif it growis we sall
Have cause to weip heirefter ane and all.
Se we remeid thairfoir furthwith, *instante*,
Nam levius laedit quicquid praevidimus ante.

251

'For clerkis sayis it is nocht sufficient   1755
To considder that is befoir thyne ee;
Bot prudence is ane inwart argument
That garris ane man provyde befoir and se
Quhat gude, quhat evill is liklie for to be
Of everilk thingis at the fynall end,   1760
And swa fra perrell the better him defend.'

252

The lark, lauchand, the swallow thus couth scorne,
And said scho fischit lang befoir the net:
'The barne is eith to busk that is unborne;
All growis nocht that in the ground is set;   1765
The nek to stoup quhen it the straik sall get
Is sone aneuch; deith on the fayest fall.'
Thus scornit thay the swallow ane and all.

1751. eit *eat* gif *if* sall *shall*
1752. weip *weep* ane *one*
1753. se *ensure* remeid *remedy*
    instante *instantly*
1754. nam levius laedit quicquid
    praevidimus ante for *what we*
    foresee does us less harm
1755. clerkis *scholars* nocht *not*
1756. that *what* ee *eyes*
1757. prudence *wisdom*
    inwart *internal*
    argument *reasoning*
1758. garris *makes* provyde *take*

care se *consider*
1759. gude *good*
1760. of *from* fynall end *very end*
1761. swa *thus*
1762. lauchand *laughing* couth
    scorne *mocked*
1763. fischit *fished*
1764. barne *child* eith *easy*
    busk *clothe*
1766. stoup *bend* quhen *when*
    straik *blow*
1767. sone aneuch *soon enough*
    fayest *those fated to die*

1753–4. 'Therefore let us ensure that we remedy the situation straight
away, immediately, for what we foresee does us less harm'.
1757–61. 'But wisdom is a process of inner reasoning which makes a man
take care in advance and consider what good and what evil is likely to
be the outcome of all things at the very end, and thus allows him to
defend himself better from danger'.
1763. 'And said she was fishing before she even had a net'.
1765. 'Not everything grows that is planted in the ground; there is time
enough to bend the neck when it is about to receive the fatal stroke; let
death befall those fated to die'.

253

Despysing thus hir helthsum document,
The foulis ferlie tuke thair flicht anone.   1770
Sum with ane bir thay braidit over the bent,
And sum agane ar to the grene wod gone.
Upon the land quhair I wes left allone,
I tuke my club and hamewart couth I carie,
Swa ferliand as I had sene ane farie.   1775

254

Thus passit furth quhill June, that jolie tyde,
And seidis that wer sawin of beforne
Wer growin hie, that hairis mycht thame hyde
And als the quailye craikand in the corne.
I movit furth, betwix midday and morne,   1780
Unto the hedge under the hawthorne grene,
Quhair I befoir the said birdis had sene.

255

And as I stude, be aventure and cace,
The samin birdis as I haif said yow air –
I hoip because it wes thair hanting place,   1785
Mair of succour or yit mair solitair –
Thay lichtit doun, and quhen thay lychtit wair
The swallow swyth put furth ane pietuous pyme,
Said: 'Wo is him can not bewar in tyme.

256

'O, blind birdis and full of negligence,   1790
Unmyndfull of your awin prosperitie,

1769. helthsum document *wise
teaching*
1770. foulis *birds* ferlie *suddenly*
1771. bir *rush* braidit *flew
quickly* bent *field*
1774. club *staff*
hamewart *homewards* couth I
carie *I went*
1775. ferliand *marvelling* as *as if*
ane farie *something from
fairyland*
1776. quhill *until* tyde *time*
1777. of beforne *previously*
1778. hairis *hares* thame
hyde *hide themselves*

1779. als *also* quailye *corncrake*
craikand *croaking*
1783. be aventure and cace *by
chance and accident*
1784. samin *same* said yow
air *told you about before*
1785. hoip *expect* hanting
place *customary haunt*
1786. mair of succour *more
sheltered* solitair *secluded*
1787. lichtit *landed*
1788. swyth *quickly* pietuous
pyme *pitiful cry*
1791. prosperitie *good*

Lift up your sicht and tak gude advertence;
Luke to the lint that growis on yone le.
Yone is the thing I bad, forsuith, that we,
Quhill it wes seid, suld rute furth of the eird;   1795
Now is it lint, now is it hie on breird.

257

'Go yit quhill it is tender, young and small,
And pull it up; let it na mair incres.
My flesche growis, my bodie quaikis all,
Thinkand on it I may not sleip in peis.'   1800
Thay cryit all and bad the swallow ceis,
And said: 'Yone lint heirefter will do gude,
For linget is to lytill birdis fude.

258

'We think, quhen that yone lint bollis ar ryip,
To mak us feist and fill us of the seid,   1805
Magre yone churll, and on it sing and pyip.'
'Weill,' quod the swallow, 'freindes, hardilie beid.
Do as ye will, bot certane, sair I dreid
Heirefter ye sall find als sour as sweit,
Quhen ye ar speldit on yone carlis speit.   1810

259

'The awner of yone lint ane fouler is,
Richt cautelous and full of subteltie.
His pray full sendill tymis will he mis
Bot gif we birdis all the warrer be.
Full mony of our kin he hes gart de,   1815

1792. sicht *eyes* advertence *heed*
1793. lint *flax* le *meadow*
1794. bad *asked* forsuith *indeed*
1795. quhill *while* rute furth *root out*
1796. hie on breird *sprouting high*
1798. na mair incres *get no bigger*
1799. growis *crawls*
1801. ceis *cease*
1803. linget *flax-seed* fude *food*
1804. think *intend* bollis *pods*
     ryip *ripe*
1805. mak us feist *feast ourselves*
1806. magre *in spite of* pyip *pipe*
1807. hardelie beid *so be it*

1808. sair *sorely*
1809. als *as much*
1810. speldit *split open*
     carlis *peasant's* speit *roasting
     spit*
1811. awner *owner* fouler *bird-
     catcher*
1812. cautelous *cunning*
     subteltie *trickery*
1813. full sendill tymis *very
     seldom* mis *miss*
1814. bot gif *unless* warrer *more
     alert*
1815. mony *many* gart de *killed*

And thocht it bot ane sport to spill thair blude;
God keip me fra him, and the halie rude.'

260
Thir small birdis, haveand bot lytill thocht
Of perrell that micht fall be aventure,
The counsell of the swallow set at nocht,   1820
Bot tuke thair flicht and furth togidder fure;
Sum to the wode, sum markit to the mure.
I tuke my staff, quhen this wes said and done,
And walkit hame, for it drew neir the none.

261
The lint ryipit, the carll pullit the lyne,   1825
Rippillit the bollis and in beitis set,
It steipit in the burne and dryit syne,
And with ane bittill knokkit it and bet,
Syne swingillit it weill and hekkillit in the flet;
His wyfe it span and twynit it in to threid,   1830
Of quhilk the fowlar nettis maid in deid.

262
The wynter come, the wickit wind can blaw,
The woddis grene were wallowit with the weit;
Baith firth and fell with froistys were maid faw,

1816. blude *blood*
1817. halie rude *holy cross*
1818. haveand *having*
1819. be aventure *by chance*
1820. counsell *advice*   set at
    nocht *disregarded*
1821. fure *went*
1822. markit *proceeded*   mure *moor*
1824. walkit *walked*   hame *home*
    the none *midday*
1825. ryipit *ripened*   pullit *pulled*
    up   lyne *flax*
1826. rippillit *combed out*

bollis *seed-pods*   in beitis *in*
bundles
1827. it steipit *soaked it*
    burne *burn; stream*   dryit *dried*
1828. bittill *mallet*   bet *beat*
1829. swingillit *scraped*
    hekkillit *combed*   flet *house*
1830. twynit *twisted*   threid *thread*
1832. can blaw *blew*
1833. wallowit *withered*   weit *wet*
    weather
1834. firth and fell *wood and hill*
    faw *to glisten*

1817. 'May God and the holy cross protect me from him'.
1825–29. 'The lint ripened, the peasant pulled up the flax, combed out
    the seed-pods and arranged the flax into bundles, steeped it in the
    stream and then dried it, and with a mallet pounded it and beat it,
    then scraped it well and put it through a flax-comb inside the house'.

Slonkis and slaik maid slidderie with the sleit;   1835
The foulis fair for falt thay fell of feit;
On bewis bair it wes na bute to byde,
Bot hyit unto housis thame to hyde.

263
Sum in the barn, sum in the stak of corne
Thair lugeing tuke and maid thair residence.   1840
The fowlar saw, and grit aithis hes sworne,
Thay suld be tane trewlie for thair expence.
His nettis hes he set with diligence,
And in the snaw he schulit hes ane plane
And heillit it all over with calf agane.   1845

264
Thir small birdis seand the calf wes glaid;
Trowand it had bene corne, thay lychtit doun,
Bot of the nettis na presume thay had,
Nor of the fowlaris fals intentioun;
To scraip and seik thair meit thay maid thame
      boun.   1850
The swallow on ane lytill branche neir by,
Dreiddand for gyle, thus loud on thame couth cry:

1835. slonkis and slaik *hollows and*   1844. schulit hes *has cleared*
  valleys slidderie *slippery*   plane *space*
  sleit *sleet*   1845. heillit *covered* calf *chaff*
1836. falt *hunger* fell of feit *fell*   1846. seand *seeing* glaid *glad*
  off their feet   1847. trowand *believing* lychtit
1837. bewis *boughs* bute *good*   doun *flew down*
1838. hyit *hastened*   1848. presume *anticipation*
  thame *themselves*   1850. scraip *scrape* meit *food*
1840. lugeing *shelter* tuke *took*   boun *ready*
1841. aithis *oaths*   1852. dreiddand for gyle *fearing a*
1842. tane *captured*   *trick* couth cry *cried*
  trewlie *certainly* expence *cost*

1836. 'The pretty birds could not stand for hunger'.
1841–2. 'The bird-catcher saw them and swore great oaths that they
  must certainly be caught for all they had cost him'.
1848–50. 'But they did not anticipate the nets, nor the bird catcher's
  devious plan; they started to scrape about and look for food'.

265

'In to that calf scraip quhill your naillis bleid;
Thair is na corne, ye laubour all in vane.
Trow ye yone churll for pietie will yow feid? 1855
Na, na, he hes it heir layit for ane trane.
Remove, I reid, or ellis ye will be slane.
His nettis he hes set full prively,
Reddie to draw; in tyme be war for thy.'

266

Grit fule is he that puttis in dangeir 1860
His lyfe, his honour, for ane thing of nocht.
Grit fule is he that will not glaidlie heir
Counsall in tyme, quhill it availl him nocht.
Grit fule is he that hes na thing in thocht
Bot thing present, and efter quhat may fall 1865
Nor of the end hes na memoriall.

267

Thir small birdis, for hunger famischit neir,
Full besie scraipand for to seik thair fude,
The counsall of the swallow wald not heir,
Suppois thair laubour dyd thame lytill gude. 1870
Quhen scho thair fulische hartis understude,
Sa indurate, up in ane tre scho flew.
With that this churll over thame his nettis drew.

1853. in to *in* quhill *until*
 bleid *bleed*
1855. trow ye *do you think* for
 pietie *out of pity*
1856. layit *laid* trane *trap*
1857. remove *fly away* reid *advise*
1858. full prively *very furtively*
1859. war *aware* for thy *therefore*
1860. fule *fool*
1861. of nocht *worth nothing*
1862. heir *hear*

1863. counsall *advice* quhill *until*
 availl *helps*
1865. efter *afterwards* quhat *what*
1866. na memoriall *no thought*
1867. thir *these* famischit
 neir *nearly starved*
1868. besie *busily*
1870. suppois *although*
1871. scho *she* fulische *foolish*
1872. sa *so* indurate *determined*

1858–9. 'He has set up his nets very furtively, ready to draw them in; so
 you had better be aware of him in time'.
1864–6. 'He is a great fool who has nothing in his head except the
 present, and gives no thought to what may happen afterwards or in the
 end'.

268

Allace, it wes grit hart sair for to se
That bludie bowcheour beit thay birdis doun,   1875
And for till heir, quhen thay wist weill to de,
Thair cairfull sang and lamentatioun.
Sum with ane staf he straik to eirth on swoun,
Of sum the heid he straik, of sum he brak the crag,
Sum half on lyfe he stoppit in his bag.   1880

269

And quhen the swallow saw that thay wer deid,
'Lo,' quod scho, 'thus it happinnis mony syis
On thame that will not tak counsall nor reid
Of prudent men or clerkis that ar wyis.
This grit perrell I tauld thame mair than thryis;   1885
Now ar thay deid, and wo is me thairfoir!'
Scho tuke hir flicht, bot I hir saw no moir.

Moralitas

270

Lo, worthie folk, Esope, that nobill clerk,
Ane poet worthie to be lawreate,
Quhen that he waikit from mair autentik werk,   1890
With uther ma, this forsaid fabill wrate,
Quhilk at this tyme may weill be applicate
To gude morall edificatioun,
Haifand ane sentence according to ressoun.

1874. allace *alas*   grit hart
   sair *heartbreaking*
1875. bowcheour *butcher*   beit *beat*
1876. for till *to*   wist *knew*   de *die*
1877. cairfull *sorrowful*   sang *song*
1878. straik *struck*   on
   swoun *stunned*
1879. heid *head*   brak *broke*
   crag *neck*
1880. on lyfe *alive*   stoppit *stuffed*
1882. syis *times*
1883. reid *advice*
1884. wyis *wise*
1885. thryis *three times*

1887. tuke hir flicht *flew away*
   moir *more*
1888. Esope *Aesop*   clerk *scholar*
1889. lawreate *laureate; crowned
   with laurel*
1890. waikit *was released*   mair
   autentik *more serious*
1891. with uther ma *among other
   things*   wrate *wrote*
1892. applicate *applied*
1893. edificatioun *instruction*
1894. haifand *possessing*
   sentence *meaning*   ressoun *reason*

1876–7. 'And to hear their sorrowful song and lamentation when they
knew for certain that they were about to die'.

271
This carll and bond, of gentrice spoliate,   1895
Sawand this calf thir small birdis to sla,
It is the feind quhilk fra the angelike state
Exylit is as fals apostata,
Quhilk day and nycht weryis not for to ga,
Sawand poysoun and mony wickit thocht   1900
In mannis saull, quhilk Christ full deir hes bocht.

272
And quhen the saull, as seid in to the eird,
Gevis consent unto delectatioun,
The wickit thocht beginnis for to breird
In deidlie sin, quhilk is dampnatioun;   1905
Ressoun is blindit with affectioun
And carnall lust growis full grene and gay,
Throw consuetude hantit from day to day.

273
Proceding furth be use and consuetude,
The sin ryipis and schame is set on syde;   1910
The feynd plettis his nettis scharp and rude,
And under plesance previlie dois hyde.
Syne on the feild he sawis calf full wyde

1895. carll *peasant*
  bond *bondman* gentrice *nobler*
  feeling spoliate *devoid*
1896. sawand *sowing* calf *chaff*
  sla *slay*
1897. feind *devil* quhilk *who*
  angelike *angelic*
1898. exylit *exiled* apostata *traitor
  to the Church*
1899. weryis not for to ga *does not
  tire of going*
1901. mannis saull *man's soul* full
  deir *at great cost*
  bocht *redeemed*
1902. eird *earth*

1903. gevis *gives*
  delectatioun *pleasures of the flesh*
1904. breird *sprout*
1905. dampnatioun *damnation*
1906. with affectioun *by desire*
1907. carnall *fleshly*
1908. consuetude *habit*
  hantit *engaged in*
1909. be *by*
1910. ryipis *ripens* on syde *aside*
1911. plettis *plaits* rude *rough*
1912. plesance *pleasure*
  previlie *secretly*
1913. syne *then* sawis *sows*
  wyde *widely*

1895. 'This peasant and bondman, devoid of nobler feeling'.
1912. 'And secretly hides them under the guise of pleasure'.

Quhilk is bot tume and verray vanitie
Of fleschlie lust and vaine prosperitie.   1915

274

Thir hungrie birdis wretchis we may call,
As scraipand in this warldis vane plesance,
Greddie to gadder gudis temporall,
Quhilk as the calf ar tume without substance,
Lytill of availl and full of variance,   1920
Lyke to the mow befoir the face of wind
Quhiskis away and makis wretchis blind.

275

This swallow, quhilk eschaipit is the snair,
The halie preichour weill may signifie,
Exhortand folk to walk and ay be wair   1925
Fra nettis of our wickit enemie
Quha sleipis not bot ever is reddie,
Quhen wretchis in this warldis calf dois scraip,
To draw his net, that thay may not eschaip.

276

Allace, quhat cair, quhat weiping is and wo,   1930
Quhen saull and bodie departit ar in twane!
The bodie to the wormis keitching go,
The saull to fyre, to everlestand pane.
Quhat helpis than this calf, thir gudis vane,

1914. tume *emptiness* verray
   vanitie *complete worthlessness*
1918. greddie *greedy*
   gadder *gather* gudis
   temporall *worldly goods*
1919. as *like*
1920. availl *profit*
   variance *changeability*
1921. mow *dust*
1922. quhiskis *whisks*
1923. eschaipit is *has escaped*
   snair *snare*

1924. halie preichour *holy
   preacher* signifie *represent*
1925. exhortand *urging*
   walk *watch* wair *alert*
1928. warldis *world's*
1929. eschaip *escape*
1930. cair *sorrow*
1931. departit *separated*
   twane *two*
1932. wormis keitching *worms'
   kitchen*
1934. gudis vane *empty possessions*

1914-15. 'Which is nothing but emptiness and the complete
worthlessness of fleshly lust and fruitless prosperity'.
1921-2. 'Like the dust which the wind whisks away, making poor
wretches blind'.

Quhen thow art put in Luceferis bag 1935
And brocht to hell, and hangit be the crag?

277

Thir hid nettis for to persave and se,
This sarie calf wyislie to understand,
Best is bewar in maist prosperitie,
For in this warld thair is na thing lestand. 1940
Is na man wait how lang his stait will stand,
His lyfe will lest, nor how that he sall end
Efter his deith, nor quhidder he sall wend.

278

Pray we thairfoir quhill we ar in this lyfe
For four thingis: the first, fra sin remufe; 1945
The secund is to seis all weir and stryfe;
The thrid is perfite cheritie and lufe;
The feird thing is, and maist for oure behufe,
That is in blis with angellis to be fallow.
And thus endis the preiching of the swallow. 1950

THE FOX, THE WOLF AND THE CADGER

279

Qwhylum thair wynnit in ane wildernes,
As myne authour expreslie can declair,

1935. Luceferis *Lucifer's*
1936. be the crag *by the neck*
1937. hid *hidden* persave *perceive*
1938. sarie *worthless* wyislic *wisely*
1939. bewar *to be wary*
  maist *greatest*
1940. lestand *lasting*
1941. wait *knows* stait *prosperity*
1942. lest *last* sall *shall*
1943. quhidder *where* wend *go*
1944. quhill *while*
1945. remufe *remove ourselves*

1946. seis *cease* weir *war*
1947. thrid *third* perfite *perfect*
  cheritie *charity* lufe *love*
1948. feird *fourth* for oure
  behufe *to our benefit*
1949. blis *bliss* fallow *companions*
1951. qwhylum *once upon a time*
  wynnit *dwelled*
1952. authour *source*
  expreslie *explicitly* can
  declair *states*

1937–41. 'It is best to be wary even in times of greatest prosperity, so
  that these hidden nets can be perceived and seen, and the worthless
  chaff wisely understood for what it is, for in this world nothing lasts
  forever. There is no man who knows how long his prosperity will
  continue'.
1948–9. 'The fourth thing, and of greatest benefit to us, is that we
  should be the companions of the angels in bliss'.

Ane revand wolf, that levit upon purches
On bestiall, and maid him weill to fair.
Wes nane sa big about him he wald spair,   1955
And he war hungrie, outher for favour or feid;
Bot in his wraith he weryit thame to deid.

280

Swa happinnit him in waithing as he went
To meit ane foxe in middis of the way.
He him foirsaw and fenyeit to be schent,   1960
And with ane bek he bad the wolf gude day.
'Welcum to me', quod he, 'thow Russell gray!'
Syne loutit doun and tuke him be the hand:
'Ryse up, Lowrence! I leif the for to stand.

281

'Quhair hes thow bene this sesoun fra my sicht?   1965
Thow sall beir office and my stewart be,
For thow can knap doun caponis on the nicht,
And lourand law thow can gar hennis de.'
'Schir,' said the foxe, 'that ganis not for me;

1953. revand *thieving*   levit *lived*
purches *robbery*
1954. on bestiall *of livestock*   maid
him weill to fair *did well for
himself*
1955. wes *there was*   spair *spare
them*
1956. and *if*   outher *either*
feid *threat*
1957. wraith *fury*   weryit *worried;
mauled*   deid *death*
1958. swa *so*   happinnit him *he
happened*   waithing *poaching*
1959. way *road*
1960. bek *bow*

1963. syne *then*   loutit *bent*   be *by*
1964. I leif the *I give you
permission*
1965. quhair *where*   hes *have*
bene *been*   sicht *sight*
1966. sall *shall*   beir *bear*
stewart *steward*
1967. knap doun *strike down*
caponis *capons; cocks*   on the
nicht *at night*
1968. lourand law *lurking low*
gar *make*   hennis *hens*   de *die*
1969. schir *sir*   ganis not *is not
suitable*

1955-7. 'If he was hungry, there was no creature round about who was
so big that he would spare them, either as a favour or on account of
threats; but in his fury he worried them to death'.
1958-9. 'So he happened, as he went poaching, to meet a fox in the
middle of the road. The fox saw the wolf coming and pretended to be
exhausted'.

And I am rad, gif thay me se onfar,   1970
That at my figure beist and bird will skar.'

282

'Na!' quod the wolf, 'Thow can in covert creip
Upon thy wame and hint thame be the heid,
And mak ane suddand schow upon ane scheip,
Syne with thy wappinnis wirrie him to deid.'   1975
'Schir,' said the foxe, 'ye knaw my roib is reid,
And thairfoir thair will na beist abyde me
Thocht I wald be sa fals as for to hyde me.'

283

'Yis,' quod the wolf, 'throw buskis and throw brais
Law can thow lour to cum to thy intent.'   1980
'Schir,' said the foxe, 'ye wait weill how it gais;
Ane lang space fra thame thay will feill my sent.
Than will thay eschaip suppois I suld be schent;
And I am schamefull for to cum behind thame,
Into the feild thocht I suld sleipand find thame.'   1985

1970. rad *afraid* gif *if* onfar *from afar*
1971. figure *appearance* beist *beast* skar *be scared*
1972. quod *said* in covert *under cover*
1973. wame *belly* hint *seize* heid *head*
1974. suddand *sudden* schow *attack* scheip *sheep*
1975. wappinnis *teeth* wirrie *worry* deid *death*
1976. roib *coat* reid *red*
1977. abyde me *remain near me*
1978. thocht *even though*
1979. yis *yes* buskis *bushes* brais *slopes*
1981. wait *know* gais *goes*
1982. lang space *long distance* feill *recognise* sent *scent*
1983. eschaip *escape* suppois *even if* schent *exhausted*
1984. schamefull *ashamed*
1985. thocht *even though* sleipand *sleeping*

1977–8. 'And therefore no animal will stay anywhere near me even if I were deceitful enough to attempt to hide myself'.
1979–80. ' "Yes you can" said the wolf, "you can crouch low in bushes and behind slopes to achieve your purpose" '.
1983. 'Then they will escape even if I exhaust myself in the process'.

284

'Na,' quod the wolf, 'thow can cum on the wind;
For everie wrink, forsuith, thow hes ane wyle.'
'Schir,' said the foxe, 'that beist ye mycht call blind
That micht not eschaip than fra me ane myle.
How micht I ane of thame that wyis begyle?   1990
My tippit twa eiris and my twa gray ene
Garris me be kend quhair I wes never sene.'

285

Than said the wolf, 'Lowrence, I heir the le,
And castys for perrellis thy ginnes to defend;
Bot all thy sonyes sall not availl the,   1995
About the busk with wayis thocht thow wend;
Falset will failye ay at the latter end.
To bow at bidding and byde not quhill thow brest,
Thairfoir I giff the counsall for the best.'

286

'Schir,' said the foxe, 'it is Lentring, ye se;   2000
I can nocht fische, for weiting of my feit,

1986. cum *approach* on the wind *up-wind*
1987. wrink *trick* forsuith *indeed* wyle *plan*
1988. mycht *could*
1989. myle *mile*
1990. that wyis *in that way* begyle *deceive*
1991. tippit *pointed* twa *two* eiris *ears* ene *eyes*
1992. kend *recognised*
1993. the *you* le *lie*
1994. castys *predict*

perrellis *trouble* ginnes *tricks*
1995. sonyes *excuses* availl *help*
1996. busk *bush* wayis *stratagems* thocht *though* wend *go*
1997. falset *falsehood* failye *fail* ay *always*
1998. bow *submit* bidding *asking* byde *wait* quhill *until* brest *break*
1999. giff *give* counsall *advice*
2000. Lentring *Lent* se *see*
2001. fische *go fishing* for weiting of *for fear of wetting* feit *feet*

1987. 'Indeed, for every trick they know, you have a cunning plan of your own'.
1989. 'That did not run a mile from me'.
1991–2. 'My two pointed ears and my two grey eyes cause me to be recognised even in places where I've never been seen before'.
1993–4. 'Then the wolf said, "I hear you telling lies, Lowrence, and predicting trouble in order to protect your own devious plans" '.
1996. 'Although you beat about the bush with all your stratagems'.
1998–9. 'Therefore, let me give you a piece of advice: it's better to do what you are told straightaway rather than waiting until you are forced to do something'.

To tak ane banestikill, thocht we baith suld de;
I have nane uther craft to win my meit.
Bot wer it Pasche, that men suld pultrie eit,
As kiddis, lambis or caponis into ply, 2005
To beir your office than wald I not set by.'

287

Than said the wolf in wraith, 'Wenis thou with wylis
And with thy mony mowis me to mat?
It is ane auld dog, doutles, that thow begylis:
Thow wenis to drau the stra befoir the cat!' 2010
'Schir,' said the foxe, 'God wait, I mene not that;
For and I did, it wer weill worth that ye
In ane reid raip had tyit me till ane tre.

288

'Bot nou I se he is ane fule perfay
That with his maister fallis in ressoning. 2015
I did bot till assay quhat ye wald say;
God wait, my mynd wes on ane uther thing.
I sall fulfill in all thing your bidding,
Quhatever ye charge on nichtis or on dayis.'
'Weill,' quod the wolf, 'I heir weill quhat thou
    sayis. 2020

2002. tak *catch*
  banestikill *stickleback*
  thocht *even though* de *die*
2003. craft *skill* meit *food*
2004. Pasche *Easter* that *when*
  pultrie *poultry*
2005. as *together with* into ply *in good condition*
2006. beir your office *act as your steward* set by *refuse*
2007. wraith *anger* wenis thou *do you expect* wylis *tricks*
2008. mowis *quibbles* mat *baffle*

2009. doutles *without doubt*
  begylis *are trying to trick*
2010. wenis *want* drau *dangle*
  stra *straw*
2011. mene *meant*
2012. and *if* weill worth *be fitting*
2013. reid raip *red rope* tyit *tied*
  till *to*
2014. fule *fool* perfay *indeed*
2015. in *into* ressoning *argument*
2016. assay *test*
2017. wait *knows*
2019. charge *command*

2012–13. 'For if I did, you'd be quite justified in tying me to a tree with
  a bloody rope'.
2016. 'I only did it to test what you would say'.

289

'Bot yit I will thow mak to me ane aith
For to be leill attour all levand leid.'
'Schir,' said the foxe, 'that ane word maks me wraith,
For nou I se ye have me at ane dreid.
Yit sall I sweir, suppois it be nocht neid,   2025
Be Juppiter and on pane of my heid,
I sall be treu to you quhill I be deid.'

290

With that ane cadgear with capill and with creillis
Come carpand furth; than Lowrence culd him spy.
The foxe the flewer of the fresche hering feillis,   2030
And to the wolf he roundis prively:
'Schir, yone ar hering the cadgear caryis by;
Thairfoir I reid that we se for sum wayis
To get sum fische aganis thir fasting dayis.

291

'Sen I am stewart I wald we had sum stuff,   2035
And ye ar silver-seik, I wait richt weill.
Thocht we wald thig, yone verray churlische chuff
He will not giff us ane hering of his creill—
Befoir yone churle on kneis thocht we wald kneill,
Bot yit I trou alsone that ye sall se   2040
Gif I can craft to bleir yone carlis ee.

2021. will *want*   aith *oath*
2022. lcill *loyal*   attour *above*
   levand leid *living creature*
2024. have . . . dreid *are suspicious
   of me*
2025. suppois *although*
   neid *necessary*
2026. be *by*   Juppiter *Jupiter*   on
   . . . heid *on pain of losing my
   head*
2027. treu *true*   deid *dead*
2028. cadgear *cadger; fish-peddler*
   capill *horse*   creillis *baskets*
2029. carpand *singing*

2030. flewer *smell*   hering *herring*
   feillis *recognises*
2031. roundis *whispers*
   prively *secretly*
2033. reid *suggest*   se *look*
2034. aganis *during*
2035. stewart *steward*   wald *wish*
   stuff *provisions*
2036. silver-seik *silver-sick,
   penniless*   wait *know*
2037. thig *beg*   chuff *peasant*
2039. churle *peasant*   kneill *kneel*
2040. trou *believe*   alsone *at once*
2041. gif *if* can craft *know tricks*
   bleir . . . ee *to deceive that fellow*

292

'Schir, ane thing is, and we get of yone pelf,
Ye man tak travell and mak us sum supple;
For he that will not laubour and help himself,
Into thir dayis he is not worth ane fle.   2045
I think to work als besie as ane be;
And ye sall follou ane lytill efterwart
And gadder hering, for that sall be your part.'

293

With that he kest ane cumpas far about,
And straucht him doun in middis of the way.   2050
As he wer deid he fenyeit him, but dout,
And than upon lenth unliklie lay;
The quhyte he turnit up of his ene tway,
His toung out hang ane handbried of his heid,
And still he lay, als straucht as he wer deid.   2055

294

The cadgear fand the foxe and he wes fane,
And till himself thus softlie can he say:
'At the nixt bait, in faith, ye sall be flane,
And of your skyn I sall mak mittenis tway.'
He lap full lichtlie about him quhair he lay,   2060

2042. and *if* get of *are to get* | him *pretended* but dout *without*
some pelf *booty* | doubt
2043. man *must* tak travell *do* | 2052. upon lenth *spread out*
some *work* supple *help* | unliklie *not a pretty sight*
2045. into thir dayis *these days* | 2053. quhyte *white* turnit *turned*
fle *fly* | ene *eyes* tway *two*
2046. think *intend* als *as* | 2054. hang *hung* handbreid *hand's*
besie *busy* | breadth
2047. follou *follow* | 2055. straucht *rigid*
2048. gadder *gather* part *job* | 2056. fand *found* fane *glad*
2049. kest *made* cumpas *circle* | 2058. nixt bait *next resting place*
2050. straucht *stretched* | flane *flayed; skinned*
middis *middle* | 2059. mittenis *mittens*
2051. as *as if* fenyeit | 2060. lap *leapt*

2049–50. 'With that he circled round at a good distance and then
stretched himself out in the middle of the road'.
2053–4. 'He rolled his eyes so that only the whites showed, his tongue
hung out a whole hand's breadth from his head'.

And all the trace he trippit on his tais;
As he had hard ane pyper play he gais.

295

'Heir lyis the devyll,' quod he, 'deid in ane dyke;
Sic ane selcouth sau I not this sevin yeir.
I trou ye have bene tussillit with sum tyke,   2065
That garris you ly sa still withoutin steir.
Schir Foxe, in faith, ye ar deir welcum heir.
It is sum wyfis malisone, I trow,
For pultrie pyking, that lychtit hes on yow.

296

'Thair sall na pedder, for purs, nor yit for glufis,   2070
Nor yit for poyntis, pyke your pellet fra me:
I sall of it mak mittenis to my lufis,
Till hald my handis hait quhairever I be;
Till Flanderis sall it never saill the se.'
With that in hy he hint be the heillis,   2075
And with ane swak he swang him on the creillis.

297

Syne be the heid the hors in hy hes hint.
The fraudfull foxe thairto gude tent hes tane,
And with his teith the stoppell, or he stint,
Pullit out, and syne the hering, ane and ane,   2080
Out of the creillis he swakkit doun gude wane.

2061. trace *road*   trippit *danced*
 tais *toes*
2062. hard *heard*   pyper *piper*
 gais *goes*
2063. lyis *lies*   quod *said*
 dyke *ditch*
2064. sic *such*   selcouth *marvel*
 sau *saw*
2065. trou *believe*
 tussillit *worried*   tyke *cur*
2066. garris *causes*   steir *movement*
2067. deir *very*
2068. wyfis *woman's*
 malisone *curse*
2069. pultrie pyking *chicken
 stealing*   lychtit *alighted*

2070. pedder *pedlar*   glufis *gloves*
2071. poyntis *trimmings*
 pyke *steal*   pellet *pelt*
2072. to my lufis *for my palms*
2073. hald *keep*   hait *hot*
2074. Flanderis *Flanders*   se *sea*
2075. in hy *in haste*   hint *seized*
 heillis *feet*
2076. swak *swing*   swang *hurled*
 creillis *baskets*
2077. be the heid *by the head*
2078. tent *heed*   hes tane *has taken*
2079. stoppell *stopper* or *before*
 stint *stopped*
2080. ane and ane *one by one*
2081. gude wane *a good number*

The wolf wes war, and gadderit spedilie.
The cadgear sang 'Huntis up, up!' upon hie.

298

Yit at ane burne the cadgear lukit about;
With that the foxe lap quyte the creillis fray.   2085
The cadgear wald have raucht the foxe ane rout,
Bot all for nocht; he wan his hoill that day.
Than with ane schout thus can the cadgear say:
'Abyde! And thou ane nekhering sall haif
Is worth my capill, creillis and all the laif.'   2090

299

'Now,' quod the foxe, 'I schreu me and we meit!
I hard quhat thou hecht to do with my skyn.
Thy handis sall never in thay mittinnis tak heit,
And thou wer hangit, carll, and all thy kyn!
Do furth thy mercat, at me thou sall nocht wyn,   2095
And sell thy hering thou hes thair till hie price;
Ellis thow sall wyn nocht on thy merchandice.'

300

The cadgear trimmillit for teyne quhair that he stude.
'It is weill worthie,' quod he, 'I want yone tyke,
That had nocht in my hand sa mekill gude   2100

2082. war *ready* gadderit *collected* *damned if*
2083. huntis *hunt is*
2084. burne *stream*
2085. lap *leapt* quyte *cleanly* fray *away from*
2086. raucht *struck* rout *blow*
2087. wan his hoill *made it back to his den*
2089. nekhering *blow on the neck* haif *have*
2090. capill *horse* laif *rest*
2091. I schreu me and *I'll be*
2092. hard *heard* hecht *promised*
2094. and *I wish* hangit *hanged*
2095. do furth *get on with* mercat *trading* at *from* wyn *profit*
2096. till *at*
2097. ellis *otherwise*
2098. trimmillit *trembled* teyne *rage*
2099. want *should have lost*
2100. sa mekill gude *so much*

2085. 'At that the fox leapt cleanly away from the baskets'.
2095–6. 'Get on with your trading, you won't make any profit out of me, and you'd better sell the herring you've got at a high price'.
2099–2101. 'I got what I deserved,' he said, 'letting that cur escape, because I didn't even have so much as a staff or pole in my hand to strike that rascal down'.

As staff or sting yone truker for to stryke!'
With that lychtlie he lap out over ane dyke
And snakkit doun ane staff, for he wes tene,
That hevie wes and of the holyne grene.

301

With that the foxe unto the wolf could wend   2105
And fand him be the hering quhair he lyis.
'Schir,' said he than, 'maid I not fair defend?
Ane wicht man wantit never and he were wyis;
Ane hardie hart is hard for to suppryis.'
Than said the wolf: 'Thow art ane berne full bald   2110
And wyse at will, in gude tyme be it tald.

302

'Bot quhat wes yone the carll cryit on hie,
And schuke his hand?' quod he. 'Hes thou no feill?'
'Schir,' said the foxe, 'that I can tell trewlie;
He said the nekhering wes intill the creill.'   2115
'Kennis thou that hering?' 'Ye, schir, I ken it weill,
And at the creill mouth I had it thryis but dout;
The wecht of it neir tit my tuskis out.

303

'Now suithlie, schir, micht we that hering fang,
It wald be fische to us thir fourtie dayis.'   2120
Than said the wolf, 'Nou God nor that I hang,
Bot to be thair I wald gif all my clays

2101. sting *pole* truker *rascal*
2102. lychtlie *nimbly*
2103. snakkit doun *broke off*
  tene *furious*
2104. holyne *holly*
2105. could wend *went*
2106. fand *found*
2107. fair defend *good defence*
2108. wicht *strong* wantit *was
  destitute* and *if* wyis *wise*
2109. hardie *courageous*
  suppryis *overpower*
2110. berne *creature* bald *bold*
2111. at will *when you want*

in gude tyme *truly* tald *told*
2112. yone *that*
2113. schuke *shook* feill *idea*
2116. kennis *know*
2117. creill mouth *rim of the
  basket* thryis *three times* but
  doubt *without doubt*
2118. wecht *weight* tit *pulled*
  tuskis *teeth*
2119. suithlie *truly* fang *get*
2120. thir *for the next*
2121. nou God nor that I
  hang *well I'll be hanged!*
2122. gif *give* clays *clothes*

2111. 'And wise when you want to be, truly let it be said'.

To se gif that my wappinnis mycht it rais.'
'Schir,' said the foxe, 'God wait, I wischit you oft,
Quhen that my pith micht not beir it onloft.   2125

304

'It is ane syde of salmond, as it wair,
And callour, pypand lyke ane pertrik ee.
It is worth all the hering ye have thair—
Ye, and we had it swa, is it worth sic thre.'
Than said the wolf, 'Quhat counsell gevis thou
          me?'   2130
'Schir,' said the foxe, 'wirk efter my devyis,
And ye sall have it, and tak you na suppryis.

305

'First, ye man cast ane cumpas far about,
Syne straucht you doun in middis of the way;
Baith heid and feit and taill ye man streik out;   2135
Hing furth your toung and clois weill your ene tway;
Syne se your heid on ane hard place ye lay;
And dout not for na perrell may appeir,
Bot hald you clois quhen that the carll cummis neir.

306

'And thocht ye se ane staf, have ye na dout,   2140
Bot hald you wonder still into that steid;
And luke your ene be clois as thay wer out,
And se that ye schrink nouther fute nor heid.
Than will the cadgear carll trou ye be deid

2123. gif *if* wappinnis *teeth*
    rais *raise*
2124. wait *knows* wischit *wished*
    for
2125. pith *strength* onloft *aloft*
2126. salmond *salmon* wair *were*
2127. callour *fresh*
    pypand *glistening* pertrik
    ee *partridge's eye*
2129. is it *it is* sic thre *three times*
    as much
2131. wirk *act* efter my
    devyis *according to my plan*

2132. suppryis *disappointment*
2133. cast ane cumpas *circle round*
2134. straucht *stretch*
2135. man *must* streik *spread*
2136. hing furth *hang out*
2137. se *see that*
2138. dout *fear*
2139. clois *still*
2141. into *in* steid *place*
2142. luke *take care* clois *closed*
2143. schrink *move*
2144. trou *think*

2138. 'And do not get frightened at any danger that might arise'.

And intill haist will hint you be the heillis,   2145
As he did me, and swak you on his creillis.'

307

'Now,' quod the wolf, 'I sweir the be my thrift,
I trou yone cadgear carll dow not me beir.'
'Schir,' said the foxe, 'onloft he will you lift
Upon his creillis, and do him lytill deir;   2150
Bot ane thing dar I suithlie to you sweir:
Get ye that hering sicker in sum place,
Ye sall not fair in fisching mair quhill Pasche.

308

'I sall say *In principio* upon yow,
And crose your corps from the top to tay;   2155
Wend quhen ye will, I dar be warrand now
That ye sall de na suddand deith this day!'
With that the wolf gird up sone and to gay,
And caist ane cumpas about the cadgear far;
Syne raucht him in the gait or he come nar.   2160

309

He laid his halfheid sicker hard and sad,
Syne straucht his four feit fra him and his heid,
And hang his toung furth as the foxe him bad.
Als styll he lay as he wer verray deid,
Rakkand nathing of the carlis favour nor feid,   2165
Bot ever upon the nekhering he thinkis,
And quyte foryettis the foxe and all his wrinkis.

2145. intill *in*
2146. swak *hurl*
2147. sweir the *tell you* be my
thrift *knowing my luck*
2148. dow not *is not able*
2150. deir *harm*
2152. sicker *safe*
2153. fair *go* quhill *until*
Pasche *Easter*
2154. In principio '*In the beginning*'
2155. crose *make the sign of the cross over* tay *toe*
2156. wend *go* warrand *surety*

2158. gird *leapt* sone *at once* to
gay *went*
2160. raucht him *threw himself*
gait *road* or *before* nar *near*
2161. halfheid *cheek* sicker
hard *very firmly* sad *heavily*
2162. straucht *stretched*
2163. bad *told*
2164. verray *truly*
2165. rakkand *caring* feid *anger*
2167. foryettis *forgets*
wrinkis *tricks*

310

With that the cadgear, als wraith as ony wind,
Come rydand on the laid, for it wes licht,
Thinkand ay on the foxe that wes behind,   2170
Upon quhat wyse revengit on him he micht;
And at the last of the wolf gat ane sicht
Quhair he in lenth lay strekit in the gait—
Bot gif he lichtit doun or nocht, God wait!

311

Softlie he said: 'I wes begylit anis.   2175
Be I begylit twyis I schrew us baith;
That evil bat it sall licht upon thy banis
He suld have had that hes done me the skaith!'
On hicht he hovit the staf, for he wes wraith,
And hit him with sic will upon the heid   2180
Quhill neir he swonit and swelt into that steid.

312

Thre battis he bure or he his feit micht find,
Bot yit the wolf wes wicht and wan away.
He mycht not se, he wes sa verray blind,
Nor wit reddilie quhether it wes nicht or day.   2185
The foxe beheld that service quhair he lay
And leuch onloft quhen he the wolf sa seis,
Baith deif and dosinnit, fall swonand on his kneis.

2168. wraith *angry*
2169. on *on top of* laid *load*
    licht *light*
2171. wysc *way* revengit *revenged*
2172. gat *caught*
2173. in lenth *at full length*
    streikit *stretched out* gait *road*
2174. gif *if* lichtit *alighted*
2175. begylit *tricked* anis *once*
2176. schrew *curse*
2177. bat *blow* banis *bones*
2178. skaith *harm*

2179. on hicht *on high*
    hovit *raised*
2180. will *gusto*
2181. swonit *passed out*
    swelt *died* steid *place*
2182. bure *suffered* or *before*
2183. wicht *strong* wan
    away *escaped*
2185. wit *knew*
2186. service *treatment*
2187. leuch *laughed* sa *saw* seis *stop*
2188. deif *deaf* dosinnit *dazed*

2174. 'God knows, he got down fast enough from that horse'.
2177–8. 'He who has done me harm should have had this terrible blow
    but now it will fall on your bones'.
2182. 'He suffered three blows before he could get to his feet'.

313

He that of ressoun can not be content,
Bot covetis all, is abill all to tyne.   2190
The foxe quhen that he saw the wolf wes schent
Said to himself: 'Thir hering sall be myne.'
I le, or ellis he wes a stewart fyne
That fand sic wayis his maister for to greif.
With all the fische thus Lowrence tuke his leif.   2195

314

The wolf wes neir weill dungin to the deid,
That uneith with his lyfe away he wan,
For with the bastoun weill brokin wes his heid.
The foxe into his den sone drew him than,
That had betraisit his maister and the man: 2200
The ane wantit the hering of his creillis,
The utheris blude wes rynnand over his heillis.

Moralitas

315

This taill is myngit with moralitie,
As I sall schaw sumquhat, or that I ceis.
The foxe unto the warld may likkinnit be;   2205
The revand wolf unto ane man, but leis;
The cadgear, deith, quhome under all man preis.

2189. of ressoun *with a reasonable amount*
2190. covetis *desires*   abill *liable*   tyne *lose*
2191. schent *beaten*
2193. le *lie*
2194. greif *harm*
2195. leif *leave*
2196. dungin *beaten*
2197. uneith *scarcely*   wan *escaped*
2198. bastoun *stick*
2199. drew him *took himself*
2200. betraist *betrayed*
2201. wantit *was missing*
2202. rynnand *running*
2203. myngit *mingled*
2204. schaw *show* or that *before*
2205. warld *world*   likkinnit *likened*
2206. revand *thieving* but leis *truly*
2207. man preis *must contend*

2193–4. 'I'd be lying if I said he wasn't a fine steward who found so many ways to harm his master'.
2197. 'That he scarcely escaped with his life'.
2207–9. 'The cadger is death, with whom everyone must contend. Every man, beast or fish in the sea that ever had life must, in accordance with nature, die'.

That ever tuke lyfe throw cours of kynd man dee,
As man and beist and fische into the see.

316

The warld, ye wait, is stewart to the man,   2210
Quhilk makis man to haif na mynd of deid,
Bot settis for winning all the craftis thay can.
The hering I likkin unto the gold sa reid,
Quhilk gart the wolf in perrell put his heid,
Richt swa the gold garris landis and cieteis   2215
With weir be waistit daylie as men seis.

317

And as the foxe with dissimulance and gyle
Gart the wolf wene to haif worschip for ever,
Richt swa this warld with vane glore for ane quhyle
Flatteris with folk as thay suld failye never;   2220
Yit suddandlie men seis it oft dissever
With thame that trowis oft to fill the sek:
Deith cummis behind and nippis thame be the nek.

318

The micht of gold makis mony men sa blind,
That settis on avarice thair felicitie,   2225
That thay foryet the cadgear cummis behind
To stryke thame, of quhat stait sa ever thay be.
Quhat is mair dirk than blind prosperitie?

2208. cours of kynd *course of nature* dee *die*
2211. haif *have* mynd *thought*
2212. settis *uses* winning *gain* craftis *skills* can *know*
2213. reid *red*
2214. gart *caused*
2215. richt swa *in the same way* cieteis *cities*
2216. weir *war* waistit *destroyed*
2217. dissimulance *deceit*
2218. wene *believe* worschip *glory*
2219. vane glore *vainglory*
2220. as *as if* failye *fail*
2221. dissever *depart*
2222. trowis *expect* sek *sack*
2225. felicitie *happiness*
2227. stait *state*
2228. mair dirk *more blind*

2212. 'But instead use all the skills they have in trying to get possessions'.
2219–22. 'In the same way this world flatters people with its vainglory for a while, making them think they will never come to grief; yet we often see it all suddenly slip away from those who expect to frequently fill up their sacks'.
2225. 'Whose happiness is derived from avarice'.
2227. 'To strike them, no matter what state they are in'.

Quhairfoir I counsell mychtie men to haif mynd
Of the nekhering interpreit in this kynd.   2230

THE FOX, THE WOLF, AND THE HUSBANDMAN

319
In elderis dayis, as Esope can declair,
Thair wes ane husband quhilk had ane pleuch to steir.
His use wes ay in morning to ryse air:
Sa happinnit him, in streiking tyme of yeir,
Airlie in the morning to follou furth his feir   2235
Unto the pleuch, bot his gadman and he.
His stottis he straucht with 'Benedicite!';

320
The caller cryit, 'How! Haik!' upon hicht,
'Hald draucht, my dowis', syne broddit thame full sair:
The oxin wes unusit, young, and licht,   2240
And for fersnes thay couth the fur forfair.
The husband than woxe angrie as ane hair,
Syne cryit, and caist his patill and grit stanis:
'The wolf', quod he, 'mot haue you all at anis!'

321
Bot yit the wolf wes neirar nor he wend,   2245
For in ane busk he lay, and Lowrence baith,

2229. mychtie *mighty* haif
mind *be mindful*
2230. interpreit *interpreted*
kynd *way*
2231. elderis dayis *the days of our
elders* Esope *Aesop*
2232. husband *husbandman;
farmer* pleuch *plough*
steir *drive*
2233. use *custom* ay *always*
air *early*
2234. happinnit him *he happened*
streiking *furrowing* yeir *year*
2235. feir *way*
2236. bot *only* gadman *goadsman*
2237. stottis *oxen* straucht *put to
work*

2238. caller *goadsman* haik *gee
up* upon hicht *loudly*
2239. hald draucht *plough on*
dowis *doves; beauties* syne *then*
broddit *goaded*
2240. unusit *inexperienced*
licht *skittish*
2241. fersnes *wildness* fur *furrow*
forfair *ruin*
2242. woxe *became* hair *hare*
2243. cryit *shouted* caist *threw*
patill *plough-staff* stanis *stones*
2244. mot *can* all at anis *all at
once*
2245. nor *than* wend *thought*
2246. busk *bush* Lowrence *the
fox* baith *too*

2241. 'And because of their wildness they ruined the furrow'.

In ane rouch rone wes at the furris end,
And hard the hecht; than Lowrence leuch full raith:
'To tak yone bud,' quod he, 'it wer na skaith.'
'Weill,' quod the wolf, 'I hecht the, be my hand,   2250
Yone carlis word as he wer king sall stand.'

322

The oxin waxit mair reulie at the last;
Syne efter thay lousit, fra that it worthit weill lait;
The husband hamewart with his cattell past.
Than sone the wolf come hirpilland in his gait   2255
Befoir the oxin, and schupe to mak debait.
The husband saw him, and worthit sumdeill agast,
And bakwart with his beistis wald haif past.

323

The wolf said, 'Quhether dryvis thou this pray?
I chalenge it, for nane of thame ar thyne!'   2260
The man thairof wes in ane felloun fray,
And soberlie to the wolf answerit syne:
'Schir, be my saull, thir oxin ar all myne:
Thairfoir I studdie quhy ye suld stop me,
Sen that I faltit neuer to you, trewlie.'   2265

2247. rouch rone *rough thicket*
　　furris *furrow's*
2248. hard *heard*　hecht *promise*
　　leuch *laughed*　full raith *at that*
2249. bud *gift*　quod *said*
　　skaith *harm*
2250. be my hand *we can shake
　　hands on it*
2251. as *as if*　sall *shall*
2252. waxit *became*　reulie *manageable*
2253. efter *afterwards*
　　lousit *unyoked*　fra that *since*
　　worthit *became*　lait *late*
2254. hamewart *homewards*
　　past *passed*
2255. sone *at once*
　　hirpilland *limping*　gait *way*

2256. schupe *shaped up*　mak
　　debait *have an argument*
2257. sumdeill agast *a bit afraid*
2258. bakwart *back the way he
　　came*
2259. quhether *where*
　　dryvis *drive*　pray *stolen cattle*
2260. thyne *yours*
2261. felloun fray *terrible dismay*
2262. soberlie *seriously*　syne *then*
2263. schir *sir*　be *by*　saull *soul*
　　thir *these*
2264. studdie *wonder*　quhy *why*
　　suld *should*
2265. sen that *since*
　　faltit *committed a fault*
　　trewlie *truly*

2249. ' "It wouldn't do any harm" he said "to take that gift" '.
2253. 'Then afterwards they unyoked the oxen from the plough, since it
　　was getting very late'.
2265. 'Since, truly, I never did anything to harm you'.

324

The wolf said, 'Carll, gaif thou not me this drift
Airlie, quhen thou wes eirrand on yone bank?
And is thair oucht, sayis thou, frear than gift?
This tarying wyll tyne the all thy thank:
Far better is frelie for to giff ane plank   2270
Nor be compellit on force to giff ane mart.
Fy on the fredome that cummis not with hart!'

325

'Schir,' quod the husband, 'ane man may say in greif,
And syne ganesay fra he avise and se.
I hecht to steill; am I thairfoir ane theif?   2275
God forbid, schir, all hechtis suld haldin be.
Gaif I my hand or oblissing,' quod he,
'Or haue ye witnes or writ for to schaw?
Schir, reif me not, bot go and seik the law'.

326

'Carll,' quod the wolf, 'ane lord, and he be leill,   2280
That schrinkis for schame, or doutis to be repruvit –
His sau is ay als sickker as his seill.

2266. carll *man* gaif *gave*
drift *team of oxen*
2267. airlie *earlier* quhen *when*
eirrand *ploughing*
2268. oucht *anything* frear *more*
generous
2269. tarying *delaying* tyne
the *lose you* thank *gratitude*
2270. frelie *willingly* giff *give*
plank *penny*
2271. nor *than* compellit *compelled*
on *by* mart *fattened ox*
2272. fy on *a curse upon*
fredome *generosity* with
hart *from the heart*

2273. say *speak* greif *anger*
2274. ganesay *unsay*
avise *reconsiders* se *sees*
2275. hecht *threaten* steill *steal*
2276. hechtis *vows* haldin be *be*
upheld
2277. oblissing *contract*
2278. writ *document* schaw *produce*
2279. reif *rob*
2280. and *if* leill *true*
2281. schrinkis for schame *shrinks*
from shame doutis *fears*
repruvit *condemned*
2282. sau *word* als *as*
sickker *good* seill *seal*

2270–1. 'It is far better to freely give a penny than to be eventually
forced to give a whole fattened ox'.
2274. 'And then take back his words because he reconsiders and sees his
error'.
2277–8. ' "Did we shake hands on it or have a contract," he said, "or
can you produce a witness or a document?" '.
2282. 'His word is always his bond' i.e. gentlemen need give no more
guarantee than their word.

Fy on the leid that is not leill and lufit!
Thy argument is fals, and eik contrufit,
For it is said in proverb: "But lawte   2285
All uther vertewis ar nocht worth ane fle." '.

327

'Schir,' said the husband, 'remember of this thing:
Ane leill man is not tane at half ane taill.
I may say and ganesay; I am na king.
Quhair is your witnes that hard I hecht thame
   haill?'   2290
Than said the wolf, 'Thairfoir it sall nocht faill.
Lowrence,' quod he, 'cum hidder of that schaw,
And say na thing bot as thow hard and saw.'

328

Lowrence come lourand, for he lufit never licht,
And sone appeirit befoir thame in that place.   2295
The man leuch na thing quhen he saw that sicht.
'Lowrence,' quod the wolf, 'thow man declair this cace,
Quhairof we sall schaw the suith in schort space.
I callit on the leill witnes for to beir:
Quhat hard thou that this man hecht me lang eir?' 2300

329

'Schir,' said the tod, 'I can not hastelie
Swa sone as now gif sentence finall,

2283. leid *man*   lufit *respected*
2284. eik *also*   contrufit *contrived*
2285. but *without*   lawte *fidelity*
2286. fle *fly*
2288. tane at *caught by*   taill *tale*
2290. hard *heard*   hecht *promised*
   haill *wholly*
2291. thairfoir *for that reason*
2292. of *from*   schaw *wood*
2293. bot as *except what*
2294. lourand *skulking*   lufit *liked*
   licht *light*

2295. appeirit *appeared*
2296. leuch na thing *didn't laugh
   at all*
2297. man declair *must settle*
   cace *case*
2298. schaw *show*   suith *truth*
   space *time*
2299. the *you*   beir *bear*
2300. lang eir *before*
2301. tod *fox*   hastelie *hastily*
2302. swa . . . now *right now*
   sentence *judgement*

2288. 'A true man is not taken in by a one-sided story'.
2291. 'Then said the wolf, "My case shall not fail on that account" '.

Bot wald ye baith submit yow heir to me,
To stand at my decreit perpetuall,
To pleis baith I suld preif, gif it may fall.'   2305
'Weill,' quod the wolf, 'I am content for me.'
The man said, 'Swa am I, however it be.'

330

Than schew thay furth thair allegeance but fabill,
And baith proponit thair pley to him compleit.
Quod Lowrence, 'Now I am ane juge amycabill: 2310
Ye sall be sworne to stand at my decreit,
Quhether heirefter ye think it soure or sweit.'
The wolf braid furth his fute, the man his hand,
And on the toddis taill sworne thay ar to stand.

331

Than tuke the tod the man furth till ane syde,   2315
And said him, 'Freind, thou art in blunder brocht;
The wolf will not forgif the ane oxe hyde.
Yit wald my self fane help the, and I mocht,
Bot I am laith to hurt my conscience ocht.
Tyne nocht thy querrell in thy awin defence.   2320
This will not throu but grit coist and expence.

2303. yow *yourselves*
2304. stand at *abide by*
    decreit *decision*
    perpetuall *perpetually*
2305. pleis *satisfy*   preif *try*
    fall *happen*
2307. be *turns out*
2308. schew *presented*
    allegeance *cases* but
    fabill *truthfully*
2309. proponit *entered* pley *plea*
    compleit *entirely*
2310. juge *judge*

amycabill *sympathetic*
2313. braid furth *proffered*
2314. on *by* taill *tail*
2316. in blunder brocht *in a bit of*
    trouble
2317. forgif the *let you off*
2318. fane *willingly* and *if*
    mocht *could*
2319. laith *loathe* hurt *betray*
    ocht *at all*
2320. tyne *lose* querrell *claim*
2321. throu *go through*
    but *without*

2303. 'But if you were both willing to submit yourselves here to my
    judgement'.
2305. 'I should try to satisfy you both, if it can be done'.
2314. 'And they are sworn, by the fox's tail, to abide by the decision.
    Then the fox took the man off to one side'.
2320–4. 'Don't lose the case by relying merely on your own powers of
    argument. This isn't going to succeed without great cost and expense.
    Don't you see how bribes carry men through, and gifts make crooked
    matters go straight? Sometimes a hen keeps a man his cow'.

332

'Seis thou not buddis beiris bernis throw,
And giftis garris crukit materis hald full evin?
Sumtymis ane hen haldis ane man in ane kow;
All ar not halie that heifis thair handis to hevin.' 2325
'Schir,' said the man, 'ye sall have sex or sevin
Richt of the fattest hennis of all the floik.
I compt not all the laif, leif me the coik.'

333

'I am ane juge,' quod Lowrence than, and leuch:
'Thair is na buddis suld beir me by the rycht. 2330
I may tak hennis and caponis weill aneuch,
For God is gane to sleip, as for this nycht;
Sic small thingis ar not sene in to his sicht.
Thir hennis', quod he, 'sall mak thy querrell sure:
With emptie hand na man suld halkis lure.' 2335

334

Concordit thus, than Lowrence tuke his leif,
And to the wolf he went in to ane ling,
Syne prevelie he plukkit him be the sleif:
'Is this in ernist', quod he, 'ye ask sic thing?
Na, be my saull, I trow it be in heithing.' 2340
Than said the wolf, 'Lowrence, quhy sayis thou sa?
Thow hard the hecht thy self that he couth ma.'

2322. seis *see* buddis *bribes*
  beiris *carry* bernis *men*
2323. garris *make* crukit
  materis *crooked matters*
  evin *straight*
2324. haldis *keeps* kow *cow*
2325. halie *holy* heifis *raise*
2326. sex *six*
2327. floik *flock*
2328. compt *care* laif *rest*
  leif *leave* coik *cock*
2329. leuch *laughed*
2330. beir me by the rycht *turn
  me from justice*

2331. caponis *capons*
  aneuch *enough*
2332. gane to sleip *gone to sleep*
2333. sic *such* in to *in* sicht *sight*
2334. thir *those*
2335. halkis *hawks*
2336. concordit *agreed* leif *leave*
2337. to ane ling *straightaway*
2338. prevelie *furtively*
  plukkit *tugged* sleif *sleeve*
2340. trow *think* heithing *jest*
2342. hecht *promise* couth
  ma *made*

2328. 'I don't care about all the rest, just leave me the cock'.

335

'The hecht', quod he, 'yone man maid at the pleuch,
Is that the cause quhy ye the cattell craif?'
Half in to heithing said Lowrence than, and leuch: 2345
'Schir, be the rude, unroikit now ye raif:
The Devill ane stirk taill thairfoir sall ye haif!
Wald I tak it upon my conscience
To do sa pure ane man as yone offence?

336

'Yit haif I commonnit with the carll', quod he.   2350
'We ar concordit upon this cunnand:
Quyte of all clamis, swa ye will mak him fre,
Ye sall ane cabok have in to your hand
That sic ane sall not be in all this land,
For it is somer cheis, baith fresche and fair: 2355
He sayis it weyis ane stane and sumdeill mair.'

337

'Is that thy counsell,' quod the wolf, 'I do,
That yone carll for ane cabok suld be fre?'
'Ye, be my saull, and I wer sworne yow to,
Ye suld nane uther counsell have for me;   2360
For gang ye to the maist extremitie,
It will not wyn yow worth ane widderit neip:
Schir, trow ye not I have ane saull to keip?'

2343. pleuch *plough*
2344. cause *reason* craif *crave*
2345. than *then* leuich *laughed*
2346. be the rude *by the cross*
  unroikit *unhinged* raif *rave*
2347. stirk *bullock's*
2349. pure *poor*
2350. commonnit *conversed*
2351. concordit *agreed*
  cunnand *plan*
2352. quyte *quit* clamis *claims*
  swa *providing*
2353. cabok *cheese*
2354. that sic ane *the like of which*
2355. somer *summer*
2356. weyis *weighs* stane *stone*
2357. counsell *advice* do *allow*
2359. and *even if*
2360. for *from*
2361. gang ye *if you go*
  maist *greatest* extremitie *extremity*
2362. widderit neip *withered
  turnip*
2363. keip *safeguard*

2346–7. 'By the cross, man, you're off your rocker: in the Devil's name,
all you'll get is a bullock's tail'.
2352. 'Providing you will make him free and quit of all claims regarding
the oxen'.
2361–2. 'For even if you take the case all the way, you won't gain as
much as a rotten turnip'.

338
'Weill,' quod the wolf, 'it is aganis my will
That yone carll for ane cabok suld ga quyte.'   2365
'Schir,' quod the tod, 'ye tak it in nane evill,
For, be my saull, your self had all the wyte.'
Than said the wolf, 'I bid na mair to flyte,
Bot I wald se yone cabok of sic pryis.'
'Schir,' said the tod, 'he tauld me quhair it lyis.'   2370

339
Than hand in hand thay held unto ane hill;
The husband till his hous hes tane the way,
For he wes fane he schaippit from thair ill,
And on his feit woke the dure quhill day.
Now will we turne unto the uther tway: 2375
Throw woddis waist thir freikis on fute can fair,
Fra busk to busk, quhill neir midnycht and mair.

340
Lowrence wes ever remembring upon wrinkis
And subtelteis, the wolf for to begyle.
That he had hecht ane caboik hc forthinkis;   2380
Yit at the last he findis furth ane wyle,
Than at himself softlie couth he smyle.
The wolf sayis, 'Lowrence, thou playis bellie blind;
We seik all nycht, bot na thing can we find.'

341
'Schir,' said the tod, 'we ar at it almaist;   2385
Soft yow ane lytill, and ye sall se it sone.'

2366. ye . . . evill *don't take it badly*
2367. wyte *blame*
2368. bid *want* flyte *argue*
2369. pryis *value*
2370. lyis *lies*
2371. held *went*
2372. tane the way *gone*
2373. fane *glad* schaippit *escaped*
2374. woke the dure *guarded the door* quhill *until*
2375. tway *two*
2376. woddis waist *wild woods* freikis *creatures* can fair *went*
2377. busk *bush*
2378. wrinkis *tricks*
2379. subtelteis *stratagems* begyle *beguile*
2380. forthinkis *regrets*
2381. findis furth *hits upon* wyle *plan*
2382. at *to*
2383. bellie blind *blind man's buff*
2386. soft yow *calm down*

2367. 'For, by my soul, you were completely in the wrong'.
2380. 'He regrets that it was a cheese he promised him'.

Than to ane manure place thay hyit in haist.
The nycht wes lycht, and pennyfull the mone.
Than till ane draw well thir senyeours past but hone,
Quhair that twa bukkettis severall suithlie hang;   2390
As ane come up ane uther doun wald gang.

342

The schadow of the mone schone in the well:
'Schir,' said Lowrence, 'anis ye sall find me leill.
Now se ye not the caboik weill your sell,
Quhyte as ane neip and round als as ane seill?   2395
He hang it yonder that na man suld it steill.
Schir, traist ye weill, yone caboik ye se hing
Micht be ane present to ony lord or king.'

343

'Na,' quod the wolf, 'mycht I yone caboik haif
On the dry land, as I it yonder se,   2400
I wald quitclame the carll of all the laif:
His dart oxin I compt thame not ane fle;
Yone wer mair meit for sic ane man as me.
Lowrence,' quod he, 'leip in the bukket sone,
And I sall hald the ane, quhill thow haue done.'   2405

344

Lowrence gird doun baith sone and subtellie;
The uther baid abufe and held the flaill.
'It is sa mekill', quod Lowrence, 'it maisteris me:

2387. manure place *manor house*
hyit in haist *go quickly*
2388. lycht *light*   pennyfull *round like a penny*   mone *moon*
2389. draw well *well*
senyeours *fine fellows*   but hone *without delay*
2390. bukkettis *buckets*
severall *separate*   suithlie *indeed*
2391. ane *one*   gang *go*
2392. schadow *reflection*
2393. anis *for once*   leill *true*
2394. weill *clearly*   sell *self*

2395. quhyte *white*   seill *seal*
2396. steill *steal*
2397. traist *believe*   hing *hanging*
2401. quitclame *release*   laif *rest*
2402. dart *draught*   compt *value*
2403. meit *food*
2404. sone *at once*
2405. have done *do the job*
2406. gird *climbed*   sone *quickly*
subtellie *dextrously*
2407. baid *waited*   flaill *winch*
2408. mekill *big*   maisteris me *is too much for me*

2390. 'Where, indeed, two separate buckets hung'.
2403. 'That's food more fitting for a man like me'.

On all my tais it hes not left ane naill.
Ye man mak help upwart, and it haill: 2410
Leip in the uther bukket haistelie,
And cum sone doun and make me sum supple!'

345

Than lychtlie in the bukket lap the loun;
His wecht but weir the uther end gart ryis:
The tod come hailland up, the wolf yeid doun.   2415
Than angerlie the wolf upon him cryis:
'I cummand thus dounwart, quhy thow upwart hyis?'
'Schir,' quod the foxe, 'thus fairis it of fortoun:
As ane cummis up, scho quheillis ane uther doun.'

346

Than to the ground sone yeid the wolf in haist;   2420
The tod lap on land, als blyith as ony bell,
And left the wolf in watter to the waist:
Quha haillit him out, I wait not, of the well.
Heir endis the text; thair is na mair to tell.
Yyt men may find ane gude moralitie   2425
In this sentence, thocht it ane fabill be.

Moralitas

347

This wolf I likkin to ane wickit man
Quhilk dois the pure oppres in everie place,
And pykis at thame all querrellis that he can,
Be rigour, reif, and uther wickitnes.   2430

2409. tais *toes*
2410. man *must* upwart *upwards*
    haill *pull*
2411. mak *give* supple *help*
2412. lap *leapt* loun *rogue*
2413. wecht *weight* but
    weir *without doubt* gart *causes*
2414. hailland *sailing* yeid *went*
2417. hyis *rise*
2418. fairis it *it happens* of
    fortoun *with fortune*
2419. quheillis *wheels*

2420. ground *bottom*
2421. blyith *happy*
2423. haillit *hauled* wait *know*
2426. sentence *tale*
2427. likkin *compare*
2428. the pure oppres *oppress the
    poor*
2429. pykis at thame *picks with
    them* querrellis *quarrels*
2430. be rigour *through harshness*
    reif *theft*

2410. 'You must help get it up, and pull it'.
2413. 'His weight, without doubt, causes the other end to go up'.

The foxe, the Feind I call into this cais,
Arctand ilk man to ryn unrychteous rinkis,
Thinkand thairthrow to lok him in his linkis.

348

The husband may be callit ane godlie man,
With quhome the Feynd falt findes, as clerkis
    reids,   2435
Besie to tempt him with all wayis that he can.
The hennis ar warkis that fra ferme faith proceidis:
Quhair sic sproutis spreidis, the evill spreit thair
    not speids,
Bot wendis unto the wickit man agane
That he hes tint his travell is full unfane.   2440

349

The wodds waist, quhairin wes the wolf wyld,
Ar wickit riches, quhilk all men gaipis to get:
Quha traistis in sic trusterie ar oft begyld,
For mammon may be callit the Devillis net,
Quhilk Sathanas for all sinfull hes set: 2445
With proud plesour quha settis his traist thairin,
But speciall grace lychtlie can not outwin.

2431. Feind *Devil* into this cais *in this instance*
2432. arctand *inciting* ilk *every* ryn *follow* unrichteous rinkis *bad courses*
2433. thairthrow *through this* lok *lock* linkis *chains*
2434. godlie *good*
2435. falt *fault* clerkis *scholars* reids *declare*
2436. besie *busy*
2437. warkis *deeds* ferme *firm* proceidis *proceed*
2438. sproutis *shoots* spreidis *grow* spreit *spirit* speids *succeed*

2439. wendis *goes*
2440. tint *wasted* travell *labours* unfane *disappointed*
2441. wodds waist *wild woods* wyld *tricked*
2442. gaipis *strive*
2443. quha *whoever* traistis in sic trusterie *puts their faith in such things*
2444. mammon *love of money* callit *called*
2445. Sathanas *Satan* set *set up*
2446. plesour *self-indulgence*
2447. but *without* lychtlie *easily* outwin *escape*

2432. 'Inciting every man to follow evil ways'.
2438. 'Where such good shoots grow, the evil spirit does not succeed'.
2440. 'Very disappointed that his efforts have been in vain'.
2445–7. 'Which Satan has set up to catch all sinful people: whoever places his trust in riches, with proud self-indulgence, cannot easily escape without special grace'.

350

The cabok may be callit covetyce,
Quhilk blomis braid in mony mannis ee.
Wa worth the well of that wickit vyce,   2450
For it is all bot fraud and fantasie,
Dryvand ilk man to leip in the buttrie
That dounwart drawis unto the pane of hell.
Christ keip all Christianis from that wickit well!

THE WOLF AND THE WETHER

351

Qwhylum thair wes, as Esope can report,   2455
Ane scheipheird dwelland be ane forrest neir,
Quhilk had ane hound that did him grit comfort.
Full war he wes to walk his fauld, but weir,
That nouther wolf nor wildcat durst appeir,
Nor foxe on feild, nor yit no uther beist,   2460
Bot he thame slew, or chaissit at the leist.

352

Sa happinnit it, as everilk beist man de,
This hound of suddand seiknes to be deid.
Bot than, God wait, the keipar of the fe
For verray wo woxe wanner nor the weid.   2465

2448. covetyce *covetousness*
2449. blomis *grows* braid *freely*
ee *eye*
2450. wa worth *a curse upon*
wickit *wicked*
2451. all bot *nothing but*
2452. dryvand *causing*
buttrie *larder*
2453. drawis *pulls*
2454. keip *protect*
2455. qwhylum *once upon a time*
Esope *Aesop*
2456. scheipheird *shepherd*
dwelland *living* be *by* neir *near*
2457. quhilk *who* did . . .
comfort *was a great comfort to him*

2458. full war *very alert*
walk *guard* fauld *fold* but
weir *without doubt*
2459. durst *dared*
2460. beist *beast*
2461. chaissit *chased away*
leist *least*
2462. sa *so* happinnit it *it
happened* everilk *every* man
de *must die*
2463. suddand *sudden*
seiknes *sickness* deid *dead*
2464. wait *knows* keipar *keeper*
fe *sheep*
2465. wanner *more withered*
nor *than* weid *weed*

2452–3. 'Causing every man to leap into the larder that pulls him
downwards to the pains of hell'.
2456. 'A shepherd living close to a forest'.
2463. 'This hound died of a sudden illness'.

'Allace,' quod he, 'now se I na remeid
To saif the selie beistis that I keip,
For with the wolf weryit beis all my scheip.'

353

It wald have maid ane mannis hart sair to se
The selie scheiphirdis lamentatioun: 2470
'Now is my darling deid, allace,' quod he,
'For now to beg my breid I may be boun,
With pyikstaff and with scrip to fair of toun;
For all the beistis befoir that bandonit bene
Will schute upon my beistis with ire and tene.'   2475

354

With that ane wedder wichtlie wan on fute:
'Maister,' quod he, 'mak merie and be blyith.
To brek your hart for baill it is na bute;
For ane deid dog ye na cair on yow kyith.
Ga fetche him hither and fla his skyn off swyth,   2480
Syne sew it on me, and luke that it be meit,
Baith heid and crag, bodie, taill, and feit.

2466. quod *said* remeid *remedy*
2467. saif *save* selie *poor*
  keip *guard*
2468. weryit *worried; mauled*
  beis *are*
2469. mannis *man's* sair *sad*
2472. breid *bread* may *can* be
  boun *get ready*
2473. pyikstaff *stick* scrip *beggar's
  bag* fair of toun *leave this
  farm*
2474. bandonit bene *were subdued*

2475. schute *rush* ire *anger*
  tene *fury*
2476. wedder *ram*
  wichtlie *bravely* wan on fute *got
  to his feet*
2477. merie *merry* blyith *happy*
2478. baill *grief* bute *remedy*
2479. cair *sorrow* kyith *show*
2480. fla *flay* swyth *quickly*
2481. syne *then* luke *take care*
  meit *close-fitting*
2482. heid *head* crag *neck*

2466–8. ' "Alas," he said, "now I can see no way to save the poor
  creatures that I guard, for all my sheep will be mauled to death by the
  wolf" '.
2472–5. 'Now I might as well get ready to beg for my bread, to leave
  this farm with a pikestaff and begging bowl; for all the wild beasts who
  were kept at bay before will now rush upon my sheep in anger and
  fury'.
2478–9. 'Breaking your heart with grief won't help matters; don't go
  showing sorrow over a dead dog'.

355

'Than will the wolf trow that I am he,
For I sall follow him fast quharever he fair.
All haill the cure I tak it upon me   2485
Your scheip to keip at midday, lait, and air:
And he persew, be God, I sall not spair
To follow him as fast as did your doig,
Swa that I warrand ye sall not want ane hoig.'

356

Than said the scheipheird, 'This come of ane gude
  wit: 2490
Thy counsall is baith sicker, leill, and trew;
Quha sayis ane scheip is daft, thay lieit of it.'
With that in hy the doggis skyn off he flew,
And on the scheip rycht softlie couth it sew.
Than worth the wedder wantoun of his weid: 2495
'Now of the wolf', quod he, 'I have na dreid.'

357

In all thingis he counterfait the dog,
For all the nycht he stude, and tuke na sleip,
Swa that weill lang thair wantit not ane hog.
Swa war he wes and walkryfe thame to keip,   2500
That Lowrence durst not luke upon ane scheip
For and he did, he followit him sa fast
That of his lyfe he maid him all agast.

2483. trow *think*
2484. fair *goes*
2485. haill *whole* cure *responsibility*
2486. lait *late* air *early*
2487. and *if* persew *pursues us*
  be *by* spair *neglect*
2488. follow *chase* doig *dog*
2489. swa *so* warrand *guarantee*
  want *lose* hoig *young sheep*
2490. wit *brain*
2491. counsall *advice* sicker *sure*
  leill *honest*
2492. lieit of it *tell a lie*
2493. in hy *quickly* flew *flayed*

2494. softlie *carefully* couth it
  sew *sewed it*
2495. worth *became*
  wantoun *insolent* weid *clothes*
2496. dreid *fear*
2497. counterfait *pretended to be*
2498. nycht *night*
2499. swa *so* weill lang *for a long
  time* wantit *went missing*
2500. war *alert* walkryfe *careful*
2501. Lowrence *the fox*
  durst *dared*
2502. and *if*
2503. agast *in fear*

2485–6. 'I accept the whole responsibility for guarding your sheep
  morning, noon and night'.
2495. 'Then the ram became insolent on account of his clothes'.

358

Was nowther wolf, wildcat, nor yit tod
Durst cum within thay boundis all about,   2505
Bot he wald chase thame baith throw rouch and snod.
Thay bailfull beistis had of thair lyvis sic dout,
For he wes mekill and semit to be stout,
That everilk beist thay dred him as the deid.
Within that woid that nane durst hald thair heid.   2510

359

Yit happinnit thair ane hungrie wolf to slyde
Out throw his scheip, quhair thay lay on ane le:
'I sall have ane,' quod he, 'quhatever betyde,
Thocht I be werryit, for hunger or I de.'
With that ane lamb in till his cluke hint he.   2515
The laif start up, for thay wer all agast,
Bot God wait gif the wedder followit fast.

360

Went never hound mair haistelie fra the hand
Quhen he wes rynnand maist raklie at the ra
Nor went this wedder baith over mois and strand,   2520
And stoppit nouther at bank, busk, nor bra,
Bot followit ay sa ferslie on his fa

2504. nowther *neither*   tod *fox*
2505. boundis *bounds*
2506. rouch and snod *rough ground and flat*
2507. bailfull *dangerous*   sic dout *such fear*
2508. mekill *big*   semit *seemed* stout *strong*
2509. dred *feared*
2510. woid *wood*   hald *hold up* heid *head*
2511. happinnit thair *there happened*   slyde *creep*
2512. le *field*

2513. ane *one*   betyde *happens*
2514. thocht *even if* de *die*
2515. in till *in*   cluke *claws* hint *seizes*
2516. laif *rest*   start *jumped*
2517. wait *knows*   gif *if*
2518. hand *hunter*
2519. rynnand *pursuing* raklie *hotly*   ra *roe-deer*
2520. nor *than*   mois *bog* strand *stream*
2521. busk *bush*   bra *hill*
2522. ay *always*   ferslie *closely* fa *foe*

2509–10. 'So that every creature feared him like the plague. None of them dared to show their faces within that wood'.
2514. 'Even if I am killed, because otherwise I'll just die of hunger anyway'.
2519–20. 'When he was most hotly pursuing the roe-deer, than this ram went over both bog and stream'.

With sic ane drift, quhill dust and dirt over-draif him,
And maid ane vow to God that he suld have him.

361

With that the wolf let out his taill on lenth,   2525
For he wes hungrie and it drew neir the ene,
And schupe him for to ryn with all his strenth;
Fra he the wedder sa neir cummand had sene,
He dred his lyfe, and he overtane had bene.
Thairfoir he spairit nowther busk nor boig,   2530
For weill he kennit the kenenes of the doig.

362

To mak him lycht, he kest the lamb him fra,
Syne lap over leis and draif throw dub and myre.
'Na,' quod the wedder, 'in faith we part not swa:
It is not the lamb, bot the, that I desyre.   2535
I sall cum neir, for now I se the tyre.'
The wolf ran till ane rekill stude behind him,
Bot ay the neirar the wedder he couth bind him.

363

Sone efter that, he followit him sa neir
Quhill that the wolf for fleidnes fylit the feild,   2540
Syne left the gait and ran throw busk and breir,
And schupe him fra the schawis for to scheild.

2523. drift *rush*   quhill *until*
over-draif *choked*
2525. on lenth *full length*
2526. ene *evening*
2527. schupe him *prepared*
himself   ryn *run*
2528. fra *because*
cummand *coming*
2529. dred *feared for*   and *if*
overtane *overtaken*
2530. spairit *shrunk from*   boig *bog*
2531. kennit *knew*
kenenes *keenness*

2532. licht *light*   kest *threw*
fra *from*
2533. lap *leapt*   leis *fields*
draif *rushed*   dub *pool*
2534. swa *so*
2535. the *you*
2536. tyre *tire*
2537. rekill *pile of stones*
2538. bind him *attach himself*
2540. fleidnes *fright*   fylit *defiled*
2541. gait *road*   breir *thicket*
2542. schupe *tried*
schawis *thickets*   scheild *protect*

2532. 'To make himself lighter he threw away the lamb'.
2538. 'But the ram was always gaining on the wolf'.
2542. 'And tried to protect himself from the thickets'.

He ran restles, for he wist of na beild;
The wedder followit him baith out and in,
Quhill that ane breir busk raif rudelie off the
    skyn.   2545

364

The wolf wes wer, and blenkit him behind,
And saw the wedder come thrawand throw the breir,
Syne saw the doggis skyn hingand on his lind.
'Na,' quod he, 'is this ye, that is sa neir?
Richt now ane hound, and now quhyte as ane
    freir.   2550
I fled over fer, and I had kennit the cais:
To God I vow that ye sall rew this rais.

365

'Quhat wes the cause ye gaif me sic ane katche?'
With that in hy he hint him be the horne:
'For all your mowis, ye met anis with your
    matche,   2555
Suppois ye leuch me all this yeir to scorne.
For quhat enchessoun this doggis skyn have ye
    borne?'
'Maister,' quod he, 'bot to have playit with yow;
I yow requyre that ye nane uther trow.'

2543. restles *without stopping*
    wist *knew* beild *refuge*
2545. breir busk *briar bush*
    raif *tore* rudelie *roughly*
2546. wer *alert* blenkit *glanced*
2547. thrawand *rushing*
2548. hingand on *hanging from*
    lind *buttocks*
2549. neir *near*
2550. richt now *a minute ago*
    quhyte *white* freir *friar*
2551. over *too* fer *far* and *if*

kennit *known* cais *case*
2552. rew *regret* rais *race*
2553. katche *chase*
2554. in hy *swiftly* hint *seized*
    be *by*
2555. mowis *tricks* anis *once*
2556. suppois *I suppose*
    leuch *mock* yeir *year*
2557. enchessoun *reason*
    borne *worn*
2558. bot *only* playit *played*
2559. requyre *ask* trow *believe*

2551. 'I ran too far, if the truth be told'.
2556. 'I suppose you'll mock me to the point of scorn for the whole
    year'.
2559. 'I beg you that you believe nothing else'.

366

'Is this your bourding in ernist than?' quod he,   2560
'For I am verray effeirit, and on flocht:
Cum bak agane, and I sall let yow se.'
Than quhar the gait wes grimmit he him brocht:
'Quhether call ye this fair play or nocht:
To set your maister in sa fell effray,   2565
Quhill he for feiritnes hes fylit up the way?

367

'Thryis, be my saull, ye gart me schute behind:
Upon my hoichis the senyeis may be sene;
For feiritnes full oft I fylit the wind.
Now is this ye? Na, bot ane hound, I wene!   2570
Me think your teith over schort to be sa kene.
Blissit be the busk that reft yow your array;
Ellis, fleand, bursin had I bene this day.'

368

'Schir,' quod the wedder, 'suppois I ran in hy,
My mynd wes never to do your persoun ill.   2575
Ane flear gettis ane follower commouly,

2560. bourding *joking* in ernist *serious*
2561. effeirit *upset* on flocht *in a flutter*
2563. grimmit *befouled* brocht *brought*
2565. set *put* sa fell effray *such terrible fear*
2566. feiritnes *terror* fylit up *befouled* way *road*
2567. thryis *three times* gart *made* schute *shoot*
2568. hoichis *hind legs*
senyeis *marks*
2570. bot *other than* wene *think*
2571. kene *fierce*
2572. blissit *blessed* reft yow *deprived you of* array *get-up*
2573. ellis *otherwise* fleand *fleeing* bursin *burst*
2574. suppois *even if* in hy *quickly*
2575. mynd *intention* ill *harm*
2576. ane flear *someone fleeing* gettis *gets*

2560. ' "Are you serious then about this being a joke?" he said'.
2563–4. 'Then he brought him to where he had befouled the road: "Do you call this a nice way to behave?" '.
2567. 'Three times, by my soul, you made me lose control of my bowels'.
2570. 'Now is this you? No, you're something other than a hound, I think'.
2573. 'Otherwise, my heart would have burst with all the running today'.
2576–7. 'Anyone running away tends to get someone chasing them, whether it's in jest or earnest, let anyone look and see'.

In play or ernist, preif quha sa ever will.
Sen I bot playit, be gracious me till,
And I sall gar my freindis blis your banis.
Ane full gude seruand will crab his maister anis.'   2580

369
'I have bene oftymis set in grit effray,
Bot, be the rude, sa rad yit wes I never
As thow hes maid me with thy prettie play:
I schot behind quhen thow overtuke me ever.
Bot sikkerlie now sall we not dissever.'   2585
Than be the crag-bane smertlie he him tuke,
Or ever he ceissit, and it in schunder schuke.

Moralitas
370
Esope, that poet, first father of this fabill,
Wrait this parabole, quhilk is convenient,
Because the sentence wes fructuous and agreabill,   2590
In moralitie exemplative prudent;
Quhais problemes bene verray excellent,
Throw similitude of figuris, to this day,
Gevis doctrine to the redaris of it ay.

2577. preif *see*
2578. sen *since* gracious *kind* me
   till *to me*
2579. gar *make* blis *bless*
   banis *bones*
2580. servand *servant*
   crab *displease*
2581. oftymis *often*
2582. be the rude *by the cross*
   rad *terrified*
2583. prettie play *clever tricks*
2584. ever *every time*
2585. sikkerlie *truly* dissever *part*
2586. crag-bane *neck bone*
   smertlie *quickly*

2587. or *before* ceissit *stopped* in
   schunder *in pieces*
2588. first father *originator*
2589. parabole *allegory*
   convenient *fitting*
2590. sentence *meaning*
   fructuous *profitable*
   agreabill *suitable*
2591. exemplative *giving example*
2592. quhais *of which*
   problemes *issues* verray *truly*
2593. similitude *relevance*
   figuris *figures*
2594. gevis doctrine *gives*
   instruction redaris *readers*

2580. 'Even a very good servant will displease his master once'.
2587. 'And shook it to pieces before he stopped'.
2591–4. 'Giving a wise example of morality; in which the issues raised
   are truly excellent, always instructing the readers through figures
   relevant to our lives today'.

371

Heir may thow se that riches of array 2595
Will cause pure men presumpteous for to be.
Thay think thay hald of nane, be thay als gay,
Bot counterfute ane lord in all degre.
Out of thair cais in pryde thay clym sa hie
That thay forbeir thair better in na steid, 2600
Quhill sum man tit thair heillis over thair heid.

372

Richt swa in service uther sum exceidis,
And thay haif withgang, welth, and cherising,
That thay will lychtlie lordis in thair deidis,
And lukis not to thair blude nor thair ofspring. 2605
Bot yit nane wait how lang that reull will ring.
Bot he was wyse that bad his sone considder:
'Bewar in welth, for hall benkis ar rycht slidder.'

373

Thairfoir I counsell men of everilk stait
To knaw thame self, and quhome thay suld
     forbeir, 2610
And fall not with thair better in debait,
Suppois thay be als galland in thair geir:

2595. riches of array *fine clothes*
2596. pure *poor*
2597. hald of nane *have no superior* als gay *as well dressed*
2598. counterfute *imitate* all degre *all respects*
2599. cais *proper place* clym *climb* hie *high*
2600. forbeir *give in to* steid *place*
2601. tit *turns* heillis *feet*
2602. richt swa *in the same way* uther sum *some others* exceidis *go too far*
2603. withgang *success* cherising *pleasure*
2604. lychtlie *make light of*

deidis *deeds*
2605. lukis *remember* blude *family line* ofspring *origins*
2606. wait *know* reull *rule* ring *prevail*
2607. bad *told* sone *son*
2608. benkis *benches* slidder *slippery*
2609. everilk *every* stait *rank in life*
2610. thame self *themselves* forbeir *respect*
2611. better *betters* in debait *into argument*
2612. galland *gallant* geir *dress*

2607. 'But he was wise who told his son to consider this: "Beware wealth, for hall benches are very slippery" '.

It settis na servand for to uphald weir,
Nor clym sa hie quhill he fall of the ledder:
Bot think upon the wolf and on the wedder.   2615

THE WOLF AND THE LAMB
374
Ane cruell wolf, richt ravenous and fell,
upon ane tyme past to ane reveir
Descending from ane rotche unto ane well;
To slaik his thrist, drank of the watter cleir.
Swa upon cace ane selie lamb come neir,   2620
Bot of his fa the wolf na thing he wist,
And in the streme laipit to cule his thrist.

375
Thus drank thay baith, bot not of ane intent:
The wolfis thocht wes all on wickitnes;
The selie lamb wes meik and innocent.   2625
Upon the rever in ane uther place
Beneth the wolf he drank ane lytill space,
Quhill he thocht gude, belevand thair nane ill.
The wolf him saw, and rampand come him till,

376
With girnand teith and angrie austre luke,   2630
Said to the lamb, 'Thow cative wretchit thing,

2613. settis *becomes* uphald weir *uphold strife*
2614. clym *climb* hie *high* ledder *ladder*
2616. richt *very* fell *cruel*
2617. past to *passed by* reveir *river*
2618. rotche *cliff* unto *into* well *pool*
2619. slaik *quench*
2620. swa *so* upon cace *by chance* selie *innocent*
2621. fa *foe* wist *knew*

2622. laipit *drank* cule *cool*
2623. ane *one*
2625. meik *meek*
2627. beneth *downstream from* lytill space *for a little time*
2628. quhill *while* thocht *thought* belevand *thinking*
2629. rampand *raging* him till *to him*
2630. girnand *bared* austre *stern* luke *look*
2631. cative *miserable* wretchit *wretched*

2613. 'It is not fitting for a servant to keep up an argument with his superior'.
2621. 'Unaware of the presence of his foe, the wolf'.
2628. 'For as long as he wanted, thinking there was no harm in it'.

How durst thow be sa bald to fyle this bruke
Quhar I suld drink with thy foull slavering?
It wer almous the for to draw and hing,
That suld presume with thy foull lippis vyle   2635
To glar my drink and this fair watter fyle.'

377

The selie lamb, quaikand for verray dreid,
On kneis fell and said, 'Schir, with your leif,
Suppois I dar not say thairof ye leid,
Bot, be my saull, I wait ye can nocht preif   2640
That I did ony thing that suld yow greif.
Ye wait alswa that your accusatioun
Failyeis fra treuth and contrair is to ressoun.

378

'Thocht I can nocht, nature will me defend,
And of the deid perfyte experience: 2645
All hevie thing man of the self discend,
Bot gif sum thing on force mak resistence;
Than may the streme on na way mak ascence
Nor ryn bakwart; I drank beneth yow far:
Ergo, for me your bruke wes never the war.   2650

2632. durst *dare* bald *bold*
  fyle *defile* bruke *stream*
2633. quhar *where*
  slavering *slobbering*
2634. wer *would be* almous *an act
  of charity* the *you* hing *hang*
2635. vyle *vile*
2636. glar *muddy*
2637. quaikand *trembling*
  dreid *fear*
2638. leif *permission*
2639. suppois *although* dar *dare*
  leid *lied*
2640. be *by* wait *know*
  preif *prove*

2641. greif *grieve*
2642. alswa *also*
2643. failyeis fra *goes astray from*
  contrair *contrary*
2644. nocht *not*
2645. deid *fact*
  experience *knowledge*
2646. man *must* the self *itself*
2647. bot gif *unless* on
  force *forcibly*
2648. on *in* mak ascence *climb
  upwards*
2649. ryn *run* bakwart *backwards*
2650. ergo *therefore* for me *on my
  account* bruke *water* war *worse*

2634. 'Hanging and drawing would be too good for you'.
2644–7. 'Though I am too weak to defend myself, nature and a perfect
  knowledge of the facts will defend me: every heavy thing must by its
  very nature move downwards, unless something forcibly holds it back'.
2649–50. 'Nor flow backwards; I drank far downstream of you: therefore,
  your water was never the worse on my account'.

379

'Alswa my lippis, sen that I wes ane lam,
Tuitchit na thing that wes contagious,
Bot sowkit milk from pappis of my dam,
Richt naturall, sweit, and als delitious.'
'Weill,' quod the wolf, 'thy language rigorus   2655
Cummis the of kynd; swa thy father before
Held me at bait, baith with boist and schore.

380

'He wraithit me, and than I culd him warne,
Within ane yeir, and I brukit my heid,
I suld be wrokkin on him or on his barne.   2660
For his exorbetant and frawart pleid
Thow sall doutles for his deidis be deid.'
'Schir, it is wrang that for the fatheris gilt
The saikles sone suld punist be or spilt.

381

'Haif ye not hard quhat Halie Scripture sayis,   2665
Endytit with the mouth of God almycht?
Of his awin deidis ilk man sall beir the pais,
As pyne for sin, reward for werkis rycht.
For my trespas, quhy suld my sone have plycht?

2651. sen *since*   lam *lamb*
2652. tuitchit *touched*
    contagious *tainted*
2653. sowkit *sucked*   pappis *teats*
    dam *mother*
2654. als *also*   delitious *delicious*
2655. quod *said*
2656. cummis . . . kynd *comes
    naturally to you*
2657. at bait *in contention*
    baith *both*   boist *threat*
    schore *menace*
2658. wraithit *angered*   culd him
    warne *warned him*
2659. yeir *year*   and *providing*
    brukit *had the use of*
2660. wrokkin *revenged*

barne *child*
2661. exorbetant *offensive*
    frawart *perverse*   pleid *dispute*
2662. doutles *without doubt*
    deidis *deeds*   deid *dead*
2663. schir *sir*   gilt *guilt*
2664. saikles *innocent*   sone *son*
    spilt *injured*
2665. hard *heard*   halie *holy*
2666. endytit *dictated*
    almycht *almighty*
2667. awin *own*   ilk *every*
    beir *bear*   pais *responsibility*
2668. pyne *punishment*   werkis
    rycht *good works*
2669. trespas *wrongdoing*
    quhy *why*   plycht *blame*

2657. 'Fought with me, using both threats and menacing behaviour'.

Quha did the mis, lat him sustene the pane.'   2670
'Yaa!' quod the wolf, 'Yit pleyis thow agane?

382
'I let the wit, quhen that the father offendis,
I will cheris nane of his successioun,
And of his barnis I may weill tak amendis
Unto the twentie degre descending doun.   2675
Thy father thocht to mak ane strang poysoun,
And with his mouth in to my watter spew.'
'Schir,' quod the lamb, 'thay twa ar nouther trew.

383
'The law sayis, and ye will understand,
Thair suld na man, for wrang nor violence,   2680
His adversar punis at his awin hand
Without proces of law and audience;
Quhilk suld have leif to mak lawfull defence,
And thairupon summond peremtourly
For to propone, contrairie, and reply.   2685

384
'Set me ane lauchfull court. I sall compeir
Befoir the lyoun, lord and leill justice,
And be my hand I oblis me rycht heir

2670. quha *whoever* the *you*
  mis *wrong*
2671. pleyis *plead* agane *against*
2672. I . . . wit *I'll have you
  know* quhen *when*
2673. cheris *hold dear*
  successioun *successors*
2674. of *from* barnis *children* tak
  amendis *seek compensation*
2675. twentie degre *twentieth
  generation*
2676. thocht *intended*
  strang *strong* poysoun *poison*
2678. thay twa *those two things*

trew *true*
2679. and *if*
2681. adversar *adversary*
  punis *punish* at *by*
2682. audience *legal hearing*
2683. leif *opportunity*
2684. summond *be summoned*
  peremtourly *peremptorily*
2685. propone *state*
  contrairie *speak in opposition*
2686. set *appoint* lauchfull *lawful*
  compeir *appear*
2687. leill justice *true judge*
2688. be *by* oblis me *promise*

2671. ' "Pah!" said the wolf, "Are you still arguing against me?" '.
2683–5. 'A man should have the opportunity to defend himself according
  to the law, and, with reference to that, receive a peremptory summons
  in order to state his case, speak in opposition, and reply to the
  charges'.

That I sall byde ane unsuspect assyis.
This is the law, this is the instant wyis.   2690
Ye suld pretend thairfoir ane summondis mak
Aganis that day, to gif ressoun and tak.'

385

'Ha,' quod the wolf, 'thou wald intruse ressoun
Quhair wrang and reif suld duell in propertie.
That is ane poynt and part of fals tressoun,   2695
For to gar reuth remane with crueltie.
Be Goddis woundis, fals tratour, thow sall de
For thy trespas, and for thy fatheris als.'
With that anone he hint him be the hals.

386

The selie lamb culd do na thing bot bleit: 2700
Sone wes he hedit, the wolf wald do na grace,
Syne drank his blude and of his flesche can eit
Quhill he wes full; syne went his way on pace.
Of his murther quhat sall we say, allace?
Wes not this reuth, wes not this grit pietie,   2705
To gar this selie lamb but gilt thus de?

2689. byde *submit to*
  unsuspect *impartial*
  assyis *inquiry*
2690. instant wyis *present custom*
2691. pretend *undertake*
  summondis *summons*
2692. aganis *for* gif *give*
  ressoun *arguments*
2693. intruse *thrust in*
2694. reif *robbery*
  propertie *possession*
2695. poynt and part *example and instance*

2696. gar *make* reuth *pity*
2697. de *die*
2698. als *also*
2699. anone *at once* hint *seized*
  hals *neck*
2700. bleit *bleat*
2701. hedit *beheaded* do *show*
  grace *mercy*
2703. on pace *swiftly*
2704. murther *murder*
2705. reuth *a shame* grit pietie *a great pity*
2706. but gilt *without guilt*

2691–2. 'You should undertake, therefore, to prepare a summons for that day, so that you can exchange arguments'.
2693–4. ' "Ha," said the wolf, "you want to thrust in arguments so that injustice and robbery can hold the floor" '.
2696. 'To try to make pity remain with cruelty'.

Moralitas

387

The pure pepill, this lamb may signifie,
As maill men, merchandis, and all laboureris,
Of quhome the lyfe is half ane purgatorie,
To wyn with lautie leving, as efferis.   2710
The wolf betakinnis fals extortioneris
And oppressouris of pure men, as we se,
Be violence, or craft in suteltie.

388

Thre kynd of wolfis in this warld now rings:
The first ar fals perverteris of the lawis,   2715
Quhilk under poleit termis falset mingis,
Lettand that all wer gospell that he schawis;
Bot for ane bud the pure man he overthrawis,
Smoirand the richt, garrand the wrang proceid;
Of sic wolfis hellis fyre sall be thair meid.   2720

389

O man of law, let be thy subteltie,
With nice gimpis and fraudis intricait,

2707. pure *poor* signifie *represent*
2708. as *such as* maill men *tenant farmers* merchandis *traders* laboureris *labourers*
2709. quhome *whom* purgatorie *purgatory*
2710. wyn *make* lautie *honesty* leving *a living* as efferis *as is fitting*
2711. betakinnis *represents* extortioneris *extortionists*
2713. be *by* craft in suteltie *devious means*
2714. kynds *kinds* rings *have power*
2715. perverteris of the lawis *corrupt lawyers*
2716. poleit *elegant* falset *falsehood* mingis *mingle*
2717. lettand *pretending* gospell *gospell truth* schawis *alleges*
2718. bud *bribe* overthrawis *destroys*
2719. smoirand *suppressing* richt *right* garrand *making* proceid *go forward*
2720. meid *reward*
2721. let be *stop* subteltie *craftiness*
2722. nice gimpis *perplexing subtleties* fraudis intricait *intricate deceptions*

2709–10. 'Whose lives are almost a purgatory, as they try to make an honest living, as they should'.
2716–8. 'Who hides his falsehood behind elegant words, acting as though everything that he alleges were the gospel truth; but all it takes is a bribe and he will destroy the poor man'.
2720. 'Hell's fire shall be the reward of such wolves'.

And think that God in his divinitie
The wrang, the richt, of all thy werkis wait.
For prayer, price, for hie nor law estait,   2725
Of fals querrellis se thow mak na defence:
Hald with the richt, hurt not thy conscience.

390

Ane uther kynd of wolfis ravenous
Ar mychtie men, haifand aneuch plentie,
Quhilkis ar sa gredie and sa covetous   2730
Thay will not thoill in peax ane pureman be:
Suppois he and his houshald baith suld de
For falt of fude, thairof thay gif na rak,
Bot over his heid his mailling will thay tak.

391

O man but mercie, quhat is in thy thocht?   2735
War than ane wolf, and thow culd understand!
Thow hes aneuch; the pure husband richt nocht,
Bot croip and calf upon ane clout of land.
For Goddis aw, how durst thow tak on hand,
And thow in barn and byre sa bene and big,   2740
To put him fra his tak and gar him thig?

2724. wait *knows*
2725. prayer *pleading*
    price *bribery* estait *rank*
2726. hald *hold*
2727. ravenous *cruel*
2728. mychtie *powerful*
    haifand *having* aneuch
    plentie *more than enough*
2730. gredie *greedy*
    covetous *avaricious*
2731. thoill *allow* peax *peace*
2732. suppois *even if* de *die*
2733. falt *lack* fude *food* gif na
    rak *pay no heed*

2734. mailling *tenant-farm*
2735. but *without* quhat is in thy
    thocht *what are you thinking
    about*
2736. war *worse* and *if*
2737. husband *farmer* richt
    nocht *almost nothing*
2738. croip and calf *crop and
    chaff* clout *patch*
2739. aw *fear* durst *dare* tak on
    hand *undertake*
2740. byre *cattle shed* bene *good*
2741. tak *leasehold farm*
    gar *make* thig *beg*

2724. 'Knows the right and the wrong of all your actions'.
2725–6. 'Take care that you do not uphold any false arguments, on account of pleading or bribery, and no matter what the person's status is'.
2731–4. 'They will not let a poor man live in peace: they take his tenant-farm by going over his head and offering the landlord higher rents, so what if the farmer and his family die of hunger, they don't care about that'.

392

The thrid wolf ar men of heritage,
As lordis that hes land be Goddis lane,
And settis to the mailleris ane village,
And for ane tyme gressome payit and tane;   2745
Syne vexis him, or half his terme be gane,
With pykit querrellis for to mak him fane
To flit or pay his gressome new agane.

394

His hors, his meir, he man len to the laird,
To drug and draw in cairt or in cariage;   2750
His servand or his self may not be spaird
To swing and sweit withoutin meit or wage:
Thus how he standis in labour and bondage
That scantlie may he purches by his maill
To leve upon dry breid and watter caill.   2755

395

Hes thow not reuth to gar thy tennentis sweit
In to thy laubour, with faynt and hungrie wame,

2742. heritage *property*
2743. hes *have* lane *gift*
2744. settis *leases* mailleris *tenant farmers*
2745. tyme *term of lease* gressome *money* payit and tane *is exchanged*
2746. vexis *torments* or *before* be gane *is passed*
2747. pykit querrellis *contrived disputes* fane *glad*
2748. flit *move*

2749. meir *mare* man len *must lend* laird *lord*
2750. drug *pull*
2751. spaird *exempt*
2752. swing *toil* meit *food*
2753. thus how *this is how*
2754. scantlie *scarcely* purches *manage* maill *farming*
2755. watter caill *cabbage broth*
2756. reuth *shame* sweit *sweat*
2757. in . . . laubour *doing your work* faynt *empty* wame *belly*

2739–41. 'As a God-fearing man, how dare you set out – you who have such a nice big barn and cattle shed of your own – to throw him out of his farm and make him beg'.
2744. 'And leases a whole village and the surrounding lands to the tenant farmers'.
2746–8. 'Then he begins to torment the farmer, before even half of his term of lease is up, contriving disputes to make him want to move or else pay his rent all over again'.
2752. 'From toiling and sweating without any food or payment'.
2753–5. 'This is how he is placed, in slave labour and bondage so that his farming scarcely provides him with enough dry bread and watery soup to live on'.

And syne hes lytill gude to drink or eit
With his menye, at evin quhen he cummis hame?
Thow suld be rad for richteous Goddis blame,　　2760
For it cryis ane vengeance unto the hevinnis hie
To gar ane pure man wirk but meit or fe.

396

O thow grit lord, that riches hes and rent,
Be nocht ane wolf, thus to devoir the pure.
Think that na thing cruell nor violent　　2765
May in this warld perpetuallie indure.
This sall thow trow and sikkerlie assure:
For till oppres, thow sall haif als grit pane
As thow the pure with thy awin hand had slane.

397

God keip the lamb, quhilk is the innocent,　　2770
From wolfis byit and fell extortioneris;
God grant that wrangous men of fals intent
Be manifest, and punischit as effeiris;
And God, as thow all rychteous prayer heiris,
Mot saif our king, and gif him hart and hand　　2775
All sic wolfis to banes out of the land.

THE PADDOCK AND THE MOUSE

398

Upon ane tyme, as Esope culd report,
Ane lytill mous come till ane rever syde.

2758. syne *afterwards*
2759. menye *family* evin *evening*
    hame *home*
2760. rad *afraid*
2761. cryis *crys* hevinnis *heavens*
2762. wirk *work* but *without*
    fe *wages*
2764. devoir *devour*
2765. think *remember*
2766. indure *endure*
2767. trow *know* sikkerlie
    assure *be sure about*
2768. for till *for if you* pane *pain*

2769. as *as if*
2770. keip *protect*
2771. fell *cruel* byit *bite*
2772. wrangous *unjust*
2773. manifest *exposed* as
    effeiris *as is fitting*
2774. heiris *hears*
2775. mot saif *save* hart *desire*
    hand *strength*
2776. banes *banish*
2777. upon ane tyme *once upon a
    time* Esope *Aesop*
2778. come till *came to* rever *river*

2760–2. 'You should be afraid of God's righteous anger, because making
    a poor man work without food or wages demands retribution from high
    heaven'.

Scho micht not waid, hir schankis wer sa schort;
Scho culd not swym; scho had na hors to ryde;   2780
Of verray force behovit hir to byde,
And to and fra besyde that revir deip
Scho ran, cryand with mony pietuous peip.

399

'Help over! Help over!' this silie mous can cry,
'For Goddis lufe, sum bodie, over the brym.'   2785
With that ane paddok, in the watter by,
Put up hir heid and on the bank can clym,
Quhilk be nature culd douk and gaylie swym.
With voce full rauk, scho said on this maneir:
'Gude morne, schir Mous! Quhat is your erand
     heir?'   2790

400

'Seis thow', quod scho, 'of corne yone jolie flat,
Of ryip aitis, of barlie, peis, and quheit?
I am hungrie, and fane wald be thair at,
Bot I am stoppit be this watter greit;
And on this syde I get na thing till eit   2795
Bot hard nuttis, quhilkis with my teith I bore:
Wer I beyond, my feist wer fer the more.

2779. scho *she*   waid *wade across*
     schankis *legs* schort *short*
2781. verray force *sheer necessity*
     behovit hir *she needed* byde *wait*
2782. fra *fro* deip *deep*
2783. cryand *crying* pietuous
     peip *pitiful peep*
2784. help over *help me over*
     silie *poor* can cry *cried*
2785. for Goddis lufe *for the love
     of God* sum bodie *somebody*
     brym *water*
2786. paddok *frog* by *nearby*
2787. heid *head* can clym *climbed*
2788. quhilk *who* douk *dive*

2789. voce *voice* full rauk *very
     hoarse* maneir *way*
2790. schir *sir* erand *business*
2791. seis thow *do you see*
     quod *said* jolie flat *nice field*
2792. ryip aitis *ripe oats*
     barlie *barley* peis *peas*
     quheit *wheat*
2793. fane *gladly*
2794. stoppit *prevented* watter
     greit *great river*
2795. till eit *to eat*
2796. bot *except for*
     quhilkis *which*
2797. feist *feast* fer *far*

2797. 'If I were over there, my dinner would be so much better'.

401

'I have no boit; heir is no maryner;
And thocht thair war, I have no fraucht to pay.'
Quod scho, 'Sister, lat be thy hevie cheir;   2800
Do my counsall, and I sall find the way,
Withoutin hors, brig, boit, or yit galay,
To bring the over saiflie, be not afeird,
And not wetand the campis of thy beird.'

402

'I haif mervell', than quod the lytill mous,   2805
'How can thow fleit without fedder or fin?
This rever is sa deip and dangerous,
Me think that thow suld drowin to wed thairin.
Tell me, thairfoir, quhat facultie or gin
Thow hes to bring the over this watter wan.'   2810
That to declair the paddok thus began:

403

'With my twa feit,' quod scho, 'lukkin and braid,
In steid of airis, I row the streme full styll,
And thocht the brym be perrillous to waid,
Baith to and fra I swyme at my awin will.   2815
I may not droun, for quhy my oppin gill
Devoidis ay the watter I resaif:
Thairfoir to droun, forsuith, na dreid I haif.'

2798. boit *boat* maryner *sailor*
2799. thocht *even if* fraucht *fare*
2800. lat be *give up* hevie
  cheir *sorrowful mood*
2801. do *follow* counsall *advice*
2802. withoutin *without*
  brig *bridge* yit galay *even galley*
2803. saiflie *safely* afeird *afraid*
2804. wetand *wetting*
  campis *whiskers* beird *beard*
2805. I haif mervell *I am amazed*
2806. fleit *float* fedder *feather*
2808. drowin *drown* to wed
  thairin *if you waded into it*

2809. facultie or gin *craft or skill*
2810. the *you* wan *dark*
2811. declair *explain*
2812. twa feit *two feet*
  lukkin *webbed* braid *broad*
2813. in steid *instead* airis *oars*
  styll *continually*
2814. thocht *although* waid *wade*
2815. fra *fro* awin *own*
2816. for quhy *because* oppin
  gill *open gills*
2817. devoidis *get rid of*
  resaiff *take in*
2818. forsuith *in truth* dreid *fear*

2799. ' "And even if there were, I don't have any money to pay the
  fare." The toad said, "Sister, don't be sad" '.

404

The mous beheld unto hir fronsit face,
Hir runkillit cheikis, and hir lippis syde,   2820
Hir hingand browis, and hir voce sa hace,
Hir loggerand leggis, and hir harsky hyde.
Scho ran abak, and on the paddok cryde:
'Gif I can ony skill of phisnomy,
Thow hes sumpart of falset and invy.   2825

405

'For clerkis sayis the inclinatioun
Of mannis thocht proceidis commounly
Efter the corporall complexioun
To gude or evill, as nature will apply:
Ane thrawart will, ane thrawin phisnomy.   2830
The auld proverb is witnes of this *lorum:*
Distortum vultum sequitur distortio morum.'

406

'Na,' quod the taid, 'that proverb is not trew,
For fair thingis oftymis ar fundin faikin;
The blaberyis, thocht thay be sad of hew,   2835
Ar gadderit up quhen primeros is forsakin;

2819. beheld unto *looked into*
    fronsit *crumpled*
2820. runkillit *wrinkled*
    syde *broad*
2821. hingand *overhanging*
    hace *hoarse*
2822. loggerand *loose-jointed*
    harsky hyde *rough skin*
2823. on *to*
2824. gif *if* can *know*
    phisnomy *physiognomy*
2825. sumpart *some*
    falset *falsehood* invy *malice*
2826. clerkis *scholars*
2827. thocht *thought*
    commouly *usually*

2828. corporall complexioun *bodily
    constitution*
2830. thrawart *perverse*
    thrawin *twisted* phisnomy *face*
2831. lorum *to conclude*
2832. distortum . . . morum *a
    distortion of character follows
    from a distorted face*
2834. fundin faikin *found to be
    deceitful*
2835. blaberyis *bilberries* sad *dull*
    hew *colour*
2836. gadderit *gathered*
    primeros *primrose*
    forsakin *ignored*

2824–5. 'If I know anything about physiognomy, you have some
    falsehood and malice in you. For scholars say that man's inclination
    towards good or evil usually depends upon his bodily constitution, as
    nature will have it: a perverse will and a twisted face go together'.

The face may faill to be the hartis takin;
Thairfoir I find this scripture in all place:
'Thow suld not juge ane man efter his face.'

407

'Thocht I unhailsum be to luke upon,   2840
I have na wyt; quhy suld I lakkit be?
Wer I als fair as jolie Absolon,
I am no causer of that grit beutie.
This difference in forme and qualitie,
Almychtie God hes causit dame Nature   2845
To prent and set in everilk creature.

408

'Of sum the face may be full flurischand,
Of silkin toung and cheir rycht amorous,
With mynd inconstant, fals, and wariand,
Full of desait and menis cautelous.'   2850
'Let be thy preiching,' quod the hungrie mous,
'And be quhat craft, thow gar me understand,
That thow wald gyde me to yone yonder land.'

409

'Thow wait,' quod scho, 'ane bodie that hes neid
To help thame self suld mony wayis cast.   2855
Thairfoir ga tak ane doubill twynit threid

2837. takin *token*
2838. scripture *motto*
2839. juge *judge* efter *according to*
2840. unhailsum *ugly*
2841. wyt *fault* lakkit *blamed*
2842. jolie *handsome*
2845. causit *caused* dame *mother*
2846. prent *imprint* everilk *every*
2847. flurischand *blossoming*
2848. toung *tongue* cheir *manner*
   amorous *lovable*

2849. wariand *fickle*
2850. desait *deceit* menis
   cautelous *cunning trickery*
2852. craft *means*
2853. gyde *convey*
2854. wait *know* ane
   bodie *anybody*
2855. thame self *themselves*
   cast *consider*
2856. ga *go* doubill twynit *with
   two strands; strong* threid *string*

2837. 'The face may fail to give a clue to the heart'.
2841–3. 'It's not my fault, so why should I be blamed? If I were as fair
   as handsome Absolom himself, I still wouldn't be responsible for that
   great beauty'.
2853–4. 'And by what means, would you have me believe, do you intend
   to convey me to that land over there'.

And bind thy leg to myne with knottis fast.
I sall the leir to swym, be not agast,
Als weill as I.' 'As thow?' than quod the mous.
'To preif that play, it wer rycht perrillous! 2860

410

'Suld I be bund and fast, quhar I am fre,
In hoip of help? Na, than I schrew us baith,
For I mycht lois baith lyfe and libertie!
Gif it wer swa, quha suld amend the skaith,
Bot gif thow sweir to me the murthour aith: 2865
But fraud or gyle to bring me over this flude,
But hurt or harme?' 'In faith,' quod scho, 'I dude.'

411

Scho goikit up, and to the hevin can cry:
'O, Juppiter, of nature god and king,
I mak ane aith trewlie to the, that I 2870
This lytill mous sall over this watter bring.'
This aith wes maid, the mous, but persaving
The fals ingyne of this foull carpand pad,
Tuke threid and band hir leg, as scho hir bad.

412

Than fute for fute thay lap baith in the brym, 2875
Bot in thair myndis thay wer rycht different:

2857. fast *secure*
2858. the leir *teach you*
2859. als *as*
2860. preif *try out* play *game*
rycht *very*
2861. bund *bound* fast *tied up*
quhar *when*
2862. hoip *hope* schrew *curse*
2863. lois *lose*
2864. gif *if* quha *who* amend the
skaith *pay damages for the
injury*

2865. bot gif *unless* murthour
aith *murder oath*
2866. but *without* flude *river*
2867. dude *do*
2868. goikit *stared foolishly* can
cry *cried*
2869. Juppiter *Jupiter*
2872. but persaving *without
perceiving*
2873. ingyne *deception* foull
carpand *lying* pad *toad*
2874. band *bound* bad *told*
2875. lap *leapt* brym *stream*

2864–7. ' "If that were the case, who would pay damages for my injuries,
unless you had already sworn a solemn oath to me without fraud or
trickery, that you would bring me across the river without any hurt or
harme?" "In faith," she said, "I'll do that".'

The mous thocht na thing bot to fleit and swym;
The paddok for to droun set hir intent.
Quhen thay in midwart of the streme wer went,
With all hir force the paddok preissit doun,   2880
And thocht the mous without mercie to droun.

413

Persavand this, the mous on hir can cry:
'Tratour to God, and manesworne unto me!
Thow swore the murthour aith richt now that I
But hurt or harme suld ferryit be and fre.'   2885
And quhen scho saw thair wes bot do or de,
Scho bowtit up and forsit hir to swym,
And preissit upon the taiddis bak to clym.

414

The dreid of deith hir strenthis gart incres,
And forcit hir defend with mycht and mane.   2890
The mous upwart, the paddok doun can pres;
Quhyle to, quhyle fra, quhyle doukit up agane.
This selie mous, this plungit in grit pane,
Gan fecht als lang as breith wes in hir breist,
Till at the last scho cryit for ane preist.   2895

2877. fleit *float*
2878. droun *drown*
2879. midwart *middle* wer
   went *had gone*
2880. force *strength*
   preissit *pressed*
2881. thocht *intended*
2882. persavand *realising*
2883. tratour *traitor*
   manesworne *forsworn*
2885. ferryit *ferried*

2887. bowtit *bobbed* forsit
   hir *forced herself*
2888. taiddis *toad's*
2889. gart *caused to*
2890. mane *power*
2892. quhyle *sometimes*
   doukit *dived*
2893. this plungit *thus plunged*
   pane *sorrow*
2894. gan fecht *fought*
   breith *breath*
2895. preist *priest*

2878. 'The frog was intent on a drowning'.
2886. 'And when she saw that there was nothing for it but to do or die'.
2889–90. 'Fear of death increased her strength, and caused her to defend
   herself with might and power'.

415
Fechtand thusgait, the gled sat on ane twist,
And to this wretchit battell tuke gude heid;
And with ane wisk, or owthir of thame wist,
He claucht his cluke betwix thame in the threid.
Syne to the land he flew with thame gude speid,   2900
Fane of that fang, pyipand with mony pew,
Syne lowsit thame, and baith but pietie slew.

416
Syne bowellit thame, that boucheour with his bill,
And bellieflaucht full fettislie thame fled,
Bot all thair flesche wald scant be half ane fill,   2905
And guttis als, unto that gredie gled.
Of thair debait, thus quhen I hard outred,
He tuke his flicht and over the feildis flaw.
Gif this be trew, speir ye at thame that saw.

Moralitas
417
My brother, gif thow will tak advertence,   2910
Be this fabill thow may persave and se
It passis far all kynd of pestilence
Ane wickit mynd with wordis fair and sle.

2896. fechtand *fighting* thusgait *in this way* gled *kite* twist *branch*
2897. wretchit *wretched* heid *heed*
2898. wisk *whoosh* or *before* owthir *either* wist *knew it*
2899. claucht his cluke *closed his talons* betwix *between* in *on*
2900. syne *then* gude speid *very quickly*
2901. fane *glad* fang *booty* pyipand *singing*
2902. lowsit *untied* but pietie *without pity*
2903. bowellit *disembowelled* boucheour *butcher*
2904. bellieflaucht *skin over head* fettislie *elegantly* fled *flayed*
2905. scant *scarcely* fill *meal*
2906. gredie gled *greedy kite*
2907. outred *settled*
2908. flaw *flew*
2909. speir ye at thame *ask those*
2910. advertence *warning*
2911. be *from* persave *perceive*
2912. passis *surpasses*
2913. sle *sly*

2896. 'While they were fighting like this, the kite sat on a branch'.
2904. 'And flayed them very elegantly by pulling the skin off over their heads in one piece'.
2907. 'In this way, I heard their quarrel was settled'.
2912–3. 'That a wicked mind hidden behind fair and sly words surpasses by far every kind of plague'.

Be war thairfore with quhome thow fallowis the,
To the wer better beir of stane the barrow,   2915
Or sweitand dig and delf quhill thow may dre,
Than to be matchit with ane wickit marrow.

418
Ane fals intent under ane fair pretence
Hes causit mony innocent for to de.
Grit folie is to gif over sone credence   2920
To all that speiks fairlie unto the.
Ane silkin toung, ane hart of crueltie,
Smytis more sore than ony schot of arrow.
Brother, gif thow be wyse, I reid the fle
To matche the with ane thrawart fenyeit marrow.   2925

419
I warne the als, it is grit nekligence
To bind the fast quhair thow wes frank and fre:
Fra thow be bund, thow may mak na defence
To saif thy lyfe nor yit thy libertie.
This simpill counsall, brother, tak of me,   2930
And it to cun perqueir se thow not tarrow:

2914. be war *beware* fallowis
the *associate*
2915. beir *carry* stane *stones*
barrow *hand-barrow*
2916. sweitand *sweating*
delf *delve* dre *endure*
2917. matchit *matched*
marrow *companion*
2919. de *die*
2920. over sone *too quickly*
credence *belief*
2922. toung *tongue*

2923. smytis *strikes* sore *painfully*
2924. gif *if* reid *advise* fle *flee*
2925. the *yourself*
thrawart *crooked*
fenyeit *deceitful*
2926. nekligence *mistake*
2927. frank *at liberty* fre *free*
2928. fra *as soon as*
2929. saif *save*
2930. counsall *advice*
2931. cun perquier *know by heart*
tarrow *delay*

2915–7. 'For you are better off carrying the barrow full of stones
yourself, or digging and delving in a sweat for as long as you can stand
it, than to be paired with a wicked companion'.
2920–21. 'It is a great mistake to believe everyone who speaks nicely to
you too quickly'.
2924–5. 'Brother, if you are wise, I advise you to refrain from associating
yourself with any crooked, deceitful companion'.
2931–2. 'And see that you don't delay in taking it to heart: it is better to
live alone in security and without strife'.

Better but stryfe to leif allane in le
Than to be matchit with ane wickit marrow.

420
This hald in mynd, rycht more I sall the tell
Quhair by thir beistis may be figurate: 2935
The paddok, usand in the flude to dwell,
Is mannis bodie, swymand air and late
In to this warld, with cairis implicate,
Now hie, now law, quhylis plungit up, quhylis doun,
Ay in perrell, and reddie for to droun;   2940

421
Now dolorus, now blyth as bird on breir;
Now in fredome, now wrappit in distres;
Now haill and sound, now deid and brocht on beir;
Now pure as Job, now rowand in riches;
Now gounis gay, now brats laid in pres;   2945
Now full as fische, now hungrie as ane hound;
Now on the quheill, now wappit to the ground.

422
This lytill mous, heir knit thus be the schyn,
The saull of man betakin may in deid:
Bundin, and fra the bodie may not twyn,   2950

2932. leif *live*   le *security*
2934. hald *keep*   rycht *even*
2935. quhair *which*   thir *these*
   figurate *represented*
2936. usand *customarily*
2937. mannis *man's*
   swymand *swimming*   air and
   late *freely*
2938. with cairis implicate *bound
   up with sorrows*
2939. hie *high*   law *low*
   quhylis *sometimes*
2941. dolorus *sorrowful*

blyth *happy*   breir *branch*
2942. wrappit in *surrounded by*
2943. haill *hale; healthy*
   brocht *carried*   beir *funeral bier*
2944. pure *poor*   rowand *rolling*
2945. gounis *gowns*   brats *rags*
   pres *cupboard*
2947. quheill *wheel*   wappit *thrown*
2948. heir *here*   knit *tied*
   schyn *leg*
2949. saull *soul*   betakin *symbolise*
   in deid *truly*
2950. bundin *bound*   twyn *separate*

2936. 'The frog, customarily living in the river'.
2945. 'One minute splendid gowns to wear, the next only rags to hang in
   the cupboard'.

Quhill cruell deith cum brek of lyfe the threid,
The quhilk to droun suld ever stand in dreid
Of carnall lust be the suggestioun,
Quhilk drawis ay the saull and druggis doun.

423

The watter is the warld, ay welterand   2955
With mony wall of tribulation,
In quhilk the saull and bodye wer steirrand,
Standand distinyt in thair opinioun:
The saull upwart, the body precis doun;
The saull rycht fane wald be brocht over, iwis,   2960
Out of this warld into the hevinnis blis.

424

The gled is deith, that cummis suddandlie
As dois ane theif, and cuttis sone the battall.
Be vigilant thairfoir and ay reddie,
For mannis lyfe is brukill and ay mortall.   2965
My freind, thairfoir, mak the ane strang castell
Of gud deidis, for deith will the assay,
Thow wait not quhen—evin, morrow, or midday.

2951. quhill *until*
2952. the quhilk *which*
2953. suggestioun *incitement*
2954. drawis *tempts* ay *always*
  druggis *drags*
2955. welterand *rough*
2956. wall *wave*
2957. wer steirrand *were in conflict*
2958. standand *standing*
  distinyt *separate*
2959. upwart *upwards*
  precis *presses*
2960. rycht fane *very gladly*

brocht over *carried across*
  iwis *indeed*
2961. hevinnis *heaven's*
2962. gled *kite*
2963. cuttis *ends* battall *battle*
2964. reddie *ready*
2965. brukill *uncertain*
2966. mak the *build yourself*
2967. deidis *deeds* the
  assay *attack you*
2968. wait *know* quhen *when*
  evin *evening* morrow *morning*

2951–4. 'Until cruel death comes and breaks the thread of life, the soul
  should always be afraid of being drowned by the incitement to evil of
  carnal lust, which always tempts the soul and drags it downwards'.

425

Adew, my freind, and gif that ony speiris
Of this fabill, sa schortlie I conclude,   2970
Say thow, I left the laif unto the freiris,
To mak a exempill and ane similitude.
Now Christ for us that deit on the rude,
Of saull and lyfe as thow art Salviour,
Grant us till pas in till ane blissit hour.   2975

2969. adew *goodbye* gif *if*
   ony *anyone* speiris *asks*
2970. of *about*
2971. laif *remainder* freiris *friars*
2972. exemple *example*

similitude *parable*
2973. deit *died* rude *cross*
2974. salviour *saviour*
2975. grant *allow* pas *pass away*
   in till *at* blissit *blessed*

2969–71. 'Goodbye, my friend, and if anyone asks you about these
   fables, which I will conclude shortly, tell them I left the rest to the
   friars'.

Orpheus and Eurydice

1

The nobilnes and grit magnificens
Of prince and lord, quha list to magnifie,
His ancestre and lineall discens
Suld first extoll, and his genolegie,
So that his harte he mycht inclyne thairby   5
The moir to vertew and to worthines,
Herand rehers his elderis gentilnes.

2

It is contrair the lawis of nature
A gentill man to be degenerat,
Nocht following of his progenitour   10
The worthy rewll and the lordly estait.
A ryall rynk for to be rusticat
Is bot a monsture in comparesoun,
Had in dispyt and full derisioun.

3

I say this be the grit lordis of Grew,   15
Quhich set thair hairt and all thair haill curage
Thair faderis steppis justly to persew,

1. grit *great* magnificens *majesty*
2. quha *whoever* list *wishes*
   magnifie *praise*
3. ancestre *ancestry* lineall
   discens *lineage*
4. extoll *praise*
   genolegie *genealogy*
5. harte *heart* inclyne *dispose*
6. moir *more* vertew *virtue*
7. herand *hearing* rehers *recounted*
   elderis *ancestors'*
   gentilnes *nobility*
8. contrair *against*
9. gentill *noble*
   degenerat *degenerate; base*
10. progenitour *ancestor*
11. rewll *conduct* estait *state*
12. ryall rynk *nobleman*
    rusticat *like a peasant*
13. bot *simply* monsture in
    comparesoun *monstrosity*
14. had *held* dispyt *contempt*
    full *foul* derisioun *derision;*
    mockery
15. Grew *Greece*
16. quhich *who* hairt *heart*
    haill *whole* curage *mind*
17. faderis *fore-fathers'*
    steppis *steps* justly *properly*
    persew *follow*

1–4. 'Whoever wishes to praise the nobility and majesty of prince and
   lord should first of all pay tribute to his ancestry and lineage and also
   to his family history'.
7. 'Hearing the nobility of his ancestors recounted'.
12–13. 'It is simply a monstrosity for a nobleman to act like a peasant'.
17. 'To follow properly in their fore-fathers' footsteps'.

Eiking the wirschep of thair he lenage,
The anseane and sad wyse men of age
Wer tendouris to the yung and insolent,   20
To mak thame in all vertewis excellent.

4

Lyk as a strand or watter of a spring
Haldis the sapour of the fontell well,
So did in Grece ilk lord and worthy king,
Of forbearis thay tuk tarage and smell;   25
Among the quhilk of ane I think to tell.
Bot first his gentill generatioun
I sall rehers, with your correctioun.

5

Upone the mont of Elicone,
The most famous of all Arrabea,   30
A goddes dwelt, excellent in bewte,
Gentill of blude, callit Memoria;
Quhilk Jupiter that goddes to wyfe can ta
And carnaly hir knew, quhilk eftir syne,
Apone a day bare him fair dochteris nyne.   35

6

The first in Grew wes callit Euterpe,
In our language 'gud delectatioun'.

18. eiking *increasing*
    wirschep *honour* he *high*
    lenage *lineage*
19. anseane *ancient* sad *solemn* of
    age *of old*
20. tendouris *guides*
    insolent *inexperienced*
21. vertewis *virtues*
22. lyk as *just as* strand *stream*
23. haldis *retains* sapour *flavour*
    fontell well *original source*
24. ilk *every*
25. forbearis *fore-bears*
    tarage *flavour* smell *aroma*
26. the quhilk *whom* ane *one*

27. generatioun *ancestry*
28. rehers *repeat* with your
    correctioun *under your correction*
29. Elecone *Helicon*
30. Arrabea *Arabia*
31. goddes *goddess* bewte *beauty*
32. blude *blood* callit *called*
33. quhilk *who* to wyfe can
    ta *took as his wife*
34. eftir syne *afterwards*
35. apone a day *one day*
    dochteris *daughters* nyne *nine*
36. Grew *Greek*
37. gud delectatioun *virtuous
    pleasure*

25. 'They inherited a sense of what was proper from their fore-bears'.
33. 'Jupiter took that goddess as his wife'

The secound maid clippit Melpomyne,
'As hony sweit in modelatioun'.
Thersycore is 'gud instruction   40
Of every thing', the thrid sister, iwis,
Thus out of Grew in Latyne translait is.

7

Caliope, that madin mervalous,
The ferd sistir, of all musik maistres
And mother to the king, schir Orpheous,   45
Quhilk throw his wyfe wes efter king of Trais;
Clio, the fyift, that now is a goddes,
In Latyne callit 'meditatioun
Of everything that hes creatioun'.

8

The sext sister is callit Herato,   50
Quhilk drawis lyk to lyk in every thing;
The sevint lady was fair Polimio,
Quhilk cowth a thowsand sangis sweitly sing;
Talia syne, quhilk can our saulis bring
In profound wit and grit agilite   55
Till undirstand and haif capacitie;

9

Urania, the nynt and last of all,
In Greik langage, quha cowth it rycht expound,

38. clippit *was called*
    Melpomyne *Melpomene*
39. as *meaning* hony *honey*
    sweit *sweet* modelatioun *making music*
40. Thersycore *Terpsichore*
41. of *in* thrid *third* iwis *truly*
42. Caliope *Calliope* madin *woman*
43. ferd *fourth* maistres *mistress*
44. schir *sir* Orpheous *Orpheus*
45. throw *through* efter *in due course* Trais *Thrace*
46. Clio *Cleo* fyift *fifth*
49. hes creatioun *has been created*

50. sext *sixth* Herato *Erato*
51. lyk *like*
52. sevint *seventh*
    Polimio *Polyhymnia*
53. cowth *could* sangis *songs*
54. Talia *Thalia* syne *next*
    saulis *souls*
55. wit *knowledge* grit *great*
    agilite *mental quickness*
56. til *to* haif *have* capacitie *full knowledge*
57. nynt *ninth*
58. cowth *could* rycht *correctly*
    expound *explain*

42. 'This is how it is translated from Greek into Latin'

Is callit 'armony celestiall',
Rejosing men with melody and sound.   60
Amang thir nyne Calliope wes cround
And maid a quene be michty god Phebus,
Of quhome he gat this prince schir Orpheous.

10

No wondir is thocht he wes fair and wyse,
Gentill and gud, full of liberalitie,   65
His fader god, and his progenetryse
A goddes, finder of all armony.
Quhen he wes borne scho set him on hir kne
And gart him souk of hir two paupis quhyte
The sweit lecour of all musik perfyte.   70

11

Incressand sone to manheid up he drew,
Of statur large and frely, fair of face;
His noble fame so far it sprang and grew,
Till at the last the michty quene of Trace,
Excelland fair, haboundand in riches,   75
A message send unto that prince so ying,
Requyrand him to wed hir and be king.

12

Euridices this lady had to name,
And quhene scho saw this prince so glorius,
Hir erand to propone scho thocht no schame;   80
With wordis sweit and blenkis amorous,
Said: 'Welcum, lord and lufe, schir Orpheus,
In this provynce ye sal be king and lord!'
Thay kissit syne, and thus thay can accord.

59. armony celestiall *heavenly harmony*
60. rejosing *gladdening*
61. thir *these*   cround *crowned*
63. of quhome *by whom*   gat *fathered*
64. thocht *though*
66. progenetryse *mother*
67. armony *harmony*
69. gart *made*   paupis *breasts* quhyte *white*
70. lecour *liquor*   perfyte *perfect*
71. incressand *growing*   sone *soon*
72. frely *noble*
75. excelland *excellingly* haboundand *abounding*
76. send *sent*   ying *young*
77. requyrand *asking*
78. Euridices *Eurydice*   had to name *was called*
80. erand *errand*   propone *propose*
81. blenkis *glances*
82. lufe *love*
84. syne *then*   can accord *made agreement*

13

Betwix Orpheus and fair Erudices,   85
Fra thai wer weddit, on fra day to day
The low of lufe cowth kyndill and incres,
With mirth and blythnes, solace, and with play.
Of wardly joy, allace, quhat sall I say?
Lyk till a flour that plesandly will spring,   90
Quhilk fadis sone and endis with murnyng.

14

I say this be Erudices the quene,
Quhilk walkit furth in to a May mornyng,
Bot with a madyn, untill a medow grene,
To tak the air and se the flouris spring.   95
Quhair in a schaw, neir by this lady ying,
A busteous hird callit Arresteus,
Kepand his beistis, lay undir a bus.

15

And quhen he saw this lady solitar,
Bairfut, with schankis quhyter than the snaw,   100
Preckit with lust, he thocht withoutin mair
Hir till oppress and till hir can he draw:
Dreidand for evill, scho fled quhen scho him saw,
And as scho ran all bairfute in a bus,
Scho strampit on a serpent vennemus.   105

---

85. betwix *between*
86. fra *from the time that*   on
    fra *and from*
87. low *flame*   cowth kyndill and
    incres *kindled and increased*
88. blythnes *happiness*
    solace *pleasure*
89. wardly *worldly*   allace *alas*
90. lyk till *like*   flour *flower*
    plesandly *pleasantly*
91. fadis *fades*   murnyng *mourning*
92. be *about*
93. in to *upon*
94. bot *only*   untill *into*

96. schaw *wood*   ying *young*
97. busteous *rough* hird *shepherd*
    Arresteus *Aristaeus*
98. kepand *tending*
    beistis *animals* bus *bush*
99. solitar *alone*
100. bairfut *barefoot*
    schankis *legs*   quhyter *whiter*
    snaw *snow*
101. preckit *pricked*   mair *delay*
102. till *to*   oppress *rape*
103. dreidand *fearing*
105. strampit *stepped*
    vennemus *poisonous*

16

This crewall venome wes so penetrife,
As natur is of all mortall pusoun,
In peisis small this quenis harte can rife,
And scho annone fell on a deidly swoun.
Seand this cais, Proserpyne maid hir boun, 110
Quhilk clepit is the goddes infernall,
Intill hir court this gentill quene can call.

17

And quhen scho vaneist was and unvisible,
Hir madyn wepit with a wofull cheir,
Cryand with mony schowt and voce terrible, 115
Quhill at the last king Orpheus can heir,
And of hir cry the caus sone cowth he speir.
Scho said, 'Allace! Euridices your quene
Is with the phary tane befoir my ene.'

18

This noble king, inflammit all in yre, 120
And rampand as a lyoun revanus,
With awful luke and ene glowand as fyre.
Sperid the maner, and the maid said thus:
'Scho strampit on a serpent venemus
And fell on swoun – with that the quene of fary 125
Clawcht hir up sone and furth with hir cowth cary.'

106. crewall *cruel*   penetrife *potent*
107. as natur is *as is the nature*
    mortall *deadly* pusoun *poison*
108. peisis *pieces* harte *heart* can
    rife *split*
109. annone *at once*
110. seand *seeing* cais *situation*
    Proserpyne *Proserpina*
    boun *ready*
111. infernall *of the underworld*
112. intill *into* can call *to call*
114. cheir *face*
115. schowt *a shout* voce *voice*
    terrible *full of terror*

116. quhill *until*   can heir *heard*
117. sone *soon*   cowth he speir *he
    asked*
119. phary *fairies*   tane *taken*
    ene *eyes*
120. inflammit *enflamed*   yre *anger*
121. rampand *raging*   lyoun *lion*
    revanus *starving*
123. sperid the maner *asked how it
    happened*
126. clawcht *snatched*
    sone *immediately*   cowth
    cary *carried*

126. 'Snatched her up immediately and carried her away with her'.

19

Quhen scho had said, the king sichit full soir;
His hairt neir brist for verry dule and wo.
Half out of mynd, he maid no tary moir,
Bot tuk his harp and on to wod cowth go,   130
Wrinkand his handis, walkand to and fro,
Quhill he mycht stand, syne sat doun on a stone
And till his harp thusgait he maid his mone:

20

'O dulful herp, with mony dully string,
Turne all thy mirth and musik in murning,   135
And seis of all thy sutell songis sweit!
Now weip with me, thy lord and cairfull king,
Quhilk lossit hes in erd all his lyking,
And all thy game thow change in gole and greit.
Thy goldin pynnis with mony teiris weit,   140
And all my pane for till report thow preis,
Cryand with me in every steid and streit:
"Quhair art thow gone, my luve *Ewridices*?" '

21

Him to rejos yit playit he a spring
Quhill that the fowlis of the wid can sing.   145
And treis dansit with thair levis grene,

127. sichit *sighed* soir *sorrowfully*
128. brist *burst* dule *grief*
129. maid no tary moir *delayed no longer*
130. wod *wood* cowth go *went*
131. wrinkand *wringing*
132. quhill *sometimes*
  syne *afterwards*
133. thusgait *in this way*
  mone *lament*
134. duleful *doleful* herp *harp*
  dully *dismal*
135. in murning *into mourning*
136. seis of *cease* sutell *beautiful*
  sweit *sweet*
137. cairfull *sorrowful*
138. quhilk *who* lossit hes *has lost* erd *earth* lyking *delight*
139. game *pleasure* in *into*
  gole *lament* greit *tears*
140. pynnis *harp pegs* teiris *tears*
  weit *make wet*
141. pane *suffering*
  preis *endeavour*
142. cryand *crying* steid *place*
144. rejos *cheer* spring *merry tune*
145. quhill *until* fowlis *birds*
  wid *wood* can sing *sang*
146. treis *tress* dansit *danced*

138. 'Who has lost all his delight in this world'.
141. 'And endeavour to record ale my suffering'.
144. 'Yet to cheer himself he played a merry tune'.

Him to devod from his grit womenting;
Bot all in vane, that vailyeit him no thing,
His hairt wes so upoun his lusty quene.
The bludy teiris sprang out of his ene,   150
Thair wes no solace mycht his sobbing ses,
Bot cryit ay, with cairis cauld and kene,
'Quhair art thow gone, my lufe Euridices?'

22

'Fair weill my place, fair weill plesandis and play,
And wylcum woddis wyld and wilsum way,   155
My wicket werd in wildirnes to ware.
My rob ryell and all my riche array
Changit sal be in rude russet of gray,
My dyademe in till a hate of hair.
My bed sal be with bever, brok and bair,   160
In buskis bene with mony busteous bes,
Withowttin song, sayand with siching sair,
'Quhair art thow gone, my luve Euridices?'

23

'I the beseik, my fair fadir Phebus,
Haif pety of thy awin sone Orpheus,   165
Wait thow nocht weill I am thy sone and chyld?
Now heir my plaint, panefull and peteus.

147. devod *distract*
    womenting *lamentation*
148. vailyeit . . . thing *did not help
    him at all*
149. upoun *set upon*
    lusty *beautiful*
150. bludy *bloody* ene *eyes*
151. solace *comfort* ses *cease*
152. ay *constantly* cairis *laments*
    cauld *gloomy* kene *bitter*
154. fair weill *farewell*
    place *palace* plesandis *pleasures*
    play *enjoyment*
155. wylcum *welcome*
    woddis *woods* wilsum *lonely*
156. werd *fate* ware *endure*

157. rob ryell *royal robe*
    array *garments*
158. in *into* rude russet *rough
    cloth*
159. dyademe *crown* hate *hat*
160. brok *badger* bair *boar*
161. buskis bene *pleasant thickets*
    busteous *wild* bes *beasts*
162. siching sair *painful sighing*
164. beseik *beseech* fadir *father*
165. haif pety of *take pity upon*
    awin *own* sone *son*
166. wait *know*
167. heir *hear* plaint *complaint*
    peteus *pitiable*

159. 'My crown shall go and my only head-dress shall be my hair'.

Direk me for this deid so dolorus,
Quhilk gois thus withouttin gilt begyld.
Lat nocht thy face with cluddis to be oursyld;   170
Len me thy lycht and lat me nocht go leis
To find that fair in fame that was nevir fyld,
My lady quene and lufe, Euridices.

24

'O Jupiter, thow god celestiall,
And grantschir to my self, on the I call   175
To mend my murning and my drery mone;
Thow gif me fors, that I nocht fant nor fall
Till I hir fynd, forsuth seik hir I sall
And nowthir stint nor stand for stok na stone.
Throw thy godheid, gyde me quhair scho is gone;   180
Gar hir appeir and put my hairt in pes.'
King Orpheus thus with his harp allone,
Soir weipit for his wyfe Euridices.

25

Quehn endit wer thir songis lamentable,
He tuk his harp and on his breist can hing,   185
Syne passit to the hevin, as sayis the fable,
To seik his wyfe, bot that velyeid no thing.

168. direk *turn*   deid *death*
dolorus *sorowful*
169. quhilk *who*   gilt *guilt*
begyld *betrayed*
170. cluddis *clouds*
oursyld *obscured*
171. len *give*   go leis *fail*
172. fair *fair one*   fame *reputation*
fyld *dishonoured*
175. grantschir *grandfather*
the *you*
176. mend *alleviate*
murning *suffering*   mone *lament*

177. fors *strength*   fant *faint*
178. forsuth *indeed*   seik *seek*
179. nowthir *neither*   stint *stop*
stok *stump*
180. godheid *divinity*   gyde *guide*
quhair *to where*
181. gar *make*   pes *peace*
184. thir *these*
185. breist *chest*   can hing *hung it*
186. syne *then*
187. velyeid no thing *did not help
at all*

168–9. 'Turn me away from this sorrowful death, I who am betrayed
through no fault of my own'.
171–2. 'Give me your light and let me not fail to find that fair lady
whose reputation was never dishonoured'.
177. 'Give me strength so that I do not faint or fall'.
179. 'And nothing is going to get in my way'.
185. 'He took his harp and slung it across his chest'.

By Wcdlingis Streit he went but tareing,
Syne come doun throw the speir of Saturne ald,
Quhilk fadir is to all the stormis cald.   190

26
Quhen scho wes socht outhrow that cauld regioun,
Till Jupiter, his grandschir, can he wend,
Quhilk rewit soir his lamentatioun,
And gart his spheir be socht fro end to end.
Scho was nocht thair, and doun he can descend   195
Till Mars, the god of battell and of stryfe,
And socht his spheir, yit gat he nocht his wyfe.

27
Than went he doun till his fadir Phebus,
God of the sone, with bemis brycht and cleir;
Bot quhen he saw his awin sone Orpheus   200
In sic a plicht, that changit all his cheir.
He gart annone ga seik throw all his spheir,
Bot all in vane, his lady come nocht thair.
He tuk his leif and to Venus can fair.

28
Quhen he hir saw, he knelit and said thus: 205
'Wait ye nocht weill I am your awin trew knycht?
In luve none leler than schir Orpheus;
And ye of luve goddas and most of micht,
Of my lady help me to get a sicht.'
'For sur,' quod scho, 'ye mone seik nedir mair.'   210
Than fra Venus he tuk his leif but mair.

188. Wedlingis Streit *the Milky
   Way* but tareing *without delay*
189. speir *sphere* Saturne *Saturn*
   ald *old*
190. quhilk *who*   cald *called*
191. socht *sought*
   outhrow *throughout* cauld *cold*
192. till *to*   can he wend *he went*
193. rewit soir *sorely pitied*
194. gart *caused* socht *searched*
196. stryfe *conflict*
197. gat *found*

199. sone *sun* bemis *beams*
201. sic *such* plicht *plight*
   cheir *appearance*
204. leif *leave* can fair *went*
205. knelit *kneeled*
206. wait *know* knycht *knight*
207. leler *more true*
208. goddas *goddess*
   most *greatest* micht *power*
210. sur *sure* quod *said* mone *must*
   nedir mair *lower down*
211. but mair *without further ado*

190. 'Who is called the father of all storms'.

29

To Mercury but tary is he gone,
Quhilk callit is the god of eloquens;
Bot of his wyfe thair gat he knawlege none.
With wofull hairt he passit doun frome thens;   215
Unto the mone he maid no residens.
Thus from the hevin he went onto the erd,
Yit be the way sum melody he lerd.

30

In his passage amang the planeitis all
He hard a hevinly melody and sound,   220
Passing all instrumentis musicall,
Causit be rollyn of the speiris round,
Quhilk armony throu all this mappamound,
Quhill moving seis, unyt perpetuall,
Quhilk of this warld Plato the saule can call.   225

31

Thair leirit he tonis proportionat,
As duplare, triplare, and emetricus,
Enolius, and eik the quadruplait,
Epoddeus rycht hard and curius.
Of all thir sex, sweit and delicius,   230

212. but tary *without delay*
213. eloquens *eloquence*
216. mone *moon* maid no
    residens *did not stay*
217. erd *earth*
218. lerd *learned*
219. passage *journey*
    planeitis *planets*
221. passing *surpassing*
222. causit *caused* rollyn *rolling*
    speiris *spheres*
223. armony *harmony*
    mappamound *world*
224. quhill *until* seis *cease* unyt

perpetuall *perpetual unison*
225. saule *soul*
226. leirit *learned* tonis
    proportionat *relationship between
    musical notes*
227. duplare *duplar*
    triplare *triplar*
    emetricus *epitritus*
228. enolius *hemiolius* eik *also*
    quadruplait *quadruplate*
229. epoddeus *epogdous*
    hard *difficult* curius *elaborate*
230. sex *six* delicius *delightful*

223–5. 'This harmony is in perpetual unison throughout the world until
the end of time, and it is this that Plato called the soul of the world'.

Rycht consonant fyfe hevinly symphonys
Componyt ar, as clerkis can devyse.

32
First diatesserone, full sweit iwis;
And dyapasone, semple and dowplait;
Dyapenty, and componyt with a dys;   235
Thir makis fyve of thre multiplicat.
This mirry musik and mellefluat,
Compleit and full of nummeris od and evin,
Is causit be the moving of the hevin.

33
Of sic musik to wryt I do bot doit,   240
Thairfoir of this mater a stray I lay,
For in my lyfe I cowth nevir sing a noit;
Bot I will tell how Orpheus tuk the way
To seik his wyfe attour the gravis gray,
Hungry and cauld, our mony wilsum wone   245
Withouttin gyd, he and his harp allone.

34
He passit furth the space of twenty dayis,
Fer and full fer, ferrer than I can tell,
And ay he fand streitis and reddy wayis,

231. consonant *in harmony*
  fyfe *five*   symphonys *chords*
232. componyt *composed*
  clerkis *scholars*   devyse *describe*
233. diatesserone *interval of a
  fourth*   iwis *indeed*
234. dyapasone *octave*
  semple *single*   dowplait *double*
235. dyapenty *interval of a fifth*
236. multiplicat *augmented*
237. mellefluat *melodious*
238. compleit *complete*
  nummeris *numbers*

239. causit be *caused by*
240. do bot doit *only talk stupidly*
241. stray *straw*
242. cowth *could*   noit *note*
244. seik *seek*   attour *over*
  gravis *groves*
245. cauld *cold*   our *over*   wilsum
  wone *lonely place*
246. gyd *guide*
247. passit furth *travelled on*
248. fer *far*
249. fand *found*   streitis *roads*
  reddy wayis *worn paths*

231–2. 'Five heavenly chords are composed, in complete harmony, as
  described by the scholars'.
240–1. 'In writing about such music I only show my ignorance, therefore
  I will stop talking about it'.

Till at the last unto the yet of hell   250
He come, and thair he fand a porter fell
With thre heidis, wes callit Serberus,
A hound of hell, a monstour mervellus.

35

Than Orpheus began to be agast
Quhen he beheld that ugly hellis hound.   255
He tuk his harp and on it playit fast,
Till at the last, throw sweitnes of the sound,
This dog slepit and fell doun on the ground.
Than Orpheus attour his wame in stall,
And neddir mair he went, as ye heir sall.   260

36

He passit furth ontill a ryvir deip,
Our it a brig, and on it sisteris thre,
Quhilk had the entre of the brig to keip:
Electo, Mygra, and Thesaphone
Turnit a quheill wes ugly for to se,   265
And on it spred a man hecht Exione,
Rolland about, rycht windir wobegone.

37

Than Orpheus playd a joly spring.
The thre susteris full fast thay fell on sleip;
The ugly quheill seisit of hir quhirling;   270
Thus left wes none the entre for to keip.
Thane Exione out of the quheill gan creip

250. yet *gate*
251. porter fell *fierce gate-keeper*
252. heidis *heads*
    Serberus *Cerberus*
254. agast *afraid*
258. slepit *fell asleep*
259. wame *belly* stall *crept*
260. neddir mair *lower down* heir
    sall *shall hear*
262. our *over* brig *bridge*
263. entre *entrance* keip *guard*
264. Electo *Alecto* Mygra *Megaera*

Thesaphone *Tisiphone*
265. quheill *wheel*
266. spred *was spread*
    hecht *called* Exione *Ixion*
267. rolland *spinning*
    windir *wondrously*
    wobegone *miserable*
268. spring *tune*
269. susteris *sisters* on sleip *asleep*
270. seisit of *ceased* hir *its*
    quhirling *whirling*
272. thane *then* gan creip *crept*

259. 'Then Orpheus crept in across his belly'.
265. 'Turned a wheel which was horrible to look at'.
271. Thus, there was no one left to guard the entrance'.

And stall away; and Orpheus annone,
Without stopping, atour the brig is gone.

38

Nocht far frome thyne he come unto a flude 275
Drubly and deip, and rythly doun can rin,
Quhair Tantelus nakit full thristy stude
And yit the wattir yeid aboif his chin.
Thocht he gaipit thair wald no drop cum in;
Quehn he dowkit the watter wald discend; 280
Thus gat he nocht his thrist to slake nor mend.

39

Befoir his face ane naple hang also,
Fast at his mowth upoun a twynid thried;
Quhen he gaipit it rollit to and fro,
And fled as it refusit him to feid. 285
Quhen Orpheus thus saw him suffir neid,
He tuk his harp and fast on it can clink:
The wattir stud, and Tantalus gat a drink.

40

Syne our a mure with thornis thik and scherp,
Wepand allone, a wilsum way he went, 290
And had nocht bene throw suffrage of his harp
With fell pikis he had bene schorne and schent.
As he blenkit besyd him on the bent,
He saw lyand speldit a wofull wycht,
Nalit full fast, and Titius he hecht. 295

273. stall *stole* annone *at once*
275. thyne *there* flude *river*
276. drubly *turbulent*
rythly *swiftly* can rin *ran*
277. Tantelus *Tantalus* nakit *naked*
thristy *thirsty* stude *stood*
278. yeid *went* aboif *above*
279. thocht *although* gaipit *opened*
his mouth
280. dowkit *bent down*
281. gat *managed* mend *assuage*
282. naple *apple* hang *hung*
283. fast at *close to*
twynid *twisted* threid *thread*

285. as *as if* feid *feed*
286. neid *hardship*
287. can clink *twanged*
289. our *across* mure *moor*
scherp *sharp*
290. wepand *weeping* wilsum *wild*
291. suffrage *support*
292. fell pikis *cruel thorns*
schorne *cut* schent *injured*
293. blenkit *looked* bent *field*
294. lyand *lying*
speldit *spreadeagled* wycht *man*
295. nalit *nailed* fast *securely*
Titius *Tityus* hecht *was called*

294. 'He saw a miserable man lying spreadeagled on the ground'.

41

And on his breist thair sat a grisly grip,
Quhilk with his bill his belly throw can boir.
Both maw, myddret, hart, lever and trip
He ruggit out; his panis was the moir.
Quhen Orpheus thus saw him suffer soir,   300
He tuke his herp and maid sweit melody:
The grip is fled and Titius left his cry.

42

Beyond this mure he fand a feirfull streit,
Myrk as the nycht, to pass rycht dengerus,
For sliddrenes skant mycht he hald his feit,   305
In quhilk thair wes a stynk rycht odius
That gydit him to hiddous hellis hous,
Quhair Rodomantus and Proserpina
Wer king and quene; and Orpheus in coud ga.

43

O dully place, and grundles deip dungeoun,   310
Furnes of fyre and stink intollerable,
Pit of dispair without remissioun,
Thy meit vennome, thy drink is pusonable,
Thy grit panis to compte unnumerable;
Quhat creature cumis to dwell in the   315
Is ay deand, and nevirmoir may de.

296. breist *chest*   grip *vulture*
297. can boir *pierced*
298. maw *stomach*
   myddret *midriff*   lever *liver*
   trip *guts*
299. ruggit *pulled*   panis *pains*
   moir *greater*
300. soir *grievously*
302. left *stopped*   cry *screaming*
303. fand *found*   feirfull
   streit *terrifying road*
304. myrk *dark*
305. sliddrenes *slipperiness*
   skant *scarcely*

306. stynk *stink*
308. Rodomantus *Rhadamanthus*
310. dully *doleful*
   grundles *bottomless*
311. furnes *furnace*
312. remissioun *abatement*
313. meit *food*
   vennome *venomous*
   pusonable *poisonous*
314. grit *great*   panis *torments*
   compte *count*
315. quhat *whatever*   the *you*
316. ay *always*   deand *dying*
   de *die*

297. 'Which pierced the man's belly with his beak'.
314. 'Your great torments are too numerous to count'.

44

Thair fand he mony cairfull king and quene,
With croun on heid of brass full hate birnand,
Quhilk in thair lyfe full maisterfull had bene,
And conquerouris of gold, riches and land. 320
Hectore of Troy and Priame thair he fand,
And Alexander for his wrang conqueist,
Antiochus als for his foull incest,

45

And Julius Cesar for his foull crewaltie,
And Herod with his brudiris wyfe he saw, 325
And Nero for his grit iniquitie,
And Pilot for his breking of the law,
Syne undir that he lukit and cowth knaw
Cresus that king, none mychtiar on mold
For cuvatyse, yet full of birnand gold. 330

46

Thair saw he Pharo, for the oppressioun
Of Godis folk on quhilk the plaigis fell,
And Sawll, for the grit abusioun
Of justice to the folk of Israell.
Thair saw he Acob and quene Jesabell, 335
Quhilk silly Nabot, that wes a propheit trew,
For his wine yaird withouttin mercy slew.

317. cairfull *sorrowful*
318. croun *crown* heid *head* hate
    birnand *burning hot*
319. maisterfull *proud* bene *been*
320. of *with*
321. Hectore *Hector* Priame *Priam*
322. wrang *wrongful*
323. als *also*
325. brudiris *brother's*
326. iniquitie *wickedness*
327. Pilot *Pilate*
328. lukit *looked* cowth
    knaw *recognised*
329. Cresus *Croesus*
    mychtiar *more powerful*
    mold *earth*
330. cuvatyse *covetousness*
    birnand *burning*
331. Pharo *Pharaoh*
332. quhilk *whom* plaigis *plagues*
333. Sawll *Saul* abusioun *abuse*
335. Acob *Ahab* Jesabell *Jezebel*
336. silly *innocent* Nabot *Naboth*
    propheit *prophet*
337. wine yaird *vineyard*

331–2. 'There he saw Pharaoh, on whom the plagues of Egypt fell
    because of his oppression of God's people'.
335–7. 'There he saw Ahab and queen Jezebel, who mercilessly killed
    innocent Naboth, who was a true prophet, because they wanted his
    vineyard'.

47

Thair saw he mony paip and cardynall,
In haly kirk quhilk did abusioun,
And bischopis in thair pontificall,   340
Be symonie and wrang intrusioun;
Abbottis and men of all religioun,
For evill disponyng of thair place and rent
In flame of fyre wer bittirly torment.

48

Syne neddir mair he went quhair Pluto was   345
And Proserpyne, and hiddirwart he drew,
Ay playand on his harp quhair he cowth pas;
Till at the last Erudices he knew,
Lene and deidlyk, and peteous paill of hew,
Rycht warsche and wane, and walluid as the weid,   350
Hir lilly lyre was lyk unto the leid.

49

Quod he: 'My lady leill and my delyt,
Full wo is me to se yow changit thus
Quhair is your rude as ros with cheikis quhyte,
Your cristell ene with blenkis amorus,   355
Your lippis reid to kiss delicius?'
Quod scho: 'As now I der nocht tell, perfay,
Bot ye sall wit the caus ane uthir day.'

338. paip *pope* cardynall *cardinal*
339. haly kirk *holy church*
    abusioun *wrong*
340. bischopis *bishops*
    pontificall *robes*
341. symonie *simony*
    intrusioun *intervention*
342. religioun *religious orders*
343. disponyng *disposing*
    place *property* rent *income*
344. torment *tormented*
345. syne *then* neddir mair *lower
    down*
346. hiddirwart *there*

347. cowth pas *went*
348. knew *recognised*
349. lene *thin* deidlyk *deathly*
    peteous *pitifully* hew *colour*
350. warsche *sickly* wane *pale*
    walluid *withered* weid *weed*
351. lyre *complexion* leid *lead*
352. quod *said* leill *true*
354. rude as ros *rosy complexion*
    cheikis *cheeks* quhyte *white*
355. ene *eyes* blenkis *glances*
357. as *for* der *dare*
    perfay *indeed*
358. wit *know*

50

Quod Pluto: 'Schir, thocht scho be lyk ane elf,
Scho hes no caus to plenye, and for quhy?   360
Scho fairis als weill daylie as dois my self,
Or King Herod for all his chevelry.
It is langour that putis hir in sic ply;
War scho at hame in hir cuntre of Trace,
Scho wald revert full sone in fax and face.'   365

51

Than Orpheus befoir Pluto sat doun,
And in his handis quhit his herp can ta
And playit mony sweit proportioun,
With baiss tonis in ypodorica,
With gemilling in yporlerica;   370
Quhill at the last for rewth and grit petie
Thay weipit soir that cowth him heir or se.

52

Than Proserpene and Pluto bad him as
His waresoun, and he wald haif rycht nocht
Bot licience with his wyfe away to pas   375
To his cuntre, that he so far had socht.
Quod Proserpyne: 'Sen I hir hiddir brocht,
We sall nocht pairte without conditioun.'
Quod he: 'Thairto I mak promissioun.'

359. thocht *although*   elf *creature
   of the otherworld*
360. plenye *complain*
361. fairis als weill *does as well*
362. chevelry *knights*
363. langour *grief*   sic ply *such a
   state*
364. war *were*   cuntre *country*
   Trace *Thrace*
365. revert *recover*   fax *hair*
367. quhit *white*   can ta *took*
368. proportioun *harmonies*
369. baiss tonis *low tones*
   ypodorica *Hypodorian mode*

370. gemilling *twinning*
   yporlerica *Hyperlerican mode*
371. quhill *until*   rewth *sympathy*
   petie *pity*
372. weipit *wept*
373. bad him as *told him to name*
374. waresoun *reward*   rycht
   nocht *nothing at all*
375. licience *permission*
377. sen *since*   hiddir *here*
378. pairte *part*
379. mak promissioun *agree*

373–6. 'Then Proserpina and Pluto told him to name his reward; and he
   wanted nothing at all except permission to go back to his own country
   with his wife, whom he had come so far to find'.

53

'Euridices than be the hand thow tak,   380
And pas thi way, bot undirneth this pane:
Gife thow turnis or blenkis behind thy bak,
We sall hir haif to hell for evir agane.'
Thocht this was hard, yit Orpheus was fane,
And on thay went, talkand of play and sport,   385
Till thay almost come to the outwart port.

54

Thus Orpheus, with inwart lufe repleit,
So blindit was with grit effectioun,
Pensyfe in hart apone his lady sweit,
Remembrit nocht his hard conditioun.   390
Quhat will ye moir? In schort conclusioun,
He blent bakwart, and Pluto come annone
And on to hell with hir agane is gone

55

Allace, it wes grit pety for to heir
Of Orpheus the weping and the wo,   395
How his lady, that he had bocht so deir,
Bot for a luk so sone wes tane him fro.
Flatlingis he fell and micht no fordir go,
And lay a quhyle in swoun and extasy
Quhen he ourcome, thus out of lufe can cry: 400

56

'Quhat art thow luve, how sall I the defyne?
Bittir and sweit, crewall and merciable,
Plesand to sum, to uthir plent and pyne;

380. be *by*
381. undirneth *under*
  pane *condition*
382. gife *if* blenkis *look*
383. haif *have*
384. fane *willing*
385. sport *amusing things*
386. outwart port *outer gate*
387. inwart lufe *inner love*
  repleit *filled*
388. effectioun *passion*
389. pensyfe *thinking*

391. quhat . . . moir *what more do
  you want to hear*
392. blent *looked* annone *at once*
396. bocht *bought*
397. tane *taken* fro *from*
398. flatlingis *prostrate*
  fordir *further*
399. swoun *swoon* extasy *faint*
400. ourcome *came round*
402. merciable *merciful*
403. plesand *pleasing*
  plent *lamentation* pyne *suffering*

Till sum constant, to uthir variable;
Hard is thy law, thy bandis unbrekable; 405
Qho servis the, thocht thay be nevir so trew,
Perchance sum tyme thay sall haif caus to rew.

57

'Now find I weill this proverb trew,' quod he,
' "Hart on the hurd and hand is on the soir;
Quhair luve gois, on fors mone turne the e." 410
I am expart and wo is me thairfoir;
Bot for a luke my lady is forloir.'
Thus chydand on with luve, our burne and bent,
A woful wedo hamewart is he went.

Moralitas

Now wirthy folk, Boece, that senatour, 415
To wryt this fenyeit fable tuk in cure
In his gay Buke of Consolatioun
For our doctrene and gud instructioun;
Quhilk in the self, suppois it fenyeid be,
And hid under the cloik of poetre, 420
Yit Maister Trivat, Doctour Nicholas,
Quhilk in his tyme a noble theologe was,

404. till *to*
405. bandis *bonds*
406. qho servis the *whoever serves you* nevir *ever* trew *true*
407. perchance *perhaps* rew *repent*
409. hurd *treasure* soir *sore*
410. on fors *by necessity* mone *must* e *eye*
411. expart *experienced*
412. forloir *lost*
413. chydand on *complaining against* our *over* burne *stream* bent *field*

414. wedo *widower* hamewart *homewards* went *gone*
415. wirthy *worthy* Boece *Boethius* senatour *senator*
416. fenyeit fable *fictitious tale* cure *responsibility*
417. gay *eloquent* buke *book*
418. doctrene *edification*
419. the self *itself* suppois *even if* fenyeid *fictional*
420. cloik *cloak*
421. Maister Trivat *Master Trivet*
422. theologe *theologian*

409–12. ' "The heart must be set on the treasure and the hand must touch the sore; in the same way, wherever love goes the eye must follow." I have experience of this and suffer because of it; my lady is lost on account of a single look.'
415–17. 'Now worthy people, Boethius, that Roman senator, was responsible for writing this fictitious tale in his eloquent book, *The Consolation of Philosophy*'.
419. 'Which, although it is fictional in itself'.

Applyis it to gud moralitie,
Rycht full of fructe and seriositie.
Fair Phebus is the god of sapience;   425
Caliope, his wyfe, is eloquence.
This twa, mareit, gat Orpheus belyfe,
Quhilk callit is the pairte intelletyfe
Of manis saule and understanding, fre
And separat fra sensualitie.   430
Euridices is our effectioun,
Be fantesy oft movit up and doun:
Quhile to ressone it castis the delyte,
Quhyle to the flesche it settis the appetyte.
Arestius, this hird that cowth persew   435
Euridices, is nocht but gud vertew,
That bissy is to keip our myndis clene;
Bot quhen we fle outthrow the medow grene
Fra vertew till this warldis vane plesans,
Myngit with cair and full of variance,   440
The serpent stangis, that is the deidly syn
That posownis the saule without and in;
And then is deid and eik oppressit doun
Till wardly lust all our affectioun.
Thane perfyte wisdome weipis wondir sair,   445

424. fructe *fruit*
seriositie *seriousness*
425. Phebus *Phoebus*
sapience *wisdom*
426. Caliope *Calliope*
427. twa *two* mareit *married*
gat *begot* belyfe *before long*
428. pairte intelletyfe *intellectual part*
429. saule *soul*
431. effectioun *desire*
432. fantesy *whim*
433. quhile *sometimes*
castis *directs*
435. hird *herdsman* cowth
persew *pursued*

436. vertew *virtue*
437. bissy *busy*
438. fle *flee* outthrow *through*
439. fra *from* vane plesans *empty pleasures*
440. myngit *mingled*
variance *inconstancy*
441. stangis *stings*
442. posownis *poisons*
without *outside*
443. eik *also* oppressit
doun *overthrown*
444. till *by* wardly *wordly*
445. peryte *perfect* wondir
sair *very bitterly*

431–4. 'Euridice is our desire, which moves upwards to divine things or
downwards to earthly things on a whim: sometimes it directs its
longing towards reason, at others it fixes its appetite on things of the
flesh'.
443–4. 'And then our desire is killed and overthrown by worldly lust.'

Seand thusgait our appetyte misfair,
And to the hevin he passit up belyfe,
Schawand to us the lyfe contemplatyfe,
The perfyte wit and eik the fervent luve
We suld haif allway to the hevin abuve.   450
Bot seildin thair our appetyte is fundin,
It is so fast within the body bundin.
Thairfoir dounwart we cast our myndis e,
Blindit with lust, and may nocht upwartis fle.
Sould our desyre be socht up in the spheiris,   455
Quhen it is tedderit in thir warldly breiris,
Quhyle on the flesch, quhyle on this wardis wrak,
And to the hevin full small intent we tak?
Schir Orpheus, thow seikis all in vane
Thy wyfe so he, thairfoir cum doun agane   460
And pas unto the monster mervellus
With thre heidis, that we call Cerberus,
Quhilk fenyeid is to haif so mony heidis
For to betakin thre maner of deidis:
The first is in the tendir yong bernage;   465
The secound deid is in the middill age;
The thrid is in greit eild quhen men ar tane.
Thus Cerberus to swelly sparis nane.
Bot quhen our mynd is myngit with sapience,

446. seand *seeing* thusgait *in this
way* misfair *go astray*
447. belyfe *straightaway*
448. schawand *showing*
contemplatyfe *contemplative*
449. wit *understanding*
451. seildin *seldom*
452. bundin *bound*
453. myndis e *mind's eye*
454. upwartis *upwards* fle *fly*
455. sould *should* socht *sought*
456. tedderit *tethered*
breiris *briars*

457. wrak *possessions*
458. intent *interest*
459. seikis *seek*
460. he *high*
462. heidis *heads*
463. fenyeid *supposed*
464. betakin *represent*
maner *kinds* deidis *death*
465. bernage *youth*
467. eild *age* tane *taken*
468. swelly *swallow* sparis *spares*
469. myngit *mingled*
sapience *wisdom*

455–8. 'Why should our desire be sought up among the spheres, when it
is tethered to these worldly briars, sometimes thinking about fleshly
things, sometimes thinking about this world's possessions, and we take
very little interest in heaven?'.

And plais upoun the herp of eloquence –   470
That is to say, makis persuasioun
To draw our will and our affectioun,
In every eild, fra syn and fowll delyte –
The dog our sawll na power hes to byte.
The secound monstouris ar the sistiris thre: 475
Electo, Migera and Thesaphany
Ar nocht ellis, in bukis as we reid,
Both wickit thocht, ill word and thrawart deid.
Electo is the bolling of the harte;
Mygera the wickit word outwart;   480
Thesaphony is operatioun
That makis fynall executioun
Of deidly syn; and thir thre turnis ay
The ugly quheill, is nocht ellis to say
Bot warldly men sumtyme ar cassin he   485
Upone the quheill in gret prosperitie,
And with a quhirle, onwarly, or thai wait,
Ar thrawin doun to pure and law estait.
Of Exione, that on the quheill wes spreid,
I sall yow tell sum pairte, as I haif red.   490
He was of lyfe brukle and lecherous,
And in that craft hardy and curagus,
That he wald luve into no lawar place

470. plais *plays*
471. makis persuasioun *provides*
    inducement
477. ellis *else* bukis *books* reid *read*
478. thrawart deid *perverse deed*
479. bolling *proud swelling*
480. outwart *outwardly expressed*
481. operatioun *action*
482. executioun *performance*
483. ay *constantly*
484. quheill *wheel*

485. cassin *placed* he *high*
487. quhirle *whirl*
    onwarly *unexpectedly* or *before*
    wait *realise*
488. thrawin *thrown* pure *poor*
    law *low* estait *condition*
490. pairte *part*
491. brukle *unstable*
492. craft *capacity* hardy *bold*
    curagus *lustful*
493. lawar *lower*

471–4. 'That is to say, it provides some inducement to attract our will
    and desire away from sin and foul pleasure, no matter what our age –
    then the dog has no power to bite our soul'.
481–4. 'Tisiphone is the action which finally brings about the deadly sin;
    and these three sisters constantly turn the ugly wheel – there is no
    more to say'.

Bot Juno, quene of nature and goddace.
And on a day he went up on the sky   495
And socht Juno, thinkand with hir to ly.
Scho saw him cum and knew his foull intent;
A rany clud doun fra the firmament
Scho gart discend and kest betwix thame two,
And in that clud his nature yeid him fro,   500
Of quhilk was generat the Sentowris,
Half man, half hors, upoun a ferly wis.
Thane for the inwart crabing and offens
That Juno tuke for his grit violens,
Scho send him doun unto the sistiris thre,   505
Upone a quheill ay turnyt for to be.
Bot quhen ressoun and perfyte sapience
Playis upone the herp of eloquens,
And persuadis our fleschly appetyte
To leif the thocht of this warldly delyte,   510
Than seisis of our hert the wicket will;
Fra frawart language than the tong is still,
Our synfull deidis fallis doun on sleip,
Than Exione out of the quheill gan creip:
That is to say, the grit solicitud,   515
Quhyle up, quhyle doun, to win this warldis gud,
Seissis furthwith, and our affectioun
Waxis quiet in contemplatioun.

494. goddace *goddess*
495. on *into*
496. socht *sought*
   thinkand *intending* ly *lie*
498. rany *rainy* clud *cloud*
499. gart *made* kest *placed*
500. nature *semen* yeid *went*
501. generat *created*
   Sentowris *Centaurs*
502. upoun *in* ferly wis *wondrous manner*
503. inwart *deep*
   crabing *displeasure*

506. ay *always* turnyt *turned*
507. sapience *wisdom*
510. leif *leave* thocht *thought*
511. seisis *ceases* wicket *wicked*
512. frawart *perverse* than *then*
   tong *tongue*
513. on sleip *asleep*
515. solicitud *concern*
516. quhyle *sometimes*
   win *acquire* gud *goods*
517. furthwith *immediately*
518. waxis *grows*

503–6. 'Then on account of the deep displeasure and offence that Juno felt at his great violence, she sent him down to the three sisters, to be turned forever upon a wheel'.
515–8. 'That is to say, the great concern man has to acquire the things of this world, as he goes up and down on Fortune's wheel, ceases immediately, and our desire grows quiet in contemplation'.

This Tantalus of quhome I spak of aire,
Quhill he levit he was a gay ostlaire,   520
And on a nycht come travilland thairby
The god of riches, and tuk harbery
With Tantalus; and he till his supper
Slew his awin sone that was him leif and deir.
Syne in a sew, with spycis soddin weill,   525
He gart the god eit up his flesche ilk deill.
For this dispyt, quhen he was deid, annone
Was dampnit in the flud of Acherone,
Till suffer hungir, thrist, nakit and cawld,
Rycht wo begone, as I befoir haif tould.   530
This hungry man and thirsty, Tantalus,
Betaknis men gredy and covetous,
The god of riches that ar ay reddy
For to ressaif and tak in harbery,
And till him sieth thair sone in pecis small,   535
That is thair flesch and blud, with grit travell
To full the bag, and nevir fund in thair hairt
Upoun thame self to spend, nor tak thair pairte.
Allace, in erd quhair is thair mair foly
Than for to want and haif haboundantly –   540

519. aire *before*
520. quhill *while*   levit *lived*   gay
    ostlaire *fine innkeeper*
521. on a nycht *one night*
    travilland *travelling*
522. tuk harbery *took lodging*
523. till *for*
524. awin *own*   sone *son*   him *to*
    him   leif *beloved*
525. syne *then*   sew *stew*
    soddin *boiled*
526. gart *made*   ilk deill *every bit*
527. dispyt *outrage*   annone *at once*

528. dampnit in *condemned to*
    flude of Acherone *river Acheron*
529. cawld *cold*
530. tould *told*
532. betaknis *signifies*
534. ressaif *receive*
535. till *for*   sieth *boil*
536. travell *effort*
537. full *fill*   fund *find*
538. pairte *share*
539. allace *alas*   erd *earth*
540. haboundantly *in abundance*

531–8. 'This hungry and thirsty man, Tantalus, signifies greedy and
    covetous men, who are always ready to receive and give shelter to the
    god of riches, and to boil up their son, who is their flesh and blood,
    for him in little pieces, all this great effort to fill up the money bag,
    and yet they never find it in their heart to spend some of that money
    on themselves, nor take their share of it'.
540–2. 'To be in need and at the same time have an abundance of
    possessions – to be poorly housed, clothed and fed, and accumulate a
    hoard of gold which will go to other men'.

Till haif distres on bed, on bak and burd,
And spair till uthir men of gold a hurde?
And in the nycht sleip soundly thay may nocht,
To gaddir geir so gredy is thair thocht.
Bot quhen that ressoun and intelligence 545
Smytis upoun the herp of conscience,
Schawand to us quhat perrell on ilk syd
That thai incur quhay will trest or confyd
Into this warldis vane prosperitie,
Quhilk hes thir sory properteis thre, 550
That is to say, gottin with grit labour,
Keipit with dreid and tynt with grit dolour,
This grit avaris, be grace quha undirstud,
I trow suld leif thair grit solicitude
Of ythand thochtis and he besines 555
To gaddir gold and syne leif in distres;
Bot he suld eit and drink quhen evir he list,
Of cuvatyse to slaik the birnand thrist.
This Titius lay nalit on the bent,
And with the grip his bowellis revin and rent; 560
Quhill he levit set his intentioun
To find the craft of divinatioun,
And lyrit it unto the spamen all,
To tell befoir sic thingis as wald befall:

541. bak *back* burd *table*
542. spair till *accumulate for*
    hurde *hoard*
544. gaddir *obtain* geir *goods*
547. ilk syd *every side*
548. quhay *who* trest *trust*
    confyd *have confidence*
550. sory *vile* properteis *attributes*
551. gottin *acquired*
552. keipit *kept* tynt *lost*
    dolour *sorrow*
553. be *by*
554. trow *believe* leif *leave*

555. ythand *constant* he
    besines *great effort*
556. leif *live*
557. list *pleases*
558. slaik *quench* birnand *burning*
559. nalit *impaled* bent *ground*
560. grip *vulture* revin and
    rent *ripped and torn*
561. quhill *while*
562. divinatioun *divination*
563. lyrit *taught*
    spamen *soothsayers*
564. befoir *in advance* sic *such*

547–9. 'Showing us what dangers those who place their trust and have confidence in this world's useless prosperity will encounter from all sides'.
553–6. 'I believe that anyone who, by the grace of God, understands this great avarice, should give up their life of great concern, where they expend constant thought and great effort to acquire gold and yet live in distress'.

Quhat lyfe, quhat deth, quhat destany and werd   565
Provydit ware unto every man on erd.
Apollo than, for this abusioun,
Quhilk is the god of divinatioun,
For he usurpit of his facultie,
Put him to hell and thair remanis he.   570
Ilk man that heiris this conclusioun
Suld dreid to sers be constillatioun
Thingis to fall under the firmament,
Till ye or na quhilk ar indefferent,
Without profixit causis and certane,   575
Quhilk nane in erd may knaw bot God allane.
Quhen Orpheus upoun his harp can play,
That is, our undirstanding, for to say,
Cryis, 'O man, recleme thi folich harte.
Will thow be God and tak on the his parte,   580
To tell thingis to cum that never wil be,
Quhilk God hes kepit in his prevetie?
Thow ma na mair offend to God of micht,
Na with thi spaying reif fra him his richt.'
This perfyte wisdome with his melody   585
Fleyis the spreit of fenyeid profecy,
And drawis upwart our affectioun
Fra witchcraft, spaying and sorsery,
And superstitioun of astrology;
Saif allanerly sic maner of thingis   590
Quhilk upoun trew and certane causis hingis,

565. werd *fate*
566. provydit ware *were ordained*
567. abusioun *outrage*
569. for *because*   facultie *power*
572. sers *discover* be
    constillatioun *from the stars*
573. fall *happen*
574. na *no*   indefferent *indifferent*
575. profixit *predetermined*
579. recleme *restrain* folich *foolish*
582. prevetie *secrecy*

583. ma *may*   God of
    micht *mighty God*
584. na *than* spaying *divination*
    reif *steal* his richt *what is
    rightfully his*
586. fleyis *flees from* spreit *spirit*
    fenyeid profecy *faked prophecy*
588. sorsery *sorcery*
590. saif allanerly *except only*
591. hingis *depend*

571–6. 'Every man who hears about Tityus' end should fear to seek
    knowledge from the stars about things that will happen on earth,
    things that are beyond human control, without predetermined and
    certain causes, that no one on earth can know except God alone'.

The quhilk mone cum, quhill thair causis indure,
On verry fors and nocht throw avanture,
As is the clippis and the conjunctioun
Of sone and mone, be calculatioun,   595
The quhilk ar fundin in trew astronomy
Be moving of the speiris in the sky.
All thir to speik it may be tollerable,
And none udir, quhilk no caussis stable.
This ugly way, this mirk and dully streit,   600
Is nocht ellis bot blinding of the spreit
With myrk cluddis and myst of ignorance,
Affetterrit in this warldis vane plesance
And bissines of temporalite.
To kene the self a styme it may nocht se,   605
For stammeris on eftir effectioun,
Fra ill to war ale thus to hale gois doun
That is wan howp, throw lang hanting of syn,
And fowll dispair that mony fallis in.
Than Orpheus, our ressoun, is full wo   610
And twichis on his harp and biddis ho
Till our desyre and fulich appetyte,
Bidis leif this warldis full delyte.
Than Pluto god, and quene of hellis fyre,
Mone grant to ressoun on fors the desyre.   615
Than Orpheus hes wone Euridices

592. mone *must* quhill *as long as*
  indure *last*
593. fors *necessity* avanture *chance*
594. clippis *eclipse*
595. sone *sun* mone *moon*
597. speiris *spheres*
598. thir *these* speik *speak about*
  tollerable *permissible*
599. udir *other* stable *fixed*
600. mirk *dark* dully *dismal*
603. affetterrit in *fettered by*
  plesance *delight*
604. bissines of
  temporalite *worldly cares*

605. kene *know* styme *little bit*
606. stammeris *staggers*
607. ill to war *bad to worse*
  ale *all* hale *hell*
608. wan howp *despair* lang *long*
  hanting of *familiarity with*
609. fallis in fall *into*
610. than *then* full wo *very sad*
611. twichis *plays* biddis ho *calls
  a halt*
613. leif *leave* full *foul*
615. mone *must* on fors *by
  necessity*
616. wone *won*

598–9. 'It is permissable to speak about all of these and no others, which
  have no fixed cause'.
605–6. 'It cannot see its way clear to understanding itself even a little bit,
  but staggers on in pursuit of its desire'.

Quhen our desyre wyth ressoun makis pes,
And seikis up to contemplatioun,
Of syn detestand the abutioun.
Bot ilk man suld be wyse and warly se   620
That he bakwart cast nocht his myndis e,
Gifand consent and dilectatioun
Of fleschly lust for the affectioun;
For thane gois bakwart to the syn agane
Our appetyte, as it befoir was slane   625
In warldly lust and vane prosperite,
And makis ressoun wedow for to be.

Now pray we God, sen our affectioun
Is allway promp and reddy to fall doun,
That he wald undirput his haly hand   630
Of mantenans, and gife us fors to stand
In perfyte luve, as he is glorius,
And thus endis the taill of Orpheus.

---

617. pes *peace*
619. abutioun *shameful practice*
620. ilk *every* warly se *watch out*
621. myndis e *mind's eye*
622. gifand *giving*
  dilectatioun *pleasure*
627. wedow *widower*

628. sen *since*
629. promp *prompt*
630. undirput *place underneath*
  haly *holy*
631. mantenans *support*
  fors *strength*

622–3. 'Giving desire permission to take pleasure in fleshly lust'.
630–1. 'That he would place his supporting, holy hand beneath us and
  give us the strength to stand'.

The Testament of Cresseid

1

Ane doolie sessoun to ane cairfull dyte
Suld correspond and be equivalent:
Richt sa it wes quhen I began to wryte
This tragedie – the wedder richt fervent,
Quhen Aries, in middis of the Lent,   5
Schouris of haill gart fra the north discend,
That scantlie fra the cauld I micht defend.

2

Yit nevertheles within myne oratur
I stude, quhen Titan had his bemis bricht
Withdrawin doun and sylit under cure;   10
And fair Venus, the bewtie of the nicht,
Uprais and set unto the west full richt
Hir goldin face, in oppositioun
Of god Phebus, direct discending doun.

3

Throwout the glas hir bemis brast sa fair   15
That I micht se on everie syde me by;
The northin wind had purifyit the air,
And sched the mistie cloudis fra the sky;
The froist freisit, the blastis bitterly
Fra Pole Artick come quhisling loud and schill,   20
And causit me remufe aganis my will.

1. doolie *dismal* sessoun *season* cairfull *sorrowful* dyte *style*
2. suld *should*
3. quhen *when*
4. wedder *weather* richt *very* fervent *fierce*
5. middis *middle*
6. schouris *showers* gart . . . discend *caused to fall*
7. scantlie *scarcely* cauld *cold*
8. oratur *oratory*
9. stude *stood* bemis *beams*
10. sylit *concealed* cure *cover*
11. bewtie *beauty*
12. uprais *ascended* full richt *straight*
15. throwout *through* brast *burst*
17. purifyit *purified*
18. sched *scattered*
19. freisit *freezes* blastis *blasts of wind*
20. quhisling *whistling* schill *shrill*
21. remufe *to go away*

1–2. 'A dismal season requires a correspondingly sorrowful tale'.

4

For I traistit that Venus, luifis quene,
To quhome sum tyme I hecht obedience,
My faidit hart of lufe scho wald mak grene,
And therupon with humbill reverence   25
I thocht to pray hir hie magnificence;
Bot for greit cald as than I lattit was,
And in my chalmer to the fyre can pas.

5

Thocht lufe be hait, yit in ane man of age
It kendillis nocht sa sone as in youtheid,   30
Of quhome the blude is flowing in ane rage,
And in the auld the curage doif and deid,
Of quhilk the fyre outward is best remeid:
To help be phisike quhair that nature faillit
I am expert, for baith I have assaillit.   35

6

I mend the fyre and beikit me about,
Than tuik ane drink my spreitis to comfort,
And armit me weill fra the cauld thairout.
To cut the winter nicht and mak it schort,
I tuik ane quair – and left all uther sport –   40
Writtin be worthie Chaucer glorious,
Of fair Creisseid and worthie Troylus.

22. traistit *trusted* luifis *love's*
    quene *queen*
23. hecht *vowed*
24. faidit *faded*
26. hie *high*
27. bot for *but because of* as
    then *at that time* lattit *prevented*
28. chalmer *chamber* can pas *went*
29. thocht *though* hait *hot* yit *yet*
30. kendillis *kindles* sone *soon*
    youtheid *youth*
31. quhome *whom* blude *blood*
    rage *furious passion*

32. auld *old* curage *sexual desire*
    doif *dull* deid *dead*
33. quhilk *which*
    outward *external* remeid
    remedy
34. phisike *medicine* faillit *fails*
35. baith *both* assaillit *tried*
36. beikit me *warmed myself*
37. tuik *took* spreitis *spirits*
38. armit me *protected myself*
40. quair *book* sport *amusement*
41. worthie *honourable*

24. 'She would make my faded heart young in love'.
27. 'But at that time I was prevented because of the terrible cold'.
32–6. 'Sexual desire is spiritless and dead in the old, and the best remedy
    for this is external heat: I am an expert at using science to help where
    nature has failed, for I have tried both'.

7

And thair I fand, efter that Diomeid
Ressavit had that lady bricht of hew,
How Troilus neir out of wit abraid,   45
And weipit soir, with visage paill of hew;
For quhilk wanhope his teiris can renew,
Quhill esperance rejoisit him agane:
Thus quhyle in joy he levit, quhyle in pane.

8

Of hir behest he had greit comforting,   50
Traisting to Troy that scho suld mak retour,
Quhilk he desyrit maist of eirdly thing,
Forquhy scho was his only paramour.
Bot quhen he saw passit baith day and hour
Of hir ganecome, than sorrow can oppres   55
His wofull hart in cair and hevines.

9

Of his distres me neidis nocht reheirs,
For worthie Chauceir, in the samin buik,
In gudelie termis and in joly veirs,
Compylit hes his cairis, quha will luik.   60
To brek my sleip ane uther quair I tuik,
In quhilk I fand the fatall destenie
Of fair Cresseid, that endit wretchitlie.

43. fand *found*
44. ressavit *received*
    hew *complexion*
45. neir *nearly* wit *mind*
    abraid *went*
46. sore *grievously* visage *face*
47. wanhope *despair* can
    renew *renewed*
48. quhill *until* esperance *hope*
    rejoisit *gladdened*
49. quhyle *sometimes* levit *lived*
50. behest *promise*
    comforting *comfort*
51. traisting *trusting* suld *should*
    mak retour *return*
52. eirdly *earthly*
53. forquhy *because*
    paramour *beloved*
55. ganecome *return* than *then*
56. cair *sorrow* heviness *dejection*
57. me neidis nocht *I do not need*
    reheirs *repeat*
58. samin *same* buik *book*
59. gudelie termis *excellent
    language* joly veirs *fine verse*
60. compylit hes *has described*
    cairis *sorrows* quha will luik *for
    whoever wishes to look*
61. breik *prevent* quair *book*
62. fatall *fateful*

57. 'It is not necessary for me to tell of his distress'

10

Quha wait gif all that Chauceir wrait was trew?
Nor I wait nocht gif this narratioun   65
Be authoreist, or fenyeit of the new
Be sum poeit, throw his inventioun
Maid to report the lamentatioun
And wofull end of this lustie Creisseid,
And quhat distres scho thoillit, and quhat deid.   70

11

Quhen Diomeid had all his appetyte
And mair fulfillit of this fair ladie,
Upon ane uther he set his haill delyte,
And send to hir ane lybell of repudie,
And hir excludit fra his companie.   75
Than desolait scho walkit up and doun,
And, sum men sayis, into the court commoun.

12

O fair Creisseid, the flour and *A per se*
Of Troy and Grece, how was thow fortunait:
To change in filth all thy feminitie,   80
And be with fleschelie lust sa maculait,
And go amang the Greikis air and lait,
Sa giglotlike, takand thy foull plesance!
I have pietie thow suld fall sic mischance!

---

64. quha *who* wait *knows* gif *if* wrait *wrote*
65. narratioun *narrative*
66. authoreist *possessed of authority* fenyeit *invented*
67. be *by* poeit *poet*
69. lustie *beautiful*
70. thoillit *suffered* deid *death*
72. mair *more* fulfillit *satisfied*
73. uther *other* haill *whole*
74. lybell of repudie *a declaration of rejection*

75. excludit fra *banished from*
77. commoun *promiscuous*
78. flour *flower* A per se *paragon*
79. fortunait *dealt with by fortune*
81. sa maculait *so stained*
82. air and lait *early and late i.e. incessantly*
83. gigotlike *like a harlot* takand *taking* plesance *pleasure*
84. pietie *pity* sic mischance *such ill fortune*

65–9. 'Nor do I know if this story has any ancient authority, or if it has instead been recently invented by some poet, created by his own imagination to describe the lamentation and woeful end of this lovely Cresseid'.

13

Yit nevertheles, quhatever men deme or say 85
In scornfull langage of thy brukkilnes,
I sall excuse, als far furth as I may,
Thy womanheid, thy wisdome and fairnes,
The quhilk Fortoun hes put to sic distres
As hir pleisit, and nathing throw the gilt 90
Of the, throw wickit langage to be spilt.

14

This fair lady, in this wyse destitute
Of all comfort and consolatioun,
Richt privelie, but fellowschip, on fute,
Disagysit passit far out of the toun 95
Ane myle or twa, unto ane mansioun
Beildit full gay, quhair hir father Calchas
Quhilk than amang the Greikis dwelland was.

15

Quhen he hir saw, the caus he can inquyre
Of hir cumming; scho said, siching full soir, 100
'Fra Diomeid had gottin his desyre
He wox werie and wald of me no moir.'
Quod Calchas, 'Douchter, weip thow not thairfoir;
Peraventure all cummis for the best.
Welcum to me! Thow art full deir ane gest.' 105

16

This auld Calchas, efter the law was tho,
Wes keiper of the tempill as ane preist
In quhilk Venus and hir sone Cupido
War honourit, and his chalmer was thame neist;

85. deme *judge*
86. brukkilnes *frailty*
87. als far furth *as far as*
88. womanheid *womanliness*
90. pleisit *pleases*   nathing *not at all*   gilt *guilt*
91. spilt *injured*
92. wyse *way*
94. richt privelie *very secretly*   but *without*
95. disagysit *disguised*
97. beildit *constructed*   full gay *very impressively*
100. siching *sighing*   soir *grievously*
101. fra *as soon as*
102. wox *grew*   werie *weary*   wald *wanted*
103. quod *said*
104. peraventure *perhaps*
105. gest *guest*
106. efter *in accordance with*   tho *then*
109. war *were*   chalmer *chamber*   thame neist *nearest to them*

To quhilk Cresseid, with baill aneuch in breist,   110
Usit to pas, hir prayeris for to say,
Quhill at the last, upon ane solempne day,

17

As custome was, the pepill far and neir,
Befoir the none unto the tempill went
With sacrifice, devoit in thair maneir.   115
Bot still Cresseid, hevie in hir intent,
Into the kirk wald not hirself present,
For giving of the pepill ony deming
Of hir expuls fra Diomeid the king;

18

Bot past into ane secreit orature   120
Quhair scho micht weip hir wofull desteny.
Behind hir back scho cloisit fast the dure
And on hir kneis bair fell doun in hy.
Upon Venus and Cupide angerly
Scho cryit out and said on this same wyse: 125
'Allace, that ever I maid yow sacrifice!

19

'Ye gave me anis ane devine responsaill
That I suld be the flour of luif in Troy;
Now am I maid ane unworthie outwaill,
And all in cair translatit is my joy.   130
Quha sall me gyde? Quha sall me now convoy,
Sen I fra Diomeid and nobill Troylus
Am clene excludit as abject odious?

110. baill *sorrow* aneuch *a great
  deal* breist *heart*
111. usit *was accustomed* pas *go*
112. quhill *until* solempne
  day *religious feast day*
114. none *noon*
115. devoit *devout*
116. hevie *sorrowful* intent *mind*
118. for giving of *for fear of
  giving* deming *suspicion*
119. expuls *expulsion*
120. orature *oratory*

122. fast *securely*
123. in hy *in haste*
125. wyse *way*
127. anis *once* devine
  responsaill *divine response*
128. luif *love*
129. outwaill *outcast*
130. translatit *transformed*
131. quha *who* gyde *guide*
  convoy *protect*
132. sen *since*
133. clene *entirely* abject *outcast*

130. 'And all my joy is transformed into sorrow'.

20

'O fals Cupide, is nane to wyte bot thow
And thy mother, of lufe the blind goddes!   135
Ye causit me alwayis understand and trow
The seid of lufe was sawin in my face,
And ay grew grene throw your supplie and grace.
Bot now, allace, that seid with froist is slane,
And I fra luifferis left and all forlane!'   140

21

Quhen this was said, doun in ane extasie,
Ravischit in spreit, intill ane dreame scho fell,
And be apperance hard, quhair scho did ly,
Cupide the king ringand ane silver bell,
Quhilk men micht heir fra hevin unto hell.   145
At quhais sound befoir Cupid appeiris
The sevin planetis discending fra thair spheiris;

22

Quhilk hes power of all thing generabill,
To reull and steir be thair greit influence
Wedder and wind and coursis variabill.   150
And first of all Saturne gave his sentence,
Quhilk gave to Cupide litill reverence,
Bot as ane busteous churle on his maneir
Come crabitlie with auster luik and cheir.

23

His face fronsit, his lyre was lyke the leid,   155
His teith chatterit and cheverit with the chin,

134. wyte *blame*
136. causit me *made me*
    trow *believe*
137. seid *seed* sawin *sown*
138. supplie *help* grace *favour*
139. allace *alas* froist *frost*
140. fra *from* luifferis *lovers*
    forlane *forgotten*
141. extasie *trance*
142. ravischit *carried away*
    spreit *spirit*
143. be appearance *seemingly*
    hard *heard* ly *lie*
147. spheiris *spheres*

148. generabill *created*
149. reull *rule* steir *govern*
150. wedder *weather* coursis
    variabill *course of fortune*
151. sentence *judgement*
153. busteous *rough*
    churle *peasant*
154. crabitlie *bad temperedly*
    auster *stern* luik *look*
    cheir *appearance*
155. fronsit *wrinkled*
    lyre *complexion* leid *lead*
156. cheverit *shivered*

His ene drowpit, how sonkin in his heid,
Out of his nois the meldrop fast can rin,
With lippis bla and cheikis leine and thin;
The ice schoklis that fra his hair doun hang   160
Was wonder greit and as ane speir als lang.

24

Atovir his belt his lyart lokkis lay
Felterit unfair, ovirfret with froistis hoir;
His garmound and his gyte full gay of gray;
His widderit weid fra him the wind out woir,   165
Ane busteous bow within his hand he boir,
Under his girdill ane flasche of felloun flanis,
Fedderit with ice and heidit with hailstanis.

25

Than Juppiter, richt fair and amiabill,
God of the starnis in the firmament   170
And nureis to all thing generabill;
Fra his father Saturne far different,
With burelie face and browis bricht and brent;
Upon his heid ane garland wonder gay,
Of flouris fair, as it had bene in May.   175

26

His voice was cleir, as cristall wer his ene,
As goldin wyre sa glitterand was his hair,
His garmound and his gyte full gay of grene,
With goldin listis gilt on everie gair;

157. ene *eyes* drowpit *drooped*
how *deeply* sonkin *sunk*
158. nois *nose* meldrop *mucus*
can rin *ran*
159. lippis *lips* bla *blue*
cheikis *cheeks* leine *lean*
160. ice schoklis *icicles*
162. atovir *over* iyart *grey*
163. felterit *tangled*
unfair *horribly* ovirfret *matted*
froistis hoir *white frost*
164. garmound *clothes* gyte *cloak*
165. widderit *tattered* weid *clothing*
out woir *fluttered about*

166. busteous *large* boir *carried*
167. girdill *belt* flasche *sheaf*
felloun *cruel* flanis *arrows*
168. fedderit *feathered*
heidit *tipped* hailstanis *hailstones*
170. starnis *stars*
171. nureis *nurturer*
generabill *capable of growth*
173. burelie *handsome*
browis *forehead* bricht *fair*
brent *high*
179. listis *edgings* gilt *gilded*
gair *gore*

179. 'With golden edgings gilded on every gore'.

Anc burelie brand about his middill bair;   180
In his richt hand he had ane groundin speir,
Of his father the wraith fra us to weir.

27
Nixt efter him come Mars, the god of ire,
Of strife, debait and all dissensioun,
To chide and fecht, als feirs as ony fyre;   185
In hard harnes, hewmound and habirgeoun,
And on his hanche ane roustie fell fachioun;
And in his hand he had ane roustie sword;
Wrything his face with mony angrie word.

28
Schaikand his sword, befoir Cupide he come,   190
With reid visage and grislie glowrand ene,
And at his mouth ane bullar stude of fome,
Lyke to ane bair quhetting his tuskis kene;
Richt tuilyeour lyke, but temperance in tene;
Ane horne he blew with mony bosteous brag,   195
Quhilk all this warld with weir hes maid to wag.

29
Than fair Phebus, lanterne and lamp of licht,
Of man and beist, baith frute and flourisching
Tender nureis, and banischer of nicht,

180. burelie brand *strong sword*
bair *bore*
181. groundin speir *sharpened spear*
182. wraith *anger*   weir *ward off*
184. debait *conflict*
dissensioun *discord*
185. chide *quarrel*   fecht *fight*
feirs *fierce*   fyre *fire*
186. harnes *armour*
hewmound *helmet*
habirgeoun *habergeon*
187. hanche *side*   roustie *rusty*

fell *cruel*   fachioun *falchion*
189. wrything *distorting*
191. glowrand *glowering*   ene *eyes*
192. bullar *bubble*   fome *foam*
193. bair *boar*   kene *sharp*
194. tuilyeour *bully*   but *without*
tene *anger*
195. bosteous brag *harsh blast*
196. weir *war*   wag *shake*
198. baith *both*   frute *fruit*
flourisching *blossom*
199. nureis *nurse*

182. 'To ward off his father's anger from us'
186. 'In hard armour, helmet and habergeon'.
187. 'And at his side a rusty, cruel falchion'.

And of the warld causing, be his moving   200
And influence, lyfe in all eirdlie thing,
Without comfort of quhome, of force to nocht
Must all ga die that in this warld is wrocht.

      30
As king royall he raid upon his chair,
The quhilk Phaeton gydit sum tyme unricht;   205
The brichtnes of his face, quhen it was bair,
Nane micht behald for peirsing of his sicht.
This goldin cart with fyrie bemis bricht
Four yokkit steidis, full different of hew,
But bait or tyring throw the spheiris drew.   210

      31
The first was soyr, with mane als reid as rois,
Callit Eoye, into the orient;
The secund steid to name hecht Ethios,
Quhitlie and paill and sumdeill ascendent;
The thrid Peros, richt hait and richt fervent;   215
The feird was blak, callit Philologie,
Quhilk rollis Phebus doun into the sey.

      32
Venus was thair present, that goddes gay,
Hir sonnis querrell for to defend and mak
Hir awin complaint, cled in ane nyce array: 220
The ane half grene, the uther half sabill blak;

201. eirdlie *earthly*   rois *rose*
202. of force *of necessity*   212. callit *called* orient *east*
    nocht *nothing*   213. to name hecht *is called*
203. ga *go* wrocht *created*   214. quhitlie *whitish* paill *pale*
204. raid *rode* chair *chariot*   sumdeill ascendent *somewhat*
205. gydit *drove* unricht *amiss*   *rising up*
207. for *for fear of*   215. thrid *third* hait *hot*
    peirsing *injuring*   fervent *fiery*
208. cart *chariot* bemis *beams*   216. feird *fourth*
209. yokkit *harnessed*   217. rollis *drives* sey *sea*
    steidis *horses* hew *colour*   220. awin *own* nyce
210. bait *stopping*   array *extravagant costume*
211. soyr *sorrel; reddish brown*

200–1. 'And engendering life in all earthly things in the world through
his movement and influence'.

Quhyte hair as gold, kemmit and sched abak;
Bot in hir face semit greit variance,
Quhyles perfyte treuth and quhyles inconstance.

33

Under smyling scho was dissimulait,   225
Provocative with blenkis amorous,
And suddanely changit and alterait,
Angrie as ony serpent vennemous,
Richt pungitive with wordis odious.
Thus variant scho was, quha list tak keip,   230
With ane eye lauch, and with the uther weip,

34

In taikning that all fleschelie paramour,
Quhilk Venus hes in reull and governance,
Is sum tyme sweit, sum tyme bitter and sour,
Richt unstabill and full of variance,   235
Mingit with cairfull joy and fals plesance,
Now hait, now cauld, now blyith, now full of wo,
Now grene as leif, now widderit and ago.

35

With buik in hand than come Mercurius,
Richt eloquent and full of rethorie,   240
With polite termis and delicious,
With pen and ink to report all reddie,

222. kemmit *combed*   sched *parted*
223. semit *seemed*
     variance *variation*
224. quhyles *sometimes*
     perfyte *perfect*   treuth *truth*
     inconstance *inconstancy*
225. dissimulait *deceitful*
226. blenkis *glances*
229. pungitive *stinging*
230. quha list tak keip *let anyone who chooses take care*
231. lauch *laugh*
232. in taikning *as a sign*

fleschelie paramour *sexual love*
233. in reull *in her power*
236. mingit *mingled*
     cairfull *sorrowfull*
     plesance *pleasure*
237. hait *hot*   cauld *cold*
     blyith *happy*
238. leif *leaf*   widderit *withered*
     ago *gone*
239. buik *book*
240. rethorie *rhetoric*
241. delicious *delightful*

222. 'Blonde hair shining like gold, combed back and parted'.
230. 'Thus, she was inconstant, let everyone beware'.
241. 'With polished and delightful forms of expression'.

Setting sangis and singand merilie;
His hude was reid, heklit atovir his croun,
Lyke to ane poeit of the auld fassoun.   245

36

Boxis he bair with fyne electuairis,
And sugerit syropis for digestioun,
Spycis belangand to the pothecairis,
Wih mony hailsum sweit confectioun;
Doctour in phisick, cled in ane skarlot goun,   250
And furrit weill – as sic ane aucht to be –
Honest and gude, and not ane word culd lie.

37

Nixt efter him come Lady Cynthia,
The last of all, and swiftest in hir spheir;
Of colour blak, buskit with hornis twa,   255
And in the nicht scho listis best appeir;
Haw as the leid, of colour nathing cleir,
For all hir licht scho borrowis at hir brother
Titan, for of hirself scho hes nane uther.

38

Hir gyte was gray and full of spottis blak,   260
And on hir breist ane churle paintit full evin,
Beirand ane bunche of thornis on his bak,
Quhilk for his thift micht clim na nar the hevin.
Thus quhen thay gadderit war, thir goddes sevin,

243. setting sangis *composing songs*
244. heklit *fringed* atouir *around*
    his croun *the crown of his head*
245. poeit *poet* fassoun *fashion*
246. electuairis *medicines*
248. pothecairis *apothecaries*
249. mony *many*
    hailsum *wholesome*
250. phisick *medicine*
251. furrit *dressed in furs* sic *such*
    aucht *ought*
255. buskit *arrayed* twa *two*

256. listis best appeir *likes best to
    appear*
257. haw *bluish-grey* leid *lead*
    nathing *not at all* cleir *clear*
260. gyte *costume*
261. churle *peasant* full evin *very
    precisely*
262. beirand *carrying*
263. thift *theft* clim na nar the
    hevin *could climb no nearer
    heaven*
264. gadderit *gathered*

244–5. 'His hood was red, fringed around the crown, like an old-
fashioned poet'.

Mercurius thay cheisit with ane assent 265
To be foirspeikar in the parliament.

39
Quha had bene thair and liken for to heir
His facound toung and termis exquisite,
Of rethorick the prettick he micht leir,
In breif sermone ane pregnant sentence wryte. 270
Befoir Cupide veiling his cap alyte,
Speiris the caus of that vocatioun,
And he anone schew his intentioun.

40
'Lo!' quod Cupide, 'quha will blaspheme the name
Of his awin god, outher in word or deid, 275
To all goddis he dois baith lak and schame,
And suld have bitter panis to his meid:
I say this by yone wretchit Cresseid,
The quhilk throw me was sum tyme flour of lufe,
Me and my mother starklie can reprufe, 280

41
'Saying of hir greit infelicitie
I was the caus, and my mother Venus.
Ane blind goddes hir cald, that micht not se,
With sclander and defame injurious.

265. cheisit *chose*
266. foirspeikar *spokesman*
267. quha *whoever* liken
  for *willing*
268. facound *eloquent*
269. prettick *practice* leir *learn*
270. sermone *words*
  pregnant *weighty*
  sentence *meaning*
271. veiling *doffing* alyte *a little*
272. speiris *asks* caus *cause*
  vocatioun *summoning*

273. anone *immediately*
  schew *made known*
  intentioun *accusation*
275. outher *either*
276. dois *does* lak *insult*
277. panis *pains* meid *reward*
278. yone *that*
280. starklie *violently* can
  reprufe *reproached*
281. infelicitie *ill fortune*
284. sclander *slander*
  defame *defamation*
  injurious *offensive*

267–70. 'Whoever had been there and willing to listen to his eloquent
  tongue and skilful words, would have learned the art of public
  speaking, how to put a weighty message in a brief speech'.
280. 'She harshly blamed me and my mother'.

Thus hir leving unclene and lecherous   285
Scho wald returne on me and my mother,
To quhome I schew my grace abone all uther.

42

'And sen ye ar all sevin deificait,
Participant of devyne sapience,
This greit injure done to our hie estait   290
Me think with pane we suld mak recompence;
Was never to goddes done sic violence.
As weill for yow as for myself I say;
Thairfoir ga help to revenge, I yow pray.'

43

Mercurius to Cupide gave answeir   295
And said, 'Schir King, my counsall is that ye
Refer yow to the hiest planeit heir,
And tak to him the lawest of degre,
The pane of Cresseid for to modifie –
As god Saturne, with him tak Cynthia.'   300
'I am content,' quod he, 'to tak thay twa.'

44

Than thus proceidit Saturne and the Mone
Quhen thay the mater rypelie had degest:
For the dispyte to Cupide scho had done
And to Venus, oppin and manifest,   305
In all hir lyfe with pane to be opprest,
And torment sair with seiknes incurabill,
And to all lovers be abhominabill.

285. leving *manner of living*
286. returne *throw back*
288. sen *considering*
  deificait *deified i.e. gods*
289. participant *having*
  devyne *divine* sapience *wisdom*
290. hie *high* estait *office*
291. pane *pain* mak
  recompence *repay*
298. lawest of degre *lowest in rank*

299. modifie *determine*
300. as *for example*
301. quod *said* thay *those*
303. rypelie *carefully*
  degest *considered*
304. dispyte *injury*
305. oppin *plain*
307. seiknes *sickness*
  incurabill *incurable*

290–1. 'I think we should repay this injury done to our high office with
  pain'.

45

This duleful sentence Saturne tuik on hand,
And passit doun quhair cairfull Cresseid lay,   310
And on hir heid he laid ane frostie wand.
Than lawfullie on this wyse can be say:
'Thy greit fairnes and all thy bewtie gay,
Thy wantoun blude, and eik thy goldin hair,
Heir I exclude fra the for evermair.   315

46

'I change thy mirth into melancholy,
Quhilk is the mother of all pensivenes;
Thy moisture and thy heit in cald and dry;
Thyne insolence, thy play and wantones
To greit diseis; thy pomp and thy riches   320
In mortall neid; and greit penuritie
Thow suffer sall and as ane beggar die.'

47

O cruell Saturne, fraward and angrie,
Hard is thy dome and to malitious!
On fair Cresseid quhy hes thow na mercie,   325
Quhilk was sa sweit, gentill and amorous?
Withdraw thy sentence and be gracious
As thow was never; sa schawis thow thy deid,
Ane wraikfull sentence gevin on fair Cresseid.

48

Than Cynthia, quhen Saturne past away,   330
Out of hir sait discendit doun belyve,

309. duleful *sorrowful*
    sentence *judgement* tuik on
    hand *took charge of*
310. passit *went* cairfull *sorrowful*
312. lawfullie *according to correct
    legal procedure* wyse *way*
314. blude *blood* eik *also*
315. heir *here* exclude *remove*
317. pensivenes *sad thoughtfulness*
319. insolence *arrogance*
    play *lasciviousness*

    wantones *wantonness*
320. discis *distress*
    pomp *splendour*
321. mortall neid *deadly need*
    penuritie *poverty*
323. fraward *adverse*
324. dome *judgement* to
    malitious *too malicious*
329. wraikfull *vengeful*
331. sait *seat* belyve *quickly*

327–9. 'Revoke your judgement, and be merciful as you have never been
    before; otherwise you show your action to be merely a vengeful
    sentence passed on fair Cresseid'.

And red ane bill on Cresseid quhair scho lay,
Contening this sentence diffinityve:
'Fra heit of bodie I the now depryve,
And to thy seiknes sall be na recure,   335
Bot in dolour thy dayis to indure.

49
'Thy cristall ene minglit with blude I mak;
Thy voice sa cleir, unplesand, hoir and hace;
Thy lustie lyre ovirspred with spottis blak,
And lumpis haw appeirand in thy face.   340
Quhair thow cummis, ilk man sall fle the place.
This sall thow go begging fra hous to hous
With cop and clapper lyke ane lazarous.'

50
This doolie dreame, this uglye visioun
Brocht to ane end, Cresseid fra it awoik,   345
And all that court and convocatioun
Vanischit away. Than rais scho up and tuik
Ane poleist glas and hir schaddow culd luik,
And quhen scho saw hir face sa deformait,
Gif scho in hart was wa aneuch, God wait!   350

51
Weiping full sair, 'Lo, quhat it is,' quod sche,
'With fraward langage for to mufe and steir
Our craibit goddis, and sa is sene on me!
My blaspheming now have I bocht full deir;
All eirdlie joy and mirth I set areir.   355

332. bill *formal document*
333. diffinityve *final*
335. recure *remedy*
336. dolour *sorrow*
338. unplesand *unpleasant*
    hoir *hoarse*   hace *rough*
339. lyre *face*   ovirspred *covered over*
340. haw *leaden*
341. ilk *each*
343. cop *cup*   lazarous *beggar*

344. doolie *dismal*
346. convocatioun *assembly*
348. poleist glas *mirror*
    schaddow *reflection*   luik *look at*
350. gif *if*   wa *miserable*
    aneuch *enough*   wait *knows*
352. fraward *bad-tempered*
    mufe *anger*   steir *provoke*
353. craibit *ill-natured*
354. bocht *paid for*
355. eirdlie *earthly*   areir *behind*

350. 'God knows she was miserable enough at heart!'.

Allace this day! Allace, this wofull tyde
Quhen I began with my goddis for to chyde!'

52

Be this was said, ane chyld come fra the hall
To warne Cresseid the supper was reddy;
First knokkit at the dure and syne culd call: 360
'Madame, your father biddis yow cum in hy.
He hes mervell sa lang on grouf ye ly,
And sayis your beedes bene to lang sumdeill;
The goddis wait all your intent full weill.'

53

Quod scho, 'Fair chyld, ga to my father deir,   365
And pray him cum to speik with me anone.'
And sa he did, and said, 'Douchter, quhat cheir?'
'Allace!' quod scho, 'Father, my mirth is gone!'
'How sa?' quod he, and scho can all expone,
As I have tauld, the vengeance and the wraik   370
For hir trespas Cupide on hir culd tak.

54

He luikit on hir uglye lipper face,
The quhylk befor was quhite as lillie flour;
Wringand his handis, oftymes he said allace
That he had levit to se that wofull hour!   375
For he knew weill that thair was na succour
To hir seiknes, and that dowblit his pane.
Thus was thair cair aneuch betwix thame twane.

55

Quhen thay togidder murnit had full lang,
Quod Cresseid: 'Father, I wald not be kend;   380
Thairfoir in secreit wyse ye let me gang

356. tyde *time*
357. chyde *quarrel*
358. be *when*   chyld *child*
360. dure *door*   syne *then*
361. in hy *quickly*
362. hes mervell *is surprised* on grouf *prostrate*
363. beedes *prayers*
364. wait *know*
366. anone *at once*

367. quhat cheir *how are you*
369. expone *explain*
370. wraik *retribution*
372. luikit *looked*   lipper *leprous*
373. quhite *white*
375. levit *lived*
376. succour *remedy*
379. murnit *lamented*
380. kend *recognised*
381. in secreit wyse *secretly*   gang *go*

Unto yone hospitall at the tounis end,
And thidder sum meit for cheritie me send
To leif upon; for all mirth in this eird
Is fra me gane – sic is my wickit weird!'   385

56

Than in ane mantill and ane baver hat,
With cop and clapper, wonder prively,
He opnit ane secreit yet and out thairat
Convoyit hir, that na man suld espy,
Unto ane village half ane myle thairby;   390
Delyverit hir in at the spittaill hous,
And daylie sent hir part of his almous.

57

Sum knew hir weill, and sum had na knawledge
Of hir becaus scho was sa deformait,
With bylis blak ovirspred in hir visage,   395
And hir fair colour faidit and alterait.
Yit thay presumit, for hir hie regrait
And still murning, scho was of nobill kin;
With better will thairfoir they tuik hir in.

58

The day passit and Phebus went to rest,   400
The cloudis blak overheled all the sky.
God wait gif Cresseid was ane sorrowfull gest,
Seing that uncouth fair and harbery!
But meit or drink scho dressit hir to ly
In ane dark corner of the hous allone,   405
And on this wyse, weiping, scho maid hir mone:

383. meit *food*
384. leif *live*   eird *earth*
385. wickit weird *cruel fate*
386. mantill *cloak*   baver *beaver*
387. wonder *very*
    prively *stealthily*
388. yet *gate*
389. convoyit *guided*   espy *see*
391. spittaill hous *leper-house*

392. almous *alms*
395. bylis *boils*
397. hie regrait *great distress*
398. still *quiet*
401. overheled *covered over*
402. wait *knows*   gest *guest*
403. fare *food*   harbery *dwelling*
404. but *without*   dressit *proceeded*
406. wyse *way*   mone *complaint*

59

'O sop of sorrow, sonkin into cair!
O cative Creisseid! For now and evermair
Gane is thy joy and all thy mirth in eird;
Of all blyithnes now art thou blaiknit bair.   410
Thair is na salve may saif the of thy sair.
Fell is thy fortoun, wickit is thy weird,
Thy blys is baneist, and thy baill on breird;
Under the eirth, God gif I gravin wer,
Quhair nane of Grece nor yit of Troy micht heird! 415

60

'Quhair is thy chalmer wantounlie besene,
With burely bed and bankouris browderit bene?
Spycis and wyne to thy collatioun,
The cowpis all of gold and silver schene;
The sweit meitis, servit in plaittis clene,   420
With saipheron sals of ane gude sessoun?
Thy gay garmentis with mony gudely goun,
Thy plesand lawn pinnit with goldin prene?
All is areir, thy greit royall renoun!

61

'Quhair is thy garding with thir greissis gay   425
And fresche flowris, quhilk the quene Floray

408. cative *wretched*
409. eird *earth*
410 blaiknit bair *made pale and bare*
411. salve *remedy* saif *cure*
412. fell *cruel* weird *fate*
413. baneist *banished* baill *sorrow* breird *grows*
414. gif *grant* gravin *buried*
415. heird *heard*
416. chalmer *chamber* wantounlie besene *luxuriously furnished*
417. burely *fine*

bankouris *coverings* browderit bene *embroidered beautifully*
418. collatioun *supper*
419. cowpis *cups* schene *bright*
420. sweit meitis *delicacies* plaittis *plates*
421. saipheron sals *saffron sauce* sessoun *flavour*
422. gudely goun *fine dress*
423. lawn *linen* prene *brooch*
424. areir *gone* renoun *reputation*
425. garding *garden* greissis *plants*

413–5. 'Your happiness is banished, and your sorrow grows; I wish to God that I were buried under the earth where no one from Grece or from Troy had heard of me'.
416–7. 'Where is your luxuriously furnished chamber, with its fine bed and beautifully embroidered covers'.

Had paintit plesandly in everie pane,
Quhair thou was wont full merilye in May
To walk and tak the dew be it was day,
And heir the merle and mavis mony ane;   430
With ladyis fair in carrolling to gane,
And se the royall rinkis in thair array,
In garmentis gay garnischit on everie grane?

62

'Thy greit triumphand fame and hie honour,
Quhair thou was callit of eirdlye wichtis flour,   435
All is decayit, thy weird is welterit so;
Thy hie estait is turnit in darknes dour;
This lipper ludge tak for thy burelie bour,
And for thy bed tak now ane bunche of stro;
For waillit wyne and meitis thou had tho   440
Tak mowlit breid, peirrie and ceder sour.
Bot cop and clapper, now is all ago.

63

'My cleir voice and courtlie carrolling,
Quhair I was wont with ladyis for to sing,
Is rawk as ruik, full hiddeous, hoir and hace;   445
My plesand port all utheris precelling,
Of lustines I was hald maist conding,

427. pane *part*
428. wont *accustomed*
429. be *as soon as*
430. heir *hear*   merle *blackbird*
  mavis *song thrush*   ane *a one*
431. carrolling *dancing and
  singing*   gane *go*
432. rinkis *men*
433. garnischit *ornamented*   on
  everie grane *in every detail*
435. eirdlye wichtis *earthly creatures*
436. weird *fortune*
  welterit *overturned*
437. estait *position*   dour *harsh*

438. lipper ludge *leper house*
  burelie bour *fine chamber*
439. stro *straw*
440. for *in place of*   waillit
  wyne *choice wine*   tho *then*
441. mowlit breid *mouldy bread*
  peirrie *perry*   ceder *cider*
442. bot *with the exception of*
445. rawk *hoarse*   ruik *rook*
  hoir *hoarse*   hace *rough*
446. port *bearing*
  precelling *surpassing*
447. lustines *loveliness*
  hald *considered*   conding *worthy*

435. 'Where you were called the flower of earthly creatures'.
436. 'All is decayed, thus has your fate revolved'.
440–1. 'In place of the choice wine and food that you had then, you
  must now take mouldy bread, perry, and sour cider'.

Now is deformit the figour of my face,
To luik on it na leid now lyking hes.
Sowpit in syte, I say with sair siching,   450
Ludgeit amang the lipper leid, 'Allace!'

64
'O ladyis fair of Troy and Grece, attend
My miserie, quhilk nane may comprehend,
My frivoll fortoun, my infelicitie,
My greit mischief, quhilk na man can amend.   455
Be war in tyme, approchis neir the end,
And in your mynd ane mirrour mak of me:
As I am now, peradventure that ye
For all your micht may cum to that same end,
Or ellis war, gif ony war may be.   460

65
'Nocht is your fairnes bot ane faiding flour,
Nocht is your famous laud and hie honour
Bot wind inflat in uther mennis eiris;
Your roising reid to rotting sall retour.
Exempill mak of me in your memour,   465
Quhilk of sic thingis wofull witnes beiris.
All welth in eird away as wind it weiris:
Be war thairfoir, approchis neir the hour:
Fortoun is fikkill quhen scho beginnis and steiris.'

448. figour *appearance*
449. leid *man*
450. sowpit in syte *immersed in sorrow*
451. ludgeit *dwelling*   leid *people*
452. attend *take note*
454. frivoll *fickle*
455. mischief *misfortune*
456. war *prepared*
458. peradventure *perhaps*
459. micht *strength*

460. war *worse*
462. laud *glory*
463. inflat *puffed*   eiris *ears*
464. roising reid *rosy complexion*
  rotting *decomposed matter*
  retour *return*
465. memour *memory*
467. welth *prosperity*   eird *earth*
  weiris *goes*
469. steiris *stirs*

458–9. 'Perhaps you might come to the same end as me, in spite of all your strength'.
464. 'Your rosy complexion shall change into rotting flesh'.
465–6. 'In your memory make an example of me, who shows the truth of these terrible things'.

66

Thus chydand with hir drerie destenye,   470
Weiping scho woik the nicht fra end to end,
Bot all in vane; hir dule, hir cairfull cry,
Micht not remeid nor yit hir murning mend.
Ane lipper lady rais and till hir wend
And said, 'Quhy spurnis thow aganis the wall   475
To sla thyself and mend nathing at all?

67

'Sen thy weiping dowbills bot thy wo,
I counsall the mak vertew of ane neid:
Go leir to clap thy clapper to and fro,
And leif efter the law of lipper leid.'   480
Thair was na buit, bot furth with thame scho yeid
Fra place to place, quhill cauld and hounger sair
Compellit hir to be ane rank beggair.

68

That samin tyme, of Troy the garnisoun,
Quhilk had to chiftane worthie Troylus,   485
Throw jeopardie of weir had strikken doun
Knichtis of Grece in number mervellous;
With greit tryumphe and laude victorious
Agane to Troy richt royallie thay raid
The way quhair Cresseid with the lipper baid.   490

470. chydand *quarrelling*	479. leir *learn*
drerie *sad*	480. leid *people*
471. woik *stayed awake*	481. buit *remedy* yeid *went*
472. dule *sorrow*	483. rank *complete*
473. remeid *remedy*	484. samin *same*
474. rais *rose* till *to* wend *went*	garnisoun *garrison*
475. spurnis *kick*	485. chiftane *commander*
476. sla *kill*	486. jeopardie of weir *daring*
477. sen *since* dowbillis *doubles*	*exploits*
bot *only*	488. laude *glory*
478. neid *necessity*	490. baid *stayed*

477. 'Since your weeping only doubles your sorrow'.
484–7. 'At the same time, the Trojan garrison which had the noble
Troilus as its commander, had struck down an astonishing number of
Greek knights through its daring exploits of arms'.

69

Seing that companie, thai come all with ane stevin.
Thay gaif ane cry and schuik coppis gude speid;
Said: 'Worthie lordis, for Goddis lufe of hevin,
To us lipper part of your almous deid!'
Than to thair cry nobill Troylus tuik heid,   495
Having pietie, neir by the place can pas
Quhair Cresseid sat, not witting quhat scho was.

70

Than upon him scho kest up baith hire ene,
And with ane blenk it come into his thocht
That he sumtime hir face befoir had sene,   500
Bot scho was in sic plye he knew hir nocht.
Yit than hir luik into his mynd it brocht
The sweit visage and amorous blenking
Of fair Cresseid, sumtyme his awin darling.

71

Na wonder was suppois in mynd that he   505
Tuik hir figure sa sone, and lo, now quhy:
The idole of ane thing in cace may be
Sa deip imprentit in the fantasy
That it deludis the wittis outwardly,
And sa appeiris in forme and lyke estait   510
Within the mynd as it was figurait.

72

Ane spark of lufe than till his hart culd spring
And kendlit all his bodie in ane fyre.

491. ane stevin *one voice*
492. gude speid *quickly*
494. part of *give a share of*
    almous deid *alms*
497. witting *knowing*
498. kest *cast* ene *eyes*
499. blenk *glance*
501. sic plye *such a condition*
505. suppois *even if*

506. tuik *thought of*
507. idole *image* in cace *by chance*
508. imprentit *fixed*
    fantasy *memory*
509. wittis outwardly *five senses*
510. lyke estait *similar condition*
511. figurait *formed*
513. kendlit *kindled*

505–11. 'It is not surprising if a picture of Cresseid came immediately
into his mind, and indeed, I will now tell you why. In some cases the
image of a thing may be so deeply fixed in the memory that the five
senses are deceived, and so an object appears in a similar form and
manner to the picture formed within the mind'.

With hait fevir ane sweit and trimbling
Him tuik, quhill he was reddie to expyre;   515
To beir his scheild his breist began to tyre;
Within ane quhyle he changit mony hew,
And nevertheles not ane ane uther knew.

73
For knichtlie pietie and memoriall
Of fair Cresseid, ane gyrdill can he tak,   520
Ane purs of gold, and mony gay jowall,
And in the skirt of Cresseid doun can swak;
Than raid away and not ane word he spak,
Pensive in hart, quhill he come to the toun,
And for greit cair oft syis almaist fell doun.   525

74
The lipper folk to Cresseid than can draw
To se the equall distribution
Of the almous; bot quhen the gold thay saw,
Ilk ane to uther prevelie can roun,
And said; 'Yone lord hes mair affectioun,   530
How ever it be, unto yone lazarous
Than to us all; we knaw be his almous.'

75
'Quhat lord is yone,' quod scho, 'have ye na feill,
Hes done to us so greit humanitie?'
'Yes,' quod a lipper man, 'I knaw him weill;   535
Schir Troylus it is, gentill and fre.'
Quhen Cresseid understude that it was he,
Stiffer than steill thair stert ane bitter stound
Throwout hir hart, and fell doun to the ground.

515. quhill *until* expyre *die*
517. ane quhyle *a short time*
    hew *colour*
519. pietie *pity*
    memoriall *remembrance*
520. gyrdill *belt*
521. jowall *jewel*
522. swak *toss*

525. oft syis *often*
529. ilk *each* prevelie *secretly* can
    roun *whispered*
531. lazarous *leper*
533. feill *idea*
536. gentill *noble* fre *generous*
538. stiffer *stronger* steill *steel*
    stert *rushed* stound *pain*

537–9. 'When Cresseid understood that it was him, a bitter pain,
    stronger than steel, rushed through her heart, and she fell down to the
    ground'.

76

Quhen scho ovircome, with siching sair and sad,   540
With mony cairfull cry and cald ochane:
'Now is my breist with stormie stoundis stad,
Wrappit in wo, ane wretch full will of wane!'
Than swounit scho oft or scho culd refrane,
And ever in hir swouning cryit scho thus: 545
'O fals Cresseid and trew knicht Troylus!

77

'Thy lufe, thy lawtie and thy gentilnes
I countit small in my prosperitie,
Sa elevait I was in wantones,
And clam upon the fickill quheill sa hie.   550
All faith and lufe I promissit to the
Was in the self fickill and frivolous:
O fals Cresseid and trew knicht Troilus!

78

'For lufe of me thow keipt gude continence,
Honest and chaist in conversatioun.   555
Of all wemen protectour and defence
Thou was, and helpit thair opinioun.
My mynd in fleschelie foull affectioun
Was inclynit to lustis lecherous:
Fy, fals Cresseid! O trew knicht Troylus!   560

79

'Lovers, be war and tak gude heid about
Quhome that ye lufe, for quhome ye suffer paine.
I lat yow wit thair is richt few thairout

541. cald *mournful* ochane *alas*
542. breist *heart* stoundis *pains*
   stad *beset*
543. will of wane *hopeless*
544. or *before* refrane *stop*
547. lawtie *loyalty*
548. countit small *considered little*
549. elevait *elevated*
   wantones *wantonness*

550. clam *climbed* quheill *wheel*
   hie *high*
552. the self *itself*
554. gude continence *good faith*
555. chaist *chaste*
   conversatioun *behaviour*
557. opinioun *reputation*
558. affectioun *desire*
563. lat *let* wit *know* thairout *in
   existence*

556–7. 'You were the protector and defender of all women, and guarded
   their reputation'.

Quhome ye may traist to have trew lufe agane;
Preif quhen ye will, your labour is in vaine.   565
Thairfoir I reid ye tak thame as ye find,
For thay ar sad as widdercok in wind.

80

'Becaus I knaw the greit unstabilnes,
Brukkil as glas, into myself, I say,
Traisting in uther als greit unfaithfulnes,   570
Als unconstant and als untrew of fay.
Thocht sum be trew, I wait richt few ar thay.
Quha findis treuth, lat him his lady ruse!
Nane but myself as now I will accuse.'

81

Quhen this was said, with paper scho sat doun,   575
And on this maneir maid hir testament:
'Heir I beteiche my corps and carioun
With wormis and with taidis to be rent;
My cop and clapper and myne ornament,
And all my gold, the lipper folk sall have,   580
Quhen I am deid, to burie me in grave.

82

'This royall ring set with this rubie reid,
Quhilk Troylus in drowrie to me send,
To him agane I leif it quhen I am deid,
To mak my cairfull deid unto him kend.   585

564. traist *trust* agane *in return*
565. preif *make trial*
566. reid *advise*
567. sad *constant*
    widdercok *weathercock*
568. unstabilnes *instability*
569. brukkill *fragile*
570. traisting *expecting to find*
    als *just as*
571. fay *fidelity*

572. thocht *though*   wait *know*
573. ruse *praise*
576. testament *will*
577. beteiche *yield* carioun *dead body*
578. taidis *toads* rent *torn apart*
579. ornament *jewels*
583. drowrie *love token* send *sent*
585. cairfull deid *sorrowfull death*
    kend *known*

566–7. 'Therefore, I advise you to take them as you find them, for they
are as constant as a weathercock in the wind'.
568–9. 'I can say this because I recognise this great instability, as fragile
as glass, in myself, and expect to find just as much infidelity in others,
as much inconstancy, and as much breaking of faith'.
585. 'To make my sorrowful death known to him'.

Thus I conclude schortlie, and mak ane end:
My spreit I leif to Diane quhair scho dwellis,
To walk with hir in waist woddis and wellis.

83

'O Diomeid, thou hes baith broche and belt
Quhilk Troylus gave me in takning   590
Of his trew lufe!' And with that word scho swelt.
And sone ane lipper man tuik of the ring,
Syne buryit hir withouttin tarying.
To Troylus furthwith the ring he bair,
And of Cresseid the deith he can declair.   595

84

Quhen he had hard hir greit infirmitie,
Hir legacie and lamentatioun,
And how scho endit in sic povertie,
He swelt for wo and fell doun in ane swoun.
For greit sorrow his hart to brist was boun;   600
Siching full sadlie, said, 'I can no moir –
Scho was untrew and wo is me thairfoir.'

85

Sum said he maid ane tomb of merbell gray,
And wrait hir name and superscriptioun,
And laid it on hir grave quhair that scho lay,   605
In goldin letteris, conteining this ressoun:
'Lo, fair ladyis! Cresseid of Troyis toun,
Sumtym countit the flour of womanheid,
Under this stane, lait lipper lyis deid.'

86

Now, worthie wemen, in this ballet schort,   610
Maid for your worschip and instructioun,

586. schortlie *briefly*	599. swelt *fainted*
587. spreit *spirit*	600. brist *burst* boun *ready*
588. waist *uninhabited*	601. can *know*
woddis *woods* wellis *streams*	603. merbell *marble*
589. broche *brooch*	604. superscriptioun *inscription*
590. in takning *as a token*	606. ressoun *statement*
591. swelt *died*	608. countit *considered*
593. syne *then* buryit *buried*	609. stane *stone* lait *former*
596. infirmitie *illness*	610. ballet *poem*
597. legacie *testament*	611. worschip *honour*

Of cheritie, I monische and exhort,
Ming not your lufe with fals deceptioun.
Beir in your mynd this sore conclusioun
Of fair Cresseid, as I have said befoir.   615
Sen scho is deid, I speik of hir no moir.

612. monische *warn*
613. ming *mingle*
616. moir *more*

Robene and Makyne

1

Robene sat on gud grene hill
Kepand a flok of fe,
Mirry Makyne said him till:
'Robene, thou rew on me!
I haif the lovit lowd and still   5
Thir yeiris two or thre;
My dule in dern bot gif thou dill,
Dowtless but dreid I de.'

2

Robene answerit, 'Be the rude,
Na thing of lufe I knaw,   10
But keipis my scheip undir yone wid—
Lo, quhair thay raik on raw.
Quhat hes marrit the in thy mude,
Makyne, to me thow schaw;
Or quhat is lufe or to be lude?   15
Fane wald I leir that law.'

3

'At luvis lair gife thou will leir,
Tak thair ane A B C:
Be heynd, courtas, and fair of feir,
Wyse, hardy and fre,   20
Se that no denger do the deir,

2. kepand *minding*   fe *sheep*
3. mirry *merry*   till *to*
4. rew *take pity*
5. lovit *loved*   lowd *openly*
   still *secretly*
6. thir *these*
7. dule *sorrow*   dern *secret*   bot
   gif *unless*   dill *assuage*
8. but dreid *without doubt*
9. answerit *answered*   be *by*
   rude *cross*
11. undir *in*   wid *wood*
12. lo *look*   quhair *where*

raik *wander*   on raw *in a line*
13. marrit *disturbed*   mude *mind*
14. schaw *reveal*
15. lude *loved*
16. fane *gladly*   leir *learn*
17. luvis *love's*   lair *teaching*
    gife *if*
19. heynd *gracious*
    courtas *courteous*   feir *behaviour*
20. hardy *brave*   fre *generous*
21. denger *disdain*   the *you*
    deir *harm*

7–8. 'Unless you assuage my sorrow in secret, without doubt and in all
   certainty, I shall die'.
21–3. 'See that no disdain does you harm, no matter what sorrow you
   suffer in private. Exert yourself with great effort and all your might'.

Quhat dule in dern thou dre.
Preis the with pane at all poweir,
Be patient and previe.'

4

Robene answerit hir agane: 25
'I wait nocht quhat is luve,
But I haif mervell in certane
Quhat makis the this wanrufe.
The weddir is fair and I am fane,
My scheip gois haill aboif;   30
And we wald play us in this plane,
Thay wald us bayth reproif.'

5

'Robene, tak tent unto my taill
And wirk all as I reid,
And thou sall haif my hairt all haill,   35
Eik and my maidinheid.
Sen God sendis bute for baill,
And for murning remeid,
In dern with the bot gif I daill,
Dowtles I am bot deid.'   40

22. quhat *whatever* dule *sorrow*
    dern *private* dre *suffer*
23. preis the *exert yourself*
    pane *effort* poweir *strength*
24. previe *discreet*
26. wait nocht *do not know*
27. I haif mervell *I am astonished*
    in certane *indeed*
28. makis the *causes you*
    wanrufe *distress*
29. weddir *weather* fane *happy*
30. gois haill *go safely* aboif *on
    high ground*
31. and *if* play us *amuse*

    ourselves plane *field*
32. bayth *both* reproif *condemn*
33. tak tent *pay attention*
    taill *words*
34. wirk *do* reid *advise*
35. sall haif *shall have*
    hairt *heart* all haill *entirely*
36. eik *also* maidinheid *virginity*
37. sen *since* bute *cure*
    baill *sorrow*
38. murning *grief* remeid *remedy*
39. in dern *in secret* bot
    gif *unless* daill *make love*
40. deid *dead*

37–40. 'Since God sends a cure for every sorrow, and a remedy for every
grief, unless I make love with you in secret, I am certain that I shall
die'.

6

'Makyne, to morne this ilk a tyde,
And ye will meit me heir,
Peraventure my scheip ma gang besyd
Quhill we haif liggit full neir.
Bot mawgre haif I and I byd   45
Fra thay begin to steir.
Quhat lyis on hairt I will nocht hyd,
Makyn, than mak gud cheir.'

7

'Robene, thow reivis me roif and rest;
I luve bot the allone'.   50
'Makyne, adew, the sone gois west,
The day is neir hand gone.'
'Robene, in dule I am so drest
That lufe wil be my bone.'
'Ga lufe, Makyne, quhairever thow list,   55
For lemman I bid none.'

8

'Robene, I stand in sic a styll,
I sich, and that full sair.'
'Makyne, I haif bene heir this quhyle—
At hame God gif I wair.'   60
'My huny Robene, talk ane quhill,
Gif thow will do no mair.'

---

41. to morne *tomorrow* ilk a
tyde *same time*
42. and *if* meit *meet*
43. peraventure *perhaps* ma *may*
gang besyd *stay nearby*
44. quhill *until* liggit *lain*
neir *close*
45. mawgre *blame* byd *stay*
46. fra *once* steir *move*
47. on *in* hyd *hide*
48. mak gud cheir *cheer up*

49. reivis me *deprive me of*
roif *peace*
51. adew *goodbye* sone *sun*
52. neir hand *almost*
53. dule *sorrow* drest *placed*
54. bone *bane*
55. ga *go* list *please*
56. lemman *lover* bid *ask for*
57. styll *state*
58. sich *sigh*
60. gif *grant*

44. 'Until we have lain very close together'.
45–6. 'But I am to blame if I linger once they have begun to move off'.
56. 'For I do not ask for any lover'.
60. 'God grant that I were at home'.

'Makyne, sum uther man begyle,
For hamewart I will fair.'

9

Robene on his wayis went   65
Als licht as leif of tre;
Mawkin murnit in hir intent
And trowd him nevir to se.
Robene brayd attour the bent,
Than Mawkyne cryit on hie:
'Now ma thow sing, for I am schent!   70
Quhat alis lufe at me?'

10

Mawkyne went hame withowttin faill,
Full wery eftir couth weip;
Than Robene in a ful fair daill   75
Assemblit all his scheip.
Be that sum pairte of Mawkynis aill
Outthrow his hairt cowd creip.
He fallowit hir fast thair till assaill,
And till hir tuke gude keip.   80

11

'Abyd, abyd, thow fair Makyne,
A word for ony thing!
For all my luve it sal be thyne,
Withowttin depairting.

63. begyle *beguile*
64. hamewart *homewards*   fair *go*
66. als *as*   licht *light*   leif *leaf*
67. murnit *mourned*   in hir
   intent *inwardly*
68. trowd *believed*
69. brayd *hurried*   attour *over*
   bent *field*
70. on hie *aloud*
71. schent *destroyed*
72. alis *ails*
73. withowttin faill *certainly*

74. wery *tired*   eftir *afterwards*
   couth weip *wept*
75. daill *dale*
77. be that *by that time*
   aill *distress*
78. outthrow *throughout*
79. fallowit *followed*   fast *quickly*
   till assaill *to woo*
80. tuke gude keip *paid close
   attention*
81. abyd *wait*
82. for ony thing *at any price*
84. depairting *division*

68. 'And thought that she would never see him again'.
72. 'What does love have against me?'
79. 'He followed her there quickly in order to woo her'.

All haill thy harte for till haif myne   85
Is all my cuvating;
My scheip to morne quhill houris nyne
Will neid of no keping.'

12

'Robene, thow hes hard soung and say
In gestis and storeis auld: 90
The man that will nocht quhen he may
Sall haif nocht when he wald.
I pray to Jesu every day,
Mot eik thair cairis cauld
That first preisis with the to play   95
Be firth, forrest or fawld.'

13

'Makyne, the nicht is soft and dry,
The wedder is warme and fair,
And the grene woid rycht neir us by
To walk attour all quhair.   100
Thair ma na janglour us espy
That is to lufe contrair;
Thairin, Makyne, bath ye and I,
Unsene we ma repair.'

14

'Robene, that warld is all away   105
And quyt brocht till ane end,

85. all haill *wholly*
86. cuvating *desire*
87. to morne *tomorrow*
   quhill *until*
89. hard soung *heard it sung*
   say *said*
90. gestis *tales*
94. mot eik *may increase* cairis
   cauld *cold sorrows*

95. preisis *tries* play *make love*
96. firth *woodland* fawld *field*
99. woid *wood*
100. attour *around* all
   quhair *everywhere*
101. ma *may* janglour *gossip*
102. contrair *hostile*
104. repair *go*
106. quyt *entirely* brocht *brought*

85–6. 'My whole desire is to have your heart entirely as my own'.
87–8. 'My sheep will not need to be tended until nine o'clock tomorrow'.
91–2. 'The man who will not take something when he can have it shall
   have nothing when he would like it'.
93–5. 'I pray to Jesus every day that he may give cold sorrows in
   abundance to whoever first attempts to make love to you'.

And never agane thairto, perfay,
Sall it be as thow wend,
For of my pane thow maid it play,
And all in vane I spend;   110
As thow hes done, sa sall I say:
Murne on, I think to mend.'

15

'Mawkyne, the howp of all my heill,
My hairt on the is sett,
And evermair to the be leill   115
Quhill I may leif, but lett;
Never to faill as utheris feill,
Quhat grace that evir I gett.'
'Robene, with the I will nocht deill.
Adew, for thus we mett.'   120

16

Malkyne went hame blyth annewche,
Attour the holtis hair.
Robene murnit and Malkyne lewche;
Scho sang, he sichit sair.
And so left him bayth wo and wewche,   125
In dolour and in cair,
Kepand his hird under a huche
Amangis the holtis hair.

107. perfay *indeed*
108. wend *believed*
109. pane *suffering*
110. spend *spent*
111. sa *so*
112. murne *mourn* think *intend*
    mend *recover*
113. howp *hope* heill *well-being*
115. leill *true*
116. quhill *while* leif *live* but
    lett *without stopping*
117. as *like* utheris feill *many
    others*

118. grace *favour*
119. deill *have dealings*
121. blyth *happy*
    annewche *enough*
122. attour *through* holtis *woods*
    hair *grey*
123. lewche *laughed*
124. scho *she* sichit *sighed*
125. bayth *both* wo *woebegone*
    wewche *hurt*
126. dolour *sorrow* cair *grief*
127. hird *flock* huche *hill*

109–10. 'Because you made a joke of my suffering, and I spent my time
    all in vain'.
118. 'No matter what favour I receive'.

The Garmont of Gud Ladeis

1

Wald my gud lady lufe me best
And wirk eftir my will,
I suld ane garmond gudliest
Gar mak hir body till.

2

Of he honour suld be hir hud   5
Upoun hir heid to weir,
Garneist with govirnance so gud
Na demyng suld hir deir.

3

Hir sark suld be hir body nixt
Of chestetie so quhyt,   10
With schame and dreid togidder mixt,
The same suld be perfyt.

4

Hir kirtill suld be of clene constance,
Lasit with lesum lufe,
The mailyeis of continuance,   15
For nevir to remufe.

1. wald *would* lufe *love*
2. wirk *act* eftir *according to*
3. garmond *suit of clothes*
   gudliest *finest*
4. gar mak *have made* till *for*
5. he *high* hud *hood*
6. heid *head* weir *wear*
7. garneist *decorated* govirnance
   so gud *very good conduct*
8. demyng *suspicion* deir *harm*
9. sark *shift; undergarment*

nixt *next to*
10. chestite *chastity* quhyt *white*
11. schame *modesty* dreid *fear of*
    dishonour mixt *blondod*
12. perfyt *perfect*
13. kirtill *gown* clene *pure*
    constance *constancy*
14. lasit *laced* lesum *lawful*
15. mailyeis *eyelets*
    continuance *steadfastness*
16. remufe *alter*

1. 'If my good lady would love me best'.
3–4. 'I should have a suit of the finest clothes made for her body'.
16. 'Never to alter'.

5

Hir gown suld be of gudlines,
Weill ribband with renowne,
Purfillit with plesour in ilk place,
Furrit with fyne fassoun.   20

6

Hir belt suld be of benignitie
Abowt hir middill meit,
Hir mantill of humilitie
To tholl bayth wind and weit.

7

Hir hat suld be of fair having,   25
And hir tepat of trewth,
Hir patelet of gud pansing,
Hir hals ribbane of rewth.

8

Hir slevis suld be of esperance
To keip hir fra dispair,   30
Hir gluvis of gud govirnance
To hyd hir fynyearis fair.

17. gudlines *goodness*
18. ribband *decorated with ribbons*
    renowne *reputation*
19. purfillit *trimmed*
    plesour *agreeableness* ilk *every*
20. furrit *furred* fyne *fine*
    fassoun *appearance*
21. benignitie *graciousness*
22. middill *waist* meit *well fitting*
23. mantill *cloak*
24. tholl *endure* weit *wet*

25. fair having *good behaviour*
26. tepat *tippet; scarf* trewth *truth*
27. patelet *collar*
    pansing *meditation*
28. hals ribbane *neck ribbon*
    rewth *pity*
29. slevis *sleeves* esperance *hope*
31. gluvis *gloves*
    govirnance *demeanour*
32. fynyearis *fingers*

18–19. 'Beautifully decorated with the ribbons of good reputation,
    trimmed all over with agreeableness'.
24. 'So that she can endure both wind and rain'.

9

Hir schone suld be of sickernes
In syne that scho nocht slyd,
Hir hois of honestie, I ges,   35
I suld for hir provyd.

10

Wald scho put on this garmond gay,
I durst sweir by my seill
That scho woir never grene nor gray
That set hir half so weill.   40

33. schone *shoes* sickernes *sureness*   38. durst *dare* seill *happiness*
34. slyd *slide*   39. woir *wore* grene *green*
35. hois *stockings* ges *guess*   40. set *suited*
36. provyd *provide*

34. 'So that she does not slide into sin'.

The Bludy Serk

1

This hindir yeir I hard be tald
Thair was a worthy king;
Dukis, erlis, and barronis bald
He had at his bidding.
The lord was anceane and ald   5
And sexty yeiris cowth ring,
He had a dochter fair to fald,
A lusty lady ying.

2

Of all fairheid scho bur the flour,
And eik hir faderis air,   10
Of lusty laitis and he honour,
Meik bot and debonair;
Scho wynnit in a bigly bour,
On fold wes none so fair,
Princis luvit hir paramour   15
In cuntreis our allquhair.

3

Thair dwelt alyt besyde the king
A fowll gyane of ane;
Stollin he hes the lady ying,
Away with hir is gane,   20

1. this hindir yeir *a long time ago*
hard *heard*
3. bald *bold*
5. anceane *ancient*   ald *old*
6. cowth ring *reigned*
7. dochter *daughter*   fald *embrace*
8. lusty *beautiful*   ying *young*
9. fairheid *beauty*   scho *she*
bur *bore*   flour *flower*
10. eik *also*   air *heir*
11. laitis *manners*   he *high*
12. meik *modest*   debonair *gracious*

13. wynnit *dwelled*   bigly *pleasant*
bour *chamber*
14. fold *earth*
15. luvit *loved*
paramour *amorously*
16. cuntreis *countries*   our
allquhair *everywhere*
17. alyt *a little*
18. gyane *giant*   of ane *paricularly*
19. stollin *abducted*
20. gane *gone*

9–10. 'She was the embodiment of beauty, and she was also her father's
heir'.
12. 'And also modest and gracious'.
17–18. 'There lived near the king a particularly foul giant'.

And kest hir in his dungering
Quhair licht scho micht se nane;
Hungir and cauld and grit thristing
Scho fand in to hir wane.

4

He wes the laithliest on to luk   25
That on the grund mycht gang,
His nailis wes lyk ane hellis cruk,
Thairwith fyve quarteris lang.
Thair wes nane that he ourtuk,
In rycht or yit in wrang,   30
Bot all in schondir he thame schuke,
The gyane wes so strang.

5

He held the lady day and nycht
Within his deip dungeoun,
He wald nocht gif of hir a sicht   35
For gold nor yit ransoun,
Bot gife the king mycht get a knycht
To fecht with his persoun,
To fecht with him both day and nycht
Quhill ane wer dungin doun.   40

6

The king gart seik baith fer and neir,
Beth be se and land,

21. kest *thrown*
    dungering *dungeon*
22. quhair *where* licht *light* se *see*
23. cauld *cold* grit *great*
    thristing *thirst*
24. fand *found* in to *in*
    wane *dwelling*
25. laithliest *most loathesome* on
    to luk *to look at*
26. grund *earth* gang *walk*
27. hellis cruk *devil's hook*
28. fyve quarteris *over a metre*

29. nane *no one* ourtuk *overtook*
31. in schondir *into pieces*
    schuke *shook*
35. gif *give*
36. ransoun *ransom*
37. bot gife *unless*
38. fecht *fight*
40. quhill *until* ane *one* dungin
    doun *defeated*
41. gart seik *ordered a search*
42. se *sea*

29–31. 'He did not pass anyone without shaking them to pieces, whether
    they had done anything wrong or not'.
35. 'He would not give anyone a sight of her'.
38. 'To fight with him in person'.

Of ony knycht gife he micht heir
Wald fecht with that gyand.
A worthy prince that had no peir   45
Hes tane the deid on hand,
For the luve of the lady cleir,
And held full trew cunnand.

7

That prince come prowdly to the toun
Of that gyane to heir,   50
And fawcht with him his awin persoun
And tuke him presoneir,
And kest him in his awin dungeoun
Allane withouttin feir,
With hungir, cauld, and confusioun,   55
As full weill worthy weir.

8

Syne brak the bour, had hame the bricht
Unto hir fadir deir;
Sa evill wondit was the knycht
That he behuvit to de;   60
Unlusum was his likame dicht,
His sark was all bludy;
In all the warld was thair a wicht
So peteous for to sy?

43. gife *if* heir *hear*
45. peir *equal*
46. tane *taken* deid *deed*
47. cleir *beautiful*
48. held *kept* trew *faithfully*
     cunnand *promise*
51. awin *own*
54. allane *alone* feir *companions*
56. worthy *noble* weir *was*

57. syne *then* brak *broke into*
     bricht *fair lady*
59. evill wondit *badly wounded*
60. behuvit to de *had to die*
61. unlusum *horrible* likame *body*
     dicht *covered*
62. sark *shirt* bludy *bloody*
63. wicht *man*
64. peteous *pitiful* sy *see*

46. 'Has accepted the challenge'.
48. 'And kept his promise faithfully'.
56. 'As the prince was very noble indeed'.
57. 'Then he broke into the chamber, and brought the fair lady home'.
61. 'His body was covered in horrible wounds'.

9

The lady murnyt and maid grit mone 65
With all hir mekle micht,
'I luvit nevir lufe bot one
That dulfully now is dicht.
God sen my lyfe wer fra me tone
Or I had sene yone sicht, 70
Or ellis in begging evir to gone
Furth with yone curtas knycht!'

10

He said, 'Fair lady, now mone I de,
Trestly ye me trow;
Tak ye my sark that is bludy, 75
And hing it forrow yow;
First think on it and syne on me
Quhen men cumis yow to wow.'
The lady said, 'Be Mary fre,
Thairto I mak a vow' 80

11

Quhen that scho lukit to the serk
Scho thocht on the persoun,
And prayit for him with all hir harte
That lowsd hir of bandoun,
Quhair scho was wont to sit full merk 85
In that deip dungeoun.
And evir quhill scho wes in quert
That was hir a lessoun.

65. murnyt *mourned* mone *lament*
66. mekle micht *strength*
68. dulfully *sadly* dicht *put to death*
69. sen *grant* tone *taken*
70. or *before* yone *that*
71. ellis *else*
72. curtas *courteous*
73. mone *must*
74. trestly *truly* trow *believe*

76. hing *hang* forrow *in front of*
78. wow *woo*
79. be *by* fre *noble*
84. lowsd *released* of bandoun *from captivity*
85. wont *accustomed* full merk *in complete darkness*
87. evir *forever* quhill *while* in quert *alive*
88. hir *to her*

69–72. 'I wish to God that I had died rather than see such a sight, or else that I should have gone begging forever with that courteous knight'.
74. 'You can believe me truly'.

12

Sa weill the lady luvit the knycht
That no man wald scho tak;   90
Sa suld we do our God of micht
That did all for us mak,
Quhilk fullely to deid wes dicht
For sinfull manis saik;
Sa suld we do both day and nycht,   95
With prayaris to him mak.

Moralitas

13

This king is lyk the Trinitie,
Baith in hevin and heir,
The manis saule to the lady,
The gyane to Lucefeir,   100
The knycht to Chryst that deit on tre
And coft our synnis deir,
The pit to hell with panis fell,
The syn to the woweir.

14

The lady was wowd, bot scho said nay   105
With men that wald hir wed;
Sa suld we wryth all syn away
That in our breist is bred.
I pray to Jesu Chryst verrey,
For us his blud that bled,   110

90. tak *accept*   102. coft *paid for*   deir *dearly*
91. do *behave*   103. panis fell *terrible torments*
93. quhilk *who*   fullely *entirely*   104. woweir *wooer*
94. saik *sake*   106. with *to*
98. heir *here*   107. wryth *turn*
99. manis *man's*   108. breist *heart*
100. Lucefeir *Lucifer*   109. verrey *himself*
101. deit *died*   tre *cross*

91–4. 'We should behave in the same way towards our mighty God who
    created everything for us, who was sentenced to death entirely for the
    sake of sinful man'.
99. 'Man's soul can be likened to the lady'.
102. 'And paid dearly for our sins'.
106. 'To men who wanted to marry her'.
110. 'Who shed his blood for us'.

To be our help on domysday
Quhair lawis ar straitly led.

15
The saule is Godis dochtir deir,
And eik his handewerk,
That was betrasit with Lucifeir   115
Quha sittis in hell full merk,
Borrowit with Chrystis angell cleir;
Hend men, will ye nocht herk?
For his lufe that bocht us deir,
Think on the bludy serk.   120

111. domysday *judgement day*   115. betrasit with *betrayed by*
112. lawis *laws*   straitly *strictly*   116. quha *who*
    led *enforced*   117. borrowit with *redeemed by*
113. dochtir *daughter*   118. hend men *good people*
114. eik *also*   handewerk *creation*   herk *listen*

117. 'Redeemed by the bright angelic form of Christ'.
119. 'For the love of him who redeemed us at great cost'.

The Annunciation

1

Forcy as deith is likand lufe,
Throuch quhom al bittir swet is;
No thing is hard, as writ can pruf,
Till him in lufe that letis.
Luf us fra barret betis: 5
Quhen fra the hevinly sete abufe
In message Gabriell couth muf,
And with myld Mary metis,
And said, 'God wele the gretis;
In the he will tak rest and rufe,   10
But hurt of syn or yit reprufe;
In him sett thi decret is.'

2

This message mervale gert that myld,
And silence held, but soundis,
As weill aferit a maid infild.   15
The angell it expoundis,
How that hir wame but woundis
Consave it suld, fra syn exild;

1. forcy *strong* deith *death*
   likand *pleasing* lufe *love*
2. throuch *through* quhom *which*
   swet *sweet*
3. writ *scripture* pruf *prove*
4. till *to* letis *thinks*
5. fra *from* barret *sorrow*
   betis *relieves*
6. quhen *when* sete *throne*
   abufe *above*
7. In message *as a messenger*
   Gabriell *Gabriel* couth
   muf *came*
8. metis *met*

9. wele *well* the *you* gretis *greets*
10. rufe *repose*
11. but *without* yit *even*
    reprufe *disgrace*
12. decret *fate*
13. mervale gert *caused to marvel*
14. held *kept* but soundis *without
    sound*
15. aferit *befitted* infild *undefiled*
16. expoundis *explains*
17. wame *womb* woundis *lesion*
18. consave *conceive* suld *should*
    exild *free*

1. 'Pleasing love is as strong as death'.
4. 'To him who thinks he is in love'.
5. 'Love relieves us from sorrow'.
10–12. 'He will take his rest and repose in you, without you being
   harmed by sin or any disgrace; your fate is sealed in him'.
13–14. 'This message made that mild one marvel, and she kept silent,
   without a sound'.

And quhen this carpin wes compilit,
Brichtnes fra bufe aboundis.   20
Than fell that gay to groundis,
Of Goddis grace na thing begild;
Wox in hir chaumer chaist with child,
With Crist our kyng that cround is.

3

Thir tithingis tauld, the messinger   25
Till hevin agane he glidis;
That princes pure withoutyn peir
Full plesandly applid is,
And blith with barne abidis.
O worthy wirschip singuler,   30
To be moder and madyn meir,
As Cristin faith confidis;
That borne was of hir sidis
Our makar, Goddis sone so deir,
Quhilk erd, wattir, and hevinnis cleir   35
Throw grace and virtu gidis.

19. carpin *speech*	28. full *very* plesandly *pleasingly*
compilit *concluded*	applid *submissive*
20. brichtnes *brightness*	29. blith *happily* barne *child*
bufe *above* aboundis *grows*	abidis *waits*
21. gay *beautiful one* groundis *the*	30. wirschip *honour*
ground	singuler *unique*
22. begild *deprived*	31. moder *mother* madyn
23. wox *became*	meir *intact virgin*
chaumer *chamber* chaist *chaste*	32. Cristin *Christian*
24. cround *crowned*	confidis *believes*
25. thir *these* tithingis *tidings*	33. sidis *body*
tauld *told*	34. makar *maker* sone *son*
26. glidis *glides*	deir *dear*
27. princes *princess*	35. quhilk *who* erd *earth*
withoutyn *without* peir *equal*	36. gidis *rules*

22. 'Not at all deprived of the grace of God'.
23. 'In her chamber she grew chaste with child'.
35–6. 'Who rules the earth, water, and the clear heavens, in his grace and
virtue'.

4

The miraclis ar mekle and meit
Fra luffis ryver rynnis;
The low of luf haldand the hete
Unbrynt full blithlie birnis;   40
Quhen Gabriell beginnis
With mouth that gudely may to grete,
The wand of Aaron, dry but wete,
To burioun nocht blynnis;
The flesch all donk within is,   45
Upon the erd na drop couth fleit;
Sa was that may maid moder swete,
And sakeles of all synnis.

5

Hir mervalus haill madinhede
God in hir bosum bracis,   50
And his divinite fra dreid
Hir kepit in all casis.
The hie God of his gracis
Himself dispisit, us to speid,
And dowtit nocht to dee on deid;   55

37. miraclis *miracles* mekle *great*
meit *fitting*
38. luffis *love's* rynnis *flow*
39. low *flame* haldand *holding*
hete *heat*
40. unbrynt *unburnt*
blithlie *brightly* brinis *burns*
42. gudely *excellent* may *maid*
grete *greet*
43. but wete *without moisture*
44. burioun *blossom* blynnis *cease*
45. flesch *fleece* donk *moist*
46. erd *earth* couth fleit *flowed*

47. sa *so* may *maid* maid *made*
moder *mother* swete *sweet*
48. sakeles *innocent* synnis *sins*
49. haill madinhede *intact virginity*
50. bosum *womb* bracis *encloses*
51. dreid *harm*
52. kepit *protects*
casis *circumstances*
53. gracis *free will*
54. dispisit *debased* speid *redeem*
55. dowtit nocht *did not hesitate*
dee *die* on deid *indeed*

38. 'Which flow from love's river'.
39–40. 'The hot flame of love burns very brightly without consuming
what it burns'.
44. 'Does not cease to blossom'.
45–6. 'The fleece was all moist inside, but not a single drop flowed upon
the earth'.
49–50. 'Her miraculous intact virginity encloses God within her womb'.
53–4. 'Exalted God debased himself of his own free will, in order to save
us'.

He panit for our peacis,
And with his blude us bacis,
Bot quhen he ras up, as we rede,
The cherite of his Godhede
Was plane in every placis.   60

6
O lady lele and lusumest,
Thy face moist fair and schene is;
O blosum blith and bowsumest,
Fra carnale cryme that clene is;
This prayer fra my splene is: 65
That all my werkis wikkitest
Thow put away and mak me chaist
Fra Termigant that teyn is,
And fra his cluke that kene is,
And syn till hevin my saule thou haist,   70
Quhair thi makar, of michtis mast,
Is kyng, and thow thair quene is.

56. panit *suffered* peacis *peace*
57. blude *blood* us bacis *saves us*
58. ras *rose* rede *read*
59. cherite *charity*
60. plane *obvious* placis *place*
61. lele *true* lusumest *loveliest*
62. moist *most* schene *beautiful*
63. blosum *blossom* blith *happy*
  bowsumest *brightest*
64. carnale cryme *fleshly sin*
65. splene *heart*

66. werkis wikkitest *most wicked
  deeds*
67. chaist *chaste*
68. Termigant *the Devil*
  teyn *angry*
69. cluke *claws* kene is *are sharp*
70. syn *then* till *to* saule *soul*
  haist *hasten*
71. makar *maker* of michtis
  mast *greatest in power*

68. 'Far from the Devil who is angry'.

The Praise of Age

1

Wythin a garth, under a rede rosere,
Ane ald man and decrepit herd I syng;
Gay was the note, swete was the voce and clere;
It was grete joy to here of sik a thing.
And, to my dome, he said in his dytyng: 5
'For to be yong I wald not, for my wis,
Of all this warld to mak me lord and king:
The more of age, the nerar hevynnis blis.

2

'False is this warld and full of variance,
Besoucht with syn and othir sytis mo;   10
Treuth is all tynt, gyle has the gouvernance,
Wrechitnes has wroht all welthis wele to wo,
Fredome is tynt and flemyt the lordis fro,
And covatise is all the cause of this;
I am content that youthede is ago: 15
The more of age, the nerar hevynnis blisse.

3

'The state of youth I repute for na gude,
For in that state sik perilis now I see

1. garth *garden*   rede *red*
   rosere *rose-bush*
2. ald *old*   herd *heard*
3. voce *voice*
4. sik *such*
5. to *in*   dome *opinion*
   dytyng *singing*
6. wis *wish*
7. warld *world*
8. nerar *nearer*   hevynnis *heaven's*
9. variance *uncertainty*
10. besoucht with *assailed by*
    sytis *sorrows*   mo *more*

11. treuth *truth*   tynt *lost*
    gyle *deceitfulness*
    gouvernance *control*
12. wrechitnes *miserliness*
    wroht *turned*   welthis
    wele *wealth's happiness*
13. fredome *generosity*   flemyt . . .
    fro *driven away from the lords*
14. covatise *greed*
15. youthede *youth*   ago *gone*
17. repute for *consider to be*
    gude *good*
18. perilis *dangers*

5–7. 'And, it seemed to me, he said in his singing: "If it were my choice,
I would not be young again even if I were to be made lord and king of
the whole world" '.
12. 'Miserliness has turned all the happiness that should come with
riches into woe'.

Bot full smal grace; the regeing of his blude
Can none gaynstand quhill that he agit be;   20
Syne of the thing that tofore joyit he
Nothing remaynis for to be callit his,
For quhy it were bot veray vanitee:
The more of age, the nerar hevynnis blisse.

            4
'Suld no man traist this wrechit warld, for quhy   25
Of erdly joy ay sorow is the end.
The state of it can no man certify:
This day a king, to morne na gude to spend.
Quhat have we here bot grace us to defend?
The quhilk God grant us, for to mend oure mys,   30
That to his glore he may oure saulis send:
The more of age, the nerar hevynnis blisse.'

19. full smal *very few*
    grace *blessings* regeing *raging*
    blude *blood*
20. gaynstand *withstand*
    quhill *until* agit *old*
21. syne *then* tofore *before* joyit
    he *he enjoyed*
23. for quhy *because* bot *only*
25. suld *should* traist *trust*

26. erdly *earthly* ay *always*
27. certify *guarantee*
28. to morne *tomorrow*
    gude *possessions*
29. quhat *what* bot *except*
30. the quhilk *which*
    mend *correct* mys *sinful ways*
31. glore *glory* saulis *souls*

18–20. 'For I now see many dangers in that state but very few blessings;
    no one can withstand the raging of his blood until he is old'.
26. 'Sorrow is always the end of earthly joy'.
27–8. 'No man can guarantee the present state of affairs: today you may
    be a king, but tomorrow have no money to spend'.

The Ressoning Betwix Aige and Yowth

Yowth

1

Quhen fair Flora, the godes of the flouris,
Baith firth and feildis freschly had ourfrete,
And perly droppis of the balmy schouris
Thir widdis grene had with thair watter wete,
Movand allone in mornyng myld I mete   5
A merry man, that all of mirth cowth mene,
Singand this sang that suttellie wes sete:
'O yowth, be glaid in to thi flouris grene!'

Aige

2

I lukit furth a litill me before:
I saw a cative on a club cumand,   10
With cheikis lene and lyart lokis hore;
His ene wes how, his voce wes hes hostand,
Wallowit and wan and waik as ony wand.
Ane bill he bure upoun his breist abone,
In letteris leill but les, with this legend: 15
'O yowth, thi flouris fedis ferly sone!'

1. quhen *when* godes *goddess*
flouris *flowers*
2. baith *both* firth *wood*
feildis *fields* ourfrete *decorated*
3. perly *pearly* schouris *showers*
4. thir *these* widdis *woods*
5. movand *travelling*
6. mirth *pleasure* cowth mene *was disposed*
7. singand *singing*
suttellie *cleverly* sete *composed*
8. be glaid in to *rejoice in*
9. lukit *looked*
10. cative *poor wretch* club *stick*

cumand *coming*
11. cheikis lene *sunken cheeks*
lyart lokis hore *silvery grey hair*
12. ene *eyes* how *hollow*
voce *voice* hes hostand *hoarse and coughing*
13. wallowit *withered* wan *faded*
waik *weak* wand *twig*
14. bill *scroll* bure *bore*
breist *chest* abone *above*
15. leill *true* but les *without lies*
legend *inscription*
16. fedis *fade* ferly sone *so very soon*

6. 'A merry man, who was disposed towards all kinds of pleasure'.
9–10. 'I looked a little way in front of me: I saw a poor wretch coming, leaning on a stick'.
14. 'He wore a placard across his chest'.

Yowth

3

This yung man lap upoun the land full lycht,
And mervellit mekle of his makdome maid;
'Waldin I am', quod he, 'and windir wycht,
With bran as bair, and breist burly and braid.   20
Na grume on grund my gardoun may degraid,
Nor of my pith may pair wirth half a prene;
My face is fair, my figour will nocht faid:
O yowth, be glaid in to thi flouris grene!'

Aige

4

This senyeour sang, bot with a sobir stevin;   25
Schakand his berd, he said, 'My bairne, lat be.
I wes within thir sexty yeiris and sevin
Ane freik on fold bayth frak, forsy, and fre;
Als glad, als gay, als yung, als yaip as ye.
Bot now that day ourdrevin is and done;   30
Luk thow my laythly lycome gif I le:
O yowth, thy flouris fadis ferly sone!'

Yowth

5

Ane uthir vers this yung man yit cowth sing:
'At luvis law a quhyle I think to leite,

17. lap *danced* lycht *nimbly*
18. mervellit *marvelled*
    mekle *greatly*
    makdome *misjudgement*
19. waldin *supple* quod *said*
    windir *amazingly* wycht *strong*
20. bran *muscles* bair *boar*
    burly *strong* braid *broad*
21. grume *man* grund *earth*
    gardoun *achievement*
    degraid *diminish*
22. pith *strength* pair *lessen*
    wirth *worth* prene *pin*
23. figour *appearance* faid *fade*

25. senyeour *elder man* sobir
    stevin *serious voice*
26. schakand *shaking* bairne *child*
27. thir *these*
28. freik *man* fold *earth*
    frak *bold* forsy *strong* fre *free*
29. als *as* yaip *eager*
30. ourdrevin *past*
31. luke *look* laythly *loathsome*
    lycome *body* gif *if* le *lie*
33. cowth sing *sang*
34. luvis *love's* quhyle *while*
    leite *linger*

18. 'And was amazed at the old man's lack of judgement'.
22. 'Nor decrease my strength by as much as half a pin'.
31. 'Take a look at my loathsome body and tell me if I lie'.
34. 'I intend to linger for a while under the law of love'.

In court to cramp clenely in my clething   35
And luke amangis thir lusty ladeis sweit;
Of marriege to mell with mowis meit,
In secreitnes quhair we may nocht be sene,
And so with birdis blythlie my baillis beit:
O yowth, be glaid in to thi flowris grene!'   40

Aige

6

This austryne man gaif answer angirly:
'For thi crampyn thow sall bayth cruk and cowr,
And thy fleschly lust thow sall defy,
And pane the sall put fra parramour.
Than will no bird be blyth of the in bour,   45
Quhen thi manheid sall mynnis as the mone.
Thow sall assay gif that my sang be sour:
O yowth, thy flouris fadis ferly sone!'

Yowth

7

This myrry man of mirth yit movit moir:
'My cors is clene without corruptioun,   50
My self is sound, but seiknes and but soir,
My wittis fyve in dew proportioun,
My curage is of clene complexioun,
My hairt is haill, my lever, and my splene;

35. cramp *prance* clenely *smartly*
36. lusty *beautiful*
37. mell *concern myself*
   mowis *pleasantries* meit *suitable*
38. secreitnes *secret*
39. birdis *ladies* blythlie *gladly*
   baillis *sorrows* beit *relieve*
41. austryne *austere*
42. for *in exchange for*
   cruk *become bent* cowr *lose your
   high spirits*
43. defy *set at nothing*
44. the *you* parramour *lover*

45. of the *with you* bour *bedroom*
46. quhen *when* manheid *virility*
   mynnis *diminish* mone *moon*
47. assay *find out* gif *if*
49. movit *spoke*
50. cors *body*
51. but *without* soir *disease*
52. wittis *five* five *senses* dew
   proportioun *suitable harmony*
53. curage *stamina*
   complexioun *health*
54. haill *perfect* lever *liver*
   splene *spleen*

39. 'And in that way relieve my sorrow with the ladies'.
44. 'And pain shall keep you away from your lovers'.
47. 'You will find out if my song is just sour grapes or not'.
53. 'My stamina has a clean bill of health'.

Thairfoir to reid this rowll I haif ressoun: 55
O yowth, be glaid in to thy flouris grene!'

Aige

8

The bevir hair said to this berly berne:
'This breif thow sall obey, sone, be thow bald;
Thy stait, thi strenth, thocht it be stark and sterne,
The feviris fell and eild sall gar the fald;   60
Thy corpis sall clyng, thi curage sall wax cald,
Thy heill sall hynk and tak a hurt bot hone;
Thy wittis fyve sall vanes, thocht thow nocht wald;
O yowth, thi flouris fadis ferly sone!'

9

This galyart grutchit and began to greif,   65
And on his wayis wrethly he went but wene;
This lene man luche na thing bot tuk his leif,
And I abaid ondir the levis grene.
Of the cedullis the suth quhen I had sene,
On trewth, me thocht that trevist in thair tone: 70
'O yowth, be glaid in to thi flouris grene!'
'O yowth, thi flouris fedis ferly sone!'

55. reid *read*   rowll *document*
57. bevir hair *grey beard*   berly
berne *handsome youth*
58. breif *document*   sone *son*
bald *assured*
59. stait *health*   thocht *although*
stark *strong*   sterne *sturdy*
60. fell *cruel*   eild *old age*
gar *make*   fald *give way*
61. corpis *body*   clyng *waste away*
wax *become*   cald *sluggish*
62. heill *health*   hynk *falter*

hurt *bad turn*   but hone *without
delay*
63. nocht wald *do not want it*
65. galyart *gallant*
grutchit *grumbled*   greif *grieve*
66. wrethly *angrily*   but
wene *without doubt*
67. lene *thin*   luche na thing *did
not laugh*   leif *leave*
68. abaid *remained*   levis *leaves*
69. cedullis *placards*   suth *truth*
70. trevist *were contrary*

59–60. 'As for your health and your strength, the cruel fevers and old
age itself will make you give way, although you are now strong and
sturdy'.
69–70. 'When I had seen the truth of the two scrolls, it seemed to me
that they were indeed contrary in their meaning'.

The Ressoning Betwix Deth and Man

Mors

1

'O mortall man, behald, tak tent to me,
Quhilk sall thi myrrour be baith day and nycht.
All erdly thing that evir tuke lyfe mon de:
Paip, empriour, king, barroun, and knycht,
Thocht thai be in thair ryell estait and hicht,   5
May nocht ganestand quhen I pleis schote this derte;
Waltownis, castellis, towiris nevir so wicht,
May nocht resist quhill it be at his hert.'

Homo

2

'Now quhat art thow that biddis me thus tak tent
And mak ane myrrour day and nycht of the,   10
Or with thi dert I suld rycht sair repent?
I trest trewly of that thow sall le.
Quhat freik on fold sa bald dar mannis me,
Or with me fecht, owthir on fute or hors?
Is none so wicht, so stark, in this cuntre,   15
Nor I sall gar him bow to me on fors.'

Mors *Death*
1. tak tent *pay attention*
2. quhilk *who* sall *ought*
3. erdly *earthly* mon de *must die*
4. paip *pope* barroun *baron*
5. thocht *although* ryell
   estait *royal position*
   hicht *exalted rank*
6. nocht *not* ganestand *withstand*
   quhen *when* pleis *please*
   schote *shoot* derte *dart*
7. waltownis *walled towns*
   nevir *ever* wicht *strong*

8. quhill *until* hert *heart*
Homo *Man*
9. biddis *tells*
10. the *you*
11. rycht sair *very painfully*
12. trest *expect* sall le *are lying*
13. freik on fold *man on earth*
    dar *dare* mannis *threaten*
14. fecht *fight* owthir *either*
    fute *foot*
15. stark *strong* cuntre *country*
16. gar *make* on fors *by force*

2. 'Who ought to be your mirror both day and night'.
6. 'Cannot withstand me when I choose to fire this dart'.
8. 'Will not be able to stop the dart before it reaches his heart'.
13. 'What man on earth would be so bold as to dare threaten me'.
15–16. 'There is no one so powerful, so strong, in this country, that I
   shall not make him bow to me by force'.

Mors

3

'My name, at me forsuth sen that thow speiris,
Tha call me Deid, suthly I the declair;
Calland all man and woman to thair beiris
Quhenevir I pleis, quhat tyme, quhat plais, or
    quhair.   20
Is nane sa stowt, sa fresch, nor yit sa fair,
So yung, so auld, so riche, nor yit so pure;
Quhairevir I pas, owthir be it lait or air,
Man put thaim heill on fors under my cure.'

Homo

4

'Sen it is swa that natur can so wirk,   25
That yung and auld, riche and pur, man de,
In my yowtheid, allace, I wes full irk,
Culd nocht tak tent to gyd and govern me
Ay gud to do, fra evill deidis to fle,
Trestand yowtheid wald with me ay abyd,   30
Fulfilland evir my sensualitie
In deidly syn and speacialy in pryd.'

Mors

5

'Thairfoir repent and remord thi conscience,
Think on thir wirdis I now upoun the cry:
O wrechit man, O full of ignorance,   35
All thi plesance thow sall deir aby;

17. forsuth *indeed*   sen *since*
    speiris *ask*
18. tha *they*   Deid *Death*
    suthly *truly*   the declair *tell you*
19. calland *culling*   all *every*
    beiris *funeral biers*
20. plais *place*   quhair *wherever*
21. stowt *strong*   fresch *lively*
22. yung *young*
23. owthir *either*   lait *late*
    air *early*
24. man *must*   heill *wholly*   on
    fors *by necessity*   cure *charge*

25. swa *so*   wirk *work*
26. man de *must die*
27. youtheid *youth*   full *very*
    irk *reckless*
28. tak tent *pay attention*
    gyd *guide*   me *myself*
29. ay *always*   deidis *deeds*   fle *flee*
30. trestand *expecting*   abyd *stay*
31. fulfilland *gratifying*
32. specialy *especially*   pryd *pride*
33. remord *examine*
34. thir *these*
36. plesance *pleasure*   aby *buy*

24. 'Must, by necessity, place themselves wholly in my charge'.
36. 'You shall pay dearly for all your pleasure'.

Dispone for the and cum with me in hy,
Edderis, askis, wirmes meit to be;
Cum quhen I call; thow may me nocht deny,
Thocht thow wer paip, empriour, and king al thre.'   40

Homo

6

'Sen it is swa fra the I may nocht chaip,
This wrechit warld for me heir I defy,
And to the, Deid, to lurk undir thi caip,
I offir me with hairt, rycht hummilly,
Beseikand God, the Devill, my enemy,   45
Na power haif my saule till assay.
Jesus, on the with peteous voce I cry,
Mercy one me to haif on Domisday.'

37. dispone for the *put your affairs
    in order* in hy *quickly*
38. edderis *adders'* askis *newts'*
    wirmes *worms'* meit *food*
41. chaip *escape*
42. defy *renounce*
43. caip *covering*

44. with hairt *sincerely*
    hummilly *humbly*
45. beseikand *beseeching*
46. saule *soul* assay *attack*
47. peteous *pitiful* voce *voice*
48. Domisday *Judgement Day*

38. 'To be the food of adders, newts and worms'.
41–2. 'Since it is the case that I cannot escape from you, I here renounce
    this wretched world'.
45–6. 'Beseeching God that the Devil, my enemy, should have no power
    to attack my soul'.

The Thre Deid Pollis

1

O sinfull man, in to this mortall se,
Quhilk is the vaill of murnyng and of cair,
With gaistly sicht behold oure heidis thre,
Oure holkit ene, oure peilit pollis bair.
As ye ar now, into this warld we wair,   5
Als fresche, als fair, als lusty to behald.
Quhan thow lukis on this suth examplair
Of thyself, man, thow may be richt unbald.

2

For suth it is that every man mortall
Mon suffer deid and de, that lyfe hes tane;   10
Na erdly stait aganis deid ma prevaill.
The hour of deth and place is uncertane,
Quhilk is referrit to the hie God allane.
Heirfoir haif mynd of deth, that thow mon dy:
This sair exampill to se quotidiane   15
Sowld caus all men fra wicket vycis fle.

3

O wantone yowth, als fresche as lusty May,
Farest of flowris, renewit quhyt and reid,

1. se *sea*
2. vaill *valley*
3. gaistly sicht *eyes of terror*
   heidis *heads*
4. holkit ene *hollowed out eyes*
   peilit pollis *peeled skulls*
5. wair *were*
6. als *as* lusty *beautiful*
7. suth exemplair *true image*
8. unbald *afraid*
9. suth *true*
10. mon *must* de *die* hes tane *has received*

11. na *no* erdly stait *earthly condition* ma prevaill *can win*
13. quhilk *that* referrit to *left to*
    hie *high* allane *alone*
14. heirfoir *therefore* haif mynd *be mindful* mon dy *must die*
15. se *see* quotidiane *every day*
16. sowld *should* fra *from*
    wicket *wicked* vycis *vices*
17. wantone *unruly* lusty *merry*
18. renewit *fresh blooming*
    quhyt *white*

9–10. 'For it is true that every mortal man who has been given life must also suffer death and die; no earthly condition can gain a victory over death'.

15–16. 'Seeing this fine example every day should cause all men to flee from wicked vices'.

Behald our heidis, O lusty gallandis gay;
Full laithly thus sall ly thy lusty heid,   20
Holkit and how, and wallowit as the weid;
Thy crampand hair and eik thy cristall ene
Full cairfully conclud sall dulefull deid;
Example heir be us it may be sene.

4

O ladeis quhyt, in claithis corruscant,   25
Poleist with perle and mony pretius stane,
With palpis quhyt and hals so elegant
Sirculit with gold and sapheris mony ane;
Your fingearis small, quhyt as quhailis bane,
Arrayit with ringis and mony rubeis reid: 30
As we ly thus, so sall ye ly ilk ane,
With peilit pollis, and holkit thus your heid.

5

O wilfull pryd, the rute of all distres,
With humill hairt upoun our pollis pens.
Man, for thy mis, ask mercy with meiknes;   35
Aganis deid na man may mak defens:
The empriour, for all his excellens,
King and quene, and eik all erdly stait,
Peure and riche, sal be but differens
Turnit in as and thus in erd translait.   40

19. gallandis *gallants, young noblemen*
20. full *very*   laithly *loathsome*   lusty *beautiful*
21. how *sunken*   wallowit *withered*   weid *weed*
22. crampand *curly*   ene *eyes*
23. cairfully *sorrowfully*   conclud *end*   sall *shall*   dulefull *dismal*
24. be *by*
25. claithis *clothes*   corruscant *bright*
26. poleist *adorned*   perle *pearls*   pretius *precious*   stane *stones*
27. palpis *breasts*   hals *neck*
28. sirculit *encircled*
29. quhailis bane *ivory*
31. ilk ane *each one*
33. rute *root*
34. humill hairt *humble heart*   pens *think*
35. mis *sin*
36. aganis *against*
38. eik *also*   all *every*   erdly *earthly*   stait *position*
39. peure *poor*   but differens *without exception*
40. in *into*   as *ash*   erd *dust*   in . . . translait *turned into*

22–3. 'Dismal death shall bring your curly hair and your crystal-clear
eyes to a very sorry end'.

6

This questioun, quha can obsolve, lat see,
Quhat phisnamour or perfyt palmester:
Quha was farest or fowlest of us thre?
Or quhilk of us of kin was gentillar?
Or maist expert in science or in lare,   , 45
In art, musik, or in astronomye?
Heir still sowld be your study and repair,
And think as thus all your heidis mon be.

7

O febill aige, ay drawand neir the dait
Of dully deid, and hes thy dayis compleit,   50
Behald our heidis with murning and regrait,
Fall on thy kneis, ask grace at God, and greit,
With orisionis and haly salmes sweit
Beseikand him on the to haif mercy,
Now of our sawlis, bydand the decreit   55
Of his Godheid, to rew and glorife.

8

Als we exhort that every man mortall,
For his saik that maid of nocht all thing,
For our sawlis pray in generall
To Jesus Chryst, of hevin and erd the king,   60
Throwch your prayar that we and ye may ring
With the hie Fader be eternitie,
The Sone alswa, the Haly Gaist conding,
Thre knit in ane be perfyt unitie.

41. obsolve *solve*
42. phisnamour *physiognomist*
    perfyt *skilful* palmester *palmist*
44. gentillar *more noble*
45. lare *learning*
46. art *rhetoric*
47. heir *here* repair *attention*
48. as thus *just like this* mon *must*
49. dait *date*
50. dully *doleful* hes . . .
    compleit *having completed*

52. grace *mercy* greit *cry*
53. orisionis *prayers* haly *holy*
    salmes *psalms*
54. beseikand *beseeching*
55. of *upon* sawlis *souls*
    bydand *awaiting* decreit *judgement*
56. Godheid *Godhead*
57. exhort *urge*
61. throwch *through* ring *prevail*
63. Sone *Son* Gaist *Spirit*
    conding *equal in rank*

41-3. 'Let us see who can solve this puzzle; what physiognomist, or
    skilful palm reader is able to tell who was the fairest or ugliest of the
    three of us'.
54. 'Beseeching him to have mercy upon you.'
58. 'For the sake of him who created everything from nothing'.

Ane Prayer for the Pest

1

O eterne God, of power infinyt,
To quhois hie knawlege na thing is obscure,
That is or was or evir sal be perfyt
Into thy sicht quhill that this warld indure,
Haif mercy of us, indigent and peure: 5
Thow dois na wrang to puneis our offens.
O Lord, that is to mankynd haill succure,
Preserve us fra this perrelus pestilens.

2

We the beseik, O lord of lordis all,
Thy eiris inclyne and heir our grit regrait.   10
We ask remeid of the in generall,
That is of help and confort desolait;
Bot thow with rewth our hairtis recreat,
We ar bot deid, but only thy clemens;
We the exhort on kneis law prostrait: 15
Preserf us fra this perellus pestilence.

3

We ar richt glaid thow puneis our trespas
Be ony kynd of uthir tribulatioun.
Wer it thy will, O lord of hevin, allais,

1. eterne *eternal* infinyt *infinite*
2. quhois *whose* hie *high*
3. sal be *shall be* perfyt *perfectly*
4. into *within* sicht *sight*
   quhill *while* warld *world*
   indure *lasts*
5. haif *have* of *on*
   indigent *needy* peure *poor*
6. dois *do* puneis *punish*
7. haill succure *only comfort*
8. preserve *save* perrelus *terrible*
   pestilens *plague*

9. beseik *beseech*
10. eiris *ears* heir *hear*
    grit *great* regrait *lament*
11. remeid *solace* the *you*
12. desolait *destitute*
13. bot *unless* rewth *pity*
    hairtis *hearts* recreat *cheer*
14. bot *without* clemens *clemency*
15. kneis *knees* law *low*
17. glaid *glad*
18. be *by* ony *any*

3–4. 'That is, or was, or shall be, all perfectly within your sight for as
long as this world lasts'.
12. 'We who are destitute of all help and comfort'.
13–14. 'Unless you cheer our hearts with your pity, we will simply die,
lacking your clemency'.

That we sowld thus be haistely put doun   20
And dye as beistis without confessioun,
That nane dar mak with uthir residence?
O blissit Jesu that woir the thorny croun,
Preserve us frome this perrellus pestilens.

4

Use derth, O lord, or seiknes and hungir soir,   25
And slaik thy plaig that is so penetryve.
Thy pepill are perreist: quha ma remeid thairfoir
Bot thow, O lord, that for thame lost thy lyve?
Suppois our syn be to the pungityve,
Oure deid ma nathing our synnys recompens.   30
Haif mercy, lord; we may not with the stryve:
Preserve us frome this perellus pestilens.

5

Haif mercy, lord; haif mercy, hevynis king;
Haif mercy of thy pepill penetent;
Haif mercy of our petous punissing;   35
Retreit the sentence of thy just jugement
Aganis us synnaris that servis to be schent;
Withowt mercy we ma mak no defens.
Thow that but rewth upoun the rude was rent,
Preserve us from this perrellus pestilens.   40

20. sowld *should* doun *down*
21. dye *die* as *like* beistis *animals*
22. nane *no one* dar *dares*
23. blissit *blessed* woir *wore*
25. derth *famine* seiknes *sickness*
    soir *terrible*
26. slaik *abate* plaig *plague*
    penetryve *cruel*
27. pepill *people*
    perreist *destroyed* ma *can*
    remeid *help*
29. suppois *even though* the *you*

pungityve *painful*
30. recompens *compensate*
31. with the *against you*
34. of *upon* penetent *penitent*
35. petous *pitiful*
    punissing *punishment*
36. retreit *retract*
37. aganis *against* servis *deserve*
    schent *destroyed*
39. but rewth *without pity*
    rude *cross* rent *torn*

22. 'Because no one dares come into contact with anyone else'.
29–30. 'Even though our sins are painful to you, our deaths cannot
    compensate in the slightest for our sins'.

6

Remember, lord, how deir thow hes us bocht
That for us synnaris sched thy pretius blude.
Now, to redeme that thow hes maid of nocht,
That is of vertew barrane and denude,
Haif rewth, lord, of thyne awin symiltude.   45
Puneis with pety and nocht with violens;
We knaw it is for our ingratitude
That we are puneist with this pestilens.

7

Thow grant us grace for till amend our mis
And till evaid this crewall suddane deid;   50
We knaw our syn is all the cause of this:
For oppin syn thair is set no remeid.
The justice of God mon puneis than be deid,
For by the law he will with non dispens;
Quhair justice laikis thair is eternall feid   55
Of God, that sowld preserf fra pestilens.

8

Bot wald the heiddismen, that sowld keip the law,
Puneis the peple for thair transgressioun,
Thair wald na deid the peple than owrthraw;
Bot thay ar gevin so planely till oppressioun   60
That God will nocht heir thair intercessioun,

41. how deir *at what great cost*
    bocht *bought*
42. pretius *precious* blude *blood*
43. maid *created* of nocht *from nothing*
44. barrane *barren*
    denude *stripped*
45. awin *own* symiltude *likeness*
46. pety *pity*
49. till *to* mis *wrongs*
50. evaid *escape from* deid *death*

52. oppin *open* remeid *solace*
53. mon *must* than *then* be
    deid *by death*
54. dispens *dispensation*
55. laikis *is lacking* feid *hostility*
56. preserf *save*
57. wald the heiddismen *if the
    leaders would* sowld *should*
58. owrthraw *destroy*
60. planely *openly*

43–5. 'Now, in order to redeem man whom you have created from
nothing, who is barren and stripped of all virtue, have pity, lord, upon
what you have made in your own image'.
49. 'Grant us the grace to make right our wrongs'.
53–4. 'The justice of God must then punish by death, for in accordance
with the law he will grant no one dispensation; where justice is absent
on earth, there you will find the eternal hostility of God, who would
otherwise save mankind from the plague'.
59. 'Then death would not destroy the people'.

Bot all are puneist for thair innobediens
By sword or deid, withowttin remissioun,
And hes just cause to send us pestilens.

9

Superne lucerne, guberne this pestilens;   65
Preserve and serve that we not sterve thairin;
Declyne that pyne be thy devyne prudens;
O trewth, haif rewth, lat not our slewth us twin.
Our syt full tyt, wer we contryt, wald blin;
Dissiver did never quha evir the besocht;   70
Send grace with space and us arrace fra syn;
Latt nocht be tynt that thow so deir hes bocht.

10

O prince preclair, this cair cotidiane,
We the exhort, distort it in exyle.
Bot thow remeid, this deid is bot ane trane   75
For to dissaif the laif and thame begyle.
Bot thow, sa wyis, devyis to mend this byle;
Of this mischief, quha ma releif us ocht

64. hes *God has*
65. superne lucerne *supreme light*
    guberne *control*
66. serve *bring comfort* that *so
    that* sterve *die*
67. declyne *diminish*
    pyne *torment* devyne *divine*
    prudens *wisdom*
68. slewth *spiritual sloth* us
    twin *separate us*
69. syt *torment* tyt *quickly*
    contryt *sorry* blin *cease*
70. dissiver *turned away*
    besocht *sought*
71. space *time* us arrace *snatch us
    away*
72. tynt *destroyed*
73. preclair *famous* cair
    cotidiane *daily suffering*
74. distort *change*
75. bot *unless* remeid *help*
    bot *only* trane *trap*
76. dissaif *deceive* laif *those left
    alive* begyle *trick*
77. wyis *wise* devyis *decide*
    mend *stop* byle *plague*
78. mischief *disaster* ocht *at all*

69–70. 'Our torment would cease very quickly, if we were sorry for our
    sins; you never turned away anyone who sought you'.
72. 'Do not allow what you have bought at so high a cost to be destroyed'.
74. 'We urge you, change it into exile instead'.
75–6. 'Unless you help, this death is nothing but a trap waiting to
    ensnare those who are not already dead and trick them too'.
78–9. 'Who can give us any relief at all from this disaster, brought on by
    our wrongful gains, unless you are willing to cover over our sins?'

For wrangus win, bot thow our syn oursyll?
Lat nocht be tynt that thow so deir hes bocht.   80

11
Sen for our vyce that justyce mon correct,
O king most hie, now pacifie thy feid.
Our syn is huge; refuge we not suspect;
As thow art juge, deluge us of this dreid;
In tyme assent, or we be schent with deid;   85
We us repent all tyme mispent forthocht.
Thairfoir evirmoir be gloir to thy Godheid:
Lat nocht be tynt that thow sa deir hes bocht.

79. wrangus win *wrongful gains*   dreid *fear*
    oursyll *conceal*   85. or *before* schent
81. sen *since* mon *must*   with *destroyed by*
82. pacifie *ease*   86. forthocht *regretfully*
83. not suspect *do not expect*   87. gloir *glory*
84. deluge *remove* of *from*

81–2. 'O king most high, since justice must correct our vices, at least
    now ease your hostility'.
86. 'We repent all the time we have spent wrongly and regretfully'.

The Abbey Walk

1

Allone as I went up and doun,
In ane abbay wes fair to se,
Thinkand quhat consolatioun
Wes best in to adversitie,
On cais I kest on syd myne e   5
And saw this writtin upoun a wall:
'Of quhat estait, man, that thow be,
Obey and thank thi God of all.

2

'Thy kindome and thy grit empyre,
Thy ryeltie nor rich array,   10
Sall nocht indure at thi desyre,
Bot as the wind will wend away;
Thy gold and all thi gudis gay,
Quhen fortoun list, will fra the fall:
Sen thow sic sampillis seyis ilk day,   15
Obey and thank thi God of all.

3

'Job was moist riche, in writ we find,
Thobe moist full of cheretie;
Job wox peur and Thoby blynd,
Baith temptit with adversitie.   20
Sen blindnes wes infirmitie,
And povertie was naturall,
Thairfoir in patience baith he and he
Obeid and thankit God of all.

5. on cais *by chance* kest *cast*
e *eye*
7. quhat *whatever* estait *rank*
8. of *for*
9. grit *great* empyre *empire*
10. ryeltie *ceremony*
11. indure *endure*
12. wend *go*
13. gudis *possessions*
14. fortoun *fortune* list *pleases*

fra the *from you*
15. sen *since* sic *such*
sampillis *examples* seyis *see*
ilk *every*
16. moist *very* writ *scripture*
17. Thobe *Tobit* cheretie *charity*
18. wox *became* peur *poor*
blynd *blind*
20. temptit with *tested by*

11. 'Shall not last as you would like them to do'.

4

'Thocht thow be blind or haif ane halt,   25
Or in thy face deformit ill,
Sa it cum nocht throw thy defalt,
Na man sowld the repreif by skill:
Blame nocht thy lord, sa is his will,
Spur nocht thy fute aganis the wall,   30
Bot with meik hairt and prayar still
Obey and thank thy God of all.

5

'God, of his justice, mon correct,
And, of his mercy, petie haif;
He is ane juge to nane suspect,   35
To puneis synfull man and saif:
Thocht thow be lord attovir the laif,
And eftirwart maid bund and thrall,
Ane peure begger with skrip and staif,
Obey and thank thy God of all.   40

6

'This changeing and grit variance
Of erdly staitis up and doun
Cumis nocht throw casualtie and chance,
As sum men sayis, withowt ressoun,
Bot be the grit provisioun   45
Of God aboif that rewill the sall:

25. thocht *even though* haif *have*
halt *limp*
26. ill *badly*
27. sa *so long as* cum *comes*
defalt *fault*
28. the repreif *rebuke you* by
skill *by rights*
29. sa *so*
30. spur *kick* fute *foot*
31. meik *humble* hairt *heart*
33. of *in* mon *must*
34. petie *pity*

35. to nane suspect *mistrusted by
no one*
36. puneis *punish* saif *save*
37. attovir *above* laif *rest*
38. eftirwart *afterwards*
bund *bondsman* thrall *slave*
39. skrip *pouch* staif *staff*
42. erdly *earthly* staitis *states*
43. casualtie *luck*
45. be *through*
provisioun *foresight*
46. rewill *rule*

26. 'Or are badly deformed in the face'.
33–4. 'God, in his justice, must correct mankind, and, in his mercy, have
pity upon them'.
36. 'Who is expected both to punish sinful man and to save him'.

Thairfoir evir thow mak the boun
To obey and thank thy God of all.

7

'In welth be meik, heiche not thyself,
Be glaid in wilfull povertie;   50
Thy power and thy warldlie pelf
Is nocht bot verry vanitie:
Remembir him that on the tre
For thy saik taistit bittir gall,
Quha hyis law and lawis he.   55
Obey and thank thy God of all.'

---

47. the *yourself* boun *ready*   vanitie *vanity itself*
49. heiche *raise up*   53. tre *tree*
50. glaid *glad* wilfull *honest*   54. saik *sake* taistit *tasted*
51. warldlie *worldly* pelf *wealth*   55. quha *who* hyis *raises*
52. nocht *nothing* verry   law *low* lawis *lowers* he *high*

47. 'Therefore always prepare yourself'.
49. 'Be humble when you are wealthy, do not raise yourself up'.
55. 'Who raises up the lowly and brings down the powerful'.

Against Hasty Credence

1

Fals titlaris now growis up full rank,
Nocht ympit in the stok of cheretie,
Howping at thair lord to gett grit thank,
Thay haif no dreid on thair nybouris to lie.
Than sowld ane lord awyse him weill and se   5
Quhen ony taill is brocht to his presence
Gif it be groundit in to veretie,
Or he thairto gif haistely creddence.

2

Ane worthy lord sowld wey ane taill wyslie,
The tailltellar, and quhome of it is tald,   10
Gif it be said for luve or for invy,
And gif the tailisman weill avow it wald;
Than eftirwart the pairteis sowld be cald
For thair excuse, to mak lawfull defence:
Thus sowld ane lord the ballance evinly hald   15
And gif not at the first haistie creddence.

3

It is no wirschep for ane nobill lord
For fals tailis to put ane trew man doun,

1. titlaris *tale-bearers* growis
up *flourish* rank *abundantly*
2. ympit in *grafted onto* stok *tree-trunk* cheretie *charity*
3. howping *hoping* at *from*
grit *great*
4. dreid *dread* on *about*
nybouris *neighbours*
5. sowld *should* avyse him *consider*
6. quhen *when* taill *tale*
7. gif *if* groundit *based* in to *on*
veretie *fact*
8. or *before* gif *gives*

haistely *hastily* creddence *belief*
9. wey *weigh up* wyslie *wisely*
10. tailltellar *teller of the tale*
quhome of *about whom*
11. invy *envy*
12. tailisman *teller* avow *swear to*
wald *would*
13. than *then* eftirwart *afterwards*
pairties *concerned parties*
cald *called*
15. ballance *scales* hald *hold*
16. gif *give*
17. wirschep *credit*

4. 'They have no qualms about lying about their neighbours'.
8. 'Before he believes it hastily'.
12. 'And if the teller would be willing to swear to the truth of the tale'.
16. 'And not hastily believe the story immediately'.
17–18. 'It is not to the credit of a noble lord that he should put a true
man down on account of false tales'.

And gevand creddence to the first recoird,
He will not heir his excusatioun.   20
The tittillaris so in his heir can roun
The innocent may get no audience:
Ryme as it may, thairin is na ressoun,
To gif till taillis hestely creddence.

4

Thir teltellaris oft tymes dois grit skaith,   25
And raissis mortall feid and discrepance,
And makis lordis with thair servandis wreith,
And baneist be withowtin cryme perchance.
It is the grund of stryfe and all distance,
Moir perrellus than ony pestillence,   30
Ane lord in flatterreris to haif plesance,
Or to gif lyaris hestely creddence.

5

O thow wyse lord, quhen that a flatterrer,
The for to pleis and hurt the innocent,
Will tell ane taill of thy familiar,   35
Thow sowld the pairteis call incontinent,
And sitt doun sadly in to jugement,
And serche the caus weill, or thow gif sentence,

19. gevand *giving* recoird *statement*
20. heir *hear*
excusatioun *explanation*
21. heir *ear* roun *whisper*
23. ryme *rhyme* ressoun *reason*
24. till *to*
25. thir *these* oft tymes *often*
dois *do* skaith *harm*
26. raissis *cause* mortall *deadly*
feid *feud* discrepance *quarrel*
27. servandis *servants*
wreith *angry*
28. baneist *dismissed*
perchance *perhaps*

29. grund *basis* stryfe *strife*
distance *disagreement*
30. moir *more*
perrellus *dangerous*
pestillence *disease*
31. flatterreris *flatterers*
plesance *pleasure*
32. lyaris *liars*
34. pleis *please*
35. of *about* familiar *friend*
36. incontinent *immediately*
37. sadly *solemnly*
38. serche *look into* caus *case*
or *before*

23. 'There is no rhyme nor reason to it'.
27–8. 'And make lords angry with their servants, and perhaps even
causes them to be dismissed without them having done wrong'.
31. 'For a lord to derive pleasure from flatterers'.
34. 'In order to please you and hurt the innocent'.

Or ellis heireftir in cais thow may repent
That thow to tailis gaif so grit creddence.   40

6

O wicket tung, sawand dissentioun,
Of fals taillis to tell that will not tyre,
Moir perrellus than ony fell pusoun,
The pane of hell thow sall haif to thi hyre;
Richt swa sall thay that hes joy or desyre   45
To gife thair eirris to heird with patience,
For of discord it kendillis mony fyre,
Throwch geving talis hestely creddence.

7

Bakbyttaris to heir it is no bourd,
For thay ar planlie curst in everie place;   50
Thre personis severall he slayis with ane wowrd:
Himself, the heirar, and the man saiklace,
Within ane hude he hes ane dowbill face,
Ane bludy tung undir a fair pretence.
I say no moir, bot God grant lordis grace   55
To gife to taillis nocht hestely creddence.

---

39. in cais *in case*
41. tung *tongue* sawand *sowing*
     dissentioun *disagreement*
42. tyre *tire*
43. fell pusoun *cruel poison*
44. pane *pain* to thi hyre *as your
     reward*
45. richt swa *in the same way*
46. eirris *ears* heird *hear*
47. kendillis *kindles*

48. throwch *through*
49. bakbyttaris *backbiters*
     bourd *joke*
50. planlie *clearly* curst *cursed*
51. severall *separate* wowrd *word*
52. heirar *hearer* saiklace *innocent*
53. ane *one* hude *hood*
     doubill *double*
54. pretence *appearance*

42. 'That will not tire of telling false tales'.
45–6. 'Those who take pleasure in such tales or want to incline their ears
     patiently to hear them shall suffer the same fate'.
49. 'Listening to backbiters is no joking matter'.
51. 'He kills three separate people with just one word.'

Sum Practysis of Medecyne

1

Guk guk, gud day, schir: gaip quhill ye get it.
Sic greting may gane weill; gud laik in your hude.
Ye wald deir me I trow, becaus I am dottit,
To ruffill me with a ryme—na, schir, be the rude.
Your saying I haif sene and on syd set it,   5
As geir of all gaddering, glaikit nocht gude;
Als your medicyne by mesour I haif meit met it,
The quhilk I stand ford ye nocht understude,
Bot wrett on as ye culd to gar folk wene
For feir my longis wes flaft,   10
Or I wes dottit or daft.
Gife I can ocht of the craft,
Heir be it sene.

2

Becaus I ken your cunnyng in to cure
Is clowtit and clampit and nocht weill cleird.   15

1. guk guk *cuckoo* schir *sir*
   gaip *gape* quhill *while*
2. sic *such* gane weill *suit well*
   laik *blame* hude *hood*
3. deir *harm* trow *think*
   dottit *foolish*
4. ruffill *confuse* ryme *rhyme* be
   the rude *by the cross*
5. haif *have* on syd *aside*
6. geir *stuff* gaddering *gathering*
   glaikit *foolish* nocht *not*
7. als *also* mesour *measuring*
   meit *measured* met *properly*
8. the quhilk *which* stand
   ford *guarantee*
9. wrett *wrote* gar *make*
   wene *believe*
10. feir *fear* longis *lungs*
    flaft *panting*
12. gife *if* can *know*
    ocht *anything* craft *craft of
    medicine*
13. sene *seen*
14. ken *know* cunnyng *knowledge*
15. clowtit *clumsy*
    clampit *botched* cleird *informed*

2. 'Such a greeting would suit you well; there's a good deal of blame in that doctor's hood of yours'.
5–6. 'I have seen what you have to say and set it aside, as rubbish gathered from all quarters, foolish not good'.
7. 'Also, by calculations of my own, I've got the exact measure of your medicine'.
9–10. 'But you kept writing as well as you could to make people believe that my lungs were panting with fear'.
14–15. 'Because I am aware that all your knowledge about curing people is clumsy and botched and not at all well informed'.

My prectik in pottingary ye trow be als pure
And lyk to your lawitnes—I schrew thame that leid.
Is nowdir fevir nor fell that our the feild fure,
Seiknes nor sairnes, in tyme gif I seid,
Bot I can lib thame and leiche thame fra lame and
    lesure,   20
With sawis thame sound mak: on your saule beid,
That ye be sicker of this sedull I send yow,
With the suthfast seggis
That glean allegeis,
With dia and dreggis   25
Of malis to mend yow.

Dia culcakit

3

Cape cukmaid, and crop the colleraige,
Ane medecyne for the maw, and ye cowth mak it
With sweit satlingis and sowrokis, the sop of the sege,
The crud of my culome, with your teith crakit,   30
Lawrean and linget seid and the luffage,

16. prectik *practice*
   pottingary *pharmacy* pure *poor*
17. lawitnes *ignorance*
   schrew *curse* leid *lied*
18. nowdir *neither* fell *torment*
   our *over* fure *went*
19. seiknes *sickness*
   sairnes *soreness* gif *if* seid *see it*
20. lib *cure* leiche *heal*
   lame *lameness* lesure *injury*
21. sawis *salves* thame . . . mak *to
   make them sound* beid *be it*
22. sicker *sure* sedull *prescription*
23. suthfast *honest* seggis *men*
24. glean *infection* allegeis *cure*

25. dia *medical preparations*
   dreggis *drugs*
26. malis *sickness*
   Dia culcakit *for the befouled-
   buttock*
27. cape *take* cukmaid *shitwort*
   crop *pluck* colleraige *arsesmart*
28. maw *stomach* couth *could*
29. satlingis *settlings; dregs*
   sowrokis *sorrel* sop *sap*
   sege *sage*
30. crud *caked dirt*
   culome *buttocks* crakit *cracked*
31. lawrean *laurel* linget
   seid *linseed* luffage *lovage*

16–17. 'You know that my own practice of pharmacy is as poor and
    ignorant as yours – I curse anyone who lies'.
22–6. 'That you make sure you get right this prescription that I'm
    sending you, with those 'honest' men of science who cure all infections,
    and relieve your sickness with their preparations and drugs'.
28. 'This is a medicine for the stomach, and you could make it'.
30. 'The crud of my buttocks, cracked with your teeth'.

The hair of the hurcheoun, nocht half deill hakkit,
With the snowt of ane selch, ane swelling to swage:
This cure is callit in our craft *dia culcakkit.*
Put all thir in ane pan with pepper and pik.   35
Syne sottin to this,
The count of ane cow kis;
Is nocht bettir iwis,
For the collik.

Dia longum

4

Recipe thre ruggis of the reid ruke,   40
The gant of ane gray meir, the claik of ane gus,
The dram of ane drekters, the douk of ane duke,
The gaw of ane grene dow, the leg of ane lows,
Fyve unce of ane fle wing, the fyn of ane fluke,
With ane seif full of slak that growis in the slus;   45
Myng all thir in ane mas with the mone cruke.
This untment is rycht ganand for your awin us,
With reid nettill seid in strang wesche to steip,
For to bath your ba cod,
Quhen ye wald nop and nod;   50
Is nocht bettir be God,
To latt yow to sleip.

32. hurcheoun *hedgehog* half
  deill *half way* hakkit *chopped*
33. selch *seal* swage *reduce*
35. thir *these* pik *pitch*
36. synne *then* sottin *add*
37. count *cunt* kis *kissed*
38. nocht *nothing*
39. collik *colic*
  Dia longum *for the long thing*
40. recipe *take* ruggis *pulls* reid
  ruke *red rook*
41. gant *yawn* meir *mare*
  claik *cry* gus *goose*
42. dram *pinch* drekters *drake's
  penis* douk *dive* duke *duck*
43. gaw *gall bladder* grene

dow *green dove* lows *louse*
44. unce *ounces* fle *fly*
  fluke *flounder*
45. seif *sieve* slak *pond weed*
  slus *mud*
46. myng *mix* in *into*
  mas *potion* mone *moon*
  cruke *crescent*
47. untment *ointment*
  ganand *good* awin *own* us *use*
48. reid *red* seid *seed* strang
  wesche *stale urine* steip *soak*
49. ba cod *scrotum*
50. nop *nap* nod *sleep*
52. latt yow to *prevent you from*
  Dia glaconium *for the folly*

32. 'The hair of a hedgehog, not finely chopped'.
46. 'Mix all these into a potion when the moon is crescent shaped'.
48. 'Soak with red nettle seeds in stale urine'.

Dia glaconicon

5

This dia is rycht deir and denteit in daill,
Caus it is trest and trew: thairfoir that ye tak
Sevin sobbis of ane selche, the quhidder of ane
  quhaill,   55
The lug of ane lempet is nocht to forsaik,
The harnis of ane haddok, hakkit or haill,
With ane bustfull of blude of the scho bak,
With ane brewing caldrun full of hait caill,
For it wil be the softar and sweittar of the smak: 60
Thair is nocht sic ane lechecraft fra Lawdian to
  Lundin.
It is clippit in our cannon
Dia glaconican,
For till fle awaye fon
Quhair fulis ar fundin.   65

Dia custrum

6

The ferd feisik is fyne and of ane felloun pryce,
Gud for haising and hosting or heit at the hairt.
Recipe thre sponfull of the blak spyce,
With ane grit gowpene of the gowk fart,
The lug of ane lyoun, the gufe of ane gryce,   70

53. dia *preparation* deir *costly*
  denteit *excellent* in daill *in part*
54. caus *because* trest *trusty* that
  ye tak *you should take*
55. sobbis *sobs;* wails selche *seal*
  quhidder *blast* quhaill *whale*
56. lug *ear* lempet *limpit* to
  forsaik *to be left out*
57. harnis *brains* hakkit *sliced*
  haill *whole*
58. bustfull *boxful* blude *blood*
  scho bak *female bat*
59. caldrun *cauldron* hait caill *hot
  cabbage*
60. smak *flavour*
61. sic *such* lechecraft *medicine*

Lawdian *Lothian*
62. clippit *called* cannon *medical
  books*
63. dia glaconicon – *for the folly*
64. fle *drive* fon *folly*
65. fulis *fools* fundin *found*
  Dia custrum *for the phlegm*
66. ferd *fourth* feisik *medicine*
  fyne *excellent* felloun *high*
67. haising *hoarseness*
  hosting *coughing* heit at the
  hairt *heartburn*
68. blak spyce *pepper*
69. gowpene *measure* gowk *cuckoo*
70. lug *ear* lyoun *lion*
  gufe *grunt* gryce *pig*

55. 'Seven sobs from a seal, and the blast from a whale's spout'.
69. 'Two big handfuls of cuckoo fart'.

Ane unce of ane oster poik at the nethir parte,
Annoyntit with nurice doung for it is rycht nyce,
Myngit with mysdirt and with mustart.
Ye may clamp to this cure, and ye will mak cost,
Bayth the bellox of ane brok,   75
With thre crawis of the cok,
The schadow of ane yule stok,
Is gud for the host.

7

Gud nycht, guk guk, for sa I began.
I haif no tome at this tyme langer to tary,   80
Bot luk on this lettir and leird gif ye can,
The prectik and poyntis of this pottingary.
Schir, minister this medecyne at evin to sum man
And or pryme be past, my powder I pary,
Thay sall blis yow or ellis bittirly yow ban,   85
For it sall fle thame in faith out of the fary.
Bot luk quhen ye gadder thir gressis and gers,
Outhir sawrand or sour,
That it be in ane gude oure:
It is ane mirk mirrour,   90
Ane uthir manis ers.

71. oster poik *oyster's stomach*
nethir *lower*
72. nuruce doung *nurse's dung*
nyce *pleasant*
73. myngit *mixed* mysdirt *mouse excrement* mustart *mustard*
74. clamp *add* and *if* will *are willing* mak cost *increase the cost*
75. bellox *bollocks* brok *badger*
76. crawis *crows*
77. stok *log*
78. host *cough*
79. gud nycht *goodnight* guk guk *cuckoo*
80. tome *leisure*
81. leird *learn* gif *if*

82. prectik *practice*
poyntis *details*
pottingary *pharmacy*
83. schir *sir* minister *administer* evin *evening*
84. or *before* pryme *sunrise* pary *bet*
85. blis *bless* ellis *else* ban *curse*
86. flc *fly* fary *illusory world*
87. luk *take care* gadder *gather* gressis *plants* gers *herbs*
88. outhir *either* sawrand *pleasant*
89. in a gude oure *at a good time*
90. mirk *dark*
91. manis *man's* ers *arse*

84–6. 'And I'm willing to bet all my powder that, before the sun rises,
they'll bless you or else bitterly curse you, for in truth it will make
them fly from this illusory world'.

The Poems of
WILLIAM DUNBAR

My Heid did Yak Yester Nicht

1

My heid did yak yester nicht,
This day to mak that I na micht;
So sair the magryme dois me menyie,
Perseing my brow as ony ganyie,
That scant I luik may on the licht.   5

2

And now, schir, laitlie eftir mes,
To dyt thocht I begowthe to dres,
The sentence lay full evill till find,
Unsleipit, in my heid behind,
Dullit in dulnes and distres.   10

3

Full oft at morrow I upryse,
Quhen that my curage sleipeing lyis.
For mirth, for menstrallie and play,
For din nor danceing nor deray,
It will not walkin me no wise.   15

---

1. heid *head* yak *ache* yester nicht *last night*
2. mak *write poetry* micht *could*
3. sair *painfully* magryme *migraine* menyie *afflict*
4. perseing *piercing* ganyie *arrow*
5. scant *scarcely* luik *look*
6. schir *sir* laitlie *not long ago* mes *mass*
7. dyt *write* begowthe *began* dres *prepare*
8. sentence *subject* evill *difficult* till *to*
9. unsleipit *not having slept* in my heid behind *at the back of my head*
10. dullit *made dull* dulnes *gloominess*
11. at morrow *in the morning* upryse *arise*
12. curage *mental ability* lyis *lies*
13. menstrallie *music* play *entertainment*
14. din *chatter* deray *revelry*
15. walkin *rouse* no wise *in any way*

2. 'So that today I could not write poetry'
8–9. 'Not having slept, the subject was very hard to grasp, lying somewhere at the back of my head'

Sir Jhon Sinclair Begowthe to Dance

1

Sir Jhon Sinclair begowthe to dance,
For he was new cum owt of France.
For ony thing that he do mycht
The an futt yeid ay onrycht
And to the tother wald nocht gree.   5
Quod an, 'Tak up the quenis knycht!'
A mirrear dance mycht na man see.

2

Than cam in Maistir Robert Schau:
He leuket as he culd lern tham a,
Bot ay his an futt did waver;   10
He stackeret lyk an strummall aver
That hopschackellt war aboin the kne.
To seik fra Sterling to Stranaver,
A mirrear daunce mycht na man see.

3

Than cam in the maister almaser,   15
An hommiltye jommeltye juffler.
Lyk a stirk stackarand in the ry,
His hippis gaff mony hoddous cry.
John Bute the fule said, 'Waes me,
He is bedirtin, fye, fy!'   20
A mirrear dance mycht na man se.

1. Jhon *John*   begowthe *began*
2. new *recently*
4. an *one*   futt *foot*   yeid *went*
   onrycht *wrong*
5. tother *other*   gree *agree*
6. quod *said*   quenis *queen's*
7. mirrear *merrier*
8. Schau *Shaw*
9. leuket as *looked as if*
   lern *teach*   a *all*
10. ay *always*   waver *shake*
11. stackeret *staggered*   strummall
    aver *clumsy old horse*

12. hopschackellt *hobbled*
    aboin *above*
13. seik *seek*   Sterling *Stirling*
    Stranaver *Strathnaver*
15. almaser *alms giver*
16. hommiltye jommeltye *higgledy-
    piggledy*   juffler *shuffler*
17. stirk *bullock*
    stackarand *blundering*   ry *rye*
18. gaff *gave*   hoddous *hiddeous*
    cry *noise*
19. fule *fool*   Waes me *woe is me*
20. bedirtin *covered in excrement*

3–5. 'No matter what he did the one foot kept going wrong, and would
     not keep in line with the other one'.
6. 'One person said, "Let the queen's knight take up the dance!" '.

4

Than cam in Dunbar the mackar;
On all the flure thair was nan frackar,
And thair he dancet the dirrye dantoun;
He hoppet lyk a pillie wanton   25
For luff of Musgraeffe, men tellis me.
He trippet quhill he tint his panton.
A mirrear dance mycht na man see.

5

Than cam in Maesteres Musgraeffe;
Scho mycht heff lernit all the laeffe.   30
Quhen I schau hir sa trimlye dance,
Hir guid convoy and contenance,
Than for hir saek I wissit to be
The grytast erle or duk in France.
A mirrear dance mycht na man see.   35

6

Than cam in Dame Dounteboir;
God waett gif that schou louket sowr.
Scho maid sic morgeownis with hir hippis,
For lachtter nain mycht hald thair lippis.
Quhen schou was danceand bisselye   40
An blast of wind son fra hir slippis.
A mirrear dance mycht na man se.

7

Quhen thair was cum in fyve or sax,
The quenis Dog begowthe to rax
And of his band he maid a bred   45

22. mackar *poet*
23. flure *floor* frackar *more agile*
25. pillie wanton *randy lecher*
26. luff *love* Musgraeffe *Musgrave*
27. quhill *until* tint *lost*
    panton *slipper*
29. maesteres *mistress*
30. heff lernit *have taught*
    laeffe *rest*
31. schau *saw* trimlye *nicely*
32. guid convoy *graceful bearing*
    contenance *manner*
33. saek *sake* wissit *wished*
34. grytast *greatest* duk *duke*

36. Dounteboir *Droopydrawers*
37. waett *knows* gif *if* louket
    sowr *looked sour*
38. sic *such* morgeownis *strange
    movements*
39. lachtter *laughter* nain *no one*
    hald *hold shut*
40. danceand *dancing*
    bisselye *energetically*
41. son *soon*
43. fyve *five* sax *six*
44. rax *stretch*
45. of *out* band *dog chain*
    bred *sudden dart*

And to the danceing soin he him med.
Quhou mastevlyk abowt yeid he!
He stinckett lyk a tyk, sum saed.
A mirrear dance mycht na man see.

46. soin *soon* him med *made his*   *mastiff* yeid *moved*
    way   48. stinckett *stank* tyk *stray dog*
47. quhou *how* mastevlyk *like a*   saed *said*

Now Fayre, Fayrest of Every Fayre

1

Now fayre, fayrest of every fayre,
Princes most plesant and preclare,
The lustyest one alyve that byne,
    Welcum of Scotlond to be quene!

2

Younge tender plant of pulcritud   5
Descendyd of imperyalle blode,
Freshe fragrant floure of fayrehede shene,
    Welcum of Scotlond to be quene!

3

Swet lusty lusum lady clere,
Most myghty kyngis dochter dere,   10
Borne of a princes most serene,
    Welcum of Scotlond to be quene!

4

Welcum the rose bothe rede and whyte,
Welcum the floure of oure delyte,
Oure spreit rejoysyng frome the sone beme,   15
    Welcum of Scotland to be quene!
    Welcum of Scotlande to be quene!

1. fayre *fair one*
2. princes *princess*
  plesant *delightful*   preclare *noble*
3. lustyest *most beautiful*   byne *is*
5. pulcritud *beauty*
6. blode *blood*
7. floure *flower*   fayrehede
  shene *dazzling loveliness*
9. lusum *fair*   clere *bright*
10. kyngis *king's* dochter
  dere *dear daughter*
13. rede *red*
15. spreit *feelings*   sone
  beme *sunbeam*

3. 'Most beautiful woman alive'.

Quhen Merche Wes with Variand Windis Past
(The Thrissill and the Rois)

1

Quhen Merche wes with variand windis past,
And Appryll had with hir silver schouris
Tane leif at Nature with ane orient blast;
And lusty May, that muddir is of flouris,
Had maid the birdis to begyn thair houris   5
Amang the tendir odouris reid and quhyt,
Quhois armony to heir it was delyt,

2

In bed at morrow sleiping as I lay,
Me thocht Aurora with hir cristall ene
In at the window lukit by the day   10
And halsit me, with visage paill and grene;
On quhois hand a lark sang fro the splene:
'Awalk, luvaris, out of your slomering,
Se how the lusty morrow dois up spring!'

3

Me thocht fresche May befoir my bed upstude   15
In weid depaynt of mony divers hew,
Sobir, benyng and full of mansuetude,
In brycht atteir of flouris forgit new,
Hevinly of color, quhyt, reid, broun and blew,
Balmit in dew and gilt with Phebus bemys,   20
Quhill all the hous illumynit of hir lemys.

1. Merche *March*
   variand *changeable*
2. schouris *showers*
3. tane leif at *taken leave of*   orient
   blast *east wind*
4. lusty *fair* muddir *mother*
5. houris *canonical hours*
6. odouris *scented flowers*
   reid *red*   quhyt *white*
7. quhois *whose* armony *harmony*
8. at morrow *in the morning*
9. me thocht *it seemed to me* ene *eyes*
10. lukit *looked* by the day *at
    daylight*
11. halsit *greeted* visage *face*

grene *fresh*
12. fro the splene *from the heart*
13. awalk *awake* luvaris *lovers*
    slomering *slumber*
15. upstude *stood*
16. weid *clothes* depaynt *coloured*
    divers *various* hew *hues*
17. sobir *mild* benyng *benign*
    mansuetude *gentleness*
18. atteir *attire* forgit *formed*
19. broun *dark-coloured*
20. balmit *bathed* gilt *gilded*
    Phebus bemys *sunbeams*
21. quhill *until* illumynit *was
    illuminated* lemys *rays of light*

4

'Slugird,' scho said, 'awalk annone for schame,
And in my honour sum thing thow go wryt.
The lark hes done the mirry day proclame,
To rais up luvaris with confort and delyt;   25
Yit nocht incresis thy curage to indyt,
Quhois hairt sum tyme hes glaid and blisfull bene,
Sangis to mak undir the levis grene.'

5

'Quhairto,' quod I, 'sall I uprys at morrow?
For in this May few birdis herd I sing.   30
Thai haif moir caus to weip and plane thair sorrow,
Thy air it is nocht holsum nor benyng.
Lord Eolus dois in thy sessone ring.
So busteous ar the blastis of his horne,
Amang thy bewis to walk I haif forborne.'   35

6

With that this lady sobirly did smyll,
And said, 'Uprys and do thy observance.
Thow did promyt in Mayis lusty quhyle
For to discryve the ros of most plesance.
Go se the birdis how thay sing and dance,   40
Illumynit our with orient skyis brycht,
Annamyllit richely with new asur lycht.'

7

Quhen this was said, departit scho, this quene,
And enterit in a lusty gairding gent;

22. slugird *sluggard* annone *at once*
23. wryt *write*
26. curage *desire* indyt *write*
28. sangis *songs* mak *compose*
29. quhairto *why* quod *said*
31. plane *complain about*
32. holsum *healthy* benyng *gentle*
33. Eolus *Aeolus* ring *reign*
34. busteous *violent*
35. bewis *branches* forborne *refrained*
36. sobirly *gently* smyll *smile*
37. do thy observance *perform your ritual*
38. promyt *promise* lusty *pleasant* quhyle *season*
39. discryve *describe* ros *rose* plesance *delight*
41. illumynit *illuminated* orient *eastern*
42. annamyllit *enamelled; coloured* asur *azure; delicate blue*
44. gairding *garden* gent *fine*

41. 'With the bright eastern sky illuminated above them'.

And than me thocht, full hestely besene   45
In serk and mantill, full haistely I went
In to this garth, most dulce and redolent
Of herb and flour and tendir plantis sweit,
And grene levis doing of dew doun fleit.

8

The purpour sone with tendir bemys reid   50
In orient bricht as angell did appeir
Throw goldin skyis putting up his heid,
Quhois gilt tressis schone so wondir cleir
That all the world tuke confort, fer and neir,
To luke upone his fresche and blisfull face,   55
Doing all sable fro the hevynnis chace.

9

And as the blisfull soune of cherarchy
The fowlis song throw confort of the licht.
The birdis did with oppin vocis cry:
'O luvaris fo, away thow dully nycht,   60
And welcum day that confortis every wicht.
Haill May, haill Flora, haill Aurora schene!
Haill princes Natur, haill Venus, luvis quene!'

10

Dame Nature gaif ane inhibitioun thair
To fers Neptunus and Eolus the bawld,   65
Nocht to perturb the wattir nor the air,
And that no schouris nor blastis cawld
Effray suld flouris nor fowlis on the fold;

45. besene *dressed*
46. serk *shirt* mantill *cloak*
47. garth *garden* dulce *sweet*
    redolent *fragrant*
49. doing . . . fleit *flowing*
50. purpour *crimson* reid *red*
53. cleir *bright*
54. confort *comfort* fer *far*
56. doing . . . chace *chasing*
    sable *darkness*
57. soune *sound* cherachy *leagues*

of angels
60. luvaris fo *enemy of lovers*
    dully *dismal*
61. wicht *creature*
62. schene *beautiful*
64. inhibitioun *prohibition*
65. fers *fierce* Neptunus *Neptune*
    bawld *bold*
66. perturb *whip up*
68. effray *disturb* fold *earth*

49. 'And dew flowing down from the green leaves'.

Scho bad eik Juno, goddas of the sky,
That scho the hevin suld keip amene and dry.   70

11
Scho ordand eik that every bird and beist
Befoir hir hienes suld annone compeir,
And every flour, of vertew most and leist,
And every herb be feild fer and neir,
As thay had wont in May fro yeir to yeir,   75
To hir thair makar to mak obediens,
Full law inclynnand with all dew reverens.

12
With that annone scho send the swyft ro
To bring in beistis of all conditioun.
The restles swallow commandit scho also   80
To feche all fowll of small and greit renown;
And to gar flouris compeir of all fassoun
Full craftely conjurit scho the yarrow,
Quhilk did furth swirk als swift as ony arrow.

13
All present wer in twynkling of ane e,   85
Baith beist and bird and flour, befoir the quene.
And first the lyone, gretast of degre,
Was callit thair, and he most fair to sene,
With a full hardy contenance and kene,
Befoir dame Natur come and did inclyne,   90
With visage bawld and curage leonyne.

69. bad *commanded* eik *also*
70. amene *pleasant*
71. ordand *decreed* beist *beast*
72. hienes *highness*
   compeir *appear*
73. vertew *magical or medicinal
   properties*
74. be feild *from field*
75. as thay had wont *as was their
   custom*
76. mak obediens *pay homage*
77. law *low* inclynnand *bowing*
   dew reverens *due respect*

78. send *sent* ro *roe; small deer*
79. conditioun *kinds*
81. renown *distinction*
82. gar *cause* compeir *make a
   formal appearance* fassoun *kinds*
83. craftely *skillfully*
   conjurit *summoned*
   yarrow *milfoil*
84. furth swirk *spring forth*
85. e *eye*
87. of degre *in rank*
89. hardy *bold* kene *fierce*
90. inclyne *bow down*

82. 'And to cause flowers of all kinds to make a formal appearance'.

14

This awfull beist full terrible wes of cheir,
Persing of luke and stout of countenance,
Rycht strong of corpis, of fassoun fair but feir,
Lusty of schaip, lycht of deliverance,   95
Reid of his cullour as is the ruby glance.
On feild of gold he stude full mychtely,
With flour delycis sirculit lustely.

15

This lady liftit up his cluvis cleir
And leit him listly lene upone hir kne,   100
And crownit him with dyademe full deir
Of radyous stonis most ryall for to se,
Saying, 'The king of beistis mak I the
And the cheif protector in woddis and schawis.
Onto thi leigis go furth and keip the lawis.   105

16

'Exerce justice with mercy and conscience,
And lat no small beist suffir skaith na skornis
Of greit beistis that bene of moir piscence.
Do law elyk to aipis and unicornis,
And lat no bowgle with his busteous hornis   110
The meik pluch ox oppres for all his pryd,
Bot in the yok go peciable him besyd.'

17

Quhen this was said, with noyis and soun of joy
All kynd of beistis in to thair degre

92. awfull *awe-inspiring*
cheir *expression*
93. persing *piercing* stout *brave*
94. corpis *body* fassoun *build* but
feir *without equal*
95. deliverance *bearing*
96. ruby glance *ruby's gleam*
98. flour delycis *fleur de lys*
sirculit *encircling*
99. cluvis *claws* cleir *bright*
100. leit *allowed* listly *gracefully*
101. dyademe *diadem;* crown
deir *precious*
102. radyous *glittering* ryall *royal*

103. schawis *groves*
104. onto *unto* leigis *subjects*
105. exerce *exercise*
107. skaith *harm* skornis *insults*
108. piscence *strength*
109. do law *enforce the law*
elyk *alike* aipis *apes*
110. bowgle *wild ox*
busteous *rough*
111. pluch *plough* pryd *pride*
112. peciable *peacefully*
114. in to thair degre *according to
their rank*

At onis cryit lawd: *Vive le roy*!   115
And till his feit fell with humilite,
And all thay maid him homege and fewte;
And he did thame ressaif with princely laitis,
Quhois noble yre is *parcere prostratis*.

18

Syne crownit scho the egle king of fowlis,   120
And as steill dertis scherpit scho his pennis,
And bawd him be als just to awppis and owlis
As unto pacokkis, papingais or crennis,
And mak a law for wycht fowlis and for wrennis,
And lat no fowll of ravyne do efferay,   125
Nor devoir birdis bot his awin pray.

19

Than callit scho all flouris that grew on feild,
Discirnyng all thair fassionis and effeiris.
Upone the awfull thrissill scho beheld,
And saw him kepit with a busche of speiris.   130
Concedring him so able for the weiris,
A radius croun of rubeis scho him gaif
And said, 'In feild go furth and fend the laif.

20

'And sen thow art a king, thow be discreit.
Herb without vertew hald nocht of sic pryce   135
As herb of vertew and of odor sweit;

115. lawd *in praise*   vive le roy *long live the king*
116. till *to*   feit *feet*
117. fewte *fealty; loyalty*
118. ressaif *receive*   laitis *manners*
119. yre *anger*   parcere prostratis *sparing to the humble*
120. syne *then*   egle *eagle*
121. steill dertis *steel spears*   scherpit *sharpened*   pennis *feathers*
122. bawd *commanded*   awppis *finches*
123. pacokkis *peacocks*   papingais *parrots*   crennis *cranes*
124. a *one*   wycht *powerful*

125. ravyne *prey*   do efferay *cause terror*
126. devoir *devour*   bot *except for*   awin pray *own prey*
128. discirnyng *examining*   fassionis *shapes*   effeiris *characteristics*
130. kepit *protected*   speiris *spears*
131. concedring *considering*   able for the weiris *fit for warfare*
132. radius *radiant*
133. fend the laif *defend the others*
134. sen *since*   discreit *of good judgement*
135. sic pryce *such value*

And lat no nettill vyle and full of vyce
Hir fallow to the gudly flour delyce,
Nor latt no wyld weid full of churlichenes
Compair hir till the lilleis nobilnes.   140

21
'Nor hald non udir flour in sic denty
As the fresche ros of cullour reid and quhyt,
For gife thow dois, hurt is thyne honesty,
Conciddering that no flour is so perfyt,
So full of vertew, plesans and delyt,   145
So full of blisfull angellik bewty,
Imperiall birth, honour and dignite.'

22
Than to the ros scho turnyt hir visage,
And said, 'O lusty dochtir most benyng,
Aboif the lilly illustare of lynnage,   150
Fro the stok ryell rysing fresche and ying,
But ony spot or macull doing spring;
Cum, blowme of joy, with jemis to be cround,
For our the laif thy bewty is renownd.'

23
A coistly croun with clarefeid stonis brycht   155
This cumly quene did on hir heid inclois,
Quhill all the land illumynit of the licht;
Quhairfoir me thocht all flouris did rejos,
Crying attonis, 'Haill be thow richest Ros,

138. hir fallow to *associate with*
    gudly *lovely*
139. weid *weed*
    churlichenes *rudeness*
140. compair hir *compare herself*
    lilleis *lily's*
141. uder *other*   denty *esteem*
143. gife *if*   honesty *honour*
147. imperiall *noblest*
149. dochtir *daughter*
    benyng *gracious*
150. aboif *above*

illustare *illustrious*
151. stok ryell *royal stock*
    ying *young*
152. but *without*   macull *blemish*
    doing spring *coming forth*
153. blowme *bloom*   jemis *gems*
154. our *above*   laif *rest*
155. coistly *precious*
    clarefeid *polished*
156. cumly *beautiful*
    inclois *encircle*
159. attonis *together*

Haill hairbis empryce, haill freschest quene
    of flouris! 160
To the be glory and honour at all houris.'

24

Thane all the birdis song with voce on hicht,
Quhois mirthfull soun wes mervelus to heir:
The mavys song, 'Haill Rois most riche and richt
That dois up flureis undir Phebus speir. 165
Haill plant of yowth, haill princes dochtir deir,
Haill blosome breking out of the blud royall,
Quhois pretius vertew is imperiall.'

25

The merle scho sang, 'Haill Rois of most delyt,
Haill of all flouris quene and soverane!' 170
The lark scho song, 'Haill Rois both reid and
    quhyt,
Most plesand flour of michty cullouris twane!'
The nychtingaill song, 'Haill naturis suffragene,
In bewty, nurtour and every nobilnes,
In riche array, renown and gentilnes.' 175

26

The commoun voce uprais of birdis small
Apone this wys: 'O blissit be the hour
That thow wes chosin to be our principall.
Welcome to be our princes of honour,
Our perle, our plesans and our paramour, 180
Our peax, our play, our plane felicite.
Chryst the conserf from all adversite!'

160. hairbis empryce *empress of
    plants*
161. the *you* houris *times*
162. song *sang* voce *voice*
    hicht *high*
164. mavys *thrush* richt *true*
165. dois up flureis *flourishes*
    Phebus speir *the sun's sphere*
166. princes *prince's* deir *dear*
167. breking out of *springing from*
    blud *blood*
168. pretius *precious*
169. merle *blackbird*

172. twane *two*
173. naturis *nature's*
    suffragene *representative*
174. nurtour *good breeding*
175. gentilnes *nobility*
177. wys *way*
178. principall *ruler*
179. princes *princess*
180. perle *pearl* plesans *delight*
    paramour *beloved*
181. peax *peace* play *delight*
    plane felicite *full joy*
182. the *you* conserf *protect*

27

Than all the birdis song with sic a schout
That I annone awoilk quhair that I lay,
And with a braid I turnyt me about   185
To se this court, bot all wer went away.
Than up I lenyt, halflingis in affrey,
And thus I wret, as ye haif hard toforrow,
Of lusty May upone the nynt morrow.

184. awoilk *awoke*   188. wret *wrote*   hard *heard*
185. braid *start*   toforrow *before*
187. lenyt *rose*   halflingis *half*   189. nynt *ninth*
    affrey *fear*

Gladethe, Thoue Queyne of Scottis Regioun

1

Gladethe, thoue queyne of Scottis regioun;
Ying tendir plaunt of plesand pulcritude,
Fresche flour of youthe, new germyng to burgeoun,
Our perle of price, our princes fair and gud,
Our charbunkle chosin of hye imperiale blud,   5
Our rois raile most reverent under croune,
Joy be and grace onto thi selcitud,
Gladethe, thoue queyne of Scottis regioun.

2

O hye triumphing peradis of joy,
Lodsteir and lamp of every lustines,   10
Of port surmounting Pollexen of Troy,
Dochtir to Pallas in angillik brichtnes,
Mastres of nurtur and of nobilnes,
Of fresch depictour princes and patroun,
O hevin in erthe of ferlifull swetnes.   15
Gladethe, thou queyne of Scottis regione.

3

Of thi fair fegour Natur micht rejoys,
That so the kervit with ale hir cuir and slicht;
Sche has the maid this verray warldis chois,

1. gladethe *rejoice* queyne *queen*
   Scottis *Scots'* regioun *country*
2. ying *young* plaunt *plant*
   pulcritude *beauty*
3. flour *flower* new *newly*
   germyng to burgeoun *beginning
   to bud*
4. perle *pearl* price *great value*
5. charbunkle *carbuncle*
   hye *noble* blud *blood*
6. rois riale *royal rose*
   reverent *respected* croune *crown*
7. selcitud *majesty*
9. peradis *paradise*
10. lodsteir *lodestar* lustines *beauty*
11. port *bearing*
    surmounting *surpassing*
    Pollexen *Polyxena*
12. dochtir *daughter*
    angillik *angelic*
13. mastres *mistress*
    nurtur *courtesy*
14. depictour *painting*
    patroun *exemplar*
15. ferlifull *wonderful*
17. of *at* fegour *image*
18. the kervit *shaped you* ale *all*
    cuir *care* slicht *skill*
19. the maid *made you* chois *most
    excellent*

7. 'May joy and grace befall thy majesty'.
14. 'Freshly painted princess and exemplar to us all'.
19. 'She has made you the most excellent creature in this world'.

Schawing one the hir craftis and hir micht,   20
To se quhow fair sche couthe depaint a wicht,
Quhow gud, how noble of ale condicioun,
Quhow womanly in every mannis sicht.
Gladethe, thoue queyne of Scottis regioun.

4

Rois red and quhit, resplendent of colour,   25
New of thi knop, at morrow fresche atyrit,
One stalk yet grene, O yong and tendir flour,
That with thi luff has ale this regioun firit.
Gret Gode us graunt that we have lang desirit—
A plaunt to spring of thi successioun,   30
Syne with ale grace his spreit to be inspirit.
Gladethe, thoue queyne of Scottis regioun.

5

O precius Margreit, plesand, cleir and quhit,
Mor blith and bricht na is the beriale schene,
Moir deir na is the diamaunt of delit,   35
Mor semly na is the sapheir one to seyne,
Mor gudely eik na is the emerant greyne,
Moir riche na is the ruby of renoune,
Fair gem of joy, Margreit, of the I meyne:
Gladethe, thoue queyne of Scottis regioun.   40

20. schawing *displaying* one the *in
you* craftis *arts* micht *power*
21. se *see* quhow *how*
couthe *could* depaint *depict*
wicht *person*
22. of *in* condicioun *respects*
23. mannis sicht *man's sight*
25. quhit *white* resplendent *bright*
26. of thi knop *budding*
morrow *morning* atyrit *adorned*
28. luff *love* firit *enflamed*
30. plaunt *offshoot*
31. syne *then* spreit *spirit*

33. plesand *pleasing*
34. mor *more* blith *happy*
na *than* beriale schene *shining
beryl*
35. deir *precious*
diamaunt *diamond* delit *delight*
36. semly *beautiful*
sapheir *sapphire* seyne *see*
37. gudely *lovely* eik *also*
emerant *emerald* greyne *green*
38. riche *splendid* of
renoune *celebrated*
39. of the I meyne *I speak of you*

28. 'Who has enflamed this whole country with love of you'.
29. 'May God in his greatness grant us what we have desired for so
long'.
36. 'More beautiful to look at than the sapphire'.
38. 'More splendid than the celebrated ruby'.

This Hindir Nycht in Dumfermeling

1

This hindir nycht in Dumfermeling
To me wes tawld ane windir thing:
That lait ane tod wes with ane lame
And with hir playit and maid gud game,
Syne till his breist did hir imbrace   5
And wald haif riddin hir lyk ane rame,
And that me thocht ane ferly cace.

2

He braisit hir bony body sweit
And halsit hir with fordir feit,
Syne schuk his taill with quhinge and yelp,   10
And todlit with hir lyk ane quhelp,
Syne lowrit on growfe and askit grace,
And ay the lame cryd, 'Lady, help!'
And that me thocht ane ferly cace.

3

The tod wes nowder lene nor skowry,   15
He wes ane lusty, reid haird lowry,
Ane lang taild beist, and grit with all.
The silly lame wes all to small
To sic ane tribbill to hald ane bace.
Scho fled him nocht, fair mot hir fall,   20
And that me thocht ane ferly cace.

1. this hindir nycht *last night*
   Dumfermeling *Dunfermline*
2. tawld *told* windir *amazing*
3. lait *lately* tod *fox* lame *lamb*
4. playit *played* game *fun*
5. syne *then* till *to*
   imbrace *embrace*
6. riddin *mounted* rame *ram*
7. me thocht *seemed to me* ferly
   cace *astonishing thing*
8. braisit *fondled* bony *lovely*
   sweit *sweet*
9. halsit *clasped* fordir feit *front
   feet*

10. schuk *shook* quhinge *whine*
11. todlit *played* quhelp *puppy*
12. lowrit on growfe *grovelled on
    the ground* grace *mercy*
15. nowder *neither* lene *skinny*
    skowry *shabby*
16. lusty *beautiful* lowry *foxy*
17. lang taild *long tailed* grit with
    all *big as well*
18. silly *innocent* to *too*
19. sic *such* tribbill *treble*
    bace *bass*
20. fair mot hir fall *may she
    prosper*

4

The tod wes reid, the lame wes quhyte,
Scho wes ane morsall of delyte.
He lovit na yowis auld, tuch and sklender:
Becaus this lame wes yung and tender,   25
He ran upoun hir with a race,
And scho schup nevir for till defend hir,
And that me thocht ane ferly cace.

5

He grippit hir abowt the west
And handlit hir as he had hest.   30
This innocent that nevir trespast
Tuke hert that scho wes handlit fast
And lute him kis hir lusty face.
His girnand gamis hir nocht agast,
And that me thocht ane ferly cace.   35

6

He held hir till him be the hals
And spak full fair, thocht he was fals,
Syne said, and swoir to hir be God,
That he suld nocht tuich hir prenecod.
The silly thing trowd him, allace.   40
The lame gaif creddence to the tod,
And that me thocht ane ferly cace.

7

I will no lesingis put in vers,
Lyk as thir jangleris dois rehers,

22. quhyte *white*	34. girnand gamis *snarling jaws*
23. morsall *morsel*	agast *frightened*
24. yowis *ewes* tuch *tough*	36. be *by* hals *neck*
sklender *scraggy*	37. spak *spoke* thocht *although*
26. race *rush*	39. tuich *touch* prenecod *pin-*
27. schup *tried*	*cushion*
29. west *waist*	40. trowd *believed* allace *alas*
30. as *as if* hest *haste*	41. gaif creddence to *trusted in*
31. trespast *did wrong*	43. lesingis *lies*
32. fast *firmly*	44. thir *these* jangleris *slanderers*
33. lute *let*	rehers *relate*

27. 'And she never tried to defend herself'.
30. 'And handled her as if he were in a hurry'.

Bot, be quhat maner, thay war mard   45
Quhen licht wes owt and durris wes bard.
I wait nocht gif he gaif hir grace,
Bot all the hollis wes stoppit hard,
And that me thocht ane ferly cace.

8

Quhen men dois fleit in joy maist far,   50
Sone cumis wo or thay be war.
Quhen carpand wer thir two most crows,
The wolf he ombesett the hous,
Upoun the tod to mak ane chace.
The lamb than cheipit lyk a mows,   55
And that me thocht ane ferly cace.

9

Throw hiddowis yowling of the wowf
This wylie tod plat doun on growf,
And in the silly lambis skin
He crap als far as he micht win   60
And hid him thair ane weill lang space.
The yowis besyd thay maid na din,
And that me thocht ane ferly cace.

10

Quhen of the tod wes hard no peip,
The wowf went all had bene on sleip,   65
And quhill the tod had strikkin ten

45. quhat *what* mard *compromised*   54. chace *attack*
46. licht *light* durris *doors*   55. cheipit *squeaked* mows *mouse*
    hard *bolted*   57. hiddowis *hideous*
47. wait *know* gif *if*   yowling *howling* wowf *wolf*
48. hollis *holes* stoppit hard *closed*   58. wylie *cunning* plat doun on
    up tight*   growf *lay flat on the ground*
50. fleit *float along* far *pleasant*   60. crap *crept* micht win *could get*
51. sone *soon* wo *woe* or *before*   61. weill lang space *very long time*
    war *aware*   62. besyd *nearby* din *noise*
52. quhen *when* carpand *talking*   64. hard *heard* peip *peep*
    crows *boldly*   65. went *supposed* on sleip *asleep*
53. ombesett *beset*   66. strikkin *copulated with*

45. 'But, no matter how it was done, they were still compromised'.
66. 'And while the fox has copulated with ten more'.

The wowf hes drest him to his den,
Protestand for the secound place.
And this report I with my pen,
How at Dumfermling fell the cace.   70

67. drest him *taken himself*
68. protestand *claiming*

68. 'Claiming only the second place'.

Schir, for Your Grace Bayth Nicht and Day

1

Schir, for your grace bayth nicht and day
Richt hartlie on my kneis I pray,
With all devotioun that I can:
God gif ye war Johne Thomsounis man.

2

For war it so, than weill war me: 5
But benefice I wald nocht be,
My hard fortoun wer endit than.
God gif ye war Johne Thomsounis man.

3

Than wald sum reuth within yow rest,
For saik of hir, fairest and best   10
In Bartane sen hir tyme began.
God gif ye war Johne Thomsounis man.

4

For it micht hurt in no degre,
That on so fair and gude as sche
Throw hir vertew sic wirschip wan,   15
Als yow to mak Johne Thomsounis man.

5

I wald gif all that ever I have,
To that conditioun, sa God me saif,
That ye had vowit to the swan
Ane yeir to be Johne Thomsounis man.   20

1. schir *sir* bayth *both*
   nicht *night*
2. richt hartlie *wholeheartedly*
   kneis *knees*
3. devotioun *devout feeling*
4. gif *grant* Johne
   Thomsounis *John Thomson's*
5. weill *well*
6. but *without*
7. fortoun *fortune* than *then*
9. reuth *pity* rest *exist*

10. saik *sake*
11. Bartane *Britain* sen *since*
14. on *one*
15. vertew *virtue* sic *such*
    wirschip *honour* wan *won*
17. gif *give*
18. to that conditioun *on the*
    condition saif *save*
19. vowit *vowed*
20. ane yeir *one year*

5. 'For were that the case, then I would be well-off'.

6

The mersy of that sweit meik rose
Suld soft yow, thirsill, I suppois,
Quhois pykis throw me so reuthles ran.
God gif ye war Johne Thomsounis man.

7

My advocat, bayth fair and sweit,   25
The hale rejosing of my spreit,
Wald speid in to my erand than,
And ye war anis Johne Thomsounis man.

8

Ever quhen I think yow harde or dour,
Or mercyles in my succour,   30
Than pray I God and sweit Sanct An,
Gif that ye war Johne Thomsounis man.

21. mersy *mercy* meik *meek*
22. soft *soften* thirsill *thistle*
    suppois *believe*
23. quhois *whose* pykis *spikes*
    reuthles *pitilessly*
25. advocat *intercessor*
26. hale *whole* rejosing *cause of*

    joy spreit *heart*
27. speid *succeed*
28. and *if* anis *once*
29. evir *always* dour *sullen*
30. succour *help*
31. Sanct An *Saint Anne*

30. 'Or merciless when it comes to helping me'.

O Lusty Flour of Yowth, Benyng and Bricht

1

O lusty flour of yowth, benyng and bricht,
Fresch blome of bewty, blythfull, brycht and schene,
Fair lufsum lady, gentill and discret,
 Yung brekand blosum yit on the stalkis grene,
 Delytsum lilly, lusty for to be sene,   5
Be glaid in hairt and expell havines;
 Bair of blis, that evir so blyth hes bene,
Devoyd langour and leif in lustines.

2

Brycht sterne at morrow that dois the nycht hyn chace,
 Of luvis lychtsum day the lyfe and gyd,   10
Lat no dirk clud absent fro us thy face,
 Nor lat no sable frome us thy bewty hyd,
 That hes no confort quhair that we go or ryd
Bot to behald the beme of thi brychtnes.
 Baneis all baill and into blis abyd;   15
Devoyd langour and leif in lustines.

3

Art thow plesand, lusty, yoing and fair,
 Full of all vertew and gud conditioun,

1. lusty *beautiful* flour *flower* benyng *gracious*
2. blome *bloom* blythfull *joyful* brycht *fair* schene *lovely*
3. lufsum *adored* gentill *noble* discret *judicious*
4. brekand *budding* yit *still* stalkis grene *green stem*
5. delytsum *delightful* sene *seen*
6. glaid *joyful* hairt *heart* havines *misery*
7. bair *bare* evir *always* blyth *happy*
8. devoyd *throw off* langour *misery* leif *live* lustines *joy*
9. sterne *star* at morrow *of*

morning nycht *night* hyn chace *chase away*
10. luvis *love's* lychtsum *bright* gyd *guide*
11. lat *let* dirk *dark* clud *cloud* absent *take*
12. sable *black* hyd *hide*
13. confort *comfort* ryd *ride*
14. bot *except*
15. baneis *banish* baill *sorrow* into *in* abyd *dwell*
17. plesand *delightful* lusty *beautiful* yoing *young*
18. vertew *virtue* conditioun *disposition*

12–13. 'Nor let any black one hide your beauty from us who have no comfort no matter where we go'.
17. 'You are delightful, beautiful, young and fair'.

Rycht nobill of blud, rycht wyis and debonair,
   Honorable, gentill, and faythfull of renoun,   20
   Liberall, lufsum and lusty of persoun,
Quhy suld thow than lat sadnes the oppres?
   In hairt be blyth and lay all dolour doun,
Devoyd langour and leif in lustines.

4

I me commend with all humilitie   25
   Unto thi bewty blisfull and bening,
To quhome I am and sall ay servand be
   With steidfast hairt and faythfull trew mening,
   Unto the deid without depairting.
For quhais saik I sall my pen addres   30
   Sangis to mak for thy reconforting,
That thow may leif in joy and lustines.

5

O fair sweit blossum, now in bewty flouris,
   Unfaidit bayth of cullour and vertew;
Thy nobill lord that deid hes done devoir,   35
   Faid nocht with weping thy vissage fair of hew;
   O lufsum lusty lady, wyse and trew,
Cast out all cair and comfort do incres;
   Exyll all sichand, on thy servand rew;
Devoyd langour and lef in lustines.   40

19. blud *blood* wyis *wise*
20. gentill *noble* renoun *reputation*
21. liberall *generous*
22. quhy *why* the *you*
23. dolour *sorrow*
27. servand *servant*
28. mening *intent*
29. deid *death*
30. quhais *whose* saik *sake*
   addres *prepare*
31. sangis *songs*
reconforting *comfort*
33. bewty flouris *the flower of beauty*
34. unfaidit *unfaded*
   cullour *appearance*
35. done devoir *destroyed*
36. faid *fade* vissage *face*
   hew *colour*
38. cair *sorrow*
39. exyll *exile* sichand *sighing*
   rew *take pity*

30–1. 'For whose sake I shall make my pen ready to compose songs to comfort you'.
35–6. 'Do not make your face with its fair complexion fade because death has destroyed your noble lord'.

Thir Ladyis Fair

1

Thir ladyis fair
That makis repair
  And in the court ar kend,
Thre dayis thair
Thay will do mair   5
  Ane mater for till end
Than thair gud men
Will do in ten
  For ony craft thay can;
So weill thay ken   10
Quhat tyme and quhen
  Thair menes thay sowld mak than.

2

With littill noy
Thay can convoy
  Ane mater fynaly   15
Richt myld and moy,
And keip it coy
  On evyns quyetly;
Thay do no mis;
Bot gif thay kis   20
  And keipis collatioun,
Quhat rek of this?
Thair mater is
  Brocht to conclusioun.

1. thir *these*
2. makis repair *attend*
3. kend *well-known*
4. thre *three*
5. mair *more*
6. till *to*
9. craft *skill*   can *possess*
10. ken *know*
11. quhen *when*
12. menes *cases*
13. noy *fuss*

14. convoy *bring*
15. fynaly *to a conclusion*
16. moy *submissive*
17. coy *quiet*
18. evyns *evenings*
19. mis *wrong*
20. gif *if*
21. keipis *take*   collatioun *intimate suppers*
22. rek *matter*

1–8. 'These fair ladies who attend the court and are well-known there, will
  conclude more business in three days than their husbands will in ten'.
22. 'What does it matter?'.

3

Wit ye weill   25
Thay haif grit feill
   Ane mater to solist,
Trest as the steill,
Syne nevir a deill
   Quhen thay cum hame ar mist.   30
Thir lairdis ar,
Me think, richt far
   Sic ladeis behaldin to
That sa weill dar
Go to the bar   35
   Quhen thair is ocht ado.

4

Thairfoir, I reid,
Gif ye haif pleid
   Or mater in to pley,
To mak remeid   40
Send in your steid
   Your ladeis grathit up gay.
Thay can defend
Evin to the end
   Ane mater furth expres;   45
Suppois thay spend
It is unkend:
   Thair geir is nocht the les.

25. wit *know*
26. grit feill *great perceptiveness*
27. solist *plead*
28. trest *true* steill *steel*
29. syne *then* deill *bit*
30. hame *home* mist *missed*
31. lairdis *lords*
32. me think *it seems to me* richt far *very much*
33. behaldin *indebted*
34. dar *dare*
35. bar *law courts*

36. ocht ado *something to be done*
37. reid *advise*
38. gif *if* pleid *lawsuit*
39. in to pley *proceeding*
40. mak remeid *get redress*
41. steid *place*
42. grathit *dressed*
45. furth *forward* expres *directly*
46. suppois *even if* spend *pay out*
47. unkend *unknown*
48. geir *possessions*

26–7. 'They have great perceptiveness as to how to plead a case'.
33. 'Indebted to such ladies'.
46–8. 'Even if they have to pay out no one will ever know about it: their things are of no less value than they were before'.

5

In quyet place
Thocht thay haif space   50
    Within les nor twa howris,
Thay can, percaice,
Purches sum grace
    At the compositouris.
Thair compositioun   55
With full remissioun
    Thair fynaly is endit;
With expeditioun
And full conditioun
    Thair seilis ar to pendit.   60

6

Al haill almoist
Thay mak the coist
    With sobir recompens;
Richt littill loist,
Thay get indoist   65
    Al haill thair evidens.
Sic ladyis wyis
Thay ar to pryis,
    To say the veretie,
Swa can devyis   70
And none suppryis
    Thame nor thair honestie.

49. quyet *quiet*	61. al haill *unscathed*
50. thocht *providing* space *opportunity*	62. coist *outlay*
51. nor *than* houris *hours*	63. sobir *certain* recompens *return*
52. percaice *perhaps*	64. loist *lost*
53. purches *obtain* grace *concession*	65. indoist *endorsed*
54. at *from* compositouris *legal officers*	66. al haill *completely* evidens *documents*
55. compositioun *settlement*	67. wyis *skilled*
56. remissioun *pardon*	68. to pryis *to be valued*
58. expeditioun *promptness*	69. veretie *truth*
59. conditioun *agreement*	70. swa *in this way* devyis *contrive*
60. seilis *seals* to pendit *attached*	71. suppryis *damage*
	72. honestie *reputation*

58–60. 'With promptness and full agreement, and their seals attached to
    make it official'.
63. 'Certain of the return of their investment'.
70–2. 'Who can bring matters about in this way without any damage to
    themselves or their reputation'.

To Dwell in Court, My Freind,
Gife that Thow List

1

To dwell in court, my freind, gife that thow list,
For gift of fortoun invy thow no degre.
Behold and heir, and lat thy tung tak rest,
In mekle speiche is pairt of vanitie,
And for no malyce preis the nevir to lie.   5
Als trubill nevir thy self, sone, be no tyd,
Uthiris to reiwll, that will not rewlit be:
He rewlis weill that weill him self can gyd.

2

Bewar quhome to thy counsale thow discure,
For trewth dwellis nocht ay for that trewth appeiris.   10
Put not thyne honour into aventeure,
Ane freind may be thy fo, as fortoun steiris.
In cumpany cheis honorable feiris,
And fra vyle folkis draw the far on syd.
The psalme sayis, *cum sancto sanctus eiris*:   15
He rewlis weill that weill him self can gyd.

1. list *desire*
2. invy *envy*   degre *high-ranking person*
3. heir *listen*   lat *let*   tung *tongue*
4. mekle *lengthy*   pairt of *some part*
5. malyce *wickedness*   preis the *urge you*
6. als *also*   sone *son*   be no tyd *at any time*
7. uthiris *others*   reiwll *rule*   rewlit be *allow themselves to be ruled*
8. gyd *guide*
9. bewar *beware*   quhome to *to whom*   counsale *opinions*   discure *disclose*
10. trewth *truth*   ay *always*   appeiris *appears*
11. into aventeure *at risk*
12. fo *enemy*   steiris *changes*
13. cheis *choose*   feiris *companions*
14. vyle *dishonourable*   draw the *withdraw yourself*   on syd *away*
15. cum sancto sanctus eiris *with the holy you will be holy*

1–2. 'If you desire to dwell in court, my friend, do not envy any high-ranking person their good fortune'.
5. 'And I urge you never to lie through wickedness'.
10. 'For truth does not always dwell where it appears to do'.

3

Haif pacience thocht thow no lordschip posseid,
For hie vertew may stand in law estait.
Be thow content, of mair thow hes no neid,
And be thow nocht, desyre sall mak debait 20
Evirmoir, till Deth say to the than: 'Chakmait!'
Thocht all war thyne this warld within so wyd,
Quha can resist the serpent of dispyt?
He rewlis weill that weill him self can gyd.

4

Fle frome the fallowschip of sic as ar defamit, 25
And fra all fals tungis fulfild with flattry,
Als fra all schrewis, or ellis thow art eschamit.
Sic art thow callit as is thy cumpany.
Fle parrellus taillis foundit of invy.
With wilfull men, son, argown thow no tyd, 30
Quhome no ressone may seis nor pacify:
He rewlis weill that weill him self can gyd.

5

And be thow not ane roundar in the nuke,
For gif thow be, men will hald the suspect.
Be nocht in countenance ane skornar, nor by luke, 35

17. thocht *although*
lordschip *property*
posseid *possess*
18. hie vertew *high virtue* law
estait *lowly position*
19. mair *more* neid *need*
20. debait *trouble*
21. Deth *Death*
chakmait *checkmate*
22. thocht *even if* wyd *wide*
23. quha *who* dispyt *hatred*
25. fle *flee* fallowschip *company*
sic *such* defamit *disreputable*
26. fulfild *filled* flattry *flattery*

27. schrewis *wicked people*
ellis *else* eschamit *disgraced*
29. parrellus *harmful*
taillis *gossip* foundit of *based
on* invy *envy*
30. wilfull *perverse* argown *argue*
tyd *time*
31. ressone *reasoned argument*
seis *stop*
33. roundar *whisperer* nuke *corner*
34. gif *if* hald the *consider you*
35. countenance *manner*
skornar *scorner* luke *look*

20–1. 'And if you are not, your desire shall cause trouble for you forever,
until Death finally says to you: "Checkmate!" '.
22. 'Even if everything within this wide world belonged to you'.
28. 'You will be known by the company you keep'.
35–6. 'Do not be a scorner in either your manner or expression, for if
you are a similar fate will befall you without doubt'.

Bot dowt siclyk sall stryk the in the neck.
Be war also to counsall or coreck
Him that extold hes far him self in pryd,
Quhair parrell is but proffeit or effect:
He rewlis weill that weill him self can gyd.   40

6

And sen thow seyis mony thingis variand,
With all thy hart treit bissines and cure.
Hald God thy freind, evir stabill be him stand,
He will the confort in all misaventeur.
And be no wayis dispytfull to the peure,   45
Nor to no man do wrang at ony tyd.
Quho so dois this, sicker I yow asseure,
He rewlis weill that sa weill him can gyd.

36. bot dowt *without doubt*
    siclyk *such like*   stryk *strike*
37. counsall *advise*   coreck *correct*
38. extold *elevated*   pryd *pride*
39. quhair *where*   parrell *danger*
    but *without*   effect *result*
41. sen *since*   seyis *sees*
    variand *changing*
42. treit bissines and cure *attend to
    your business and tasks*

43. hald *keep*   stabill *steadfast*
    be *by*
44. the confort *support you*
    misaventeur *misfortune*
45. no wayis *in no way*
    dispytfull *uncharitable*
    peure *poor*
46. wrang *wrong*
47. quho *who*   sicker *truly*
    asseure *assure*

37. 'Be careful also about advising or correcting'.

How Sowld I Rewill Me or Quhat Wyis

1

How sowld I rewill me or quhat wyis,
I wald sum wyisman wald devyis.
I can not leif in no degre,
Bot sum my maneris will dispyis.
Lord God, how sall I governe me?   5

2

Gif I be galland, lusty and blyth,
Than will thay say on me full swyth,
That, 'Owt of mynd yone man is he,
Or sum hes done him confort kyth.'
Lord God, how sall I governe me?   10

3

Gife I be sorrowfull and sad,
Than will thay say that I am mad,
I do bot drowp, as I wold die,
Thus will thay say, baith man and lad.
Lord God, how sall I governe me?   15

4

Gife I be lusty in array,
Than luve I parramouris, thay say,
Or in my hairt is prowd and hie,
Or ellis I haif it sum wrang way.
Lord God, how sall I governe me?   20

1. sowld *should* rewill me *behave*
   quhat wyis *in what way*
2. wald *wish* wyisman *wise man*
   wald devyis *would prescribe*
3. leif *live* no degre *any fashion*
4. maneris *behaviour*
   dispyis *despise*
5. sall *shall*
6. gif *if* galland *gallant*
   lusty *cheerful* blyth *happy*
7. on *of* full swyth *very quickly*

8. yone *that*
9. sum *someone* done . . .
   kyth *given* confort *comfort*
13. drowp *droop* as *as if*
14. baith *both*
16. lusty in array *well dressed*
17. luve I parramouris *I have
   lovers*
18. hairt *heart* hie *haughty*
19. haif *have*

8–9. 'That man is out of his mind, or else someone has shown him a
good time'.
13–14. 'They'll all say, both man and boy, that I'm just drooping
around, as if I'm about to die'.
19. 'Or else I got my clothes in some unacceptable way'.

5

And gif I be nocht weill besene,
Than twa and twa sayis thame betwene,
That 'Evill he gydis, yone man, trewlie,
Lo, be his claithis it may be sene!'
Lord God, how sall I governe me?   25

6

Gif I be sene in court ovirlang,
Than will thay murmour thame ammang,
My freyndis ar not worth a fle,
That I sa lang but guerdon gang.
Lord God, how sall I governe me?   30

7

In court rewaird gif purches I,
Than haif thay malyce and invy,
And secreitly thay on me lie
And dois me hinder prevely.
Lord God, how sall I governe me?   35

8

I wald my gyding war devysit:
Gif I spend littill I am dispysit;
Gif I be nobill, gentill and fre,
A prodigall man I am so prysit.
Lord God, how sall I governe me?   40

21. gif *if* weill besene *well dressed*
22. twa and twa *pairs of them*
23. gydis *goes*
24. lo *look* be *by* claithis
    clothes sene *seen*
26. ovirlang *too long*
27. thame ammang *among
    themselves*
28. freyndis *friends* fle *fly*
29. but guerdon *without reward*

gang *go*
31. purches *obtain*
32. invy *envy*
33. on me lie *lie about me*
34. prevely *secretly*
36. gyding *behaviour*
    devysit *prescribed*
38. gentill *courtly* fre *generous*
39. prodigall *extravagant*
    prysit *considered*

22–3. 'Then pairs of them say to one another, that "Truly, he's going to
the bad, that man" '.
31. 'If I obtain reward at court'.
36. 'I wish that my behaviour could be prescribed'.
39. 'I am considered to be an extravagant man'.

9

Now juge thay me, baith gude and ill,
And I may no mans tung hald still,
To do the best my mynd sal be,
Latt every man say quhat he will.
The gratious God mot governe me.   45

---

42. tung *tongue* hald *hold*   44. gratious *merciful*
43. mynd *intention*

43–5. 'My intention shall be to do the best I can, let every man say
whatever he wishes. May merciful God govern me'.

Musing Allone this Hinder Nicht

1

Musing allone this hinder nicht
Of mirry day quhen gone was licht,
Within ane garth undir a tre
I hard ane voce that said on hicht,
May na man now undemit be.   5

2

For thocht I be ane crownit king
Yit sall I not eschew deming:
Sum callis me guid, sum sayis thai lie,
Sum cravis of God to end my ring,
So sall I not undemit be.   10

3

Be I ane lord and not lord lyk,
Than every pelour and purspyk
Sayis, land war bettir warit on me;
Thocht he dow not to leid a tyk,
Yit can he not lat deming be.   15

4

Be I ane lady fresche and fair
With gentillmen makand repair,
Than will thay say, baith scho and he,
That I am jaipit lait and air;
Thus sall I not undemit be.   20

1. this hinder nicht *the other night*
2. mirry *happy*   quhen *when*
   licht *light*
3. garth *garden*   tre *tree*
4. hard *heard*   voce *voice*   on
   hicht *from on high*
5. undemit *unjudged*
6. thocht *even if*   crownit *crowned*
7. eschew *escape*
   deming *judgement*
8. guid *good*
9. cravis of *begs*   ring *reign*

10. sall *shall*
11. be I *if I were*   lyk *resembling*
12. than *then*   pelour *thief*
    purspyk *pick-pocket*
13. warit *cursed*
14. thocht *although*   dow not *is not*
    fit   leid *lead*   tyk *stray dog*
16. fresche *lovely*
17. makand repair *keeping company*
18. scho *she*
19. jaipit *seduced*   lait and air *late
    and early*

5. 'No one now can be left unjudged'.
11. 'If I were a lord but did not seem like one'.
15. 'That still won't stop him making judgements'.
19. 'That I am being seduced every hour of the day'.

5

Be I ane courtman or ane knycht
Honestly cled, that cumis me richt,
Ane prydfull man than call thay me;
Bot God send thame a widdy wicht
That can not lat sic demyng be.   25

6

Be I bot littill of stature
Thay call me catyve createure;
And be I grit of quantetie
Thay call me monstrowis of nature;
Thus can I not undemit be.   30

7

And be I ornat in my speiche
Than Towsy sayis I am sa streiche,
I speik not lyk thair hous menyie.
Suppois hir mowth misteris a leiche
Yit can I not undemit be.   35

8

Bot wist thir folkis that uthir demis
How that thair sawis to uthir semis,
Thair vicious wordis and vanite,
Thair tratling tungis that all furth temis,
Sum wald lat thair demyng be.   40

21. courtman *courtier*
    knycht *knight*
22. cled *dressed* that cumis me
    richt *as is fit and proper*
23. prydfull *proud*
24. widdy wicht *strong withy*
27. catyve *miserable*
29. monstrowis *monstrous*
31. ornat *rhetorical*

32. streiche *genteel*
33. menyie *retinue*
34. suppois *even if* misteris *needs*
    leiche *doctor*
36. wist *knew* thir *these*
37. sawis *words*
39. tratling tungis *chattering*
    tongues temis *empty*

33. 'I don't speak like anyone in their household'.
36–40. 'But if these people who judge others knew how their remarks
    seemed to other people, their vicious words and vanity, their chattering
    tongues that pour everything out, then some would stop their judging'.

9

War nocht the mater wald grow mair
To wirk vengeance on ane demair,
But dout I wald caus mony de,
And mony catif end in cair
Or sum tyme lat thair deming be.   45

10

Gude James the ferd, our nobill king,
Quhen that he was of yeiris ying
In sentens said full subtillie:
Do weill, and sett not by demyng,
For no man sall undemit be.   50

11

And so I sall with Goddis grace
Keip his command in to that cace,
Beseiking ay the Trinitie
In hevin that I may haif ane place;
For thair sall no man demit be.   55

41. war nocht *were it not that*
    mater *matter* mair *bigger*
42. wirk *take* demair *judge*
43. but dout *without doubt*
    caus *make* de *die*
44. catif *wretch* cair *sorrow*

46. gude *good* ferd *fourth*
47. of yeiris ying *young in years*
48. sentens *theme* subtillie *cleverly*
49. sett not *set no store by*
52. cace *matter*
53. beseiking *praying*

41–3. 'Were it not for the fact that taking revenge on one of these judges
    would just make the matter worse, without doubt I'd kill many of
    them'.
48. 'Very cleverly took this as his theme'.

Madam, Your Men Said Thai Wald Ryd

1

Madam, your men said thai wald ryd
And latt this Fasterennis Evin ower slyd;
  Bott than thair wyffis cam furth in flockis
And baid tham betteis soin abyd
  Att haem, and lib tham of the pockis.   5

2

Nou propois thai, sen ye dwell still,
Of Venus feest to fang ane fill,
  Bott in the felde preif thai na cockis:
For till hef riddin hed bein les ill
  Nor latt thair wyffis breid the pockis.   10

3

Sum of your men sic curage hed,
Dame Venus fyre sa hard tham sted,
  Thai brak up durris and raef up lockis
To get ane pamphelet on a pled,
  That thai mycht lib tham of the pockis.   15

4

Sum that war ryatous as rammis
Ar nou maid tame lyk ony lammis,

1. ryd *ride out*
2. latt *let* Fasterennis
Evin *Fastern's Eve* ower
slyd *slip by*
3. than *then* wyffis *wives*
4. baid *told* betteis *remedies*
soin *soon* abyd *submit to*
5. haem *home* lib *cure*
pockis *syphilis*
6. propois thai *they intend*
sen *since* dwell *stay* still *in the
same place*
7. feest *feast* fang ane fill *take*

their fill
8. felde *battlefield* preif *prove*
cockis *cocks*
9. till *to* riddin *rode*
10. nor *than* breid *contract*
11. sic *such* curage *sexual desire*
12. fyre *fire* sted *beset*
13. brak up *broke down*
durris *doors* raef up *broke
through*
14. pamphelet *wench* pled *excuse*
16. ryatous *wanton* rammis *rams*
17. maid *made* lammis *lambs*

4–5. 'And told them to submit to treatment at once at home, and cure
themselves of the syphilis'.
9–10. 'For it would have been better for them to have ridden out than to
let their wives contract syphilis'.

And settin down lyk sarye crockis,
And hes forsaekin all sic gammis
     That men callis libbin of the pockis.   20

5

Sum thocht tham selffis stark lyk gyandis
Ar nou maid waek lyk willing wandis,
     With schinnis scharp and small lyk rockis;
And gottin thair bak in bayth thair handis
     For over oft libbin of the pockis.   25

6

I saw coclinkis me besyd
The young men to thair howses gyd,
     Had bettir lugget in the stockis;
Sum fra the bordell wald nocht byd
     Quhill that thai gatt the Spanyie pockis.   30

7

Thairfoir, all young men, I you pray,
Keip you fra harlottis nycht and day.
     Thai sall repent quhai with tham yockis;
And be war with that perrellous play
     That men callis libbin of the pockis.   35

18. settin *settle* sarye *wretched*   small *narrow* rockis *rocks*
    crockis *old ewes*   25. over oft *too frequent*
19. forsaekin *given up*   26. coclinkis *prostitutes*
    gammis *games*   28. lugget *lodged*
20. callis *call* libbin *treatment*   29. bordell *brothel* byd *stay away*
21. thocht *thought* stark *strong*   30. quhill *until* Spanyie *Spanish*
    gyandis *giants*   32. keip you *keep yourselves*
22. waek *weak* willing   nycht *night*
    wandis *bendable twigs*   33. quhai *whoever* yockis *copulates*
23. schinnis scharp *bony shins*   34. war *careful* perrellous *dangerous*

21. 'Some who thought of themselves as strong like giants'.
23. 'With bony, skinny shins like rocks'.
24. 'And whose backs are only two hands broad'.
28. 'They would have been better off spending the night in the stocks'.
33. 'Whoever has sex with them will regret it'.

Of Februar the Fyiftene Nycht (The Dance of the Sevin Deidly Synnis)

1

Of Februar the fyiftene nycht,
Full lang befoir the dayis lycht,
   I lay in till a trance,
And than I saw baith hevin and hell;
Me thocht amangis the feyndis fell   5
   Mahoun gart cry ane dance
Of schrewis that wer nevir schrevin,
Aganis the feist of Fasternis Evin
   To mak thair observance.
He bad gallandis ga graith a gyis,   10
And kast up gamountis in the skyis,
   That last came out of France.

2

'Lat se,' quod he, 'now quha begynnis?'
With that the fowll sevin deidly synnis
   Begowth to leip at anis.   15
And first of all in dance wes Pryd,
With hair wyld bak and bonet on syd,
   Lyk to mak waistie wanis.

1. Februar *February*
   fyiftene *fifteenth* nycht *night*
2. dayis lycht *dawn*
3. in till *in*
4. baith *both*
5. me thocht *it seemed to me*
   amangis *among* feyndis fell *cruel fiends*
6. gart cry *had called for*
7. schrewis *sinners*
   schrevin *absolved from sin*
8. aganis *ready for* feist *festival*
   Fasternis Evin *Shrove Tuesday*
9. observance *ritual*
10. bad *ordered* gallandis *young men* graith *prepare*
   gyis *masquerade*
11. gamountis *leaps*
13. lat se *let us see* quod *said*
   quha *who* begynnis *should begin*
14. fowll *foul* deidly synnis *deadly sins*
15. begowth *began* leip *caper*
   anis *once*
16. Pryd *Pride*
17. wyld bak *cascading behind*
   bonet *cap* on syd *at an angle*
18. lyk *likely* waistie wanis *ruined dwellings*

8–9. 'Ready to perform their ritual on the festival of Shrove Tuesday'.
11–12. 'And throw themselves with great leaps into the sky, the latest thing from France'.

And round abowt him, as a quheill,
Hang all in rumpillis to the heill   20
   His kethat for the nanis.
Mony prowd trumpour with him trippit,
Throw skaldand fyre ay as thay skippit
   Thay gyrnd with hiddous granis.

3

Heilie harlottis on hawtane wyis   25
Come in with mony sindrie gyis,
   Bot yit luche nevir Mahoun
Quhill preistis come in with bair schevin nekkis,
Than all the feyndis lewche and maid gekkis,
   Blak Belly and Bawsy Brown.   30

4

Than Yre come in with sturt and stryfe,
His hand wes ay upoun his knyfe,
   He brandeist lyk a beir.
Bostaris, braggaris and barganeris
Eftir him passit in to pairis,   35
   All bodin in feir of weir.
In jakkis and stryppis and bonettis of steill,
Thair leggis wer chenyeit to the heill,

19. as *like*   quheill *wheel*
20. rumpillis *folds*   heill *heel*
21. kethat *coat*   for the
   nanis *indeed*
22. trumpour *impostor*
   trippit *capered*
23. skaldand fyre *scalding fire*
   ay *continually*
24. gyrnd *cried*   granis *groans*
25. heilie harlottis *proud rascals*
   hawtane wyis *haughty manner*
26. sindrie *different*   gyis *costumes*
27. luche *laughed*
28. quhill *until*   preistis *priests*
   schevin *shaved*   nekkis *necks*

29. than *then*   lewche *laughed*
   maid gekkis *made gestures*
31. Yre *Ire*   sturt *quarrelling*
   stryfe *strife*
32. ay *always*
33. brandeist *acted*   beir *bear*
34. bostaris *boasters*
   braggaris *braggarts*
   barganeris *wranglers*
35. in to pairis *in pairs*
36. bodin *armed*   feir of
   weir *warlike manner*
37. jakkis *jerkins*   stryppis *splints*
   bonettis of steill *steel helmets*
38. leggis *legs*   chenyeit *chained*

19–21. 'And, indeed, his coat spread out round about him like a wheel,
with great folds of cloth draped down to his heels'.
38. 'Their legs were clad in chainmail right down to the heel'.

Frawart wes thair affeir.
Sum upoun uder with brandis beft,   40
Sum jaggit uthiris to the heft,
    With knyvis that scherp cowd scheir.

5
Nixt in the dance followit Invy,
Fild full of feid and fellony,
    Hid malyce and dispyte;   45
For pryvie hatrent that tratour trymlit.
Him followit mony freik dissymlit,
    With fenyeit wirdis quhyte,
And flattereris in to menis facis,
And bakbyttaris of sindry racis   50
    To ley that had delyte,
And rownaris of fals lesingis.
Allace, that courtis of noble kingis
    Of thame can nevir be quyte.

6
Nixt him in dans come Cuvatyce,   55
Rute of all evill and grund of vyce,
    That nevir cowd be content.
Catyvis, wrechis and ockeraris,

39. frawart *troublesome*
affeir *behaviour*
40. uder *one another*
brandis *swords*   beft *struck*
41. jaggit *stabbed*   heft *hilt*
42. knyvis *knives*   scherp *sharply*
scheir *cut*
43. Invy *Envy*
44. fild *filled*   feid *hostility*
fellony *cruelty*
45. hid *hidden*   dispyte *animosity*
46. pryvie hatrent *secret hatred*
tratour *traitor*   trymlit *shook*
47. freik dissymlit *deceitful man*

48. fenyeit *guileful*   wirdis
quhyte *insincere words*
49. menis facis *men's faces*
50. bakbyttaris *backbiters*
sindry *various*   racis *races*
51. ley *lie*
52. rownaris *whisperers*
lesingis *lies*
54. quyte *rid*
55. dans *dance*
Cuvatyce *Covetousness*
56. rute *root*   grund *foundation*
58. catyvis *villains*   wrechis *wretches*
ockeraris *money-lenders*

40. 'Some struck one another with swords, some stabbed others right up
to the hilt'.
46. 'That traitor shook with secret hatred'.
49–50. 'And those who flatter men to their faces, and then slander them
in secret'.
53–4. 'Alas, that the courts of noble kings can never be rid of them'.

Hudpykis, hurdaris and gadderaris
    All with that warlo went.   60
Out of thair throttis thay schot on udder
Hett moltin gold, me thocht a fudder,
    As fyreflawcht maist fervent.
Ay as thay tomit thame of schot,
Feyndis fild thame new up to the thrott,   65
    With gold of allkin prent.

                    7

Syne Sweirnes, at the secound bidding,
Come lyk a sow out of a midding,
    Full slepy wes his grunyie.
Mony sweir bumbard belly huddroun,   70
Mony slute daw and slepy duddroun
    Him servit ay with sounyie.
He drew thame furth in till a chenyie,
And Belliall with a brydill renyie
    Evir lascht thame on the lunyie.   75
In dance thay war so slaw of feit,
Thay gaif thame in the fyre a heit
    And maid thame quicker of counyie.

59. hudpykis *misers*
    hurdaris *hoarders*
    gadderaris *money-grubbers*
60. warlo *demon*
61. throttis *throats*
    schot *vomitted* on udder *on
    others*
62. hett *hot* moltin *molten*
    fudder *cart-load*
63. as *like* fyreflawcht *lightning*
    fervent *hot*
64. tomit thame *emptied themselves*
65. new *anew*
66. of allkin prent *of every
    currency*
67. Sweirnes *Sloth*

68. midding *dunghill*
69. grunyie *grunt*
70. mony *many a* sweir *indolent*
    bumbard *slothful* belly
    huddroun *big glutton*
71. slute daw *dirty layabout* slepy
    duddroun *dozy sloven*
72. him servit *served him*
    sounyie *excuse*
73. chenyie *chain*
74. Belliall *Belial* brydill
    renyie *bridle and reins*
75. lascht *whipped* lunyie *loins*
76. slaw *slow* feit *feet*
77. gaif *gave* heit *heat*
78. of counyie *in the dance*

67–8. 'Then Sloth, after he'd been called twice, emerged like a sow from
    a dunghill'.
72. 'Served him with constant excuses for their slackness'.

8

Than Lichery, that lathly cors,
Come berand lyk a bagit hors,   80
   And Ydilnes did him leid.
Thair wes with him ane ugly sort,
And mony stynkand fowll tramort
   That had in syn bene deid.
Quhen thay wer entrit in the dance   85
Thay were full strenge of countenance,
   Lyk turkas birnand reid.
All led thay uthir by the tersis,
Suppois thay fycket with thair ersis,
   It mycht be na remeid.   90

9

Than the fowll monstir Glutteny,
Of wame unsasiable and gredy,
   To dance he did him dres.
Him followit mony fowll drunckart,
With can and collep, cop and quart,   95
   In surffet and exces.
Full mony a waistles wallydrag
With wamis unweildable did furth wag,
   In creische that did incres.
'Drynk!' ay thay cryit, with mony a gaip.   100

79. Lichery *Lichery* lathly
   cors *loathesome body*
80. berand *carrying on*
   bagit *enlarged; aroused*
81. Ydilnes *Idleness* leid *lead*
82. sort *lot*
83. stynkand *stinking* fowll *foul*
   tramort *corpse*
84. bene deid *died*
86. strenge *strange*
87. turkas *tongs* birnand
   reid *glowing red*
88. uthir *one another* tersis *penises*
89. suppois *although*
   fycket *fidgeted* ersis *arses*

90. remeid *remedy*
91. Glutteny *Gluttony*
92. wambe *belly*
   unsasiable *insatiable*
93. him dres *prepare*
94. drunckart *drunkard*
95. collep *tankard* cop *cup*
   quart *quart-pot*
96. surffet *surfeit*
97. waistles *fat* wallydrag *good-
   for-nothing*
98. unweildable *cumbersome*
   wag *stagger*
99. creische *grease*
100. gaip *gape*

90. 'It didn't do any good'.
100. ' "Drink!" they constantly cried, with many a mouth opened
   greedily'.

The feyndis gaif thame hait leid to laip,
Thair lovery wes na les.

10

Na menstrallis playit to thame, but dowt,
For glemen thair wer haldin owt
   Be day and eik by nycht;   105
Except a menstrall that slew a man,
Swa till his heretage he wan,
   And entirt be breif of richt.

11

Than cryd Mahoun for a heleand padyane:
Syne ran a feynd to feche Makfadyane,   110
   Far northwart in a nuke.
Be he the correnoch had done schout
Erschemen so gadderit him abowt,
   In hell grit rowme thay tuke.
Thae tarmegantis with tag and tatter   115
Full lowd in Ersche begowth to clatter
   And rowp lyk revin and ruke.
The devill sa devit wes with thair yell
That in the depest pot of hell
   He smorit thame with smuke.   120

---

101. hait leid *hot lead* laip *drink*
102. lovery *bounty* les *less*
103. menstrallis *minstrels* but
   dowt *without doubt*
104. glemen *entertainers* haldin
   owt *kept out*
105. eik *also*
106. slew *killed*
107. swa till *so that*
   heretage *inheritance*
   wan *received*
108. entirt *entered* breif of
   richt *writ of legal right*
109. heleand padyane *highland
   pageant*
111. northwart *northwards*

nuke *corner*
112. be *when* correnoch *outcry*
113. Erschemen *Highlanders*
   gadderit *gathered*
114. rowme *space* tuke *took*
115. thae *those* tarmegantis *devils*
   tag *rags*
116. Ersche *Gaelic*
   begowth *began* clatter *chatter*
117. rowp *croak* revin *raven*
   ruke *rook*
118. sa devit *so deafened*
119. pot *pit*
120. smorit *smothered*
   smuke *smoke*

114. 'They took up a lot of space in hell'.
115. 'Those devils in rags and tatters'.

12

Nixt that a turnament wes tryid,
That lang befoir in hell wes cryid
    In presens of Mahoun,
Betwix a telyour and ane sowtar,
A pricklous and ane hobbell clowttar,   125
    The barres wes maid boun.
The tailyeour baith with speir and scheild
Convoyit wes unto the feild,
    With mony lymmar loun:
Of seme byttaris and beist knapparis,   130
Of stomok steillaris and clayth takkaris,
    A graceles garisoun.

13

His baner born wes him befoir,
Quhairin wes clowttis ane hundreth scoir,
    Ilk ane of divers hew;   135
And all stowin out of sindry webbis,
For quhill the Greik sie fillis and ebbis,
    Telyouris will nevir be trew.
The tailyour on the barrowis blent;
Allais, he tynt all hardyment,   140
    For feir he chaingit hew.
Mahoun come furth and maid him knycht,

121. turnament *tournament*
    tryid *attempted*
122. cryid *announced*
124. telyour *tailor* sowtar *cobbler*
125. pricklous *louse-killer* hobbell
    clowttar *shoe-patcher*
126. barres *enclosure* boun *ready*
127. speir *spear*
128. convoyit *escorted*
    feild *battlefield*
129. lymmar loun *villainous rascal*
130. seme byttaris *seam biters*
    beist knapparis *thread snappers*
131. stomok steillaris *stomacher
    stealers* clayth takkaris *cloth
    thieves*
132. graceles *unattractive*

garisoun *company*
133. born *carried*
134. clowttis *rags* hundreth
    scoir *two thousand*
135. ilk ane *each one* divers
    hew *different colour*
136. stowin *stolen* sindry *various*
    webbis *pieces of cloth*
137. quhill *until* Greik
    sie *Mediterranean* fillis and
    ebbis *ebbs and flows*
138. trew *honest*
139. barrowis *enclosures*
    blent *looked*
140. tynt *lost* hardyment *courage*
141. feir *fear* chaingit
    hew *changed colour*

133. 'His banner was carried in front of him'.
139. 'The tailor looked towards the enclosures'.

Na ferly thocht his hart wes licht
That to sic honour grew.

14

The tailyeour hecht hely befoir Mahoun   145
That he suld ding the sowtar doun,
    Thocht he wer strang as mast.
Bot quhen he on the barrowis blenkit
The telyouris curage a littill schrenkit,
    His hairt did all ourcast.   150
And quhen he saw the sowtar cum
Of all sic wirdis he wes full dum,
    So soir he wes agast.
For he in hart tuke sic a scunner
Ane rak of fartis lyk ony thunner   155
    Went fra him, blast for blast.

15

The sowtar to the feild him drest,
He wes convoyid out of the west,
    As ane defender stout.
Suppois he had na lusty varlot,   160
He had full mony lowsy harlott
    Round rynnand him aboute.
His baner wes a barkit hyd,
Quhairin Sanct Girnega did glyd,
    Befoir that rebald rowt.   165
Full sowttarlyk he wes of laitis,
For ay betwix the harnes plaitis
    The uly birstit out.

143. na ferly thocht *no wonder
    that* licht *happy*
144. sic *such*
145. hecht hely *promised solemnly*
146. ding *strike*
147. strang *strong*
149. schrenkit *diminished*
150. hairt *heart* ourcast *flip over*
152. wirdis *words* dum *silent*
153. soir *greatly* agast *terrified*
154. tuke sic a scunner *was so upset*
155. rak of fartis *explosion of farts*
    thunner *thunder*
157. him drest *took himself*
158. convoyid *escorted*

159. stout *brave*
160. suppois *even if* lusty
    varlot *fair attendant*
161. lowsy harlott *lice-infested
    rogue*
162. rynnand *running*
163. barkit hyd *tanned hide*
164. Sanct *Saint* glyd *fly*
165. rebald rowt *scurrilous
    company*
166. sowttarlyk *like a cobbler*
    laitis *behaviour*
167. ay *always* harnes
    plaitis *plates of armour*
168. uly *oil* birstit *burst*

16

Apon the telyour quhen he did luke,
His hairt a litill dwamyng tuke,   170
   He mycht nocht rycht upsitt.
In to his stommok was sic ane steir,
Of all his dennar, that cost him deir,
   His breist held never a bitt.
To comfort him or he raid forder,   175
The devill of knychtheid gaif him order,
   For stynk than he did spitt,
And he about the devillis nek
Did spew agane ane quart of blek.
   Thus knychtly he him quitt.   180

17

Than fourty tymis the feynd cryd, 'Fy!'
The sowtar rycht effeiritly
   Unto the feild he socht.
Quhen thay wer servit of thair speiris,
Folk had ane feill be thair effeiris,   185
   Thair hairtis wer baith on flocht.
Thai spurrit thair hors on adir syd,
Syne thay attour the grund cowd glyd,
   And tham togidder brocht.
The tailyeour was no thing weill sittin,   190
He left his sadill all beschittin,
   And to the grund he socht.

170. dwamyng *faintness*
171. upsitt *sit up*
172. steir *turmoil*
173. dennar *dinner* deir *a lot*
175. or *before* raid forder *rode further*
176. knychtheid *knighthood* gaif *gave*
177. stynk *stench*
179. blek *blacking*
180. knychtly *in knightly fashion* quitt *repaid*
181. tymis *times*

182. effeiritly *fearfully*
183. socht *went*
184. servit of *provided with*
185. feill *suspicion* be *by* effeiris *behaviour*
186. on flocht *in a flutter*
187. spurrit *spurred* adir *either*
188. attour *across*
190. no thing *not at all* weill sittin *well seated*
191. beschittin *covered in excrement*
192. socht *fell*

169–70. 'When he looked at the tailor, he became a little faint at heart'.
172–4. 'There was such turmoil in his stomach that he wasn't able to keep down his dinner, which had cost him so much'.
176. 'The devil gave him the order of knighthood'.
187. 'On either side they spurred on their horses'.

18

His harnas brak and maid ane brattill,
The sowtaris hors start with the rattill
    And round about cowd reill.   195
The beist, that frayit wes rycht evill,
Ran with the sowtar to the devill,
    And he rewardit him weill.
Sum thing frome him the feynd eschewit,
He trowit agane to be bespewit,   200
    So stern he wes in steill.
He thocht he wald agane debait him.
He turnd his ers and all bedret him,
    Quyte our from nek till heill.

19

He lowsit it of with sic a reird,   205
Baith hors and man flawe to the eird,
    He fartit with sic ane feir.
'Now haif I quitt the', quod Mahoun.
The new maid knycht lay into swoun,
    And did all armes forswer.   210
The devil gart thame to dungeoun dryve
And thame of knychtheid cold depryve,
    Dischargeing thame of weir;
And maid thame harlottis agane for evir,
Quhilk still to keip thay had fer levir,   215
    Nor ony armes beir.

193. harnas *harness* brak *broke*
    brattill *clatter*
194. start *bolted* rattill *racket*
195. cowd reill *reeled*
196. beist *animal* frayit *frightened*
    rycht evill *very badly*
199. eschewit *withdrew*
200. trowit *expected*
    bespewit *vomitted upon*
201. steill *steel*
202. debait him *defend himself*
203. ers *arse* bedret him *covered
    him in excrement*
204. quyte *entirely* till *to* heill *heel*

205. lowsit it of *let it loose* reird *noise*
206. flawe *flew* eird *earth*
207. fartit *farted* with . . . feir *in
    such a way*
208. quitt the *repaid you* quod *said*
209. new maid *newly created* into
    swoun *in a faint*
210. armes *deeds of arms*
    forswer *renounce*
211. gart *caused*
212. cold depryve *deprived*
213. of weir *from battle*
215. still *name* fer levir *far rather*
216. nor *than*

199. 'The fiend withdrew from him a little'.
211. 'The devil had them taken to a dungeon'.
215–6. 'A name which they had much rather have than bear any weapons'.

20

I had mair of thair werkis writtin,
Had nocht the sowtar bene beschittin,
 With Belliallis ers unblist.
Bot that sa gud ane bourd me thocht,   220
Sic solace to my hairt it rocht,
 For lawchtir neir I brist,
Quhairthrow I walknit of my trance.
To put this in rememberance,
 Mycht no man me resist,   225
To dyte how all this thing befell,
Befoir Mahoun, the heir of hell.
 Schirris, trow it gif ye list!

217. werkis *deeds*
219. unblist *accursed*
220. bourd *jest* me thocht *it seemed to me*
221. solace *pleasure* rocht *brought*
222. lawchtir *laughter*
 neir *nearly* brist *burst*
223. quhairthrow *whereupon*
 walknit of *awakened from*
225. resist *prevent*
226. dyte *write* befell *happened*
228. schirris *sirs* trow *believe* gif ye list *if you please*

224–6. 'No man could prevent me from committing this to memory, and recording how all these things happened'.

Betwix Twell Houris and Ellevin

1

Betwix twell houris and ellevin
I dremed ane angell came fra hevin
With plesand stevin sayand on hie:
Telyouris and sowtaris, blist be ye.

2

In hevin hie ordand is your place,   5
Aboif all sanctis in grit solace,
Nixt God grittest in dignitie:
Tailyouris and sowtaris, blist be ye.

3

The caus to yow is nocht unkend;
That God mismakkis ye do amend   10
Be craft and grit agilitie:
Tailyouris and sowtaris, blist be ye.

4

Sowtaris, with schone weill maid and meit,
Ye mend the faltis of ill maid feit,
Quhairfoir to hevin your saulis will fle: 15
Telyouris and sowtaris, blist be ye.

5

Is nocht in all this fair a flyrok
That hes upoun his feit a wyrok,

1. betwix *between* twell *twelve*
   ellevin *eleven*
2. dremed *dreamed* hevin *heaven*
3. pleasand *pleasing* stevin *voice*
   hie *high*
4. telyouris *tailors*
   sowtaris *cobblers* blist *blessed*
5. ordand *ordained*
6. aboif *above* sanctis *saints*
   solace *happiness*

7. dignitie *rank*
9. unkend *unknown*
10. mismakkis *does wrong*
11. be craft *with skill*
    agilitie *cleverness*
13. schone *shoes* meit *fittingly*
14. faltis *defects* feit *feet*
15. saulis *souls* fle *fly*
17. flyrok *deformed person*
18. wyrok *corn*

1. 'Between eleven and twelve o'clock'.
7. 'The highest in rank next to God'.
10. 'Whatever God does wrong you put right'.
17–20. 'There isn't a deformed person in all the land with a corn on his foot, swollen toes or chilblains of any kind, but you can hide them all, a blessing upon you'.

Knowll tais nor mowlis in no degrie,
Bot ye can hyd thame, blist be ye.   20

6

And ye tailyouris, with weil maid clais
Can mend the werst maid man that gais
And mak him semely for to se:
Telyouris and sowtaris, blist be ye.

7

Thocht God mak ane misfassonit man   25
Ye can him all schaip new agane,
And fassoun him bettir be sic thre:
Telyouris and sowtaris, blist be ye.

8

Thocht a man haif a brokin bak,
Haif he a gude telyour, quhattrak,   30
That can it cuver with craftis slie:
Telyouris and sowtaris, blist be ye.

9

Of God grit kyndnes may ye clame,
That helpis his peple fra cruke and lame,
Supportand faltis with your supple: 35
Tailyouris and sowtaris, blist be ye.

---

19. knowll tais *swollen toes*
    mowlis *chilblains* degrie *kind*
20. hyd *hide*
21. weil maid *well made*
    clais *clothes*
22. werst *worst* gais *goes*
23. semely *attractive* for to se *to look at*
25. thocht *although*
    misfassonit *misshapen*
26. schaip *form*

27. fassoun *make*
29. brokin bak *deformed back*
30. haif he *if he has* quhattrak *no matter*
31. cuver *conceal* craftis
    slie *expert skill*
33. clame *claim*
34. cruke *deformity* lame *lameness*
35. supportand *rectifying*
    faltis *defects* supple *help*

27. 'And make him look three times better than he did before'.

10

In erd ye kyth sic mirakillis heir,
In hevin ye salbe sanctis full cleir,
Thocht ye be knavis in this cuntre:
Telyouris and sowtaris, blist be ye.   40

37. in erd *on earth* kyth *reveal*   38. salbe *shall be* sanctis *saints*
    mirakillis *miracles*   cleir *bright*
                                            39. knavis *rogues* cuntre *country*

37–8. 'You reveal such miracles here on earth that you are bound to be
resplendent saints in heaven'.

Lang Hef I Maed of Ladyes Quhytt

Lang hef I maed of ladyes quhytt;
Nou of ane blak I will indytt
   That landet furth of the last schippis,
Quhou fain wald I descryve perfytt
   My ladye with the mekle lippis: 5

Quhou schou is tute mowitt lyk ane aep,
And lyk a gangarall onto graep,
   And quhou hir schort catt nois up skippis,
And quhou schou schynes lyk ony saep,
   My ladye with the mekle lippis.   10

Quhen schou is claid in reche apparrall
Schou blinkis als brycht as ane tar barrell;
   Quhen schou was born the son tholit clippis,
The nycht be fain faucht in hir querrell,
   My ladye with the mekle lippis.   15

Quhai for hir saek with speir and scheld
Preiffis maest mychttelye in the feld
   Sall kis and withe hir go in grippis,
And fra thyne furth hir luff sall weld,
   My ladye with the mekle lippis.   20

1. maed *composed poetry* of *about*
quhytt *white*
2. nou *now* blak *black woman*
indytt *write*
3. landet furth of *disembarked
from* schippis *ships*
4. quhou *how* fain *gladly*
descryve *describe*
  perfytt *perfectly*
5. mekle *big*
6. schou *she* tute mowitt *with
protruding lips* aep *ape*
7. gangarall *toad* graep *touch*
8. catt *cat-like* nois *nose* up
skippis *turns up*

9. schynes *glistens* saep *soap*
11. claid *dressed* reche *rich*
12. blinkis *gleams* brycht *brightly*
13. quhen *when* son *sun* tholit
clippis *suffered an eclipse*
14. nycht *night* be fain *gladly*
faucht *fought* querrell *cause*
16. quhai *whoever* saek *sake*
scheld *shield*
17. preiffis *proves himself*
mychtellye *bravely*
feld *battlefield*
18. go in grippis *wrestle*
19. fra thyne furth *thenceforth*
luff *love* weld *enjoy*

6–7. 'How she has protruding lips like an ape, and is like a toad to the touch'.

And quhai in felde receaves schaem
And tynis thair his knychtlie naem
    Sall cum behind and kis hir hippis
And nevir to uther confort claem:
My ladye with the mekle lippis.   25

21. felde *battlefield*   naem *reputation*
    schaem *dishonour*   23. hippis *buttocks*
22. tynis *loses*   knychtlie *knightly*   24. confort *pleasure*   claem *claim*

24. 'And never claim any more pleasure from her than that'.

Now Lythis of ane Gentill Knycht

1

Now lythis of ane gentill knycht,
Schir Thomas Norny, wys and wycht,
    And full of chevelry,
Quhais father was ane giand keyne;
His mother was ane farie queyne,   5
    Gottin be sossery.

2

Ane fairar knycht nor he was ane
On ground may nothair ryd nor gane,
    Na beire buklar nor brand,
Or com in this court, but dreid;   10
He did full mony valyeant deid
    In Rois and Murray land.

3

Full mony catherein hes he chaist,
And cummerid mony Helland gaist
    Amang thay dully glennis.   15
Of the glen Quhettane twenti scoir
He drave as oxin him befoir,
    This deid thocht na man kennis.

1. lythis *listen* of *about*
    gentill *noble* knycht *knight*
2. schir *sir* wys *skilled*
    wycht *strong*
3. chevelry *chivalry*
4. quhais *whose* giand keyne *fierce giant*
5. farie queync *fairy queen*
6. gottin *begotten* sossery *sorcery*
7. nor *than*
8. nothair *neither* ryd *ride*
    gane *go*
9. na *nor* beire *bore*
    buklar *shield* brand *sword*
10. com in *entered* but

dreid *without doubt*
11. valyeant deid *valiant deeds*
12. Rois *Ross* Murray
    land *Moray*
13. catherein *Highland robber*
    chaist *chased away*
14. cummerid *disturbed* Helland
    gaist *Highland ghost*
15. thay *those* dully
    glennis *gloomy glens*
16. glen Quhettane *clan Chattan*
    scoir *score*
17. drave *drove*
18. deid *deed* thocht *although*
    kennis *knows*

7–8. 'A fairer knight than him never rode nor walked the earth'.
16–18. 'He drove four hundred members of clan Chattan in front of him like oxen, although this deed is not widely known'.

4

At feastis and brydallis up aland
He wan the gre and the garland,   20
  Dansit non so on deis.
He hes at werslingis bein ane hunder,
Yet lay his body never at under,
  He knawis gif this be leis.

5

Was never wyld Robein under bewch   25
Nor yet Roger of Clekniskleuch
  So bauld a berne as he;
Gy of Gysburne na Allan Bell,
Na Simonis sonnes of Quhynfell
  At schot war never so slie.   30

6

This anterous knycht, quhar ever he went,
At justing and at tornament
  Evermor he wan the gre;
Was never of half so gryt renowne
Schir Bevis the knycht of Southe Hamptowne,   35
  I schrew him gif I le.

7

Thairfoir Quenetyne was bot a lurdane
That callit him ane full plum jurdane,

---

19. feastis *feasts*
  brydallis *weddings* aland *in the country*
20. wan *won* gre *prize*
21. dansit *danced* deis *platform*
22. werslingis *wrestling matches*
  bein *been* hunder *hundred*
23. at under *under his opponent*
24. knawis *knows* gif *if* leis *a lie*
25. Robein under bewch *Robin Hood*
27. bauld *brave* berne *man*
28. Gy of Gysburne *Guy of Gisburne* na *nor*
29. Simonis sonnes of

Quhynfell *the sons of Simon of Whinfell*
30. schot *archery* slie *skilful*
31. anterous *adventurous*
32. justing *jousting*
  tornament *tournament*
34. gryt *great*
35. Southe
  Hamptowne *Southampton*
36. schrew *curse* le *lie*
37. Quenetyne *Quintin*
  lurdane *rascal*
38. callit *called* full *foul*
  plum *fat* jurdane *chamber-pot*

21. 'No one could dance up on the dais like him'.

This wyse and worthie knycht.
He callit him fowlar than a full,   40
He said he was ane licherus bull,
    That croynd baith day and nycht.

8

He wald hef maid him Curris knef.
I pray God better his honour saif
    Na to be lychtleit swa.   45
Yet this far furth I dar him prais:
He fyld never sadell in his dais,
    And Curry befyld twa.

9

Quhairfoir ever at Pesche and Yull
I cry him lord of evere full   50
    That in this regeone dwellis;
And verralie that war gryt rycht,
For, of ane hy renowned knycht,
    He wanttis no thing bot bellis.

40. fowlar *more vile*   full *fool*
41. licherus *lecherous*
42. croynd *bellowed*
43. hef *have*   Curris knef *Curry's attendant*
44. saif *save*
45. na *than*   lychtleit *insulted* swa *in this way*
46. this far furth *to this extent* dar *dare*
47. fyld *dirtied*   sadell *saddle*

dais *life*
48. befyld *dirtied*   twa *two*
49. Pesche *Easter*   Yull *Christmas*
50. cry *proclaim*   evere full *every fool*
51. regeone *country*
52. verralie *truly*   war *would be* gryt rycht *entirely fitting*
53. hy *noble*
54. wanttis *lacks*   bellis *bells*

In Vice Most Vicius He Excellis

1

In vice most vicius he excellis
That with the vice of tressone mellis.
   Thocht he remissioun
   Haif for prodissioun,
   Schame and susspissioun   5
   Ay with him dwellis.

2

And he evir odious as ane owle,
The falt sa filthy is and fowle:
   Horrible to natour
   Is ane tratour,   10
   As feind in fratour
   Undir a cowle.

3

Quha is a tratour or ane theif,
Upoun him self turnis the mischeif.
   His frawdfull wylis   15
   Himself begylis,
   As in the Ilis
   Is now a preif.

1. vicius *wicked* excellis *excells*
2. tressone *treason* mellis *gets involved*
3. thocht *even if* remissioun *pardon*
4. prodissioun *treachery*
6. ay *always*
7. evir *forever* owle *owl*
8. falt *crime*
9. natour *nature*
10. tratour *traitor*
11. feind *demon* fratour *monastery*
12. cowle *cowl*
13. quha *whoever*
14. mischeif *harm*
15. frawdfull wylis *fraudulent tricks*
16. begylis *deceive*
17. Ilis *Western Isles*
18. preif *proof*

8. 'The crime is so filthy and foul'.
11–12. 'Like a demon in a monastery wearing a cowl'.
17–18. 'As is now proved in the Western Isles'.

4

The fell strong tratour, Donald Owyr,
Mair falsett hes nor udir fowyr   20
  Round ylis and seyis.
  In his suppleis,
  On gallow treis
  Yitt does he glowir.

5

Falsett no feit hes nor deffence,   25
Be power, practik nor puscence.
  Thocht it fra licht
  Be smord with slicht,
  God schawis the richt
  With soir vengence.   30

6

Of the falis fox dissimulatour
Kynd hes all reffar, theiff and tratour:
  Eftir respyt
  To wirk dispyt
  Moir appetyt   35
  He hes of natour.

19. fell *cruel* strong *guilty*   puscence *violence*
    Donald Owyr *Donald Dubh*   27. licht *light*
20. falsett *falseness* nor *than*   28. smord *hidden* slicht *cunning*
    udir *other* fowyr *four*   29. schawis *reveals* richt *truth*
21. ylis *islands* seyis *seas*   30. soir *terrible*
22. in *with* suppleis *supporters*   31. dissimulatour *dissembling*
23. gallow treis *the gallows*   32. reffar *robber*
24. glowir *grimace*   33. respyt *reprieve*
25. feit *firm foundations*   34. wirk dispyt *cause harm*
26. be *through* practik *stratagems* 36. of natour *by nature*

20–4. 'Has more falseness about him than any four others among his
    supporters from around the islands and seas, who now grimace high up
    on the gallows'.
31–2. 'Every robber, thief and traitor has the character of the false,
    dissembling fox'.

7

War the fox tane a thowsand fawd
And grace him gevin als oft for frawd,
   War he on plane,
   All war in vane,   40
   Frome hennis agane
   Micht non him hawd.

8

The murtherer ay murthour mais,
And evir quhill he be slane he slais.
   Wyvis thus makis mokkis,   45
   Spynnand on rokkis:
   Ay rynnis the fox
   Quhill he fute hais.

37. war *were* tane *captured*
   fawd *times*
38. grace *pardon* gevin *given* als
   oft *as often* frawd *deceit*
39. on plane *out in the open*
40. in vane *useless*
41. hennis *hens*
42. hawd *hold*
43. murtherer *murderer* murthour
   mais *commits murder*

44. quhill *until* slane *killed*
   slais *kills*
45. wyvis *women* makis
   mokkis *make derisive remarks*
46. spynnand *spinning*
   rokkis *distaffs*
47. rynnis *runs*
48. quhill *while* fute *foot*

40–2. 'All would be in vain, no one could hold him back from the hens
   again'.
47–8. 'The fox will keep running while he still has a foot'.

Renownit, Ryall, Right Reverend and Serene
(The Ballade of Barnard Stewart)

The ballade of ane right noble victorius and myghty   i
lord, Barnard Stewart, lord of Aubigny, erle of Beaumont   ii
Roger and Bonaffre, consaloure and chamerlane ordinare   iii
to the maist hee, maist excellent and maiste crystyn prince iv
Loys, king of France, knyght of his ordoure, capitane   v
of the kepyng of his body, conquereur of Naplis and   vi
umquhile constable general of the same. Compilit be   vii
Maistir Willyam Dumbar at the said lordis cumyng to   viii
Edinburghe in Scotland send in ane ryght excellent   ix
embassat fra the said maist crystin king to our maist   x
souverane lord and victorius prince, James the ferde   xi
kyng of Scottis.   xii

1

Renownit, ryall, right reverend and serene
Lord, hie tryumphing in wirschip and valoure,
Fro kyngis downe most cristin knight and kene,
Most wyse, most valyand, moste laureat hie victour,
Onto the sterris upheyt is thyne honour.   5
In Scotland welcum be thyne excellence
To king, queyne, lord, clerk, knight and servatour,
Withe glorie and honour, lawde and reverence.

2

Welcum, in stour most strong, incomparable knight,
The fame of armys and floure of vassalage;   10

iii. consaloure *counsellor*   1. ryall *royal* reverend *revered*
   chamerlane ordinare *official*   2. hie *noble* wirschip *honour*
   chamberlain   3. downe *descended* kene *bold*
iv. hee *high* Crystyn *Christian* 4. valyand *valiant*
v. Loys *Louis* ordoure *order*   laureat *honoured*
vi. kepyng *protection*   5. onto *unto* sterris *stars*
   Naplis *Naples*   upheyt *exalted*
vii. umquhile *formerly*   7. queyne *queen* servatour *servant*
   compilit *composed*   8. lawde *praise*
ix. send *sent*   9. stour *combat*
x. embassat *embassy*   10. armys *warfare* floure *flower*
xi. ferde *fourth*   vassalage *military prowess*

10. 'The pride and joy of warfare and the greatest in military prowess'.

Welcum, in were moste worthi, wyse and wight;
Welcum, the soun of Mars of moste curage;
Welcum, moste lusti branche of our linnage,
In every realme oure scheild and our defence;
Welcum, our tendir blude of hie parage,   15
With glorie and honour, lawde and reverence.

3

Welcum, in were the secund Julius,
The prince of knightheyd and flour of chevalry;
Welcum, most valyeant and victorius;
Welcum, invincible victour moste wourthy;   20
Welcum, our Scottis chiftane most dughti;
With sowne of clarioun, organe, song and sence.
To the atonis, lord, 'Welcum!', all we cry,
With glorie and honour, lawde and reverence.

4

Welcum, oure indeficient adjutorie,   25
That evir our naceoun helpit in thare neyd,
That never saw Scot yit indigent nor sory
Bot thou did hym suport with thi gud deid.
Welcum, therfor, abufe all livand leyd,
Withe us to live and to maik recidence,   30
Quhilk never sall sunye for thi saik to bleid,
To quham be honour, lawde and reverence.

5

Is none of Scotland borne fathfull and kynde,
Bot he of naturall inclinacioune
Dois favour the withe all his hert and mynde,   35

11. were *war* wight *courageous*
12. soun *son*
13. lusti *flourishing* linnage *lineage*
15. tendir blude *near kinsman*
    parage *rank*
18. knightheyd *knighthood*
21. dughti *valiant*
22. sowne *sound* clarioun *trumpet*
    sence *incense*
23. the *you* atonis *in unison*
25. indeficient *unfailing*

adjutorie *supporter*
26. naceoun *nation* neyd *need*
27. indigent *disadvantaged*
    sory *wretched*
28. gud deid *good deeds*
29. abufe *above* livand leyd *living
    creature*
30. recidence *residence*
31. quhilk *who* sunye *hesitate*
    bleid *bleed*
35. favour the *support you*

26. 'Who always helped our nation in its time of need'.
31. 'Who shall never hesitate to shed their blood for your sake'.

Withe fervent, tendir, trew intencioun
And wald of inwart hie effectioun,
But dreyd of danger, de in thi defence,
Or dethe or schame war done to thi persoun,
To quham be honour, lawde and reverence.   40

6

Welcum, thow knight moste fortunable in feild;
Welcum, in armis moste aunterus and able
Undir the soun that beris helme or scheild;
Welcum, thow campioun in feght unourcumable;
Welcum, most dughti, digne and honorable,   45
And moist of lawde and hie magnificence,
Nixt undir kingis to stand incomparable,
To quham be honour, lawde and reverence.

7

Throw Scotland, Ingland, France and Lumbardy
Fleys on weyng thi fame and thi renoune,   50
And our all cuntreis undirnethe the sky,
And our all strandis fro the sterris doune.
In every province, land and regioun
Proclamit is thi name of excellence,
In every cete, village and in toune,   55
Withe gloire and honour, lawd and reverence.

37. inwart *heartfelt*
    effectioun *affection*
38. but *without* dreyd *fear* de *die*
39. or *before*
41. fortunable *successful*
    feild *battlefield*
42. armis *arms*
    aunterus *adventurous*
43. soun *sun* beris *bear*
    helme *helmet*
44. campioun *champion*
    feght *battle*
    unourcumable *unbeatable*

45. digne *worthy*
46. moist *most*
49. Ingland *England*
    Lumbardy *Lombardy*
50. fleys *flies* weyng *wing*
    renounc *reputation*
51. our *throughout*
    cuntreis *countries*
52. strandis *shores* sterris *stars*
    doune *down*
54. proclamit *proclaimed*
55. cete *city*
56. gloire *glory*

43. 'Of all those under the sun who bear helmet or shield'.
50. 'Your fame and reputation wing their way'.
52. 'And throughout all shores from here to the stars'.

8

O feyrse Achill in furius hie curage,
O strong, invincible Hector undir scheild,
O vailyeant Arthur in knyghtli vassalage,
Agamenon in governance of feild,　　　　　60
Bold Henniball in batall to do beild,
Julius in jupert in wisdom and expence,
Most fortunable chiftane bothe in yhouth and eild,
To the be honour, lawde and reverence.

9

At parlament thow suld be hye renownit,　　　　65
That did so mony victoryse opteyn.
Thi cristall helme withe lawry suld be crownyt,
And in thi hand a branche of olyve greyn.
The sweird of conquis and of knyghtheid keyn
Be borne suld highe before the in presence,　　　　70
To represent sic man as thou has beyn,
With glorie and honour, lawde and reverence.

10

Hie furius Mars, the god armipotent,
Rong in the hevin at thyne nativite;
Saturnus doune withe fyry eyn did blent　　　　75

57. feyrse *fierce* Achill *Achilles*
59. vailyeant *valiant* knyghtli
vassalage *knightly prowess*
60. Agamenon *Agamemnon*
governance *control*
61. Henniball *Hannibal* beild *bold
deeds*
62. jupert *enterprise*
expence *planning*
63. yhouth *youth* eild *age*
65. hye renownit *highly acclaimed*
66. victoryse *victories*
opteyn *obtain*

67. cristall *gleaming* lawry *laurel*
crownyt *crowned*
68. greyn *green*
69. sweird *sword*
conquis *conquest* keyn *fierce*
70. borne *carried*
71. represent *indicate* sic *such*
beyn *been*
73. armipotent *powerful in arms*
74. rong *reigned* hevin *heavens*
nativite *birth*
75. Saturnus *Saturn* fyry
eyn *fiery eyes* blent *look*

57–9. 'O you are like fierce Achilles in your furious lofty courage, you
are a strong, invincible Hector beneath your shield, o valiant Arthur in
your knightly prowess'.
68. 'And a green olive branch placed in your hand'.
70–1. 'Should be carried high before you, to indicate the kind of man
that you have been'.

Throw bludy visar men manasing to gar de;
On the fresche Venus keist hir amourouse e;
On the Marcurius furtheyet his eloquence;
Fortuna major did turn hir face on the,
Wyth glorie and honour, lawde and reverence. 80

11
Prynce of fredom and flour of gentilnes,
Sweyrd of knightheid and choise of chevalry,
This tyme I lefe, for grete prolixitnes,
To tell quhat feildis thow wan in Pikkardy,
In France, in Bertan, in Naplis and Lumbardy, 85
As I think eftir withe all my diligence,
Or thow departe, at lenthe for to discry,
With glorie and honour, lawd and reverence.

12
B in thi name betaknis batalrus,
A able in feild, R right renoune most hie, 90
N nobilnes and A for aunterus,
R ryall blude, for dughtines is D,
V valyeantnes, S for strenewite:
Quhoise knyghtli name so schynyng in clemence,
For wourthines in gold suld writtin be, 95
With glorie and honour, lawd and reverence.

76. visar *visor* manasing *threatening* gar de *cause to die*
77. on the *upon you* fresche *lovely* keist cast e *eye*
78. Marcurius *Mercury* furtheyet *poured*
81. gentilnes *nobility*
82. sweyrd *sword* choise *most excellent*
83. lefe *give up* prolixitnes *extensiveness*
84. wan *won* Pikkardy *Picardy*
85. Bertan *Britain*
86. think *intend*
87. or *before* discry *describe*
89. betaknis *signifies* batalrus *bellicose; warlike*
90. right *rightful*
91. aunterus *adventurous*
92. ryall *royal* dughtines *doughtiness; bravery*
93. valyeantnes *valour* strenewite *strength; vigour*
94. quhoise *whose* clemence *mercy*

76. 'Through his blood-stained visor, threatening to cause the deaths of men'.
83–7. 'For the time being I must refrain, because of the extensive nature of the exercise, from telling of the battlefields you won in Picardy, France, Britain, Naples and Lombardy, battles which I afterwards intend to describe diligently and at length, before you depart'.
95. 'Should be written in gold because of its worthiness'.

Illuster Lodovick, of France Most Cristin King

1

Illuster Lodovick, of France most cristin king,
Thow may complain with sighis lamentable
The death of Bernard Stewart, nobill and ding,
In deid of armes most anterous and abill,
Most mychti, wyse, worthie and confortable   5
Thy men of weir to governe and to gy.
For him, allace, now may thow weir the sabill,
Sen he is gon, the flour of chevelrie.

2

Complaine sould everie noble valiant knycht
The death of him that douchtie was in deid,   10
That many ane fo in feild hes put to flight
In weris wicht, be wisdome and manheid.
To the Turk sey all land did his name dreid,
Quhois force all France in fame did magnifie.
Of so hie price sall nane his place posseid,   15
For he is gon, the flour of chevilrie.

3

O duilfull death, O dragon dolorous,
Quhy hes thow done so dulfullie devoir

1. illuster Lodovick *illustrious*
Louis cristin *Christian*
2. complain *lament*
lamentable *pitiful*
3. ding *worthy*
4. deid of armes *battle*
anterous *adventurous* abill *able*
5. mychti *mighty* wyse *wise*
confortable *encouraging*
6. weir *war* gy *guide*
7. allace *alas* weir *wear*
sabill *sable black; mourning
clothes*

8. sen *since* flour *flower*
chevelrie *chivalry*
10. douchtie *valiant* deid *deed*
11. ane fo *a foe* feild *battlefield*
12. weris wicht *fierce battles*
manheid *courage*
13. Turk sey *Turkish sea* dreid *dread*
14. force *power*
15. price *merit* posseid *occupy*
17. duilfull *mournful*
dolorous *sorrowful*
18. done . . . devoir *devoured*
dulfullie *unkindly*

10. 'The death of him who was valiant in his deeds'.
12. 'In fierce battles, through his wisdom and courage'.
13–4. 'His name was feared in all countries as far as the Black Sea, and
his power enhanced the reputation of France'.
15. 'No one of such high merit will be found to occupy his place'.

The prince of knychtheid, nobill and chevilrous,
The witt of weiris, of armes and honour,   20
The crop of curage, the strenth of armes in stoir,
The fame of France, the fame of Lumbardy,
The schois of chiftanes, most awfull in airmour,
The charbuckell cheif of every chevelrie?

4

Pray now for him all that him loveit heir,   25
And for his saull mak intercessioun
Unto the lord that hes him bocht so deir,
To gif him mercie and remissioun;
And namelie we of Scottis natioun,
Intill his lyff quhom most he did affy,   30
Foryett we nevir into our orisoun
To pray for him, the flour of chevelrie.

19. knychtheid *knighthood*   chevelrie *fighting force*
20. witt *great strategist*   26. saull *soul* mak
    weiris *wars*   intercessioun *pray*
21. crop of curage *greatest in*   27. bocht *redeemed* so deir *at such*
    courage* stoir *combat*   great price*
22. Lumbardy *Lombardy*   28. gif *grant* remissioun *pardon*
23. schois *most excellent*   29. namelie *especially*
    chiftanes *leaders* awfull *awe-*   Scottis *Scottish*
    inspiring* airmour *armour*   30. lyff *life* affy *trust*
24. charbuckell cheif *choice ruby*   31. foryett *forget* orisoun *prayers*

25. 'All those who loved him here on earth should pray for him now'.
30. 'Whom he trusted most during his life'.
31–2. 'May we never forget when saying our prayers to pray for him, the
    flower of chivalry'.

I Maister Andro Kennedy

1

I maister Andro Kennedy
Curro quando sum vocatus.
Gottin with sum incuby
Or with sum freir *infatuatus,*
In faith I can nought tell redly   5
Unde aut ubi fui natus.
Bot in treuth I trow trewly
Quod sum dyabolus incarnatus.

2

Cum nichill sit cercius morte
We mon all de, man, that is done.   10
Nescimus quando vel qua sorte
Na blind Allane wait of the mone.
Ego pacior in pectore,
This night I myght not sleip a wink.
Licet eger in corpore,   15
Yit wald my mouth be wet with drink.

3

Nunc condo testamentum meum.
I leif my saull for evirmare,
Per omnipotentem deum,
In to my lordis wyne cellar,   20

1. maister *master*
2. curro quando sum vocatus *run when I am called*
3. gottin *begotten* incuby *incubus*
4. freir infatuatus *foolish friar*
5. redly *for certain*
6. unde aut ubi fui natus *from whom or where I was born*
7. treuth *truth* trow *believe*
8. quod sum dyabolus incarnatus *that I am the devil incarnate*
9. cum nichill sit cercius morte *since nothing is more certain than death*
10. mon *must* de *die*
done *inevitable*
11. nescimus quando vel qua sorte *we do not know when or how*
12. na *than* Allane *Allan* wait *knows* mone *moon*
13. ego pacior in pectore *I suffer in my heart*
15. licet eger in corpore *although my body is destitute*
17. nunc condo testamentum meum *now I make my last will and testament*
18. leif *leave* saull *soul*
19. per omnipotentem deum *through almighty God*

11–12. 'We do not know when or how any more than blind Allan knows about the moon'.
16. 'My mouth would still like to be wet with drink'.

Semper ibi ad remanendum
Quhill domisday, without dissever,
Bonum vinum ad bibendum
With sweit Cuthbert that lufit me nevir.

4

Ipse est dulcis ad amandum.   25
He wald oft ban me in his breith,
Det michi modo ad potandum,
And I forgif him laith and wraith,
Quia in cellario cum cervisia
I had lever lye, baith air and lait,   30
Nudus solus in camesia
Na in my lordis bed of stait.

5

A barell bung ay at my bosum,
Of warldis gud I bad na mair.
Corpus meum ebriosum   35
I leif on to the toune of Air,
In a draf mydding for evir and ay,
Ut ibi sepeliri queam,
Quhar drink and draf may ilka day
Be cassyne *super faciem meam.*   40

21. semper ibi ad remanendum *to remain there always*
22. quhill *until*
    domisday *doomsday*
    dissever *separation*
23. bonum vinum ad bibendum *in order to drink good wine*
24. luffit *loved*
25. ipse est dulcis ad amandum *he himself is sweet to love*
26. ban *curse* breith *anger*
27. det michi modo ad potandum *he only needs to give me something to drink*
28. forgif *forgive* laith *ill-will* wraith *anger*
29. quia in cellario cum cervisia *since in the cellar with the beer*
30. lever *rather* lye *lie* air *early*

lait *late*
31. nudus solus in camesia *naked apart from my shirt*
32. na *than* stait *state*
33. barell bung *barrel stopper* bosum *chest*
34. warldis gud *worldly goods* bad *desired*
35. corpus meum ebriosum *my drunken body*
36. leif *leave* toune *town* Air *Ayr*
37. draf *malt dregs* mydding *midden* ay *always*
38. ut ibi sepeliri queam *so that I may be buried there*
39. ilka *every*
40. cassyne *thrown* super faciem meam *over my face*

24. 'With sweet Cuthbert who never loved me'.
34. 'I desired no more worldly goods than that'.

6

I leif my hert that nevir wes sicir
Sed semper variabile,
That nevir mare wald flow nor flicir,
Consorti meo Jacobe,
Thought I wald bynd it with a wicir.   45
Verum deum renui,
Bot and I hecht to teme a bicker
Hoc pactum semper tenui.

7

Syne leif I the best aucht I bocht
(*Quod est Latinum propter 'caupe'?*)   50
To hede of kyn; bot I wait nought
Quis est ille, than I schrew my scawpe.
I callit my lord my heid, but hiddill,
Sed nulli alii hoc dixerunt.
We weir als sib as seve and riddill,   55
In una silva que creverunt.

8

Omnia mea solacia
(Thai wer bot lesingis, all and ane)

41. sicir *faithful*
42. sed semper variabile *but always fickle*
43. mare *more*   flow *beat*
    flicir *quiver*
44. consorti meo Jacobe *to my partner Jacoba*
45. thought *although*   wicir *willow twig*
46. verum deum renui *I rejected the true God*
47. and *if*   hecht *promised* teme *empty*   bicker *glass*
48. hoc pactum semper tenui *I always stayed faithful to that agreement*
49. aucht *thing*   bocht *bought*
50. quod est Latinum propter

'caupe' *what is the Latin for 'caupe'?*
51. hede *head*   kyn *family* wait *know*
52. quis est ille *who he is* schrew *curse*   scawpe *scalp*
53. but hiddill *without hiding it*
54. sed nulli alii hoc dixerunt *but none of the others called him this*
55. als sib *as alike*   seve *sieve* riddill *riddle; sieve*
56. in una silva que creverunt *which grew in the same wood*
57. omnia mea solacia *all my pleasures*
58. bot *nothing but*   lesingis *lies* all and ane *one and all*

49–52. 'Next I leave the best thing I ever bought (what is the Latin for 'old cow?') to the head of my family; but I don't know who he is, so I curse my own head'.

Cum omni fraude et fallacia
I leif the maister of Sanct Antane,   60
Willelmo Gray, sine gratia,
Myne awne deir cusing, as I wene,
Qui nunquam fabricat mendatia
Bot quhen the holyne growis grene.

9

My fenyening and my fals wynyng   65
Relinquo falsis fratribus,
For that is Goddis awne bidding:
Dispersit, dedit pauperibus.
For menis saulis thai say thai sing,
Mencientes pro muneribus.   70
Now god gif thaim ane evill ending
Pro suis pravis operibus.

10

To Jok Fule my foly fre
Lego post corpus sepultum.
In faith I am mair fule than he,   75
Licet ostendit bonum vultum.
Of corne and catall, gold and fe

59. cum omnia fraude et
  fallacia *with every kind of fraud
  and deceit*
60. Sanct Antane *St Antony's*
61. Willelmo Gray, sine
  gratia *William Gray, without
  thanks*
62. awne *own* deir *dear*
  cusing *cousin* wene *believe*
63. qui nunquam fabricat
  mendatia *who never tells lies*
64. bot *except* holyne *holly*
  grene *green*
65. fenyening *lying* wynyng *profit*
66. relinquo falsis fratribus *I
  bequeath to the flase friars*
67. bidding *command*
68. dispersit, dedit pauperibus *he*

  shared out, he gave to the poor
69. saulis *souls*
70. mencientes pro
  muneribus *telling lies to get
  money*
71. gif *give*
72. pro suis pravis operibus *in
  return for their evil deeds*
73. Jok Fule *Jock the Fool*
  foly *stupidity* fre *generously*
74. lego post corpus sepultum *I
  bequeath after the burial of my
  body*
75. mair fule *a greater fool*
76. licet ostendit bonum
  vultum *granted, he has a good
  appearance*
77. fe *wealth*

69. 'They say that they sing for the sake of men's souls'.
73–4. 'I generously bequeath my stupidity to Jock the Fool after the
  burial of my body'.

Ipse habet valde multum,
And yit he bleris my lordis e
Fingendo eum fore stultum.   80

11

To master Johne Clerk syne
Do et lego intime
Goddis malisone and myne.
Ipse est causa mortis mee.
War I a dog and he a swyne   85
Multi mirantur super me,
Bot I suld ger that lurdane quhryne
Scribendo dentes sine de.

12

Residuum omnium bonorum
For to dispone my lord sall haif,   90
Cum tutela puerorum,
Ade, Kytte and all the laif.
In faith I will na langar raif.
Pro sepultura ordino
On the new gys, sa God me saif,   95
Non sicut more solito.

78. ipse habet valde multum *he himself certainly has a great deal*
79. bleris my lordis e *deceives my lord*
80. fingendo eum fore stultum *by pretending to be a fool*
81. syne *next*
82. do et lego intime *I cordially give and bequeath*
83. malisone *curse*
84. ipse est causa mortis mee *he is the cause of my death*
85. war I *if I were* swyne *pig*
86. multi mirantur super me *many people would marvel at me*
87. ger *make* lurdane *villain* quhryne *squeal*

88. scribendo dentes sine de *for writing 'dentes' without a 'd'*
89. residuum omnium bonorum *all the rest of my worldly goods*
90. dispone *dispose*
91. cum tutela puerorum *with the guardianship of my children*
92. Ade *Adam* Kytte *Kitty* laif *rest*
93. raif *rant*
94. pro sepultura ordino *I arrange for my funeral*
95. on *in* gys *fashion* sa God me saif *may God save me*
96. non sicut more solito *not according to the usual practice*

89–90. 'My lord shall have all the rest of my worldly goods to dispose of as he pleases'.

13

In die mee sepulture
I will nane haif bot our awne gyng,
Et duos rusticos de rure
Berand a barell on a styng,   100
Drynkand and playand cop-out-evin,
Sicut egomet solebam.
Singand and gretand with hie stevin,
Potum meum cum fletu miscebam.

14

I will na preistis for me sing: 105
Dies illa, dies ire,
Na yit na bellis for me ring
Sicut semper solet fieri,
Bot a bag pipe to play a spryng
Et unum ail wosp *ante me;*   110
In stayd of baneris for to bring
Quatuor lagenas cervisie,
Within the graif to set sic thing
In modum crucis juxta me,
To fle the fendis than hardely sing   115
De terra plasmasti me.

97. in die mee sepulture *on the day of my funeral*
98. our awne gyng *our own group*
99. et duos rusticos de rure *and two peasants from the country*
100. berand *carrying* styng *pole*
101. drynkand *drinking* cop-out-evin *drain-the-cup*
102. sicut egomet solebam *just as I used to myself*
103. gretand *crying* hie stevin *loud voice*
104. potum meum cum fletu miscebam *I mixed my drink with tears*
105. preistis *priests*
106. dies illa, dies ire *that day, the day of wrath*
107. bellis *bells*
108. sicut semper solet fieri *as is always the custom*
109. spryng *jig*
110. et unum *and at the same time* ail wosp *sign of an ale house* ante me *in front of me*
111. in stayd *instead*
112. quatuor lagenas cervisie *four jugs of beer*
113. graif *grave* sic thing *such things*
114. in modum crucis juxta me *next to me in the shape of the cross*
115. fle *scare away* fendis *demons* than *then* hardely *boldly*
116. de terra plasmasti me *you have created me from the earth*

98. 'I want no one there except close friends'.
105. 'I will have no priests singing for me'.
111–4. 'Instead of banners bring four jugs of beer, and set these down next to me in the grave in the sign of the cross'.

Schir Johine the Ros, ane Thing Thair is Compild
(The Flyting of Dumbar and Kennedie)

The Flyting of Dumbar and Kennedie
Heir efter followis jocound and mirrie

1

Schir Johine the Ros, ane thing thair is compild
In generale be Kennedy and Quinting,
Quhilk hes thameself aboif the sternis styld.
Bot had thay maid of mannace ony mynting
In speciall, sic stryfe sould rys but stynting;   5
Howbeit with bost thair breistis wer als bendit
As Lucifer that fra the hevin discendit,
Hell sould nocht hyd thair harnis fra harmis hynting.

2

The erd sould trymbill, the firmament sould schaik,
And all the air in vennaum suddane stink,   10
And all the divillis of hell for redour quaik,
To heir quhat I suld wryt with pen and ynk;
For and I flyt, sum sege for schame sould sink,
The se sould birn, the mone sould thoill ecclippis,
Rochis sould ryfe, the warld sould hald no grippis,   15
Sa loud of cair the commoun bell sould clynk.

1. Schir Johine the Ros *Sir John Ross*   thing *document*   compild *composed*
2. in generale *in general terms*   be *by*
3. quhilk *who*   thameself *themselves*   aboif *above*   sternis *planets*   styld *praised*
4. manace . . . mynting *any attempt at threats*
5. in speciall *directed at individuals*   stryfe *conflict*   rys *arise*   but stynting *without stopping*
6. howbeit *although*   bost *boasting*   bendit *stretched with pride*
8. hyd *protect*   harnis *brains*   harmis hynting *receiving injury*
9. erd *earth*   trymbill *tremble*   firmament *vault of heaven*   schaik *shake*
10. in vennaum *with venom*   suddane *suddenly*
11. divillis *devils*   redour *terror*
13. and *if*   sege *man*
14. se *sea*   birn *burn*   mone *moon*   thoill ecclippis *suffer an eclipse*
15. rochis *rocks*   ryfe *split in two*   warld *world*   hald no grippis *fall apart*
16. of cair *for sorrow*   commoun *public*   clynk *clang*

3. 'Who have praised themselves in the highest possible terms'.

3

Bot wondir laith wer I to be ane baird.
Flyting to use richt gritly I eschame.
For it is nowthir wynnyng nor rewaird,
Bot tinsale baith of honour and of fame,   20
Incres of sorrow, sklander and evill name.
Yit mycht thay be sa bald in thair bakbytting,
To gar me ryme and rais the feynd with flytting
And throw all cuntreis and kinrikis thame proclame.

Quod Dumbar to Kennedy

4

Dirtin Dumbar, quhome on blawis thow thy boist,   25
Pretendand the to wryte sic skaldit skrowis?
Ramowd rebald, thow fall doun att the roist,
My laureat lettres at the and I lowis.
Mandrag, mymmerkin, maid maister bot in mows,
Thrys scheild trumpir with ane threidbair goun,   30
Say, 'Deo mercy', or I cry the doun,
And leif thy ryming, rebald, and thy rowis.

17. wondir laith *extremely reluctant*
   baird *bard; travelling poet*
18. I eschame *I am ashamed*
19. nowthir *neither*
   wynnyng *profit*
20. bot *but* tinsale *loss*
   fame *reputation*
21. incres *increase*
   sklander *slander*
22. bald *bold* bakbytting *backbiting*
23. gar *cause* ryme *compose*
   verses rais *call up* feynd *fiend*
24. cuntreis *countries*
   kinrikis *kingdoms*
   proclame *denounce* Quod
   Dumbar *Said Dunbar*
25. dirtin *filthy* blawis *blows*
   boist *boast*
26. pretendand the *taking it upon*
   yourself skaldit *scabby*
   skrowis *scrolls*
27. ramowd rebald *foul-mouthed*
   rascal roist *roast; feast [of*
   words]
28. laureat lettres *acclaimed verses*
   and *if* lowis *fire*
29. mandrag *mandrake*
   mymmerkin *dwarf*
   maister *master of arts* in
   mows *as a joke*
30. thrys *three times*
   scheild *exposed*
   trumpir *imposter* ane *one*
31. Deo mercy *mercy, for God's*
   sake cry the doun *will denounce*
   you
32. leif *give up* rowis *papers*

18. 'I am greatly ashamed to engage in flyting'.
25–8. 'Filthy Dunbar, to whom do you think you are boasting, taking it
   upon yourself to write such scabby scrolls? Foul-mouthed rascal, you
   will fall down at this feast of words if I fire my acclaimed verses at
   you'.

5

Dreid, dirtfast dearch, that thow hes dissobeyit
My cousing Quintene and my commissar.
Fantastik fule, trest weill thow sal be fleyit.   35
Ignorant elf, aip, owll irregular,
Skaldit skaitbird and commoun skamelar,
Wanfukkit funling, that natour maid ane yrle,
Baith Johine the Ros and thow sall squeill and skirle,
And evir I heir ocht of your making mair.   40

6

Heir I put sylence to the in all pairtis:
Obey and ceis the play that thow pretendis,
Waik walidrag and verlot of the cairtis,
Se sone thow mak my commissar amendis
And lat him lay sax leichis on thy lendis,   45
Meikly in recompansing of thi scorne,
Or thow sall ban the tyme that thow wes borne,
For Kennedy to the this cedull sendis.

Quod Kennedy to Dumbar

Juge in the nixt quha gat the war

7

Iersche brybour baird, vyle beggar with thy brattis,
Cuntbittin crawdoun, Kennedy, coward of kynd,   50

33. dreid *be afraid* dirtfast
dearch *filthy dwarf*
34. cousing *cousin*
commissar *deputy*
35. fantastik *deluded* fule *fool*
trest weill *rest assured*
fleyit *scared away*
36. aip *ape* irregular *lawless*
37. skaldit *scabby*
skaitbird *vulture*
skamelar *scavenger*
38. wanfukkit *misbegotten*
funling *foundling* natour *nature*
yrle *dwarf*
39. squeill *squeal* skirle *shriek*
40. and *if* ocht . . . mair *any
more* making *verse*
41. put sylence to the *silence you*
pairtis *respects*
42. ceis *cease* play *game*

pretendis *have undertaken*
43. waik *weak* walidrag *good-for-
nothing* verlot of the cairtis *cart
boy*
44. se *see that* mak . . .
amendis *compensate*
45. sax *six* leichis *lashes*
lendis *buttocks*
46. in recompansing *as
compensation*
47. ban *curse*
48. the *you* cedull *document*
Juge judge nixt *next* quha *who*
war *worse*
49. iersche *highland*
brybour *vagabond* baird *bard*
brattis *rags*
50. cuntbitten *impotent*
crawdoun *renegade; coward* of
kynd *by nature*

Evill farit and dryit, as Densmen on the rattis,
Lyk as the gleddis had on thy gulesnowt dynd,
Mismaid monstour, ilk mone owt of thy mynd,
Renunce, rebald, thy rymyng, thow bot royis.
Thy trechour tung hes tane ane Heland strynd,   55
Ane Lawland ers wald mak a bettir noyis.

8

Revin, raggit ruke, and full of rebaldrie,
Scarth fra scorpioun, scaldit in scurrilitie,
I se the haltane in thy harlotrie
And in to uthir science no thing slie,   60
Of every vertew voyd, as men may sie.
Quytclame clergie and cleik to the ane club,
Ane baird blasphemar in brybrie ay to be,
For wit and woisdome ane wisp fra the may rub.

9

Thow speiris, dastard, gif I dar with the fecht.   65
Ye, Dagone dowbart, thairof haif thow no dowt.
Quhairevir we meit, thairto my hand I hecht
To red thy rebald rymyng with a rowt.

51. evill farit *ugly* dryit *dried up*
Densmen *Danes* rattis *wheels*
52. lyk as *as if* gleddis *kites*
gulesnowt *yellow nose*
dyned *dined*
53. mismaid *deformed* ilk
mone *each moon*
54. renunce *give up* rebald *knave*
bot *only* royis *rave*
55. trechour *treacherous*
tung *tongue* tane *taken on*
Heland strynd *Highland sound*
56. Lawland *Lowland* ers *arse*
noyis *noise*
57. revin *raven* ruke *rook*
rebaldrie *obscenity*
58. scarth *monster* fra *[sprung]*
from scaldit *inflamed*
scurrilitie *coarse jokes*
59. haltane *haughty*

harlotrie *promiscuous lifestyle*
60. science *knowledge* no
thing *not at all* slie *skilled*
61. voyd *devoid; empty* sie *see*
62. quytclame clergie *give up*
learning cleik *grab*
63. blasphemar *evil speaking*
brybrie *destitution*
64. wisp *small bunch of straw*
rub *brush*
65. speiris *ask* dastard *coward*
gif *if* fecht *fight*
66. ye *yes* dagone *idolatrous*
dowbart *fool* dowt *doubt*
67. meit *meet* thairto my hand I
hecht *I pledge my hand to this;*
give my word
68. red *get rid of* with a rowt *at*
one stroke

62–4. 'Give up your attempts at learning and grab hold of a club, you
will always be a destitute, evil-speaking bard, for a wisp of straw would
be enough to brush away your wit and wisdom'.

Throw all Bretane it sal be blawin owt
How that thow, poysonit pelour, gat thy paikis. 70
With ane doig leich I schepe to gar the schowt,
And nowther to the tak knyfe, swerd nor aix.

10

Thow crop and rute of tratouris tressonable,
The fathir and moder of morthour and mischeif,
Dissaitfull tyrand with serpentis tung unstable, 75
Cukcald, cradoun, cowart and commoun theif,
Thow purpest for to undo our lordis cheif
In Paislay with ane poysone that wes fell,
For quhilk, brybour, yit sall thow thoill a breif.
Pelour, on the I sall it preif mysell. 80

11

Thocht I wald lie, thy frawart phisnomy
Dois manifest thy malice to all men.
Fy, tratour theif, fy, Ganyelon, fy, fy!
Fy, feyndly front far fowlar than ane fen,
My freyindis thow reprovit with thy pen. 85
Thow leis, tratour, quhilk I sall on the preif,
Suppois thy heid war armit tymis ten,
Thow sall recry it, or thy croun sall cleif.

69. Bretane *Brtain* blawin owt *proclaimed*
70. poysonit *venomous* pelour *plunderer* thy paikis *the thrashing due to you*
71. doig leich *dog leash* schepe *intend* gar *make*
72. nowther *neither* aix *axe*
73. crop and rute *supreme example* tratouris tressonable *treacherous traitors*
74. morthour *murder*
75. dissaitful *deceitful* tyrand *tyrant* tung *tongue*
76. cukcald *cuckold; deceived husband* cradoun *coward*
77. purpest for *intended* undo *destroy* lordis cheif *foremost lords*

78. Paislay *Paisley* poysone *poison* fell *deadly*
79. brybour *vagabond* yit *yet* thoill a breif *receive a summons*
80. pelour *criminal* preif *prove* mysell *myself*
81. thocht *although* frawart *ugly* phisnomy *face*
82. manifest *reveal*
83. fy *fie* Ganyelon *Ganelon*
84. feyndly front *fiendish forehead* fen *midden; dunghill*
85. freyindis *friends* reprovit *accused*
86. leis *lie* preif *prove*
87. suppois *even if* heid *head* armit tymis ten *ten times more protected*
88. recry *retract* croun *crown (of head)* cleif *split*

72. 'And take neither knife, sword, nor axe to you'.
80. 'Criminal, I shall prove the charge against you myself'.

12

Or thow durst move thy mynd malitius,
Thow saw the saill abone my heid up draw.   90
Bot Eolus, full woid, and Neptunus,
Mirk and moneles, us met with wind and waw,
And mony hundreth myll hyne cowd us blaw,
By Holland, Seland, Yetland and Northway coist,
In sey desert quahir we wer famist aw.   95
Yit come I hame, fals baird, to lay thy boist.

13

Thow callis the rethore with thy goldin lippis.
Na, glowrand, gaipand fule, thow art begyld.
Thow art bot gluntoch, with thy giltin hippis,
That for thy lounry mony a leisch hes fyld.   100
Wan-visaged widdefow, out of thy wit gane wyld,
Laithly and lowsy, als lathand as ane leik,
Sen thow with wirschep wald sa fane be styld,
Haill, soverane senyeour, thy bawis hingis throw thy breik.

14

Forworthin fule, of all the warld reffuse,   105
Quhat ferly is thocht thow rejoys to flyte?
Sic eloquence as thay in Erschry use,

89. or *before* durst *dared*
malitius *malicious*
90. up draw *raised*
91. Eolus *Aeolus* woid *stormy*
Neptunus *Neptune*
92. mirk *dark* moneles *without a moon* waw *waves*
93. myll *miles* hyne *from here*
cowd us blaw *blew us*
94. Seland *Zeeland*
Yetland *Shetland* Northway
coist *coast of Norway*
95. sey desert *empty sea* famist
aw *all starved*
96. hame *home* lay *put a stop to*
97. callis the *call yourself*
rethore *poet*
98. glowrand *staring*
gaipand *gawping*

begyld *deceived*
99. gluntoch *bare-kneed*
giltin *gilded*
100. lounry *villainy* leisch *lash*
hes fyld *has defiled*
101. wan-visaged *pale-faced*
widdefow *gallows-bird*
102. laithly *loathesome* lowsy *lice
ridden* lathand *worthless*
leik *leek*
103. wirschep *honour* wald sa
fane *want so much*
styld *addressed*
104. senyeour *lord* bawis *testicles*
hingis *are hanging* breik *breeches*
105. forworthin *deformed* of *by*
reffuse *rejected*
106. ferly *wonder*
107. sic *such* Erschry *Gaelic*

89-90. 'You waited until you saw me about to embark on a sea voyage
before you set in motion your malicious plan'.

In sic is sett thy thraward appetyte.
Thow hes full littill feill of fair indyte.
I tak on me, ane pair of Lowthiane hippis   110
Sall fairar Inglis mak and mair parfyte
Than thow can blabbar with thy Carrik lippis.

15

Bettir thow ganis to leid ane doig to skomer,
Pynit pykpuris pelour, than with thy maister pingill.
Thow lay full prydles in the peis this somer   115
And fane at evin for to bring hame a single,
Syne rubb it at ane uther auld wyvis ingle.
Bot now in winter for purteth thow art traikit,
Thow hes na breik to latt thy bellokis gyngill;
Beg the ane bratt, or, baird, thow sall go naikit.   120

16

Lene, larbar loungeour, lowsy in lisk and lonye,
Fy, skolderit skyn, thow art bot skyre and skrumple:
For he that rostit Lawrance had thy grunye.
And he that hid Sanct Johnis ene with ane wimple,
And he that dang Sanct Augustyne with ane rumple   125
Thy fowll front had, and he that Bartilmo flaid.
The gallowis gaipis eftir thy graceles gruntill,
As thow wald for ane haggeis, hungry gled.

108. thraward *perverse*
109. full *very*   feill of *feel for*
    indyte *writing*
110. tak on me *vow*
    Lowthaine *Lothian*   hippis *hips*
111. Inglis *English*   parfyte *perfect*
112. Carrik *Carrick*   lippis *lips*
113. bettir thow ganis *you are*
    better suited   skomer *defecate*
114. pynit pykpuris *emaciated*
    pickpocket   pingill *battle*
115. prydles *without pride*
    peis *peas*   somer *summer*
116. fane *happy*   evin *evening*
    single *small bundle of corn*
117. syne *then*   rubb it *prepare it*
    ingle *fire*
118. purteth *poverty*   traikit *worn out*
119. breik *breeches*   latt *stop*
    bellokis *testicles*   gyngill *jingling*
120. ane bratt *some rags*
    baird *bard*   naikit *naked*
121. lene *skinny*   larbar *impotent*
    loungeour *layabout*   lisk *groin*
    lonye *loin*
122. skolderit *scorched*
    skyre *lines*   skrumple *wrinkles*
123. rostit *roasted*
    Lawrance *Lawrence*
    grunye *snout*
124. Sanct Johnis ene *St John's*
    eyes   wimple *veil*
125. dang *hit*   Sanct Augustyne *St*
    Augustine   rumple *tail of a fish*
126. front *forehead*
    Bartilmo *Bartholomew*
    flaid *flayed*
127. gallowis *gallows*   gaipis *gapes*
    in hunger   gruntill *snout*
128. haggeis *haggis*   gled *kite*

17

Commirwarld crawdoun, na man comptis the ane kers.
Sweir swappit swanky, swynekeper ay for swaittis,   130
Thy commissar, Quintyne, biddis the cum kis his ers.
He luvis nocht sic ane forlane loun of laittis,
He sayis thow skaffis and beggis mair beir and aitis
Nor ony cripill in Karrik land abowt.
Uther pure beggaris and thow for wage debaittis,   135
Decrepit karlingis on Kennedy cryis owt.

18

Mater annuche I haif, I bid not fenyie,
Thocht thow, fowll trumpour, thus upoun me leid.
Corrupt carioun, he sall I cry my senyie.
Thinkis thow nocht, how thow come in grit neid,   140
Greitand in Galloway lyk to ane gallow breid,
Ramand and rolpand, beggand koy and ox?
I saw the thair in to thy wathemanis weid,
Quhilk wes nocht worth ane pair of auld gray sox.

19

Ersch katherene, with thy polk breik and rilling,   145
Thow and thy quene as gredy gleddis ye gang

129. commirwarld *burdensome*
   crawdoun *coward* comptis
   the *thinks you are worth*
   kers *cress*
130. sweir *lazy* swappit *big*
   swanky *fellow*
   swynekeper *swineherd*
   swaittis *small beer*
132. luvis *loves* forlane . . .
   laittis *despicable manners*
   loun *rascal*
133. skaffis *scrounge* beir *barley*
   aitis *oats*
134. nor *than*
135. uther *other* pure *poor* for wage
   debaittis *struggle for the spoils*
136. karlingis *old women* cryis
   owt *shout out*
137. mater annuche *enough*

   material bid *seek* fenyie *feign*
138. trumpour *cheat*
   upoun *about* leid *lied*
139. corrupt carioun *rotten corpse*
   he *loudly* senyie *war-cry*
140. thinkis *remember* come *came*
141. greitand *weeping* ane gallow
   breid *someone bound for the
   gallows*
142. ramand *shouting*
   rolpand *roaring* koy *cow*
143. wathemanis weid *outlaw's
   clothes*
144. sox *socks*
145. Ersche katherene *Highland
   robber* polk *sack* breik *misshapen*
   rilling *clumsy shoes*
146. quene *woman* gleddis *kites*
   gang *go*

137–8. 'I have enough material on you, I don't need to go inventing any,
even though you, foul cheat, have lied about me'.

With polkis to mylne, and beggis baith meill and schilling.
Thair is bot lys and lang nailis yow amang,
Fowll heggirbald, for henis thus will ye hang.
Thow hes ane perrellus face to play with lambis.   150
Ane thowsand kiddis, wer thay in faldis full strang,
Thy lymmair luke wald fle thame and thair damis.

20

In till ane glen thow hes, owt of repair,
Ane laithly luge that wes the lippir menis.
With the ane sowtaris wyfe, of blis als bair,   155
And lyk twa stalkaris steilis in cokis and henis.
Thow plukkis the pultre and scho pullis of the penis.
All Karrik cryis, 'God gif this dowsy be drownd!'
And quhen thow heiris ane guse cry in the glenis,
Thow thinkis it swetar than secrrind bell of sound.   160

21

Thow Lazarus, thow laithly lene tramort,
To all the warld thow may example be,
To luk upoun thy gryslie peteous port;
For hiddowis, haw and holkit is thyne ee,
Thy cheikbane bair and blaiknit is thy ble.   165

147. mylne *mill* beggis *beg*
meill *oatmeal* schilling *husks*
148. lys *lice* lang nailis *long nails*
149. heggirbald *villain* henis *hens*
150. perrellus *dangerous*
151. kiddis *kids; young goats*
faldis *enclosures*
152. lymmair luke *evil appearance*
fle *scare* damis *mothers*
153. in till *in* glen *glen; valley*
154. laithly luge *horrible hut* wes
the lipper menis *belonged to the*
lepers
155. sowtaris *shoemaker's* of blis
als bare *without any happiness*
156. twa *two* stalkaris *poachers*
steilis in *creep up on* cokis *cocks*
157. plukkis *snatch*
pultre *poultry* pullis of the
penis *plucks out the feathers*
158. gif *grant* dowsy *idiot*
159. guse *goose*
160. swetar *sweeter* secrrind
bell *sacring bell*
161. laithly *loathsome* lene
skinny tramort *putrefying*
corpse
163. peteous *deplorable*
port *appearance*
164. haw *leaden* holkit *hollow*
ee *eyes*
165. thy cheikbane bair *your*
cheekbones protrude
blaiknit *pale* ble *complexion*

149–52. 'Foul hedge-creeper, you will hang for stealing hens. You have
too dangerous a face to go playing with the lambs. Your evil
appearance would scare away a thousand kids and their mothers even if
they were in the strongest enclosures'.
160. 'You think it is a sweeter sound than the sacring bell'.

Thy choip, thy choll garris men for to leif chest,
Thy gane, it garris us think that we mon de.
I conjure the, thow hungert Heland gaist.

22
The larbar lukis of thy lang lenye craig,
Thy pure pynit thrott, peilit and owt of ply,   170
Thy skolderit skin, hewd lyk ane saffrone bag,
Garris men dispyt thar flesche, thow spreit of Gy.
Fy, feyndly front, fy, tykis face, fy, fy!
Ay loungand lyk ane loikman on ane ledder,
With hingit luik, ay wallowand upone wry,   175
Lyk to ane stark theif glowrand in ane tedder.

23
Nyse nagus nipcaik with thy schulderis narrow,
Thow lukis lowsy, loun of lounis aw,
Hard hurcheoun hirpland, hippit as ane harrow,
Thy rigbane rattillis and thy ribbis on raw,   180
Thy hanchis hirklis with hukebanis harth and haw,
Thy laithly lymis ar lene as ony treis.
Obey, theif baird, or I sall brek thy gaw.
Fowll carrybald, cry mercy on thy kneis.

166. choip *jaw* choll *jowl*
   garris *makes* leif chest *live
   sinlessly*
167. gane *face* mon de *must die*
168. conjure the *tell you*
   hungert *starving*
   Heland *Highland* gaist *ghost*
169. larbar *weak* lukis *looks*
   lenye craig *skinny neck*
170. pure *pitiful* pynit
   thrott *scraggy throat*
   peilit *meagre* ply *condition*
171. skolderit *scorched*
   hewd *coloured* saffrone *saffron*
172. dispyt *despise* spreit of
   Gy *spirit of Guy*
173. feyndly front *fiendish
   forehead* tykis face *mongrel face*
174. loikman *hangman*
   ledder *ladder*

175. hingit luik *hung expression*
   wallowand upone wry *twisted to
   one side*
176. stark *dyed-in-the-wool*
   glowrand *staring* tedder *noose*
177. nyse nagus nipcaik *foolish,
   stingy cake pincher*
178. loun of lounis aw *wretch of
   all wretches; consummate wretch*
179. hurcheoun *hedgehog*
   hirpland *limping* hippit *with
   hips* harrow *hare*
180. rigbane *backbone* on raw *in a
   row*
181. hanchis hirklis *haunches
   crouch together* hukebanis *hip-
   bones* harth *rough* haw *blue*
182. lymis *limbs* treis *twigs*
183. brek thy gaw *break your spirit*
184. carrybald *monster*

24

Thow pure, pynhippit, ugly averill,   185
With hurkland banis holkand throw thy hyd,
Reistit and crynit as hangitman on hill,
And oft beswakkit with ane ourhie tyd,
Quhilk brewis mekle barret to thy bryd.
Hir cair is all to clenge thy cabroch howis,   190
Quhair thow lyis sawsy in saphron, bak and syd,
Powderit with prymros, savrand all with clovis.

25

Forworthin wirling, I warne the, it is wittin
How, skyttand skarth, thow hes the hurle behind.
Wan wraiglane wasp, ma wormis hes thow beschittin   195
Nor thair is gers on grund or leif on lind.
Thocht thow did first sic foly to me fynd,
Thow sall agane with ma witnes than I.
Thy gulsoch gane dois on thy bak it bind,
Thy hostand hippis lattis nevir thy hos go dry.   200

26

Thow held the burch lang with ane borrowit goun
And ane caprowsy, barkit all with sweit,

185. pynhippit *bony hipped*
averill *old cart-horse*
186. hurkland banis *buckling*
bones holkand *poking* hyd *hide;*
skin
187. reistit *smoke-dried*
crynit *shrivelled* hangit
man *hanged man*
188. beswakkit *drenched*
ourhic *too high* tyd *tide*
189. brewis *causes* barret *distress*
bryd *bride*
190. clenge *clean* cabroch *lean*
howis *houghs*
191. sawsy in saphron *in a saffron*
sauce
192. powderit with
prymros *sprinkled with powdered*
primrose savrand *flavouring*
clovis *cloves*

193. forworthin wirling *deformed*
wretch wittin *known*
194. skyttand skarth *shitting*
monster hurle behind *diarrhoea*
195. wan *wretched*
wraiglane *wriggling* ma *more*
beschittin *excreted*
196. nor *than* gers *grass* lind *tree*
197. fynd *attribute*
198. thow sall agane *you shall have*
it back again witnes *witnesses*
199. gulsoch gane *jaundiced ugly face*
200. hostand *spluttering* lattis
nevir *never allow* hos *hose;*
men's stockings
201. held *frequented*
burch *borough; town* lang *for a*
long time goun *gown*
202. caprowsy *little cape*
barkit *hardened* sweit *sweat*

199. 'Your ugly jaundiced face makes the filth stick to your own back'.

And quhen the laidis saw the sa lyk a loun,
Thay bickerit the with mony bae and bleit.
Now upaland thow leivis on rubbit quheit, 205
Oft for ane caus thy burdclaith neidis no spredding,
For thow hes nowthir for to drink nor eit,
Bot lyk ane berdles baird that had no bedding.

27

Strait Gibbonis air, that nevir ourstred ane hors,
Bla, berfute berne, in bair tyme wes thow borne. 210
Thow bringis the Carrik clay to Edinburgh cors,
Upoun thy botingis hobland, hard as horne.
Stra wispis hingis owt, quhair that the wattis ar worne.
Cum thow agane to skar us with thy strais,
We sall gar scale our sculis all the to scorne, 215
And stane the up the calsay quhair thow gais.

28

Of Edinburgh the boyis as beis owt thrawis,
And cryis owt, 'Hay, heir cumis our awin queir clerk!'
Than fleis thow lyk ane howlat chest with crawis,
Quhill all the brachis at thy botingis dois bark. 220
Than carlingis cryis, 'Keip curches in the merk.
Our gallowis gaipis, lo, quhair ane greceles gais!'

203. laidis *boys* the *you* loun *loon*
204. bickerit *attacked* bae and bleit *baa and bleat (like sheep)*
205. upaland *in the country* leivis *live* rubbit quheit *rubbed wheat*
206. for ane cause *for one good reason* burdclaith *tablecloth*
208. berdles *beardless*
209. Strait Gibbonis air *Stingy Gibbon's heir* ourstred *rode*
210. bla *blue with cold* berfute *barefoot man* bair tyme *hard times*
211. cors *cross*
212. botingis *boots* hobland *hobbling*

213. stra *straw* wispis *wisps* hingis *hang* wattis *melts*
214. skar *scare* strais *straw*
215. gar scale *dismiss* sculis *schools*
216. stane the *hit you with stones* calsay *pavement* gais *walk*
217. beis *bees* thrawis *swarm*
219. howlat *owl* chest with *chased by* crawis *crows*
220. brachis *hounds*
221. carlingis *old women* curches *head-dresses* in the merk *in the dark; hidden*
222. gallowis *washing-line* gaipis *is empty* greceles *evil man*

214. 'We shall dismiss our schools to allow all the children to mock you'.
221–4. 'Then the old women cry out: 'Keep your fine clothes hidden. Our washing-lines are gaping empty. Look, there goes the evil man!' Another one says, 'I see he needs a shirt, I advise you, neighbour, take your linen clothes off the line'.

Ane uthir sayis, 'I se him want ane sark,
I reid yow, cummer, tak in your lynning clais.'

29

Than rynis thow doun the gait with gild of boyis,   225
And all the toun tykis hingand in thy heilis.
Of laidis and lownis thair rysis sic ane noyis
Quhill runsyis rynis away with cairt and quheilis
And cager aviris castis bayth coillis and creilis,
For rerd of the and rattling of thy butis.   230
Fische wyvis cryis 'Fy!' and castis doun skillis and skeilis,
Sum claschis the, sum cloddis the on the cutis.

30

Loun, lyk Mahoun, be boun me till obey,
Theif, or in greif mischeif sall the betyd.
Cry grace, tykis face, or I the chece and fley,   235
Oule, rare and yowle, I sall defowll thy pryd,
Peilit gled, baith fed and bred of bichis syd,
And lyk ane tyk, purspyk, quhat man settis by the?
Forflittin, countbittin, beschittin, barkit hyd,
Clym-ledder, fyle-tedder, foule edder, I defy the.   240

223. him want *he lacks* sark *shirt*
224. reid *advise*
      cummer *neighbour* lynning
      clais *linen clothes*
225. rynis *run* gait *road*
      gild *clamour*
226. tykis *tykes; stray dogs* heilis *heels*
227. lownis *ruffians* sic *such*
228. quhill *until* runsyis *horses*
      rynis *run* cairt *cart*
      quheilis *wheels*
229. cager aviris *peddlars' cart-
      horses* castis *throw off* coillis
      and creilis *coal and baskets*
230. rerd *noise* butis *boots*
231. skillis *baskets* skeilis *tubs*
232. sum *one* claschis *strikes*
      cloddis *throws clods* cutis *ankles*
233. Mahoun *Muhammad*
      boun *ready* me till obey *to obey
      me*

234. greif *distress* the betyd *befall
      you*
235. grace *mercy* chece *chase*
      fley *frighten you off*
236. oule *owl* rare *screech*
      yowle *howl* defowll *trample
      down*
237. peilit gled *plucked kite*
      bred *nourished* bichis *bitch's*
238. purspyk *pickpocket* settis by
      the *respects you*
239. forflitten *abused*
      countbitten *impotent*
      beschitten *filthy* barkit
      hyd *tanned hide*
240. clym-ledder *climber of the
      gallows ladder* fyle-
      tedder *despoiler of the hangman's
      noose* foule edder *foul snake*

31

Mauch muttoun, byt-buttoun, peilit gluttoun, air to Hilhous,
Rank beggar, ostir-dregar, flay-fleggar in the flet.
Chittirlilling, ruch rilling, lik-schilling in the milhous,
Baird rehator, theif of nator, fals tratour, feyindis gett,
Filling of tauch, rak-sauch, cry crauch, thow art
  oursett.   245
Muttoun-dryver, girnall-ryver, yadswyvar, fowll fell the!
Herretyk, lunatyk, purspyk, carlingis pet,
Rottin crok, dirtin dok, cry cok, or I sall quell the!

Quod Dumbar to Kennedy

241. mauch muttoun *maggoty sheep* byt-buttoun *button-biter* peilit gluttoun *destitute glutton* air to Hilhous *heir to Hillhouse*
242. rank *out-and-out* ostir-dregar *oyster-dredger* flay-fleggar in the flet *chasing your own fleas in the hall*
243. chittirlilling *pig's guts* ruch rilling *shaggy shoes* lik-schilling *husk-licker*
244. baird rehator *villainous bard* of nator *by nature* feyindis gett *devil's spawn*
245. filling of tauch *lump of animal fat* rak-sauch *gallows-bird* cry crauch *admit defeat* oursett *conquered*
246. muttoun dryver *sheep-stealer* girnall-ryver *granary-raider* yadswyvar *mare-buggerer* fowll fell the *a curse upon you*
247. herretyk *heretic* lunatyk *lunatic* purspyk *pickpocket* carlingis pet *old woman's fart*
248. rottin crok *diseased ewe* dirtin dok *dirty arse* cry cok *admit defeat* quell *destroy*

Schir, I Complane of Injuris

1

Schir, I complane of injuris:
A refing sonne of rakyng Muris
Hes magellit my making throw his malis
And present it in to yowr palis.
Bot sen he ples with me to pleid,   5
I sall him knawin mak hyne to Calis,
Bot gif yowr henes it remeid.

2

That fulle dismemberit hes my meter
And poysonid it with strang salpeter,
With rycht defamows speiche of lordis,   10
Quhilk with my collouris all discordis,
Quhois crewall sclander servis ded,
And in my name all leis recordis.
Your grace beseik I of remeid.

3

He has indorsit myn indyting   15
With versis of his awin hand wryting,
Quhairin baithe sclander is and tressoun.

1. schir *sir* complane *complain* injuris *injustices*
2. refing *thieving* sonne *son* rakyng Muris *the vagabond Mure*
3. magellit *mangled* making *poetry* malis *wickedness*
4. present *presented* palis *palace*
5. sen *since* ples *wants* pleid *dispute*
6. knawin *notorious* hyne *from here* Calis *Calais*
7. bot gif *unless* henes *highness* remeid *remedies*
8. fulle *fool* meter *verse*
9. poysonid *poisoned* strang salpeter *strong saltpetre*
10. rycht defamows *very defamatory* speiche *speech*
11. quhilk *which* collouris *style* discordis *disagrees*
12. crewall *cruel* sclander *slander* servis ded *deserves the death penalty*
13. leis *lies* recordis *relates*
14. beseik I *I beseech you* of remeid *for redress*
15. indorsit *written on the back of* indyting *poetry*
16. awin *own*

5–7. 'But since he wants to dispute with me, I shall make his name notorious from here to Calais, unless your highness remedies the situation'.
11. 'Which is completely at odds with my style'.
13. 'And relates all these lies in my name'.

Of ane wod fuill, far owt of seasoun,
He wantis nocht bot a rowndit heid,
For he has tynt baith wit and ressoun.   20
Yowr grace beseik I of remeid.

4

Punes him for his deid culpabile,
Or gar deliver him a babile,
That Cuddy Rug, the Drumfres fuill,
May him resave agane this Yuill,   25
All roundit, in to yallow and reid,
That ladis may bait him lyk a buill,
For that to me war sum remeid.

18. wod fuill *mad fool*
19. wantis nocht *lacks nothing*
    rowndit heid *cropped head*
20. tynt *lost*   baith *both*
22. punes *punish*   deid
    culpabile *shameful deed*
23. gar *cause*   babile *fool's sceptre*

24. that *so that*
    Drumfres *Dumfries*
25. resave *welcome*
    Yuill *Christmas*
26. roundit *close-cropped*
    yallow *yellow*   reid *red*
27. ladis *boys*   buill *bull*

18–19. 'He's only lacking the close-cropped head for him to look like a
    mad fool, well outwith the season for it'.
23. 'Or have him given a fool's sceptre'.

Quhy Will Ye, Merchantis of Renoun

1

Quhy will ye, merchantis of renoun,
Lat Edinburgh, your nobill toun,
For laik of reformatioun
The commone proffeitt tyine and fame?
 Think ye not schame,   5
That onie uther regioun
Sall with dishonour hurt your name?

2

May nane pas throw your principall gaittis,
For stink of haddockis and of scattis,
For cryis of carlingis and debaittis,   10
For feusum flyttingis of defame.
 Think ye not schame,
Befoir strangeris of all estaittis,
That sic dishonour hurt your name?

3

Your Stinkand Stull, that standis dirk, 15
Haldis the lycht fra your parroche kirk.
Your foirstair makis your housis mirk,
Lyk na cuntray bot heir at hame.
 Think ye not schame,
Sa litill polesie to work,   20
In hurt and sklander of your name?

1. renoun *distinction*
2. lat *let*
3. laik *lack*
4. tyine *lose* fame *reputation*
6. onie *any*
8. gaittis *streets*
9. scattis *skates (fish)*
10. carlingis *old women*
 debaittis *arguments*
11. feusum *foul* flyttingis *abusive exchanges* of defame *defamatory*

13. estaittis *ranks*
14. sic *such*
15. Stinkand Stull *Stinking Style*
 dirk *dark*
16. haldis *keeps* lycht *light*
 parroche kirk *parish church*
17. foirstair *external staircase*
 mirk *gloomy*
18. cuntray *country* hame *home*
20. polesie *improvement*
21. sklander *slander*

4. 'Lose the prosperity of the community and its good reputation'
8. 'No one can pass through your main streets'.

4

At your hie croce, quhar gold and silk
Sould be, thair is bot crudis and milk;
And at your trone bot cokill and wilk,
Pansches, pudingis of Jok and Jame.   25
　　Think ye not schame,
Sen as the world sayis that ilk,
In hurt and sclander of your name?

5

Your commone menstrallis hes no tone
Bot 'Now the day dawis' and 'Into Joun'.   30
Cunningar men man serve Sanct Cloun,
And nevir to uther craftis clame.
　　Think ye not schame,
To hald sic mowaris on the moyne,
In hurt and sclander of your name?   35

6

Tailyouris, soutteris and craftis vyll
The fairest of your streitis dois fyll,
And merchandis at the Stinkand Styll
Ar hamperit in ane hony came.
　　Think ye not schame   40
That ye have nether witt nor wyll,
To win yourself ane bettir name?

22. hie *high*　croce *market cross*
23. crudis *curds; the cheese part of milk*
24. Trone *weighing house*
　　bot *only*　cokill and wilk *cockles and whelks*
25. pansches *tripe*
　　pudingis *sausages*
27. sen *since*　ilk *same*
29. commone *public*
　　menstrallis *minstrals; musicians*
　　tone *tune*
30. dawis *dawns*　Joun *June*

31. cunningar *more skilfull*
　　man *must*　Sanct Cloun *St Cloun*
32. clame *lay claim*
34. hald *employ*　mowaris on the moyne *howlers at the moon*
36. tailyouris *tailors*
　　soutteris *cobblers*　vyll *base; vile*
37. dois fyll *defile*
39. hamperit *cramped*　hony came *honeycomb*
41. witt *wisdom*　wyll *desire*

27. 'Since the whole world says the same thing'.

7

Your burgh of beggeris is ane nest,
To schout thai swentyouris will not rest.
All honest folk they do molest,   45
Sa piteuslie thai cry and rame.
    Think ye not schame,
That for the poore hes nothing drest,
In hurt and sclander of your name?

8

Your proffeit daylie dois incres,   '   50
Your godlie workis les and les.
Through streittis nane may mak progres,
For cry of cruikit, blind and lame.
    Think ye not schame,
That ye sic substance dois possess,   55
And will not win ane bettir name?

9

Sen for the court and the Sessioun,
The great repair of this regioun
Is in your burgh, thairfoir be boun
To mend all faultis that ar to blame,   60
    And eschew schame.
Gif thai pas to ane uther toun,
Ye will decay and your great name.

---

44. thai swentyouris *those*
    vagabonds
46. piteuslie *pitifully*   rame *shout*
48. hes nothing drest *no provision*
    has been made
50. incres *increase*
51. godlie workis *good deeds*
    les *less*
52. mak progres *proceed*
53. cruikit *crippled*

55. substance *riches*
57. sen for *because*
    Sessioun *Court of Session*
58. repair *resort*
59. boun *prepared*
60. mend *correct*   faultis *defects*
61. eschew *avoid*
62. gif *if*
63. decay *decline*

43–4. 'Your burgh is a nest of beggars, and those vagabonds will not
    stop shouting'.
51. 'Your good deeds become fewer and fewer'.
57–60. 'Since the whole region resorts to your town, because the court
    and the Court of Session are here, be prepared therefore to correct all
    the defects for which you are to blame'.

10

Thairfoir strangeris and leigis treit,
Tak not over mekill for thair meit,   65
And gar your merchandis be discreit.
That na extortiounes be, proclame
   All fraud and schame.
Keip ordour and poore nighbouris beit,
That ye may gett ane bettir name.   70

11

Singular proffeit so dois yow blind,
The common proffeit gois behind.
I pray that lord remeid to fynd
That deit into Jerusalem,
   And gar yow schame,   75
That sumtyme ressoun may yow bind,
For to win bak to yow guid name.

64. leigis *loyal subjects*
65. tak *charge* over mekill *too much* meit *food*
66. gar *make* discreit *of sound judgment*
67. that *so that* extortiounes *extortions*
69. ordour *order* beit *assist*

71. singular proffeit *private gain*
72. common proffeit *the good of the community* gois behind *is disregarded*
73. remeid *remedy*
74. deit *died*
75. schame *feel shame*
76. ressoun *good sense* bind *govern*

64. 'Therefore welcome strangers and loyal subjects'.
67–8. 'Publicly proclaim all fraud and shameful behaviour in order to avoid extortion'.

This Nycht in My Sleip I wes Agast

1

This nycht in my sleip I wes agast:
Me thocht the Devill wes tempand fast
The peple with aithis of crewaltie,
Sayand, as throw the mercat he past,
'Renunce thy God and cum to me'.   5

2

Me thocht as he went throw the way
Ane preist sweirit be God verey
Quhilk at the alter ressavit he;
'Thow art my clerk', the Devill can say,
'Renunce thy God and cum to me'.   10

3

Than swoir ane courtyour, mekle of pryd,
Be Chrystis windis bludy and wyd,
And be his harmes wes rent on tre;
Than spak the Devill hard him besyd,
'Renunce thy God and cum to me'.   15

4

Ane merchand his geir as he did sell
Renuncit his pairt of hevin and hell;
The Devill said, 'Welcum mot thow be,
Thow sal be merchand for mysell;
Renunce thy God and cum to me'.   20

---

1. nycht *night*
2. me thocht *it seemed to me*
   tempand *tempting*
3. aithis of crewaltie *violent oaths*
4. sayand *saying* mercat *market
   place* past *passed*
5. renunce *renounce*
7. sweirit *swore* verey *true*
8. quhilk *whom* ressavit *greeted*
9. clerk *cleric* can say *said*

11. courtyour *courtier*
    mekle *great* pryd *pride*
12. Chrystis windis *Christ's
    wounds* wyd *wide*
13. harmes *pains* rent *torn apart*
    tre *cross*
14. hard *close*
16. merchand *merchant* geir *wares*
18. mot *may*
19. mysell *myself*

7. 'A priest swore by the one true God'.
13. 'And by his pains, who was torn apart on the cross'.
18–19. 'The Devil said, "You are welcome, you shall be my very own
    merchant" '.

5

Ane goldsmith said, 'The gold is sa fyne
That all the workmanschip I tyne;
The Feind ressaif me gif I le'.
'Think on', quod the Devill, 'that thow art myne;
Renunce thy God and cum to me'.   25

6

Ane tailyour said, 'In all this toun
Be thair ane better weilmaid goun,
I gif me to the Feynd all fre'.
'Gramercy telyour', said Mahoun,
'Renunce thy God and cum to me'.   30

7

Ane sowttar said, 'In gud effck,
Nor I be hangit be the nek
Gife bettir butis of ledder ma be'.
'Fy', quod the Feynd, 'thow sairis of blek;
Ga clenge the clene and cum to me'.   35

8

Ane baxstar sayd, 'I forsaik God
And all his werkis evin and od,
Gif fairar stuff neidis to be'.
The Dyvill luche and on him cowld nod:
'Renunce thy God and cum to me'.   40

21. fyne *good*
22. tyne *lose*
23. ressaif *take*   gif *if*   le *lie*
26. tailyour *tailor*
27. be thair *if there is*   weilmaid
    goun *skilfully made gown*
28. gif me *give myself up*   all
    fre *freely*
29. gramercy *thank you*
31. sowttar *shoemaker*   in gud
    effek *in truth*
32. nor *may*   hangit *hung*

33. gife *if*   butis *boots*
    ledder *leather*
34. quod *said*   sairis *smell*
    blek *polish*
35. clenge the clene *scrub yourself
    clean*
36. baxstar *baker*
37. werkis *works*   evin and
    od *every one*
38. neidis *needs*
39. luche *laughed*   on him cowld
    nod *nodded to him*

22. 'That all my labour is lost'.
38. 'If anyone ever needs better stuff than this'.

9

Ane fleschour swoir be the sacrament
And be Chrystis blud maist innocent,
Nevir fatter flesch saw man with e:
The Devill said, 'Hald on thy intent;
Renunce thy God and cum to me'.　　　　45

10

The maltman sais, 'I God forsaik,
And that the Devill of hell me taik
Gif ony bettir malt may be,
And of this kill I haif inlaik'.
'Renunce thy God and cum to me'.　　　　50

11

Ane browstar swoir the malt wes ill,
Baith reid and reikit on the kill,
That, 'It will be na aill for me,
Ane boll will nocht sex gallonis fill'.
'Renunce thy God and cum to me'.　　　　55

12

The smyth swoir, 'Be rude and raip,
In till a gallowis mot I gaip
Gif I ten dayis wan pennyis thre,
For with that craft I can nocht thraip'.
'Renunce thy God and cum to me'.　　　　60

41. fleschour *butcher*
42. blud *blood*　maist *most*
43. e *eye*
44. intent *purpose*
46. maltman *maltster*　sais *says*
49. kill *kiln*　inlaik *shortcoming*
51. browstar *brewer*　ill *bad*
52. reid *red*　reikit *fumigated*

53. that *so that*　aill *ale*
54. boll *measure*　sex *six*
56. smyth *blacksmith*　rude *cross*
　　raip *rope*
57. gaip *gape*
58. wan *earn*
59. thraip *struggle on*

44. 'The Devil said, "Hold onto that thought" '.
47. 'And swear that the Devil of hell can take me'.
49. 'And if my kiln is deficient in any way'.
54. 'One measure will not produce six gallons'.
56–8. 'May I hang open-mouthed on the gallows if I earn as much as three pennies in ten days'.

13

Ane menstrall said, 'The Feind me ryfe
Gif I do ocht bot drynk and swyfe'.
The Devill said, 'Hardly mot it be,
Exers that craft in all thy lyfe,
Renunce thy God and cum to me'.   65

14

Ane dysour said with wirdis of stryfe
The Devill mot stik him with a knyfe
Bot he kest up fair syisis thre.
The Devill said, 'Endit is thy lyfe;
Renunce thy God and cum to me'.   70

15

Ane theif said, 'God, that evir I chaip,
Nor ane stark widdy gar me gaip,
Bot I in hell for geir wald be'.
The Devill said, 'Welcum in a raip.
Renunce thy God and cum to me'.   75

16

The fische wyffis flett and swoir with granis
And to the feind, saule, flesch and banis
Thay gaif thame with ane schowt on hie.
The Devill said, 'Welcum all att anis.
Renunce thy God and cum to me'.   80

61. menstrall *minstrel* me
ryfe *tear me apart*
62. ocht bot *anything except*
swyfe *copulate*
63. hardly mot it be *so be it*
64. exers *practise*
66. dysour *gambler* wirdis of
stryfe *fighting words*
67. stik *stab*
68. bot *unless* kest up *threw*
syisis *sixes* thre *three*
69. endit *ended*

71. chaip *escape*
72. stark *strong* widdy *withy*
gar *make*
73. geir *wealth*
74. raip *rope*
76. fische wyffis *fish-wives*
flett *spoke abusively*
granis *groans*
77. saule *soul* banis *bones*
78. gaif thame *gave themselves*
schout on hie *loud shout*
79. all att anis *all together*

71–3. 'A thief said, "God, may I always manage to escape, and don't
ever let me hang open-mouthed from a strong withy, unless I am to be
wealthy in hell" '.

17

Me thocht the devillis als blak as pik
Solistand wer as beis thik,
Ay tempand folk with wayis sle,
Rownand to Robene and to Dik,
'Renunce thy God and cum to me'.   85

81. devillis *devils* als *as* pik *pitch*
82. solistand *inciting* wer *trouble*
    beis thik *busy as bees*

83. tempand *tempting* wayis
    sle *devious ways*
84. rownand *whispering*
    Robene *Robin* Dik *Dick*

Ane Murlandis Man of Uplandis Mak

1

Ane murlandis man of uplandis mak
At hame thus to his nychtbour spak:
'Quhat tydingis, gossep, peax or weir?'
The tother rownit in his eir:
'I tell yow this undir confessioun;   5
Bot laitly lichtit of my meir
I come of Edinburch fra the Sessioun.'

2

'Quhat tythingis hard ye thair, I pray yow?'
The tother answerit, 'I sall say yow,
Keip this all secreit, gentill brother.   10
Is na man thair that trestis ane uther.
Ane commoun doar of transgressioun
Of innocent folkis prevenis a futher:
Sic tydingis hard I at the Sessioun.

3

'Sum with his fallow rownis him to pleis,   15
That wald for invy byt of his neis;
His fa sum by the oxstar leidis;

1. murlandis *from the moors;*
   country uplandis mak *rustic*
   appearance
2. hame *home*
   nychtbour *neighbour* spak *spoke*
3. quhat *what* tydingis *news*
   gossep *neighbour* weir *war*
4. rownit *whispered* eir *ear*
5. undir confessioun *in confidence*
6. laitly *recently*
   lichtit *dismounted* meir *mare*
7. Edinburch *Edinburgh*
   Sessioun *law courts*
8. hard *heard* pray *ask*

9. tother *other* say *tell*
10. gentill *noble*
11. trestis *trusts*
12. ane *one* doar of
    transgressioun *wrongdoer*
13. prevenis *gets the better*
    futher *cartload; large number*
14. sic *such*
15. sum *one* fallow *companion*
    pleis *please*
16. invy *envy* byt of *bite off*
    neis *nose*
17. fa *enemy* oxstar *arm*
    leidis *leads*

6–7. 'I have come from the law courts in Edinburgh and have only just
    dismounted from my mare'.
11. 'There isn't a single man there who trusts another one'.
13. 'Gets the better of a whole cartload of innocent people'.
15–16. 'One man whispers with his companion to please him when in
    reality he would like to bite off his nose with envy'.

Sum patteris with his mowth on beidis
That hes his mynd all on oppressioun;
Sum beckis full law and schawis bair heidis,   20
Wald luke full heich war not the Sessioun.

4

'Sum bydand the law layis land in wed;
Sum super expendit gois to his bed;
Sum speidis for he in court hes menis.
Of parcialitie sum complenis,   25
How feid and favour flemis discretioun;
Sum speikis full fair and falsly fenis.
Sic tythingis hard I at the Sessioun.

5

Sum castis summondis and sum exceptis;
Sum standis besyd and skaild law keppis;   30
Sum is continuit, sum wynnis, sum tynis;
Sum makis him mirry at the wynis;
Sum is put out of his possessioun;
Sum herreit and on creddens dynis.
Sic tydingis hard I at the Sessioun.   35

---

18. patteris *mutters*
mowth *mouth* beidis *rosary beads*
19. oppressioun *evil deeds*
20. beckis *bow* law *low*
schawis *show* bair heidis *bare heads*
21. luke *look* heich *high*
22. bydand *awaiting* layis *puts*
wed *mortgage*
23. super expendit *bankrupt*
24. speidis *succeeds* menis *friends*
25. parcialitie *favouritism*

complenis *complains*
26. feid *hatred* flemis *drive out*
discretioun *judgement*
27. fenis *deceives*
29. castis *reject*
summondis *summonses*
exceptis *object*
30. besyd *nearby*
skaild *fragments* keppis *catches*
31. continuit *adjourned* tynis *loses*
32. mirry *merry* wynis *wine*
34. herreit *is reduced to poverty*
on creddens dynis *dines on credit*

18. 'One man mutters aloud as he says his rosary who is really intent on evil deeds'.
20–1. 'Some who bow very low and respectfully take off their hats would be looking very haughty if it were not for the courts'.
22. 'One man has to mortgage his land as he waits for the law to take its course'.
30. 'One man stands nearby and picks up some fragments of law'.

6

Sum sweiris and forsaikis God;
Sum in ane lambskin is ane tod;
Sum in his toung his kyndnes tursis;
Sum cuttis throttis, and sum pykis pursis;
Sum gois to gallous with processioun; 40
Sum sanis the sait, and sum thame cursis.
Sic tydingis hard I at the Sessioun.

7

Religious men of divers placis
Cumis thair to wow and se fair facis;
Baith Carmeleitis and Cordilleris 45
Cumis thair to genner and get ma freiris,
And ar unmyndfull of thair professioun.
The yungar at the eldar leiris.
Sic tydingis hard I at the Sessioun.

8

Thair cumis yung monkis of he complexioun, 50
Of devoit mynd, luve and affectioun,
And in the courte thair hait flesche dantis,
Full faderlyk with pechis and pantis;
Thay ar so humill of intercessioun,
All mercyfull wemen thair eirandis grantis. 55
Sic tydingis hard I at the Sessioun.

36. sweiris *swears*
forsaikis *renounces*
37. tod *fox*
38. toung *tongue* tursis *packs up*
39. cuttis throttis *cuts throats*
pykis pursis *picks pockets*
40. gois *goes* gallous *gallows*
41. sanis *blesses* sait *court*
cursis *curses*
43. divers *different* placis *places*
44. cumis *come* wow *woo* se *see*
facis *faces*
45. Carmeleitis *Carmelites*

Cordilleris *Franciscans*
46. genner *engender* get *beget*
ma *more* freiris *friars*
48. yungar *younger* leiris *learns*
50. monkis *monks* he *rosy*
51. devoit *pious*
52. hait *hot* dantis *subdue*
53. faderlyk *fatherly* pechis *puffs*
54. humill of intercessioun *humble
in their entreaties*
55. wemen *women*
eirandis *business*

38. 'One man is kind only in his words'.
48. 'The younger one learns from his elders'.
55. 'All mercifull women consent to their business'.

Blyth Aberdeane, Thow Beriall of all Tounis

1

Blyth Aberdeane, thow beriall of all tounis,
The lamp of bewtie, bountie and blythnes,
Unto the heaven ascendit thy renoun is
Of vertew, wisdome and of worthines;
He nottit is thy name of nobilnes.   5
Into the cuming of oure lustie quein,
The wall of welth, guid cheir and mirrines,
Be blyth and blisfull, burgh of Aberdein.

2

And first hir mett the burges of the toun,
Richelie arrayit, as become thame to be;   10
Of quhom they cheset four men of renoun,
In gounes of velvot, young, abill and lustie,
To beir the paill of velves cramase
Abone hir heid, as the custome hes bein.
Gryt was the sound of the artelyie: 15
Be blyth and blisfull, burgh of Aberdein.

1. blyth *happy*
   Aberdeane *Aberdeen*
   beriall *beryl; paragon*
   tounis *towns*
2. bewtie *beauty*
   bountie *goodness*
   blythnes *happiness*
3. renoun *reputation*
4. of *for* vertew *virtue*
   worthines *excellence*
5. he *highly* nottit *celebrated*
   name *reputation*
   nobilnes *nobility*
6. into *upon* cuming *arrival*
   lustie *beautiful* quein *queen*
7. wall *source* welth *well-being*

guid cheir *good cheer*
8. blisfull *joyful* burgh *town*
9. burges *burgesses*
10. richelie *splendidly*
    arrayit *dressed* become thame *it
    befitted them*
11. quhom *whom* cheset *chose*
    renoun *good reputation*
12. gounes *gowns* velvot *velvet*
    lustie *handsome*
13. beir *bear* paill *canopy* velves
    cramase *crimson velvet*
14. abone *over* heid *head*
    bein *been*
15. gryt *great* artelyie *artillery*

3–4. 'Your reputation for virtue, wisdom and excellence has ascended to
heaven itself'.

6–8. 'Be happy and joyful, borough of Aberdeen, upon the arrival of our
beautiful queen, the source of all well-being, good cheer and
merriness'.

9. 'First to meet her were the burgesses of the town'.

3

Ane fair processioun mett hir at the port,
In a cap of gold and silk, full pleasantlie,
Syne at hir entrie with many fair disport
Ressaveit hir on streittis lustilie;   20
Quhair first the salutatioun honorabilly
Of the sweitt Virgin guidlie mycht be seine,
The sound of menstrallis blawing to the sky:
Be blyth and blisfull, burgh of Aberdein.

4

And syne thow gart the orient kingis thrie   25
Offer to Chryst with benyng reverence
Gold, sence and mir with all humilitie,
Schawand him king with most magnificence;
Syne quhow the angill, with sword of violence,
Furth of the joy of paradice putt clein   30
Adame and Ev for innobedience:
Be blyth and blisfull, burch of Aberdein.

5

And syne the Bruce that evir was bold in stour
Thow gart as roy cum rydand under croun,
Richt awfull, strang and large of portratour,   35

17. port *gate*
18. cap *cape*   pleasantlie *joyfully*
19. syne *then*   entrie *entrance*
    disport *entertainment*
20. ressaveit *received*
    streittis *streets*   lustilie *gaily*
21. salutatioun *greeting*
22. guidlie *well*   seine *seen*
23. menstrallis *minstrels*
    blawing *blowing trumpets*
25. gart *caused*   orient *eastern*
    thrie *three*
26. benyng *gracious*
27. sence *incense*   mir *myrrh*
28. schawand *showing*
29. quhow *how*   angill *angel*
30. putt *drove*   clein *completely*
31. innobedience *disobedience*
32. burch *town*
33. stour *battle*
34. roy *king*   rydand *riding*
    croun *crown*
35. awfull *awe-inspiring*
    strang *strong*   portratour *stature*

21–2. 'Where the honourable salutation to the sweet Virgin could first be
    seen well performed'.
25–8. 'And then you had the three eastern kings offer gold, incense and
    myrrh to Christ with gracious reverence and complete humility,
    showing him to be the most magnificent of kings'.
30–1. 'Drove Adam and Eve completely from the joy of paradise on
    account of their disobedience'.
34. 'You had come riding out as king wearing his crown'.

As nobill, dreidfull, michtie campioun.
The royall Stewartis syne, of great renoun,
Thow gart upspring with branches new and greine,
Sa gloriouslie quhill glaidid all the toun:
Be blyth and blisfull, burch of Aberdein.   40

6

Syne come thair four and twentie madinis ying,
All claid in greine, of mervelous bewtie,
With hair detressit, as threidis of gold did hing,
With quhyt hattis all browderit rycht bravelie,
Playand on timberallis and singand rycht sweitlie.   45
That seimlie sort, in ordour weill besein,
Did meit the quein, hir halsand reverentlie:
Be blyth and blisfull, burch of Aberdein.

7

The streittis war all hung with tapestrie,
Greit was the pres of peopill, dwelt about,   50
And pleasant padgeanes playit prattelie.
The legeis all did to thair lady loutt,
Quha was convoyed with ane royall routt
Of gryt barrounes and lustie ladyis schene.
'Welcum, our quein!', the commones gaif ane schout: 55
Be blyth and blisfull, burch of Aberdein.

36. dreidfull *fearsome*
    michtie *mighty*
    campioun *champion*
37. Stewartis *Stewarts*
    renoun *distinction*
38. upspring *spring up*
    greine *green*
39. quhill *until* glaidid *rejoiced*
41. madinis ying *young maidens*
42. claid *dressed* bewtie *beauty*
43. detressit *unbound*
    threidis *threads* hing *hang*
44. quhyt *white* hattis *hats*
    browderit *embroidered*
    bravelie *finely*
45. playand *playing*
    timberallis *tambourines*

46. seimlie sort *excellent company*
    ordour *order* besein *arranged*
47. halsand *greeting*
49. streittis *streets*
50. pres *crowd* dwelt about *who lived nearby*
51. padgeanes *plays*
    playit *performed*
    prattelie *skilfully*
52. legeis *subjects* loutt *bow*
53. quha *who* convoyed *escorted*
    routt *retinue*
54. barrounes *barons* lustie *lovely*
    schene *beautiful*
55. commones *common people*
    schout *shout*

46–7. 'That excellent company, well arranged in order, met the queen, greeting her with reverence'.

8

At hir cuming great was the mirth and joy,
For at thair croce aboundantlie rane wyne.
Untill hir ludgeing the toun did hir convoy,
Hir for to treit thai sett thair haill ingyne.   60
Ane riche present thai did till hir propyne,
Ane costlie coup that large thing wald contene,
Coverit and full of cunyeit gold rycht fyne:
Be blyth and blisfull, burch of Aberdein.

9

O potent princes, pleasant and preclair,   65
Great caus thow hes to thank this nobill toun,
That for to do the honnour did not spair
Thair geir, riches, substance and persoun,
The to ressave on maist fair fasoun.
The for to pleis thay socht all way and mein.   70
Thairfoir sa lang as quein thow beiris croun,
Be thankfull to this burch of Aberdein.

58. croce *market cross*   princes *princess*
    rane *flowed* wyne *wine*   pleasant *delightful*
59. untill *to* ludgeing *lodging* preclair *illustrious*
60. treit *entertain* haill   67. the *you* spair *hold back*
    ingyne *ingenuity*   68. geir *possessions*
61. did . . . propyne *gave*   substance *wealth* persoun *selves*
62. coup *goblet* contene *hold*   69. ressave *receive* fasoun *fashion*
63. coverit *with a lid*   70. pleis *please* socht *sought*
    cunyeit *coined*   mein *means*
65. potent *powerful*   71. beiris *bear*

60. 'They applied all their ingenuity to entertaining her'.
70. 'They tried in every way to please you'.

We that are Heir in Hevynnis Glorie

We that ar heir in hevynnis glorie
To you that ar in purgatorie
Commendis us on hartlie wys:
I mene we folk in paradys,
In Edinburgh with all merynes, 5
To yow at Striveling in distres,
Quhair nowdir plesour nor delyt is,
For pietie this epistell wrytis.
O ye heremytis and ankirsadillis
That takkis your pennance at your tabillis 10
And eitis no meit restorative,
Nor drinkis no wyne confortative
Nor aill, bot that is thin and small,
With few coursis in your hall,
But cumpany of lordis and knychtis 15
Or ony uther gudlie wychtis,
Solitar walking your alone,
Seing no thing bot stok and stone,
Out of your panefull purgatorie,
To bring yow to the blys and glorie 20
Of Edinburcht, the myrrie town,
We sall begin ane cairfull sown,
Ane dirige, devoit and meik,
The lord of blys doing beseik,
Yow to delyver out of your noy 25
And bring yow sone to Edinburgh joy,

1. hevynnis *heaven's*
2. purgatorie *purgatory*
3. commendis us *send greetings*
   hartlie wys *heartfelt manner*
6. Striveling *Stirling*
7. nowdir *neither* plesour *pleasure*
8. for pietie *out of compassion*
   epistell *letter*
9. heremytis *hermits*
   ankirsadillis *anchorites*
10. pennance *penance*
11. eitis *eat* meit *food*
    restorative *giving health and strength*
12. wyne *wine*
    confortative *comforting*
13. aill *ale* bot that *except that* small *weak*
14. coursis *courses at dinner*
15. but *without*
16. gudlie wychtis *fine people*
17. solitar *solitary* your alone *on your own*
21. Edinburcht *Edinburgh* myrrie *happy*
22. cairfull *sorrowful* sown *song*
23. dirige *dirge; funeral hymn* devoit *devout* meik *humble*
24. doing beseik *beseeching*
25. noy *distress*
26. sone *soon*

For to be merye amangis us.
The dirige begynnis thus:

Lectio prima

The Fader, the Sone, the Holie Gaist,
The blissit Marie, virgen chaist,   30
Of angellis all the ordour nyne,
And all the hevinlie court divyne,
Sone bring yow fra the pyne and wo
Of Striveling, everie court mans foo,
Agane to Edinburchtis joy and blys,   35
Quhair wirschip, welthe and weilfair is,
Play, plesance eik and honestie.
Say ye amen, for chirritie.
Tu autem, domine.

Responsio

Tak consolatioun in your payne,   40
In tribulatioun tak consolatioun,
Out of vexatioun cum hame agayne,
Tak consolatioun in your payne.
Iube, domine etc.
Out of distres of Stirling town   45
To Edinburgh blys God mak yow bown.

Lectio secunda

Patriarchis, prophetis, apostillis deir,
Confessouris, virgynis and martyris cleir
And all the hevinlie court celestiall,

27. amangis *amongst*
Lectio prima *first lesson*
29. Holie Gaist *Holy Spirit*
30. chaist *chaste*
31. ordour nyne *nine orders*
33. pyne *pain*
34. foo *foe*
35. agane *back*
36. wirschip *honour*
37. eik *also* honestie *virtue*
38. chirritie *charity*
39. Tu autem domine *Do thou, O Lord, [have mercy on us]*

Responsio *Response*
40. consolatioun *consolation; comfort*
41. tribulatioun *tribulation; distress*
44. Iube, domine etc *give [blessing], O Lord*
46. bown *ready to go*
Lectio secunda *second lesson*
47. patriarchis *patriarchs; figures of the Old Testament*
apostillis *apostles*
48. confessouris *saints*
martyris *martyrs* cleir *bright*

31. 'All the nine orders of angels'

Devoitlie we upone thame call   50
That sone out of your paynis fell
Ye may in hevin heir with us dwell,
To eit swan, cran, peirtrik and pluver,
And everie fische that swowmis in rever,
To drink withe us the new fresche wyne   55
That grew apone the revar of Ryne,
Fresche fragrant claretis out of France,
Of Angeo and of Orliance,
With mony ane cours of grit daynte.
Say ye amen, for chirrite.   60
Tu autem, domine.

Responsio

God and Sanct Geill heir yow convoy,
Baythe sone and weill, God and sanct Geill,
To sonce and seill, solace and joy,
God and Sanct Geill heir yow convoy.   65
Iube, domine.
Out of Stirling paynis fell,
In Edinburgh joy sone mot ye dwell.

Lectio tertia

We pray to all the sanctis in hevin,
That ar abuif the sternis sevin,   70
Yow to delyver out of your pennance:
That ye may sone play, sing and dance
And in to Edinburgh mak gud cheir,
Quhair welthe and weilfair is, but weir.
And I that dois your paynis discryve   75
Thinkis for to visie yow belyve,

51. fell *cruel*
53. eit *eat* cran *crane*
    peirtrik *partridge* pluver *plover*
54. swowmis *swims* rever *river*
56. revar of Ryne *banks of the
    Rhine*
57. claretis *clarets*
58. Angeo *Anjou*
    Orliance *Orleans*
59. daynte *delicacy*

61. Sanct Geill *St Giles*
    convoy *bring*
64. sonce *abundance*
    seill *prosperity* solace *comfort*
68. mot *may*
70. abuif *above* sternis *planets*
74. but weir *without doubt*
75. discryve *describe*
76. thinkis for *intend* visie *visit*
    belyve *soon*

61. 'May God and St Giles bring you here'

Nocht in desert with yow to dwell
Bot as the angell Gabriell
Dois go betweyne fra hevynis glorie
To thame that ar in purgatorie,   80
And in thair tribulatioun
To gif thame consolatioun,
And schaw thame, quhone thair pane is past,
They sall to hevin cum at the last,
And how nane servis to have sweitnes   85
That never taistit bittirnes.
And thairfoir how ye sould considdir
Of Edinburgh blys quhone ye cum hiddir,
Bot gif ye taistit had befoir
Of Stirling toun the paynis soir?   90
And thairfoir tak in patience
Your pennance and your abstinence,
And ye sall cum, or Yule begyn,
In to the blys that we are in,
Quhilk grant the glorious Trinite.   95
Say ye amen, for chirrite.
Tu autem, domine.

83. quhone *when*   90. soir *grievous*
85. servis *deserves*   93. or *before* Yule *Christmas*
87. considdir *be able to judge*   95. Trinite *Trinity*
89. bot gif *unless*

95. 'May the glorious Trinity grant this'

Responsio
Cum hame and dwell no mair in Stirling,
Fra hyddows hell cum hame and dwell,
Quhair fische to sell is nane bot spyrling,   100
Cum hame and dwell na mair in Stirling.
Iube, domine.

Et ne nos inducas in tentationem de Stirling
Sed libera nos a malo eiusdem.
Requiem Edinburgi dona eis, domine,   105
Et lux ipsius luceat eis.
A porta tristitiae de Stirling
Erue, domine, animas et corpora eorum.
Credo gustare vinum Edinburgi
In villa viventium.   110
Requiescant statim in Edinburgo. Amen.
Domine, exaudi orationem meam
Et clamor meus ad te veniat.
Oremus.   114
Deus, qui iustos et corde humiles ex eorum tribulatione
liberare dignatus es, libera famulos tuos apud villam de
Stirling versantes a penis et tristitiis eiusdem, et ad Edinburgi
gaudia feliciter perducas. Amen.

99. hyddows *hideous*
100. spyrling *smelt; little fish*

100. 'Where the only fish for sale are smelt'
103–18. 'And do not lead us into the temptation of Stirling but deliver
  us from its evil. Give them the peace of Edinburgh, Lord, and let its
  light shine upon them. From the sad gate of Stirling, Lord, bring forth
  their souls and bodies. I believe I shall taste the wine of Edinburgh in
  the land of the living. May they soon be at rest in Edinburgh. Amen.
Lord, hear my prayer and let my cry come to thee.
Let us pray.
God, who deigns to free the just and humble at heart from their
  tribulation, free your servants who dwell in the town of Stirling from
  its pains and sorrows, and bring them rejoicing to the joys of
  Edinburgh. Amen.

As Yung Awrora with Cristall Haile
(A Ballat of the Abbot of Tungland)

1

As yung Awrora with cristall haile
In orient schew hir visage paile,
A swevyng swyth did me assaile
    Of sonis of Sathanis seid.
Me thocht a Turk of Tartary   5
Come throw the boundis of Barbary
And lay forloppin in Lumbardy
    Full lang in waithman weid.

2

Fra baptasing for to eschew,
Thair a religious man he slew   10
And cled him in his abeit new,
    For he cowth wryte and reid.
Quhen kend was his dissimulance
And all his cursit govirnance,
For fcir he fled and come in France,   15
    With littill of Lumbard leid.

3

To be a leiche he fenyt him thair,
Quhilk mony a man micht rew evirmair,
For he left nowthir seik nor sair
    Unslane, or he hyne yeid;   20

1. Awrora *Aurora* haile *drops*
2. orient *the east* schew *showed* visage *face*
3. swevyng *vision* swyth *quickly*
4. sonis *sons* Sathanis seid *Satan's lineage*
5. me thocht *it seemed to me*
6. come throw *came from* boundis *lands* Barbary *the Barbarians*
7. forloppin *as a renegade* Lumbardy *Lombardy*
8. waithman weid *outlaw's dress*
9. baptasing *baptism* eschew *avoid*
10. religious man *man in holy orders* slew *killed*
11. cled him *clothed himself* abeit *habit; robe*
12. cowth *knew how to* reid *read*
13. kend *discovered* dissimulance *deception*
14. govirnance *behaviour*
15. feir *fear*
16. leid *language*
17. leiche *doctor* fenyt him *pretended*
18. rew *regret*
19. seik *sick* sair *suffering*
20. unslane *alive* or *before* hyne *there* yeid *left*

Vane organis he full clenely carvit;
Quhen of his straik so mony starvit,
Dreid he had gottin that he desarvit
    He fled away gud speid.

4

In Scotland than, the narrest way,   25
He come his cunnyng till assay.
To sum man thair it was no play,
    The preving of his sciens.
In pottingry he wrocht grit pyne,
He murdreist mony in medecyne;   30
The jow was of a grit engyne,
    And generit was of gyans.

5

In leichecraft he was homecyd.
He wald haif, for a nycht to byd,
A haiknay and the hurt manis hyd,   35
    So meikle he was of myance.
His yrnis was rude as ony rawchtir.
Quhair he leit blude, it was no lawchtir.
Full mony instrument for slawchtir
    Was in his gardevyance.   40

21. vane organis *jugular veins*
    carvit *slit*
22. straik *stroke*   starvit *died*
23. dreid *afraid*   desarvit *deserved*
24. gud speid *quickly*
25. narrest way *quickest route*
26. cunnyng *craft*   assay *try out*
27. play *game*
28. preving *testing*
    sciens *knowledge*
29. pottingry *pharmacy*
    wrocht *caused*   pyne *pain*
30. murdreist *murdered* in *with*
31. jow *infidel* engyne *ingenuity*

32. generit *begotten*   gyans *giants*
33. leichecraft *medicine*
    homecyd *homicidal*
34. haif *demand*   to byd *in
    attendance*
35. haiknay *fine horse* hyd *skin*
36. meikle *great*   myance *influence*
37. yrnis *surgical instruments*
    rude *rudimentary*   rawchtir *roof-
    beam*
38. leit blude *let blood*
    lawchtir *laughing matter*
39. slawchtir *slaughter*
40. gardevyance *trunk*

23–4. 'Afraid that he was about to get what he deserved, he quickly ran
away'
34–5. 'In return for one night's attendance on a patient, he would
demand a fine horse and the sick man's own skin'.

6

He cowth gif cure for laxatyve,
To gar a wicht hors want his lyve.
Quha evir assay wald, man or wyve,
   Thair hippis yeid hiddy giddy.
His practikis nevir war put to preif,   45
Bot suddane deid or grit mischeif.
He had purgatioun to mak a theif
   To dee withowt a widdy.

7

Unto no mes pressit this prelat,
For sound of sacring bell nor skellat.   50
As blaksmyth bruikit was his pallatt,
   For battering at the study.
Thocht he come hame a new maid channoun,
He had dispensit with matynnis channoun,
On him come nowther stole nor fannoun,   55
   For smowking of the smydy.

8

Me thocht seir fassonis he assailyeit
To mak the quintessance and failyeit,
And quhen he saw that nocht availyeit
   A fedrem on he tuke,   60
And schupe in Turky for to fle.

41. laxatyve *diarrhoea*
42. gar *make* wicht *strong* want *lose*
43. assay *try it* wyve *woman*
44. yeid hiddy giddy *went helter skelter*
45. practikis *medical skills* put to preif *put to the test*
46. bot *without* deid *death* mischeif *harm*
47. purgatioun *laxatives*
48. dee *die* widdy *hangman's noose*
49. mes *mass* pressit *hurried* prelat *high-ranking priest*
50. sacring bell *consecration bell* skellat *hand bell*
51. bruikit *blackened* pallatt *head*
52. study *anvil*
53. new maid *newly made* channoun *canon*
54. matynnis channoun *canon law; law of the church*
55. stole nor fannoun *priest's vestments*
56. for *because of* smydy *smithy; blacksmith's workshop*
57. seir *different* fassonis *methods* assailyeit *tried*
58. quintessance *'fifth essence'* failyeit *failed*
59. nocht availyeit *nothing succeeded*
60. fedrem *coat of feathers*
61. schupe *prepared* fle *fly*

41-2. 'His cure for diarrhoea would have killed a strong horse'
60-1. 'He put on a coat of feathers, and got ready to fly to Turkey'

And quhen that he did mont on he,
All fowill ferleit quhat he sowld be,
    That evir did on him luke.

9

Sum held he had bene Dedalus,   65
Sum the Menatair marvelus,
Sum Martis blaksmyth, Vulcanus,
    And sum Saturnus kuke.
And evir the tuschettis at him tuggit,
The rukis him rent, the ravynis him druggit,   70
The hudit crawis his hair furth ruggit,
    The hevin he micht not bruke.

10

The myttane and Sanct Martynis fowle
Wend he had bene the hornit howle,
Thay set aupone him with a yowle,   75
    And gaif him dynt for dynt.
The golk, the gormaw and the gled
Beft him with buffettis quhill he bled,
The sparhalk to the spring him sped,
    Als fers as fyre of flynt.   80

11

The tarsall gaif him tug for tug,
A stanchell hang in ilka lug,

62. mont on he *climb up high*
63. all fowill *every bird*
    ferleit *wondered*
64. luke *look*
65. held *thought*
    Dedalus *Daedalus*
66. Menatair *Minotaur*
67. Martis *Mars'*
    Vulcanus *Vulcan*
68. Saturnus kuke *Saturn's cook*
69. tuschettis *lapwings*
    tuggit *tugged*
70. rukis *rooks* rent *tore at*
    ravynis *ravens* druggit *pulled*
71. hudit crawis *hooded crows*
    ruggit *pulled violently*

72. hevin *sky* bruke *enjoy*
73. myttane *bird of prey* Sanct
    Martynis *Saint Martin's*
74. wend *thought* hornit
    howle *horned owl*
75. yowle *yowl; scream*
76. dynt *blow*
77. golk *cuckoo*
    gormaw *cormorant* gled *kite*
78. beft *hit* quhill *until*
79. sparhalk *sparrow hawk*
    spring *attack*
80. fers *fierce* fyre *fire* flynt *flint*
81. tarsall *tercel; male hawk*
82. stanchell *kestrel* hang *hung*
    ilka lug *each ear*

The pyot furth his pennis did rug,
  The stork straik ay but stynt.
The bissart, bissy but rebuik, 85
Scho was so cleverus of hir cluik
His bawis he micht not langer bruik,
  Scho held thame at ane hint.

12

Thik was the clud of kayis and crawis,
Of marleyonis, mittanis and of mawis, 90
That bikkrit at his berd with blawis,
  In battell him abowt.
Thay nybbillit him with noyis and cry,
The rerd of thame rais to the sky,
And evir he cryit on Fortoun, 'Fy!' 95
  His lyfe was in to dowt.

13

The ja him skrippit with a skryke
And skornit him, as it was lyk.
The egill strong at him did stryke
  And rawcht him mony a rowt. 100
For feir uncunnandly he cawkit,
Quhill all his pennis war drownd and drawkit.
He maid a hundreth nolt all hawkit
  Beneth him with a spowt.

83. pyot *magpie* pennis *feathers*
  rug *pull*
84. straik *struck [him]* ay *constantly*
  but stynt *without stopping*
85. bissart *buzzard* bissy *busy*
  but rebuik *without rebuke*
86. cleverus *piercing* cluik *talons*
87. bawis *testicles* bruik *enjoy the
  possession*
88. ane hint *one grasp*
89. thik *thick* clud *cloud*
  kayis *jackdaws* crawis *crows*
90. marleyonis *merlins; small
  falcons* mittanis *birds of prey*
  mawis *gulls*
91. bikkrit *attacked* berd *beard*
  blawis *blows*

93. nybbillit *nibbled* noyis *noise*
94. rerd of thame *noise they made*
96. in to dowt *in danger*
97. ja *jay* skrippit *mocked*
  skryke *screech*
98. skornit *scorned* as . . . lyk *as it
  seemed*
99. egill *eagle*
100. rawcht *gave* rowt *blow*
101. feir *fear*
  uncunnandly *uncontrollably*
  cawkit *defecated*
102. quhill *until* pennis *feathers*
  drawkit *drenched*
103. nolt *cattle* hawkit *dirty*
104. a spowt *one burst*

83. 'The magpie pulled out his feathers'

14

He schewre his feddreme, that was schene,   105
And slippit owt of it full clene,
And in a myre up to the ene
    Amang the glar did glyd.
The fowlis all at the fedrem dang,
As at a monster thame amang,   110
Quhill all the pennis of it owtsprang
    In till the air full wyde.

15

And he lay at the plunge evirmair,
So lang as any ravin did rair.
The crawis him socht with cryis of cair   115
    In every schaw besyde.
Had he reveild bene to the ruikis,
Thay had him revin all with thair cluikis.
Thre dayis in dub amang the dukis
    He did with dirt him hyde.   120

16

The air was dirkit with the fowlis,
That come with yawmeris and with yowlis,
With skryking, skrymming and with scowlis,
    To tak him in the tyde.
I walknit with the noyis and schowte,   125
So hiddowis beir was me abowte.
Sensyne I curs that cankerit rowte,
    Quhairevir I go or ryde.

105. schewre *slit*
    feddreme *feathery coat*
    schene *beautiful*
106. full clene *entirely*
107. myre *bog*   ene *eyes*
108. glar *mud*   glyd *glide*
109. dang *struck*
110. owtsprang *flew out*
113. at the plunge *in the pool*
114. rair *croak*
116. schaw *wood*
117. reveild *revealed*
118. revin *torn apart*   cluikis *claws*

119. dub *pond*   dukis *ducks*
121. dirkit *darkened*
122. yawmeris *yammering; yells*
123. skryking *shrieking*
    skrymming *darting about*
    scowlis *hostile looks*
124. in the tyde *at any time*
125. walknit *awoke*
    schowte *shouting*
126. beir *racket; din*
127. sensyne *since then*
    cankerit *evil*   rowte *crowd*
128. go *walk*

117–8. 'If the rooks had seen him, they would have torn him apart with
    their claws'

Lucina Schyning in Silence of the Nycht

1

Lucina schyning in silence of the nycht,
The hevyn all being full of sterris bricht,
To bed I went, bot thair I tuke no rest.
With havie thocht so sair I wes opprest
That sair I langit eftir the dayis licht.   5

2

Of Fortoun I complenit havalie
That scho to me stude so contrariouslie,
And at the last, quhone I had turnit oft,
For werynes on me a slumer soft
Come with a dreming and a fantasie.   10

3

Me thocht dame Fortoun with a fremmit cheir
Stude me beforne and said on this maneir:
'Thow suffir me to wirk gif thow do weill,
And preis the not to stryve aganis my quheill
Quhilk everie warldlie thing dois turne and steir.   15

2. sterris *stars*
4. havie thocht *burdensome thoughts*   sair *grievously*
5. sair *sorrowfully* langit eftir *longed for* dayis licht *daylight*
6. of *about* complenit *complained* havalie *greatly*
7. contrariouslie *in opposition*
8. turnit oft *tossed and turned*
9. slumer *slumber*
10. dreming *dream* fantasie *vision*
11. me thocht *it seemed to me* fremmit cheir *strange expression*
12. me beforne *before me* maneir *manner*
13. suffir *allow* wirk *work* gif *if* weill *well*
14. preis *attempt* aganis *against* quheill *wheel*
15. warldlie *worldly* steir *guide*

7. 'That she stood so much in opposition to me'.
9–10. 'Through tiredness a soft slumber full of dreams and visions overcame me'.
13–15. 'You must allow me to do my work if you want to do well, and don't attempt to strive against my wheel which turns and guides the progress of everything in the world'.

4

'Full mony ane I set upone the heycht,
And makis mony full law doun to lycht.
Upone my stagis or that thow do ascend,
Traist wele thi trouble is neir at ane end,
Seing thir takynnis; quhairfoir thow mark
    thame richt.   20

5

'Thy trublit gaist sall never be degest
Nor thow in to no benefice possest;
Quhill that ane abbot him cleythe in eirnis pennys
And fle up in the air amang the crennys,
And as a falcoun fair fro eist to west.   25

6

'He sall ascend as ane horrible griphoun.
Him meit sall in the air ane scho dragoun.
Thir terribill monsturis sall togiddir thrist,
And in the cluddis get the Antechrist,
Quhill all the air infect of thair poysoun.   30

7

'Undir Saturnis fyrie regioun
Symon Magus sall meit him and Mahown,
And Merleyn at the mune sall him be bydand,

16. mony ane *many a person*
    heycht *top*
17. makis *make*   law *low*
    lycht *descend*
18. stagis *steps*   or that *before*
19. traist *trust*   neir *nearly*
20. seing *when you see*   thir *these*
    takynnis *signs*   mark *interpret*
    richt *correctly*
21. trublit gaist *troubled spirit*
    degest *calm*
22. possest *possessed*
23. quhill that *until*   him
    cleythe *clothe himself*   eirnis

pennys *eagle's feathers*
24. fle *fly*   crennys *cranes*
25. fair *go*
26. as *like*   griphoun *griffin*
27. scho dragoun *she-dragon*
28. togiddir thrist *copulate together*
29. cluddis *clouds*   get *beget*
30. quhill *until*   infect of *is
    infected with*
31. Saturnis *Saturn's*   fyrie *fiery*
32. Mahown *Muhammad*
33. Merleyn *Merlin*   mune *moon*
    him be bydand *be awaiting him*

17. 'And cause very many to descend very low'.
22. 'Nor you possessed of any benefice'.
27. 'A she-dragon shall encounter him in the air'.

And Jonet the wedo on a busum rydand
Of wytchis with ane wondrus garesoun.   35

8
'And syne thai sall discend with reik and fyre,
And preiche in eird the Antechristis impyre,
And than it sal be neir the warldis end.'
With that this ladie did schortlie fra me wend.
Sleipand and walkand wes frustrat my desyre.   40

9
Quhone I awoyk, my dreme it wes so nyce,
Fra everie wicht I hid it as a vyce,
Quhill I hard tell be mony suthfast wy,
Fle wald ane abbot up into the sky
And all his feddrem maid wes at devyce.   45

10
Within my hert confort I tuke full sone.
'Adew,' quod I, 'my drerie dayis ar done.
Full weill I wist to me wald never cum thrift
Quhill that twa munis were first sene in the lift
Or quhill ane abbot flew abone the moyne.'   50

34. wedo *widow*
    busum *broomstick* rydand *riding*
35. wondrus *amazing*
    garesoun *band*
36. syne *then* reik *smoke*
37. preiche *proclaim* in eird *on
    earth* impyre *reign*
38. sal be *shall be* warldis *world's*
39. schortlie *soon* wend *go*
40. sleipand *sleeping*
    walkand *waking*
    frustrat *frustrated*
41. awoyk *awoke* nyce *strange*

42. wicht *person*
43. quhill *until* hard tell *heard it
    said* suthfast wy *truthful person*
44. fle *fly*
45. feddrem *plumage* at
    devyce *skilfully*
47. adew *farewell* quod *said*
    drerie *sad* done *over*
48. wist *knew* thrift *wealth*
49. twa munis *two moons*
    sene *seen* lift *sky*
50. abone *above* moyne *moon*

34–5. 'And the widow Janet riding on a broomstick with an amazing
    band of witches'.

This Nycht Befoir the Dawing Cleir

1

This nycht befoir the dawing cleir
Me thocht Sanct Francis did to me appeir
With ane religious abbeit in his hand,
And said: 'In this go cleith the my servand.
Reffus the warld, for thow mon be a freir.'   5

2

With him and with his abbeit bayth I skarrit,
Lyk to ane man that with a gaist wes marrit.
Me thocht on bed he layid it me abone,
Bot on the flure delyverly and sone
I lap thairfra and nevir wald cum nar it.   10

3

Quoth he, 'Quhy skarris thow with this holy weid?
Cleith the thairin, for weir it thow most neid.
Thow that hes lang done Venus lawis teiche
Sall now be freir and in this abbeit preiche.
Delay it nocht, it mon be done but dreid.'   15

4

Quod I, 'Sanct Francis, loving be the till,
And thankit mot thow be of thy gude will

1. dawing cleir *bright dawn*
2. me thocht *it seemed to me*
Sanct *Saint*
3. abbeit *habit; costume*
4. cleith *clothe*   servand *follower*
5. reffus *reject*   warld *world*
mon *must*   freir *friar*
6. bayth *too*   I skarrit *I was
frightened*
7. gaist *ghost*   marrit *startled*
8. layid *lay*   abone *above*
9. flure *floor*   delyverly *quickly*
sone *at once*
10. lap *leapt*   thairfra *from it*
nar *near*
11. quoth *said*   quhy *why*
weid *garment*
12. weir *wear*   most neid *must*
13. lang *long*   done . . .
teiche *taught*   lawis *laws*
14. preiche *preach*
15. but dreid *without doubt*
16. quod *said*   loving be the
till *may you be praised*
17. mot *may*

4. 'And said, "Go clothe yourself in this as my follower" '.
8. 'It seemed to me that he laid it upon me on the bed'.
13. 'You who have taught people about the laws of Venus for so long'.
17–19. 'And may you be thanked for your good will towards me, being
so generous with your clothes, but it has never before entered my head
to wear them'.

To me, that of thy clathis ar so kynd,
Bot thame to weir it nevir come in my mynd.
Sweit confessour, thow tak it nocht in ill.   20

5
'In haly legendis haif I hard, all evin,
Ma sanctis of bischoppis nor freiris be sic sevin.
Of full few freiris that hes bene sanctis I reid;
Quhairfoir ga bring to me ane bischopis weid,
Gife evir thow wald my sawle yeid unto hevin.'   25

6
'My brethir oft hes maid the supplicationis
Be epistillis, sermonis and relationis
To tak the abyte, bot thow did postpone.
But forder proces cum on thairfoir annone.
All sircumstance put by and excusationis.'   30

7
'Gif evir my fortoun wes to be a freir,
The dait thairof is past full mony a yeir;
For into every lusty toun and place
Of all Yngland, frome Berwick to Kalice,
I haif into thy habeit maid gud cheir.   35

18. clathis *clothes* kynd *generous*
19. come *came*
20. thow tak it nocht in ill *do not take it the wrong way*
21. haly legendis *holy saints' lives* hard *heard* all evin *in truth*
22. ma *more* bischoppis *bishops* nor *than* sic *such*
23. reid *read*
24. quhairfoir *therefore*
25. gife *if* wald *wished* sawle *soul* yeid *went*
26. brethir *brother friars* the supplicationis *appeals to you*
27. be epistillis *by letters*

relationis *moral tales*
28. postpone *put it off*
29. but *without* forder proces *more ado* annone *at once*
30. sircumstance *long stories* excusationis *excuses*
31. fortoun *destiny*
32. dait thairof *time for it* full mony a yeir *many years ago*
33. lusty toun *pleasant town* place *home*
34. Yngland *England* Kalice *Calais*
35. maid gud cheir *enjoyed myself*

21–3. 'In truth, in the holy saints' lives I have heard, there were seven times more saints among bishops than among the friars. I read about very few friars who have been saints'.
29–30. 'Therefore, get on with it at once without further delay. Forget about all your long stories and excuses'.

8

'In freiris weid full fairly haif I fleichit;
In it haif I in pulpet gon and preichit
In Derntoun kirk and eik in Canterberry,
In it I past at Dover our the ferry
Throw Piccardy, and thair the peple teichit.   40

9

'Als lang as I did beir the freiris style,
In me, God wait, wes mony wrink and wyle.
In me was falset with every wicht to flatter,
Quhilk micht be flemit with na haly watter.
I wes ay reddy all men to begyle.'   45

10

This freir that did Sanct Francis thair appeir,
Ane fieind he wes in liknes of ane freir.
He vaneist away with stynk and fyrie smowk.
With him, me thocht, all the hous end he towk,
And I awoik as wy that wes in weir.   50

36. fleichit *flattered*
37. pulpet *pulpit* preichit *preached*
38. Derntoun kirk *Darlington
   church* eik *also*
   Canterberry *Canterbury*
39. our *over on*
40. teichit *taught*
41. freiris style *name of friar*
42. wait *knows* wrink *trick*
43. falset *falsehood* wicht *person*
44. quhilk *which* flemit *driven
   away* haly watter *holy water*
45. ay *always* begyle *deceive*
47. fieind *devil*
48. vaneist *vanished* fyrie
   smowk *fiery smoke*
49. end *side* towk *took*
50. awoik *awoke* wy *man*
   weir *confusion*

46–7. 'This friar who appeared there as Saint Francis, was really a devil
in the likeness of a friar'.
49–50. 'It seemed to me that he took the whole side of the house with
him, and I awoke like a man in a state of confusion'.

Of Benefice, Sir, at Everie Feist

1

Of benefice, sir, at everie feist
Quha monyast hes makis maist requeist.
Get thai not all, thai think ye wrang thame.
Ay is the ovirword of the geist:
Giff thame the pelffe to pairt amang thame.   5

2

Sum swelleis swan, sum swelleis duke,
And I stand fastand in a nuke,
Quhill the effect of all thai fang thame.
Bot lord! how petewouslie I luke,
Quhone all the pelfe thai pairt amang thame.   10

3

Of sic hie feistis of sanctis in glorie,
Baithe of commoun and propir storie,
Quhair lairdis war patronis, oft I sang thame,
Charitas, pro dei amore;
And yit I gat na thing amang thame.   15

4

This blynd warld ever so payis his dett:
Riche befoir pure spraidis ay thair net,

1. feist *feast*
2. quha *who* monyast *most* requeist *demand*
3. get thai not *if they do not get*
4. ay *always* ovirword *meaning* geist *story*
5. giff *give* pelffe *booty* pairt *share*
6. sum *one* swelleis *swallows* duke *duck*
7. fastand *starving* nuke *corner*
8. quhill *while* effect *greatest* share fang *seize*
9. petewouslie *pitifully* luke *look*
11. sic *such* sanctis in glorie *saints in glory*
12. commoun *general* propir storie *individual office*
13. lairdis *lords* patronis *patrons* thame *to them*
14. charitas, pro dei amore *charity, for the love of God*
15. gat *got*
16. warld *world* dett *debt*
17. pure *poor* spraidis *spreads*

1–2. 'At every feast, sir, those who already have the most make the most demands for benefices'.
4. 'It's always the same story'.
8. 'While they seize the greatest share for themselves'.
11. 'On the high feast days of the saints in glory'.
16. 'This blind world always pays his debts like that'.

To fische all watiris dois belang thame.
Quha na thing hes can na thing gett,
Bot ay as syphir set amang thame.   20

5
Swa thai the kirk have in thair cure,
Thai fors bot litill how it fure,
Nor of the buikis or bellis, quha rang thame.
Thai pans not of the prochin pure,
Hed thai the pelfe to pairt amang thame.   25

6
So warryit is this warldis rent
That men of it ar never content,
Of deathe quhill that the dragoun stang thame.
Quha maist hes than sall maist repent,
With largest compt to pairt amang thame.   30

18. fische *fish* dois belang
    thame *is their privilege*
19. quha *whoever*
20. syphir *cipher; zero*
21. swa *so* kirk *church*
    cure *control*

22. fors *would care* fure *fares*
23. buikis *books* bellis *bells*
24. pans *would think* prochin
    pure *poor parishioners*
26. warryit *cursed* rent *wealth*
30. compt *reckoning*

19–20. 'Whoever has nothing, gets nothing, but instead is always treated
    like nothing by everyone else'.
28. 'Until the dragon of death stings them'.
29–30. 'Whoever has most shall then repent most, with the largest
    reckoning of all to be shared amongst them'.

Schir, at this Feist of Benefice

1

Schir, at this feist of benefice
Think that small partis makis grit service,
And equale distributioun
Makis thame content that hes ressoun,
And quha hes nane ar plesit na wyis. 5

2

Schir, quhiddir is it mereit mair
To gif him drink that thristis sair,
Or fill a fow man quhill he birst,
And lat his fallow de a thrist,
Quhilk wyne to drink als worthie war? 10

3

It is no glaid collatioun,
Quhair ane makis myrrie, ane uther lukis doun,
Anc thristis, ane uther playis cop out.
Lat anis the cop ga round about,
And wyn the covanis banesoun. 15

1. schir *sir* feist *feast*
   benefice *benefices*
2. think *consider* partis *portions*
   grit *great*
4. ressoun *reason*
5. quha *whoever* plesit *pleased*
   wyis *way*
6. quhiddir *ask yourself whether*
   mereit mair *of greater merit*
7. gif *give* thristis sair *has a
   terrible thirst*
8. fow *full* quhill *until*

birst *bursts*
9. lat *let* fallow *companion* de a
   thrist *die of thirst*
10. quhilk *who* als *as* war *was*
11. glaid *happy* collatioun *meal*
12. myrrie *merry* lukis doun *is
    downcast*
13. playis cop out *competes at
    draining the glass*
14. anis *once* ga *go*
15. wyn *gain* covanis *company's*
    banesoun *blessing*

2. 'Consider that small portions mean a greater number are served'.
4–5. 'Makes those who are of a reasonable disposition content, and those
   who are not reasonable are never pleased anyway'.
10. 'Who was just as worthy to drink the wine'.
14. 'Let the cup circulate to everyone once'.

Complane, I Wald, Wist I Quhome Till

Complane I wald, wist I quhome till
Or unto quhome darect my bill:
Quhidder to God that all thing steiris,
All thing seis and all thing heiris,
And all thing wrocht in dayis seveyne;   5
Or till his moder, quein of heveyne;
Or unto wardlie prince heir downe,
That dois for justice weir a crownne –
Of wrangis and of gryt injuris
That nobillis in thar dayis induris,   10
And men of vertew and cuning,
Of wit and wysdome in gydding,
That nocht cane in this cowrt conquys
For lawte, luiff nor lang servys.
Bot fowll jow jowrdane-hedit jevellis,   15
Cowkin kenseis and culroun kevellis,
Stuffettis, strekouris and stafische strummellis,
Wyld haschbaldis, haggarbaldis and hummellis,
Druncartis, dysouris, dyowris, drevellis,

1. wald *would* wist *knew* quhome till *to whom*
2. darect *direct* bill *letter*
3. quhidder *whether* steiris *governs*
4. seis *sees* heiris *hears*
5. wrocht *created* seveyne *seven*
6. till *to* moder *mother* quein *queen*
7. wardlie *worldly* heir *here*
8. weir *wear*
9. wrangis *wrongs* gryt *great* injuris *injustices*
10. nobillis *noblemen* dayis *lifetimes* induris *endure*
11. vertew *virtue* cuning *learning*
12. wit *intelligence* gydding *conduct*

13. nocht *nothing* cane *can* conquys *obtain*
14. lawte *loyalty* luiff *love*
15. jow *infidel* jowrdane *chamber-pot* jevellis *ruffians*
16. cowkin kenseis *dirty rogues* culroun kevellis *rascally knaves*
17. stuffettis *lackeys* strekouris *dogs* stafische strummellis *unruly beasts*
18. haschbaldis *hooligans* haggarbaldis *ruffians* hummellis *ineffectual beasts*
19. druncartis *drunkards* dysouris *gamblers* dyowris *bankrupts* drevellis *wasters*

1–2. 'I would complain, if I knew who to, or to whom I should direct my letter'.
7–8. 'Or to some worldly prince down here, who wears a crown to administer justice'.
9–10. 'About the wrongs and injustices that noblemen have to endure in their lives now'.
15. 'But foul, infidel rascals with heads like chamber-pots'.

Misgydit memberis of the Devellis,   20
Mismad mandragis of mastis strynd,
Crawdones, couhirttis and theiffis of kynd,
Blait-mouit bladyeanes with bledder cheikis,
Clubfacet clucanes, with clutit breikis,
Chuff midding churllis, cuming of cart fillaris,   25
Gryt glaschewe-hedit gorge-millaris,
Evill, horrible monsteris, fals and fowll:
Sum causles clekis till him ane cowll,
Ane gryt convent fra syne to tys,
And he himself exampill of vys,   30
Enterand for geir and no devocioun.
The devill is glaid of his promocioun.
Sum ramyis ane rokkat fra the roy,
And dois ane dastart destroy,
And sum that gaittis ane personage   35
Thinkis it a present for a page,
And on no wayis content is he

20. misgydit *misguided*
    memberis *agents* Devellis *Devil*
21. mismad *deformed*
    mandragis *mandrakes*
    mastis *mastiffs*
    strynd *temperament*
22. crawdones *faint-hearts*
    couhirttis *cowards* theiffis of
    kynd *born thieves*
23. blait-mouit *loose-lipped*
    bladyeanes *clowns*
    bledder *bladder*
24. clubfacet *club-faced*
    clucanes *yokels* clutit
    breikis *patched breeches*
25. chuff *rough* midding
    churllis *dunghill peasants* cart

fillaris *dung carters*
26. gryt *great* glaschewe-
    hedit *fishy-headed* gorge-
    millaris *gluttons*
28. causles *without right*
    clekis *grabs* cowll *cowl*
29. convent *monastery* syne *sin*
    tys *draw away*
30. vys *vice*
31. enterand *entering* geir *money*
33. ramyis *pesters* rokkat *bishop's
    vestment* roy *king*
34. dastart *coward*
35. gaittis *receives*
    personage *parson's benefice*
36. page *knave*
37. on no wayis *in no way*

21. 'Deformed mandrakes with the temperament of mastiffs'.
23. 'Loose-lipped clowns with cheeks like full bladders'.
25. 'Rough dunghill peasants, descended from dung-carters'.
28–31. 'One grabs a cowl for himself without any right, in order to draw
    a great monastery away from sin, and yet he himself is the embodiment
    of vice, entering the Church for money and not religious reasons'.
33. 'One pesters the king for a bishop's vestment'.
36. 'Thinks it is a gift fit only for a knave'.

'My lord' quhill that he callit be.
Bot quhow is he content or nocht,
Dem ye abowt in to yowr thocht,   40
The lerit sone of erle or lord,
Upone this ruffie to remord,
That with ald castingis hes him cled,
His erandis for to ryne and red
And he is maister native borne   45
And all his eldaris him beforne,
And mekle mair cuning, be sic thre,
Hes to posseid ane dignite,
Saying his odius ignorance
Panting ane prelottis countenance,   50
Sa far above him set at tabell,
That wont was for to muk the stabell:
Ane pykthank in a prelottis clais,
With his wawill feit and wirrok tais,
With hoppir hippis and henches narrow,   55
And bausy handis to bere a barrow,
With lut schulderis and luttard bak,
Quhilk Natur maid to beir a pak,

38. quhill *until*
39. quhow *whether*
40. dem *judge*   abowt *around*
41. lerit *learned*   sone *son*
42. ruffie *villain*   remord *bitterly contemplate*
43. ald *old*   castingis *cast-off clothing*   cled *dressed*
44. erandis *errands*   ryne *run*   red *perform*
45. maister *university graduate*
46. eldaris *ancestors*   him beforne *before him*
47. mekle mair *much more*   cuning *learned*   sic *such*
48. posseid *possess*   dignite *ecclesiastical office*

49. saying *seeing*
50. panting *putting on*   prelottis countenance *prelate's manner*
51. tabell *table*
52. wont was *was accustomed*   muk *muck out*
53. pykthank *sycophant*   clais *clothes*
54. wawill feit *deformed feet*   wirrok tais *toes with corns*
55. hoppir hippis *hips like a hopper*   henches *haunches*
56. bausy *clumsy*   handis *hands*
57. lut *stooping*   luttard *crooked*
58. quhilk *which*   pak *peddlar's pack*

38. 'Until he can be called "my lord" '.
39–44. 'But you can make up your own mind whether or not the learned son of an earl or lord is content to contemplate this villain, who has dressed him up in old cast-offs, to run and perform his errands'.
47–8. 'And is much more learned – three times as much – so that he should be the one to possess ecclesiastical office'.

With gredy mynd and glaschane gane,
Mell-hedit lyk ane mortar stane, 60
Fenyeing the feris of ane lord,
And he ane strumbell, I stand ford;
And ever moir as he dois rys,
Nobles of bluid he dois dispys
And helpis for to hald thame downe 65
That thay rys never to his renowne.
Thairfoir, O prince maist honorable,
Be in this meter merciabill
And to thy auld servandis haff e,
That lang hes lipinit into the. 70
Gif I be ane of tha mysell,
Throw all regiones hes bein hard tell,
Of quhilk my wrytting witnes beris.
And yete thy danger ay me deris.
Bot efter danger cumis grace, 75
As hes bein herd in mony plece.

59. gredy *greedy* glaschane
gane *fishy face*
60. mell-hedit *blockheaded*
stane *stone*
61. fenyeing *imitating*
feris *manners*
62. strumbell *dumb beast* stand
ford *guarantee*
63. rys *rise up the ranks*
64. nobles of bluid *those of noble
blood* dispys *despise*
65. hald *keep*
66. renowne *distinction*
67. maist *most*

68. meter *matter*
merciabill *merciful*
69. servandis *servants* haff e *take
care*
70. lipinit into the *relied upon you*
71. gif *whether* tha *those* my
sell *myself*
72. regiones *countries* bein *been*
hard *heard*
73. witnes beris *bears witness*
74. yete *yet* danger *displeasure*
ay *always* deris *hurts*
75. cumis *comes*
76. herd *heard* plece *place*

66. 'So that they never rise to his level'.
71–3. 'As to whether I am one of those myself, it has been said that I am
throughout all parts of the world, and my writing bears witness to it'.

Schir, Yit Remember As Befoir

1

Schir, yit remember as befoir
How that my youthe is done forloir
In your service with pane and greif;
Gud conscience cryis reward thairfoir.
Exces of thocht dois me mischief.   5

2

Your clarkis ar servit all aboute
And I do lyke ane rid halk schout,
To cum to lure that hes na leif,
Quhair my plumis begynnis to mowt.
Exces of thocht dois me mischeif.   10

3

Foryet is ay the falcounis kynd,
Bot ever the myttell is hard in mynd;
Quhone the gled dois the peirtrikis preif
The gentill goishalk gois undynd.
Exces of thocht dois me mischeif.   15

4

The pyat withe the pairtie cote
Feynyeis to sing the nychtingale note,
Bot scho can not the corchet cleif

1. schir *sir*
2. is done forloir *has been lost*
3. pane *pain*
4. cryis *demands*
5. mischief *harm*
6. clarkis *scholars* servit *looked after*
7. rid halk *red hawk* schout *cry out*
8. leif *permission*
9. quhair *when* plumis *feathers* mowt *moult*
11. foryet *forgotten* ay *always*
kynd *species*
12. myttell *lesser bird* hard in mynd *remembered*
13. quhone *when* gled *kite* peirtrikis *partridges* preif *taste*
14. gentill *noble* goishalk *goshawk* undynd *without dinner*
16. pyat *magpie* pairtie cote *coat of two colours*
17. feynyeis *pretends* note *song*
18. the corchet cleif *split the crotchet*

7–9. 'And I cry out like a red hawk, which doesn't have permission to come in to the lure, even though my feathers are beginning to moult'.
13–14. 'When the kite gets a taste of the partridges the noble goshawk has to go without his dinner'.

For hasknes of hir carleche throte.
Exces of thocht dois me mischeif. 20

5

Ay fairast feddiris hes farrest foulis,
Suppois thai have na sang bot yowlis,
In sylver caiges thai sit but greif.
Kynd native nestis dois clek bot owlis.
Exces of thocht dois me mischeif. 25

6

O gentill egill, how may this be,
Quhilk of all foulis dois heast fle?
Your leggis quhy do ye not releif
And chirreis thame eftir thair degre?
Exces of thocht dois me mischeif. 30

7

Quhone servit is all uther man,
Gentill and sempill, of everie clan,
Raf Coilyearis kynd and Johnne the Reif,
No thing I gett nor conqueis can.
Exces of thocht dois me mischeif. 35

8

Thocht I in courte be maid refuse
And have few vertewis for to ruse,
Yit am I cum of Adame and Eve

19. hasknes *harshness*
carleche *rough*
21. fairast *fairest*
feddiris *feathers* farrest *furthest*
foulis *birds*
22. suppois *even if* yowlis *yowling*
23. caiges *cages* but greif *without
any cares*
24. kynd *natural* clek *hatch*
26. egill *eagle*
27. quhilk *which* foulis *birds*

heast fle *fly the highest*
28. leggis *subjects* releif *help*
29. chirreis *cherish* eftir *as befits*
degre *rank*
32. sempill *lowly*
33. Raf Coilyearis *Rauf Coilyear's*
Johnne the Reif *John the Reeve*
34. conqueis can *can acquire*
36. be maid refuse *am refused*
37. vertewis *virtues* for to ruse *to
boast of*

21. 'Birds from far-off lands always have the finest feathers'.
24. 'The nests that nature provides in this country are only good for
hatching owls'.
28. 'Why do you not help your subjects?'

And fane wald leif as utheris dois.
Exces of thocht dois me mischeif.　　　　　40

9

Or I suld leif in sic mischance,
Gif it to God war na grevance,
To be ane pykthank I wald preif,
For thai in warld wantis na plesance.
Exces of thocht dois me mischeif.　　　　　45

10

In sum pairt of my selffe I pleinye:
Quhone utheris dois flattir and feynye,
Allace, I can bot ballattis breif.
Sic barnheid leidis my brydill reynye.
Exces of thocht dois me mischeif.　　　　　50

11

I grant my service is bot lycht.
Thairfoir, of mercye and not of rycht,
I ask you, schir, no man to greif,
Sum medecyne gif that ye mycht.
Exces of thocht dois me mischeif.　　　　　55

12

Nane can remeid my maledie
Sa weill as ye, schir, veralie:
With ane benefice ye may preif,

39. fane wald leif *would like to
live*　utheris dois *others do*
41. or *before*　leif *live*　sic
mischance *such misery*
42. gif *if*　grevance *offence*
43. pykthank *sycophant*　preif *try*
44. wantis *lack*　plesance *pleasure*
46. pleinye *blame*
47. utheris *others*　feynye *deceive*
48. allace *alas*　bot *only*　ballattis

breif *write poems*
49. barnheid *childish innocence*
brydill reynye *bridle rein*
51. bot lycht *only slight*
53. greif *grieve*
54. gif *if*
56. nane *no one*　remeid *cure*
maledie *illness*
57. veralie *truly*
58. preif *prove it*

41–3. 'If it were not an offense against God, I would try to be a
sycophant rather than living in such misery'.
46. 'To some extent I blame myself'.
49. 'Such childish innocence leads me by the bridle'.
53. 'I ask you, sir, without harming anyone'.
58. 'You can prove that this is the case with a benefice'.

And gif I mend not haistalie,
Exces of thocht lat me mischeif.   60

13

I wes in youthe on nureice kne
Cald 'dandillie, bischop, dandillie.'
And quhone that age now dois me greif
A sempill vicar I can not be.
Exces of thocht dois me mischeif.   65

14

Jok that wes wont to keip the stirkis
Can now draw him ane cleik of kirkis,
With ane fals cairt in to his sleif,
Worthe all my ballattis under the byrkis.
Exces of thocht dois me mischeif.   70

15

Twa curis or thre hes uplandis Michell,
With dispensationis in ane knitchell,
Thocht he fra nolt had new tane leif.
He playis with 'totum' and I with 'nychell'.
Exces of thocht dois me mischeif.   75

16

How sould I leif, and I not landit,
Nor yit withe benefice am blandit?
I say not, schir, yow to repreif,
Bot doutles I go rycht neirhand it.
Exces of thocht dois me mischeif.   80

59. haistalie *quickly*
60. lat *let*
61. nureice kne *nurse's knee*
62. cald *called*
63. age *old age*
64. sempill *simple*
66. Jok *Jock* was wont to *used to*
keip *look after* stirkis *bullocks*
67. cleik of kirkis *handful of churches*
68. cairt *card* sleif *sleeve*
69. ballattis *poems* byrkis *birch*
trees
71. twa curis *two benefices* uplandis Michell *country Michael*
72. knitchell *bundle*
73. thocht *even though* nolt *cattle* tane leif *taken leave*
74. totum *all* nychell *nothing*
76. leif *live* landit *in possession of lands*
77. blandit *soothed*
78. repreif *rebuke*
79. rycht neirhand it *very close to it*

68. 'With a cheating card up his sleeve'.
73. 'Even though he has only just parted from his cows'.

17

As saule in to purgatorie,
Leifand in pane with hoip of glorie,
So is my selffe, ye may beleif,
In hoip, schir, of your adjutorie.
Exces of thocht dois me mischeif.   85

Schir, Ye have Mony Servitouris

Schir, ye have mony servitouris
And officiaris of dyvers curis:
Kirkmen, courtmen and craftismen fyne,
Doctouris in jure and medicyne,
Divinouris, rethoris and philosophouris,   5
Astrologis, artistis and oratouris,
Men of armes and vailyeand knychtis
And mony uther gudlie wichtis,
Musicianis, menstralis and mirrie singaris,
Chevalouris, cawandaris and flingaris,   10
Cunyouris, carvouris and carpentaris,
Beildaris of barkis and ballingaris,
Masounis lyand upon the land,
And schipwrichtis hewand upone the strand,
Glasing wrichtis, goldsmythis and lapidaris,   15
Pryntouris, payntouris and potingaris;
And all of thair craft cunning,
And all at anis lawboring,
Quhilk pleisand ar and honorable
And to your hienes profitable,   20
And richt convenient for to be
With your hie regale majestie,
Deserving of your grace most ding

1. schir *sir* servitouris *servants*
2. officiaris *officials* dyvers curis *different responsibilities*
3. kirkmen *men of the church*
4. doctouris in *doctors of* jure *law*
5. divinouris *practitioners of divination* rethoris *rhetoricians*
6. astrologis *astrologers* artistis *learned men* oratouris *orators*
7. vailyeand *valiant* knychtis *knights*
8. gudlie wichtis *good people*
9. menstralis *minstrals* mirrie singaris *merry singers*
10. chevalouris *horsemen* cawandaris *hurlers* flingaris *flingers*
11. cunyouris *coin makers*
carvouris *carvers*
12. beildaris *builders* barkis *small boats* ballingaris *little ships*
13. masounis *masons* lyand *living*
14. hewand *cutting wood* strand *shore*
15. glasing wrichtis *glass makers* lapidaris *jewellors*
16. pryntouris *printers* payntouris *painters* potingaris *apothecaries*
17. cunning *skilled*
18. at anis *together* lawboring *working*
19. pleisand *pleasing*
20. hienes *highness*
21. richt convenient *very fitting*
22. hie *high*
23. ding *worthy*

Bayth thank, rewarde and cherissing.
And thocht that I amang the laif   25
Unworthy be ane place to have
Or in thair nummer to be tald,
Als lang in mynd my work sall hald,
Als haill in everie circumstance,
In forme, in mater and substance,   30
But wering or consumptioun,
Roust, canker or corruptioun,
As ony of thair werkis all,
Suppois that my rewarde be small.
Bot ye sa gracious ar and meik,   35
That on your hienes followis eik
Ane uthir sort more miserabill,
Thocht thai be nocht sa profitable:
Fenyeouris, fleichouris and flatteraris,
Cryaris, craikaris and clatteraris,   40
Soukaris, groukaris, gledaris, gunnaris,
Monsouris of France, gud clarat cunnaris,
Inopportoun askaris of Yrland kynd
And meit revaris, lyk out of mynd,

24. thank *gratitude*
    cherissing *solicitude*
25. thocht *although* laif *others*
27. nummer *number* tald *counted*
28. als *as* mynd *memory*
    hald *stay*
29. haill *complete*
    circumstance *respect*
31. but *without* wering *wearing*
    out consumptioun *destruction*
32. roust *rust* canker *decay*
33. werkis *works*
34. suppois *even though*
35. meik *modest*
36. eik *also*
37. uthir *other* miserabill *wretched*

39. fenyeouris *liars*
    fleichouris *hypocrites*
40. cryaris *whingers*
    craikaris *clamourers*
    clatteraris *chatterers*
41. soukaris *parasites*
    groukaris *scroungers*
    gledaris *scavengers*
    gunnaris *gunners*
42. monsouris *monsieurs*
    clarat *claret* cunnaris *tasters*
43. inopportoun *importunate*
    askaris *beggars* Yrland
    kynd *Irish stock*
44. meit *food* revaris *stealers*

25–6. 'And although I am not worthy to have a place amongst all these
    others'.
28. 'My work shall stay just as long in the memory'.
36–7. 'That another, more wretched, sort of people also follow your
    highness' court'.
44. 'And people who steal food, as if they were out of their minds'.

Scaffaris and scamleris in the nuke 45
And hall huntaris of draik and duik,
Thrimlaris and thristaris, as thay war woid,
Kokenis, and kennis na man of gude,
Schulderaris and schovaris that hes no schame
And to no cunning that can clame, 50
And can non uthir craft nor curis
Bot to mak thrang, schir, in your duris,
And rusche in quhair thay counsale heir
And will at na man nurtir leyr;
In quintiscence eik ingynouris joly, 55
That far can multiplie in folie,
Fantastik fulis, bayth fals and gredy,
Of toung untrew and hand evill diedie.
Few dar of all this last additioun
Cum in tolbuyth without remissioun. 60
And thocht this nobill cunning sort,
   Quhom of befoir I did report,
Rewardit be, it war bot ressoun;

45. scaffaris *beggars*
   scamleris *spongers* nuke *corner*
46. huntaris *hunters* draik *drake*
   duik *duck*
47. thrimlaris *pushers*
   thristaris *thrusters* as *as if*
   woid *mad*
48. kokenis *rogues*
   kennis *acquaintances*
49. schulderaris *people who*
   shoulder their way in
   schovaris *shovers*
50. cunning *skill* clame *claim*
51. can *know* curis *office*
52. mak thrang *crowd* schir *sir*
   duris *doors*

53. quhair *where* counsale *private*
   conversation heir *hear*
54. nurtir *good manners* leyr *learn*
55. quintiscence *alchemy*
   ingynouris joly *presumptuous*
   contrivers
56. folie *folly*
57. fantastik fulis *crazy fools*
   gredy *greedy*
58. toung *tongue* evill diedic *doing*
   evil
59. dar *dare*
60. tolbuyth *tolbooth*
   remissioun *pardon*
61. cunning *skilled*
63. bot ressoun *only reasonable*

46. 'And hunters who only go as far as the banqueting hall in their
   search for drake and duck'.
48. 'Rogues, and those who are not acquainted with any good people'.
50. 'And can lay claim to no skill'.
54. 'And will learn good manners from no one'.
56. 'Who can produce great amounts of folly'.
59–60. 'Of this last group, few would dare to come to the tolbooth
   without a pardon'.
62. 'Of whom I spoke earlier'.

Thairat suld no man mak enchessoun.
Bot quhen the uther fulis nyce   65
That feistit at Cokelbeis gryce
Ar all rewardit and nocht I,
Than on this fals warld I cry, fy!
My hart neir bristis than for teyne,
Quhilk may nocht suffer nor sustene   70
So grit abusioun for to se
Daylie in court befoir myn e.
And yit more pacience wald I have,
Had I rewarde amang the laif:
It wald me sumthing satisfie   75
And les of my malancolie,
And gar me mony falt ourse
That now is brayd befoir myn e.
My mind so fer is set to flyt
That of nocht ellis I can endyt.   80
For owther man my hart to breik
Or with my pen I man me wreik.
And sen the tane most nedis be –
In to malancolie to de
Or lat the vennim ische all out –   85
Be war anone, for it will spout,
Gif that the tryackill cum nocht tyt
To swage the swalme of my dispyt.

64. enchessoun *objection*
65. nyce *silly*
66. feistit *feasted* Cokelbeis gryce *Colkelbie's sow*
68. warld *world* fy *fie!*
69. neir bristis *nearly breaks* than *then* teyne *anger*
70. sustene *endure*
71. grit abusioun *great abuse* se *see*
72. e *eye*
74. laif *rest*
75. sumthing *to some extent*
76. les of *relieve me of* malancolie *melancholy*
77. gar *cause* falt *fault*

ourse *overlook*
78. brayd *plainly*
79. fer *much* flyt *flyte*
80. ellis *else* endyt *compose*
81. owther *either* man *must* breik *break in pieces*
82. me wreik *avenge myself*
83. sen *since* tane *one* nedis *needs*
84. de *die*
85. lat *let* vennim *venom* ische *pour*
86. be war *beware* anone *at once*
87. gif *if* tryackill *remedy* tyt *quickly*
88. swage *heal* swalme *swelling* dispyt *hatred*

80. 'That I can't compose verse about anything else'.
83–5. 'And since one of these things must come about – to die in a state of melancholy or else let the venom all pour out'.

Be Divers Wyis and Operatiounes

Be divers wyis and operatiounes
Men makis in court thair solistationes:
Sum be service and diligence,
Sum be continuall residence.
Sum on his substance dois abyd,   5
Quhill fortoune do for him provyd.
Sum singis, sum dances, sum tellis storyis,
Sum lait at evin bringis in the moryis.
Sum flirdis, sum fenyeis and sum flatteris,
Sum playis the fuill and all owt clatteris.   10
Sum man, musand be the waw,
Luikis as he mycht nocht do with aw.
Sum standis in a nuk and rownes,
For covetyce ane uthair neir swownes.
Sum beris as he wald ga wud   15
For hait desyr of warldis gud.
Sum at the mes leves all devocion
And besy labouris for premocione.
Sum hes thair advocattis in chalmir,
And takis thameself thairof no glawmir.   20

1. be *by* divers *diverse*
wyis *means*
operatiounes *methods*
2. makis *make* solistationes
petitions for preferment
3. sum *one* be *by*
4. residence *attendance at court*
5. substance *resources* dois
abyd *lives*
6. quhill *until*
8. lait *late* at evin *in the evening*
moryis *morris dance*
9. flirdis *chatters* fenyeis *pretends*
10. fuill *fool* all owt
clatteris *prattles out everything*
11. musand *pondering* be the
waw *beside the wall*

12. luikis *looks* as *as if* with
aw *along with the rest*
13. nuk *corner* rownes *whispers*
14. covetyce *covetousness* ane
uthair *another* neir *nearly*
swownes *faints*
15. beris *behaves* ga wud *go mad*
16. hait *burning* warldis
gud *worldly goods*
17. mes *mass* leves *abandons*
devocion *spiritual meditation*
18. besy *busily*
premocione *promotion*
19. hes *meets with*
advocattis *intercessors* in
chalmir *in private*
20. thairof *for it* glawmir *scandal*

5–6. 'One man has to live on his own resources for a while, until fortune
provides for him'.
11–12. 'One man, standing thinking beside the wall, looks as if he could
not act like all the others'.
20. 'And suffer no scandal on that account themselves'.

My sempillnes, amang the laif,
Wait of na way, sa God me saif,
Bot with ane hummble cheir and face
Refferis me to the kyngis grace.
Methink his graciows countenance   25
In ryches is my sufficiance.

21. sempillnes *simplicity*   laif *rest*
22. wait *knows*   saif *save*
23. cheir *expression*
24. referris me *submit myself*
25. methink *it seems to me*
26. sufficiance *sufficiency*

23–4. 'Except to submit myself to the king's favour with a humble
    expression and face'.
26. 'Is sufficient riches for me'.

Of Every Asking Followis Nocht

1

Of every asking followis nocht
Rewaird, bot gif sum caus war wrocht.
And quhair caus is, men weill ma sie,
And quhair nane is, it wil be thocht:
In asking sowld discretioun be.   5

2

Ane fule, thocht he haif caus or nane,
Cryis ay, 'Gif me!' in to a drene;
And he that dronis ay as ane bee
Sowld haif ane heirar dull as stane:
In asking sowld discretioun be.   10

3

Sum askis mair than he deservis;
Sum askis far les than he servis;
Sum schames to ask, as braidis of me,
And all withowt reward he stervis:
In asking sowld discretioun be.   15

4

To ask but service hurtis gud fame;
To ask for service is not to blame;

1. asking *request*
2. bot gif *unless* caus *reason*
   wrocht *given*
3. quhair *where* weill *well* ma
   sie *can see it*
4. thocht *considered*
6. fule *fool* thocht *whether*
   haif *has*
7. cryis *cries* ay *constantly*
   gif *give* in to *a*
   drene *monotonously*
8. dronis *drones* as *like*
9. haif *have* heirar *listener*
   stanc *stone*
12. servis *deserves*
13. schames *is ashamed* braidis *is
    the case*
14. stervis *dies*
16. but *without* hurtis *harms*
    fame *reputation*
17. service *payment for service*
    blame *culpable*

1–2. 'Reward does not follow every request, only if some good reason is
given'.
5. 'Requests should always be made with discretion'.
9. 'Deserves to have a listener as deaf as a post'.
16–17. 'To ask someone for reward without having served them harms
one's good reputation; there is no harm in asking for payment for
services rendered'.

To serve and leif in beggartie
To man and maistir is baith schame:
In asking sowld discretioun be.   20

5

He that dois all his best servyis
May spill it all with crakkis and cryis,
Be fowll inoportunitie;
Few wordis may serve the wyis:
In asking sowld discretioun be.   25

6

Nocht neidfull is, men sowld be dum;
Na thing is gottin but wordis sum;
Nocht sped but diligence we se;
For nathing it allane will cum:
In asking sowld discretioun be.   30

7

Asking wald haif convenient place,
Convenient tyme, lasar and space
But haist or preis of grit menyie,
But hairt abasit, but toung rekles:
In asking sowld discretioun be.   35

8

Sum micht haif 'ye' with littill cure,
That hes oft 'nay' with grit labour;
All for that tyme not byd can he,
He tynis baith eirand and honour:
In asking sowld discretioun be.   40

18. leif *live* beggartie *poverty*
22. spill *spoil* crakkis *shouts*
24. wyis *wise*
26. neidfull *necessary* dum *silent*
27. but *without*
28. sped *succeed* se *see*
32. lasar *leisure*
33. haist *haste* preis *throng*

grit *great* menyie *company*
34. hairt *heart* abasit *cast down*
    toung *tongue*
36. ye *yes* cure *trouble*
37. nay *no*
38. byd *wait*
39. tynis *loses* eirand *errand*

19. 'Shames both the man and his master'.
23. 'By making foul demands at the wrong moment'.
28. 'We see nothing succeed without hard work'.
36–9. 'One might have been told "yes" with little trouble, who has often
    expended great effort only to be told "no"; he loses both his request
    and his honour all because he could not bide his time'.

9

Suppois the servand be lang unquit,
The lord sumtyme rewaird will it.
Gife he dois not, quhat remedy?
To fecht with fortoun is no wit:
In asking sowld discretioun be.   45

41. suppois *although*   43. gife *if*
    servand *servant*   unquit *unpaid*   44. fecht *fight*   wit *use*

44. 'There is no point in trying to fight against fortune'.

To Speik of Gift or Almous Deidis

1

To speik of gift or almous deidis.
Sum gevis for mereit and for meidis,
Sum warldly honour to uphie
Gevis to thame that nothing neidis:
In geving sowld discretioun be.   5

2

Sum gevis for pryd and glory vane,
Sum gevis with grugeing and with pane,
Sum gevis in practik for supple,
Sum gevis for twyis als gud agane:
In geving sowld discretioun be.   10

3

Sum gevis for thank and sum chereit,
Sum gevis money and sum gevis meit,
Sum gevis wordis fair and sle.
Giftis fra sum ma na man treit:
In geving sowld discretioun be.   15

4

Sum is for gift sa lang requyrd
Quhill that the crevar be so tyrd
That, or the gift deliverit be,

1. gift *gifts* almous deidis *giving alms*
2. sum *one* gevis *gives* mereit *virtue* meidis *reward*
3. warldly *worldly* uphie *exalt*
4. neidis *need*
5. geving *giving*
6. glory vane *vainglory*
7. with grugeing *grudgingly* pane *pain*
8. in practik *in a practical way*
supple *self-advantage*
9. for twyis *twice* als gud *as good*
11. thank *gratitude* chereit *charity*
12. meit *food*
13. sle *cunning*
14. treit *favour*
16. requyrd *asked*
17. quhill *until* crevar *suppliant* tyrd *tired*
18. or *before*

3–4. 'One, to exalt his own honour in the world, gives to those who need nothing'.
5. 'Discretion should be shown in one's gifts'.
14. 'Gifts from one will do no one any good'.
16. 'One is asked so long for the gift'.

The thank is frustrat and expyrd:
In geving sowld discretioun be.   20

5

Sum gevis to littill full wretchitly
That his giftis ar not set by
And for a huidpyk haldin is he,
That all the warld cryis on him, 'Fy!':
In geving sowld discretioun be.   25

6

Sum in his geving is so large
That all ourlaidin is his berge;
Than vyce and prodigalite
Thairof his honour dois dischairge:
In geving sowld discretioun be.   30

7

Sum to the riche gevis geir
That micht his giftis weill forbeir,
And thocht the peur for falt sowld de
His cry nocht enteris in his eir:
In geving sowld discretioun be.   35

8

Sum givis to strangeris with faces new
That yisterday fra Flanderis flew,
And to awld servandis list not se
War thay nevir of sa grit vertew:
In geving sowld discretioun be.   40

19. frustrat *frustrated* expyrd *at an end*
21. to *too* wretchitly *miserably*
22. set by *worth anything*
23. huidpyk *miser*
24. fy *shame*
26. large *generous*
27. ourlaidin *overloaded* berge *barge*
28. than *then* prodigalite *squander*

29. dischairge *relieve*
31. geir *wealth*
32. forbeir *do without*
33. thocht *although* peur *poor man* falt *want* de *die*
34. eir *ear*
37. Flanderis *Flanders*
38. awld *old* servandis *servants* list *choose* se *see*

23. 'And he is regarded as a miser'.
29. 'Relieve him of his honour'.
38–9. 'And choose not to see their old servants no matter how virtuous they have been'.

9

Sum gevis to thame can ask and plenyie,
Sum gevis to thame can flattir and fenyie,
Sum gevis to men of honestie
And haldis all janglaris at disdenyie:
In geving sowld discretioun be.   45

10

Sum gettis giftis and riche arrayis
To sweir all that his maister sayis,
Thocht all the contrair weill knawis he;
Ar mony sic now in thir dayis:
In geving sowld discretioun be.   50

11

Sum gevis gudmen for thair kewis,
Sum gevis to trumpouris and to schrewis,
Sum gevis to knaiffis autoritie;
Bot in thair office gude fundin few is:
In geving sowld discretioun be.   55

12

Sum givis parrochynnis full wyd,
Kirkis of Sanct Barnard and Sanct Bryd,
To teiche, to rewill and to ovirsie,
That hes na witt thameselfe to gyde:
In geving sowld discretioun be.   60

41. plenyie *complain*
42. fenyie *deceive*
44. janglaris *gossips* at
    disdenyie *in contempt*
46. arrayis *garments*
48. thocht *even though*
    contrair *contrary*
49. sic *such* thir *these*
51. gudmen *good men* kewis *good
    conduct*
52. trumpouris *cheats*

schrewis *scoundrels*
53. knaiffis *rogues* autoritie *power*
54. office *official role*
    fundin *found*
56. parrochynnis *parishes*
    wyd *wide*
57. kirkis *churches* Sanct
    Barnard *St Bernard* Bryd *Bride*
58. teiche *teach* rewill *rule*
    ovirsie *oversee*
59. witt *brains* gyde *rule*

47–8. 'For swearing that all his master says is true, even though he
knows well that the opposite is the case'.
53. 'One gives power to rogues'.
54. 'But few are found to be good at their jobs'.
59. 'Who don't even have the brains to take care of themselves'.

Eftir Geving I Speik of Taking

1

Eftir geving I speik of taking,
Bot littill of ony gud forsaiking.
Sum takkis our littill awtoritie
And sum our mekle, and that is glaiking:
In taking sowld discretioun be.   5

2

The clerkis takis beneficis with brawlis,
Sum of Sanct Petir and sum of Sanct Pawlis;
Tak he the rentis, no cair hes he
Suppois the Divill tak all thair sawlis:
In taking sowld discretioun be.   10

3

Barronis takis fra the tennentis peure
All fruct that growis on the feure
In mailis and gersomes rasit ouirhie,
And garris thame beg fra dure to dure:
In taking sowld discretioun be.   15

4

Sum takis uthir mennis takkis
And on the peure oppressioun makkis,
And nevir remembris that he mon die
Quhill that the gallowis gar him rax:
In taking sowld discretioun be.   20

---

1. geving *giving*
2. bot *without* forsaiking *giving up*
3. takkis *takes* our *too*
   awtoritie *power*
4. mekle *much* glaiking *folly*
5. discretioun *good judgement*
6. takis *take* beneficis *benefices*
   brawlis *uproar*
7. sanct *saint* Pawlis *Paul's*
8. rentis *money* cair *care*
9. suppois *even if* Divill *Devil*
   sawlis *souls*
11. barronis *barons* tennentis
    peure *poor tenant farmers*
12. fruct *produce* feure *furrow*
13. mailis *rents* gersomes *deposits*
    rasit *raised* ouirhie *too high*
14. garris *makes* dure *door*
16. uthir *other* mennis *men's*
    takkis *farms*
18. mon *must*
19. quhill that *until* gar *make*
    rax *stretch*

---

2. 'Without giving up anything of value'.
8–9. 'Providing he takes in the money, he doesn't care if the Devil takes all their souls'.

5

Sum takis be sie and sum be land
And nevir fra taking can hald thair hand
Quhill he be tit up to ane tre,
And syne thay gar him undirstand:
In taking sowld discretioun be.   25

6

Sum wald tak all his nychbouris geir;
Had he of man als littill feir
As he hes dreid that God him see,
To tak than sowld he nevir forbeir:
In taking sowld discretioun be.   30

7

Sum wald tak all this warldis breid
And yit not satisfeit of thair neid
Throw hairt unsatiable and gredie;
Sum wald tak littill, and can not speid:
In taking sowld discretioun be.   35

8

Grit men for taking and oppressioun
Ar sett full famous at the sessioun,
And peur takaris ar hangit hie,
Schamit for evir and thair successioun:
In taking sowld discretioun be.   40

---

21. be sie *by sea*
22. hald *hold back*
23. tit *tied* tre *tree*
24. syne *then*
26. nychbouris *neighbour's*
    geir *possessions*
27. als *as* feir *fear*
28. dreid *dread*
29. forbeir *refrain*
31. warldis *world's* breid *bread*

32. satisfeit *satisfied*
33. hairt *heart* gredie *greedy*
34. speid *succeed*
36. grit *great*
37. sett *placed* full famous *very
    respectably* sessioun *session court*
38. peur takaris *poor takers* hangit
    hie *hanged on high*
39. schamit *shamed*
    successioun *descendants*

32. 'And still not feel that their desire had been satisfied'.

This Waverand Warldis Wretchidnes

1

This waverand warldis wretchidnes,
The failyeand and frutles bissines,
The mispent tyme, the service vane,
For to considder is ane pane.

2

The slydand joy, the glaidnes schort,   5
The feynyeid luif, the fals confort,
The sweit abayd, the slichtfull trane,
For to considder is ane pane.

3

The sugurit mouthis with myndis thairfra,
The figurit speiche with faceis twa,   10
The plesand toungis with hartis unplane,
For to considder is ane pane.

4

The labour lost and liell service,
The lang availl on humill wyse,
And the lytill rewarde agane,   15
For to considder is ane pane.

5

Nocht I say all be this cuntre,
France, Ingland, Ireland, Almanie,

1. waverand *changeable*
   warldis *world's*
2. failyeand *unsuccessful*
   frutles *fruitless* bissines *activity*
3. mispent *misspent* vane *useless*
4. pane *pain*
5. slydand *transient*
   glaidnes *happiness* schort *brief*
6. feynyeid luif *false love*
   confort *pleasure*
7. abayd *delay* slichtfull
   trane *cunning trick*
9. sugurit *sweet* thairfra *from
   there*
10. figurit *eloquent* faceis twa *two
   faces*
11. hartis unplane *dishonest hearts*
13. liell *loyal*
14. availl *attendance* humill
   wyse *humble fashion*
15. agane *in return*
17. be *about* cuntre *country*
18. Almanie *Germany*

4. 'It is a painful thing to consider'.
9. 'The sweet-sounding mouths with minds very far from sweet'.
17. 'I am not talking only about this country'.

Bot als be Italie and Spane,
Quhilk to considder is ane pane.   20

6

The change of warld fro weill to wo,
The honorable use is all ago,
In hall and bour, in burgh and plane,
For to considder is ane pane.

7

Belief dois liep, traist dois nocht tarie,   25
Office dois flit and courtis dois vary,
Purpos dois change as wynd or rane,
Quhilk to considder is ane pane.

8

Gud rewle is banist our the bordour,
And rangat ringis but ony ordour,   30
With reird of rebaldis and of swane,
Quhilk to considder is ane pane.

9

The pepill so wickit ar of feiris,
The frutles erde all witnes beiris,
The ayr infectit and prophane,   35
Quhilk to considder is ane pane.

19. als *also*
21. weill *happiness*
22. use *way of life*   ago *gone*
23. bour *chamber*   burgh *town*
     plane *country*
25. dois liep *bounds away*
     traist *trust*   tarie *wait around*
26. office *authority*   flit *depart*
     courtis *courtesy*   vary *change*
27. purpos *resolve*   rane *rain*
29. rewle *behaviour*

banist *banished*   our *over*
     bordour *border*
30. rangat ringis *riot reigns*
     but *without*   ordour *order*
31. reird *commotion*
     rebaldis *rogues*   swane *peasants*
33. pepill *people*   of feiris *in
     behaviour*
34. erde *soil*
35. ayr *air*   prophane *polluted*

25. 'Belief in others bounds away, trust does not wait around'.
33–5. 'The fruitless soil, the infected and polluted air, both bear witness
     to the wicked behaviour of the people'.

10

The temporale stait to gryp and gather,
The sone disheris wald the father,
And as ane dyvour wald him demane,
Quhilk to considder is ane pane.   40

11

Kirkmen so halie ar and gude
That on thair conscience, rowme and rude,
May turne aucht oxin and ane wane,
Quhilk to considder is ane pane.

12

I knaw nocht how the kirk is gydit,   45
Bot beneficis ar nocht leill devydit:
Sum men hes sevin and I nocht ane,
Quhilk to considder is ane pane.

13

And sum unworthy to browk ane stall
Wald clym to be ane cardinall.   50
Ane bischoprik may nocht him gane,
Quhilk to considder is ane pane.

14

Unwourthy I, amang the laif,
Ane kirk dois craif and nane can have.
Sum with ane thraif playis passage plane,   55
Quhilk to considder is ane pane.

---

37. temporale stait *earthly estate*
gryp *seize*
38. sone *son*   disheris wald *would
disinherit*
39. dyvour *bankrupt*   demane *ill-
treat*
41. kirkmen *churchmen*   halie *holy*
42. rowme *big*   rude *rough*
43. aucht *eight*   wane *wagon*
45. gydit *governed*

46. leill devydit *fairly distributed*
47. ane *one*
49. browk *own*
50. clym *rise up*
51. bischoprik *bishopric*   gane *be
enough*
53. laif *rest*
54. craif *desire*
55. thraif *large number*
passage *dice*   plane *openly*

51. 'A bishopric would not be enough for him'.
55. 'One man who has been given a large number of churches is seen
openly gambling'.

15

It cumis be king, it cumis be quene,
Bot ay sic space is us betwene,
That nane can schut it with ane flane,
Quhilk to considder is ane pane.   60

16

It micht have cuming in schortar quhyll
Fra Calyecot and the new fund yle,
The partis of transmeridiane,
Quhilk to considder is ane pane.

17

It micht be this, had it bein kynd,   65
Cuming out of the desertis of Ynde,
Our all the grit se occeane,
Quhilk to considder is ane pane.

18

It micht have cuming out of all ayrtis:
Fra Paris and the orient partis,   70
And fra the ylis of Aphrycane,
Quhilk to consydder is ane pane.

19

It is so lang in cuming me till,
I dreid that it be quyt gane will,
Or bakwart it is turnit agane,   75
Quhilk to considder is ane pane.

57. cumis be *comes from*
58. ay *always* sic *such*
59. schut *shoot* flane *arrow*
61. cuming *come* quhyll *time*
62. Calyecot *Calicut* new fund
yle *newly discovered island*
63. partis *regions*
transmeridiane *the southern
hemisphere*
65. be this *by this time*

kynd *normal*
66. cuming *have come* Ynde *India*
67. our *over* grit se occeane *great
sea*
69. ayrtis *directions*
70. orient partis *eastern lands*
71. Aphrycane *Africa*
73. me till *to me*
74. dreid *fear* quyt *entirely* gane
will *gone astray*

57–9. 'It could come from the king, it could come from the queen, but I
am still such a long way from getting my church that no one could
even shoot it with an arrow from here'.
75. 'Or that it has turned back to port again'.

20

Upon the heid of it is hecht
Bayth unicornis and crownis of wecht.
Quhen it dois cum, all men dois frane,
Quhilk to considder is ane pane. 80

21

I wait it is for me provydit,
Bot sa done tyrsum it is to byd it,
It breikis my hairt and birstis my brane,
Quhilk to considder is ane pane.

22

Greit abbais grayth I nill to gather, 85
Bot ane kirk scant coverit with hadder,
For I of lytill wald be fane,
Quhilk to considder is ane pane.

23

And for my curis in sindrie place,
With help, schir, of your nobill grace, 90
My sillie saule sall never be slane,
Na for sic syn to suffer pane.

24

Experience dois me so inspyr,
Of this fals failyeand warld I tyre,

77. heid *head* hecht *promised*
78. unicornis *unicorns; gold coins*
crownis of wecht *heavy crowns*
79. frane *ask*
81. wait *know* me
provydit *arranged for me*
82. sa done tyrsum *so very
tiresome* byd *await*
83. birstis *tears apart* brane *brain*
85. abbais *abbeys'* grayth *wealth*
nill *do not wish*

86. bot *only* scant coverit *poorly
thatched* hadder *heather*
87. fane *glad*
89. curis *benefices* sindrie *different*
90. schir *sir*
91. sillie saule *innocent soul*
slane *condemned*
92. na *nor* syn *sin* pane *torment*
93. inspyr *influence*
94. failyeand *declining* tyre *grow
tired*

77–9. 'Coins and heavy gold money have been promised upon its safe
arrival; everyone asks when it is coming'.
85. 'I do not wish to acquire the wealth of great abbeys'.
89–92. 'Thanks to your noble favour, sir, my innocent soul shall never
be condemned for having benefices in different places, nor ever suffer
torment for that sin'.

That evermore flytis lyk ane phane,   95
Quhilk to considder is ane pane.

25
The formest hoip yit that I have
In all this warld, sa God me save,
Is in your grace, bayth crop and grayne,
Quhilk is ane lessing of my pane.   100

95. flytis *changes*   98. sa God me save *may God*
    phane *weathervane*   *protect me*
97. formest hoip *greatest hope* 99. crop *top of plant* grayne *seed*
                                  100. lessing *alleviation*

99. 'Is in your favour, from beginning to end'.

This Hinder Nycht, Half Sleiping As I Lay

1

This hinder nycht, half sleiping as I lay,
Me thocht my chalmer in ane new aray
Was all depent with many divers hew
Of all the nobill storyis, ald and new,
Sen oure first father formed was of clay.   5

2

Me thocht the lift all bricht with lampis lycht,
And thairin enterrit many lustie wicht,
Sum young, sum old, in sindry wyse arayit.
Sum sang, sum danceit, on instrumentis sum playit,
Sum maid disportis with hartis glaid and lycht.   10

3

Thane thocht I thus: this is ane felloun phary,
Or ellis my witt rycht woundrouslie dois varie.
This seimes to me ane guidlie companie,
And gif it be ane feindlie fantasie,
Defend me Jhesu and his moder Marie!   15

4

Thair pleasant sang nor yett thair pleasant toun
Nor yett thair joy did to my heart redoun.
Me thocht the drerie damiesall, Distres,
And eik hir sorie sister, Hevines,
Sad as the leid in baid lay me abone.   20

1. this hinder nycht *last night*
2. me thocht *it seemed to me*
   chalmer *room*   aray *arrangement*
3. depent *decorated*   divers
   hew *different colours*
4. ald *old*
5. sen *since*
6. lift *sky*   lampis lycht *lamplight*
7. thairin *inside*   lustie wicht *fair person*
8. sindry wyse *different ways*
   arayit *dressed*
10. disportis *entertainments*
    hartis *hearts*   lycht *joyful*
11. felloun phary *great vision*

12. ellis *else*   witt *mind*
    varie *wander*
13. guidlie *distinguished*
14. gif *if*   feindlie fantasie *diabolic illusion*
15. moder *mother*
16. sang *song*   yett *even*
    toun *music*
17. redoun *penetrate*
18. drerie damiesall *mournful damsel*   Distres *Grief*
19. eik *also*   sorie *sorrowful*
    Hevines *Misery*
20. sad *heavy*   leid *lead*   baid *bed*
    abone *above*

5

And Langour satt up at my beddis heid.
With instrument full lamentable and deid
Scho playit sangis, so duilfull to heir,
Me thocht ane houre seimeit ay ane yeir.
Hir hew was wan and wallowed as the leid.   25

6

Thane com the ladyis danceing in ane trace,
And Nobilnes befoir thame come ane space,
Saying withe cheir bening and womanly:
'I se ane heir in bed oppressit ly,
My sisteris, go and help to gett him grace.'   30

7

With that anon did start out of a dance
Twa sisteris callit Confort and Pleasance,
And with twa harpis did begin to sing;
Bot I thairof mycht tak na rejoseing,
My heavines opprest me with sic mischance.   35

8

Thay saw that I not glader wox of cheir,
And thairof had thai winder all, but weir,
And said ane lady that Persaveing hecht,
'Of hevines he fiellis sic a wecht,
Your melody he pleisis not till heir.   40

21. Langour *Wretchedness*
  heid *head*
22. lamentable *sad*   deid *funereal*
23. duilfull *doleful*   heir *hear*
24. ane houre *one hour*   seimeit
  ay *seemed like*   yeir *year*
25. hew *complexion*
  wallowed *discoloured*   leid *lead*
26. com *came*   trace *procession*
27. ane space *a little way*
28. cheir bening *kind expression*
29. se *see*   ane *someone*   oppressit
  ly *lies afflicted*

31. anon *at once*   start *move*
32. twa *two*   Confort *Delight*
  Plesance *Pleasure*
33. harpis *harps*
34. thairof *in that*   rejoseing *cheer*
35. sic mischance *such misery*
36. wox *became*   cheir *mood*
37. winder *astonishment*   but
  weir *without doubt*
38. Persaveing hecht *was called*
  Perceptiveness
39. fiellis *feels*   wecht *weight*
40. pleisis *chooses*   till *to*

27. 'And Nobility came a little way in front of them'.
29. 'I see someone here lying afflicted in bed'.
36. 'They saw that my mood did not improve'.
40. 'He chooses not to hear your melody'.

9

'Scho and Distres, hir sister, dois him greve.'
Quod Nobilnes, 'Quhow sall he thame eschew?'
Thane spak Discretioun, ane lady richt bening:
'Wirk eftir me, and I sall gar him sing,
And lang or nicht gar Langar tak hir leve.'   45

10

And then said Witt, 'Gif thai work not be the,
But onie dout thai sall not work be me.'
Discretioun said, 'I knaw his melody,
The strok he feillis of melancholie,
And, Nobilnes, his lecheing lyis in the.   50

11

'Or evir this wicht at heart be haill and feir,
Both thow and I most in the court appeir,
For he hes lang maid service thair in vane;
With sum rewaird we mane him quyt againe,
Now in the honour of this guid New Yeir.'   55

12

'Weill worth the, sister,' said Considerance,
'And I sall help for to mantene the dance.'
Thane spak ane wicht callit Blind Effectioun:
'I sall befoir yow be with myne electioun,
Of all the court I have the governance.'   60

41. greve *grieve*
42. quod *said* quhow *how*
    eschew *escape*
43. Discretioun *Discernment*
44. wirk eftir me *act according to
    my instructions* gar *make*
45. lang or *long before* leve *leave*
46. gif *if* be the *for you*
47. but onie dout *without any
    doubt*
48. melody *affliction*
49. strok *blow*

50. lecheing *cure* the *you*
51. or evir *before* wicht *person*
    haill *whole* feir *healthy*
52. most *must*
54. mane *must* quyt *repay*
56. weill worth the *may you
    prosper*
    Considerance *Consideration*
57. mantene *continue*
58. Effectioun *Affection*
59. electioun *candidate*
60. governance *control*

45. 'And make Wretchedness take her leave long before night comes'.

13

Thane spak ane constant wycht callit Ressoun,
And said, 'I grant yow hes beine lord a sessioun
In distributioun, bot now the tyme is gone.
Now I may all distribute myne alone.
Thy wrangous deidis did evir mane enschesoun.   65

14

'For tyme war now that this mane had sumthing,
That lange hes bene ane servand to the king,
And all his tyme nevir flatter couthe nor faine,
Bot humblie into ballat wyse complaine
And patientlie indure his tormenting.   70

15

'I counsall him be mirrie and jocound.
Be Nobilnes his help mon first be found.'
'Weill spokin, Ressoun, my brother', quod Discretioun,
'To sett on dies with lordis at the sessioun
Into this realme yow war worth mony ane pound.'   75

16

Thane spak anone Inoportunitie:
'Ye sall not all gar him speid without me,
For I stand ay befoir the kingis face.
I sall him deif or ellis myself mak hace,
Bot gif that I befoir him servit be.   80

62. grant *admit* beine *been* a sessioun *for a time*
64. myne alone *on my own*
65. wrangous deidis *evil deeds* evir mane *everyone* enschesoun *blame*
67. servand *servant*
68. couthe *could* faine *feign*
69. bot *only* ballat wyse *the poetic form*
70. indure *endure*

71. counsall *advise* mirrie *merry* jocound *cheerful*
72. be *by means of* mon *must*
74. sett *sit* dies *dais* sessioun *law court*
75. into *to* realme *land*
76. spak *spoke* Inoportunitie *Persistent Demand*
77. speid *succeed*
79. deiff *deafen* hace *hoarse*
80. bot gif *unless* servit be *be provided for*

65. 'Everyone found fault with your evil deeds'.
66. 'For it is time now that this man received something'.
74–5. 'It would be a very valuable thing for this country to have you sitting up on the dais with the lords in the law courts'.
79–80. 'I shall deafen him or make myself hoarse in the attempt, unless I am provided for before him'.

17

'Ane besy askar soonner sall he speid
Na sall twa besy servandis, out of dreid;
And he that askis not tynes bot his word,
Bot for to tyne lang service is no bourd.
Yett thocht I nevir to do sic folie deid.'   85

18

Thane com anon ane callit Schir Johne Kirkpakar,
Of many cures ane michtie undertaker.
Quod he, 'I am possest in kirkis sevin,
And yitt I think thai grow sall till ellevin,
Or he be servit in ane, yone ballet maker.   90

19

'And then, schir, bet the kirk, sa mot I thryff,
I haif of busie servandis foure or fyve,
And all direct unto sindrie steidis,
Ay still awaitting upoun kirkmenes deidis,
Fra quham sum tithingis will I heir belyff.'   95

20

Quod Ressoun than, 'The ballance gois unevin,
That thow, allece, to serff hes kirkis sevin,

81. besy askar *busy petitioner*
82. na *than* servandis *servants*
    out of dreid *without doubt*
83. not tynes *loses nothing*
84. tyne *waste* bourd *joke*
85. thocht *intended* folie
    deid *foolish deed*
86. Schir Johne Kirkpakar *Sir
    John Churchacquirer*
87. cures *benefices* michtie
    undertaker *wealthy collector*
88. possest in *in possession of*
90. or *before* servit in *provided*

with yone *that* ballet
maker *poet*
91. bet *destroy* mot I thryff *may I
    prosper*
93. direct *dispatched* sindric
    steidis *various places*
94. kirkmenes deidis *churchmen's
    deaths*
95. fra quham *from whom*
    tithingis *news* heir *hear*
    belyff *soon*
96. ballance *scales*
97. allece *alas* serff *serve*

81–4. 'A constant petitioner will succeed in his claims sooner than two
    attentive servants, without any doubt; and he who asks for things loses
    nothing except his words, but to waste a period of long service is no
    joke'.
91. 'And then, sir, so long as I prosper, let the church go to ruin'.
96–8. 'Then said Reason, "The scales are not balanced when you, alas,
    have to serve seven churches as their priest, while seven men just as
    deserving of a church have none" '.

And sevin als worth kirk not haifand ane.
With gredines I sie this world ourgane,
And sufficience dwellis nocht bot in heavin.'   100

21

'I have not wyt thairof,' quod Temperance,
'For thocht I hald him evinlie the ballance,
And but ane cuir full micht till him wey,
Yett will he tak ane uther and gar it swey.
Quha best can rewll wald maist have governance.'   105

22

Patience to me, 'My freind,' said, 'Mak guid cheir,
And on the prince depend with humelie feir.
For I full weill dois knaw his nobill intent:
He wald not, for ane bischopperikis rent,
That yow war unrewairdit half ane yeir.'   110

23

Than as ane fary thai to duir did frak,
And schot ane gone that did so ruidlie rak
Quhill all the aird did raird the ranebow under.
On Leith sandis me thocht scho brak in sounder,
And I anon did walkin with the crak.   115

---

98. als worth *as worthy of*
    haifand *having*
99. gredines *greed* sie *see*
    ourgane *overcome*
100. sufficience *contentment* nocht
    bot *only*
101. wyt *blame*
102. thocht *although* him *for him*
103. till *for* wey *weigh*
104. swey *tilt*
105. rewll *rule*
106. mak guid cheir *cheer up*

107. humelie feir *humble behaviour*
109. bischopperikis *bishopric's*
111. as *like* fary *vision* duir *door*
    frak *rush*
112. schot *shot* gone *gun* ruidlie
    rak *violently explode*
113. quhill *until* aird *earth*
    raird *resound*
114. sandis *sands* brak in
    sounder *broke apart*
115. walkin *awaken* crak *explosion*

102–3. 'For although I hold the scales evenly for him, and a single
benefice would weigh enough for him'.
105. 'Whoever can rule best should have the most power'.
109–110. 'He would not want it to happen, not even for all the money
from a bishopric, that you should go unrewarded for a full six months'.

My Prince in God Gif The Guid Grace

1

My prince in God gif the guid grace,
Joy, glaidnes, confort and solace,
Play, pleasance, myrth and mirrie cheir,
In hansill of this guid New Yeir.

2

God gif to the ane blissed chance   5
And of all vertew aboundance,
And grace ay for to perseveir,
In hansill of this guid New Yeir.

3

God give the guid prosperitie,
Fair fortoun and felicitie,   10
Evir mair in earth quhill thow ar heir,
In hansell of this guid New Yeir.

4

The heavinlie lord his help the send,
Thy realme to reull and to defend,
In peace and justice it to steir,   15
In hansell of this guid New Yeir.

5

God gif the blis quharevir thow bownes,
And send the many Fraunce crownes,
Hie liberall heart and handis not sweir,
In hansell of this guid New Yeir.   20

1. gif the *grant you* guid
   grace *good favour*
2. confort *pleasure*
   solace *enjoyment*
3. plesance *joy* myrth *mirth*
   mirrie cheir *good cheer*
4. in hansill *as a gift*
5. blissed chance *good fortune*
6. vertew *virtue*

7. ay *always* perseveir *persevere*
10. felicitie *happiness*
11. quhill *while* heir *here*
14. reull *rule*
15. steir *govern*
17. quharevir *wherever* bownes *go*
18. Fraunce crownes *French coins*
19. hie *noble* liberall *generous*
    sweir *slow*

6. 'And abundance of every virtue'.
19. 'A noble, generous heart and hands that are not slow to give'.

Schir, Lat it Never in Toune Be Tald

Schir, lat it never in toune be tald
That I suld be ane Yowllis yald.

1

Suppois I war ane ald yald aver,
Schott furth our clewch to squische the clever,
And hed the strenthis of all Strenever,   5
I wald at Youll be housit and stald.
Schir, lat it never in toune be tald
That I suld be ane Yowllis yald.

2

I am ane auld hors, as ye knaw,
That ever in duill dois drug and draw.   10
Gryt court hors puttis me fra the staw,
To fang the fog be firthe and fald.
Schir, lat it never in toune be tald
That I suld be ane Yowllis yald.

3

I hef run lang furth in the feild   15
On pastouris that ar plane and peld.
I mycht be now tein in for eild,
My bekis ar spruning he and bald.
Schir, lat it never in toun be tald
That I suld be ane Yowllis yald.   20

1. schir *sir* tald *proclaimed*
2. Yowllis *Yule; Christmas*
   yald *neglected old horse*
3. suppois *even if* ald *old* yald
   aver *neglected cart-horse*
4. schott furth *driven out*
   our *over* clewch *cliff*
   squische *squash* clever *clover*
5. hed *possess* strenthis *wastelands*
   Strenever *Strath Naver*
6. wald *would like* housit *housed*
   stald *stabled*

10. duill *sorrow* drug *drag*
11. gryt *big* puttis me *pushes me*
    staw *stall*
12. fang *take* fog *winter grass*
    firthe *wood* flad *field*
15. hef *have* furth *out*
16. pastouris *pastures*
    plane *smooth* peld *stripped bare*
17. tein in *taken in* for eild *on
    account of old age*
18. bekis *teeth* spruning *falling
    out* he *big* bald *fierce*

1–2. 'Sir never let it be proclaimed in the town that I should be a
neglected old horse at Christmas'.
18. 'My big, fierce teeth are falling out'.

4

My maine is turned in to quhyt,
And thairof ye hef all the wyt:
Quhen uthair hors hed brane to byt,
I gat bot gris, grype gif I wald.
Schir, lat it never in towne be tald   25
That I suld be ane Yowllis yald.

5

I was never dautit in to stabell.
My lyf hes bein so miserabell,
My hyd to offer I am abell,
For evill schoud strae that I reiv wald.   30
Schir, lat it never in towne be tald
That I suld be ane Yowllis yald.

6

And yett, suppois my thrift be thyne,
Gif that I die your aucht within
Lat nevir the soutteris have my skin,   35
With uglie gumes to be gnawin.
Schir, lat it nevir in toun be tald
That I sould be ane Yowllis yald.

7

The court hes done my curage cuill
And maid me ane forriddin muill.   40
Yett to weir trapperis at the Yuill,

21. maine *mane* quhyt *white*
22. thairof *for that* wyt *blame*
23. uthair *other* brane *bran*
    byt *bite*
24. bot *only* gris *grass* grype *giff
    I wald* if I was able to get hold of
    any*
27. dautit *petted* stabell *stable*
29. hyd *skin* offer *sell* abell *ready*
30. evill schoud strae *poor quality
    straw* reiv *devour*

33. thrift *resources* thyne *few*
34. gif *if* aucht *possession*
35. soutteris *shoemakers*
36. gumes *gums* gnawin *chewed*
39. done . . . cuill *cooled*
    curage *high spirits*
40. forriddin *hard-ridden*
    muill *mule*
41. weir *wear* trapperis *horse-
    covers*

29–30. 'I am ready to sell my own skin for poor quality straw that I
    would devour'.
41–2. 'Yet, I'd be happy to be whipped all over if it meant I could wear
    new horse-coverings at the Christmas feast'.

I wald be spurrit at everie spald.
Schir, lett it nevir in toun be tald
That I sould be ane Yuillis yald.

8
Now lufferis cummis with larges lowd.   45
Quhy sould not palfrayis thane be prowd,
Quhen gillettis wil be schomd and schroud,
That riddin ar baith with lord and lawd?
Schir, lett it nevir in toun be tald
That I sould be ane Yuillis yald.   50

9
Quhen I was young and into ply
And wald cast gammaldis to the sky,
I had beine bocht in realmes by,
Had I consentit to be sauld.
Schir, lett it nevir in toun be tauld   55
That I sould be ane Yuillis yald.

10
With gentill hors quhen I wald knyp,
Thane is thair laid on me ane quhip.
To colleveris than man I skip,
That scabbit ar, hes cruik and cald.   60
Schir, lett it nevir in toun be tald
That I sould be ane Yuillis yald.

---

42. spurrit *spurred*   spald *limb*
45. lufferis *liverymen*
    larges *generosity*   lowd *loud*
46. sould *should*   palfrayis *riding
    horses*   prowd *proud*
47. gillettis *mares*
    schomed *groomed*
    schroud *adorned*
48. lawd *lad*
51. into ply *in good condition*

52. gammaldis *leaps*
53. realmes *countries*   by *nearby*
54. sauld *sold*
57. gentill *noble*   knyp *graze*
58. quhip *whip*
59. colleveris *horses that carry
    coal*   man *must*
60. scabbit *scabby*   cruik *lameness*
    cald *sickness*

53. 'I could have been bought by neighbouring realms'.
57–8. 'When I try to graze with the noble horses then a whip is laid on
    me'.

11

Thocht in the stall I be not clappit,
As cursouris that in silk beine trappit,
With ane new hous I wald be happit   65
Aganis this Crysthinmes for the cald.
Schir, lett it nevir in toun be tald
That I sould be ane Yuillis yald.

Respontio regis
Efter our wrettingis, thesaurer,
Tak in this gray hors, auld Dumbar,   70
Quhilk in my aucht with service trew
In lyart changeit is his hew.
Gar hows him new aganis this Yuill
And busk him lyk ane bischopis muill,
For with my hand I have indost   75
To pay quhatevir his trappouris cost.

63. clappit *patted*
64. cursouris *coursers; large, fast
horses*   trappit *adorned*
65. hous *horse-cover*
happit *wrapped up warmly*
66. aganis *ready for*
Respontio regis *the king's answer*
69. efter *in accordance with*

wrettingis *written instructions*
thesaurer *treasurer*
71. aucht *possession*
72. lyart *grey*   hew *colour*
73. gar hows him *have him clothed*
74. busk *dress finely*   muill *mule*
75. indost *authorized*
76. trappouris *trappings*

The Wardraipper of Venus Boure

1

The wardraipper of Venus boure,
To giff a doublett he is als doure
As it war of an futt-syd frog:
Madame, ye heff a dangerous dog.

2

Quhen that I schawe to him your markis,   5
He turnis to me again and barkis
As he war wirriand an hog:
Madame, ye heff a dangerous dog.

3

Quhen that I schawe to him your wrytin,
He girnis that I am red for bytin;   10
I wald he had an havye clog:
Madame, ye heff an dangerous dog.

4

Quhen that I speik till him freindlyk,
He barkis lyk an midding tyk
War chassand cattell throu a bog: 15
Madam, ye heff a dangerous dog.

5

He is an mastive, mekle of mycht,
To keip your wardroippe over nycht
Fra the grytt sowdan Gog Magog:
Madam, ye heff a dangerous dog.   20

1. wardraipper *wardrobe master*
   boure *chamber*
2. giff *give* doublett *doublet; short
   jacket* doure *sullen*
3. futt syd *ankle-length* frog *cloak*
4. heff *have*
5. schawe *show* markis *seal*
7. wirriand *worrying* hog *sheep*
9. wrytin *writing*
10. girnis *snarls* that *so that* red
    for bytin *in fear of being bitten*

11. wald *wish* havye *heavy*
    clog *block of wood*
13. freindlyk *in a friendly manner*
14. midding tyk *midden mongrel*
15. chassand *chasing*
17. mastive *mastiff* mekle *great*
    mycht *power*
18. keip *guard*
    wardroippe *wardrobe*
    nycht *night*
19. grytt *great* sowdan *sultan*

2–3. 'He is as sullen about giving away a doublet as he would be for an
    ankle-length cloak'.
11. 'I wish he were tied to a heavy block of wood'.

6

He is over mekle to be your messan.
Madam, I red you, get a less an.
His gang garris all your chalmeris schog.
Madam, ye heff a dangerous dog.

21. over mekle *too big*
    messan *lapdog*
22. red *advise* less an *smaller one*

23. gang *walk* garris *causes*
    chalmeris *rooms* schog *to shake*

O Gracious Princes Guid and Fair

1

O gracious Princes guid and fair,
Do weill to James, your wardraipair,
Quhais faythfull bruder maist freind I am:
He is na dog, he is a lam.

2

Thocht I in ballet did with him bourde,   5
In malice spack I nevir an woord,
Bot all, my dame, to do you gam:
He is na dog, he is a lam.

3

Your hienes can nocht gett an meter
To keip your wardrope, nor discreter   10
To rewle your robbis and dres the sam:
He is na dog, he is a lam.

4

The wyff that he had in his innis,
That with the taingis wald braek his schinnis,
I wald schou drownet war in a dam: 15
He is na dog, he is a lam.

5

The wyff that wald him kuckald mak,
I wald schou war, bayth syd and back,
Weill batteret with an barrou tram:
He is na dog, he is a lam.   20

3. bruder *brother* frein *friendly*
4. lam *lamb*
5. ballet *poem* bourde *jest*
6. spack *spoke*
7. dame *lady* do you
gam *entertain you*
9. hienes *highness* an meter *more
suitable person*
10. discreter *more discreet*
11. rewle *look after* robbis *robes*

dres *dresses* the sam *together*
13. wyff *woman* innis *house*
14. taingis *fire tongs* braek *break*
schinnis *shins*
15. wald *wish*
16. kuckald *cuckold; deceived
husband*
19. batteret *beaten* barrou
tram *shaft of a wheelbarrow*

3. 'Whose faithful and most friendly brother I am'.

6

He hes sa weill doin me obey
In till all thing, thairfoir I pray,
That nevir dolour mak him dram:
He is na dog, he is a lam.

21. doin me obey *obeyed me*
22. in till all thing *in all respects*
23. dolour *sorrow*   dram *dejected*

23. 'That sorrow never make him feel dejected'.

Sanct Salvatour, Send Silver Sorrow

1

Sanct Salvatour, send silver sorrow!
It grevis me both evin and morrow,
Chasing fra me all cheritie.
It makis me all blythnes to borrow,
My panefull purs so priclis me.   5

2

Quhen I wald blythlie ballattis breif,
Langour thairto givis me no leif.
War nocht gud howp my hart uphie,
My verry corpis for cair wald cleif.
My panefull purs so prikillis me.   10

3

Quhen I sett me to sing or dance
Or go to plesand pastance,
Than pansing of penuritie
Revis that fra my remembrance.
My panefull purs so prikillis me.   15

4

Quhen men that hes pursis in tone
Pasis to drynk or to disjone,
Than mon I keip ane gravetie
And say that I will fast quhill none.
My panefull purs so priclis me.   20

1. Sanct Salvatour *Holy Saviour*
2. grevis *distresses* evin *evening*
   morrow *morning*
3. cheritie *charity*
4. blythnes *happiness*
5. purs *purse* so priclis me *causes
   me so much pain*
6. quhen *when* blythile *happily*
   ballattis breif *write poems*
7. langour *misery* leif *permission*
8. war *were* howp *hope*
   uphie *raise*

9. corpis *body* cair *sorrow*
   cleif *split in two*
12. plesand *pleasant*
    pastance *pastime*
13. than *then* pansing *thinking*
    penuritie *poverty*
14. revis *removes*
16. in tone *in tune; healthy*
17. pasis *go* disjone *breakfast*
18. mon *must* gravetie *serious
    expression*
19. quhill *until* none *noon*

1. 'Holy Saviour, let silver be cursed'.
4. 'It means that I have to borrow all my happiness'.
8. 'If it were not for good hope raising my spirits'.
13–14. 'Then the thought of my poverty removes that idea from my mind'.

5

My purs is maid of sic ane skyn,
Thair will na cors byd it within:
Fra it as fra the feynd thay fle.
Quhaevir tyne, quhaevir win,
My panefull purs so priclis me.   25

6

Had I ane man of ony natioun,
Culd mak on it ane conjuratioun
To gar silver ay in it be,
The devill suld haif no dominatioun
With pyne to gar it prickill me.   30

7

I haif inquyrit in mony a place
For help and confort in this cace,
And all men sayis, my lord, that ye
Can best remeid for this malice,
That with sic panis prickillis me.   35

21. sic *such* skyn *skin*
22. cors *coin* byd *remain*
23. fra *from* feynd *devil* fle *flee*
24. tyne *loses*
26. ony *any*
27. conjuratioun *magic spell*
28. gar *make* ay *always*

30. pyne *pain*
31. inquyrit *inquired*
32. confort *consolation* cace *matter*
34. remeid *provide a cure*
    malice *disease*
35. panis *pains*

24. 'No matter who loses no matter who wins'.

My Lordis of Chalker, Pleis Yow to Heir

1

My lordis of chalker, pleis yow to heir
My coumpt, I sall it mak yow cleir,
But ony circumstance or sonyie;
For left is nether corce nor cunyie
Of all that I tuik in the yeir.   5

2

For rekkyning of my rentis and roumes
Yie neid not for to tyre your thowmes,
Na for to gar your countaris clink,
Na paper for to spend nor ink,
In the ressaveing of my soumes.   10

3

I tuik fra my lord thesaurair
Ane soume of money for to wair.
I cannot tell yow how it is spendit,
Bot weill I waitt that it is endit,
And that me think ane coumpt our sair.   15

1. chalker *exchequer* pleis *if it
please* heir *hear*
2. coumpt *account* yow cleir *clear
to you*
3. but *without*
circumstance *digression*
sonyie *excuse*
4. corce *copper* cunyie *coin*
5. tuik *received* yeir *year*
6. rekkyning *reckoning*
rentis *wealth* roumes *estates*
7. tyre *tire* thowmes *thumbs*

8. na *nor* gar *make*
countaris *counters*
9. spend *use up*
10. ressaveing *receipt*
soumes *sums*
11. thesaurair *treasurer*
12. wair *spend*
14. waitt *know* endit *gone*
15. me think *seems to me*
coumpt *account* our sair *too
painful*

10. 'In calculating the sums that I've received'.

4

I trowit, the tyme quhen that I tuik it,
That lang in burgh I sould have bruikit.
Now the remanes ar eith to turs:
I have na preiff heir bot my purs,
Quhilk wald not lie and it war luikit.   20

16. trowit *believed*   quhen *when*
17. lang *long*   burgh *town*
    bruikit *kept it*
18. remanes *remains*   eith to
    turs *easily carried*

19. preiff *proof*   heir *here*
    purs *purse*
20. quhilk *which*   and *if*
    luikit *looked into*

16. 'I believed, at the time that I received it, that I would have it a long
time in that town'.

I Thocht Lang Quhill Sum Lord Come Hame

1
I thocht lang quhill sum lord come hame,
Fra quhom faine kyndnes I wald clame.
His name of confort I will declair:
Welcome, my awin lord thesaurair!

2
Befoir all rink of this regioun,   5
Under our roy of most renoun,
Of all my mycht, thocht it war mair,
Welcom, my awin lord thesaurair!

3
Your nobill payment I did assay,
And ye hecht sone, without delay,   10
Againe in Edinburgh till repair:
Welcom, my awin lord thesaurair!

4
Ye keipit tryst so winder weill,
I hald yow trew as ony steill;
Neidis nane your payment till dispair.   15
Welcom, my awin lord thesaurair!

1. thocht lang *thought it long*
   quhill *until*   sum *a certain*
   hame *home*
2. quhom *whom*   faine *gladly*
   kyndnes *generosity*   clame *lay claim to*
3. confort *comfort*
4. awin *own*   thesaurair *treasurer*
5. all *every*   rink *knight*
   regioun *country*
6. roy *king*
7. of *with*   mycht *power*
   thocht *even if*
9. assay *try to obtain*
10. hecht *promised*   sone *soon*
11. againe . . . till repair *to return*
13. tryst *promise*   winder
    weill *amazingly well*
14. hald *consider*   trew *true*
    steill *steel*
15. neidis nane *no one needs*

1–2. 'It seemed like a long time to me until a certain lord came home, from whom I was only too willing to claim some generosity'.
3. 'I will openly declare his name to be a comfort'.
7. 'With all my power, even if it were greater'.
11. 'To return to Edinburgh'.
14. 'No one needs to despair of ever receiving payment from you'.

5

Yett in a pairt I was agast,
Or ye the narrest way had past
Fra toun of Stirling to the air.
Welcom, my awin lord thesaurair!   20

6

Thane had my dyt beine all in duill,
Had I my wage wantit quhill Yuill,
Quhair now I sing with heart onsair,
Welcum, my awin lord thesaurair!

7

Welcum, my benefice and my rent,   25
And all the lyflett to me lent;
Welcum, my pensioun most preclair!
Welcum, my awin lord thesaurair!

8

Welcum als heartlie as I can,
My awin dear maister, to your man   30
And to your servand singulair!
Welcum, my awin lord thesaurair!

17. in a pairt *to some extent*
    agast *anxious*
18. or *in case* narrest way *most
    direct route*
19. air *circuit court*
21. dyt *writing* beine *been*
    duill *misery*
22. wantit *lacked* Yuill *Christmas*

23. quhair *whereas* onsair *joyful*
25. benefice *pension* rent *income*
26. lyflett *means of living*
    lent *given*
27. preclair *splendid*
29. als *as* heartlie *heartily*
31. servand singulair *special
    servant*

18–19. 'In case you had taken the most direct route from the town of
    Stirling to the circuit court'.
21–2. 'If I had had to do without my money until Christmas, then all my
    writing would have been miserable'.

To Speik of Science, Craft or Sapience

1

To speik of science, craft or sapience,
Of vertew morall, cunnyng or doctrene,
Of jure, of wisdome or intelligence,
Of everie study, lair or disciplene –
All is bot tynt or reddie for to tyne,　　　　　　　　5
Not using it as it sould usit be,
The craft exerceing, considdering not the fyne:
A paralous seiknes is vane prosperite.

2

The curious probatioun logicall,
The eloquence of ornat rethorie,　　　　　　　　10
The naturall science philosophicall,
The dirk apperance of astronomie,
The theologis sermoun, the fablis of poetrie,
Without gud lyfe all in the selfe dois de,
As Maii flouris dois in September dry.　　　　　　15
A paralous lyfe is vane prosperite.

3

Quhairfoir, ye clarkis grittest of constance,
Fullest of science and of knawlegeing,
To us be myrrouris in your governance
And in our darknes be lamps in schyning,　　　　20
Or than in frustar is your lang leirning.

<table>
<tr><td>1. science learning　craft skill
　sapience wisdom</td><td>10. ornat ornate　rethorie rhetoric</td></tr>
<tr><td>2. vertew virtue
　cunnyng knowledge
　doctrene instruction</td><td>12. dirk dark
13. theologis sermoun theologian's
　sermon　fablis fictions</td></tr>
<tr><td>3. jure jurisprudence; law</td><td>14. de die</td></tr>
<tr><td>4. lair subject</td><td>15. Maii May　dois . . . dry wither</td></tr>
<tr><td>5. tynt wasted　tyne go to waste</td><td>17. clarkis scholars　grittest of
　constance of greatest constancy in</td></tr>
<tr><td>7. exerceing practising　fyne end</td><td>　learning</td></tr>
<tr><td>8. paralous seiknes dangerous
　sickness　vane fruitless; empty</td><td>18. knawlegeing knowledge</td></tr>
<tr><td>9. curious subtle　probatioun proof</td><td>19. governance behaviour
21. or than otherwise　frustar vain</td></tr>
</table>

8. 'Empty prosperity is a dangerous sickness'.
19–20. 'Be mirrors to us in your behaviour, and shining lamps in our darkness'

Gif to your sawis your deidis contrair be,
Your maist accusar sal be your awin cunning.
A paralus seiknes is vane prosperite.

22. gif *if*   sawis *talk*   deidis *deeds*
    contrair *at variance*
23. maist accusar *greatest accuser*

22–3. 'If your deeds are the opposite of what you preach, then your own
    knowledge will be your greatest accuser'

He that Hes Gold and Grit Riches

1

He that hes gold and grit riches
And may be into mirrynes,
And dois glaidnes fra him expell
And levis in to wretchitnes,
He wirkis sorrow to himsell.   5

2

He that may be but sturt or stryfe
And leif ane lusty plesand lyfe,
And syne with mariege dois him mell
And bindis him with ane wicket wyfe,
He wirkis sorrow to himsell.   10

3

He that hes for his awin genyie
Ane plesand prop, but mank or menyie,
And schuttis syne at ane uncow schell
And is forfairn with the fleis of Spenyie,
He wirkis sorrow to himsell.   15

4

And he that with gud lyfe and trewth,
But varians or uder slewth,

1. grit *great*
2. may *can* mirrynes *merriness*
3. glaidnes *happiness* fra *from*
4. levis *lives* in to *in*
   wretchitnes *misery*
5. wirkis *causes* him sell *himself*
6. but *without* sturt *quarrel*
   stryfe *strife*
7. leif *live* lusty *cheerful*
   plesand *pleasant*
8. syne *then* mariege *marriage*
   him mell *involve himself*
9. bindis him *binds himself*

   with *to* wicket *wicked*
11. hes *has* awin *own*
    genyie *arrow-shaft*
12. prop *target* mank *flaw*
    menyie *fault*
13. schuttis *shoots*
    uncow *unknown* schell *target*
14. forfairn *ruined* fleis of
    Spenyie *syphilis*
16. trewth *loyalty*
17. varians *hostility* uder *other*
    slewth *sin*

2. 'And can live a life of merriness'.
11–15. 'He that has a pleasing target of his own for his arrow-shaft,
   without any flaw or fault, and then shoots his bolt at some other target,
   and comes down with syphilis, brings his troubles on himself'.

Dois evir mair with ane maister dwell
That nevir on him will haif no rewth,
He wirkis sorrow to himsell.   20

5
Now all this tyme lat us be mirry,
And sett nocht by this warld a chirry.
Now quhill thair is gude wyne to sell,
He that dois on dry breid wirry,
I gif him to the devill of hell!   25

---

18. maister *master*   chirry *cherry*
19. rewth *pity*   23. quhill *while*   wyne *wine*
21. mirry *merry*   24. breid *bread*   wirry *chew*
22. sett *value*   warld *world*   25. gif *give*

19. 'Who will never take pity on him'.
22. 'And not give a cherry for this world'.
23–5. 'If anyone chooses to chew on dry bread while there is good wine
to be had, let him go to the Devil'.

Man, Sen Thy Lyfe is Ay in Weir

1

Man, sen thy lyfe is ay in weir
And deid is evir drawand neir,
The tyme unsicker and the place,
Thyne awin gude spend quhill thow hes space.

2

Gif it be thyne, thyself it usis;   5
Gif it be nocht, the it refusis –
Ane uthir of it the proffeit hes:
Thyne awin gud spend quhill thow hes spais.

3

Thow may to day haif gude to spend
And hestely to morne fra it wend   10
And leif ane uthir thy baggis to brais:
Thyne awin gude spend quhill thow hes space.

4

Quhill thow hes space se thow dispone
That for thy geir, quhen thow art gone,
No wicht ane uder slay nor chace: 15
Thyne awin gude spend quhill thow hes space.

5

Sum all his dayis dryvis our in vane,
Ay gadderand geir with sorrow and pane,

1. sen *since* weir *doubt*
2. deid *death* drawand *drawing*
3. unsicker *uncertain*
4. awin *own* gude *goods*
    quhill *while* space *time*
5. gif *if* usis *make use of*
6. the *you* refusis *leave behind*
7. proffeit *benefit*
10. hestely *hastily* to
    morne *tomorrow* wend *go*

11. leif *leave* baggis *money bags*
    brais *embrace*
13. se *see that* dispone *take care*
14. geir *possessions* quhen *when*
15. wicht *man* uder *other*
    chace *chase away*
17. dryvis our *spends*
18. ay *always*
    gadderand *accumulating*
    pane *pain*

4. 'Spend your own money while you have the time'.
5–7. 'If it is your own, you make use of it yourself; if it is not yours, you
    have to leave it behind – someone else has the benefit of it'.
17. 'One person spends all his days uselessly'.

And nevir is glaid at Yule nor Pais:
Thyne awin gude spend quhill thow hes space.   20

6
Syne cumis ane uder glaid of his sorrow
That for him prayit nowdir evin nor morrow,
And fangis it all with mirrynais:
Thyne awin gude spend quhill thow hes space.

7
Sum grit gud gadderis and ay it spairis,   25
And eftir him thair cumis yung airis
That his auld thrift settis on ane es:
Thyne awin gude spend quhill thow hes space.

8
It is all thyne that thow heir spendis,
And nocht all that on the dependis,   30
Bot his to spend it that hes grace:
Thyne awin gud spend quhill thow hes spais.

9
Trest nocht ane uthir will do the to
It that thyself wald nevir do,
For gife thow dois, strenge is thy cace: 35
Thyne awin gud spend quhill thow hes space.

10
Luke how the bairne dois to the muder,
And tak example be nane udder
That it nocht eftir be thy cace,
Thyne awin gud spend quhill thow hes space.   40

19. glaid *happy* Yule *Christmas*   spairis *hoards it*
    Pais *Easter*   26. yung airis *young heirs*
21. syne *then* cumis *comes*   27. auld *previous* es *ace*
22. prayit *prayed* nowdir *neither*   31. grace *good fortune*
    evin *evening* morrow *morning*   33. trest *trust* the to *to you*
23. fangis *seizes*   35. strenge *strange* cace *situation*
    mirrynais *cheerfulness*   37. luke *look* bairne *child*
25. grit gud *great wealth* it   muder *mother*

27. 'Who gamble all his years of thrift on one ace'.
29–30. 'Everything that you spend on earth is your own, and does not
   belong to those who depend on you'.
34. 'What you yourself would never do'.
39. 'So that it does not become your situation afterwards'.

Quhome to Sall I Complene My Wo

1

Quhome to sall I complene my wo
And kyth my kairis on or mo?
I knaw nocht amang riche nor pure
Quha is my freynd, quha is my fo,
For in this warld may none assure.   5

2

Lord how sall I my dayis dispone?
For lang service rewarde is none,
And schort my lyfe may heir indure
And lossit is my tyme bygone;
Into this warld ma none assure.   10

3

Oft falsatt rydis with ane rowt
Quhen trewth gois on his fute abowt
And lak of spending dois him spur;
Thus quhat to do I am in dowt:
Into this warld may none assure.   15

4

Nane heir bot riche men hes renoun
And bot pure men ar pluckit doun

1. quhome *whom*
   complene *complain* wo *suffering*
2. kyth *reveal* kairis *sorrows*
   on *one* mo *more*
3. knaw nocht *do not know*
   pure *poor*
4. quha *who* freynd *friend*
5. warld *world* assure *trust*
6. dispone *spend*
7. lang *long*
8. schort *short time* heir *here*

indure *last*
9. lossit *wasted* bygone *gone by*
11. oft *often* falsatt *falsehood*
    rydis *rids* rowt *company*
12. quhen *when* on his fute
    abowt *about on foot*
13. spending *money* spur *sting*
14. dowt *doubt*
16. nane *no one* bot *except*
    renoun *honour*
17. pluckit doun *pulled down*

1–2. 'To whom shall I complain about my suffering and reveal the full extent of my sorrows'.
5. 'For no one can place their trust in this world'.
8–9. 'My life here may last just a short time, and the time gone by is already wasted'.
16. 'No one here is honoured except the rich'.

And nane bot just men tholis injure;
Sa wit is blindit and ressoun:
Into this warld may none assure. 20

5

Vertew the court hes done dispyis,
Ane rebald to renoun dois ryis,
And cairlis of nobillis hes the cure,
And bumbardis brukis the benifyis:
Into this warld may none assure. 25

6

All gentrice and nobilitie
Ar passit out of he degre;
On fredome is laid foirfaltour;
In princis is thair no pety:
For in this warld may none assure. 30

7

Is non so armit in to plait
That can fra truble him debait;
May no man lang in welth indure
For wo that evir lyis at the wait:
Into this warld may none assure. 35

18. tholis *suffer* injure *injustice*
19. sa *so* wit *understanding*
    blindit *blinded*
21. vertew *virtue* done
    dispyis *despised*
22. rebald *rogue*
    renoun *distinction* dois ryis *rises*
23. cairlis *peasants*
    nobillis *noblemen* cure *authority*
24. bumbardis *layabouts*
    brukis *get* benifyis *benefices*

26. gentrice *gentility*
27. passit *passed* he degre *high
    rank*
28. fredome *generosity*
    foirfaltour *forfeiture*
29. pety *compassion*
31. armit *armed* plait *armour*
32. debait *defend*
33. welth *prosperity* indure *last*
34. for *on account of* at the
    wait *in ambush*

21. 'The court has despised virtue'.
23–4. 'And peasants have authority over noblemen, and layabouts get the
    benefices'.
26–8. 'Those of high rank no longer possess gentility and nobility;
    generosity has been forfeited'.
31–2. 'No one is so well equipped with armour that he can defend
    himself against all troubles'.

8

Flattry weiris ane furrit goun
And falsett with the lordis dois roun
And trewth standis barrit at the dure
And exul is honour of the toun:
Into this warld may none assure.   40

9

Fra everilk mowth fair wirdis proceidis;
In every hairt disceptioun breidis;
Fra everylk e gois lukis demure
Bot fra the handis gois few gud deidis:
Into this warld may none assure.   45

10

Toungis now ar maid of quhyte quhaill bone
And hairtis ar maid of hard flynt stone
And ene ar maid of blew asure
And handis of adamant laith to dispone:
Into this warld may none assure.   50

11

Yit hairt with hand and body all
Mon anser deth quhen he dois call
To compt befoir the juge future;
Sen all ar deid or than de sall,
Quha suld in to this warld assure?   55

36. flattry *flattery*   weiris *wears*
   furrit goun *fur-trimmed gown*
37. falsett *falsehood* dois
   roun *whispers*
38. barrit *shut out*   dure *door*
39. exul *exiled*
41. everik *every* wirdis *words*
   proceidis *come forth*
42. hairt *heart*
   disceptioun *deception*
   breidis *breeds*
43. e *eye* lukis *looks*

44. deidis *deeds*
46. toungis *tongues* quhyte *white*
   quhaill bone *whale bone*
48. ene *eyes* blew asure *blue lapis
   lazuli*
49. adamant *diamond*
   laith *reluctant* dispone *distribute*
52. mon anser *must answer*
   deth *death*
53. compt *account* juge *judge*
54. sen *since* deid *dead* de
   sall *shall die*

39. 'And honour is exiled from the town'.

12

No thing bot deth this schortly cravis,
Quhair fortoun evir as fo dissavis
With freyndly smylingis of ane hure
Quhais fals behechtis as wind hyne wavis:
Into this warld may none assure.   60

13

O quha sall weild the wrang possessioun
Or the gold gatherit with oppressioun
Quhen the angell blawis his bugill sture,
Quhilk unrestorit helpis no confessioun?
Into this warld may none assure.   65

14

Quhat help is thair in lordschippis sevin
Quhen na hous is bot hell and hevin,
Palice of licht or pitt obscure
Quhair youlis ar hard with horreble stevin?
Into this warld may none assure.   70

15

Ubi ardentes anime,
Semper dicentes sunt, Ve, ve!
Sall cry Allace, that wemen thame bure,
O quante sunt iste tenebre!
Into this warld may none assure.   75

56. schortly *soon* cravis *desires*
57. fo *enemy* dissavis *deceives*
58. smylingis *smiles* hure *whore*
59. quhais *whose*
behechtis *promises* hyne
wavis *pass away*
61. quha *who* weild *enjoy* wrang
possessioun *ill-gotten gains*
62. gatherit *acquired*
oppressioun *extortion*
63. blawis *blows* bugill *trumpet*
sture *loudly*
64. unrestorit *unrestored*
66. lordschippis sevin *seven estates*
68. palice *palace* obscure *dark*
69. youlis *howls* hard *heard*
stevin *sound*
71. ubi ardentes anime *where*
burning souls
72. semper dicentes sunt, Ve,
ve *are always saying, Woe, woe*
73. allace *alas* thame bure *bore them*
74. O quante sunt iste tenebre *O,*
how great is that darkness

56. 'This world desires nothing except death to come to us soon'.
59. 'Whose false promises pass away like the wind'.
64. 'Which confession cannot make better because the goods have not
been returned to their rightful owners'.
67. 'When there is no true home except hell or heaven'.

16

Than quho sall wirk for warldis wrak
Quhen flude and fyre sall our it frak,
And frely fruster feild and fure
With tempest kene and hiddous crak?
Into this warld may none assure.   80

17

Lord, sen in tyme sa sone to cum
De terra surrecturus sum,
Reward me with non erdly cure –
Bot me ressave *in regnum tuum*
In to this warld may non assure.   85

76. wirk *work* wrak *rubbish*
77. flude *flood* our it frak *consume it*
78. frely *freely* fruster *destroy* fure *furrow*
79. kene *fierce* crak *thunder crack*

81. sen *since* sone *soon*
82. de terra surrecturus sum *I am to rise from the earth*
83. erdly cure *earthly office*
84. me ressave *receive me* in regnum tuum *into your kingdom*

Foure Maner of Men ar Evill to Pleis

1

Foure maner of men ar evill to pleis:
Ane is that riches hes and eis,
Gold, silver, corne, cattell and ky,
And wald haif pairt fra uthiris by.

2

Ane uthir is of land and rent   5
So grit a lord and so potent
That he may not it rewill nor gy,
And yit wald haif fra uthiris by.

3

The thrid dois eik so dourly drink
And aill and wyne within him sink   10
Quhill in his wame no rowme be dry,
And yit wald haif fra uthiris by.

4

The last, that hes of nobill blude,
Ane lusty lady fair and gude,
Boith vertewis, wyis and womanly,   15
Bot yit wald haif ane uthir by.

5

In erd no wicht I can persaif
Of gude so grit aboundance haif,

1. maner *kinds* evill to pleis *hard to please*
2. ane *one* eis *comfort*
3. cattell *livestock* ky *cows*
4. pairt *share* uthiris *others* by *besides*
5. rent *property*
6. grit *great* potent *powerful*
7. it rewill *manage it* gy *govern*
9. third *third* eik *also*

10. dourly *sullenly*
10. aill *ale* wyne *wine*
11. quhill *until* wame *belly* rowme *space*
13. blude *blood*
14. lusty *beautiful* gude *good*
15. vertewis *virtuous* wyis *wise*
17. in erd *on earth* wicht *creature* persaif *perceive*
18. aboundance *abundance*

2. 'One is the man who has riches and comfort'.
4. 'And wants a share from others besides'.
16. 'But yet would have another one besides'.
18. 'Having such a great abundance of goods'.

Nor in this warld so welthfull wy,
Bot yit he wald haif uthir by. 20

6
Bot yit of all this gold and gud,
Or uthir conyie, to conclude:
Quha evir it haif, it is not I;
It gois fra me to uthiris by.

19. welthfull *wealthy* wy *man*
20. conyie *coins*
21. quha evir *whoever*

Fredome, Honour and Nobilnes

1

Fredome, honour and nobilnes,
Meid, manheid, mirth and gentilnes,
Ar now in court reput as vyce;
And all for caus of cuvetice.

2

All weilfair, welth and wantones 5
Ar chengit in to wretchitnes,
And play is sett at littill price;
And all for caus of covetyce.

3

Halking, hunting and swift hors rynning
Ar chengit all in wrangus wynnyng, 10
Thair is no play bot cartis and dyce;
And all for caus of covetyce.

4

Honorable houshaldis ar all laid doun;
Ane laird hes with him bot a loun
That leidis him eftir his devyce; 15
And all for caus of covetyce.

5

In burghis, to landwart and to sie,
Quhair was plesour and grit plentie,

1. fredome *generosity*
2. meid *merit* manheid *manliness*
   mirth *cheerfulness*
   gentilnes *gentility*
3. reput *considered* vyce *vice*
4. for cause *because*
   cuvetice *covetousness*
5. weilfair *happiness* welth *well-being* wantones *delight*
6. chengit *transformed*
7. play *entertainment* price *value*
9. halking *hawking* rynning *racing*
10. in *into* wrangus
    wynnyng *wrongful profit*
11. cartis *cards* dyce *dice*
13. houshaldis *households* laid
    doun *brought down*
14. laird *lord* loun *rogue*
15. leidis *leads* devyce *design*
17. burghis *towns* to landwart *in the country* to sie *by the sea*
18. quhair *where*
    plesour *enjoyment* plentie *plenty*

15. 'Who leads him along as he pleases'.

Vennesoun, wyld fowill, wyne and spyce,
Ar now decayid thruch covetyce.　　　　　　20

6

Husbandis that grangis had full grete,
Cattell and corne to sell and ete,
Hes now no beist bot cattis and myce;
And all thruch caus of covettyce.

7

Honest yemen in every toun,　　　　　　25
War wont to weir baith reid and broun,
Ar now arrayit in raggis with lyce;
And all for caus of cuvetyce.

8

And lairdis in silk harlis to the heill,
For quhilk thair tennents sald somer meill　　30
And leivis on rutis undir the ryce;
And all for caus of cuvetyce.

9

Quha that dois deidis of petie
And leivis in pece and cheretie
Is haldin a fule, and that full nyce;　　　　35
And all for caus of cuvetyce.

---

19. vennesoun *venison*
fowill *fowl*　wyne *wine*
spyce *spices*
20. decayid *fallen away*
thruch *through*
21. husbandis *farmers*
grangis *granaries*　grete *great*
22. ete *eat*
23. beist *beast*　cattis *cats*
25. yemen *freeholders*
26. wont *accustomed*　reid *red*

27. arrayit *dressed*　raggis *rags*
29. harlis *sweep*　heill *heel*
30. quhilk *which*　sald *sold*　somer
meill *summer oatmeal*
31. leivis *live*　rutis *roots*
ryce *brushwood*
33. quha that *whoever*
deidis *deeds*　petie *compassion*
34. pece *peace*　cheretie *charity*
35. haldin *considered*　fule *fool*
nyce *ridiculous*

29. 'And lords sweep by in silk down to the ground'.
35. 'Is considered a fool, and a ridiculous one at that'.

10

And quha can reive uthir menis rowmis
And upoun peur men gadderis sowmis
Is now ane active man, and wyice;
And all for caus of cuvetyce.   40

11

Man, pleis thy makar and be mirry,
And sett not by this warld a chirry;
Wirk for the place of paradyce,
For thairin ringis na cuvettyce.

37. reive *steal* menis *men's*   41. pleis *please* makar *maker*
    rowmis *property*   mirry *merry*
38. peur *poor* gadderis *collect*   42. warld *world* chirry *cherry*
    sowmis *amounts*   43. wirk *strive*
39. active *industrious* wyice *wise* 44. ringis *reigns*

38. 'And collect money from poor men'.
42. 'And don't give a cherry for the things of this world'.

Quho Thinkis that He Hes Sufficence

1

Quho thinkis that he hes sufficence
Of gudis hes no indigence.
Thocht he have nowder land nor rent,
Grit mycht nor hie magnificence,
He hes anewch that is content.   5

2

Quho had all riches unto Ynd,
And wer not satefeit in mynd,
With povertie I hald him schent:
Of covatyce sic is the kynd.
He hes anewch that is content.   10

3

Thairfoir, I pray yow, bredir deir,
Not to delyt in daynteis seir;
Thank God of it is to the sent,
And of it glaidlie mak gud cheir.
Anewch he hes that is content.   15

4

Defy the warld, feynyeit and fals,
Withe gall in hart and hunyt hals.

---

1. quho *whoever* sufficence *enough*
2. gudis *possessions*
   indigence *poverty*
3. thocht *although*
   nowder *neither* rent *income*
4. grit mycht *great power* hie *high*
5. anewch *enough*
6. Ynd *India*
7. satefeit *satisfied*
8. hald *consider* schent *destroyed*

9. covatyce *covetousness* sic *such*
   kynd *nature*
11. bredir *brother*
12. daynteis seir *many luxuries*
13. the *you*
14. of *for* mak gud cheir *be cheerful*
16. defy *renounce* warld *world*
    feynyeit *deceitful*
17. gall *bitterness* hunyt
    hals *honeyed voice*

6. 'Whoever possessed all the world's riches from here to India'.
8–9. 'I consider him to be destroyed by poverty: such is the nature of covetousness'.
12–13. 'Are not served with many luxuries, thank God for what he has sent you'.

Quha maist it servis sall sonast it repent,
Of quhais subchettis sour is the sals.
He hes aneuch that is content.   20

5

Giff thow hes mycht, be gentill and fre,
And gif thow standis in povertie,
Of thine awin will to it consent
And riches sall returne to the.
He hes aneuch that is content.   25

6

And ye and I, my bredir all,
That in this lyfe hes lordschip small,
Lat langour nane in us be lent.
Gif we not clym, we tak no fall.
He hes aneuch that is content.   30

7

For quho in warld moist covatus is
In warld is purast man, iwis,
And neidfullest in his intent,
For of all gudis no thing is his,
That of no thing can be content.   35

18. maist *most* sonast *soonest*   28. lat *let* langour *misery* lent *set*
19. subchettis *luxurious dishes*   29. clym *climb*
21. giff *if* gentill *noble*   31. moist *most* covatus *envious*
    fre *generous*   32. purast *poorest* iwis *indeed*
22. standis *are*   33. neidfullest *most needy*
23. awin *own*   intent *mind*
26. bredir *brothers*   34. gudis *possessions*
27. lordschip small *little property*

18. 'Whoever serves the world most shall repent it most'.
19. 'The world serves up luxurious dishes but the sauce is sour'.
23. 'Accept it of your own free will'.
28. 'Let us not be unhappy'.
31–2. 'For whoever in the world is the most envious is indeed the
    poorest man in the world'.

Full Oft I Mus and Hes in Thocht

1

Full oft I mus and hes in thocht
How this fals warld is ay on flocht,
Quhair nothing ferme is nor degest;
And quhen I haif my mynd all socht
For to be blyth me think it best.   5

2

This warld evir dois flicht and vary;
Fortoun sa fast hir quheill dois cary
Na tyme bot turne can it tak rest,
For quhois fals change suld none be sary;
For to be blyth me thynk it best.   10

3

Wald man considdir in mynd rycht weill
Or Fortoun on him turn hir quheill
That erdly honour may nocht lest,
His fall less panefull he suld feill;
For to be blyth me think it best.   15

4

Quha with this warld dois warsill and stryfe
And dois his dayis in dolour dryfe,
Thocht he in lordschip be possest
He levis bot ane wrechit lyfe;
For to be blyth me think it best.   20

1. mus *reflect* hes in
   thocht *contemplate*
2. warld *world* ay *continually*
   on flocht *in a state of flux*
3. quhair *where* ferme *constant*
   degest *settled*
4. quhen *when* socht *searched*
5. blyth *happy*
6. flicht *fluctuate*
7. quheill *wheel* dois cary *drives*
8. bot *without*
9. quhois *whose*

change *changeability*
sary *unhappy*
11. wald man *if man would*
12. or *before*
13. erdly *earthly* lest *last*
14. feill *feel*
16. quha *whoever* warsill *wrestle*
   stryfe *strive*
17. dolour *sorrow* dryfe *spends*
18. thocht *even though*
   lordschip *landed property*
19. levis *lives* bot *nothing but*

5. 'It seems best to me to be happy'.
7–8. 'Fortune drives her wheel so fast that at no time can it lie still without turning'.
12. 'Before Fortune turns him on her wheel'.
17–18. 'And spends his days in sorrow, even though he possesses landed property'.

5

Of warldis gud and grit riches
Quhat fruct hes man but mirines?
Thocht he this warld had eist and west
All wer povertie but glaidnes;
For to be blyth me thynk it best.   25

6

Quho suld for tynsall drowp or de,
For thyng that is bot vanitie,
Sen to the lyfe that evir dois lest
Heir is bot twynklyng of ane e;
For to be blyth me think it best.   30

7

Had I for warldis unkyndnes
In hairt tane ony havines,
Or fro my plesans bene opprest,
I had bene deid lang syne, dowtles;
For to be blyth me think it best.   35

8

How evir this warld do change and vary,
Lat us in hairt nevir moir be sary,
Bot evir be reddy and addrest
To pas out of this frawdfull fary;
For to be blyth me think it best.   40

21. warldis gud *worldly goods*
22. fruct *benefit* mirines *happiness*
24. but glaidnes *without gladness*
26. tynsall *loss* drowp *droop*
    de *die*
28. sen *since* to *compared to*
29. heir *here* twynkling *blinking*
    e *eye*
31. had I *if I had*

32. in hairt tane *taken to heart*
    havines *dejection*
33. plesans *pleasure*
    opprest *crushed*
34. lang syne *long since*
    dowtles *without doubt*
37. lat *let* sary *sorry*
38. addrest *prepared*
39. frawdfull fary *deceitful world*

21–2. 'Of what benefit are worldly goods and great riches to a man
    without happiness?'.
24. 'It would all be poverty unless he also had gladness'.
26–9. 'Why should someone droop or die for something that is mere
    vanity, since in comparison with eternal life this earthly life is gone in
    the blinking of an eye'.
33. 'Or if I had been crushed by sorrow and deprived of pleasure'.

Be Mery, Man, and Tak Nocht Fer in Mynd

1

Be mery, man, and tak nocht fer in mynd
The wavering of this wrechit vale of sorow;
To God be hummle and to thi frend be kyind,
And with thi nichtbour glaidlie len and borow:
His chance this nycht, it may be thine tomorow.　　　5
Be mery, man, for any aventure;
For be wismen it has bene said afforow:
Without glaidnes avalis no tresure.

2

Mak gude cheir of it that God the sendis,
For warldis wrak but weilfar nocht avalis;　　　　10
No thing is thine sauf onlie that thow spendis,
The remanent of all thow brukis with balis.
Seik to solace quhen saidnes the assalis,
Thy lyfe in dolour ma nocht lang indure;
Quharfor of confurt set up all thi salis:　　　　15
Without glaidnes avalis no tresure.

3

Follow pete, flie trubill and debait,
With famous folkis hald thi company;

1. fer *so much*
2. wavering *instability*
   wrechit *miserable*
3. hummle *humble*　frend *friend*
   kyind *kind*
4. nichtbour *neighbour*
   glaidlie *happily*　len *lend*
5. chance *fate*　nycht *night*
6. mery *cheerful*　aventure *event*
7. be *by*　wismen *wise men*
   afforow *before now*
8. glaidnes *happiness*　avalis *helps*
9. mak gude cheir *be glad*　the
   sendis *sends you*
10. warldis wrak *worldly dross*

but *without*　weilfar *happiness*
11. sauf *except*　onlie *only*
   spendis *give away*
12. remanent *rest*　brukis *enjoy*
   balis *sorrows*
13. seik to solace *seek consolation*
   quhen *when*　saidnes *sadness*
   the assalis *assails you*
14. dolour *sorrow*　ma *can*　lang
   indure *last long*
15. quharfor *therefore*
   confurt *consolation*　salis *sails*
17. pete *compassion*　flie *flee*
   trubill *trouble*　debait *strife*
18. famous *reputable*

5. 'What is his fate tonight, may be yours tomorow'.
6. 'Be cheerful, man, no matter what happens'.
8. 'Treasure is of no use without happiness'.
18. 'Keep company with people of good reputation'.

Be cheritable and hummle of estait,
For warldis honour lestis bot ane cry; 20
For truble in erd tak no malancoly.
Be rich in patiens, gife thoue in gudis be pur;
Quha levis mery, he levis michtely:
Without glaidnes avalis no tresur.

4

Thow seis the wrechis set with sorow and care 25
To gaddir gudis all thar liffis spaice,
And quhen thar baggis ar full tharself ar bar,
And of thar riches bot the keping hes
Quhill uthiris cum to spend it that hes grace
Quhilk of the wynning no labour hed na cur. 30
Thairfoir be glaid, and spend with mirrie face:
Without glaidnes avalis no tresure.

5

Thocht all the wrak that evir hed levand wicht
War onlie thine, no mor thi pert dois fall
Bot met and clacht, and of the laif ane sicht, 35
Yit to the juge thow sall mak compt of all.

19. estait *behaviour*
20. lestis *lasts*
21. in erd *on earth*
  malancoly *sadness*
22. patiens *patience* gife *if*
  gudis *wealth* pur *poor*
23. quha *whoever* levis *lives*
  michtely *with power*
25. seis *see* wrechis *wretches*
  set *beset*
26. gaddir *acquire* liffis
  spaice *lifetime*
27. thar *their* baggis *bags*

tharself *themselves*
28. bot *only* keping *guarding*
29. quhill *until* uthiris *others*
  grace *benefit*
30. cur *concern*
33. thocht *although* levand *living*
  wicht *creature*
34. pert *share*
35. met *food* clacht *clothes*
  laif *rest* sicht *glimpse*
36. juge *judge* mak compt
  of *account for*

20. 'For the honour of this world lasts only as long as a cry'.
21. 'Do not be sad about any earthly trouble'.
27–30. 'And when their money bags are full they themselves are
  emotionally destitute, and only have the trouble of guarding their
  riches until others come who did not have the effort or concern of
  acquiring it but who have the benefit of spending it'.
33–5. 'Even if all the rubbish that any living creature ever had was yours
  alone, no more really belongs to you than your food and clothing, with
  only a glimpse of all the rest'.

Ane raknyng richt cummis of ane ragment small.
Be just and joyus, and do to none injur,
And treuth sall mak the strang as ony wall:
Without glaidnes avalis no tresure.   40

---

37. raknyng *account* cummis
   of *comes from* ragment
   small *short list*

38. none *no one* injur *harm*
39. treuth *truth* strang *strong*

37. 'A short account leads to a correct bill'.

In to thir Dirk and Drublie Dayis

1

In to thir dirk and drublie dayis,
Quhone sabill all the hevin arrayis
With mystie vapouris, cluddis and skyis,
Nature all curage me denyis
Of sangs, ballattis and of playis.   5

2

Quhone that the nycht dois lenth in houris,
With wind, with haill and havy schouris,
My dule spreit dois lurk for schoir;
My hairt for langour dois forloir,
For laik of symmer with his flouris.   10

3

I walk, I turne, sleip may I nocht;
I vexit am with havie thocht;
This warld all ovir I cast about,
And ay the mair I am in dout,
The mair that I remeid have socht.   15

4

I am assayit on everie syde.
Despair sayis ay, 'In tyme provyde,

1. in to *in* thir *these* dirk *dark* drublie *gloomy*
2. quhone *when* sabill *black* arrayis *dresses*
3. cluddis *clouds*
4. curage *inclination*
5. ballattis *poems* playis *entertainment*
6. lenth *lengthen*
7. havy schouris *heavy showers*
8. dule spreit *doleful spirit* dois lurk *shrinks* schoir *threatening*
9. hairt *heart* langour *misery*
10. laik *absence* symmer *summer* flouris *flowers*
11. walk *lie awake*
12. vexit *troubled* havie thocht *oppressive thoughts*
13. cast about *reflect upon*
14. ay *always* mair *more* in dout *perplexed*
15. remeid *remedy* socht *sought*
16. assayit *assailed*
17. provyde *make provision*
   dois forloir *becomes forlorn*

2–5. 'When the entire heavens are dressed in black with misty vapours, both the clouds and the sky itself, nature deprives me of all inclination for songs, poems and entertainment'.
8. 'My doleful spirit shrinks from the threatening weather'.
15. 'The more I have sought a remedy'.
17. 'Despair keeps saying, "Make provision for the future before it is too late"'.

And get sum thing quhairon to leif,
Or with grit trouble and mischeif
Thow sall in to this court abyd.'   20

5

Than Patience sayis, 'Be not agast,
Hald hoip and treuthe within the fast,
And lat Fortoun wirk furthe hir rage,
Quhone that no rasoun may assuage,
Quhill that hir glas be run and past.'   25

6

And Prudence in my eir sayis ay,
'Quhy wald thow hald that will away,
Or craif that thow may have no space,
Thow tending to ane uther place,
A journay going everie day?'   30

7

And than sayis Age, 'My freind, cum neir,
And be not strange, I the requeir.
Cum, brodir, by the hand me tak.
Remember thow hes compt to mak
Of all thi tyme thow spendit heir.'   35

18. quhairon *on which* leif *live*
19. grit *great* mischeif *hardship*
20. sall *shall* abyd *live*
21. agast *afraid*
22. hald *hold* hoip *hope* the *you*
    fast *securely*
23. lat *let* wirk furthe *vent*
24. quhone *since* rasoun *rational
    argument* assuage *soothe*
25. glas *time*
26. eir *ear*

27. quhy *why* that *that which*
28. craif *crave*
29. tending *travelling*
30. journay *day's travel*
31. neir *near*
32. strange *standoffish* the
    requeir *request you*
33. brodir *brother*
34. compt to mak *to make an
    account*

22–5. 'Keep hope and truth securely within your heart, and let Fortune
    vent her anger against you, since no rational argument will soothe her,
    until her time has run its course'.
27–30. 'Why do you want to hold onto something which will leave you,
    or crave something that you will not have for long, you who are
    travelling to another place, closer by a whole day's journey every day?'.

8

Syne Deid castis upe his yettis wyd,
Saying, 'Thir oppin sall the abyd;
Albeid that thow wer never sa stout,
Undir this lyntall sall thow lowt.
Thair is nane uther way besyde.'   40

9

For feir of this all day I drowp:
No gold in kist nor wyne in cowp,
No ladeis bewtie nor luiffis blys
May lat me to remember this,
How glaid that ever I dyne or sowp.   45

10

Yit quhone the nycht begynnis to schort
It dois my spreit sum pairt confort,
Of thocht oppressit with the schowris.
Cum, lustie symmer, with thi flowris,
That I may leif in sum disport.   50

36. Deid *Death* upe *open*
yettis *gates* wyd *wide*
37. thir *these* oppin *open* the
abyd *await you*
38. albeid *albeit* stout *brave*
39. lyntall *lintel; door frame*
lowt *stoop*
41. feir *fear* drowp *droop*
42. kist *chest* cowp *cup*
43. ladeis bewtie *lady's beauty*

luiffis blys *love's bliss*
44. lat *prevent*
45. glaid *gladly* sowp *drink*
46. schort *shorten*
47. spreit *mind* sum pairt *to some
extent* confort *comfort*
48. schowris *showers*
49. lustie symmer *pleasant
summer*
50. leif *live* disport *delight*

37–9. 'Saying, "These open gates shall await you; no matter how fierce
you may be, you must bow your head under this doorway" '.
45. 'No matter how gladly I ever wine and dine'.
47–8. 'It comforts my mind to some extent, which has been oppressed by
the showers of thought'.

I Seik Aboute this Warld Onstable

1

I seik aboute this warld onstable
To find a sentence conveniable,
Bot I can not in all my witt
Sa trew a sentence find of it,
As say it is dissavable.   5

2

For yistirday I did declair
How that the sasoun soft and fair
Come in als fresche as pacok feddir.
This day it stangis lyke ane eddir,
Concluding all in my contrair.   10

3

Yistirday fair up sprang the flowris,
This day thai ar all slane with schouris;
And foulis in forrest that sang cleir
Now walkis with ane drerie cheir,
Full caild ar bayth thair beddis and bowris.   15

4

So nixt to symmer wyntir bene,
Nixt eftir confort cairis kene,

1. seik *seek* onstable *unstable*
2. sentence *judgement*
   conveniable *appropriate*
3. witt *knowledge*
4. trew *true*
5. dissavable *deceitful*
6. yistirday *yesterday*
7. sasoun *season*
8. come in *began* als *as*
   fresche *lovely* pacok
   feddir *peacock feather*
9. this day *today* stangis *stings*
   eddir *adder*
10. in my contrair *against me*
11. flowris *flowers*
12. schouris *showers*
13. foulis *birds* cleir *brightly*
14. walkis *awaken* drerie
    cheir *sorrowful mood*
15. full caild *very cold*
    bayth *both* bowris *bowers*
16. nixt *next* symmer *summer*
    bene *is*
17. confort *pleasure* cairis
    kene *bitter sorrow*

3–5. 'But with all my knowledge I cannot find a truer judgement than to say that it is deceitful'.
10. 'Ending the matter entirely differently from what I said'.
16–17. 'So next to summer comes winter, and after pleasure comes bitter sorrow'.

Nixt dirk mydnycht the myrthfull morrow,
Nixt eftir joy ay cumis sorrow:
So is this warld and ay hes bene.   20

---

18. dirk mydnycht *dark midnight*   19. ay *always*
      myrthfull morrow *joyful morning*   20. hes bene *has been*

Of Lentren in the First Mornyng

1

Of Lentren in the first mornyng,
Airly as did the day up spring,
Thus sang ane bird with voce up plane:
'All erdly joy returnis in pane.

2

'O man, haif mynd that thow mon pas,   5
Remembir that thow art bot as,
And sall in as revert agane:
All erdly joy returnis in pane.

3

'Haif mynd that eild ay followis yowth,
Deth followis lyfe with gaipand mowth,   10
Devoring fruct and flowring grane:
All erdly joy returnis in pane.

4

'Welth, wardly gloir and riche array
Ar all bot thornis laid in thy way,
Ourcoverd with flouris, laid in a trane: 15
All erdly joy returnis in pane.

5

'Come nevir yit May so fresche and grene,
Bot Januar come als, wod and kene;
Wes nevir sic drowth bot anis come rane:
All erdly joy returnis in pane.   20

1. Lentren *Lent*
2. airly *early* up spring *dawn*
3. voce *voice* up plane *clearly*
4. erdly *earthly* returnis in *turns into* pane *pain*
5. haif mynd *be aware* mon pas *must pass away*
6. as *ash*
7. in *to*
9. eild *old age* ay *always* yowth *youth*
10. gaipand *gaping*
11. devoring *devouring* fruct *fruit* grane *plants*
13. wardly gloir *worldly glory*
14. bot *only* thornis *thorns*
15. ourcoverd *covered over* flouris *flowers* trane *trap*
17. come *came* yit *yet* grene *green*
18. Januar *January* als *also* wod *furious* kene *bitter*
19. sic *such* drowth *drought* anis *one day*

1. 'On the first morning of Lent'.
7. 'And shall return to ash again'.
19. 'There was never such a drought that the rain did not come one day'.

6

'Evirmair unto this warldis joy
As nerrest air succeidis noy;
Thairfoir quhen joy ma nocht remane,
His verry air succeidis, pane.

7

'Heir helth returnis in seiknes,   25
And mirth returnis in havines,
Toun in desert, forrest in plane:
All erdly joy returnis in pane.

8

'Fredome returnis in wrechitnes
And trewth returnis in dowbilnes,   30
With fenyeit wirdis to mak men fane:
All erdly joy returnis in pane.

9

'Vertew returnis in to vyce
And honour in to avaryce;
With cuvatyce is consciens slane: 35
All erdly joy returnis in pane.

10

'Sen erdly joy abydis nevir
Wirk for the joy that lestis evir,
For uder joy is all bot vane:
All erdly joy returnis in pane.'   40

21. evirmair *always*
    warldis *world's*
22. nerrest air *immediate heir*
    noy *distress*
23. quhen *when* ma nocht *cannot*
24. verry *rightful* pane *pain*
25. heir *here* returnis in *turns
    into* seiknes *sickness*
26. mirth *happiness* havines *misery*
27. toun *town* in *into*
    plane *wasteland*
29. fredome *generosity*

wrechitnes *miserliness*
30. trewth *truth*
    dowbilnes *duplicity*
31. fenyeit wirdis *deceitful words*
    fane *glad*
33. vertew *virtue*
34. avaryce *greed*
35. cuvatyce *covetousness*
37. sen *since* erdly *earthly*
    abydis *lasts*
38. lestis evir *lasts forever*
39. uder *other* vane *useless*

21–4. 'Distress always inherits the world's joy as the immediate heir;
therefore, when joy cannot stay any longer it is pain, his rightful heir,
who follows him'.
35. 'Conscience is killed by covetousness'.

Memento, Homo, Quod Cinis Es

1

Memento, homo, quod cinis es:
Think, man, thow art bot erd and as.
Lang heir to dwell na thing thow pres,
For as thow come sa sall thow pas.
Lyk as ane schaddow in ane glas   5
Hyne glydis all thy tyme that heir is.
Think, thocht thy bodye ware of bras,
Quod tu in cinerem reverteris.

2

Worthye Hector and Hercules,
Forcye Achill and strong Sampsone,   10
Alexander of grit nobilnes,
Meik David and fair Absolone
Hes playit thair pairtis and all are gone,
At will of God, that all thing steiris.
Think, man, exceptioun thair is none,   15
Sed tu in cinerem reverteris.

3

Thocht now thow be maist glaid of cheir,
Fairest and plesandest of port,
Yit may thow be within ane yeir
Ane ugsum, uglye tramort.   20
And sen thow knawis thy tyme is schort,

1. memento homo quod cinis
es *remember, man, that thou art
ash*
2. bot *nothing but*   erd *earth*
as *ash*
3. na thing *not at all*   pres *try*
4. come *came*   sall *shall*   pas *pass
away*
5. schaddow *reflection*   glas *mirror*
6. hyne *from here*   glydis *drifts*
7. thocht *even if*   bras *brass*
8. quod tu in cinerem
reverteris *that you must return to
ashes*
10. forcye *powerful*

Achill *Achilles*
Sampsone *Samson*
12. meik *humble*
Absolone *Absolon*
13. playit thair pairtis *played their
parts*
14. steiris *rules*
16. sed *but*
17. thocht *although*   maist *most*
glaid of cheir *joyful*
18. plesandest *most pleasing*
port *appearance*
19. yeir *year*
20. ugsum *repulsive*   tramort *corpse*
21. sen *since*

3. 'There is no point in you trying to stay here long'.
5–6. 'All your time here on earth drifts away like a reflection in a mirror'.

And in all houre thy lyfe in weir is,
Think, man, amang all uthir sport
Quod tu in cinerem reverteris.

4

Thy lustye bewte and thy youth   25
Sall feid as dois the somer flouris,
Syne sall the swallow with his mouth
The dragone, Death, that all devouris.
No castell sall the keip, nor touris,
Bot he sall seik the with thy feiris.   30
Thairfore remembir at all houris
Quod tu in cinerem reverteris.

5

Thocht all this warld thow did posseid,
Nocht eftir death thow sall possess,
Nor with the tak bot thy guid deid,   35
Quhen thow dois fro this warld the dres.
Go speid the, man, and the confes,
With humill hart and sobir teiris,
And sadlye in thy hart inpres
Quod tu in cinerem reverteris.   40

6

Thocht thow be taklit nevir so sure,
Thow sall in deathis port arryve,

22. all *every* weir *uncertainty*
23. sport *enjoyment*
25. lustye bewte *pleasing beauty*
26. feid *fade* somer
    flouris *summer flowers*
27. syne *then*
29. castell *castle* the keip *protect
    you* touris *towers*
30. seik the *seek you*
    feiris *companions*
33. posseid *possess*

34. nocht *nothing*
35. guid deid *good deeds*
36. quhen *when* the dres *take
    yourself*
37. speid the *hurry* the
    confes *make your confession*
38. humill *humble* sobir
    teiris *solemn tears*
39. inpres *imprint*
41. taklit *fitted with rigging*
    sure *securely*

23. 'Think, man, in the midst of all your fun and games'.
27–8. 'Then the dragon, Death, who devours all things, shall swallow
    you with his mouth'.
41–4. 'No matter how securely you are fitted with rigging, you will end
    up in death's port anyway, where nothing can survive the storm, but is
    violently broken into pieces'.

Quhair nocht for tempest may indure,
Bot ferslye all to speiris dryve.
Thy ransonner with woundis fyve   45
Mak thy plycht anker and thy steiris,
To hald thy saule with him on lyve,
Cum tu in cinerem reverteris.

43. quhair *where* nocht *nothing*
44. ferslye *violently*
    speiris *fragments* dryve *break*
45. ransonner *redeemer*
46. plycht anker *main anchor*
    steiris *rudder*

47. hald *keep* saule *soul* on
    lyve *alive*
48. cum tu in cinerem
    reverteris *when you must return
    to ashes*

45–7. 'Make your redeemer with the five wounds your main anchor and
your rudder, so that he keeps your soul alive with him'.

O Wreche, Be War, this Warld Will Wend the Fro

1

O wreche, be war, this warld will wend the fro,
Quhilk hes begylit mony greit estait.
Turne to thy freynd, beleif nocht in thy fo.
Sen thow mon go, be grathing to thy gait,
Remeid in tyme and rew nocht all to lait.   5
Provyd thy place, for thow away man pas
Out of this vaill of trubbill and dissait:
Vanitas vanitatum et omnia vanitas.

2

Walk furth, pilgrame, quhill thow hes dayis licht,
Dres fra desert, draw to thy dwelling place.   10
Speid home, for quhy anone cummis the nicht,
Quhilk dois the follow with ane ythand chaise.
Bend up thy saill and win thy port of grace,
For and the deith ourtak the in trespas,
Than may thow say thir wourdis with allace: 15
Vanitas vanitatum et omnia vanitas.

3

Heir nocht abydis, heir standis nothing stabill;
This fals warld ay flittis to and fro:

1. wreche *wretch* war *ready*
   warld *world* wend the fro *pass
   from you*
2. quhilk *which* begylit *deceived*
   greit estait *powerful person*
3. freynd *friend* beleif nocht *do
   not trust* fo *enemy*
4. sen *since* mon *must* be
   grathing to thy gait *prepare for
   your journey*
5. remeid *amend* rew *repent* to
   lait *too late*
6. provyd *prepare* man *must*
7. vaill *valley* dissait *deceit*
8. vanitas vanitatum et omnia

vanitas *vanity of vanities, all is
vanity*
9. quhill *while* dayis licht *daylight*
10. dres fra *turn from*
11. speid *hurry* for quhy *because*
   anone *soon* nicht *night*
12. ythand chaise *unflagging
   pursuit*
13. bend *draw* win *reach*
14. and *if* deith *death*
   ourtak *overtake* trespas *sin*
15. thir *these* allace *sorrow*
17. nocht *nothing* abydis *lasts*
18. flittis *shifts*

3. 'Turn to God, do not trust in the Devil'.
5. 'Amend your ways in time and do not repent too late'.
14. 'For if death should overtake you in a state of sin'.

Now day up bricht, now nycht als blak as sabill,
Now eb, now flude, now freynd, now cruell fo,   20
Now glaid, now said, now weill, now into wo,
Now cled in gold, dissolvit now in as;
So dois this warld transitorie go:
Vanitas vanitatum et omnia vanitas.

19. day up *daybreak* als *as*
    sabill *sable*
20. eb *ebb* flude *flow*

21. glaid *happy* said *sad*
22. cled *dressed*
    dissolvit *dissolved* in as *into dust*

Quhat is this Lyfe Bot ane Straucht Way to Deid

Quhat is this lyfe bot ane straucht way to deid,
Quhilk hes a tyme to pas and nane to dwell,
A slyding quheill us lent to seik remeid,
A fre chois gevin to paradice or hell,
A pray to deid, quhome vane is to repell,   5
A schoirt torment for infineit glaidnes,
Als schort ane joy for lestand hevynes.

1. quhat *what* lyfe *life* straucht
   way *direct route* deid *death*

2. quhilk *which* pas *go*
   dwell *linger*

3. slyding quheill *turning wheel*
   lent *bestowed* remeid *salvation*

4. fre chois *free choice* gevin *given*

5. pray *prey* vane *useless*

6. schoirt *short* for *in return for*
   infineit *infinite*

7. als *as* lestand
   hevynes *everlasting sorrow*

3. 'A turning wheel bestowed upon us so that we can seek salvation'.
5. 'Prey to death, whom it is useless to try to repel'.

I that in Heill Wes and Gladnes
(The Lament for the Makars)

1
I that in heill wes and gladnes
Am trublit now with gret seiknes
And feblit with infermite:
Timor mortis conturbat me.

2
Our plesance heir is all vane glory;   5
This fals warld is bot transitory,
The flesch is brukle, the fend is sle:
Timor mortis conturbat me.

3
The stait of man dois change and vary;
Now sound, now seik, now blith, now sary,   10
Now dansand mery, now like to dee:
Timor mortis conturbat me.

4
No stait in erd heir standis sickir;
As with the wynd wavis the wickir,
So waveris this warldis vanite: 15
Timor mortis conturbat me.

5
On to the ded gois all estatis,
Princis, prelotis and potestatis,
Baith riche and pur of al degre:
Timor mortis conturbat me.   20

1. heill *health*
2. trublit *afflicted*   seiknes *sickness*
3. feblit *weakened*   infermite *illness*
4. timor mortis conturbat me *I am disturbed by the fear of death*
5. plesance *pleasure*   heir *here* vane glory *empty pride*
6. bot *merely*
7. brukle *frail*   fend *devil*   sle *sly*
9. stait *condition*
10. sound *healthy*   seik *sick* blith *happy*   sary *sorrowful*
11. dansand mery *dancing merrily* like *likely*   dee *die*
13. erd *earth*   sickir *secure*
14. wavis *waves*   wickir *willow*
15. waveris *fluctuates* warldis *world's*
17. ded *death*   estatis *ranks of society*
18. princis *princes*   prelotis *church dignitaries*   potestatis *rulers*
19. baith *both*   pur *poor*   al degre *every rank*

13–5. 'No position here on earth stands secure: the vain things of this world fluctuate like a willow in the wind'.

6

He takis the knychtis in to feild,
Anarmit under helme and scheild;
Victour he is at all mellie.
Timor mortis conturbat me.

7

That strang unmercifull tyrand   25
Takis on the moderis breist sowkand
The bab full of benignite.
Timor mortis conturbat me.

8

He takis the campion in the stour,
The capitane closit in the tour,   30
The lady in bour full of bewte,
Timor mortis conturbat me.

9

He sparis no lord for his piscence,
Na clerk for his intelligence;
His awfull strak may no man fle: 35
Timor mortis conturbat me.

10

Art magicianis and astrologgis,
Rethoris, logicianis and theologgis,
Thame helpis no conclusionis sle:
Timor mortis conturbat me.   40

21. knychtis *knights* in to feild *on the battlefield*
22. anarmit *armed* under *beneath* helme *helmet*
23. mellie *combat*
25. strang *strong* unmercifull *merciless* tyrand *tyrant*
26. moderis breist *mother's breast* sowkand *sucking*
27. bab *baby* benignite *innocence*
29. campion *hero* stour *battle*
30. capitane *captain* closit *enclosed* tour *tower*
31. bour *bedroom* bewte *beauty*
33. piscence *power*
35. strak *stroke* fle *flee*
37. art magicianis *magicians* astrologgis *astrologers*
38. rethoris *rhetoricians* logicianis *logicians* theologgis *theologians*
39. conclusionis sle *clever arguments*

23. 'He is the victor in every fight'.
26–7. 'Takes even the innocent baby sucking at its mother's breast'.
39. 'No clever arguments can help them'.

11

In medicyne the most practicianis,
Lechis, surrigianis and phisicianis,
Thameself fra ded may not supple:
Timor mortis conturbat me.

12

I se that makaris, amang the laif,   45
Playis heir ther pageant, syne gois to graif.
Sparit is nought ther faculte.
Timor mortis conturbat me.

13

He has done petuously devour
The noble Chaucer, of makaris flour,   50
The monk of Bery, and Gower, all thre:
Timor mortis conturbat me.

14

The gud Syr Hew of Eglintoun,
And eik Heryot, and Wyntoun
He has tane out of this cuntre: 55
Timor mortis conturbat me.

15

That scorpion fell has done infek
Maister Johne Clerk and James Afflek
Fra balat making and trigide:
Timor mortis conturbat me.   60

41. most practicianis *greatest practitioners*
42. lechis *doctors*
surrigianis *surgeons*
phisicianis *physicians*
43. ded *death* supple *rescue*
45. se *see* makaris *poets* laif *rest*
46. syne *then* gois *go* graif *grave*
47. sparit *spared* faculte *profession*
49. done . . . devour *devoured*
petuously *lamentably*

50. flour *flower*
51. Bery *Bury St Edmunds*
thre *three*
53. Syr Hew of Eglintoun *Sir Hugh of Eglinton*
54. eik *also*
55. tane *taken* cuntre *country*
57. fell *cruel* done infek *poisoned*
58. Afflek *Auchinleck*
59. balat *poetry* making *composing* trigide *tragedies*

43. 'Cannot rescue themselves from death'.
46. 'Act out their pageants here and then go to their grave'.
49–50. 'He has lamentably devoured noble Chaucer, the flower of all poets'.

16

Holland and Barbour he has berevit.
Allace, that he nought with us levit
Schir Mungo Lokert of the Le:
Timor mortis conturbat me.

17

Clerk of Tranent eik he has tane,   65
That maid the anteris of Gawane;
Schir Gilbert Hay endit has he:
Timor mortis conturbat me.

18

He has blind Hary and Sandy Traill
Slaine with his schour of mortall haill,   70
Quhilk Patrik Johnestoun myght nought fle:
Timor mortis conturbat me.

19

He has reft Merseir his endite,
That did in luf so lifly write,
So schort, so quyk, of sentence hie: 75
Timor mortis conturbat me.

20

He has tane Roull of Aberdene,
And gentill Roull of Corstorphin,
Two better fallowis did no man se:
Timor mortis conturbat me.   80

---

61. berevit *carried off*
62. allace *alas* levit *left*
63. Schir Mungo Lokert of the Le *Sir Mungo Lockhart of the Lee*
66. anteris *adventures* Gawane *Gawain*
70. schour *shower* mortall haill *deadly hail*

71. quhilk *which* Patrik Johnestoun *Patrick Johnston*
73. reft *robbed* Merseir *Mersar* endite *writing*
74. luf *love* lifly *vividly*
75. schort *succinct* quyk *lively* sentence hie *noble substance*
77. Aberdene *Aberdeen*
79. fallowis *fellows*

73. 'He has robbed Mersar of his ability to write'.

21

In Dunfermelyne he has done roune
With maister Robert Henrisoun.
Schir Johne the Ros enbrast has he:
Timor mortis conturbat me.

22

And he has now tane, last of aw,   85
Gud gentill Stobo and Quintyne Schaw,
Of quham all wichtis has pete;
Timor mortis conturbat me.

23

Gud maister Walter Kennedy
In poynt of dede lyis veraly.   90
Gret reuth it wer that so suld be:
Timor mortis conturbat me.

24

Sen he has all my brether tane,
He will naught lat me lif alane.
On forse I man his nyxt pray be: 95
Timor mortis conturbat me.

25

Sen for the ded remeid is none,
Best is that we for dede dispone,
Efter our deid that lif may we:
Timor mortis conturbat me.   100

---

81. Dunfermelyne *Dunfermline*
    done roune *discoursed*
82. Henrisoun *Henryson*
83. Johne the Ros *John Ross*
    enbrast *embraced*
85. aw *all*
87. wichtis *people* pete *compassion*
90. in poynt *on the point*
    dede *death* veraly *truly*

91. reuth *pity*
93. sen *since* brether *brothers*
    tane *taken*
94. lif *live* alane *alone*
95. on forse *inevitably* man *must*
    nyxt *next* pray *victim*
97. ded *death* remeid *remedy*
98. dispone *prepare*
99. lif *live*

95. 'I must inevitably be his next victim'.
97–9. 'Since there is no cure for death, it is best that we prepare
ourselves for it, so that after death we can live forever'.

Hale, Sterne Superne, Hale, in Eterne

1

Hale, sterne superne, hale, in eterne
  In Godis sicht to schyne;
Lucerne in derne for to discerne
  Be glory and grace devyne.
Hodiern, modern, sempitern,   5
  Angelicall regyne,
Our tern inferne for to dispern,
  Helpe, rialest rosyne.
Ave Maria, gracia plena.
  Haile, fresche flour femynyne,   10
Yerne us guberne, virgin matern,
  Of reuth baith rute and ryne.

2

Haile, yhyng benyng fresche flurising,
  Haile, Alphais habitakle.
Thy dyng ofspring maid us to syng   15
  Befor his tabernakle.
All thing maling we doune thring
  Be sicht of his signakle,

1. hale *hail* sterne superne *heavenly star* eterne *eternity*
2. sicht *sight* schyne *shine*
3. lucerne *lamp* derne *darkness* discerne *see*
4. be *by* devyne *divine*
5. hodiern *today* modern *the present age* sempitern *all eternity*
6. regyne *queen*
7. tern inferne *infernal gloom* dispern *drive away*
8. rialest *most royal* rosyne *rose*
9. Ave Maria, gracia plena *Hail Mary, full of grace*
10. flour femynyne *flower of women*
11. yerne *diligently* guberne *govern* matern *maternal*
12. reuth *pity* rute *root* ryne *bark*
13. yhyng *young* benyng *gracious* flurising *flower*
14. Alphais habitakle *dwelling of God*
15. dyng *worthy*
17. maling *evil* doune thring *overthrow*
18. be sicht *at the sight* signakle *sign of the cross*

1–2. 'Hail, heavenly star, hail, destined to shine in God's sight for eternity'.
3–4. 'The lamp which lets us see in the darkness by glory and divine grace'.
12. 'The source of all pity'.

Quhilk king us bring unto his ryng,
   Fro dethis dirk umbrakle.   20
Ave Maria, gracia plena.
   Haile, moder and maide but makle,
Bricht syng, gladyng our languissing
   Be micht of thi mirakle.

        3
Haile, bricht be sicht in hevyn on hicht,   25
   Haile, day sterne orientale,
Our licht most richt in clud of nycht,
   Our dirknes for to scale.
Haile, wicht in ficht, puttar to flicht
   Of fendis in battale,   30
Haile, plicht but sicht, hale, mekle of mycht,
   Haile, glorius virgin, hale
Ave Maria, gracia plena.
   Haile, gentill nychttingale,
Way stricht, cler dicht, to wilsome wicht   35
   That irke bene in travale.

        4
Hale, qwene serene, hale, most amene,
   Haile, hevinlie hie emprys,
Haile, schene, unseyne with carnale eyne,

19. ryng *kingdom*
20. dirk *dark* umbrakle *shadow*
22. moder *mother* maide *virgin*
   but makle *without blemish*
23. syng *sign* gladyng *gladdening*
   languissing *suffering*
24. be *by* micht *power*
   mirakle *miracle*
25. be sicht *in appearance* on
   hicht *on high*
26. sterne *star* orientale *in the east*
27. richt *true* clud *cloud*
   nycht *night*
28. scale *disperse*

29. wicht *courageous* ficht *battle*
   flicht *flight*
30. fendis *fiends*
31. plicht but sicht *unseen anchor*
   mekle *great*
35. stricht *straight* dicht *marked*
   wilsome wicht *wandering man*
36. irke bene *is weary*
   travale *travelling*
37. amene *delightful*
38. hie *high* emprys *empress*
39. schene *beautiful one*
   unseyne *unseen* carnale
   eyne *human eyes*

19–20. 'May that king bring us into his kingdom, away from the dark
   shadow of death'.
26. 'Hail, day star in the east'.
35–6. 'A straight road, clearly marked, for the wandering man who is
   tired of travelling'.

Haile, ros of paradys, 40
Haile, clene bedene ay till conteyne,
Haile, fair fresche flour delyce,
Haile, grene daseyne, hale fro the splene,
Of Jhesu genitrice.
Ave Maria, gracia plena. 45
Thow bair the prince of prys,
Our teyne to meyne and ga betweyne
As humile oratrice.

5

Hale, more decore than of before
And swetar be sic sevyne, 50
Our glore forlore for to restor
Sen thow art qwene of hevyn.
Memore of sore, stern in aurore,
Lovit with angellis stevyne,
Implore, adore, thow indeflore, 55
To mak our oddis evyne.
Ave Maria, gracia plena.
With lovingis lowde ellevyn,
Quhill store and hore my youth devor,
Thy name I sall ay nevyne. 60

40. ros *rose*
41. clene bedene *completely pure*
till conteyne *to continue*
42. flour delyce *fleur-de-lys*
43. grene daseyne *fresh daisy*
fro *from* splene *heart*
44. genitrice *mother*
46. bair *bore* prys *glory*
47. teyne *affliction* meyne *take
pity on* ga *go*
48. humile *humble*
oratrice *intercessor*
49. decore *beautiful* of
before *before*

50. swetar *sweeter* be sic
sevyne *seven times*
51. glore *glory* forlore *lost*
52. sen *since*
53. memore *mindful* sore *sorrow*
stern *star* in aurore *at dawn*
54. lovit *praised* stevyne *voices*
55. indeflore *undeflowered one*
56. oddis *odds* evyne *even*
58. lovingis *praise* lowde *loud*
ellevyn *indeed*
59. quhill *until* store *struggle*
hore *old age* devor *destroy*
60. nevyne *recite*

44. 'Mother of Jesus'.
47–8. 'To take pity on our affliction and plead for us as a humble
intercessor'.
58–60. 'I shall always recite your name with loud praise indeed, until
life's struggle and old age destroy my youth'.

6

Empryce of prys, imperatrice,
　Bricht polist precious stane,
Victrice of vyce, hie genitrice
　Of Jhesu, lord soverayne,
Our wys pavys fro enemys,　　　　　　　　　　65
　Agane the feyndis trayne,
Oratrice, mediatrice, salvatrice,
　To God gret suffragane.
Ave Maria, gracia plena.
　Haile, sterne meridiane,　　　　　　　　　　70
Spyce, flour delice of paradys,
　That bair the gloryus grayne.

7

Imperiall wall, place palestrall
　Of peirles pulcritud,
Tryumphale hall, hie trone regall　　　　　　　75
　Of Godis celsitud,
Hospitall riall, the lord of all
　Thy closet did include,
Bricht ball cristall, ros virginall,
　Fulfillit of angell fude.　　　　　　　　　　80
Ave Maria, gracia plena.
　Thy birth has with his blude
Fra fall mortall originall
　Us raunsound on the rude.

61. imperatrice *empress*
62. polist *polished*　stane *stone*
63. victrice *conqueror*　hie *high*
　genitrice *mother*
64. soverayne *supreme*
65. wys *wise*　pavys *shield*
66. agane *against*　feyndis *fiend's*
　trayne *deception*
67. oratrice *intercessor*
　mediatrice *mediator*
　salvatrice *saviour*
68. suffragane *helper*
70. sterne meridiane *midday star*
71. spyce *spice*
72. bair *bore*　grayne *seed*

73. place palestrall *magnificent
　palace*
74. peirles *unequalled*
　pulcritud *beauty*
75. trone *throne*
76. celsitud *majesty*
77. hospitall riall *royal shelter*
78. closet *inner room*
　include *enclose*
80. fulfillit *completely filled*
　fude *food*
82. birth *child*
84. raunsound *redeemed*
　rude *cross*

Rorate, Celi, Desuper

1

Rorate, celi, desuper!
Hevins, distill your balmy schouris,
For now is rissin the brycht day ster
Fro the ros, Mary, flour of flouris.
The cleir sone quhome no clud devouris,   5
Surmunting Phebus in the est,
Is cumin of his hevinly touris,
Et nobis puer natus est.

2

Archangellis, angellis and dompnationis,
Tronis, potestatis and marteiris seir,   10
And all ye hevinly operationis,
Ster, planeit, firmament and speir,
Fyre, erd, air and watter cleir,
To him gife loving, most and lest,
That come in to so mcik mancir   15
Et nobis puer natus est.

3

Synnaris, be glaid and pennance do
And thank your makar hairtfully,
For he that ye mycht nocht cum to
To yow is cumin full humly,   20

1. Rorate, celi, desuper *Rain down dew, o heavens, from above*
2. distill *let fall in drops* schouris *showers*
3. ster *star*
4. fro *from* ros *rose* flour *flower*
5. cleir *bright* sone *sun* quhome *whom* clud *cloud*
6. surmunting *surpassing* Phebus *Phoebus* est *east*
7. is cumin of *has come from* touris *towers*
8. Et nobis puer natus est *And unto us a child is born*
9. archangellis *archangels*

dompnationis *dominations*
10. tronis *thrones* potestatis *powers* marteiris seir *many martyrs*
11. operationis *forces*
12. speir *sphere*
13. fyre *fire* erd *earth*
14. gife loving *give praise*
15. come *came* meik maneir *humble way*
17. synnaris *sinners* glaid *glad*
18. makar *creator* hairtfully *wholeheartedly*
20. is cumin *has come* humly *humbly*

19–20. 'For he to whom you could not come has come to you in all humility'.

Your saulis with his blud to by
And lous yow of the feindis arrest,
And only of his awin mercy,
Pro nobis puer natus est.

4

All clergy, do to him inclyne   25
And bow unto that barne benyng,
And do your observance devyne
To him that is of kingis king.
Ensence his altar, reid and sing
In haly kirk with mynd degest,   30
Him honouring attour all thing,
Qui nobis puer natus est.

5

Celestiall fowlis in the are,
Sing with your nottis upoun hicht,
In firthis and in forrestis fair   35
Be myrthfull now at all your mycht,
For passit is your dully nycht.
Aurora hes the cluddis perst,
The son is rissin with glaidsum lycht
Et nobis puer natus est.   40

6

Now spring up, flouris, fra the rute,
Revert yow upwart naturaly,
In honour of the blissit frute
That rais up fro the rose Mary.

21. saulis *souls* blud *blood*
    by *redeem*
22. lous *free* feindis *fiend's*
    arrest *imprisonment*
23. of *on account of* awin *own*
25. inclyne *bow down*
26. barne benyng *gracious child*
27. observance devyne *religious worship*
29. ensence *perfume with incense*
    reid *read*
30. haly kirk *holy church*
    degest *solemn*
31. attour *above*
32. Qui nobis puer natus est *the*

child who is born unto us
33. fowlis *birds* are *air*
34. nottis *songs* hicht *high*
35. firthis *woods*
36. myrthfull *joyful* at *with*
    mycht *power*
37. passit *passed* dully
    nycht *gloomy night*
38. cluddis *clouds* perst *pierced*
39. glaidsum lycht *joyful light*
41. rute *root*
42. revert yow upwart *turn upwards*
43. blissit frute *blessed fruit*
44. rais *rose*

Lay out your levis lustely, 45
Fro deid tak lyfe now at the lest,
In wirschip of that prince wirthy,
Qui nobis puer natus est.

7

Syng, hevin imperiall, most of hicht,
Regions of air, mak armony. 50
All fische in flud and foull of flicht,
Be myrthfull and mak melody.
All, *gloria in excelsis* cry,
Hevin, erd, se, man, bird and best;
He that is crownit abone the sky, 55
Pro nobis puer natus est.

45. levis *leaves* lustely *beautifully*
46. deid *death* the lest *last*
47. wirschip *honour*
    wirthy *worthy*
49. imperiall *majestic* hicht *height*
50. armony *music*
51. flud *river* foull *bird* of

flicht *in flight*
53. gloria in excelsis *glory in the highest*
54. erd *earth* se *sea* best *beast*
55. abone *above*
56. pro nobis puer natus est *for our sake a child is born*

49. 'Sing, majestic heaven, most high'.

Amang Thir Freiris, Within ane Cloister

1

Amang thir freiris, within ane cloister,
I enterit in ane oritorie,
And knelit doun with ane *pater noster*
Befoir the michtie king of glorie,
Haveing his passioun in memorie;   5
Syn to his mother I did inclyne,
Hir halsing with ane *gaude flore*,
And sudandlie I sleipit syne.

2

Methocht Judas with mony ane Jow
Tuik blissit Jesu our salvatour,   10
And schot him furth with mony ane schow,
With schamefull wourdis of dishonour;
And lyk ane theif or ane tratour
Thay leid that hevinlie prince most hie,
With manassing attour messour,   15
O mankynd, for the luif of the.

3

Falslie condamnit befoir ane juge,
Thay spittit in his visage fayr,
And as lyounis with awfull ruge
In yre thay hurlit him heir and thair,   20
And gaif him mony buffat sair

1. thir *these* freiris *friars*
2. oritorie *oratory*
3. knelit *knelt* pater noster *Our Father*
4. michtie *mighty* glorie *glory*
5. passioun *suffering*
6. syn *then* inclyne *bow*
7. hir halsing *greeting her* gaude flore *hymn of joy*
8. sudandlie *suddenly* sleipit *slept*
9. methocht *it seemed to me* Jow *Jew*
10. tuik *took* blissit *blessed* Jesu *Jesus* salvatour *saviour*
11. schot *drove* schow *shove*
12. wourdis *words*
13. tratour *traitor*
14. leid *led* hie *noble*
15. manassing *threats* attour messour *beyond all measure*
16. luif *love* the *you*
17. condamnit *condemned* juge *judge*
18. spittit *spat* visage *face*
19. lyounis *lyons* awfull ruge *terrifying roar*
20. yre *anger* hurlit *threw* heir *here*
21. gaif *gave* buffat sair *painful blow*

14. 'They led that most noble, heavenly prince'.

That it wes sorow for to se.
Of all his claythis thay tirvit him bair,
O mankynd, for the luif of the.

4

Thay terandis, to revenge thair tein,   25
For scorne thai cled him in to quhyt
And hid his blythfull glorious ene,
To se quham angellis had delyt;
Dispituouslie syn did him smyt,
Saying, 'Gif sone of God thow be,   30
Quha straik the now thow tell us tyt',
O mankynd, for the luif of the.

5

In tene thay tirvit him agane,
And till ane pillar thai him band.
Quhill blude birst out at everie vane,   35
Thay scurgit him bayth fut and hand.
At everic straik ran furth ane strand
Quhilk mycht have ransonit warldis thre.
He baid in stour quhill he mycht stand,
O mankynd, for the luif of the.   40

22. se *see*
23. claythis *clothes* tirvit *stripped*
25. thay terandis *those villains*
    revenge *vent* tein *anger*
26. cled *dressed* quhyt *white*
27. blythfull *joyful* ene *eyes*
28. quham *whom* delyt *delight*
29. dispituouslie *pitilessly*
    smyt *strike*
30. gif *if* sone *son*
31. quha *who* straik *struck* tyt *at
    once*
33. tene *anger*

34. till *to* band *tied*
35. quhill *until* blude *blood*
    birst *burst* vane *vein*
36. scurgit *scourged* bayth *both*
    fut *foot*
37. straik *stroke* strand *stream of
    blood*
38. quhilk *which*
    ransonit *redeemed*
    warldis *worlds*
39. baid *remained* in stour *in
    combat* quhill *while*

27–8. 'And blindfolded his joyful, glorious eyes, which the angels had
    such delight in seeing'.
30–1. 'Saying, "If you are the son of God, tell us at once who strikes
    you now" '.
39. 'He remained in combat while he could still stand'.

6

Nixt all in purpyr thay him cled,
And syn with thornis scharp and kene
His saikles blude agane thay sched,
Persing his heid with pykis grene;
Unneis with lyf he micht sustene   45
That croune on thrungin with crueltie
Quhill flude of blude blindit his ene,
O mankynd, for the luif of the.

7

Ane croce that wes bayth large and lang,
To beir thay gaif this blissit lord,   50
Syn fullelie, as theif, to hang
Thay harlit him furth with raip and corde.
With bluid and sweit was all deflorde
His face, the fude of angellis fre,
His feit with stanis was revin and scorde,   55
O mankynd, for the luif of the.

8

Agane thay tirvit him bak and syd,
Als brim as ony baris woid.
The clayth that claif to his cleir hyd
Thay raif away with ruggis rude,   60

41. nixt *next* purpyr *purple*
42. kene *cruel*
43. saikles *innocent* sched *shed*
44. persing *piercing* heid *head*
pykis grene *fresh thorns*
45. unneis *scarcely* sustene *endure*
46. on thrungin *pressed on*
47. quhill *until* flude *flow*
ene *eyes*
49. croce *cross*
50. beir *carry* gaif *gave*
51. fullelie *in a foul manner*
52. harlit *dragged* raip *rope*

53. sweit *sweat* deflorde *disfigured*
54. fude *food* fre *noble*
55. stanis *stones* revin *torn*
scorde *cut*
57. tirvit *stripped* bak and
syd *completely*
58. als *as* brim *fierce* baris
woid *crazed boars*
59. clayth *cloth* claif *stuck* cleir
hyd *fair skin*
60. raif *tore* ruggis rude *violent
tugs*

46–7. 'That crown was cruelly pressed on until the flow of blood blinded
his eyes'.
49–50. 'They gave this blessed lord a cross to carry, that was both large
and long'.
51–2. 'Then, in a foul manner, they dragged him out with ropes and
cords, to hang him up like a thief'.

Quhill fersly followit flesche and blude,
That it was pietie for to se.
Na kynd of torment he ganestude,
O mankynd, for the luif of the.

9

On to the crose of breid and lenth   65
To gar his lymmis langar wax,
Thay straitit him with all thair strenth
Quhill to the rude thay gart him rax,
Syn tyit him on with greit irne takkis,
And him all nakit on the tre,   70
Thay raissit on loft be houris sax,
O mankynd, for the luif of the.

10

Quhen he was bendit so on breid
Quhill all his vanis brist and brak,
To gar his cruell pane exceid   75
Thay leit him fall doun with ane swak,
Quhill cors and corps and all did crak.
Agane thay rasit him on hie,
Reddie may turmentis for to tak,
O mankynd, for the luif of the.   80

11

Betwix two theiffis the spreit he gaif
On to the fader most of micht.
The erde did trimmill, the stanis claif,
The sone obscurit of his licht,

61. fersly *roughly*
62. pietie *pity* se *see*
63. ganestude *resisted*
65. breid *breadth*
66. gar *make* lymmis *limbs*
    langar *longer* wax *grow*
67. straitit *pulled*
68. rude *cross* gart *made* rax *stretch*
69. tyit *tied* irne *iron* takkis *nails*
70. nakit *naked* tre *tree*
71. on loft *on high* be houris
    sax *at the sixth hour*
73. bendit *stretched* on breid *fully*
74. vanis *veins* brist *burst*

brak *broke*
75. exceid *increase*
76. swak *thud*
77. cors *cross* corps *body*
78. rasit *raised*
79. may *more* turmentis *torments*
    tak *endure*
81. betwix *between* the spreit he
    gaif *he gave up his spirit*
82. fader *father* most *greatest*
    micht *power*
83. erde *earth* trimmill *tremble*
    stanis *stones* claif *split apart*
84. sone *sun* obscurit *darkened*

The day wox dirk as ony nicht,   85
Deid bodies rais in the cite.
Goddis deir sone all thus was dicht,
O mankynd, for the luif of the.

12

In weir that he wes yit on lyf
Thay rane ane rude speir in his syde,   90
And did his precious body ryff
Quhill blude and watter did furth glyde.
Thus Jesus with his woundis wyde
Ane marter sufferit for to de,
And tholit to be crucifyid,   95
O mankynd, for the luif of the.

13

Methocht Compassioun, wode of feiris,
Than straik at me with mony ane stound,
And soir Contritioun, bathit in teiris,
My visage all in watter drownit,   100
And Reuth in to my eir ay rounde:
'For schame allace, behald, man, how
Beft is with mony ane wound
Thy blissit salvatour Jesu.'

14

Than rudelie come Remembrance   105
Ay rugging me withouttin rest,
Quhilk crose and nalis, scharp scurge and lance,

85. wox *became* dirk *dark*
86. deid *dead* rais *rose up*
87. dicht *treated*
89. in weir *uncertain* yit *still* on
   lyf *alive*
90. rane *thrust* rude *rough*
91. ryff *tear*
92. quhill *so that* furth glyde *flow
   out*
94. marter *martyr* de *die*
95. tholit to be *endured being*
97. methocht *it seemed to me*
   wode *angry* of feiris *in manner*

98. straik *struck* stound *pang*
99. soir *sorrowful* bathit *bathed*
   teiris *tears*
100. visage *face*
101. Reuth *Pity* eir *ear*
   ay *constantly* rounde *whispered*
102. allace *alas*
103. beft *beaten*
104. salvatour *saviour*
105. rudlie *roughly*
106. rugging *pulling*
107. quhilk *who* crose *cross*
   nalis *nails* scurge *scourge*

94. 'Suffered to die as a martyr'.

And bludy crowne befoir me kest.
Than Pane with passioun me opprest,
And evir did Petie on me pow   110
Saying, 'Behald how Jowis hes drest
Thy blissit salvatour Chryst Jesu.'

15

With greiting glaid be than come Grace,
With wourdis sweit saying to me,
'Ordane for him ane resting place,   115
That is so werie wrocht for the,
That schort, within thir dayis thre
Sall law undir thy lyntell bow,
And in thy hous sall herbrit be
Thy blissit salvatour Chryst Jesu.'   120

16

Than swyth Contritioun wes on steir
And did eftir Confessioun ryn,
And Conscience me accusit heir
And kest out mony cankerit syn.
To rys Repentence did begin,   125
And out at the yettis did schow.
Pennance did walk the hous within,
Byding our salvitour Chryst Jesu.

17

Grace become gyd and governour
To keip the hous in sicker stait,   130
Ay reddie till our salvatour,

108. kest *threw*
109. Pane *Pain* passioun *torment*
110. Petie *Pity* pow *pull*
111. Jowis *Jews* drest *treated*
113. glaid *glad*
115. ordane *prepare*
116. werie *weary* wrocht *made*
117. schort *shortly* thir *these*
118. law *low* lyntell *doorway*
   bow *stoop*
119. herbrit *lodged*

121. swyth *swiftly* on steir *in motion*
122. ryn *run*
123. accusit *accused*
124. cankerit *malignant*
125. rys *rise*
126. yettis *gates* schow *push*
128. byding *awaiting*
129. gyd *guide*
130. sicker stait *secure state*
131. till *for*

116. 'Who has been made so weary for your sake'.

Quhill that he come, air or lait.
Repentence ay with cheikis wait
No pane nor pennence did eschew,
The hous within evir to debait,   135
Onlie for luif of sweit Jesu.

18

For grit terrour of Chrystis deid
The erde did trymmill quhair I lay,
Quhairthrow I waiknit in that steid,
With spreit halflingis in effray.   140
Than wrayt I all without delay
Richt heir as I have schawin to yow,
Quhat me befell on Gud Fryday
Befoir the crose of sweit Jesu.

132. air *early*
133. cheikis wait *wet cheeks*
134. eschew *avoid*
135. debait *protect*
137. Chrystis deid *Christ's death*
139. quhairthrow *on account of*

which waiknit *awakened*
steid *place*
140. spreit *spirit* halflingis *half*
effray *fear*
141. wrayt *wrote*
142. heir *here* schawin *shown*

Done is a Battell on the Dragon Blak

1

Done is a battell on the dragon blak,
Our campioun Chryst confoundit hes his force,
The yettis of hell ar brokin with a crak,
The signe triumphall rasit is of the croce.
The divillis trymmillis with hiddous voce,   5
The saulis ar borrowit and to the blis can go,
Chryst with his blud our ransonis dois indoce:
Surrexit dominus de sepulchro.

2

Dungin is the deidly dragon, Lucifer,
The crewall serpent with the mortall stang,   10
The auld kene tegir, with his teith on char,
Quhilk in a wait hes lyne for us so lang,
Thinking to grip us in his clowis strang.
The mercifull lord wald nocht that it wer so;
He maid him for to felye of that fang: 15
Surrexit dominus de sepulchro.

3

He for our saik that sufferit to be slane
And lyk a lamb in sacrifice wes dicht,
Is lyk a lyone rissin up agane
And as a gyane raxit him on hicht.   20

1. on *against*
2. campioun *champion*
   confoundit *overthrown*
3. yettis *gates*
4. signe triumphall *victorious
   battle-standard* rasit *raised*
   croce *cross*
5. divillis *devils*
   trymmillis *tremble* voce *voice*
6. saulis *souls* borrowit *redeemed*
7. blud *blood* ransonis *ransoms*
   indoce *affirm*
8. Surrexit dominus de sepulchre *the
   Lord is risen from the tomb*
9. dungin *beaten*
10. crewall *cruel* mortall
    stang *deadly sting*
11. kene *fierce* tegir *tiger* on
    char *bared*
12. wait *ambush* lyne *lain in wait*
13. clowis *claws*
14. wald nocht *did not wish*
15. felye of *lose* fang *prey*
18. dicht *treated*
19. lyone *lion*
20. gyane *giant* raxit
    him *stretched himself* on
    hicht *on high*

4. 'The victorious battle standard of the cross is raised'.

Sprungin is Aurora, radius and bricht,
On loft is gone the glorius Appollo;
The blisfull day departit fro the nycht:
Surrexit dominus de sepulchro.

4
The grit victour agane is rissin on hicht   25
That for our querrell to the deth wes woundit.
The sone that wox all paill now schynis bricht,
And, dirknes clerit, our fayth is now refoundit.
The knell of mercy fra the hevin is soundit,
The Cristin ar deliverit of thair wo;   30
The Jowis and thair errour ar confoundit:
Surrexit dominus de sepulchro.

5
The fo is chasit, the battell is done ceis,
The presone brokin, the jevellouris fleit and flemit,
The weir is gon, confermit is the peis,   35
The fetteris lowsit and the dungeoun temit,
The ransoun maid, the presoneris redemit,
The feild is win, ourcumin is the fo,
Dispulit of the tresur that he yemit:
Surrexit dominus de sepulchro.   40

21. sprungin *risen* radius *radiant*
22. on loft *on high*
23. departit *is separated*
26. querrell *cause*
27. sone *sun* wox *grew* paill *pale*
28. dirknes *darkness* clerit *cleared away* refoundit *re-established*
29. knell *ringing bell*
30. Cristin *Christians*
31. Jowis *Jews* confoundit *cast down*
33. chasit *chased away* done ceis *finished*

34. presone *prison*
jevellouris *jailers* fleit *frightened off* flemit *banished*
35. weir *war* gon *ended*
confermit *established* peis *peace*
36. fetteris *fetters; chains*
lowsit *loosened* temit *emptied*
37. redemit *redeemed*
38. feild *battle* win *won*
ourcumin *overcome*
39. dispulit *deprived*
tresur *treasure* yemit *guarded*

To The, O Marcifull Salviour Myn, Jesus
(The Tabill of Confessioun)

1

To the, O marcifull salviour myn, Jesus,
My king, my lord and my redemer sweit,
Befor thy bludy figour dolorus
I schryve me cleyne, with humile spreit and meik,
That ever I did unto this hour compleit,   5
Baith in word, in wark and in entent.
Falling on face full law befor thy feit,
I cry the marcy and laser to repent.

2

To the, my meik sweit salviour, I me schrife,
And dois me in thy marcy maist excelling,   10
Of the wrang spending of my wittis five,
In hering, seing, tuiching, gusting, smelling,
Ganestanding, greving, offending and rebelling
Aganis my lord God omnipotent.
With teris of sorrow fra myn ene distelling   15
I cry the marcy and laser to repent.

3

I, wrachit synnar, vile and full of vice,
Of the sevin deidly synnis dois me schrif:
Of prid, invy, of ire and covatice,

1. the *thee*   salviour *saviour*
2. redemer sweit *sweet redeemer*
3. bludy figour *blood-stained image*   dolorus *sorrowful*
4. schryve me *confess*   cleyne *fully*   humilc *humble*   spreit *humble spirit*   meik *meek*
5. compleit *completely*
6. baith *both*   wark *deed*   entent *thought*
7. law *low*   feit *feet*
8. laser *time*
10. dois me in *surrender myself to*   excelling *exceptional*
11. wrang spending *wrongful use*   wittis *senses*
12. hering *hearing*   tuiching *touch*   gusting *taste*
13. ganestanding *opposing*   greving *grieving*
14. aganis *against*
15. teris *tears*   ene *eyes*   distelling *dropping*
17. wrachit *wretched*
18. deidly *deadly*   synnis *sins*
19. prid *pride*   invy *envy*   ire *wrath*   covatice *covetousness*

5. 'Of everything I have ever done until now'.
8. 'I appeal to you for mercy and for the time to repent'.

Of lichory, gluttony, with sleuth ay till ourdrife,   20
Exercing vicis ever in all my life,
For quhilk, allace, I servit to be schent:
Rew on me, Jesu, for thy woundis five,
I cry the marcy and laser to repent.

4

I schrif me, lord, that I abusit have   25
The sevin deidis of marcy corporall:
The hungry meit, nor thristy drink I gaif,
Vesyit the seik, nor redemit the thrall,
Herbreit the wilsum, nor nakit cled at all,
Nor yit the deid to bery tuke I tent.   30
Thow that put marcy abone thi werkis all,
I cry the marcy and laser to repent.

5

In the sevin deidis of marcy spirituall:
To the ignorant nocht gaif I my teching,
Synneris correctioun, nor distitud consall,   35
Nor unto wofull wrachis conforting,
Nor unto saulis support of my praying,
Nor wes to ask forgevinnes pacient,
Nor to forgif my nychtburis offending.
I cry the marcy and laser to repent.   40

20. lichory *lechery* sleuth *sloth*
    till ourdrife *to waste time*
21. exercing *practising* vicis *vices*
22. quhilk *which* allace *alas*
    servit *deserve* schent *punished*
23. rew *take pity*
25. I schrif me *I confess*
    abusit *neglected*
26. deidis *acts* marcy
    corporall *physical mercy*
27. meit *food* gaif *gave*
28. vesyit *visited* seik *sick*
    redemit *redeemed* thrall *prisoner*
29. herbreit *sheltered*

wilsum *homeless* nakit
cled *clothed the naked*
30. deid *dead* bery *bury* tent *care*
31. abone *above*
35. distitud consall *advice to the
    destitute*
36. wofull wrachis *sorrowful
    wretches* conforting *comfort*
37. saulis *souls*
38. forgevinnes *forgiveness*
    pacient *patient*
39. forgif *forgive* nychtburis
    offending *neighbours' offenses*

20–1. 'Of lechery, gluttony, always ready to waste time with sloth,
      constantly engaged in vice throughout my life'.
27. 'I did not give food to the hungry, nor drink to the thirsty'.
30. 'Nor did I even take care to see that the dead were buried'.
33. 'As for the seven deeds of spiritual mercy'.
38. 'Nor was I patient towards those requiring forgiveness'.

6

Lord, I have done full litill reverence
Unto the sacramentis sevin of gret renoun:
To that hie eucarist moist of exellence,
Baptasing, pennence and confirmacioun,
Matremony, ordour and extreme uncioun.   45
Heirof sa fer as I wes necligent,
With hert contrit and teris falling doun,
I cry the marcy and laser to repent.

7

Thy ten commandmentis: a God for to honour,
Nocht tane in vane, na manslaar to be,   50
Fader and moder to worschip at all houre,
To be no theif, the haly day to uphie,
Nychtburis to luf, fals witnes for to fle,
To leif adultre, to covat na manis rent:
In all thir, Lord, culpabill knaw I me.   55
I cry the marcy and laser to repent.

8

In the twelf artickillis of the treuth: a God to trow,
The Fader that all wrocht and comprehendit,
And in his only sone, blissit Jesu,

41. full litill *very little*
42. renoun *distinction*
43. hie eucarist *holy eucharist*
    moist *greatest*
44. baptasing *baptism*
    confirmacioun *confirmation*
45. ordour *ordination*
    uncioun *unction*
46. heirof *in this* sa fer as *in so
    far as* necligent *neglectful*
47. hert contrit *contrite heart*
    teris *tears*
49. a *one*
50. tane *taken* manslaar *murderer*

51. fader *father* moder *mother*
    worschip *honour* houre *times*
52. haly day *sabbath* uphie *observe*
53. luf *love* fle *flee*
54. leif *avoid* adultre *adultery*
    covat *covet* manis rent *man's
    goods*
55. thir *these* knaw I me *I know I
    am*
57. twelf artickillis *twelve articles*
    treuth *creed* trow *believe*
58. all wrocht *created everything*
    comprehendit *included*
59. sone *son* blissit *blessed*

50. 'His name not to be taken in vain, not to be a murderer'.
57. 'In the twelve articles of the creed: to believe in one God'.

Of Mary borne, on croce deid and discendit,   60
The thrid day rais, to the Faderis rycht hand ascendit,
Of quik and ded to cum and hald jugement:
Into thir pointis, O Lord, quhare I offendit,
I cry the marcy and laser to repent.

9

I trow into the blissit Haly Spreit,   65
And in the kirk, to do as it commandis,
And in the day of dome that we sall ris compleit,
And tak oure flesche agane, baith feit and handis,
All to be saif, into the stait of grace that standis.
Plane I revoik in thir quhair I myswent,   70
Befoir the juge and lord of sey and landis.
I cry the marcy and laser to repent.

10

I synnit, Lord, nocht being strang as wall
In hope, faith and fervent cherite,
Nocht with the fair foure vertuis cardinall   75
Agins vicis sure anarmyng me;
With fortitud, prudence and temporance, thir thre,
With justice ever in word, werk, and in entent:
To the, Crist Jesu, casting up myn ee,
I cry the marcy and laser to repent.   80

60. borne *born* croce *cross*
    deid *died* discendit *descended*
61. rais *rose* rycht *right*
62. quik *living*
63. quhare *wherever*
65. trow into *believe in*
    Spreit *Spirit*
66. kirk *church*
67. dome *judgement* ris
    compleit *rise complete*
69. saif *saved* standis *endures*
70. plane *fully* revoik *recant*

myswent *erred*
71. juge *judge* sey *sea*
73. synnit *sinned* strang as
    wall *strong as a wall*
74. cherite *charity*
75. vertuis cardinall *cardinal
    virtues*
76. sure *securely*
    anarmyng *arming*
77. fortitud *fortitude*
    temporance *temperance*
79. ee *eyes*

60–2. 'Born of Mary, who died on the cross and descended into hell, he
    rose again on the third day, and ascended to the right hand of the
    father, he will come again and judge the living and the dead'.
75–6. 'Not securely arming myself against sin with the four fair cardinal
    virtues'.

11

In the sevin commandis of the kirk, that is to say,
Thy teind to pay, and cursing to eschew,
To keipe the festuall and the fasting day,
The mes on Sonday, the parroche kirk persew,
To proper curat to mak confessioun trew,   85
Anis in the yer to tak the sacrament:
Into thir pointis quhair I have offendit, sair I rew.
I cry the marcy and laser to repent.

12

Of syn also into the Haly Spreit,
Of schrift postponit, of syn aganis natour,   90
Of incontricioun, of confessour undiscreit,
Of ressait synfull of my salvature,
Of undone pennence and satisfactioun sure,
Of the sevin giftis the Haly Gaist me sent,
Of *pater noster* and sevin peticionis pure,   95
I cry the marcy and laser to repent.

13

Nocht thankand the of gratitud and grace,
That thou me wrocht and bocht me with thi ded,
Of this schort lyfe remembring nocht the space,
The hevinns blis, the hellis hiddous feid: 100

82. teind *tithe* eschew *avoid*
83. festuall *feast days*
84. mes *mass* parroche *parish*
  persew *attend*
85. curat *priest* trew *proper*
86. anis *once* yer *year*
87. sair I rew *I sorely repent*
89. of *for* into *against*
90. schrift *confession*
  postponit *postponed* aganis
  natour *unnatural*
91. incontricioun *lack of
  contrition* undiscreit *unfit*

92. ressait synfull *reception in a
  state of sin* salvature *saviour*
93. satisfactioun *reparation*
  sure *complete*
94. gaist *ghost*
95. peticionis *clauses*
97. thankand the *thanking you*
  of *with*
98. wrocht *created*
  bocht *redeemed* ded *death*
99. space *time*
100. hellis hiddous feid *terrifying
  hostility of hell*

93. 'For the penance and complete reparation I have left undone'.
99. 'For not remembering how brief this short life is'.

Bot mor trespas, my synnis to remeid,
Concluding never, all throu myn entent.
Thow quhois blud on rude for me ran reid,
I cry the marcy and laser to repent.

14

I knaw me vicius, Lord, and rycht culpabill   105
In aithis, swering, lessingis and blasflemyng,
Of frustrat speiking, in court, in kirk, in tabill,
In word, in will, in wantones expremyng,
Prising myself, and evill my nychtburis demyng,
And so in idilnes my dais I have myspent.   110
Thow that wes rent on rude for my redeming,
I cry the marcy and laser to repent.

15

I have synnit in discimilit thochtis joly,
Up to the hevin extollit in myn entencioun,
In hie exaltit arrogance and folly,   115
Imprudence, derisioun, scorne and vilipencioun,
Presumpcioun, inobedience and contempcioun,
In fals vanglore and deidis necligent.
O thow that deit for my redempcioun,
I cry the marcy and laser to repent.   120

101. bot *without* trespas *misdeeds*
remeid *atone for*
102. concluding *resolving*
entent *intent*
103. quhois *whose* rude *cross*
reid *red*
105. vicius *wicked*
106. aithis *oaths* lessingis *lies*
blasflemyng *blasphemy*
107. frustrat *unnecessary* in
tabill *at table*
108. wantones expremyng *wanton
expression*
109. prising *praising*
demyng *judging*

110. dais *days* myspent *wasted*
111. rent *torn apart* for my
redeming *in order to redeem me*
113. discimilit *deceitful*
joly *conceited*
114. extollit *exalted*
entencioun *mind*
115. hie *high*
116. derisioun *disdain*
vilipencioun *contempt*
117. contempcioun *disregard for
authority*
118. vanglore *vainglory*
119. deit *died*

101–2. 'Never resolving, with my whole intent, to atone for my sins
without further misdeeds'.
109. 'Praising myself, and judging my neighbours harshly'.

16

I have synnit also in reif and opprecioun,
In wrangus gudis taking and posceding,
Contrar my ressoun, conscience and discrecioun,
In prodigall spending, but reuth of pure folkis neding,
In foule descepcioun, in fals invencionis breding,   125
To conqueir honour, tresour, land or rent,
In fleschely lust abone messour exceding:
I cry the marcy and laser to repent.

17

Of mynd dissimilit, Lord, I me confes,
Of feid under ane freindlie continance,   130
Of parsiall juging and perverst wilfulnes,
Of flattering wordis for finyng of substance,
Of fals seling for wrang deliverance,
At counsall, sessioun and at perliament.
Of everilk gilt and wickit governance   135
I cry the marcy and laser to repent.

18

I schrif me of all cursit cumpany,
In all tyme witting and unwiting me;
Of cryminall caus and deid of fellony,
Of tiranny or vengabill cruelte.   140

---

121. reif *theft* opprecioun *violence*
122. wrangus gudis *wrongful goods* posceding *possessing*
123. contrar *against*
124. prodigall *wasteful* but reuth *without pity* pure *poor* neding *need*
125. descepcioun *deception* fals invencionis breding *spreading false gossip*
126. conqueir *acquire*   rent *possessions*
127. messour *measure*
129. dissimilit *deceitful*
130. feid *hatred* continance *appearance*

131. parsiall juging *biased judgement* perverst *wicked*
132. finyng *obtaining* substance *wealth*
133. fals seling *using false seals* deliverance *judgement*
134. sessioun *law courts*
135. everilk gilt *every crime* governance *action*
137. cursit *evil*
138. witting *knowing*
139. caus *fault* deid of fellony *act of cruelty*
140. tiranny *violence* vengabill *vindictive*

---

127. 'Exceeding the bounds with my fleshly lust'.
132. 'Of using flattering words in order to obtain wealth'.
138. 'At all times, whether I was aware of it or not'.

Of ded or slauchter culpabill gif I be,
In ony wise, deid, counsall or consent,
O deir Jesu that for me deit on tre,
I cry the marcy and laser to repent.

19

Thoucht I have nocht thi precius feit to kis,   145
As had the Magdalyn quhen scho did marcy craife,
I sall as scho weipe teris for my mys,
And every morrow seik the at thi graife.
Thairfore forgif me, as thow hir forgaif,
That seis my hert as hirris penitent.   150
Thy precius body in breist or I ressaif,
I cry the marcy and laser to repent.

20

Thou mak me, Jesu, unto the to remember.
I ask thy passioun in me so to abound
Quhill nocht in me unmannyit be a member,   155
Bot felling wo with the of every wound.
At every straik mak throu my hert a stound
That ever did strenye thi fair flesche innocent,
Sa at na part be of my body sound.
I cry the marcy and laser to repent.   160

141. ded *death*   gif *if*
142. wise *way*
143. tre *tree; cross*
145. thoucht *although*
146. Magdalyn *Magdalene*
  quhen *when*   scho *she*   craife *beg for*
147. weipe *weep*   mys *sin*
148. morrow *morning*   seik *seek* graife *tomb*
150. seis *sees*   hirris *hers*

151. breist *breast*   or *before* ressaif *receive*
154. passioun *suffering*
155. quhill *until* unmannyit *uninjured* member *limb*
156. felling wo *feeling pain*
157. straik *stroke*   stound *pain*
158. strenye *torture*
159. at *that*   sound *whole*

150. 'Who sees my heart as penitent as hers'.
151. 'Before I receive your precious body in my breast'.
154–6. 'I ask that your suffering should abound in me until not one of my limbs feels uninjured, and that I should feel pain with you from every wound'.
159. 'So that no part of my body is unharmed'.

21
Of all thir synnis that I heir expreme
And hes foryet, to the, Lord, I me schrife,
Appelling fra thy justice court extreme
Unto thi court of marcy exultive.
Thou mak my schip in blissit port arrive,   165
That saillis heir in stormes violent,
And saife me, Jesu, for thy woundis five,
I cry the marcy and laser to repent.

161. expreme *declare*
162. hes foryet *have forgotten*
163. appelling *appealing* justice
court extreme *rigorous court of
justice*

164. exultive *exultant*
165. schip *ship*
166. saillis *sails*
167. saife *save*

O Synfull Man, thir ar the Fourty Dayis
(The Maner of Passyng to Confessioun)

1

O synfull man, thir ar the fourty dayis
That every man sulde wilfull pennence dre.
Oure lorde Jesu, as haly writ sayis,
Fastit himself, oure exampill to be.
Sen sic ane mychty king and lorde as he   5
To fast and pray was so obedient,
We synfull folk sulde be more deligent.

2

I reid the, man, of thi transgressioun
With all thi hert that thou be penitent.
Thow schrive the clene and mak confessioun   10
And se thairto thou be deligent,
With all thi synnis into thi mynde presente,
That every syn be the selfe be schawin,
To thyne confessour it ma be kend and knawin.

3

Apon thi body gif thou hes ane wounde   15
That caussis the gret panis for to feill,
Thair is no leiche ma mak the haill and sounde
Quhill it be sene and clengit every deill;

1. thir *these*
2. wilfull *voluntary*
  pennence *penance* dre *endure*
3. haly writ *holy scripture*
4. fastit *fasted*
5. sen *since* sic *such*
7. deligent *diligent*
8. reid the *advise you*
  transgressioun *sin*
9. hert *heart*
10. schrive the *confess yourself*
  clene *fully*
11. se thairto *see to it*

12. synnis *sins*
13. be the selfe *by yourself*
  schawin *shown*
14. ma *can* kend *imparted*
  knawin *made known*
15. apon *upon* gif *if* ane *a*
16. caussis the *causes you*
  panis *pains* feill *feel*
17. leiche *doctor* haill *hale*
  sounde *healthy*
18. quhill *until* sene *seen to*
  clengit *cleansed* deill *part*

8–9. 'I advise you, man, that you should be sorry for your sins with all your heart'.
12–13. 'With all your sins brought to mind, so that each sin can be disclosed by you'.
16. 'That causes you to feel great pain'.

Rycht swa thi schrift, bot it be schawin weill,
Thow art not abill remissioun for to get,   20
Wittandlie and thou ane syn foryet.

4

Of twenty wonddis and ane be left unhelit,
Quhat avalis the leiching of the laif?
Richt swa thi schrift, and thair be oucht conselit,
It avalis not thi sely saule to saif,   25
Nor yit of God remissioun for to have.
Of syn gif thou wald have deliverance
Thow sulde it tell with all the circumstance.

5

Se that thi confessour be wys and discreit,
That can the discharge of every doute and weir,   30
And power hes of thi synnes compleit.
Gif thou can not schaw furth thi synnes perqueir
And he be blinde and can not at the speir,
Thow ma rycht weill in thi mynde consydder
That ane blynde man is led furth be ane uther.   35

6

And sa I halde that ye ar baith begylde:
He can not speir nor thou can not him tell

---

19. rycht swa *in the same way*
    schrift *confession* bot *unless*
20. abill *able* remissioun *pardon*
21. wittandlie *knowingly* and *if*
    foryet *omit*
22. wonddis *wounds*
    unhelit *unhealed*
23. avalis *helps* leiching *healing*
    laif *remainder*
24. and *if* oucht *anything*
    conselit *concealed*

25. sely saule *poor soul* saif *save*
27. gif *if*
28. circumstance *detail*
29. wys *wise*
30. the discharge *free you*
    doute *doubt* weir *uncertainty*
32. schaw furth *reveal*
    perqueir *perfectly*
33. at the speir *question you*
36. halde *believe* begylde *deceived*
37. speir *ask*

---

21. 'If you knowingly omit any of your sins'.
22-3. 'If even one of twenty wounds is left unhealed, what use is the healing of the rest?'.
25. 'Then that confession will not help at all to save your poor soul'.
27. 'If you wish to be delivered from your sin'.
32. 'And has complete authority in the matter of your sins'.
35. 'That it is like the blind leading the blind'.

Quhen nor how thi conscience thou hes fylde.
Thairfor I reid that thou excus thi sell
And rype thi mynde, how every thing befell,⁣   40
The tyme, the place, and how and in quhat wys,
So that thi confessioun ma thi synnes pryce.

7

Avys the weill, or thou cum to the preist,
Of all thi synnes, and namelie of the maist,
That thai be reddy prentit in thi breist.⁣   45
Thow sulde not cum to schryfe the in haist,
And syne sit doun abasit as ane beist.
With humyll hert and sad contrycioun
Thow suld cum to thine confessioun.

8

With thine awin mouth thi synnes thou suld tell;⁣   50
Bot sit and hier the preist hes not ado.
Quha kennes thi synnes better na thi sell?
Thairfor I reid the, tak gude tent thairto.
Thow knawis best quhair bindis the thi scho.
Thairfor be wys afor, or thow thair cum,⁣   55
That thou schaw furth thi synnes, all and sum.

---

38. quhen *when* fylde *defiled*
39. reid *advise* thi sell *yourself*
40. rype *examine* befell *happened*
41. quhat wys *what way*
42. ma *can* pryce *assess*
43. avys the *consider* or *before*
    preist *priest*
44. namelie *especially*
    maist *greatest*
45. prentit in *imprinted on*
    breist *heart*
46. schryfe the *confess* haist *haste*
47. syne *then* abasit *abashed*

beist *beast*
48. humyll *humble* sad *solemn*
    contrycioun *contrition*
50. awin *own*
51. ado *to do*
52. quha *who* kennes *knows*
    na *than* thi sell *yourself*
53. reid the *advise you* tak gude
    tent *pay attention*
54. bindis *pinches* scho *shoe*
55. wys *wise* afor *in advance*
    or *before*
56. all and sum *one and all*

39. 'Therefore I advise you that you seek forgiveness properly'.
42. 'So that your confession is made in a way that allows your sins to be properly assessed'.
51. 'The priest has nothing to do except sit and listen'.
54. 'You know best where your own shoe pinches'.

9

Quhair seldin compt is tane and hes a hevy charge
And syne is rekles in his governance
And on his conscience he takis all to large
And on the end hes no rememberance,   60
That man is abill to fall ane gret mischance.
The synfull man that all the yeir oursettis,
Fra Pasche to Pasche, rycht mony a thing foryettis.

10

I reid the, man, quhill thou art stark and young,
With pith and strenth into thi yeris grene,   65
Quhill thou art abill baith in mynde and toung,
Repent the, man, and kepe thi conscience clene.
Till byde till age is mony perrell sene:
Small merit is of synnes for to irke
Quhen thou art ald and ma na wrangis wyrke.   70

57. seldin *seldom* compt *account*
    tane *taken* charge *duty*
58. rekles *careless*
    governance *conduct*
59. to large *too much*
61. abill *likely*
    mischance *misfortune*
62. yeir *year* oursettis *puts off*
    [confession]
63. Pasche *Easter* foryettis *forgets*

64. quhill *while* stark *strong*
65. pith *vigour* yeris grene *green
    years; youth*
68. till byde *to wait* age *old age*
    perrell *danger* sene *seen*
69. irke *grow tired*
70. ald *old* na wrangis
    wyrke *commit no sins*

57–61. 'Where a man seldom takes stock of his sins and there is a heavy
    duty to pay on them, and is then careless in his conduct and allows too
    much to weigh upon his conscience alone, so that in the end he has no
    memory of all his sins, great misfortune is likely to befall that man'.
68. 'Waiting until old age is obviously very dangerous'.

Salviour, Suppois My Sensualite

Salviour, suppois my sensualite
Subject to syn hes maid my saule of sys,
Sum spark of lycht and spiritualite
Walkynnis my witt, and ressoun biddis me rys.
My corrupt conscience askis, clips and cryis   5
First grace, syne space for to amend my mys,
Substance with honour, doing none suppryis,
Freyndis, prosperite; heir peax, syne hevynis blys.

1. salviour *saviour*
   suppois *although*
2. syn *sin* saule *soul* of sys *often*
3. lycht *light*
4. walkynnis *awakens*
   witt *understanding*
   ressoun *reason* rys *rise*
5. askis *asks for* clips *calls out*

   for cryis *cries for*
6. grace *mercy* syne *then*
   space *time* mys *sin*
7. substance *wealth* none *no one*
   suppryis *harm*
8. freyndis *friends* heir *here*
   peax *peace* hevynis
   blys *heaven's bliss*

2. 'Has often made my soul subject to sin'.

In May as that Aurora did Up Spring

1

In May as that Aurora did up spring,
With cristall ene chasing the cluddis sable,
I hard a merle with mirry notis sing
A sang of lufe with voce rycht confortable,
Agane the orient bemis amiable,   5
Upone a blisfull brenche of lawry grene.
This wes hir sentens sweit and delectable:
'A lusty lyfe in luves service bene.'

2

Undir this brench ran doun a revir bricht
Of balmy liquour, cristallyne of hew,   10
Agane the hevinly aisur skyis licht,
Quhair did upone the tother syd persew
A nychtingall with suggurit notis new,
Quhois angell fedderis as the pacok schone.
This wes hir song and of a sentens trew: 15
'All luve is lost bot upone God allone.'

3

With notis glaid and glorius armony
This joyfull merle so salust scho the day
Quhill rong the widdis of hir melody,
Saying, 'Awalk, ye luvaris, o this May!   20

2. ene *eyes* cluddis *clouds*
sable *black*
3. hard *heard* merle *blackbird*
mirry *merry*
4. lufe *love* voce *voice*
confortable *delightful*
5. agane *towards* orient *eastern*
bemis *beams* amiable *lovely*
6. brenche *branch* lawry *laurel*
7. sentens *meaning*
delectable *pleasing*
8. lusty *pleasant* luves *love's*
bene *is*
9. revir *river*

10. balmy *fragrant* liquour *water*
hew *colour*
11. agane *against* aisur *azure; blue*
12. tother *other* syd *side*
persew *answer*
13. nychtingall *nightingale*
suggurit *sweet*
14. fedderis *feathers*
pacok *peacock*
17. armony *music*
18. salust *greeted*
19. rong *rang* widdis *woods*
20. awalk *awake* luvaris *lovers*
o *on*

8. 'It is a pleasant life in the service of love'.

Lo, fresche Flora hes flurest every spray
As Natur hes hir taucht, the noble quene.
The feild bene clothit in a new array.
A lusty lyfe in luvis service bene.'

4

Nevir swetar noys wes hard with levand man   25
Na maid this mirry gentill nychtingaill.
Hir sound went with the rever as it ran,
Outthrow the fresche and flureist lusty vaill.
'O merle,' quod scho, 'O fule, stynt of thy taill,
For in thy song gud sentens is thair none;   30
For boith is tynt the tyme and the travaill
Of every luve bot upone God allone.'

5

'Seis', quod the merle, 'thy preching, nychtingale!
Sall folk thair yewth spend in to holines?
Of yung sanctis growis auld feyndis, but fable;   35
Fy, ypocreit, in yeiris tendirnes
Agane the law of kynd thow gois expres,
That crukit aige makis on with yewth serene,
Quhome Natur of conditionis maid dyvers.
A lusty lyfe in luves service bene.'   40

6

The nychtingaill said, 'Fule, remembir the
That both in yewth and eild and every hour

21. flurest *caused to bloom*
    spray *twig*
23. bene *is*
25. noys *sound* hard *heard* with
    levand *by living*
26. na *than*
28. outthrow *throughout*
    flureist *flowering* vaill *valley*
29. fule *fool* stynt of *stop*
    taill *speech*
31. tynt *lost* travaill *trouble*
33. seis *cease* quod *said*

34. yewth *youth* in to *in*
35. sanctis *saints* feyndis *fiends*
    but fable *without doubt*
36. fy *shame* ypocreit *hypocrite*
    tendirnes *immaturity*
37. agane *against* kynd *nature*
    expres *directly*
38. crukit *crooked* makis on *makes
    one; becomes the same*
39. conditionis *states*
    dyvers *different*

36–9. 'Shame upon you, hypocrite, in your youth you go directly against
the law of nature so that crooked age becomes the same thing as serene
youth, states that Nature intended to be different'.

The luve of God most deir to man suld be,
That him of nocht wrocht lyk his awin figour
And deit himself fro deid him to succour.   45
O quhithir wes kythit thair trew lufe or none?
He is most trew and steidfast paramour.
All luve is lost bot upone him allone.'

7

The merle said, 'Quhy put God so grit bewte
In ladeis with sic womanly having,   50
Bot gife he wald that thay suld luvit be?
To luve eik Natur gaif thame inclynnyng,
And he, of Natur that wirker wes and king,
Wald no thing frustir put nor lat be sene
In to his creature of his awin making.   55
A lusty lyfe in luves service bene.'

8

The nychtingall said, 'Nocht to that behufe
Put God sic bewty in a ladeis face,
That scho suld haif the thank thairfoir or lufe,
Bot he, the wirker, that put in hir sic grace.   60
Of bewty, bontie, riches, tyme or space,
And every gudnes that bene to cum or gone,
The thank redoundis to him in every place.
All luve is lost bot upone God allone.'

9

'O nychtingall, it wer a story nyce,   65
That luve suld nocht depend on cherite,

---

44. of nocht *from nothing*
   wrocht *created* awin figour *own*
   image
45. deit *died* succour *rescue*
46. quhithir *whether* kythit *shown*
47. paramour *lover*
49. bewte *beauty*
50. having *behaviour*
51. bot gife *unless*
52. eik *also* inclynnyng *inclination*

53. wirker *creator*
54. frustir *useless*
57. behufe *purpose*
59. thank *praise* thairfoir *for it*
61. bontie *goodness*
62. gudnes *virtue* gone *go*
63. redoundis *belongs*
65. wer *would be* nyce *silly*
66. cherite *charity*

65–6. 'O nightingale, it would be a silly thing to say that love should not
   rest upon charity'.

And gife that vertew contrair be to vyce,
Than lufe mon be a vertew, as thinkis me,
For ay to lufe invy mone contrair be.
God bad eik lufe thy nychtbour fro the splene,   70
And quho than ladeis swetar nychtbouris be?
A lusty lyfe in lufes service bene.'

10

The nychtingaill said, 'Bird, quhy dois thow raif?
Ane man may in his lady tak sic delyt
Him to foryet that hir sic vertew gaif,   75
And for his hevin ressaif hir cullour quhyt.
Hir goldin-tressit hairis redomyt,
Lyk to Appollois bemis thocht thay schone,
Suld nocht him blind fro lufe that is perfyt.
All lufe is lost bot upone God allone.'   80

11

The merle said, 'Lufe is caus of honour ay,
Luve makis cowardis manheid to purchas,
Luve makis knychtis hardy at assey,
Luve makis wrechis full of lergenes,
Luve makis sweir folkis full of bissines,   85
Luve makis sluggirdis fresche and weill besene,
Luve changis vyce in vertewis nobilnes.
A lusty lyfe in luvis service bene.'

67. gife *if* contrair be *is contrary*
68. mon *must* as thinkis me *as it seems to me*
69. invy *envy*
70. bad *commanded* eik *also* nychtbour *neighbour* fro *from* splene *heart*
73. raif *rave*
75. foryet *forget* gaif *gave*
76. ressaif *accepts* cullour *complexion* quhyt *white*
77. redomyt *beautiful*

78. Appollois *Apollo's* bemis *beams* thocht *though*
79. perfyt *perfect*
82. manheid *bravery* purchas *acquire*
83. knychtis *knights* hardy *bold* assey *attack*
84. lergenes *generosity*
85. sweir *lazy* bissines *activity*
86. sluggirdis *sluggards* besene *arrayed*
87. in *into* vertewis *virtuous*

67–9. 'And if virtue is the opposite of vice, then love must be a virtue, it seems to me, for love must always be the opposite of envy'.
71. 'And who are sweeter neighbours than the ladies?'
74–6. 'A man may take such pleasure in his lady that he forgets Him who gave her such beauty and accepts her white complexion for his heaven'.
78. 'Though they shone like the beams of Apollo'.

12

The nychtingaill said, 'Trew is the contrary:
Sic frustir luve it blindis men so far,   90
In to thair myndis it makis thame to vary.
In fals vane glory thai so drunkin ar,
Thair wit is went, of wo thai ar nocht war
Quhill that all wirchip away be fro thame gone,
Fame, guddis, and strenth: quhairfoir weill say
                            I dar,   95
All luve is lost bot upone God allone.'

13

Than said the merle, 'Myn errour I confes.
This frustir luve all is bot vanite.
Blind ignorance me gaif sic hardines
To argone so agane the varite.   100
Quhairfoir I counsall every man that he
With lufe nocht in the feindis net be tone,
Bot luve the luve that did for his lufe de.
All lufe is lost bot upone God allone.'

14

Than sang thay both with vocis lowd and cleir.   105
The merle sang, 'Man, lufe God that hes the wrocht',
The nychtingall sang, 'Man, lufe the Lord most deir
That the and all this warld maid of nocht'.
The merle said, 'Luve him that thy lufe hes socht
Fra hevin to erd and heir tuk flesche and bone'.   110
The nychtingall sang, 'And with his deid the bocht:
All luve is lost bot upone him allone.'

90. frustir *vain*	100. argone *argue* agane *against*
91. vary *go astray*	varite *truth*
92. vane glory *vainglory*	101. counsall *advise*
93. went *gone* war *aware*	102. feindis *fiend's* tone *captured*
94. quhill that *until*	103. de *die*
wirchip *honour*	109. socht *sought*
95. guddis *possessions* weill . . .	110. erd *earth* heir *here*
dar *I dare well say*	111. deid *death* the
98. vanite *vanity*	bocht *redeemed you*
99. hardines *boldness*	

101–2. 'Therefore I advise every man to take care that he is not captured
in the fiend's net by love'.
103. 'But love the beloved one who died for the love of him'.]

15

Thane flaw thir birdis our the bewis schene,
Singing of lufe amang the levis small,
Quhois ythand pleid in to my thocht is grene,   115
Bothe sleping, walking, in rest and in travall.
Me to reconfort most it dois availl,
Agane for lufe quhen lufe I can find none,
To think how song this merle and nychtingaill:
All lufe is lost bot upone God allone.   120

113. flaw *flew* thir *these* our *over*
     bewis *branches* schene *beautiful*
114. small *delicate*
115. ythand *sustained*
     pleid *debate* grene *fresh*

116. travall *work*
117. renconfort *comfort* availl *help*
118. agane *in return*
119. song *sang*

118. 'When I can find no love in return for my love'.

Ryght as the Stern of Day Begouth to Schyne
(The Goldyn Targe)

1

Ryght as the stern of day begouth to schyne,
Quhen gone to bed war Vesper and Lucyne,
I raise and by a rosere did me rest.
Up sprang the goldyn candill matutyne,
With clere depurit bemes cristallyne,   5
Glading the mery foulis in thair nest.
Or Phebus was in purpur cape revest
Up raise the lark, the hevyns menstrale fyne,
In May in till a morow myrthfullest.

2

Full angellike thir birdis sang thair houris   10
Within thair courtyns grene in to thair bouris,
Apparalit quhite and rede wyth blomes swete;
Anamalit was the felde wyth all colouris.
The perly droppis schuke in silvir schouris,
Quhill all in balmc did branch and levis flete.   15
To part fra Phebus did Aurora grete;
Hir cristall teris I saw hyng on the flouris,
Quhilk he for lufe all drank up wyth his hete.

1. ryght *just* stern *star*
   begouth *began*
2. quhen *when* war *were*
   Lucyne *Lucina*
3. raise *rose* rosere *rose bush*
4. candill *candle* matutyne *of the
   morning*
5. depurit *pure* bemes *beams*
6. glading *gladdening* foulis *birds*
7. or *before* Phebus *Phoebus*
   purpur cape *crimson cloak*
   revest *dressed*
8. hevyns *heavens'* menstrale
   fyne *fine minstrel*
9. in till *upon* morow *morning*

myrthfullest *most joyful*
10. angellike *angelically*
    thir *these* houris *hours*
11. courtyns *curtains*
    bouris *chambers*
12. apparalit *arrayed*
    quhite *white* blomes *flowers*
13. anamalit *enamelled* felde *field*
14. perly *pearly* schuke *scattered*
    schouris *showers*
15. quhill *until* levis *leaves*
    flete *flow*
16. grete *weep*
17. teris *tears* hyng *hang*
18. quhilk *which* lufe *love* hete *heat*

11–12. 'In their chambers draped with green curtains, decorated in white
and red with sweet flowers'.
15. 'Until the branches and leaves all flowed with balm'.
16. 'Aurora wept at parting from Phoebus'.

3

For mirth of May wyth skippis and wyth hoppis
The birdis sang upon the tender croppis   20
With curiouse note, as Venus chapell clerkis.
The rosis yong, new spreding of thair knopis,
War powderit brycht with hevinly beriall droppis,
Throu bemes rede birnyng as ruby sperkis.
The skyes rang for schoutyng of the larkis,   25
The purpur hevyn, ourscailit in silvir sloppis,
Ourgilt the treis branchis, lef and barkis.

4

Down throu the ryce a ryvir ran wyth stremys,
So lustily agayn thai lykand lemys
That all the lake as lamp did leme of licht,   30
Quhilk schadowit all about wyth twynkling glemis.
The bewis bathit war in secund bemys
Throu the reflex of Phebus visage brycht.
On every syde the hegies raise on hicht,
The bank was grene, the bruke was full of bremys,   35
The stanneris clere as stern in frosty nycht.

5

The cristall air, the sapher firmament,
The ruby skyes of the orient
Kest beriall bemes on emerant bewis grene.

20. croppis *young shoots*
21. curiouse note *skilful music*
22. new *newly* spreding
of *spreading forth* knopis *buds*
23. powderit brycht *brightly dusted* beriall *sparkling*
24. birnyng *gleaming* sperkis *sparks*
25. schoutyng *calling*
26. ourscailit *sprinkled* sloppis *clouds*
27. ourgilt *gilded* barkis *bark*
28. ryce *greenery* stremys *currents*
29. lustily *prettily* agayn *against* thai *those* lykand lemys *pleasant rays*
30. lake *water* leme *gleam* of licht *with light*
31. schadowit *was reflected* glemis *gleams*
32. bewis *boughs* bathit war *were bathed*
33. reflex *reflection* visage *face*
34. hegies *hedges* raise on hicht *grew high*
35. bruke *brook* bremys *bream; fish*
36. stanneris *pebbles*
37. sapher firmament *sapphire sky*
38. orient *east*
39. kest *cast* emerant *emerald*

21. 'With skilful music, like clerks in the chapel of Venus'.
24. 'Through sunbeams gleaming red like sparks of rubies'.
36. 'The pebbles on the bottom as clearly visible as stars on a frosty night'.

The rosy garth, depaynt and redolent,   40
With purpur, azure, gold and goulis gent
Arayed was by dame Flora, the quene,
So nobily that joy was for to sene;
The roch agayn the rivir resplendent,
As low enlumynit all the leves schene.   45

6

Quhat throu the mery foulys armony
And throu the ryveris soune rycht ran me by,
On Florais mantill I slepit as I lay;
Quhare sone in to my dremes fantasy
I saw approch agayn the orient sky   50
A saill als quhite as blossum upon spray,
Wyth merse of gold brycht as the stern of day,
Quhilk tendit to the land full lustily,
Als falcoun swift desyrouse of hir pray.

7

And hard on burd unto the blomyt medis   55
Amang the grene rispis and the redis
Arrivit sche; quharfro anon thare landis
Ane hundreth ladyes, lusty in to wedis,
Als fresch as flouris that in May up spredis,
In kirtillis grene, withoutyn kell or bandis.   60

40. garth *garden* depaynt *brightly coloured* redolent *fragrant*
41. goulis *red* gent *pretty*
42. quene *queen*
43. nobily *splendidly*
44. roch *rocks* resplendent *shining*
45. low *flame* enlumynit *lit up* leves schene *beautiful leaves*
46. quhat throu *what with* foulys *birds'* armony *harmony*
47. ryveris *river's* soune *sound* rycht *right*
48. Florais mantill *Flora's cloak* slepit *slept*
49. dremes *dream's*
50. agayn *against* orient *eastern*
51. quhite *white* spray *branch*

52. merse *top-castle*
53. tendit to *headed towards* lustily *speedily*
54. desyrouse *desirous* pray *prey*
55. hard on burd *close at hand* blomyt medis *flowering meadows*
56. rispis *sedge* redis *reeds*
57. arrivit *arrived* quharfro *from which* anon *at once* landis *disembarks*
58. hundreth ladyes *hundred ladies* lusty in to wedis *beautifully dressed*
59. up spredis *blossom*
60. kirtillis *dresses* kell *cap* bandis *headbands*

43. 'So splendidly that it was a joy to behold'.
47. 'And on account of the sound of the river that ran right by me'.

Thair brycht hairis hang gletering on the strandis,
In tressis clere wyppit wyth goldyn thredis,
With pappis quhite and mydlis small as wandis.

8

Discrive I wald, bot quho coud wele endyte
How all the feldis wyth thai lilies quhite   65
Depaynt war brycht, quhilk to the hevyn did glete?
Noucht thou, Omer, als fair as thou coud wryte,
For all thine ornate stilis so perfyte.
Nor yit thou, Tullius, quhois lippis swete
Of rethorike did in to termes flete.   70
Your aureate tongis both bene all to lyte
For to compile that paradise complete.

9

Thare saw I Nature and Venus, quene and quene,
The fresch Aurora and lady Flora schene,
Juno, Appollo and Proserpyna,   75
Dyane, the goddesse chaste of woddis grene,
My lady Cleo, that help of makaris bene,
Thetes, Pallas and prudent Minerva,
Fair feynit Fortune and lemand Lucina.
Thir mychti quenis in crounis mycht be sene,   80
Wyth bemys blith, bricht as Lucifera.

61. hairis *hair*   hang *hung*
    strandis *shore*
62. clere *bright*   wyppit *bound*
    thredis *ribbons*
63. pappis *breasts*   mydlis *waists*
    small *slender*   wandis *wands*
64. descrive *describe*   quho *who*
    endyte *put into verse*
65. feldis *fields*   thai *those*
66. depaynt *decorated*   glete *glitter*
67. noucht *not*   Omer *Homer*
68. stilis *writing*   perfyte *perfect*
70. rethorike *rhetoric*   flete *flow*
71. aureate tongis *golden tongues*

bene *are* to lyte *inadequate*
72. compile *describe*
    complete *perfect*
73. quene *queen*
74. fresch *lovely*   schene *beautiful*
75. Appollo *Apolleine*
    Proserpyna *Proserpina*
76. Dyane *Diana*   woddis *woods*
77. makaris *poets*
79. feynit *deceitful*   lemand *shining*
80. thir *these*   mychti *mighty*
    crounis *crowns*   sene *seen*
81. bemys blith *sunny beams*

69–70. 'Nor even you, Tullius, from whose sweet lips terms of rethoric
flowed'.
77. 'My lady Clio, who is the helper of poets'.

10

Thare saw I May, of myrthfull monethis quene,
Betwix Aprile and June, hir sistir schene,
Within the gardyng walking up and doun,
Quham of the foulis gladdith all bedene;   85
Scho was full tender in hir yeris grene.
Thare saw I Nature present hir a goun,
Rich to behald and nobil of renoun,
Of eviry hew under the hevin that bene,
Depaynt and broud be gude proporcion.   90

11

Full lustily thir ladyes all in fere
Enterit within this park of most plesere,
Quhare that I lay, ourhelit wyth levis ronk.
The mery foulis blisfullest of chere
Salust Nature, me thoucht, on thair manere;   95
And eviry blome on branch and eke on bonk
Opnyt and spred thair balmy levis donk,
Full low enclynyng to thair quene so clere,
Quham of thair noble norising thay thonk.

12

Syne to dame Flora on the samyn wyse   100
Thay saluse and thay thank a thousand syse,
And to dame Venus, lufis mychti quene,

82. myrthfull *joyful*
    monethis *months*
83. betwix *between*   sistir *sisters*
84. gardyng *garden*
85. quham of *for whom*
    gladdith *rejoice*   bedene *greatly*
86. tender *young*   yeris *years*
87. goun *gown*
88. nobil *splendid*   of renoun *by
    reputation*
89. hew *colour*
90. broud *embroidered*   be gude
    proporcion *in good proportion*
91. in fere *in a group*
92. plesere *delight*

93. ourhelit *hidden*   lcvis
    ronk *thick leaves*
94. blisfullest *happiest*   chere *mood*
95. salust *greeted*
96. blome *flower*   eke *also*
    bonk *bank*
97. opnyt *opened*   donk *moist*
98. enclynyng *bowing*   clere *bright*
99. norising *nourishment*
    thonk *thank*
100. syne *then*   samyn wyse *same
     way*
101. saluse *greet*   syse *times*
102. lufis *love's*

82. 'There I saw May, queen of the joyful months'.
85. 'At whose presence all the birds greatly rejoice'.

Thay sang ballettis in lufe, as was the gyse,
With amourouse notis lusty to devise,
As thay that had lufe in thair hertis grene.   105
Thair hony throtis, opnyt fro the splene,
With werblis swete did perse the hevinly skyes,
Quhill loud resownyt the firmament serene.

13

Ane othir court thare saw I consequent:
Cupide, the king, wyth bow in hand ybent   110
And dredefull arowis grundyn scharp and square.
Thare saw I Mars, the god armypotent,
Awfull and sterne, strong and corpolent.
Thare saw I crabbit Saturn, ald and haire –
His luke was lyke for to perturb the aire.   115
Thare was Mercurius, wise and eloquent,
Of rethorike that fand the flouris faire.

14

Thare was the god of gardingis, Priapus,
Thare was the god of wildernes, Phanus,
And Janus, god of entree delytable.   120
Thare was the god of fludis, Neptunus,
Thare was the god of wyndis, Eolus,
With variand luke rycht lyke a lord unstable.

103. ballettis in lufe *love songs*
gyse *custom*
104. notis *notes* devise *describe*
105. hertis grene *youthful hearts*
106. hony throtis *honey throats*
opnyt *opened* splene *heart*
107. werblis *singing* perse *pierce*
108. quhill *until*
resownyt *resounded*
109. consequent *next*
110. ybent *bent*
111. grundyn scharp *filed to a
sharp point* square *strong*
112. armypotent *mighty in battle*
113. awfull *awe-inspiring*
corpolent *powerfully built*

114. crabbit *bad-tempered*   ald *old*
haire *grey*
115. luke *look* lyke *likely*
perturb *disturb*
116. Mercurius *Mercury*
117. fand *found*
118. gardingis *gardens*
119. Phanus *Faunus*
120. entree *entry*
delytable *delightful*
121. fludis *rivers*
Neptunus *Neptune*
122. wyndis *winds*
123. variand *changeable*
unstable *untrustworthy*

117. 'Who invented the fair flowers of rhetoric'.
120. 'And Janus, delightful god of entrances'.

Thare was Bacus, the gladder of the table,
There was Pluto, the elrich incubus, 125
In cloke of grene – his court usit no sable.

15

And eviry one of thir in grene arayit
On harp or lute full merily thai playit,
And sang ballettis with michty notis clere.
Ladyes to dance full sobirly assayit, 130
Endlang the lusty ryvir so thai mayit,
Thair observance rycht hevynly was to here.
Than crap I throu the levis and drew nere,
Quhare that I was rycht sudaynly affrayit,
All throu a luke, quhilk I have boucht full dere. 135

16

And schortly for to speke, be lufis quene
I was aspyit. Scho bad hir archearis kene
Go me arrest, and thay no tyme delayit.
Than ladyes fair lete fall thair mantillis grene,
With bowis big in tressit hairis schene 140
All sudaynly thay had a felde arayit.
And yit rycht gretly was I noucht affrayit,
The party was so plesand for to sene.
A wonder lusty bikkir me assayit.

124. Bacus *Bacchus*
  gladder *rejoicer*
125. elrich *elvish*
126. cloke *cloak* usit *wore*
  sable *black*
130. sobirly *solemnly*
  assayit *proceeded*
131. endlang *along* mayit *did a May dance*
132. observance *ritual* here *hear*
133. crap *crept*
134. affrayit *frightened*
135. throu *on account of*

boucht *paid for* dere *dearly*
136. be *by* lufis *love's*
137. aspyit *seen* bad *commanded*
  archearis kene *fierce archers*
139. than *then* lete fall *threw off*
140. tressit hairis *braided hair*
141. felde *battlefield*
  arayit *prepared*
142. affrayit *afraid*
143. party *troop* sene *see*
144. wonder lusty *amazingly fierce* bikkir *onslaught* me assayit *assailed me*

124. 'There was Bacchus, who made those at table glad'.
140. 'With large bows in the possession of those with beautiful braided hair'.

17

And first of all with bow in hand ybent   145
Come dame Beautee, rycht as scho wald me schent.
Syne folowit all hir dameselis yfere,
With mony diverse awfull instrument.
Unto the pres Fair Having wyth hir went,
Fyne Portrature, Plesance and Lusty Chere.   150
Than come Reson with schelde of gold so clere,
In plate and maille as Mars armypotent.
Defendit me that nobil chevallere.

18

Syne tender Youth come wyth hir virgyns ying,
Grene Innocence and schamefull Abaising,   155
And quaking Drede wyth humble Obedience.
The goldyn targe harmyt thay no thing.
Curage in thame was noucht begonne to spring,
Full sore thay dred to done a violence.
Swete Womanhede I saw cum in presence;   160
Of artilye a warld sche did in bring,
Servit wyth ladyes full of reverence.

19

Scho led wyth hir Nurture and Lawlynes,
Contenence, Pacience, Gude Fame and Stedfastnes,

145. ybent *bent*
146. rycht as *as if* me
   schent *destroy me*
147. syne *then* dameselis *women*
   yfere *together*
148. awfull *terrible*
   instrument *weapon*
149. pres *thick of battle*
   Having *Behaviour*
150. Portrature *Appearance*
   Plesance *Delight* Lusty
   Chere *Lovely Expression*
151. schelde *shield*
152. plate *armour* maille *chain-
   mail* as *like*
153. chevallere *knight*

154. ying *young*
155. schamefull *modest*
   Abaising *reserve*
156. Drede *Apprehension*
157. targe *shield*
158. curage *desire*
159. dred *feared* done *do*
   violence *violent act*
160. Womanhede *Womanliness*
161. artilye *artillery* warld *large
   amount*
163. Nurture *Breeding*
   Lawlynes *Humility*
164. Contenence *Chastity* Gude
   Fame *Good Reputation*
   Stedfastnes *Fidelity*

157. 'They could not harm the golden shield at all'.
161. 'She brought in a large amount of artillery'.

Discrecion, Gentrise and Considerance,   165
Levefull Company and Honest Besynes,
Benigne Luke, Mylde Chere and Sobirnes.
All thir bure ganyeis to do me grevance,
Bot Reson bure the targe wyth sik constance,
Thair scharp assayes mycht do no dures   170
To me, for all thair awfull ordynance.

20

Unto the pres persewit Hie Degree:
Hir folowit ay Estate and Dignitee,
Comparison, Honour and Noble Array,
Will, Wantonnes, Renoun and Libertee,   175
Richesse, Fredom and eke Nobilitee.
Wit ye, thay did thair baner hye display.
A cloud of arowis, as hayle schour, lousit thay
And schot quhill wastit was thair artilye,
Syne went abak reboytit of thair pray.   180

21

Quhen Venus had persavit this rebute,
Dissymilance scho bad go mak persute
At all powere to perse the goldyn targe;
And scho that was of doubilnes the rute
Askit hir choise of archeris in refute.   185

165. Discrecion *Judgement*   Wantonnes *Playfulness*
  Gentrise *Nobility*   Renoun *Reputation*
  Considerance *Consideration*   176. Richesse *Wealth*
166. Levefull *Proper*   Fredom *Generosity* eke *also*
  Besynes *Diligence*   177. wit *know*
167. Benigne *Kind*   178. hayle schour *shower of hail*
  Sobirnes *Seriousness*   lousit *fired*
168. bure *carried* ganyeis *arrows* 179. quhill *until* wastit *used up*
  grevance *harm*   180. went abak *retreated*
169. sik *such* constance *steadfastness*   reboytit *deprived*
170. assayes *attacks* dures *injury* 181. persavit *perceived*
171. ordynance *military appearance*   rebute *repulse*
172. persewit *advanced* Hie   182. Dissymilance *Deceit*
  Degree *High Rank*   persute *persuit*
173. Estate *Social Position*   183. all powere *full force*
  Dignitee *Good Standing*   perse *pierce*
174. Comparison *Distinction*   184. doubilnes *duplicity* rute *root*
175. Will *Desire*   185. in refute *for protection*

185. 'Asked to choose the archers for her protection'.

Venus the best bad hir go wale at large.
Scho tuke Presence, plicht anker of the barge,
And Fair Callyng, that wele a flayn coud schute,
And Cherising for to complete hir charge.

22

Dame Hamelynes scho tuke in company,   190
That hardy was and hende in archery,
And broucht dame Beautee to the felde agayn
With all the choise of Venus chevalry.
Thay come and bikkerit unabaisitly,
The schour of arowis rappit on as rayn.   195
Perilouse Presence, that mony syre has slayn,
The bataill broucht on bordour hard us by;
The salt was all the sarar, suth to sayn.

23

Thik was the schote of grundyn dartis kene,
Bot Resoun with the scheld of gold so schene   200
Warly defendit, quho so evir assayit.
The awfull stoure he manly did sustene,
Quhill Presence kest a pulder in his ene,
And than as drunkyn man he all forvayit.
Quhen he was blynd the fule wyth him thay playit, 205
And banyst hym amang the bewis grene.
That sory sicht me sudaynly affrayit.

186. wale *choose* at large *freely*
187. Presence *Physical Presence*
  barge *ship*
188. Callyng *Greeting*
  flayn *arrow* schute *shoot*
189. Cherising *Affection*
  charge *task*
190. Hamelynes *Intimacy*
191. hardy *brave* hende *skilled*
193. choise *best* chevalry *knights*
194. bikkerit *assaulted*
  unabaisitly *fearlessly*
195. rappit on *pelted down*
  rayn *rain*
196. syre *man*

197. on bordour *to the edge of the field*
198. salt *assault* sarar *fiercer*
  suth *true* sayn *say*
199. grundyn *sharpened*
  dartis *spears*
201. warly *valiantly* quho so
  evir *no matter who*
202. stoure *conflict*
203. kest *threw* pulder *powder*
  ene *eyes*
204. forvayit *went astray*
205. fule *fool*
206. banyst *banished* bewis *boughs*
207. sicht *sight*

197–8. 'Brought the battle close to us at the edge of the field; the assault was the fiercer, if the truth be told'.
205. 'When he was blind they made a fool of him'.

24

Than was I woundit to the deth wele nere
And yoldyn as a wofull prisonnere
To lady Beautee in a moment space. 210
Me thoucht scho semyt lustiar of chere
Efter that Resoun tynt had his eyne clere
Than of before and lufliare of face.
Quhy was thou blyndit, Resoun, quhi, allace?
And gert ane hell my paradise appere, 215
And mercy seme quhare that I fand no grace.

25

Dissymulance was besy me to sile,
And Fair Calling did oft apon me smyle,
And Cherising me fed wyth wordis fair.
New Acquyntance enbracit me a quhile 220
And favouryt me, quhill men mycht go a myle,
Syne tuke hir leve; I saw hir nevir mare.
Than saw I Dangere toward me repair.
I coud eschew hir presencc be no wyle,
On syde scho lukit wyth ane fremyt fare. 225

26

And at the last Departing coud hir dresse,
And me delyverit unto Hevynesse

208. wel nere *very nearly*
209. yoldyn *surrendered*
210. in a moment space *in the space of a moment*
211. semyt *seemed* lustiar *nicer* chere *expression*
212. tynt *lost*
213. lufliare *lovelier*
214. quhy *why* allace *alas*
215. gert *caused*
216. seme *seem* quhare *where* fand *found*
217. besy *busy* sile *deceive*
218. smyle *smile*

220. Acquyntance *Acquaintance* enbracit *embraced* quhile *while*
221. myle *mile*
222. tuke hir leve *went away* mare *more*
223. Dangere *Disdain* repair *come*
224. eschew *avoid* wyle *clever trick*
225. on syde *askance* fremyt fare *hostile expression*
226. Departing *Parting* hir dresse *prepare herself*
227. delyverit *delivered* Hevynesse *Depression*

212. 'After Reason had lost the clarity of his vision'.
215–6. 'And caused a hell to appear to be my paradise, and there seem to be mercy where in fact I found no favour'.
221. 'And treated me well, but this only lasted for the length of time it would take a man to walk a mile'.

For to remayne, and scho in cure me tuke.
Be this the lord of wyndis, with wodenes,
God Eolus, his bugill blew, I gesse,   230
That with the blast the levis all toschuke.
And sudaynly in the space of a luke
All was hyne went, thare was bot wildernes,
Thare was no more bot birdis, bank and bruke.

27
In twynklyng of ane eye to schip thai went,   235
And swyth up saile unto the top thai stent,
And with swift course atour the flude thai frak.
Thai fyrit gunnis with powder violent,
Till that the reke raise to the firmament.
The rochis all resownyt wyth the rak,   240
For rede it semyt that the raynbow brak.
Wyth spirit affrayde apon my fete I sprent,
Amang the clewis so careful was the crak.

28
And as I did awake of my sweving,
The joyfull birdis merily did syng   245
For myrth of Phebus tender bemes schene.
Swete war the vapouris, soft the morowing,
Halesum the vale depaynt wyth flouris ying,
The air attemperit, sobir and amene.
In quhite and rede was all the felde besene,   250

228. in cure me tuke *took charge of me*
229. be *at*   wodenes *fierceness*
230. gesse *suppose*
231. levis *leaves*
    toschuke *shuddered*
233. hyne went *gone*   bot *only*
234. bot *except*   bruke *river*
236. swyth *at once*   top *masthead*
    stent *raised*
237. atour *over*   flude *sea*
    frak *sped*
238. fyrit *fired*   powder *gunpowder*
239. reke *smoke*
240. rochis *cliffs*

resownyt *resounded*   rak *gunfire*
241. rede *noise*   brak *broke*
242. sprent *leapt*
243. clewis *cliffs*
    careful *distressing*   crak *sound of explosives*
244. sweving *vision*
247. vapouris *mists*
    morowing *morning*
248. halesum *wholesome*
    depaynt *decorated*
249. attemperit *temperate*
    sobir *mild*   amene *delightful*
250. quhite *white*   besene *arrayed*

236. 'And at once they raised up the sail to the very top of the mast'.

Throu Naturis nobil fresch anamalyng
In mirthfull May of eviry moneth quene.

29

O reverend Chaucere, rose of rethoris all
(As in oure tong ane flour imperiall)
That raise in Britane evir, quho redis rycht,   255
Thou beris of makaris the tryumph riall,
Thy fresch anamalit termes celicall
This mater coud illumynit have full brycht.
Was thou noucht of oure Inglisch all the lycht,
Surmounting eviry tong terrestriall   260
Alls fer as Mayes morow dois mydnycht?

30

O morall Gower and Ludgate laureate,
Your sugurit lippis and tongis aureate
Bene to oure eris cause of grete delyte.
Your angel mouthis most mellifluate   265
Oure rude langage has clere illumynate
And fair ourgilt oure spech, that imperfyte
Stude or your goldyn pennis schupe to write.
This ile before was bare and desolate
Of rethorike or lusty fresch endyte.   270

251. anamalyng *enamelling*
253. reverend *revered*
    Chaucere *Chaucer* rethoris *poets*
254. tong *tongue* flour *flower*
    imperiall *pre-eminent*
255. raise *flourished* redis *reads*
256. beris *bear* tryumph
    riall *kingly honour*
257. anamalit *enamelled*
    celicall *heavenly*
258. illumynit *illuminated*
259. Inglisch *English* lycht *light*
260. surmounting *surpassing*

terrestriall *earthly*
261. alls fer *as far*
262. Ludgate *Lydgate*
    laureate *crowned with laurel*
263. sugurit *sweet* aureate *golden*
264. bene *are* eris *ears*
265. mellifluate *honey-sweet*
266. rude *crude*
267. ourgilt *gilded*
268. or *before* pennis *quill pens*
    schupe *began*
269. ile *island*
270. endyte *poetry*

253–5. 'O revered Chaucer, for whoever reads properly, you are the rose
    amongst all poets who ever flourished in Britain (as you are a pre-
    eminent flower in our language)'.
259–61. 'Were you not the leading light of our English, surpassing every
    earthly tongue in the same was as a May morning surpasses midnight?'
267–8. 'And beautifully gilded our speech, that existed only in an
    imperfect form before your golden pen began to write'.

31

Thou lytill quair, be evir obedient,
Humble, subject and symple of entent
Before the face of eviry connyng wicht.
I knaw quhat thou of rethorike hes spent;
Of all hir lusty rosis redolent   275
Is non in to thy gerland sett on hicht.
Eschame tharof and draw the out of sicht.
Rude is thy wede, disteynit, bare and rent,
Wele aucht thou be aferit of the licht.

271. quair *book*
272. subject *submissive*
    symple *modest*   entent *intention*
273. connyng wicht *learned person*
275. redolent *fragrant*
276. gerland *garland*   on hicht *on high*

277. eschame *be ashamed*   draw
    the *withdraw yourself*
278. wede *garment*
    disteynit *dirty*   bare *threadbare*
    rent *torn*
279. aucht *ought*   aferit *afraid*

274. 'I know what effort you have spent on poetry'.

Sen that I am a Presoneir

1

Sen that I am a presonier
Till hir that farest is and best,
I me commend fra yeir till yeir
In till hir bandoun for to rest.
I govit on that gudliest,   5
So lang to luk I tuk laseir,
Quhill I wes tane withouttin test
And led furth as a presoneir.

2

Hir sweit having and fresche bewte
Hes wondit me but swerd or lance;   10
With hir to go commandit me
Ontill the castell of pennance.
I said, 'Is this your govirnance,
To tak men for thair luking heir?'
Bewty sayis, 'Ya, ser, perchance   15
Ye be my ladeis presoneir.'

3

Thai had me bundin to the yet
Quhair Strangenes had bene portar ay
And in deliverit me thairat;
And in thir termis can thai say,   20
'Do wait and lat him nocht away'.
Quo Strangenes unto the porteir,

1. sen *since*   presoneir *prisoner*
2. till *of*   farest *fairest*
3. me commend *offer myself*
   yeir *year*   till *to*
4. in till *under*   bandoun *authority*
5. govit *gazed*   gudliest *loveliest
   one*
6. laseir *opportunity*
7. quhill *until*   tane *taken*
   test *trial*
9. having *manner*   bewte *beauty*
10. wondit *wounded*   but *without*

swerd *sword*
12. ontill *to*
13. govirnance *custom*
14. luking *looking*   heir *here*
15. ya *yes*   ser *sir*
17. bundin *bound*   yet *gate*
18. Strangenes *Disdain*
    portar *porter*   ay *always*
20. thir *these*   termis *words*
21. do wait *keep watch*   lat *let*
    away *run away*
22. quo *said*   unto *as*

11. 'She commanded me to go with her'.
22–4. 'Disdain, in his capacity as porter, said: "I do declare, you are too
poor a prisoner for my lady" '.

'Ontill my lady, I dar lay,
Ye be to pure a presoneir.

4

Thai kest me in a deip dungeoun   25
And fetterit me but lok or cheyne.
The capitane, hecht Comparesone,
To luke on me he thocht greit deyne.
Thocht I wes wo I durst nocht pleyne
For he had fetterit mony a feir;   30
With petous voce thus cuth I sene,
'Wo is a wofull presoneir'.

5

Langour wes weche upoun the wall
That nevir sleipit bot evir wouke;
Scorne wes bourdour in the hall   35
And oft on me his babill schuke,
Lukand with mony a dengerous luke:
'Quhat is he yone, that methis us neir?
Ye be to townage, be this buke,
To be my ladeis presoneir'.   40

6

Gud Houp rownit in my eir
And bad me baldlie breve a bill,
With Lawlines he suld it beir,

23. dar lay *dare declare*   *awake*
24. to pure *too poor*   35. Scorne *Contempt*
25. kest *threw*   bourdour *jester*
26. fetterit *fettered*   but *without*   36. babill *bauble* schuke *shook*
    cheyne *chain*   37. lukand *looking*
27. hecht *called*   dengerous *disdainful*
    Comparesone *Comparison*   38. yone *there* methis *comes*
28. deyne *scorn*   39. to townage *too uncourtly*
29. thocht *although* wo *unhappy*   be *by* buke *book*
    durst *dared* pleyne *complain*   41. Gud Houp *Good Hope*
30. feir *fellow*   rownit *whispered* eir *ear*
31. petous voce *pitiful voice*   42. bad *told* baldlie *boldly*
    cuth *could* sene *say*   breve *write* bill *letter*
33. Langour *Misery* weche *guard*   43. Lawlines *Humility* beir *carry*
34. sleipit *slept* wouke *stayed*

28. 'Thought it was beneath his dignity to look at me'.

With Fair Service send it hir till.
I wouk and wret hir all my will.   45
Fair Service fur withouttin feir
Sayand till hir with wirdis still,
'Haif pety of your presoneir'.

7

Than Lawlines to Petie went
And said till hir in termis schort,   50
'Lat we yone presoneir be schent,
Will no man do to us support;
Gar lay ane sege unto yone fort'.
Than Petie said, 'I sall appeir';
Thocht saysis, 'I hecht, com I ourthort,   55
I houp to lows the presoneir'.

8

Than to battell thai war arreyit all,
And ay the vawart kepit Thocht;
Lust bur the benner to the wall
And Bissines the grit gyn brocht.   60
Skorne cryis out, sayis, 'Wald ye ocht?'
Lust sayis, 'We wald haif entre heir';
Comparisone sayis, 'That is for nocht;
Ye will nocht wyn the presoneir'.

44. hir till *to her*
45. wret *wrote* will *desire*
46. fur *went* feir *fear*
47. wirdis still *soft words*
48. haif pety of *have pity on*
49. Petie *Pity*
50. termis schort *brief words*
51. lat we *if we let*
    schent *destroyed*
53. gar *cause* sege *siege*
54. appeir *present myself*
55. Thocht *Thought*
    hecht *promise* com I ourthort *if*

I get across
56. houp *hope* lows *free*
57. to *for* arreyit *ready*
58. vawart *vanguard* kepit *kept back*
59. bur *carried* benner *banner*
60. Bissines *Diligence* grit gyn *great siege engine*
    brocht *brought*
61. Skorne *Scorn* wald ye ocht *what do you want*
62. entre *entry*
63. for nocht *pointless*

52. 'No one will ever help us'.
53. 'Have that fort placed under siege'.

9

Thai thairin schup for to defend,   65
And thai thairfurth sailyeit ane hour;
Than Bissines the grit gyn bend,
Straik doun the top of the foir tour.
Comparisone began to lour
And cryit furth, 'I yow requeir   70
Soft and fair and do favour
And tak to yow the presoneir'.

10

Thai fyrit the gettis deliverly
With faggottis wer grit and huge,
And Strangenes quhair that he did ly   75
Wes brint in to the porter luge.
Lustely thay lakit bot a juge,
Sik straikis and stychling wes on steir,
The semeliest wes maid assege
To quhome that he wes presoneir.   80

11

Thrucht Skornes nos thai put a prik;
This he wes banist and gat a blek.
Comparisone wes erdit quik
And Langour lap and brak his nek.
Thai sailyeit fast, all the fek;   85
Lust chasit my ladeis chalmirleir;

65. schup *prepared*
66. sailyeit *attacked*
67. bend *bent*
69. straik *struck* foir tour *front tower*
69. lour *cower*
70. yow requeir *ask you*
71. favour *act of goodwill*
73. fyrit *set fire to* gettis *gates* deliverly *quickly*
74. faggottis *bundles of sticks*
76. brint *burnt* porter luge *gatehouse*
77. lustely *cheerfully* lakit bot *did without* juge *judge*

78. sik *such* straikis *wounds* stychling *thrusting* on steir *in the fray*
79. semeliest *most beautiful one* maid assege *besieged*
81. thrucht *through* nos *nose* prik *skewer*
82. this *thus* banist *banished* blek *black*
83. erdit *buried*
84. lap *jumped* brak *broke*
85. sailyeit *attacked* fek *main group*
86. chasit *chased* chalmirleir *chambermaid*

82. 'Thus he was banished and had a black mark against him'.

Gud Fame wes drownit in a sek:
Thus ransonit thai the presoneir.

12

Fra Sklandir hard Lust had undone
His enemeis, he him aganis   90
Assemblit ane semely sort full sone,
And rais, and rowttit all the planis:
His cusing in the court remanis,
Bot jalous folkis and geangleiris
And fals Invy that no thing lanis   95
Blew out on Luvis presoneir.

13

Syne Matremony that nobill king
Was grevit, and gadderit ane grit ost
And all enermit, without lesing,
Chest Sklander to the west se cost.   100
Than wes he and his linege lost;
And Matremony withowttin weir
The band of freindschip hes indost
Betwix Bewty and the presoneir.

14

Be that of eild wes Gud Famis air   105
And cumyne to continuatioun,
And to the court maid his repair

87. drownit *drowned* sek *sack*	97. syne *then*
88. ransonit *saved*	98. grevit *annoyed*
89. hard *heard* undone *defeated*	gadderit *assembled* ost *army*
90. aganis *against*	99. enermit *armed* lesing *lying*
91. semely sort *excellent company*	100. chest *chased* se cost *sea coast*
full sone *at once*	102. weir *doubt*
92. rais *rose* rowttit *rode over*	103. indost *endorsed*
planis *battlefields*	105. be that *by that time* eild *age*
93. cusing *cousin*	air *heir*
94. jalous *jealous*	106. cumyne to *come into*
geangleiris *gossips*	continuatioun *inheritance*
95. Invy *Envy* lanis *keeps secret*	107. repair *stay*
96. blew out on *denounced*	

89–91. 'When Lust heard from Slander that he had defeated his enemies,
he at once assembled an excellent company against him'.
105. 'By that time, Good Reputation's heir had reached maturity'.

Quhair Matremony than woir the crowne.
He gat ane confirmatioun,
All that his modir aucht but weir,   110
And baid still, as it wes resoune,
With Bewty and the presoneir.

108. woir *wore*   110. modir *mother* aucht *owned*
109. gat *obtained*   111. baid *remained*
    confirmatioun *document*   resoune *reasonable*

My Hartis Tresure and Swete Assured Fo

1

My hartis tresure and swete assured fo,
The finale endar of my lyfe for ever,
The creuell brekar of my hart in two,
To go to deathe this I deservit never.
O man slayar quhill saule and life dissever,   5
Stynt of your slauchtir; allace, your man am I,
A thowsand tymes that dois yow mercy cry.

2

Have mercie, luif; have mercie, ladie bricht.
Quhat have I wrocht aganis your womanheid
That ye murdir me, a saikles wicht,   10
Trespassing never to yow in word nor deid?
That ye consent thairto, O God forbid!
Leif creuelte and saif your man, for schame,
Or throucht the warld quyte losit is your name.

3

My deathe chasis my lyfe so besalie   15
That wery is my goist to fle so fast.
Sic deidlie dwawmes so mischeifaislie

1. hartis *heart's* assured
   fo *unquestionable enemy*
2. finale *complete* endar *one who
   brings to an end*
3. creuell *cruel*
4. this *thus*
5. quhill *until* saule *soul*
   dissever *separate*
6. stynt of *cease*
   slauchtir *slaughter* allace *alas*
7. cry *beg*
8. luif *beloved* bricht *beautiful*
9. quhat *what* wrocht *done*
   aganis *against*
   womanheid *womanliness*

10. saikles wicht *innocent man*
11. deid *deed*
12. thairto *to it*
13. leif *abandon* creuelte *cruelty*
    saif *save*
14. throucht *throughout*
    warld *world* quyte losit *entirely
    ruined* name *reputation*
15. chasis *chases*
    besalie *persistently*
16. wery *tired* goist *spirit* fle *flee*
17. sic *such* deidlie *deadly*
    dwawmes *faints*
    mischeifaislie *harmfully*

2. 'Lady who completely ends my life forever'.
7. 'Who begs you for mercy a thousand times'.
9. 'What have I done to harm your womanliness?'.
15–16. 'My death chases after my life so persistently that my spirit is
weary from fleeing so fast'.

Ane hundrithe tymes hes my hairt ovirpast,
Me think my spreit rynnis away full gast,
Beseikand grace on kneis yow befoir,　　　20
Or that your man be lost for evermoir.

4

Behald my wod intollerabill pane,
For evermoir quhilk sal be my dampnage.
Quhy undir traist your man thus have ye slane?
Lo, deithe is in my breist with furious rage,　　　25
Quhilk may no balme nor tryacle asswage
Bot your mercie, for laik of quhilk I de.
Allace, quhair is your womanlie petie?

5

Behald my deidlie passioun dolorous;
Behald my hiddows hew and wo, allace!　　　30
Behald my mayne and murning mervalous,
Withe sorrowfull teris falling frome my face.
Rewthe, luif, is nocht, helpe ye not in this cace.
For how sould ony gentill hart indure
To se this sycht on ony creature?　　　35

6

Quhyte dow, quhair is your sobir humilnes?
Swete gentill turtour, quhair is your pete went?

---

18. hundrithe *hundred*
    hairt *heart*　ovirpast *passed over*
19. me think *it seems to me*
    spreit *spirit*　rynnis *runs*　full
    gast *terrified*
20. beseikand grace *begging for
    mercy*
21. or that *before*　evermoir *ever
    more*
22. behald *behold*　wod *mad*
    pane *pain*
23. quhilk *which*　sal be *shall be*
    dampnage *destruction*
24. quhy *why*　traist *trust*
25. breist *breast*
26. balme *ointment*

tryacle *medicine*　asswage *relieve*
27. bot *except for*　laik *lack*　de *die*
28. petie *pity*
29. passioun *suffering*
    dolorous *sorrowful*
30. hiddows hew *hideous colour*
31. mayne *grief*　murning
    mervalous *astonishing mourning*
32. teris *tears*
33. rewthe *pity*　cace *case*
34. sould *could*　indure *bear*
35. sycht *sight*
36. quhyte dow *white dove*　sobir
    humilnes *quiet humility*
37. turtour *turtle-dove*　pete *pity*
    went *gone*

26. 'Which no ointment or medicine can relieve'.
33. 'There is no pity in this world, beloved, unless you help in this instance'.

Quhair is your rewthe, the frute of nobilnes,
Of womanheid the tresour and the rent?
Mercie is never put out of meik intent,   40
Nor out of gentill hart is fundin petie,
Sen mercyles may no weycht nobill be.

7

In to my mynd I sall you mercye cry
Quhone that my toung sall faill me to speik;
And quhill that Nature me my sycht deny,   45
And quhill my ene for pane incluse and steik,
And quhill the dethe my hart in sowndir breik,
And quhill my mynd may think and toung may steir:
And syne fairweill, my hartis lady deir!

38. frutc *fruit*
39. tresour *treasure* rent *wealth*
40. put out *expelled from* meik
    intent *modest disposition*
41. fundin *found*
42. sen *since* mercyles *without*
    mercy weycht *person*
43. in to *in*

44. quhone *when* toung *tongue*
    me to speik *to speak for me*
45. quhill *until* sycht *eyesight*
46. ene *eyes* pane *pain*
    incluse *close up* steik *shut*
47. in sowndir breik *breaks asunder*
48. quhill *as long as* steir *stir*
49. syne *then* hartis *heart's*

41–2. 'Nor is a noble heart ever found to be without mercy, since
    without mercy no one can ever be truly noble'.
45. 'Until Nature robs me of my eyesight'.

Sweit Rois of Vertew and of Gentilnes

1

Sweit rois of vertew and of gentilnes,
Delytsum lyllie of everie lustynes,
Richest in bontie and in bewtie cleir
And everie vertew that is deir,
Except onlie that ye ar mercyles.   5

2

In to your garthe this day I did persew;
Thair saw I flowris that fresche wer of hew,
Baithe quhyte and rid, moist lusty wer to seyne,
And halsum herbis upone stalkis grene,
Yit leif nor flour fynd could I nane of rew.   10

3

I dout that Merche with his caild blastis keyne
Hes slane this gentill herbe that I of mene,
Quhois petewous deithe dois to my hart sic pane
That I wald mak to plant his rute agane,
So confortand his levis unto me bene.   15

1. rois *rose* vertew *virtue*
gentilnes *nobility*
2. delytsum *delightful* lyllie *lily*
lustynes *loveliness*
3. bontie *goodness* bewtie *beauty*
cleir *shining*
4. deir *precious*
5. onlie *only*
6. garthe *garden* persew *enter*
7. hew *colour*
8. quhyte *white* rid *red*

moist *most* lusty *lovely*
seyne *see*
9. halsum *health-giving*
10. rew *rue*
11. dout *fear* Merche *March*
caild *cold* keyne *fierce*
12. that I of mene *of which I speak*
13. petewous *piteous*
14. mak *try* rute *root*
15. confortand *encouraging*
bene *are*

10. 'Yet I could not find a leaf or flower of rue'.

Be Ye ane Luvar, Think Ye Nocht Ye Suld

1

Be ye ane luvar, think ye nocht ye suld
Be weill advysit in your governing?
Be ye nocht sa, it will on yow be tauld;
Bewar thairwith for dreid of misdemyng.
Be nocht a wreche, nor skerche in your spending,   5
Be layth alway to do amis or schame;
Be rewlit rycht and keip this doctring:
Be secreit, trew, incressing of your name.

2

Be ye ane lear, that is werst of all;
Be ye ane tratlar, that I hald als evill;   10
Be ye ane janglar, and ye fra vertew fall;
Be nevir mair on to thir vicis thrall.
Be now and ay the maistir of your will;
Be nevir he that lesing sall proclame;
Be nocht of langage quhair ye suld be still: 15
Be secreit, trew, incressing of your name.

3

Be nocht abasit for no wicket tung,
Be nocht sa set as I haif said yow heir,

1. be ye *if you are* luvar *lover*
2. weill advysit *well considered*
   governing *behaviour*
3. sa *so* on yow be tauld *be
   counted against you*
4. bewar *beware* dreid *fear*
   misdemyng *wrong judgement*
5. wreche *wretch* skerche *miser*
6. layth *loathe* amis *wrong*
   schame *anything shameful*
7. be rewlit rycht *listen to good
   advice* keip *keep*
   doctring *teaching*
8. secreit *discreet* trew *faithful*
   incressing of *enhancing*

name *reputation*
9. lear *liar* werst *worst*
10. tratlar *gossip* hald *consider*
    als *just as*
11. janglar *slanderer* fra *from*
    vertew *virtue*
12. nevir mair *never again*
    vicis *vices* thrall *captive*
13. ay *always* maistir *master*
14. he *the one* lesing *lie*
15. of langage *talkative*
    quhair *where* still *silent*
17. abasit *cast down* for *on
    account of* tung *tongue*
18. sa set *so regarded* heir *here*

11. 'If you are a slanderer, then you yourself fall from grace'.
12. 'Never again allow yourself to be enslaved by these vices'.
14. 'Never be the one to tell a lie'.
18. 'Do not let yourself be regarded as any of the things I have described here'.

Be nocht sa lerge unto thir sawis sung,
Be nocht our prowd, thinkand ye haif no peir;   20
Be ye so wyis that uderis at yow leir,
Be nevir he to sklander nor defame,
Be of your lufe no prechour as a freir:
Be secreit, trew, incressing of your name.

19. lerge *lavish*   sawis *speeches*   leir *learn*
20. our *too*   thinkand *thinking*   22. sklander *slander*
    peir *equal*   23. lufe *love*   prechour *preacher*
21. wyis *wise*   uderis *others*   freir *friar*

19. 'Do not be too lavish to those who sing your praises'.
21. 'Be so wise that others learn from you'.
23. 'Do not proclaim your love like a preaching friar'.

Quha Will Behald of Luve the Chance

1

Quha will behald of luve the chance
With sweit dissavyng countenance,
In quhais fair dissimulance
   May none assure;
Quhilk is begun with inconstance   5
And endis nocht but variance.
Scho haldis with continuance
   No serviture.

2

Discretioun and considerance
Ar both out of hir govirnance,   10
Quhairfoir of it the schort plesance
   May nocht indure.
Scho is so new of acquentance,
The auld gais fra remembrance.
Thus I gife our the observans   15
   Of luvis cure.

3

It is ane pount of ignorance
To lufe in sic distemperance,

1. quha *whoever*
  chance *unpredictability*
2. dissavyng *deceitful*
3. quhais *whose*
  dissimulance *deception*
4. assure *trust*
5. quhilk *which*
  inconstance *inconstancy*
6. nocht *not* but *without*
7. haldis *holds*
  continuance *steadfastness*
8. serviture *servitude*
9. considerance *consideration*
10. govirnance *control*
11. quhairfoir *therefore*
  plesance *pleasure*
12. indure *last*
13. acquentance *acquaintance*
14. auld *old* gais *goes*
15. gife our *give up*
  observans *observation*
16. luvis cure *love's office*
17. pount *sign*
18. lufe *love* sic
  distemperance *such chaos*

1–2. 'Anyone who wants to can see how unpredictable love is with her sweit deceitful countenance'.
4. 'No one can place their trust'.
6. 'And does not end without variance'.
7–8. 'She is not a slave to steadfastness'.
13–16. 'She is so busy with her new acquaintances, the old ones are forgotten, so I'm going to give up attending to love's business'.

Sen tyme mispendit may avance
   No creature.   20
In luve to keip allegance,
It war als nys an ordinance
As quha wald bid ane deid man dance
   In sepulture.

19. sen *since* mispendit *misspent*   ordinance *idea*
    avance *promote*   23. quha *who* deid *dead*
21. allegance *fidelity*   24. sepulture *sepulchre*
22. als *as* nys *foolish*

19–20. 'Since time spent badly can do no creature good'.
21–4. 'Fidelity in love is as foolish an idea as telling a dead man to dance
   in his tomb'.

Apon the Midsummer Evin, Mirriest of Nichtis
(The Tretis of the Twa Mariit Wemen and the Wedo)

Apon the Midsummer Evin, mirriest of nichtis,
I muvit furth allane in meid as midnicht wes past,
Besyd ane gudlie grein garth, full of gay flouris,
Hegeit of ane huge hicht with hawthorne treis,
Quhairon ane bird on ane bransche so birst out hir notis   5
That never ane blythfullar bird was on the beuche hard.
Quhat throw the sugurat sound of hir sang glaid
And throw the savour sanative of the sweit flouris,
I drew in derne to the dyk to dirkin efter mirthis.
The dew donkit the daill, and dynnit the feulis.   10
I hard, under ane holyn hevinlie grein hewit,
Ane hie speiche at my hand with hautand wourdis.
With that in haist to the hege so hard I inthrang
That I was heildit with hawthorne and with heynd leveis.
Throw pykis of the plet thorne I presandlie luikit,   15
Gif ony persoun wald approche within that plesand garding.
I saw thre gay ladeis sit in ane grein arbeir,
All grathit in to garlandis of fresche gudlie flouris.
So glitterit as the gold wer thair glorius gilt tressis,

1. Midsumer Evin *Midsummer Eve*   mirriest *merriest*
2. allane *alone*   meid *meadow*
3. gudlie *beautiful*   garth *enclosed garden*   flouris *flowers*
4. hegeit *hedged*   hicht *height*
5. birst out *poured forth*   notis *notes*
6. blythfullar *more joyful*   beuche *branch*   hard *heard*
7. quhat *partly*   throw *on account of*   sugurat *sweet*   sang *song*   glaid *glad*
8. savour *scent*   sanative *healing*
9. in derne *silently*   dyk *wall*   to dirkin *to hide away*   mirthis *entertainment*
10. donkit *dampened*   daill *dale*   dynnit *sang loudly*   feulis *birds*
11. hard *heard*   holyn *holly tree*   hevinlie *splendid*   grein *green*   hewit *coloured*
12. hie *loud*   speiche *conversation*   at my hand *nearby*   hautand *haughty*
13. hege *hedge*   inthrang *pushed in*
14. heildit *hidden*   heynd leveis *pleasant leaves*
15. pykis *spaces*   plet thorne *intertwined thorns*   presandlie *quickly*   luikit *looked*
16. gif *[to see]* if   garding *garden*
17. arbeir *arbour, a shady recess in a garden*
18. grathit *adorned*   gudlie *pretty*
19. glitterit *glittering*   gilt tressis *golden tresses*

10. 'The dale became damp with morning dew, and the birds sang loudly.'

Quhill all the gressis did gleme of the glaid hewis.   20
Kemmit war thair cleir hair and curiouslie sched,
Attour thair schulderis doun schyre schyning full bricht,
With curches cassin thair abone of kirsp cleir and thin.
Thair mantillis grein war as the gress that grew in May sessoun,
Fetrit with thair quhyt fingaris about thair fair sydis.   25
Of ferlifull fyne favour war thair faceis meik,
All full of flurist fairheid as flouris in June –
Quhyt, seimlie and soft as the sweit lillies,
Now upspred upon spray as new spynist rose;
Arrayit ryallie about with mony riche vardour   30
That nature full nobillie annamalit with flouris,
Of alkin hewis under hevin that ony heynd knew,
Fragrant, all full of fresche odour, fynest of smell.
Ane cumlie tabil coverit wes befoir tha cleir ladyis,
With ryalle cowpis apon rawis, full of ryche wynis.   35
And of thir fair wlonkes, twa weddit war with lordis,
Ane was ane wedow, iwis, wantoun of laitis.
And as thai talk at the tabill of mony taill sindry,
Thay wauchtit at the wicht wyne and waris out wourdis;
And syn thai spak more spedelie and sparit no matiris.   40

20. gressis *plants* gleme *gleam*
    glaid *glad* hewis *colours*
21. kemmit *combed* cleir *fair*
    curiouslie *carefully* sched *parted*
22. attour *over* doun
    schyre *straight down*
23. curches *head-coverings*
    cassin *thrown* abone *over*
    kirsp *fine fabric*
    cleir *transparent*
24. mantillis *mantles, sleeveless
    cloaks* grein *green*
25. fetrit *fastened* quhyt *white*
    sydis *sides*
26. ferlifull *wonderfully* fyne
    favour *fine appearance*
    meik *meek*
27. flurist fairheid *blossoming
    beauty*
28. seimlie *fine*
29. upspred *spread open*
    spray *stem* new spynist *newly*

opened
30. ryallie *richly* riche *splendid*
    vardour *plant*
31. nobillie *excellently*
    annamalit *enamelled*
32. alkin *all kinds of* heynd *noble
    person*
34. cumlie *fair* tabil *table*
    coverit *covered with a cloth*
    cleir *bright*
35. cowpis *goblets* apon rawis *in
    rows* wynis *wines*
36. thir *those* wlonkes *ladies*
    twa *two* weddit *married*
37. wedow *widow* iwis *indeed*
    wantoun *playful* laitis *behaviour*
38. taill *tale* sindry *different*
39. wauchtit at *downed*
    wicht *strong* waris out *spout out*
40. syn *then* sparit *refrained from*
    matiris *topic*

Aude viduam iam cum interrogatione sua
'Bewrie,' said the wedo, 'ye woddit wemen ying,
Quhat mirth ye fand in maryage sen ye war menis wyffis.
Reveill gif ye rewit that rakles conditioun,
Or gif that ever ye luffit leyd upone lyf mair
Nor thame that ye your fayth hes festinit for ever,   45
Or gif ye think, had ye chois, that ye wald cheis better.
Think ye it nocht ane blist band that bindis so fast,
That none undo it a deill may bot the deith ane?'

Responsio prime uxoris ad viduam
Than spak ane lusty belyf with lustie effeiris:
'It that ye call the blist band that bindis so fast   50
Is bair of blis and bailfull, and greit barrat wirkis.
Ye speir, had I fre chois, gif I wald cheis bettir?
Chenyeis ay ar to eschew and changeis ar sweit.
Sic cursit chance till eschew, had I my chois anis,
Out of the cheinyeis of ane churle I chaip suld for evir.   55
God gif matrimony wer made to mell for ane yeir!
It war bot merrens to be mair bot gif our myndis pleisit.
It is agane the law of luf, of kynd, and of nature,

41. bewrie *reveal* woddit *married* ying *young*
42. fand *have found* sen *since* war *have been* menis wyffis *the wives of men*
43. reveill *reveal* gif *whether* rewit *regret* rakles conditioun *reckless agreement*
44. luffit *loved* leyd upone lyf *any living creature* mair *more*
45. nor thame *than those* festinit *pledged*
46. chois *a choice*
47. think . . . nocht *don't you think* blist *blessed*
48. a deill *a bit* bot *except for*
ane *alone*
49. lusty *beautiful woman* belyf *at once* effeiris *bearing*
51. bair *bare* bailfull *miserable* barrat *distress* wirkis *causes*
52. speir *ask*
53. chenyeis *chains* to eschew *to be avoided*
54. sic *such* chance *fate* chois *opportunity to choose* anis *once*
55. churle *churl, a coarse man* chaip *escape*
56. gif *grant* mell *copulate*
57. merrens *annoyance* bot gif *unless*

43–5. 'Tell me whether or not you regret that reckless marriage agreement you made, or if you ever loved any living creature more than those to whom you have pledged your fidelity forever'.
47–8. 'Don't you think it a blessed band that binds so securely that nothing can undo it in the slightest except death alone?'
54–5. 'If I had the opportunity to choose just once, to avoid such an accursed fate, I would escape forever from the churl's chains'.

Togidder hartis to strene that stryveis with uther.
Birdis hes ane better law na bernis be meikill, 60
That ilk yeir, with new joy joyis ane maik
And fangis thame ane fresche feyr, unfulyeit and constant,
And lattis thair fulyeit feiris flie quhair thai pleis.
Cryst gif sic ane consuetude war in this kith haldin!
Than weill war us wemen that evir we war born. 65
We suld have feiris as fresche to fang quhen us likit
And gif all larbaris thair leveis quhen thai lak curage.
Myself suld be full semlie in silkis arrayit,
Gymp, jolie and gent, richt joyus and gent.
I suld at fairis be found, new faceis to se, 70
At playis and at preichingis and pilgrimages greit,
To schaw my renone royaly quhair preis was of folk,
To manifest my makdome to multitude of pepill
And blaw my bewtie on breid quhair bernis war mony,
That I micht cheis and be chosin and change quhen me
lykit. 75
Than suld I waill ane full weill our all the wyd realme
That suld my womanheid weild the lang winter nicht;
And quhen I gottin had ane grome ganest of uther,
Yaip and ying, in the yok ane yeir for to draw,
Fra I had preveit his pith the first plesand moneth, 80

59. strene *force* stryveis
    with *struggle against*
60. birdis *birds* na bernis *than
    men* be meikill *by far*
61. ilk *every* joyis *enjoy*
    maik *mate*
62. fangis *take* feyr *mate*
    unfulyeit *fresh*
63. fulyeit *tired* feiris *companions*
64. consuetude *custom*
    kith *country* haldin *observed*
65. weill war *it would be fortunate*
66. fang *take*
67. gif *give* larbaris *impotent men*
    leveis *leave* curage *sexual vigour*
69. gymp *graceful* jolie *gay*
    gent *elegant*
70. fairis *fairs* faceis *faces*

71. preichingis *public sermons*
72. schaw *show* renone *distinction*
    quhair *wherever* preis *a crowd*
73. manifest *show* makdome *figure*
74. blaw *make known*
    bewtie *beauty* on breid *abroad*
    bernis *people*
76. waill *choose* full weill *very
    well* our *throughout*
77. womanheid *womanliness*
    weild *possess*
78. grome *man* ganest of
    uther *more suitable than any other*
79. yaip *keen* ying *young*
    yok *yoke*
80. fra *after* preveit *tested* pith
    vigour plesand *pleasant*
    moneth *month*

60–2 'Birds have a far better law than people do, which enjoy a new
mate with new joy every year and take a fresh companion, vigorous
and constant'.

Than suld I cast me to keik in kirk and in markat,
And all the cuntre about, kyngis court and uther,
Quhair I ane galland micht get aganis the nixt yeir
For to perfurneis furth the werk quhen failyeit the tother:
A forky fure, ay furthwart and forsy in draucht,   85
Nother febill nor fant nor fulyeit in labour,
Bot als fresche of his forme as flouris in May,
For all the fruit suld I fang, thocht he the flour burgeoun.'

Aude ut dicet de viro suo
'I have ane wallidrag, ane worme, ane auld wobat carle,
A waistit wolroun na worth bot wourdis to clatter,   90
Ane bumbart, ane dron bee, ane bag full of flewme,
Ane scabbit skarth, ane scorpioun, ane scutarde behind.
To se him scart his awin skyn grit scunner I think.
Quhen kissis me that carybald, than kyndillis all my sorow.
As birs of ane brym bair his berd is als stif,   95
Bot soft and soupill as the silk is his sary lume.
He may weill to the syn assent, bot sakles is his deidis.
With gor his twa grym ene ar gladderit all about
And gorgeit lyk twa gutaris that war with glar stoppit.

81. cast me *apply myself*
    keik *look*   kirk *church*
82. cuntre *country*   uther *elsewhere*
83. galland *young man*
    aganis *ready for*   nixt *next*
84. perfurneis furth *perform*
    failyeit *loses strength*
85. forky fure *strong man*
    furthwart *to the fore*   forsy in
    draucht *forceful at the plough*
86. nother *neither*   fant *faint*
    fulyeit *wearied*
87. forme *body*
88. fang *take*   thocht *even though*
    flour burgeoun *makes the flowers
    bud*
89. wallidrag *worthless man*
    wobat *hairy caterpillar*
    carle *churl*
90. waistit *wasted*

wolroun *animal*   na worth *good
for nothing*   clatter *chatter*
91. bumbart *idler*   dron bee *drone*
    flewme *phlegm*
92. scabbit skarth *scabby monster*
    scutarde *skitterer*
93. scart *scratch*
    scunner *nauseating*
94. carybald *monster*
    kyndillis *aroused*
95. birs *bristles*   brym bair *wild
    boar*   berd *beard*
96. soupill *bending*   sary *pathetic*
    lume *tool, penis*
97. assent *agree*   sakles *innocent
    is are*
98. gor *slime*   grym *fierce*
    ene *eyes*   gladderit *smeared*
99. gorgeit *clogged*   gutaris *gutters*
    glar *filthy debris*   stoppit *choked*

93. 'It makes me sick to see him scratch his own skin'.
95. 'His beard is as prickly as the bristles on a wild boar'.

Bot quhen that glowrand gaist grippis me about,   100
Than think I hiddowus Mahowne hes me in armes.
Thair ma na sanyne me save fra that auld Sathane,
For thocht I croce me all cleine fra the croun doun,
He wil my corse all beclip and clap me to his breist.
Quhen schaiffyn is that ald schaik with a scharp rasour, 105
He schovis on me his schevill mouth and schendis my lippis,
And with his hard hurcheone skyn sa heklis he my chekis
That as a glemand gleyd glowis my chaftis.
I schrenk for the scharp stound, bot schout dar I nought,
For schore of that auld schrew, schame him betide.   110
The luf blenkis of that bogill fra his blerde ene,
As Belzebub had on me blent, abasit my spreit.
And quhen the smy on me smyrkis with his smakes molet
He fepillis like a farcy aver that flyrit on a gillot.
Quhen that the sound of his saw sinkis in my eris,   115
Than ay renewis my noy or he be neir cumand.
Quhen I heir nemmyt his name than mak I nyne crocis
To keip me fra the cummerans of that carll mangit,
That full of eldnyng is and anger and all evill thewis.
I dar nought luke to my luf, for that lene gib;   120
He is sa full of jelusy and engyne fals,
Ever ymagynyng in mynd materis of evill,
Compasand and castand cacis a thousand,

100. glowrand *glowering* gaist *ghost*
102. ma *may* sanyne *making the sign of the cross* Sathane *Satan*
103. croce me *bless myself* all cleine *completely* croun *head*
104. corse *body* beclip *embrace* clap *clasp*
105. schaiffyn *shaved* schaik *man*
106. schovis *shoves* schevill *twisted* schendis *hurts*
107. hurcheone *hedgehog* skyn *skin* heklis *scratches*
108. glemand gleyd *glowing coal* chaftis *jaws*
109. for *from* stound *pain*
110. schore *threatening* schrew *troublemaker* schame him betide *shame on him*
111. luf *love* blenkis *glances*

bogill *hobgoblin* blerde *bleary*
112. as *as if* blent *looked* abasit *subdue* spreit *spirit*
113. smy *rogue* smyrkis *simpers* smakes *rascally* molet *muzzle*
114. fepillis *sticks out his lower lip* farcy *diseased* aver *old horse* flyrit *leered* gillot *filly, young female horse*
115. saw *talking*
116. noy *annoyance* or *before*
117. nemmyt *mentioned*
118. cummerans *annoyance* carll *man* mangit *crazy*
119. eldnyng *jealousy* thewis *ways*
120. gib *cat*
121. engyne *ingenuity*
123. castand *devising* cacis *scenarios*

103. 'The sign of the cross cannot protect me from that old devil'.
114. 'He sticks out his lower lip like a diseased old nag leering at a filly'.

How he sall tak me with a trawe at trist of ane othir.
I dar nought keik to the knaip that the cop fillis 125
For eldnyng of that ald schrew that ever on evill thynkis.
For he is waistit and worne fra Venus werkis,
And may nought beit worth a bene in bed of my mystirs.
He trowis that young folk I yerne yeild for he gane is,
Bot I may yuke all this yer, or his yerd help. 130
Ay quhen that caribald carll wald clym on my wambe,
Than am I dangerus and daine and dour of my will.
Yit leit I never that larbar my leggis ga betwene,
To fyle my flesche na fummyll me without a fee gret,
And thoght his pen purly me payis in bed, 135
His purse pays richely in recompense efter.
For or he clym on my corse, that carybald forlane,
I have condition of a curche, of kersp allther fynest,
A goun of engranyt claith right gaily furrit,
A ring with a ryall stane or other riche jowell, 140
Or rest of his rousty raid, thoght he wer rede wod.
For all the buddis of Johne Blunt, quhen he abone clymis
Me think the baid deir aboucht, sa bawch ar his werkis –
And thus I sell him solace, thoght I it sour think.
Fra sic a syre God yow saif, my sweit sisteris deir!' 145
Quhen that the semely had said hir sentence to end,

124. tak me *catch me*   trawe *trick*
trist *secret meeting*
125. dar *dare*   keik *glance*
knaip *boy*   cop *cup*
128. beit *attend*   bene *bean*
mystirs *sexual needs*
129. trowis *thinks*   yerne *gladly*
yeild *yield*   gane *impotent*
130. yuke *itch*   or *before*   yerd *penis*
131. caribald *monstrous*
clym *climb*   wambe *belly*
132. dangerus *disdainful*
daine *contemptuous*
dour *stubborn*
133. larbar *impotent good-for-nothing*
134. fyle *defile*   fummyll *fumble with*
135. pen *penis*   purly *poorly*

137. or *before*   forlane *despicable*
138. I have condition *I have the promise*   curche *kerchief*
kersp *voile, fine fabric*   allther *of the*
139. goun *dress*   engranyt claith *scarlet cloth*
furrit *trimmed with fur*
140. ryall *precious*   jowell *jewel*
141. rest *stop*   rousty raid *clumsy riding*   thought *even though*
rede wod *furious*
142. buddis *bribes*   abone *on top*
143. baid *bargain*   aboucht *paid for*   bawch *poor*
145. syre *man*   saif *save*
146. semely *beautiful one*
sentence *speech*

124. 'How he shall trap me secretly meeting another man'.
128. 'And his attention to my sexual needs isn't worth a bean'.
141. 'Or else he can stop his clumsy riding, even if it makes him mad'.

Than all thai leuch apon loft with latis full mery
And raucht the cop round about, full of riche wynis,
And ralyeit lang, or thai wald rest, with ryatus speche.

Hic bibent et inde vidua interrogat alteram mulierem et illa
respondet ut sequitur
The wedo to the tothir wlonk warpit thir wordis: 150
'Now, fair sister, fallis yow but fenying to tell.
Sen man ferst with matrimony yow menskit in kirk,
How haif ye farne, be your faith, confese us the treuth,
That band to blise or to ban, quhilk yow best thinkis,
Or how ye like lif to leid in to lell spousage?   155
And syne myself ye exeme on the samyn wise,
And I sall say furth the suth, dissymyland no word.'
The plesand said, 'I protest, the treuth gif I schaw,
That of your toungis ye be traist.' The tothir twa grantit.
With that sprang up hir spreit be a span hechar.   160
'To speik', quod scho, 'I sall nought spar, ther is no spy neir.
I sall a ragment reveil fra rute of my hert,
A roust that is sa rankild quhill risis my stomok.
Now sall the byle all out brist, that beild has so lang.
For it to beir on my breist wes berdin our hevy.   165
I sall the venome devoid with a vent large,

147. leuch apon loft *laughed*
     loudly latis *demeanour*
148. raucht *handed*
149. ralyeit *joked* ryatus *noisy,*
     wanton
150. wedo *widow* wlonk *fair lady*
     warpit *uttered* thir *these*
151. fallis yow *it is your turn*
     but *without* fenying *lying*
152. sen *since* ferst *first*
     menskit *honoured* kirk *church*
153. farne *fared* confese *confess*
154. blise *bless* ban *curse*
     quhilk *whichever*
155. lell *lawful* spousage *marriage*
156. syne *then* exeme *examine*
     samyn *same* wise *way*

157. suth *truth* dissymyland *falsifying*
158. plesand *pleasing one*
     protest *ask* schaw *tell*
159. traist *trustworthy* grantit *agreed*
160. spreit *spirits* span *hand's*
     breadth hechar *higher*
161. quod *said* spar *hold back*
162. ragment *long catalogue*
     rute *root, bottom*
163. roust *festering bitterness*
     rankild *painful* risis *turns*
164. byle *boil* brist *burst*
     beild *built up*
165. beir *bear* breist *breast*
     berdin *burden* our *over, too*
166. venome *poison* devoid *release*
     vent *discharge* large *heavy*

152–3. 'How have you fared since you first honoured a man with your
     hand in matrimony in church?'
155. 'Or how you like living a life of lawfull matrimony'.
160. 'With that her confidence increased a great deal'.

And me assuage of the swalme that swellit wes gret.
My husband wes a hur maister, the hugeast in erd.
Tharfor I hait him with my hert, sa help me our Lord.
He is a young man, ryght yaip, bot nought in youth
                                 flouris,   170
For he is fadit full far and feblit of strenth.
He wes as flurising fresche within this few yeris,
Bot he is falyeid full far and fulyeid in labour.
He has bene lychour so lang quhill lost is his natur,
His lume is waxit larbar and lyis in to swoune.   175
Wes never sugeorne wer set na on that snaill tyrit,
For efter sevin oulkis rest it will nought rap anys.
He has bene waistit apone wemen or he me wif chesit,
And in adultre in my tyme I haif him tane oft.
And yit he is als brankand with bonet on syde,   180
And blenkand to the brichtest that in the burgh dwellis,
Alse curtly of his clething and kemmyng of his hair,
As he that is mare valyeand in Venus chalmer.
He semis to be sumthing worth, that syphyr in bour,
He lukis as he wald luffit be, thoght he be litill of valour. 185
He dois as dotit dog that damys on all bussis,

167. assuage *relieve*
swalme *growth* swellit *swelled*
168. hur maister *man who went to
prostitutes* hugeast *greatest* in
erd *on earth*
170. yaip *quick* youth flouris *the
flower of youth*
171. fadit *faded* feblit *become feeble*
172. flurising *flower*
173. falyeid *lost strength*
fulyeid *exhausted*
174. lychour *lecherous*
quhill *until* natur *sexual power*
175. waxit *become*
larbar *impotent* lyis *lies*
swoune *swoon*
176. sugeorne *rest* wer *worse*
set *spent* na *than* snail *slug*
tyrit *weary*

177. oulkis *weeks* rap *drive in*
anys *once*
178. or *before* wif *as his wife*
chesit *chose*
179. adultre *adultery* haif him
tane *have caught him*
180. brankand *proud* bonet *hat*
on syde *at a jaunty angle*
181. blenkand *casting glances*
brichtest *most beautiful women*
182. alse *as* curtly *courtly*
clething *clothes* kemmyng *combing*
183. mare *more* valyeand *bold*
chalmer *chamber*
184. syphyr *cipher, nothing*
bour *bedroom*
185. luffit *loved*
186. dotit *stupid* damys *makes
water* bussis *bushes*

171–2. 'He was like a fresh flower only a few years ago, but now his strength
has declined so much and he is exhausted from his sexual labours'.
176–7. 'Rest was never wasted more than on that weary slug, for even
after seven weeks' rest it will not stay hard even once'.

And liftis his leg apon loft thoght he nought list pische.
He has a luke without lust and lif without curage.
He has a forme without force and fesson but vertu,
And fair wordis but effect, all fruster of dedis.   190
He is for ladyis in luf a right lusty schadow,
Bot in to derne at the deid he sal be drup fundin.
He ralis and makes repet with ryatus wordis,
Ay rusing him of his radis and rageing in chalmer.
Bot God wait quhat I think, quhen he so thra spekis   195
And (how it settis him!) so syde to sege of sic materis:
Bot gif himself of sum evin mycht ane say amang thaim,
Bot he nought ane is, bot nane of naturis possessoris.
Scho that has ane auld man nought all is begylit;
He is at Venus werkis na war na he semys.   200
I wend I josit a gem, and I haif geit gottin.
He had the glemyng of gold and wes bot glase fundin.
Thought men be ferse, wele I fynd, fra falye ther curage –
Thar is bot eldnyng and anger ther hertis within.
Ye speik of berdis on bewch, of blise may thai sing,   205
That on Sanct Valentynis day ar vacandis ilk yer.
Hed I that plesand prevelege, to part quhen me likit,
To change and ay to cheise agane, than chastite adew!

187. apon loft *up*   nought list *does not want*   pische *piss*
188. curage *sexual desire*
189. forme *good body*   force *strength*   fesson *fair appearance*   but *without*   vertu *power*
190. but effect *without actions*   fruster *useless*
191. schadow *image*
192. derne *private*   at the deid *in the act*   drup *droopy*
193. ralis *jokes*   repet *a lot of noise*   ryatus *extravagant*
194. rusing him *boasting*   radis *rides, copulation*   rageing *sexual activity*
195. wait *knows*   thra *boldly*
196. settis *suits*   syde *widely*
197. sege *people*   sic *such*
197. evin *evening*   say *attempt*
198. bot *without*   nane *any*   possessoris *powers*
199. all *entirely*   begylit *deceived*
200. na war na *no worse than*
201. wend *believed*   josit *had*   geit *jet*
202. glase *glass*
203. ferse *bold*   fra *afterwards*   falye *fails*
204. eldnyng *jealousy*
205. berdis *birds*   bewch *branch*
206. Sanct *Saint*   vacandis *free to take a new mate*   ilk *every*
207. prevelege *privilege*   part *depart*   me likit *it pleased me*
208. cheise *choose*   adew *goodbye*

197–8. 'He boasts "if only he could have a go at one of them some night", but he is not one of those, he is a man without any sexual power'.

Than suld I haif a fresch feir to fang in myn armys.
To hald a freke quhill he faynt may foly be calit. 210
Apone sic materis I mus at mydnyght full oft
And murnys so in my mynd, I murdris myselfin.
Than ly I walkand for wa and walteris about,
Wariand oft my wekit kyn that me away cast,
To sic a craudoune but curage that knyt my cler bewte, 215
And ther so mony kene knyghtis this kenrik within.
Than think I on a semelyar, the suth for to tell,
Na is our syre be sic sevin. With that I sych oft.
Than he ful tenderly dois turne to me his tume person,
And with a yoldin yerd dois yolk me in armys, 220
And sais, "My soverane sweit thing, quhy sleip ye no betir?
Me think ther haldis yow a hete, as ye sum harme alyt."
Quod I, "My hony, hald abak and handill me nought sair.
A hache is happinnit hastely at my hert rut."
With that I seme for to swoune, thought I na swerf tak, 225
And thus beswik I that swane with my sweit wordis.
I cast on him a crabit e quhen cleir day is cummyn,
And lettis it is a luf blenk quhen he about glemys;
I turne it in a tender luke that I in tene warit,
And him behaldis hamely with hertly smyling. 230
I wald a tender peronall that myght na put thole,

209. feir *mate* fang *take*
210. freke *man* faynt *grows weak*
    foly *foolishness* calit *called*
211. mus *think*
212. murnys *grieve*
    murdris *torment*
213. walkand *awake* wa *grief*
    walteris *toss and turn*
214. wariand *cursing*
    wekit *wicked* kyn *family*
215. craudoune *coward* but
    curage *impotent* knyt *joined*
    cler *bright*
216. kene *brave* kenrik *kingdom*
217. semelyar *more handsome man*
    suth *truth*
218. na *than* sic *times* sych *sigh*

219. tume *feeble*
220. yoldin *subdued* yerd *penis*
    yolk *clasp*
222. haldis . . . hete *you have a
    fever* harme *sickness*
    alyt *suffered*
223. hony *honey* sair *painfully*
224. hache *pain* rut *root*
225. na swerf tak *I do not faint*
226. beswik *deceive* swane *man*
227. crabit *bad-tempered* e *eye*
228. lettis *pretend* glemys *looks*
229. tene *anger* warit *gave*
230. hamely *kindly*
    hertly *heartfelt*
231. wald *wish that* peronall *girl*
    put *thrust* thole *endure*

215–6. 'Who joined my bright beauty to such an impotent coward when
there were so many brave knights within this kingdom'.
217–8. 'Then, to tell the truth, I think about a man seven times more
handsome than my husband. At this I sigh a great deal'.

That hatit men with hard geir for hurting of flesch,
Had my gud man to hir gest, for I dar God swer,
Scho suld not stert for his straik a stray breid of erd.
And syne I wald that ilk band that ye so blist call   235
Had bund him so to that bryght quhill his bak werkit,
And I wer in a beid broght with berne that me likit.
I trow that bird of my blis suld a bourd want.'
Onone quhen this amyable had endit hir speche,
Loud lauchand, the laif allowit hir mekle.   240
Thir gay wiffis maid game amang the grene leiffis,
Thai drank and did away dule under derne bewis,
Thai swapit of the sweit wyne, thai swan quhit of hewis,
Bot all the pertlyar, in plane, thai put out ther vocis.

Nunc bibent et inde prime due interrogant viduam et de
sua responsione et quomodo erat
Than said the weido: 'Iwis, ther is no way othir: 245
Now tydis me for to talk, my taill it is nixt.
God my spreit now inspir and my speche quykkin,
And send me sentence to say substantious and noble,
Sa that my preching may pers your perverst hertis
And mak yow mekar to men in maneris and conditiounis. 250
I schaw yow, sisteris, in schrift, I wes a schrew ever,

232. hatit *hated* geir *gear, sexual*
    equipment
233. to hir gest *as her lover*
234. stert *flinch* straik *thrust* stray
    . . . erd *straw's breadth of ground*
235. syne *since* ilk *same*
236. bund *bound* bryght *fair girl*
    quhill *until* werkit *ached*
237. beid *bed* berne *man*
238. trow *believe* bird *girl*
    blis *blessed state* bourd *share*
239. onone *at once*
    amyable *amiable one*
240. lauchand *laughing* laif *others*
    allowit *praised* mekle *much*
241. game *sport* leiffis *leaves*
242. did away *cast off*
    dule *sorrow* derne *shady*
    bewis *branches*

243. swapit of *knocked back*
    thai *those* quhit *white*
    hewis *complexion*
244. pertlyar *more boldly* in
    plane *plainly*
245. weido *widow* iwis *truly*
246. tydis me *it is my turn*
    taill *tale*
247. spreit *mind* inspir *inspire*
    quykkin *give life to*
248. sentence *meaningful themes*
    substantious *weighty*
249. pers *pierce* perverst *perverse*
250. mekar *more humble*
    maneris *manners*
    conditiounis *dispositions*
251. schaw yow *reveal to you*
    schrift *confession* schrew *bad*
    woman

234. 'His thrust wouldn't make her flinch even a straw's breadth'.
238. 'I think that girl would want a share of my blessed state'.

Bot I wes schene in my schrowd and schew me innocent;
And thought I dour wes and dane, dispitois and bald,
I wes dissymblit suttelly in a sanctis liknes.
I semyt sober and sweit and sempill without fraud,   255
Bot I couth sexty dissaif that suttillar wer haldin.
Unto my lesson ye lyth and leir at me wit,
Gif you nought list be forleit with losingeris untrew:
Be constant in your governance and counterfeit gud maneris,
Thought ye be kene, inconstant and cruell of mynd.   260
Thought ye as tygris be terne, be tretable in luf,
And be as turtoris in your talk, thought ye haif talis brukill.
Be dragonis baith and dowis ay in double forme,
And quhen it nedis yow, onone note baith ther stranthis.
Be amyable with humble face, as angellis apperand,   265
And with a terrebill tail be stangand as edderis.
Be of your luke like innocentis, thoght ye haif evill myndis.
Be courtly ay in clething and costly arrayit –
That hurtis yow nought worth a hen, yowr husband pays for all.
Twa husbandis haif I had, thai held me baith deir;   270
Thought I dispytit thaim agane, thai spyit it na thing.
Ane wes a hair hogeart that hostit out flewme.
I hatit him like a hund, thought I it hid preve.

252. schene *beautiful*
schrowd *gown*   schew
me *appeared*
253. dour *sullen*   dane *haughty*
dispitois *pitiless*   bald *bold*
254. dissymblit *disguised*
suttelly *cleverly*   sanctis *saint's*
255. sober *mild*   sempill *innocent*
256. sexty *sixty*   dissaif *deceive*
suttillar *cleverer*
haldin *considered*
257. lyth *listen*   leir *learn*
258. list *want*   forleit
with *abandoned by*
losingeris *flatterers*
259. governance *behaviour*
260. thought *even though*
kene *fierce*
261. tygris *tigers*   terne *ferocious*
tretable *submissive*

262. turtoris *turtle doves*   talis *tails
(sexual parts)*   brukill *easily
yielding*
263. dragonis *dragons*   dowis *doves*
264. it nedis yow *you require*
onone *at once*   note *use*
stranthis *strengths*
265. apperand *appearing*
266. stangand *stinging*
edderis *adders*
268. costly arrayit *expensively
dressed*
269. nought worth a hen *not in the
slightest*
271. dispytit *despised*   spyit *saw*
272. hair hogeart *grey-haired old
man*   hostit *coughed*
flewme *phlegm*
273. hatit *hated*   hund *hound*
preve *secretly*

262. 'And be like turtle-doves in your speech even though your tails are
fickle'.

With kissing and with clapping I gert the carill fon,
Weill couth I krych his cruke bak and kemm his kewt
noddill,   275
And with a bukky in my cheik bo on him behind,
And with a bek gang about and bler his ald e,
And with a kyind contynance kys his crynd chekis,
In to my mynd makand mokis at that mad fader,
Trowand me with trew lufe to treit him so fair.   · 280
This couth I do without dule and na dises tak,
Bot ay be mery in my mynd and myrthfull of cher.
I had a lufsummar leid my lust for to slokyn,
That couth be secrete and sure and ay saif my honour,
And sew bot at certane tymes and in sicir placis.   285
Ay quhen the ald did me anger with akword wordis,
Apon the galland for to goif it gladit me agane.
I had sic wit that for wo weipit I litill,
Bot leit the sweit ay the sour to gud sesone bring.
Quhen that the chuf wald me chid with girnand chaftis, 290
I wald him chuk, cheik and chyn, and cheris him so mekill
That his cheif chymys he had chevist to my sone,
Suppos the churll wes gane chaist or the child wes gottin.
As wis woman ay I wrought and not as wod fule,
For mar with wylis I wan na wichtnes of handis.   295

*   *   *

274. clapping *fondling* gert . . .
      fon *made the fool besotted*
275. claw *scratch* cruke *crooked*
      kemm *comb* kewt
      noddill *cropped hair*
276. bukky . . . cheik *tongue in*
      cheek bo *make a face*
277. bek *curtsy* gang *go* bler . . .
      e *beguile his old eye, hoodwink*
      him
278. contynance *countenance*
      crynd *shrivelled*
279. makand mokis *mocking*
      fader *old man*
280. trowand *believing*
281. dule *grief* dises *distress*
282. cher *mood*
283. lufsummar *more lovable*
      leid *man* slokyn *satisfy*
284. sure *dependable*

285. sew *come to me* sicir *safe*
286. ald *old one* akword *bad-*
      tempered
287. galland *young man* goif *gaze*
      gladit *gladenned*
289. sesone *seasoning, flavour*
290. chuf *churlish man* chid *scold*
      girnand chaftis *snarling jaws*
291. chuk *fondle* cheris *cherish*
      mekill *much*
292. cheif chymys *manor house*
      chevist *bequethed* sone *son*
293. suppos *although* gane *gone*
      or *before* gottin *conceived*
294. wrought *behaved* wod
      fule *mad fool*
295. mar *more* wylis *cunning*
      wan *won* na *than*
      wichtnes *strength*

280. 'Who believed I must love him truly to treat him so well'.

'Syne maryt I a merchand, myghti of gudis.
He wes a man of myd eld and of mene statur;
Bot we na fallowis wer in frendschip or blud,
In fredome na furth bering na fairnes of persoune –
Quhilk ay the fule did foryet for febilnes of knawlege.   300
Bot I sa oft thoght him on, quhill angrit his hert,
And quhilum I put furth my voce and peddir him callit.
I wald ryght tuichandly talk, be I wes twyse maryit,
For endit wes my innocence with my ald husband.
I wes apperand to be pert within perfit eild: 305
Sa sais the curat of our kirk, that knew me full ying.
He is our famous to be fals, that fair worthy prelot.
I sal be laith to lat him le quhill I may luke furth.
I gert the buthman obey – ther wes no bute ellis –
He maid me ryght hie reverens fra he my rycht knew,   310
For, thocht I say it myself, the severance wes mekle
Betwix his bastard blude and my birth noble.
That page wes never of sic price for to presome anys
Unto my persone to be peir, had pete nought grantit.
Bot mercy in to womanheid is a mekle vertu,   315
For never bot in a gentill hert is generit ony ruth.
I held ay grene in to his mynd that I of grace tuk him,
And that he couth ken himself I curtasly him lerit.

296. syne *then*   maryt *married*
    merchand *merchant*
297. myd eld *middle age*   mene
    statur *moderate height*
298. na *not*   fallowis *equals*
    frendschip *kindred*   blud *blood*
299. fredome *gentility*   na *nor*
    furth bering *conduct*
300. foryet *forget*
    febilnes *inadequacy*
    knawlege *intelligence*
301. thoght him on *reminded him*
    of it
302. quhilum *sometimes*
    voce *voice*   peddir *pedlar*
303. tuichandly *cuttingly*
305. apperand *seeming*   pert *clever,*
    forward   perfit eild *maturity*
306. sais *says*   curat *priest*
    ying *young*

307. our famous *too respectable*
    prelot *clergyman*
308. laith *reluctant*   le *tell a lie*
    furth *around*
309. gert *made*   buthman *stall-*
    keeper   no bute ellis *no other*
    way for it
310. hie reverens *great respect*
    fra *when*   my rycht knew *knew*
    what was due to me
311. severance *difference*   mekle *great*
313. page *knave*   sic price *worth so*
    much   presome *presume*   anys *once*
314. peir *equal*   pete *pity*
316. bot *except*   gentill *noble*
    generit *produced*   ruth *pity*
317. held ay grene *kept it always*
    fresh   of grace *out of pity*
318. that *so that*   ken *know*
    curtasly *courteously*   lerit *taught*

306. 'I was likely to be very knowledgeable by the time I was grown up'.
308. 'I would be very sorry to make him a liar while I live'.

He durst not sit anys my summondis, for or the secund charge
He wes ay redy for to ryn, so rad he wes for blame.   320
Bot ay my will wes the war of womanly natur:
The mair he loutit for my luf, the les of him I rakit,
And eik – this is a ferly thing – or I him faith gaif
I had sic favour to that freke, and feid syne forevir.
Quhen I the cure had all clene and him ourcummyn haill, 325
I crew abone that craudone as cok that wer victour.
Quhen I him saw subject and sett at myn bydding,
Than I him lichtlyit as a lowne and lathit his maneris.
Than woxe I sa ummerciable, to martir him I thought,
For as a best I broddit him to all boyis laubour.   330
I wald haif riddin him to Rome with raip in his heid,
Wer not ruffill of my renoune and rumour of pepill.
And yit hatrent I hid within my hert all,
Bot quhilis it hepit so huge quhill it behud out.
Yit tuk I never the wosp clene out of my wyde throte,   335
Quhill I oucht wantit of my will or quhat I wald desir.
Bot quhen I severit had that syre of substance in erd,

319. durst *dared* sit *ignore*
   anys *once* summondis *summons*
   or *before* charge *command*
320. rad *afraid*
321. war *worse*
322. loutit *humbled himself* les . . .
   rakit *the less I cared about him*
323. eik *also* ferly *strange*
   or *before* him faith gaif *pledged
   myself to him*
324. sic favour to *such good will*
   towards feid *hatred*
   syne *afterwards*
325. cure *mastery* all
   clene *completely*
   ourcummyn *overcome*
   haill *wholly*
326. crew *crowed* abone *over*
   craudone *coward* cok *cock*
327. subject *submissive*

328. lichtlyit *despised*
   lowne *wretch* lathit *loathed*
   maneris *behaviour*
329. woxe *became*
   ummerciable *pitiless*
   martir *torment*
330. best *beast* broddit *goaded*
   boyis *menial*
331. raip *rope*
332. wer not *were it not for*
   ruffil *damage* pepill *people*
333. hatrent *hatred*
334. quhilis *sometimes* hepit *built
   up* quhill *until* behud *was
   forced*
335. wosp *stopper* throte *throat*
336. quhill *while* oucht *anything*
   wantit *lacked*
337. severit *parted* syre *fellow*
   substance in erd *worldly goods*

321. 'But my womanly nature always made my feelings for him worse'.
331–2. 'I would have ridden him to Rome with a rope round his head, if
   it hadn't been for the damage to my reputation and for what people
   would have said'.

And gottin his biggingis to my barne and hie burrow landis,
Than with a stew stert out the stoppell of my hals,
That he all stunyst throu the stound as of a stele wappin. 340
Than wald I efter lang first sa fane haif bene wrokin
That I to flyte wes als fers as a fell dragoun.
I had for flattering of that fule fenyeit so lang,
Mi evidentis of heritagis or thai wer all selit,
My breist that wes gret beild bowdyn wes sa huge, 345
That neir my baret out birst or the band makin.
Bot quhen my billis and my bauchlis wes all braid selit,
I wald na langar beir on bridill bot braid up my heid;
Thar myght na molet mak me moy na hald my mouth in.
I gert the renyeis rak and rif in to sondir, 350
I maid that wif carll to werk all womenis werkis,
And laid all manly materis and mensk in this eird.
Than said I to my cummaris in counsall about,
"Se how I cabeld yone cout with a kene brydill.
The cappill that the crelis kest in the caf mydding 355
Sa curtasly the cart drawis and kennis na plungeing.
He is nought skeich na yit sker na scippis nought on syd."
And thus the scorne and the scaith scapit he nothir.

338. biggingis *buildings*
barne *child* hie burrow
landis *tenements in the town*
339. stew *stench* stert out *flew
out* stoppell *stopper* hals *throat*
340. stunyst *was stunned*
stound *shock* stele wappin *steel
weapon*
341. first *delay* fane *gladly*
wrokin *avenged*
342. flyte *scold* fers *fierce*
fell *cruel*
343. fenyeit *pretended*
344. evidentis of
heritagis *documents of
inheritance* or *until* selit *sealed*
345. beild *inflamed*
bowdyn *swollen*
346. baret *anger* or *before*
band *contract* makin *was made*
347. billis and . . . bauchlis *legal
documents* braid selit *bound up*

and sealed
348. beir on bridill *put up with the
bridle* braid *tossed*
349. molet *bit* moy *submissive*
350. gert *made* renyeis *reins*
rak *strain* rif *break*
351. wif carll *womanish man*
352. laid *he laid aside*
mensk *dignity* eird *earth*
353. cummaris *friends*
354. cabeld *tied up* cout *colt*
kene *strong*
355. cappill *horse* crelis *creels,
baskets* caf mydding *dung heap*
356. curtasly *well behaved* kennis
na *is not given to*
plungeing *throwing its head down*
357. skeich *likely to shy*
sker *ready to break loose*
scippis *skips*
358. scaith *humiliation*
scapit *escaped* nothir *neither*

344. 'Until my inheritance documents were all signed and sealed'.

He wes no glaidsum gest for a gay lady,
Tharfor I gat him a gam that ganyt him bettir.   360
He wes a gret goldit man and of gudis riche.
I leit him be my lumbart to lous me all misteris,
And he wes fane for to fang fra me that fair office,
And thoght my favoris to fynd throw his feill giftis.
He grathit me in a gay silk and gudly arrayis,   365
In gownis of engranyt claith and gret goldin chenyeis,
In ringis ryally set with riche ruby stonis,
Quhill hely raise my renoune amang the rude peple.
Bot I full craftely did keip thai courtly wedis
Quhill efter dede of that drupe that docht nought in
                                        chalmir.   370
Thought he of all my clathis maid cost and expense,
Ane othir sall the worschip haif that weildis me eftir.
And thoght I likit him bot litill, yit for luf of othris
I wald me prunya plesandly in precius wedis,
That luffaris myght apon me luke and ying lusty
                                        gallandis,   375
That I held more in daynte and derer be ful mekill
Ne him that dressit me so dink – full dotit wes his heyd!
Quhen he wes heryit out of hand to hie up my honoris,
And payntit me as pako, proudest of fedderis,
I him miskennyt, be Crist, and cukkald him maid.   380
I him forleit as a lad and lathlyit him mekle.

359. glaidsum *happy*   gest *lover*
360. gat *got* gam *job* ganyt *suited*
361. gret goldit *very wealthy*
    gudis *goods*
362. lumbart *banker* lous . . .
    misteris *to free me from business*
363. fane *happy* fang *take*
364. feill *many*
365. grathit *clothed* arrayis *dresses*
366. engranyt *dyed scarlet*
    chenyeis *chains*
368. hely *greatly*
    renoune *reputation* rude *common*
369. wedis *clothes*
370. dede *death* drupe *droopy*
    one docht nought *was useless*
    chalmir *bedroom*
371. maid cost and expense *paid for*

372. worschip *honour*
    weildis *possesses*
374. me prunya *deck myself out*
375. luffaris *lovers* gallandis *men*
376. daynte *favour* derer *dearer*
377. ne *than* dink *daintily*
    dotit *stupid* heyd *head*
378. heryit *plundered* out of
    hand *entirely* hie up *raise up*
    honoris *social position*
379. pako *peacock*
    fedderis *feathers*
380. miskennyt *neglected*
    cukkald *cuckold, a deceived
    husband*
381. forleit *rejected* lad *servant*
    lathlyit *loathed*

I thought myself a papingay and him a plukit herle.
All thus enforsit he his fa and fortifyit in strenth,
And maid a stalwart staff to strik himselfe doune.
Bot of ane bowrd in to bed I sall you breif yit: 385
Quhen he ane hal year wes hanyt and him behuffit rage,
And I wes laith to be loppin with sic a lob avoir,
Alse lang as he wes on loft I lukit on him never,
Na leit never enter in my thoght that he my thing persit;
Bot ay in mynd ane othir man ymagynit that I haid,   390
Or ellis had I never mery bene at that myrthles raid.
Quhen I that grome geldit had of gudis and of natur,
Me thoght him gracelese on to goif, sa me God help.
Quhen he had warit all on me his welth and his substance,
Me thoght his wit wes all went away with the laif.   395
And so I did him dispise, I spittit quhen I saw
That superspendit evill spreit spulyeit of all vertu.
For weill ye wait, wiffis, that he that wantis riches
And valyeandnes in Venus play is ful vile haldin.
Full fruster is his fresch array and fairnes of persoune, 400
All is bot frutlese his effeir and falyeis at the upwith.
I buskit up my barnis likc baronis sonnis,
And maid bot fulis of the fry of his first wif.
I banyst fra my boundis his brethir ilkane,
His frendis as my fais I held at feid evir.   405
Be this ye beleif may, I luffit nought himself,

382. papingay *parrot* plukit
  herle *plucked heron*
383. enforsit *gave strength to*
  fa *enemy*
384. stalwart *strong*
385. bowrd *joke* breif *tell*
386. hal *whole* hanyt *held back*
  behuffit *needed* rage *sex*
387. laith *unwilling*
  loppin *mounted* lob avoir *clumsy
  cart-horse*
388. on loft *on top*
389. persit *penetrated*
391. raid *ride*
392. grome *man* geldit *gelded,
  castrated (of a horse)*
  natur *sexual potency*
393. gracelese . . . goif *unattractive*

to look at
394. warit *spent*
395. laif *rest*
397. superspendit *bankrupt*
  spreit *devil* spulyeit *robbed*
  vertu *manliness*
398. wait *know* wantis *lacks*
399. valyeandnes *strength*
400. fruster *useless*
401. effeir *equipment* falyeis *fails*
  upwith *climax*
402. buskit *dressed*
  barnis *children* baronis *baron's*
403. fulis *fools* fry *spawn*
404. banyst *banished*
  boundis *lands* brethir *brothers*
  ilkane *each one*
405. fais *foes* held at feid *despised*

385. 'But let me tell you about one joke I played on him in bed'.

For never I likit a leid that langit till his blude.
And yit thir wismen, thai wait that all wiffis evill
Ar kend with ther conditionis and knawin with the samin.

'Deid is now that dyvour and dollin in erd.   410
With him deit all my dule and my drery thoghtis.
Now done is my dolly nyght, my day is upsprungin.
Adew, dolour, adew, my daynte now begynis.
Now am I a wedow, iwise, and weill am at ese.
I weip as I wer woful bot wel is me forevir.   415
I busk as I wer bailfull bot blith is my hert.
My mouth it makis murnyng and my mynd lauchis.
My clokis thai ar caerfull in colour of sabill,
Bot courtly and ryght curyus my corse is ther undir.
I drup with a ded luke in my dule habit,   420
As with manis daill I had done for dayis of my lif.
Quhen that I go to the kirk cled in cair weid,
As foxe in a lambis fleise fenye I my cheir.
Than lay I furth my bright buke on breid on my kne,
With mony lusty letter ellummynit with gold,   425
And drawis my clok forthwart our my face quhit,
That I may spy unaspyit a space me beside.
Full oft I blenk by my buke and blynis of devotion,

407. leid *person* langit *belonged*
408. wait *know* wiffis evill *wicked wives*
409. kend *recognised*
     conditionis *actions* samin *same*
410. dyvour *bankrupt*
     dollin *buried* erd *earth*
411. deit *died* dule *sorrow*
412. dolly *mournful*
413. adew *goodbye* dolour *sorrow*
     daynte *delight*
414. iwise *indeed* ese *ease*
416. busk *dress* bailfull *in mourning* blith *happy*
417. lauchis *laughs*
418. caerfull *sorrowful looking*
     sabill *sable, black*
419. courtly *elegant*

curyus *beautiful* corse *body*
420. drup *droop* ded *funereal*
     dule habit *mourning clothes*
421. as *as if* manis daill *men's dealing, sexual intercourse*
422. kirk *church* cair
     weid *mourning dress*
423. fleise *fleece* fenye *feign*
     cheir *expression*
424. on breid *wide open*
425. lusty *beautiful*
     ellummynit *illuminated*
426. forthwart *forward* our *over*
     quhit *white*
427. unaspyit *unseen*
428. blenk by *look away from*
     blynis of *cease*

408–9. 'Wise men know that wicked wives are to be recognised by such behaviour as this'.

To se quhat berne is best brand or bredest in schulderis,
Or forgeit is maist forcely to furnyse a bancat 430
In Venus chalmer valyeandly withoutin vane ruse.
And as the new mone all pale oppressit with change
Kythis quhilis her cleir face through cluddis of sable,
So keik I through my clokis and castis kynd lukis
To knychtis and to cleirkis and cortly personis. 435
Quhen frendis of my husbandis behaldis me on fer,
I haif a watter spunge for wa within my wyde clokis.
Than wring I it full wylely and wetis my chekis.
With that watteris myn ene and welteris doune teris.
Than say thai all that sittis about, "Se ye nought, allace, 440
Yone lustlese led, so lelely scho luffit hir husband.
Yone is a pete to enprent in a princis hert,
That sic a perle of plesance suld yone pane dre."
I sane me as I war ane sanct and semys ane angell,
At langage of lichory I leit as I war crabit. 445
I sith without sair hert or seiknes in body,
According to my sable weid I mon haif sad maneris,
Or thai will se all the suth; for certis we wemen
We set us all for the syght, to syle men of treuth.
We dule for na evill deid, sa it be derne haldin. 450
Wise wemen has wayis and wonderfull gydingis
With gret engyne to bejaip ther jolyus husbandis,
And quyetly with sic craft convoyis our materis,

429. berne *man* brand *muscled*
 bredest *broadest*
430. forgeit *formed* maist
 forcely *best* furnyse *lay out*
 bancat *banquet*
431. chalmer *chamber*
 valyeandly *boldly* ruse *boast*
432. oppressit *afflicted*
433. kythis *shows*
 quhilis *sometimes* cluddis *clouds*
434. keik *keek, peep*
435. cleirkis *clerks* cortly *courtly*
436. on fer *from afar*
437. watter spunge *wet sponge*
 wa *grief*
438. wylely *cunningly*
439. welteris *roll* teris *tears*
441. lustlese *joyless* led *creature*
 lelely *loyally* luffit *loved*

442. pete *pitiful sight*
 enprent *imprint*
443. perle *pearl* plesance *delight*
 pane *pain* dre *suffer*
444. sane me *cross myself*
 sanct *saint* semys *look like*
445. lichory *lechery* leit *behave*
 crabit *offended*
446. sich *sigh*
447. according to *as befits* mon *must*
448. se *see* suth *truth*
449. syle *deceive*
450. dule *grieve* derne haldin *kept
 secret*
451. gydingis *ways of acting*
452. engyne *ingenuity* bejaip *fool*
 joylus *jealous*
453. quyetly *quietly*
 convoyis *conduct* materis *business*

That under Crist no creatur kennis of our doingis.
Bot folk a cury may miscuke that knawlege wantis,   455
And has na colouris for to cover ther awne kindly fautis;
As dois thir damysellis for derne dotit lufe,
That dogonis haldis in dainte and delis with thaim so lang,
Quhill al the cuntre knaw ther kyndnes and faith.
Faith has a fair name bot falsheid faris beittir.   460
Fy on hir that can nought feyne, her fame for to saif!
Yit am I wise in sic werk and wes all my tyme.
Thoght I want wit in warldlynes I wylis haif in luf,
As ony happy woman has that is of hie blude.
Hutit be the halok lase a hunder yeir of eild!   465
I have ane secrete servand, rycht sovir of his toung,
That me supportis of sic nedis quhen I a syne mak.
Thoght he be sympill to the sicht he has a tong sickir,
Full mony semelyar sege wer service dois mak.
Thoght I haif cair under cloke the cleir day quhill nyght,   470
Yit haif I solace under serk quhill the sone ryse.
Yit am I haldin a haly wif our all the haill schyre.
I am sa peteouse to the pur, quhen ther person is mony.
In passing of pilgrymage I pride me full mekle,
Mair for the prese of peple na ony perdoun wynyng.   475
Bot yit me think the best bourd quhen baronis and knychtis

454. kennis *knows*
455. cury *dish* miscuke *spoil in cooking* wantis *is lacking in*
456. colouris *disguises* kindly *natural*
457. damysellis *young ladies* derne *secret* dotit *stupid*
458. dogonis *worthless men* dainte *favour* delis with *have dealings with*
459. quhill *until* cuntre *country* kyndnes *love*
461. fy *fie (a term of disgust)* fame *reputation* saif *save*
462. wes *was*
463. want *lack* warldlynes *worldly matters* wylis *wiles* haif *have*
464. happy *fortunate* hie *noble*
465. hutit *hooted at, mocked*

halok *guileless* lase *lass, girl*
466. sovir *trustworthy*
467. syne *sign*
468. sickir *secure*
469. semelyar *more handsome* sege *man* wer *worse*
470. thoght *even though* cair *sorrow* quhill *until*
471. solace *consolation* serk *underwear* sone *sun*
472. haldin *considered to be* haill *whole* schyre *district*
473. peteouse *compassionate* pur *poor* ther . . . mony *there are many people about*
474. passing of *going on* pride me *pride myself*
475. prese *crowd* na *than*
476. bourd *fun*

465. 'May the guileless girl be mocked for her stupidity until she is a hundred'.

And othir bachilleris blith, blumyng in youth,
And all my luffaris lele my lugeing persewis,
And fyllis me wyne wantonly with weilfair and joy.
Sum rownis and sum ralyeis and sum redis ballatis,   480
Sum raiffis furth rudly with riatus speche,
Sum plenis and sum prayis, sum prasis mi bewte,
Sum kissis me, sum clappis me, sum kyndnes me proferis.
Sum kerffis to me curtasli, sum me the cop giffis,
Sum stalwardly steppis ben with a stout curage,   485
And a stif standand thing staiffis in mi neiff,
And mony blenkis ben our, that but full fer sittis,
That mai for the thik thrang nought thrif as thai wald.
Bot with my fair calling I comfort thaim all:
For he that sittis me nixt I nip on his finger,   490
I scrf him on the tothir syde on the samin fasson,
And he that behind me sittis I hard on him lene,
And him befor with my fut fast on his I stramp,
And to the bernis far but sweit blenkis I cast.
To every man in speciall speke I sum wordis,   495
So wisly and so womanly quhill warmys ther hertis.
Thar is no liffand leid so law of degre
That sall me luf unluffit, I am so loik hertit.
And gif his lust so be lent in to my lyre quhit
That he be lost or with me lig, his lif sall not danger.   500
I am so mercifull in mynd, and menys all wichtis,
My sely saull sal be saif quhen Sabot all jugis.

478. lele *faithful* lugeing *house*
    persewis *visit*
479. fyllis me wyne *pour me wine*
    weilfair *good times*
480. rownis *talk softly*
    ralyeis *joke* redis ballatis *read poetry*
481. raiffis *talk loudly*
    rudly *roughly* riatus *lascivious*
482. plenis *complain* bewte *beauty*
483. clappis *embrace* proferis *offer*
484. kerffis to me *carves [the meat] for me* cop *cup* giffis *gives*
485. stalwardly *boldly* ben *inside*
    stout *strong* curage *sexual desire*
486. standand *erect*
    staiffis *thrusts* neiff *fist*

487. our *over* blenkis *glances*
488. thrang *crowd* thrif *succeed*
    wald *would like*
489. fair calling *courteous welcome*
493. stramp *stamp*
494. bernis *men* far *far off*
497. liffand leid *living man*
    law *low* degre *rank*
498. unluffit *without love in return* loik hertit *warm hearted*
499. lent *inclined* lyre *skin*
    quhit *white*
500. or *unless* lig *lie* danger *be in danger*
501. menys *take pity on* wichtis *men*
502. sely *innocent* saull *soul* sal be *shall be* saif *safe* Sabot *God*

487. 'And many glance inside who are only permitted to sit far away'.

Ladyis, leir thir lessonis and be no lassis fundin.
This is the legeand of my lif, thought Latyne it be nane.'

Quhen endit had hir ornat speche this eloquent wedow, 505
Lowd thai lewch all the laif and loffit hir mekle,
And said thai suld exampill tak of her soverane teching
And wirk efter hir wordis, that woman wes so prudent.
Than culit thai ther mouthis with confortable drinkis,
And carpit full cummerlik, with cop going round. 510
Thus draif thai our that deir nyght with danceis full noble,
Quhill that the day did up daw and dew donkit flouris.
The morow myld wes and meik the mavis did sing,
And all remuffit the myst and the meid smellit.
Silver schouris doune schuke as the schene cristall, 515
And berdis shoutit in schaw with ther schill notis.
The goldin glitterand gleme so gladit ther hertis,
Thai maid a glorius gle amang the grene bewis.
The soft sowch of the swyr and soune of the stremys,
The sweit savour of the sward and singing of foulis 520
Myght confort ony creatur of the kyn of Adam,
And kindill agane his curage, thoght it wer cald sloknyt.
Than rais thir ryall rosis in ther riche wedis,
And rakit hame to ther rest through the rise blumys;
And I all prevely past to a plesand arber, 525
And with my pen did report ther pastance most mery.
Ye auditoris most honorable that eris has gevin
Onto this uncouth aventur quhilk airly me happinnit,
Of thir thre wanton wiffis that I haif writtin heir,
Quhilk wald ye waill to your wif, gif ye suld wed one? 530

503. leir *learn* lassis *girls*
505. ornat *splendid*
506. lewch *laughed* laif *rest*
 loffit *praised*
507. soverane *matchless*
508. efter *according to*
509. culit *refreshed*
 confortable *fortifying*
510. carpit *talked*
 cummerlik *intimately*
511. draif thai our *they passed*
512. up daw *dawn* donkit *bathed*
513. morow *morning*
 meik *modestly* mavis *thrush*
514. remuffit *vanished*
 meid *meadow*

515. schuke *fell* schene *bright*
516. berdis *birds* schaw *wood*
 schill *shrill*
518. gle *melody* bewis *branches*
519. sowch *murmuring breeze*
 swyr *valley* soune *sound*
520. sward *grass* foulis *birds*
522. sloknyt *extinguished*
523. rais *rose* rosis *roses*
524. rakit *went* rise
 blumys *blossoming branches*
525. prevely *secretly* arber *garden*
526. pastance *pastime*
528. uncouth *strange* airly *in the
 early hours*
530. waill *choose*

503. 'Ladies, learn these lessons and don't be found to be silly girls'.

In Secreit Place this Hyndir Nycht

1

In secreit place this hyndir nycht
I hard ane beyrne say till ane bricht:
'My huny, my hart, my hoip, my heill,
I have bene lang your luifar leill
And can of yow get confort nane.   5
How lang will ye with danger deill?
Ye brek my hart, my bony ane.'

2

His bony beird wes kemmit and croppit,
Bot all with cale it was bedroppit,
And he wes townysche, peirt and gukit.   10
He clappit fast, he kist and chukkit,
As with the glaikis he wer ovirgane.
Yit be his feirris he wald have fukkit:
'Ye brek my hart, my bony ane.'

3

Quod he: 'My hairt, sweit as the hunye,   15
Sen that I borne wes of my mynnye,
I never wowit weycht bot yow.
My wambe is of your luif sa fow

1. this hyndir nycht *the other night*
2. hard *heard* beryne *man* till *to*
   bricht *fair lady*
3. huny *honey* hart *sweetheart*
   hoip *hope* heill *well-being*
4. bene lang *long been* luifar
   leill *faithful lover*
5. confort *comfort*
6. danger *disdain* deill *deal*
7. brek *break* bony *pretty*
   ane *one*
8. beird *beard* kemmit *combed*
   croppit *trimmed*
9. cale *broth* bedroppit *spattered*
10. townysche *a 'towny'*
    peirt *forward* gukit *foolish*
11. clappit *embraced* kist *kissed*
    chukkit *groped*
12. glaikis *desire*
    ovirgane *overcome*
13. yit *yet* feirris *behaviour*
    fukkit *had sex*
15. quod *said*
16. sen *since* mynnye *mother*
17. wowit *wooed* weycht *anyone*
18. wambe *belly* luif *love*
    fow *full*

5. 'And yet can get no comfort from you'.
6. 'How long do you intend to be disdainful towards me?'
11–13. 'He held her fast, he kissed and groped her, as if he were
overcome by his desire. Yet his behaviour showed that what he really
wanted was to have sex'.

That as ane gaist I glour and grane.
I trymble sa, ye will not trow,   20
Ye brek my hart, my bony ane.'

4

'Tehe!' quod scho, and gaif ane gawfe.
'Be still, my tuchan and my calfe,
My new spanit howffing fra the sowk,
And all the blythnes of my bowk.   25
My sweit swanking, saif yow allane
Na leyd I luiffit all this owk.
Full leif is me yowr graceles gane.'

5

Quod he: 'My claver and my curldodie,
My huny soppis, my sweit possodie,   30
Be not oure bosteous to your billie,
Be warme hairtit and not evill willie.
Your heylis, quhyt as quhalis bane,
Garris ryis on loft my quhillelillie.
Ye brek my hart, my bony ane.'   35

6

Quod scho: 'My clype, my unspaynit gyane,
With moderis mylk yit in your mychane,

19. as *like* gaist *ghost*
    glour *stare* grane *groan*
20. trymble *tremble* sa *so much*
    trow *believe*
22. tehe *teehee* scho *she*
    gaif *gave* gawfe *guffaw*
23. tuchan *dummy* calfe *calf*
24. new *newly* spanit *weaned*
    howffing *oaf* sowk *breast*
25. blythnes *pleasures* bowk *body*
26. swanking *young man*
    saif *except*
27. leyd *lad* luiffit *loved*
    owk *week*
28. leif *dear* graceles *unattractive*

gane *ugly face*
29. claver *clover* curldodie *ribwort*
30. soppis *sops* possodie *refreshment*
31. oure *too* bosteous *harsh*
    billie *friend*
32. hairtit *hearted* evill willie *ill-disposed*
33. heylis *heels* quhyt *white*
    quhalis bane *ivory*
34. garris ryis *cause to rise* on
    loft *into the air* quhillelillie *penis*
36. clype *big lad*
    unspaynit *unweaned* gyane *giant*
37. moderis *mother's* yit *still*
    mychane *mouth*

24–5. 'My oaf newly weaned from the breast and all the other pleasures
of my body'.
26–8. 'My sweet young man, I have loved no lad all this week except for
you alone. Your ugly mug is very dear to me'.

My belly huddrun, my swete hurle bawsy,
My huny gukkis, my slawsy gawsy,
Your musing waild perse ane harte of stane. 40
Tak gud confort, my grit heidit slawsy,
Full leif is me your graceles gane.'

7

Quod he: 'My kid, my capirculyoun,
My bony baib with the ruch brylyoun,
My tendir gyrle, my wallie gowdye, 45
My tyrlie myrlie, my crowdie mowdie,
Quhone that oure mouthis dois meit at ane,
My stang dois storkyn with your towdie.
Ye brek my hairt, my bony ane.'

8

Quod scho: 'Now tak me be the hand, 50
Welcum, my golk of Marie land,
My chirrie and my maikles munyoun,
My sowklar, sweit as ony unyoun,
My strumill stirk, yit new to spane.
I am applyit to your opunyoun, 55
I luif rycht weill your graceles gane.'

38. belly huddrun *heifer-belly*
hurle bawsy *clumsy clot*
39. huny gukkis *sweet fool* slawsy
gawsy *rosy-cheeked sluggard*
40. musing *complaining*
perse *pierce* stane *stone*
41. grit heidit slawsy *big-headed
sluggard*
43. kid *little goat*
capirculyoun *wood grouse*
44. baib *baby* ruch *rough*
brylyoun *shaggy shoes*
45. gyrle *girl* wallie gowdye *pretty
goldie*
46. tyrlie myrlie *itsy-bitsy*

crowdie mowdie *mouldy porridge*
47. quhone *when* dois meit *meet
at ane together*
48. stang *penis* storkyn *stiffen*
towdie *buttocks*
51. golk *cuckoo* Marie
land *fairyland*
52. chirrie *cherry* maikles
munyoun *matchless lover*
53. sowklar *suckling pig*
unyoun *onion*
54. strumill stirk *gawky bullock*
spane *weaning*
55. applyit *inclined*
opunyoun *proposal*

55. 'I am inclined to accept your proposal'.

9

He gaif to hir ane apill rubye.
Quod scho, 'Gramercye, my sweit cowhubye!'
And thai tway to ane play began,
Quhilk men dois call the 'dery dan',   60
Quhill that thair myrthis met baythe in ane.
'Wo is me,' quod scho, 'Quhair will ye, man?
Best now I luif that graceles gane.'

57. gaif *gave* apill rubye *ruby-red apple*
58. gramercye *thank you* cowhubye *simpleton*
59. thai tway *the two of them*

60. dery dan *'rumpy pumpy';* *copulation*
61. quhill that *until* myrthis *pleasures* ane *one*
62. quhair will ye *where are you going*

59–61. 'And the two of them began to play the one game, which people call "rumpy pumpy", until their pleasures coincided'.

Now Cumis Aige Quhair Yewth hes Bene

Now cumis aige quhair yewth hes bene
And trew luve rysis fro the splene.

1

Now culit is dame Venus brand,
Trew luvis fyre is ay kindilland,
And I begyn to undirstand   5
In feynit luve quhat foly bene.
Now cumis aige quhair yewth hes bene
And trew luve rysis fro the splene.

2

Quhill Venus fyre be deid and cauld,
Trew luvis fyre nevir birnis bauld.   10
So as the ta lufe waxis auld,
The tothir dois incres moir kene.
Now cumis aige quhair yewth hes bene
And trew lufe rysis fro the splene.

3

No man hes curege for to wryte   15
Quhat plesans is in lufe perfyte,
That hes in fenyeit lufe delyt;
Thair kyndnes is so contrair clene.
Now cumis aige quhair yewth hes bene
And trew lufe rysis fro the splene.   20

1. quhair *where*   yewth *youth*
2. trew luve *true love*   rysis *rises*
   fro *from*   splene *heart*
3. culit *cooled*   brand *firebrand*
4. ay *always*   kindilland *ablaze*
6. feynit *false*   foly *folly*
   bene *there is*
9. quhill *until*   deid *dead*
   cauld *cold*
10. birnis bauld *burns brightly*

11. ta *one*   waxis *grows*   auld *old*
12. tothir *other*   dois incres *grows*
    moir kene *more fervent*
15. curege *ability*
16. plesans *joy*   perfyte *perfect*
17. that *who*   fenyeit *false*
    delyt *pleasure*
18. kyndnes *natures*   contrair *at
    variance*   clene *completely*

4. 'The fire of the one true love is always ablaze'.
16. 'What joy there is in perfect love'.
18. 'Their natures are so completely at variance'.

4

Full weill is him that may imprent,
Or onywayis his hairt consent
To turne to trew luve his intent,
And still the quarrell to sustene.
Now cumis aige quhair yewth hes bene   25
And trew lufe rysis fro the splene.

5

I haif experience by my sell.
In luvis court anis did I dwell,
Bot quhair I of a joy cowth tell,
I culd of truble tell fyftene.   30
Now cumis aige quhair yewth hes bene
And trew lufe rysis fro the splene.

6

Befoir quhair that I wes in dreid,
Now haif I confort for to speid;
Quhair I had maugre to my meid,   35
I trest rewaird and thankis betwene.
Now cumis aige quhair yewth hes bene
And trew lufe rysis fro the splene.

7

Quhair lufe wes wont me to displeis,
Now find I in to lufe grit eis;   40

---

21. imprent *remain firm*
22. onywayis *in any way*
    hairt *heart*   consent *induce*
23. intent *mind*
24. quarrell *grievance*
    sustene *endure*
27. by my sell *of my own*
28. anis *once*
29. quhair *whereas*   a *one*
    cowth *could*
30. truble *tribulation*

33. quhair *where*   dreid *fear*
34. confort *encouragement*
    speid *succeed*
35. maugre *ill-will*   to *as*
    meid *reward*
36. trest *expect*
    thankis *appreciation*   betwene *too*
39. wont *accustomed*
    displeis *distress*
40. in to *in*   grit *great*
    eis *contentment*

---

24. 'And still endure the grievances caused by fleshly desire'.
29–30. 'But whereas I could tell one story about love's joys, I could tell
    fifteen about its tribulations'.
36. 'I now expect a reward and appreciation too'.

Quhair I had denger and diseis,
My breist all confort dois contene.
Now cumis aige quhair yewth hes bene
And trew lufe rysis fro the splene.

8

Quhair I wes hurt with jelosy   45
And wald no luver wer bot I,
Now quhair I lufe I wald all wy
Als weill as I luvit, I wene.
Now cumis aige quhair yewth hes bene
And trew lufe rysis fro the splene.   50

9

Befoir quhair I durst nocht for schame
My lufe discure nor tell hir name,
Now think I wirschep wer and fame
To all the warld that it war sene.
Now cumis aige quhair yewth hes bene   55
And trew lufe rysis fro the splene.

10

Befoir no wicht I did complene,
So did hir denger me derene,
And now I sett nocht by a bene
Hir bewty nor hir twa fair ene.   60
Now cumis aige quhair yewth hes bene
And trew lufe rysis fro the splene.

41. denger *disdain* diseis *hardship*   fame *distinction*
42. confort *joy* contene *contain*   54. sene *seen*
47. all wy *every creature*   57. wicht *person*
48. als *as* wene *believe*   complene *complain*
51. durst nocht *did not dare*   58. denger *disdain* derene *assail*
52. discure *reveal*   59. sett *value* bene *bean*
53. wirschep *honour*   60. twa *two* ene *eyes*

46. 'And wished no lover but I existed'.
48. 'Loved as much as I do, I believe'.
54–5. 'Now I think it would be an honour and distinction if it were
   obvious to the whole world'.
57. 'Before I complained to nobody'.
59–60. 'And now I don't care at all for her beauty or her two pretty
   eyes'.

11

I haif a luve farar of face,
Quhome in no denger may haif place,
Quhilk will me guerdoun gif and grace,   65
And mercy ay quhen I me mene.
Now cumis aige quhair yewth hes bene
And trew lufe rysis fro the splene.

12

Unquyt I do no thing nor sane,
Nor wairis a luvis thocht in vane.   70
I sal be als weill luvit agane,
Thair may no jangler me prevene.
Now cumis aige quhair yewth hes bene
And trew luve rysis fro the splene.

13

Ane lufe so fare, so gud, so sweit,   75
So riche, so rewthfull and discreit,
And for the kynd of man so meit
Nevir moir sal be nor yit hes bene.
Now cumis aige quhair yewth hes bene
And trew lufe rysis fro the splene.   80

14

Is none sa trew a luve as he
That for trew lufe of us did de.
He suld be luffit agane, think me,
That wald sa fane our luve obtene.
Now cumis aige quhair yewth hes bene   85
And trew lufe rysis fro the splene.

---

63. farar *fairer*
65. guerdoun gif *give reward*
    grace *favour*
66. ay *always* me mene *bewail my
    fate*
69. unquyt *unrewarded* sane *say*
70. wairis *expend*
71. sal be *shall be* agane *in return*

72. jangler *detractor*
    prevene *supplant*
75. fare *fair*
76. rewthfull *compassionate*
    discreit *judicious*
77. kynd *nature* meit *fitting*
82. de *die*
84. sa fane *so gladly* obtene *obtain*

64. 'Who has no dealings with disdainful behaviour'.
69–70. 'Everything I do and say is rewarded, and I do not have a loving
    thought in vain'.

15

Is non but grace of God, iwis,
That can in yewth considdir this.
This fals, dissavand warldis blis
So gydis man in flouris grene.   90
Now cumis aige quhair yewth hes bene
And trew luve rysis fro the splene.

87. but *without* iwis *indeed*   blis *worldly joy*
88. yewth *youth* considdir *realise* 90. gydis *rules* flouris grene *green*
89. dissavand *deceitful* warldis   *flowers; youth*

87–90. 'Indeed, there is no one who is able to realise this in his youth
without the grace of God, this false, deceitful, worldly joy has such
control over man when he is young'.

Rycht Airlie on Ask Weddinsday

1

Rycht airlie on Ask Weddinsday
Drynkand the wyne satt cumeris tway;
The tane cowth to the tother complene:
Graneand and suppand cowd scho say:
'This lang Lentern makis me lene.'   5

2

On cowch besyd the fyre scho satt,
God wait gif scho wes grit and fatt;
Yit to be feble scho did hir fene.
And ay scho said, 'Cummer, latt preif of that:
This lang Lentern makis me lene.'   10

3

'My fair sweit cummer,' quod the tuder,
'Ye tak that nigirtnes of your muder;
All wyne to test scho wald disdane
Bot mavasy, scho bad nane uder:
This lang Lentern makis me lene.   15

4

'Cummer, be glaid both evin and morrow
Thocht ye suld bayth beg and borrow,
Fra our lang fasting ye yow refrene

1. rycht airlie *very early* Ask
   Weddinsday *Ash Wednesday*
2. drynkand *drinking* wyne *wine*
   cumeris tway *two female friends*
3. tane *one* cowth *could*
   tother *other*
4. graneand *groaning*
   suppand *sipping* scho *she*
5. lang *long* Lentern *Lent*
   lene *skinny*
6. cowch *bed*
7. wait *knows* gif *if* grit *big*

8. feble *delicate* hir fene *pretend*
9. ay *constantly* latt preif of *let us
   prove*
11. quod *said* tuder *other*
12. tak *inherit* nigirtnes *leanness*
    muder *mother*
13. test *taste*
14. bot mavasy *except malmsey*
    bad *wanted*
16. evin *evening* morrow *morning*
17. thocht *even if*
18. yow refrene *abstain*

3. 'One complained to the other'.
7. 'God knows, she was a big fat woman'.
17–18. 'Even if you have to both beg and borrow, make sure that you
   abstain from this long fast'.

And latt your husband dre the sorrow:
This lang Lentern makis me lene.'   20

5

'Your counsale, cummer, is gud,' quod scho;
'All is to tene him that I do;
In bed he is nocht wirth a bene.
Fill fow the glas and drynk me to;
This lang Lentern makis me lene.'   25

6

Of wyne out of ane choppyne stowp
Thay drank twa quartis sowp and sowp,
Of drowth sic exces did thame strene;
Be than to mend thay had gud howp:
This lang Lentroun makis me lene.   30

19. latt *let* dre *endure*
21. counsale *advice*
22. tene *annoy*
23. nocht wirth a bene *not worth a bean; useless*
24. fow *to the brim*

26. choppyne stowp *half-pint glass*
27. twa quartis *four pints*
    sowp *sip*
28. drowth *thirst* sic exces *such excess* strene *afflict*
29. be than *by then* howp *hope*

22. 'Everything I do is intended to annoy him'.
27–9. 'They drank four pints, matching one another sip for sip, such a terrible thirst afflicted them; by that time they had good hope of a recovery'.

Now of Wemen this I Say, for Me

Now of wemen this I say, for me:
Of erthly thingis nane may bettir be.
Thay suld haif wirschep and grit honoring
Of men, aboif all uthir erthly thing.
Rycht grit dishonour upoun him self he takkis,   5
In word or deid, quha evir wemen lakkis,
Sen that of wemen cumin all ar we.
Wemen ar wemen and sa will end and de.
Wo wirth the fruct wald put the tre to nocht,
And wo wirth him rycht so that sayis ocht   10
Of womanheid that may be ony lak,
Or sic grit schame upone him for to tak.
Thay us consaif with pane, and be thame fed
Within thair breistis thair we be boun to bed.
Grit pane and wo and murnyng mervellus   15
Into thair birth thay suffir sair for us.
Than meit and drynk to feid us get we nane,
Bot that we sowk out of thair breistis bane.
Thay ar the confort that we all haif heir,
Thair may no man be till us half so deir.   20
Thay ar our verry nest of nurissing –
In lak of thame quha can say ony thing,

1. wemen *women*   for me *for my own part*
2. nane *none*
3. haif *receive*   wirschep *respect*   grit *great*
4. of *from*   aboif *above*
5. takkis *brings*
6. lakkis *disparages*
7. sen *since*   cumin *come*
8. de *die*
9. wo wirth *woe betide*   fruct *fruit*   put . . . to nocht *destroy*
10. rycht so *in the same way*   ocht *anything*
11. womanheid *womanliness*

lak *criticism*
12. sic *such*
13. us consaif *conceive us*   pane *pain*   be thame *by them*
14. within *upon*   breistis *breasts*   boun *ready*
15. murnyng mervellus *terrible agony*
16. into *in*   birth *childbearing*   sair *painfully*
17. than *then*   meit *food*   feid *feed*   nane *none*
18. sowk *suck*   bane *comfortable*
20. till *to*
21. verry *true*   nurissing *nursing*

5–7. 'Anyone who disparages women, by word or deed, brings very great dishonour upon himself, since we all came forth from women'.
9. 'Woe betide the fruit that would destroy the tree on which it grew'.
12. 'Or who brings such great shame upon himself'.
14. 'Upon their breasts where we are ready to lie'.

That fule his nest he fylis, and forthy
Exylit he suld be of all gud cumpany.
Thair suld na wyis man gif audience 25
To sic a fule without intelligence.
Chryst to his fader he had nocht ane man;
Se quhat wirschep wemen suld haif than.
That sone is lord, that sone is king of kingis,
In hevin and erth his majestie ay ringis. 30
Sen scho hes borne him in hir halines,
And he is well and grund of all gudnes,
All wemen of us suld haif honoring,
Service and luve, aboif all uthir thing.

23. fule *fool* fylis *defiles*
    forthy *therefore*
24. exylit *excluded*
25. wyis *wise* gif *give*
26. fule *fool*
27. fader *father*
28. wirschep *honour*

29. sone *son*
30. ay ringis *reigns forever*
31. sen *since* scho *she*
    halines *holiness*
32. well *source* grund *foundation*
33. of *from*
34. luve *love*

23–4. 'That fool defiles his own nest, and therefore he should be
    excluded from all good company'.
27. 'Christ did not take a man as his father'.

GAVIN DOUGLAS

The Palis of Honoure
THE PROLOGUE

Quhen pale Aurora with face lamentable
Hir russat mantill, borderit all with sable,
Lappit about be hevinlye circumstance
The tender bed and arres honorable
Of Flora, quene till flouris amyable,   5
In May, I rays to do my observance
And entrit in a garding of plesance
With sole depaint, as Paradys amyable,
And blisfull bewes with blomed variance,

So craftely Dame Flora had overfret   10
Hir hevinly bed, powderit with mony a set
Of ruby, topas, perle and emerant,
With balmy dewe bathit and kyndly wet,
Quhil vapours hote, right fresche and wele ybet,
Dulce of odour, of flewour most fragrant,   15
The silver droppis on dayseis distillant,

1. quhen *when*
  lamentable *sorrowful*
2. russat *russet; reddish*
  mantill *cloak* borderit *trimmed*
  sable *black*
3. lappit *wrapped* be *with*
  hevinlye circumstance *divine
  formality*
4. tender *soft* arres
  honorable *noble tapestry*
5. quene *queen* till *of*
  flouris *flowers* amyable *lovely*
6. rays *rose* observance *ritual*
7. entrit *entered* garding *garden*
  plesance *pleasure*
8. with *by* sole *sun*

depaint *painted*
paradys *paradise*
9. blisfull *beautiful* bewes *boughs*
  blomed variance *variety of
  blossoms*
10. craftely *skilfully*
  overfret *decorated*
11. powderit *spangled* set *cluster*
12. topas *topaz* emerant *emerald*
13. dewe *dew* bathit *bathed*
  kyndly *suitably*
14. quhil *while* right *very*
  ybet *constituted*
15. dulce *sweet* flewour *scent*
16. dayseis *daisies*
  distillant *trickling*

1–6. In May, when pale, sorrowful-faced Aurora enveloped the soft bed
   and noble tapestry of Flora, queen of the lovely flowers, in her russet
   cloak, all trimmed with black, with an air of divine formality, I rose to
   perform my ritual.
8. 'Painted by the sun, as lovely as paradise.
16–18. 'Were trickling upon the dasies in silver drops, and were poured
   over the garden paths by fresh green branches, with smoky incense
   chasing away the mists'.

Quhilk verdour branches over the alars yet,
With smoky sence the mystis reflectant.

The fragrant flouris, blomand in their seis,
Overspred the leves of Naturis tapestreis,   20
Above the quhilk, with hevinly armoneis,
the birdes sat on twistes and on greis,
Melodiously makand thair kyndely gleis,
Quhois schill notis fordinned al the skyis.
Of reparcust ayr, the eccon cryis   25
Amang the branchis of the blomed treis;
And on the laurers, silver droppis lyis.

Quhyll that I rowmed in that paradice
Replennessed and full of all delice,
Out of the sea Eous alift his heid –   30
I meyne the hors quhilk drawis at device
The assiltre and goldin chaire of pryce
Of Tytan, quhilk at morowe semis reid.
The new colour that all the night lay deid
Is restored. Baith fowlis, flowris, and ryce   35
Reconfort was throw Phebus gudlyheid.

17. quhilk *which* verdour *vibrant green* alars *garden paths* yet *poured*
18. sence *incense* mystis *mists* reflectant *diverting*
19. blomand *blooming* seis *places*
20. leves *leaves* Naturis *Nature's*
21. the quhilk *which* armoneis *harmonies*
22. twistes *twigs* greis *branches*
23. makand *performing* kyndely gleis *natural songs*
24. quhois *whose* schill notis *shrill notes* fordinned *resounded throughout*
25. reparcust *reverberating* eccon *echo* cryis *sounds*
26. blomed treis *trees in blossom*
27. laurers *laurels* lyis *lie*
28. quhyll that *while* rowmed *roamed*
29. replennessed *replenished* delice *delight*
30. alift *lifted*
31. meyne *mean* drawis *pulls* at device *with perfect skill*
32. assiltre *axletree* chaire *chariot* of pryce *of great worth*
33. Tytan *Titan* morowe *morning* semis *appears* reid *red*
34. deid *dead*
35. fowlis *birds* ryce *branches*
36. reconfort *refreshed* Phebus *Phoebus'* gudlyheid *benevolence*

36. 'Have been refreshed through the benevolence of Phoebus'.

The dasy and the maryguld onlappit
Quhilkis all the nicht lay with thair levis happit
Thaim to preserve fra rewmes pungitive.
The umbrate treis that Tytan about wappit   40
War portrait and on the erth yschappit
Be goldin bemes vivificative
Quhois amene hete is most restorative.
The gershoppers amangis the vergers gnappit
And beis wrocht materiall for thair hyve.   45

Richt halsom was the sessoun of the yeir.
Phebus furth yet depured bemes cleir
Maist nutrityve tyll all thynges vigitant.
God Eolus of wynd list nocht appeir,
Nor ald Saturne with his mortall speir   50
And bad aspect, contrar til every plant.
Neptunus nolde within that palace hant.
The beriall stremes rynnyng men micht heir
By bonkis grene with glancis variant.

For till beholde that hevinly place complete –   55
The purgit ayr with new engendrit hete,

37. maryguld *marigold*
    onlappit *unfold*
38. nicht *night* levis *petals*
    happit *wrapped up*
39. thaim *them* preserve
    fra *protect from* rewmes
    pungitive *piercing vapours*
40. umbrate *shady*
    wappit *wrapped*
41. portrait *painted*
    yschappit *outlined*
42. bemes vivificative *life-giving*
    beams
43. amene hete *pleasant heat*
44. gershoppers *grasshoppers*
    amangis *in* vergers *gardens*
    gnappit *nibbled*
45. beis *bees* wrocht *made* hyve *hive*
46. halsom *wholesome*
47. furth . . . depured *poured*

forth cleir *bright*
48. nutrityve *nourishing*
    vigitant *growing*
49. Eolus *Aeolus* list nocht *chose
    not to*
50. ald Saturne *old Saturn*
    mortall speir *deadly spear*
51. aspect *astrological influence*
    contrar til *unfavourable to*
52. Neptunus *Neptune*
    nolde *would not* palace *enclosed
    garden* hant *dwell*
53. beriall stremes *crystal-clear
    streams* heir *hear*
54. bonkis *banks* glancis
    variant *glancing sunlight*
55. complete *entirely*
56. purgit *purified*
    engenderit *generated* hete *heat*

39. 'To protect themselves from the piercing night vapours'.

The soyl enbroude with colour, ure and stone,
The tender grene, the balmy droppes swete –
So rejoysit and confort wes my sprete
I not wes it a vision or fanton.   60
Amyd the buskys rowmyng myn allone
Within that garth of all plesans replete,
A voce I hard, preclare as Phebus schone

Syngand, 'O May thow myrrour of soles,
Maternall moneth, lady and maistres,   65
Tyl every thing adoun respirature,
Thyn hevinly werk and worthy craftines
The small herbis constrenis tyl encres.
O verray ground tyl werking of nature
Quhois hie curage and assucuryt cure   70
Causis the erth his fruitis tyll expres,
Dyffundant grace on every creature.

'Thy godly lore, cunnyng incomparabyl,
Dantis the savage bestis maist unstabyl
And expellis all that nature infestis.   75
The knoppit syonys with levys agreabyl

57. soyl *soil* enbroude *embroidered*
ure *ore* stone *jewels*
59. rejoysit *gladdened*
confort *comforted* sprete *spirit*
60. not *did not know*
fanton *illusion*
61. buskys *bushes*
rowmyng *roaming* myn
allone *by myself*
62. garth *garden* plesans *delights*
replete *full*
63. voce *voice* hard *heard*
preclare *clear* schone *shone*
64. syngand *singing*
myrrour *mirror* soles *delight*
65. moneth *month*
maistres *mistress*
66. tyl *of* adoun *down here*

respirature *reviver*
67. werk *work* craftines *skill*
68. herbis *plants*
constrenis *compels* encres *grow*
69. ground tyl *foundation of*
70. quhois *whose* hie curage *noble*
vigour assucuryt cure *assured*
care
71. frutis *fruits* expres *produce*
72. dyffundant *pouring forth*
73. godly lore *excellent teaching*
cunnyng incomparabyl
incomparable skill
74. dantis *subdues* bestis *beasts*
unstabyl *unstable*
75. infestis *infests*
76. knoppit syonys *budding shoots*
levys agreabyl *lovely leaves*

60. 'I did not know whether it was a vision or an illusion'.
63. 'I heard a voice, as clear as the beams of Phoebus'.
67–8. 'Your heavenly work and valuable skill compel the little plants to
grow'.

For tyl revert and burgione ar maid abyll.
Thy myrth refreschis birdis in thair nestis,
Quhilkis the to pryse and Nature never restis,
Confessand you maist potent and lovabyll   80
Amang the brownys of the olyve twystes.

'In the is rute and augment of curage.
In the enforcis Martis vassalage.
In the is amorus luf and armony
With incrementis fresche in lusty age.   85
Quha that constrenit ar in luffis rage,
Addressand thaim with observans ayrly,
Weil auchtyst the tyl glore and magnify.'
And with that word I rasyt my vissage
Sore effrayit, half in a frenisye.   90

'O Nature Queen and O ye lusty May,'
Quod I tho, 'quhow lang sall I thus forvay,
Quhilk yow and Venus in this garth deservis?
Reconsell me out of this gret affray
That I maye synge yow laudis day be day.   95
Ye that al mundane creaturis preservis

77. revert *recover*
   burgione *flourish* abyll *able*
78. myrth *joy*
79. the to pryse *to praise you*
80. confessand *declaring*
   potent *powerful*
81. brownys *twigs* olyve
   twystes *olive branches*
82. the *you* rute *root*
   augment *increase* curage *vigour*
83. enforcis *increases* Martis
   vassalage *service to Mars*
84. amorus luf *amorous love*
   armony *harmony*
85. incrementis fresche *new
   growth* lusty age *age of vigorous
   youth*
86. quha *whoever* constrenit
   ar *are constrained* luffis

rage *love's passion*
87. addressand thaim *preparing
   themselves* observans ayrly *early
   morning ritual*
88. auchtyst *ought* glore *glorify*
   magnify *praise*
89. rasyt *raised* vissage *head*
90. effrayit *afraid* frenisye *frenzy*
91. lusty *beautiful*
92. quod *said* tho *then*
   quhow *how* lang *long* forvay *go
   astray*
93. quhilk *who* deservis *serves*
94. reconsell me *bring me back*
   gret affray *great alarm*
95. laudis *songs of praise* be *by*
96. mundane *earthly*
   preservis *protects*

77. 'Are enabled to recover and flourish'.
79. 'Who never stop praising you and Nature'.
88. 'Ought to glorify and praise you well'.

Confort your man that in this fanton stervis
With sprete arrasyt and every wit away,
Quakyng for fere, baith puncys, vane and nervis.'

My fatall werd, my febyl wit I wary,   100
My dasyt heid, quham lake of brane gart vary
And not sustene so amyabyll a soun.
With ery curage, febyl strenthis sary,
Bownand me hame and list no langer tary,
Out of the ayr come ane impressioun   105
Throw quhois lycht in extasy or swoun,
Amyd the virgultis all in tyl a fary
As femynine so feblyt fell I doun.

And with that gleme so dasyt wes my mycht
Quhill thair remanit nothir voce nor sycht,   110
Breth, motione, nor hetis naturale.
Saw nevir man so faynt a levand wycht,
And na ferly, for over excelland lycht

97. confort *comfort* fanton *dream*
    stervis *suffers*
98. sprete *spirit* arrasyt *snatched
    away* every wit away *out of his
    wits*
99. fere *fear* puncys *pulses*
    vane *veins*
100. fatall werd *preordained
    destiny* febyl *feeble* wary *curse*
101. dasyt heid *confused mind*
    quham *which* lake *lack*
    brane *intelligence* gart *caused to*
    vary *wander*
102. sustene *allow to continue*
    soun *sound*
103. ery *fearful* curage *mind*
    strenthis *spirit* sary *miserable*
104. bownand me *preparing*

myself list *wish*
105. impressioun *flash of light*
106. lycht *light* swoun *swoon*
107. virgultis *bushes* in tyl *in*
    fary *daze*
108. femynine *woman*
    feblyt *enfeebled*
109. gleme *bright light*
    dasyt *numbed* mycht *power*
110. quhill *until*
    remanit *remained*
    nothir *neither* voce *voice*
    sycht *sight*
111. breth *breath* hetis
    naturale *natural warmth*
112. levand wicht *living creature*
113. na ferly *no wonder* over
    excelland *too-great* lycht *light*

101–2. 'My confused mind, which lack of intelligence caused to wander
instead of listening to such a beautiful sound'.
103–4. 'With fearful mind, and miserable, enfeebled spirit, preparing
myself to go home and not wishing to delay any longer'.
108. 'I fell down as weak as a woman'.
112. 'No one ever saw a living creature faint like that'.

Corruppis the wit and garrys the blud availe
On tyl the hart that it no danger ale –   115
Quhen it is smorit, membris wyrkes not richt:
The dredfull terrour sua did me assaile.

Yyt at the last – I not quhou long a space –
A lytell hete aperyt in my face
Quhilk had tofore beyn pale and voyde of blud.   120
Tho in my sweven I met a ferly cace:
I thought me set within a desert place,
Amyd a forest by a hydous flud
With grysly fysche, and shortly tyl conclud
I shall descryve, as God wil geve me grace,   125
Myn avision in rurell termes rude.

THE FIRST PARTE

Thow barrant wyt overset with fantasyis,
Schaw now the craft that in thy memor lyis,
Schaw now thy shame, schaw now thy bad nystee,
Schaw thyn endyt, repruf of rethoryis,   130
Schaw now thy beggit termis mare than thryis,
Schaw now thy ranys and thyn harlottree,

114. corruppis *corrupts*
     garrys *makes* blud *blood*
     availe *descend*
115. hart *heart* that *so that*
     ale *harms*
116. smorit *smothered*
     membris *limbs* wyrkes *work*
     richt *properly*
117. sua *in this way*
118. not *do not know* quhou *how*
     space *time*
119. hete *heat; colour*
     aperyt *appeared*
120. tofore *before* voyde *empty*
121. tho *then* sweven *dream*
     met *encountered* ferly
     cace *amazing thing*
122. me set *I was set down*

desert *uninhabited*
123. hydous flud *hideous river*
124. grysly fysche *horrible fish*
     conclud *conclude*
125. descryve *describe*
126. avision *vision* rurell termes
     rude *rough country words*
127. barrant *barren* wyt *wit*
     overset with *overcome by*
128. schaw *show* craft *skill*
     memor *memory* lyis *lies*
129. bad nystee *wicked folly*
130. endyt *writing* repruf *shame*
     rethoryis *rhetoricians*
131. beggit termis *borrowed
     phrases* thryis *three times*
132. ranys *ranting*
     harlottree *ribaldry*

115. 'Into the heart so that it is not harmed'.
131. 'Show now the phrases you have already borrowed more than three
     times'.

Schaw now thy dull exhaust inanytee,
Schaw furth thy cure and wryte their frenesyis
Quhilkis of thy sempyll cunnyng nakyt the.   135

My ravyst sprete in that deserte terrybill
Approchit nere that ugly flude horrybill,
Lyk tyll Cochyte the ryver infernall,
Wyth vyle wattyr quhilk maid a hydduus trubbyll
Rynnand overhed, blud red, and – impossybyll   140
That it had byn a ryver naturall –
With brayis bare, raif rochis lyke to fall,
Quhareon na gers nor herbys wer visibyll,
Bot skauppis brynt with blastis boryall.

Thys laythly flude rumland as thondyr routyt   145
In quham the fysche yelland as elvys schoutyt.
Thair yelpis wylde my hering all fordevyt.
Tha grym monsturis my spretis abhorryt and doutyt.
Not throu the soyl bot muskan treis sproutyt,
Combust, barrant, unblomyt and unlevyt;   150

133. exhaust *worn-out*
    inanytee *inanity*
134. cure *diligence*   their
    frenesyis *these frenzies*
135. sempyll cunnyng *simple
    ability*   nakyt the *stripped you*
136. ravyst sprete *entranced spirit*
137. nere *near*   flude *river*
138. lyk tyll *like*   Cochyte *Cocytus*
139. quhilk *which*
    trubbyll *disturbance*
140. rynnand overhed *rushing
    headlong*   blud *blood*
141. byn *been*
142. brayis *banks*   raif *loose*
    rochis *rocks*   lyke *likely*
143. quhareon *upon which*
    gers *grass*   herbys *plants*

144. bot *only*   skauppis *bare rock*
    brynt *parched*   blastis boryall *blasts
    of wind from the north*
145. laythly *loathsome*
    rumland *rumbling*
    thondyr *thunder*   routyt *roared*
146. quham *which*   fysche *fish*
    schoutyt *shouted*
147. hering *hearing*   fordevyt *deafened*
148. tha *those*   spretis *senses*
    abhorryt *abhorred*
    doutyt *dreaded*
149. not *nothing*   soyl *soil*   muskan
    treis *decaying trees*
    sproutyt *grew*
150. combust *scorched*
    barrant *bare*   unblomyt *without
    blossom*   unlevyt *without leaves*

134–5. 'Reveal your diligence and write down these frenzies which have
    stripped you of what simple ability you had'.
145–9. 'This loathsome river roared like rumbling thunder in which the
    fish shouted out like yelling elves. Their wild yelps completely
    deafened me. My senses abhorred and dreaded those grim monsters.
    Nothing grew in that soil except decaying trees'.

Ald rottyn runtis quhairin no sap was levyt
Moch, all wast, widdrit, with granis moutyt:
A ganand den quhair morthurars men revyt.

Quhairfore myselvyn was richt sore agast.
This wyldernes abhomynable and wast,   155
In quhome na thing wes Nature confortand,
Was dyrk as royk the quhilk the see upcast.
The quhislyng wynd blew mony byttir blast,
Runtis ratlit and uneth myght I stand:
Out throu the wode I crap on fut and hand.   160
The ryvar stank, the treis clattryt fast,
The soil was not bot marres, slyik, and sand.

And not but caus my spretis were abaysit
All solitare in that desert arrasyt.
'Allas,' I said, 'is non other remede?   165
Cruel Fortoun, quhy hes thow me betrasyt?
Quhy hes thow thus my fatall end compasyt?
Allas, allas, sall I thus sone be dede
In this desert, and wait non uther rede,
Bot be devoryt wyth sum best ravanus?   170

151. ald *old* runtis *stumps*
  levyt *left*
152. moch *dank* widdrit *withered*
  granis moutyt *seeds fallen off*
153. ganand *fitting*
  morthurars *murderers*
  revyt *robbed*
154. myselvyn *I myself*
  sore *terribly* agast *afraid*
156. confortand *comforting*
157. dyrk *dark* royk *fog* see *sea*
158. quhislyng *whistling*
159. runtis *tree stumps*
  ratlit *shook* uneth *scarcely*
160. wode *wood* crap *crept* on

fut and hand *on all fours*
162. not bot *nothing but*
  marres *marsh* slyik *mud*
163. but caus *without cause*
  abaysit *confused*
164. in *into* arrasyt *snatched away*
165. remede *remedy*
166. Fortoun *Fortune*
  betrasyt *betrayed*
167. fatall *destined*
  compasyt *planned*
168. sone *soon* dede *dead*
169. wait *know* rede *remedy*
170. devoryt *devoured* with *by*
  best *beast*

153. 'A fitting place for murderers to rob people'.
156–7. 'In which Nature comforted no living thing, was as dark as the
  fog that rolls in from the sea'.
165. ' "Alas," I said, "is there no other help for me?" '.
169–70. 'In this deserted place, and know no other end to my troubles
  than to be devoured by some ravenous beast'.

I wepe, I wale, I plene, I cry, I plede:
Inconstant warld and quheil contrarius!

'Thy transitory plesans quhat avaylys?
Now thare, now heir, now hie and now devalys;
Now to, now fro, now law, now magnifyis;   175
Now hote, now cald, now lauchys, now bewalys;
Now seik, now hail, now wery, now not alys;
Now gud, now evyll, now wetis, and now dryis;
Now thow promittis and rycht now thou denyis;
Now wo, now weill, now ferm, now frevilus;   180
Now gam, now gram, now lovys, now defyis:
Inconstant warld and quheil contrarius!

'Ha! quha suld haif affyans in thy blys?
Ha! quha suld haif fyrm esperans in this
Quhilk is, allace, sa freuch and variant?   185
Certis none. Sum hes? No wicht, suythly, yis!
Than hes myself bene gylty? Ya iwys.
Thairfore, allace, sall danger thus me dant?
Quhyddyr is bycum sa sone this duyly hant
And veyr translat in wyntyr furyus?   190
Thus I bewale my faitis repugnant:
Inconstant warld and quheil contrarius!'

171. wepe *weep* wale *wail*
plene *lament* plede *plead*
172. warld *world* quheil
contrarius *perverse wheel*
173. avaylys *use*
174. heir *here* hie *high*
devalys *sinks down*
175. law *low* magnifyis *great*
176. cald *cold* lauchys *laughs*
bewalys *laments*
177. seik *sick* hail *healthy*
wery *tired* not alys *nothing is
wrong*
178. wetis *wet*
179. promittis *promise*
denyis *renegue*

180. ferm *steadfast* frevilus *fickle*
181. gam *play* gram *sorrow*
lovys *flatters* defyis *despises*
183. affyans *confidence*
184. fyrm esperans *firm belief*
185. allace *alas* sa freuch *so frail*
variant *inconstant*
186. certis *certainly* sum *someone*
wicht *creature* suythly *truly*
187. ya iwys *yes indeed*
188. dant *subdue*
189. quhyddyr *why* bycum *come*
duyly hant *gloomy place*
190. veyr *spring* translat in *turned
into*
191. faitis *fate*

173. 'What use are your transitory pleasures?'.
183. 'Ha! who should trust in the good times you bring?'.
189. 'Why has this gloomy place come upon me so soon?'.

Bydand the deid thus in myn extasy,
A dyn I hard approchyng fast me be
Quhilk movit fra the plage septentrionall 195
As heyrd of bestis stampyng with loud cry.
Bot than, God wate, how afferyt wes I
Traistand tyl be stranglyt with bestiall.
Amyd a stok richt prevaly I stall
Quhare lukand out anone I dyd espy 200
Ane lusty rout of bestis rationall –

Of ladyis fair and gudly men arrayit
In constant weid, that weil my spretis payit,
Wyth degest mynd quhairin all wyt aboundyt.
Full sobyrly thair haknais thay assait 205
Eftyr the feitis auld, and not forvayt.
Thair hie prudence schew furth, and nothyng roundit,
With gude effere, quhare at the wod resoundyt.
In stedfast ordour, to vysy onaffrayit
Thay rydyng furth with stabylnes ygroundyt. 210

193. bydand *awaiting* the
deid *death* exstasy *trance*
194. dyn *noise* hard *heard* fast
me by *close beside me*
195. movit *moved* plage
septentrionall *northern region*
196. as *like* heyrd *herd*
bestis *beasts*
197. bot *only* wate *knows*
afferyt *afraid*
198. traistand *expecting*
stranglyt *killed* with bestiall *by beasts*
199. amyd *inside* stok *hollow tree*
prevaly *stealthily* stall *crept*
200. lukand *looking*
anone *suddenly* espy *see*
201. lusty rout *fine company*
202. gudly *handsome*

arrayit *dressed*
203. constant weid *similar clothing* payit *pleased*
204. degest *serious* quhairin *in which* aboundyt *abounded*
205. sobyrly *solemnly*
haknais *saddle-horses* assait *tried out*
206. feitis auld *traditional ways* forvayt *go astray*
207. prudence *wisdom* roundit *whispered*
208. effere *manner* resoundyt *echoed*
209. ordour *order* vysy *look about* onaffrayit *unafraid*
210. stabylnes *thoroughness* ygroundyt *trained*

205–6. 'They solemnly put their horses through their paces in accordance with the old practices, and did not make any mistakes'.
207–8. 'Their words of lofty wisdom were disclosed, and nothing was whispered, in a fine manner, at which the wood echoed'.
210. 'They went riding forth, thoroughly well trained'.

Amyddys quham, borne in ane goldyn chare
Ovyrfret with perle and stonys maist preclare,
That drawin wes by haiknays four, mylk quhyt,
Was set a quene, as lylly swete of sware,
In purpur robe hemmid with gold ilk gare   215
Quhilk jemmyt claspes closyd all parfyte.
A diademe maist pleasandly polyte
Set on the tressys of her gyltyn hare,
And in her hand a sceptre of delyte.

Syne next her, rayed in granyt violate,   220
Twelf damysylles, ilk ane in theyr estate
Quhilkis semyt of hyr consell most secre
And nixt thaym wes a lusty rout, God wate:
Lordis, ladyis, and mony fair prelate,
Baith borne of hie estate and law degre,   225
Furth with thair quene thay al bypassyt me.
Ane esy pase thay rydyng furth the gate
And I abaid alone within the tre.

And as the rout wes passyt one and one
And I remanand in the tre alone,   230

211. quham *whom*   borne *carried*
    chare *chariot*
212. ovyrfret *decorated*
    stonys *jewels*   preclare *brilliant*
213. drawin *pulled*
    haiknays *horses*   mylk quhyt *milk
    white*
214. lylly swete *lily fair*
    sware *neck*
215. purpur *purple*   ilk gare *each
    gore*
216. jemmyt claspes *jewelled
    clasps*   parfyte *perfectly*
217. diademe *crown*
    polyte *polished*
218. gyltyn hare *golden hair*

219. of delyte *delightful*
220. syne *then*   rayed *dressed*
    granyt violate *violet coloured
    robes*
221. damysylles *damsels*
    estate *rank*
222. semyt *seemed*   consell *council*
    secre *intimate*
223. lusty route *fine company*
    wate *knows*
224. prelate *church dignitary*
225. law degre *low rank*
227. esy pase *easy pace*   gate *way*
228. abaid *waited*
229. one and one *one by one*

214–6. 'Sat a queen, with a throat as fair as a lily, in a purple robe on
    which each gore was trimmed with gold, and which was perfectly
    fastened with jewelled clasps'.
221–2. 'Twelve damsels, each arranged according to her rank, who
    seemed to be most intimate members of her council'.
227. 'Unhurriedly, they went riding on their way'.

Out throw the wode come rydand cativis twane,
Ane on ane asse, a wedy about his mone,
The tothir raid ane hiddows hors apone.
I passyt furth and fast at thaym did frane
Quhat men thay wer. Thay answeryt me agane,   235
'Our namys ben Achitefel and Synone
That by our suttell menys feil hes slane.'

'Wait ye,' quod I, 'quhat signifyis yon rout?'
Synon sayd 'Ya!', and gave ane hyddows schout.
'We wrechys bene abject thairfra, iwys.   240
Yone is the Quene of Sapience, but dout,
Lady Minerve, and yone twelf hir about
Ar the prudent Sibillais ful of blys,
Cassandra, eik Delbora and Circis,
The fatale systeris twynand our weirdes out,   245
Judith, Jael, and mony a prophetis

'Quhilkis groundyt ar in fyrm intelligens.
And thair is als in to yone court gone hens
Clerkis divine with problewmys curius
As Salomon the well of sapiens   250
And Arestotyl, fulfyllet of prudens,
Salust, Senek and Titus Livius,

231. come rydand *came riding*
cativis twane *two wretches*
232. ane *one* asse *donkey*
wedy *rope* mone *mane*
233. tothir *other* raid *rode*
hiddows *hideous* apone *upon*
234. passyt furth *came out*
fast *eagerly* frane *ask*
235. agane *in return*
236. namys *names* ben *are*
Achitefel *Ahithophel*
Synone *Sinon*
237. suttell menys *cunning means*
feil *many* slane *slain*
238. wait ye *do you know?*
quod *said* rout *company*
239. schout *shout*
240. abject thairfra *thrown out of
there* iwys *indeed*
241. Sapience *Wisdom* but
dout *without doubt*

242. Minerve *Minerva*
243. Sibillais *Sybils*
244. eik *also* Delbora *Deborah*
Circis *Circe*
245. fatale systeris *fateful sisters*
twynand *spinning*
weirdes *destinies*
246. prophetis *prophetess*
247. groundyt *based* fyrm
intelligens *secure understanding*
248. als *also* hens *hence*
249. divine *of sacred knowledge*
problewmys curius *puzzling
questions*
250. as *such as* Salomon *Solomon*
well *source* sapiens *wisdom*
251. Arestotyl *Aristotle*
fulfyllet *full* prudens *wisdom*
252. Senek *Seneca* Titus
Livius *Livy*

Picthagoras, Porphure, Permenydus,
Melysses with his sawis but defence,
Sidrag, Secundus and Solenyus,   255

'Ptholomeus, Ipocras, Socrates,
Empedocles, Neptennebus, Hermes,
Galien, Averroes and Plato,
Enoth, Lameth, Job and Diogenes,
The eloquent and prudent Ulisses,   260
Wyse Josephus and facund Cicero,
Melchisedech, with othyr mony mo.
Thair viage lyis throwout this wildernes.
To the Palice of Honour all thay go,

'Is situat from hens liggis ten hundyr.   265
Our horsys oft or we be thair wyll fundyr.
Adew, we may no langer heir remane.'
'Or that ye passe,' quod I, 'tell me this wondyr,
How that ye wrechyt cativis thus at undyr
Ar sociat with this court soverane?'   270
Achitefell maid this answer agane:
'Knawis thou not? Haill, erd quake, and thundyr
Ar oft in May, with mony schour of rane.

'Rycht so we bene in tyll this company.
Our wyt aboundit, and usyt wes lewdly.   275
My wysdome ay fulfyllyt my desyre

253. Pichthagoras *Pythagoras*
    Porphure *Porphyry*
    Permenydus *Parmenides*
254. Melysses *Melissus* sawis but
    defence *incontrovertible sayings*
255. Sidrag *Shadrach*
    Solenyus *Solinus*
256. Ptholomeus *Ptolemy*
    Ipocras *Hippocrates*
257. Neptennebus *Nactanabus*
258. Galien *Galen*
259. Enoth *Enoch* Lamet *Lamech*
260. Ulisses *Ulysses*
261. facund *eloquent*
262. Melchisedech *Melchizedek*

mo *more*
263. viage *route* lyis *passes*
265. situat *situated* liggis ten
    hundyr *a thousand leagues*
266. or *before* fundyr *stumble*
267. adew *goodbye*
268. or that *before*
269. cativis *rascals* at undyr *in
    your lowly position*
270. sociat *associated* soverane *royal*
272. erd quake *earthquake*
273. schour *shower* rane *rain*
274. rycht so *in the same way*
275. usyt *used* lewdly *wickedly*
276. ay *always*

266. 'Our horses will often go lame before we get there'.

As thou may in the Bybyl weil aspy,
How Davidis prayer put my counsell by.
I gart his sonne aganys hym conspyre,
The quhilk wes slane. Quhairfore up be the swyre   280
Myself I hangit, frustrat sa fowlily.
This Synon wes a Greik that rasyt fyre

'First in to Troy, as Virgyll dois report.
Sa tratourlyk maid him be draw overwhort
Quhill in he brocht the hors with men of armys   285
Quhairthrow the towne distroit wes at schort.'
Quod I, 'Is this your destany and sort?
Cursit be he that sorowis for your harmys,
For ye bene schrewis baith, be Goddis armys!
Ye will optene nane entres at yone port   290
Bot gif it be throw sorcery or charmys.'

'Ingres tyll have,' quod thay, 'we not presume.
It sufficis us tyl se the Palice blume
And stand on rowme quhare bettyr folk bene charrit.
For tyll remane, adew, we have na tume.   295
This ilk way cummis the courtis, be our dume,

277. Bybyl *Bible* weil aspy *well see*
278. counsell *advice*
279. gart *made* aganys *against*
280. the quhilk *who* quhairfore *for that reason* be *by* swyre *neck*
281. hangit *hanged* frustrat *thwarted* fowlily *badly*
282. Greik *Greek* rasyt *started*
283. Virgyll *Virgil*
284. tratourlyk *treacherously* draw *brought* overwhort *across*
285. men of armys *armed men*
286. quhairthrow *through which* distroit *destroyed*
287. sort *fate*
288. cursit *cursed* harmys *afflictions*
289. schrewis *villains* be Goddis armys *by God's wounds*
290. optene *obtain* entres *entry* port *gate*
291. bot gif *unless*
292. ingres *entrance* presume *expect*
293. sufficis us *is enough for us* blume *flourish*
294. on rowme *at a distance* charrit *turned away*
295. tume *time*
296. ilk *same* cummis *comes* be our dume *by our reckoning*

278. 'How David's prayer caused my advice to be ignored'.
284. 'Who treacherously had himself taken to the other side'.
292. ' "We do not expect," they said, "to gain entrance" '.
294. 'And stand at a distance where better people than us have been turned away'.

Of Diane and Venus that feil hes marryt.'
With that thay raid away as thay war skarryt,
And I agayne, maist lyk ane elrych grume,
Crap in the muskane akyn stok mysharrit.   300

Thus wrechitly I maid my resydence,
Imagynand feil syse for sum defence
In contrar savage bestis maist cruell,
For na remeid bot deid be violence,
Sumtyme, asswagis febill indegence.   305
Thus in a part I reconfort mysell
Bot that so lityll wes I dar nocht tell:
The stychlyng of a mows out of presence
Had bene to me mare ugsum than the hell.

Yit glaid I wes that I with thaym had spokkyn.   310
Had not bene that, certis my hart had brokkyn
For megirnes and pusillamytee.
Remanand thus within the tre al lokkyn,
Dissyrand fast sum signys or sum tokkyn
Of Lady Venus and of hir companee,   315
A hart transformyt ran fast by the tree
With houndis rent, on quham Diane wes wrokkyn.
Tharby I understude that sche wes nee.

297. Diane *Diana* feil *many*
  marryt *harmed*
298. raid *rode* as *as if* skarryt *scared*
299. maist *very* elrych grume *elf-man*
300. crap *crept* muskane *rotten*
  akyn stok *oak-stump*
  mysharrit *decrepit*
302. imagynand *devising* feil
  syse *many ways*
303. in contrar *against*
304. remeid *remedy* bot *except*
  deid *death*
305. asswagis *alleviates*
  indegence *destitution*

306. in a part *somewhat* reconfort
  mysell *console myself*
307. dar *dare*
308. stychlyng *squeaking*
309. ugsum *horrible*
310. glaid *glad*
311. certis *for certain*
312. megirnes *weakness*
  pusillamytee *timidity*
313. lokkyn *enclosed*
314. dissyrand *desiring* signys *signs*
316. fast *close*
317. rent *torn apart*
  wrokkyn *avenged*
318. nee *near*

297. 'Of Diana and Venus who have harmed many'.
304–9. 'For sometimes death by violence is the only remedy which comes
  along for those in a state of feeble destitution. Thus I consoled myself
  somewhat, but in fact it was such little comfort that I scarcely dare
  mention it: the squeaking of some unseen mouse would at that time
  have seemed to me more horrible than hell itself.

Thay had tofore declarit hir cummyng:
Mare perfytly forthy I knew the syng. 320
Wes Action quhilk Diane nakyt watyt
Bathyng in a well and eik hir madynnys yyng.
The goddes wes commovyt at this thing
And hym in forme hes of a hart translatit.
I saw, allace, his houndis at him slatit. 325
Bakwert he blent to gyf thaym knawlegyng
Tha raif thair lord, mysknew hym at thaym batit.

Syne ladyis come with lusty giltyn tressys,
In habit wild maist lyke till fostaressys,
Amyddys quham heich on ane eliphant 330
In syng that sche in chastite incressys
Raid Diane that ladyis hartis dressys
Tyl be stabil and na way inconstant.
God wait that nane of thaym is variant:
All chast and trew virginite professys. 335
I not, bot few I saw with Diane hant.

319. tofore *before*
320. forthy *therefore*   syng *sign*
321. Action *Actaeon*
   watyt *watched*
322. eik *also*   madynnys
   yyng *young maidens*
323. commovyt *incensed*
324. translatit *transformed*
325. at him slatit *set upon him*
326. bakwert *backwards*
   blent *glanced*
327. tha raif *they tore to pieces*
   mysknew *did not know*   batit *fed*
328. syne *then*   lusty *beautiful*

giltyn tressys *golden hair*
329. habit wild *outdoor clothes*
   fostaressys *women foresters*
330. amyddys *amidst*   heich *high*
331. in syng *as a sign*   in chastite
   incressys *grows in chastity*
332. raid *rode*   hartis *hearts*
   dressys *prepares*
333. stabil *faithful*
334. wait *knows*   nane *none*
   variant *fickle*
335. chast *chaste*
336. not *do not know*
   hant *accompany*

321. 'It was Actaeon who watched Diana while she was naked'.
324. 'And transformed him into a hart'.
326–7. 'He glanced behind him to let them know that they were tearing
their lord to pieces, but they did not recognise the one who had fed
them'.
332–3. 'Rode Diana who prepares the hearts of ladies to be faithful and
not at all inconstant'.
335–6. 'All profess chastity and true virginity. I don't know about that,
but I saw very few women with Diana'.

Intil that court I saw anone present
Jeptyis douchtir, a lusty lady gent
Offeryt tyl God in hir virginite.
Pollixena, iwys, wes not absent;　　　　　　340
Panthessile with mannys hardyment,
Effygyn and Virgenius douchter fre,
With uthyr flouris of feminyte,
Baith of the New and the Ald Testament,
All on thay raid and left me in the tre.　　　　　345

In that desert dispers in sondyr skattryt
Wer bewis bare quham rane and wynde on battryt.
The water stank, the feild was odious
Quhar dragonys, lessertis, askis, edders swattryt
With mouthis gapand, forkyt tayles tattryt,　　　　350
With mony a stang and spoutis vennomous
Corruppyng ayr be rewme contagious.
Maist gros and vyle enposonyt clowdis clatteryt,
Rekand lyk hellys smoke sulfuryus.

My dasyt hed fordullit dissyly　　　　　　355
I rasyt up, half in a letergy,
As dois a catyve ydronken in slepe

337. intil *in*　anone *soon*
338. Jeptyis douchtir *Jephthah's daughter*　gent *noble*
339. offeryt *offered*
340. Pollixena *Polixena*
341. Panthessile *Penthesileia*
mannys hardyment *manly courage*
342. Effygyn *Iphigenia*
Virgenius *Virginius'*　fre *noble*
343. uthyr *other*　flouris *flowers*
346. dispers *dispersed*
skattryt *scattered*
347. bewis *branches*
quham *which*　rane *rain* on
battryt *battered*
348. feild *land*
349. lessertis *lizards*　askis *asps*
edders *adders*　swattryt *wallowed*

350. gapand *gaping*　forkyt
tayles *forked tails*
tattryt *tattered*
351. stang *sting*　spoutis *squirt*
352. corruppyng ayr *contaminating the air*　rewme
contagious *noxious vapour*
353. gros *large*
enposonyt *poisoned*
clatteryt *rattled*
354. rekand *reeking*
sulfuryus *sulphurous*
355. dasyt hed *dazed head*
fordullit dissyly *made dizzily stupid*
356. rasyt *raised*　letergy *lethargy*
357. catyve *wretch*
ydronken *drunken*

353–4. 'Very large and vile clouds full of poison clattered past, reeking like sulphurous smoke from hell'.
357. 'As a drunken wretch does from his sleep'.

And so opperyt tyl my fantasy
A schynand lycht out of the northest sky.
Proportion sounding dulcest hard I pepe   360
The quhilk with cure till heir I did tak kepe.
In musyk nowmer full of harmony
Distant on far wes caryit be the depe.

Farther by wattyr folk may soundis here
Than by the erth, the quhilk with poris sere   365
Up drynkis ayr that movit is by sound
Quhilk in compact wattir of ane rivere
May nocht entre bot rynnys thare and here
Quhil it at last be caryit on the ground;
And thocht throw dyn, be experience is found,   370
The fysch ar causyt within the rivere stere,
Inoth the wattyr the nois dois not abound.

Violent dyn the ayr brekkis and deris,
Syne gret motion of ayr the watyr steris.
The wattyr steryt, fischis for ferdnes fleis.   375
Bot, out of dout, no fysch in wattyr heris
For, as we se, rycht few of thaym has eris;
And eik, forsuyth, bot gyf wyse clerkis leis,

358. opperyt *appeared*
     fantasy *mind*
359. schynand lycht *shining light*
360. proportion *measure*
     dulcest *sweetest* hard *heard*
     pepe *peep*
361. cure *attentiveness* kepe *care*
362. nowmer *number*
363. caryit *carried* depe *deep*
364. here *hear*
365. poris sere *many pores*
368. entre *enter* rynnys *runs*

369. quhil *until*
370. thocht *although* dyn *noise*
371. stere *to move*
372. inoth *within*
373. brekkis *breaks* deris *disturbs*
374. steris *stirs up*
375. ferdnes *fear* fleis *move away*
376. heris *hears*
377. rycht *very* eris *ears*
378. forsuyth *indeed* bot
     gyf *unless* leis *lie*

360–3. 'I heard the sweetest sounding measure go "peep", to which I took care to listen with attentiveness. A number full of harmony in music was carried by the deep water from afar'.

369–72. 'Until it is at last carried to dry land; and although, as observation has taught us, it is noise which causes the fish to move in the water, there is no noise within the water itself'.

373–5. 'Violent noise breaks and disturbs the air; then the great motion of air stirs up the water; the water is stirred up, and the fishes move away in fear'.

Thair is nane ayr inoth watters nor seis,
But quhilk na thing may heir, as wyse men leiris,   380
Lyik as but lycht thair is na thyng that seis.

Anewch of this, I not quhat it may mene.
I wyll returne till declare all bedene
My dreidfull dreme with grysly fantasyis.
I schew tofore quhat I had hard and sene,   385
Perticularly sum of my paynfull tene.
But now God wate quhat ferdnes on me lyis!
Lang ere I said – and now this tyme is twyis –
A sound I hard, of angellys as it had bene,
With armony fordynnand all the skyis   390

So dulce, so swete and so melodius
That every wycht thair with mycht be joyous
Bot I and cativis dullit in dispare.
For quhen a man is wreth or furius,
Malancolyk for wo or tedius,   395
Than is al plesance till hym maist contrare
And semblably than so did wyth me fare:
This melody intonyt hevinly thus
For profund wo constrenyt me mak care.

379. nane ayr *no air*   seis *seas*
380. but quhilk *without which*
    leiris *teach*
381. lyik as *just as*   seis *sees*
382. anewch *enough*   not *do not*
    know *mean*   mene *mean*
383. all bedene *straightaway*
385. schew *showed*   tofore *before*
386. tene *trouble*
387. wate *knows*   ferdnes *terror*
388. lang ere *earlier*   twyis *twice*
389. as *as if*
390. armony *harmony*
    fordynnand *resounding through*

391. dulce *pleasing*
392. wycht *creature*
393. bot *except*   dullit *made dull*
    dispare *despair*
394. wreth *angry*
395. malancolyk *melancholy*
    tedius *bored*
396. than *then*   plesance *pleasure*
    contrare *contrary*
397. semblably *similarly*   fare *go*
398. intonyt *sung*
399. constrenyt *constrained*   mak
    care *lament*

381. 'Just as nothing can see without light'.
396–7. 'Then all pleasurable things are at odds with his nature, and so
    things went similarly with me then'.
399. 'Caused me to lament through profound sorrow'.

And murnand thus as ane maist wofull wicht, 400
Of the maist plesand court I had a sycht
In warld adoun sen Adam wes create.
Quhat sang? quhat joy? quhat armony? quhat lycht?
Quhat myrthfull solace, plesance all at ryght?
Quhat fresch bewte? quhat excelland estate? 405
Quhat swete vocis? quhat wordis suggurate?
Quhat fair debatis? quhat lufsum ladyis bricht?
Quhat lusty gallandis did on thair servyce wate?

Quhat gudly pastance and quhat menstraly?
Quhat game thay maid? In faith, not tell can I. 410
Thocht I had profund wit angelicall
The hevinly soundis of thair armony
Has dymmyt so my drery fantasy,
Baith wit and reason, half is lost of all.
Yit as I knaw, als lychtly say I sall: 415
That angellyk and godly company
Tyll se me thocht a thyng celestiall.

Procedand furth wes draw ane chariote
Be cursuris twelf trappit in gren velvote.
Of fyne gold wer juncturis and harnasyngis, 420
The lymnuris wer of byrnyst gold, God wate.

400. murnand *mourning*
maist *most*
401. sycht *sight*
402. adoun *here below* sen *since*
create *created*
403. quhat sang *what song*
404. myrthfull solace *joyful
delight* at ryght *in good order*
405. bewte *beauty*
estate *appearance*
406. vocis *voices* suggurate *sweet*
407. debatis *discussions*
lufsum *lovable*
408. lusty gallandis *handsome
gentlemen* wate *wait*
409. gudly pastance *excellent*

recreation menstraly *minstrelsy*
410. game *amusement*
411. thocht *even if*
413. dymmyt *dimmed*
415. lychtly *readily*
416. godly *fine*
417. tyll se *to see*
418. procedand furth *coming
nearer* draw *pulled*
419. cursuris twelf *twelve war-
horses* trappit *adorned*
velvote *velvet*
420. juncturis *metal links*
harnasyngis *harness*
421. lymnuris *shafts*
byrnyst *burnished*

401–2. 'I caught sight of the most pleasant court to exist in the world
here below since Adam was created'.
415. 'Yet as I remember it, as readily shall I tell it'.

Baith extre and quhelis of gold, I hote.
Of goldyn cord wer lyamys, and the stryngis
Festnyt conjunct in massy goldyn ryngis.
Evyr hamys convenient for sic note   425
And raw silk brechamys ovyr thair halsys hyngis.

The body of the cart of evir bone
With crysolytis and mony pretious stone
Wes all ovirfret in dew proportioun
Lyke sternys in the firmament quhilkis schone.   430
Reperalit wes that godlyk plesand wone,
Tyldyt abone and to the erth adoun
In rychest claith of gold of purpur broun,
But fas nor othyr frenyeis had it none
Save plate of gold anamallyt all fassioun   435

Quhairfra dependant hang thair megyr bellys,
Sum round, sum thraw, in sound the quhilkis excellis.
All wer of gold of Araby maist fyne
Quhilkis with the wynd concordandly so knellys
That to be glad thair sound al wycht compellys.   440
The armony wes so melodius fyne
In mannys voce and instrument divine,
Quhare so thay went, it semyt nothyng ellys
Bot jerarchyes of angellys, ordours nyne.

422. extre *axle-tree*
    quhelis *wheels* hote *dare say*
423. lyamys *reins* stryngis *traces*
424. festnyt conjunct *fastened
    together* massy *solid*
425. evyr hamys *ivory yokes* sic
    note *such work*
426. brechamys *collars*
    halsys *necks* hyngis *hang*
427. evir *ivory*
428. crysolytis *chrysolites*
    pretious *precious*
429. ovirfret *decorated*
    dew *rightful*
430. sternys *stars*
431. reperalit *fitted out* godlyk *fit
    for a god* wone *dwelling*
432. tyldyt *curtained* abone *above*

433. claith *cloth* purpur
    broun *dark purple*
434. fas *tassles* frenyeis *trimmings*
435. save *except*
    anamallyt *enamelled* all
    fassioun *in all kinds of patterns*
436. dependant *hanging down* thair
    megyr bellys *these delicate bells*
437. thraw *twisted*
438. of Araby *from Arabia*
439. concordandly *harmoniously*
    knellys *ring*
440. wycht *creature* compellys *compels*
442. mannys *man's*
443. quhare so *wherever*
    semyt *seemed*
444. jerarchyes *hierarchies*
    ordours *orders*

440. 'That their sound compels every creature to be happy'.

Amyd the chare fulfillyt of plesance,   445
A lady sat, at quhais obeysance
Wes all that rout; and wondyr is till here
Of hir excelland lusty countenance.
Hir hie bewte, quhilk mayst is til avance,
Precellys all, thair may be na compere.   450
For lyk Phebus in hiest of his spere
Hir bewtye schane, castand so gret a glance
All farehed it opprest, baith far and nere.

Scho wes peirles of schap and portrature.
In her had Nature fynesyt hir cure.   455
As for gud havyngis, thair wes nane bot sche;
And hir array wes so fyne and so pure
That quhairof wes hir rob I am not sure,
For nocht bot perle and stonys mycht I se
Of quham the brychtnes of hir hie bewtie   460
For till behald my sycht myght not endure
Mair than the brycht sonne may the bakkis e.

Hir hair as gold or topasis wes hewyt.
Quha hir beheld, hir bewtie ay renewyt.
On heid sche had a crest of dyamantis.   465

445. chare *chariot* fulfillyt of
plesance *abounding with delight*
446. quhais obeysance *whose
command*
447. rout *company* till here *to
hear*
448. excelland lusty *exceedingly
lovely*
449. hie bewte *lofty beauty* til
avance *to be praised*
450. precellys *surpasses*
compere *equal*
451. Phebus *Phoebus* in hiest *at
the zenith* spere *sphere*
452. schane *shone* castand *giving*
glance *flash of light*
453. farehed *beauty*

opprest *overwhelmed* nere *near*
454. peirles *unequalled*
schap *figure* portrature *features*
455. fynesyt *perfected* cure *task*
456. gud havyngis *good manners*
457. array *clothing*
458. quhair of *of what material*
rob *gown*
459. nocht *nothing* perle *pearls*
stonys *precious stones* se *see*
460. quham *which*
461. sycht *sight*
462. bakkis e *eye of the bat*
463. topasis *topazes* hewyt *coloured*
464. quha *whoever* renewit *revived*
465. heid *head* crest of
dyamantis *crown of diamonds*

456. 'As for good manners, no one seemed well-mannered in comparison
to her'.
462. 'Any more than the eye of the bat can endure the bright sun'.
464. 'Whoever beheld her was revived by her beauty'.

Thair wes na wycht that gat a sycht eschewyt;
Wer he nevir sa constant nor weil thewyt,
Na he was woundit and him hir servant grantis.
That hevinly wycht hir cristall eyn so dantis
For blenkis swete nane passit unpersewyt   470
Bot gyf he wer preservit as thir sanctis.

I wondryt sore and in mynd did stare
Quhat creature that mycht be wes so fare,
Of sa peirles excelent womanheid.
And, farlyand thus, I saw within the chare   475
Quhare that a man wes set with lymmes square,
His body weil entalyeit every steid:
He bare a bow with dartis haw as leid;
His clethyng wes als grene as ane hountare
Bot he forsuyth had none eyn in his hed.   480

I understude by signis persavabill
That wes Cupyd the god maist dissavabill,
The lady, Venus, his mother, a goddes.
I knew that wes the court so variabill
Of erdly luf quhilk sendill standis stabill.   485
Bot yit thair myrth and solace nevertheles

466. wycht *creature*
     eschewyt *escaped*
467. weil thewyt *self-disciplined*
468. na *but* grantis *acknowledges*
469. eyn *eyes* dantis *vanquish*
470. blenkis *glances*
     unpersewyt *unassailed*
471. bot gyf *unless*
     preservit *protected* sanctis *saints*
472. wondryt sore *wondered
     greatly* did stare *was amazed*
474. sa peirles *such matchless*
     womanheid *femininity*
475. farlyand *wondering*
476. lymmes square *strong limbs*
477. entalyeit *formed* steid *part*
478. bare *carried* dartis *arrows*
     haw *grey* leid *lead*
479. als *as* hountare *hunter*
480. forsuyth *in truth* none
     eyn *no eyes*
481. signis persavabill *visible signs*
482. Cupyd *Cupid*
     dissavabill *deceitful*
484. variabill *changeable*
485. erdly luf *earthly love*
     sendill *seldom*
486. solace *delight*

466–71. 'No man who caught a glimpse of her escaped; no matter how
     faithful or self-disciplined he was, he was wounded and acknowledged
     himself to be her servant. The crystal eyes of that heavenly creature so
     vanquished everyone that no one could pass unassailed by those sweet
     glances unless he were protected like the saints'.
473. 'What creature this could be who was so fair'.

In musik, tone, and menstraly expres.
So craftely with corage aggreabill,
Hard never wicht sik melody, I ges.

Acumpanyit lusty yonkers with all.   490
Fresche ladyis sang in voce virgineall
Concordes swete, divers entoned reportis.
Proportionis fyne with sound celestiall –
Duplat, triplat diatesseriall,
Sesque altra and decupla resortis,   495
Diapason of mony syndry sortis –
War songin and plait be seir cunnyng menstrall
On luf ballattis with mony fair disportis.

In modulation hard I play and syng
Faburdoun, priksang, discant, conturyng,   500
Cant organe, figuration, and gemmell.
On croud, lute, harp, with mony gudly spryng.
Schalmis, clarionis, portativis hard I ryng,
Monycord, orgain, tympane, and symbell,
Sytholl, psalttry, and vocis swetc as bell,   505

487. tone *pitch*
menstraly *minstrelsy*
expres *expressed*
488. craftely *skilfully* corage
aggreabill *pleasing spirit*
489. hard *heard* sik *such*
ges *suppose*
490. acumpanyit *accompanied*
yonkers *young men*
491. fresche *beautiful* voce
virgineall *maidenly voices*
492. concordes *harmonies*
divers *various* entoned
reportis *sung responses*
493. proportionis *intervals*
494. duplat *double* triplat *triplat*
diatesseriall *with intervals of a
fourth*
495. sesque altra *intervals of a
fifth* decupla resortis *repeats*
496. diapason *octaves*
syndry *different*
497. songin *sung* plait *played*

seir *many a* cunnyng *skilful*
498. on luf ballattis *in love songs*
disportis *amusements*
499. modulation *carefully composed
music*
500. faburdoun *extemporised
harmony* priksang *written song*
discant *melodious accompaniment*
conturyng *singing an
accompaniment*
501. cant organe *polyphony*
figuration *polyphonic variation*
gemmell *two-part harmony*
502. croud *fiddle* gudly
spryng *lively tune*
503. schalmis *reed pipes*
clarionis *trumpets*
portativis *small organs*
504. monycord *clavichord*
orgain *organ* tympane *drum*
505. sytholl *citole*
psalttry *psaltery* vocis *voices*

Soft releschyngis in dulce delyveryng,
Fractyonis divide at rest or clos compell.

Not Pan of Archaid so plesandly plays,
Nor King David, quhais playng, as men sayis,
Conjurit the spreit the quhilk Kyng Saul
         confoundit,   510
Nor Amphion with mony subtile layis
Quhilk Thebes wallit with harpyng in his dayis,
Nor he that first the subtile craftis foundit
Was not in musik half so weil igroundit
Nor knew thair mesure tent dele be no wayes. 515
At thair resort baith hevyn and erd resoundit.

Na mare I understude thir noumeris fyne
Be God than dois a gekgo or a swyne,
Save that me think swete soundis gude to heir.
Na mair heiron my labour will I tyne.   520
Na mair I wyl thir verbillys swete diffyne,
How that thair musik tones war mair cleir
And dulcer than the movyng of the speir
Or Orpheus harp of Trace with sound divyne.
Glaskeryane maid na noyes compeir.   525

506. releschyngis *singing* dulce
 delyveryng *clear enunciation*
507. fractyonis *short notes* divide
 at *divided by* clos
 compell *driven close together*
508. Archaid *Arcadia*
510. conjurit *entranced*
 spreit *spirit*
 confoundit *tormented*
511. subtile layis *skilful songs*
512. quhilk *who* wallit *fortified*
 harpyng *harp playing*
513. craftis *arts* foundit *created*
514. igroundit *accomplished*
515. tent dele *a tenth part* be no
 wayes *in no way*

516. resort *assemblage*
 hevyn *heaven*
517. noumeris fyne *subtle
 harmonies*
518. be *from* gekgo *cuckoo*
 swyne *pig*
519. save *except* gude *good*
520. heiron *on this* tyne *waste*
521. verbillys *singing*
 diffyne *describe*
522. cleir *clear*
523. dulcer *sweeter* speir *sphere*
524. Trace *Thrace*
525. Glaskeryane *Glasgerion*
 noyes *sound* compeir *equal*

510. 'Entranced the evil spirit which tormented King Saul'.
512. 'Who, in his day, fortified Thebes with his harp playing'.
515. 'Nor, indeed, knew a tenth part of what they knew'.
525. 'Glasgerion made no sound equal to them'.

Thay condescend sa weil in ane accord
That by na juynt thair soundis bene discord,
In every key thay werren sa expert.
Of thair array gyf I suld mak record –
Lusty spryngaldis and mony gudly lord,   530
Tendyr yonglyngis with pietuous virgin hart,
Eldar ladyis knew mair of lustis art,
Divers utheris quhilkis me not list remord,
Quhais lakkest weid was silkis ovirbrouderit

In vesturis quent of mony syndry gyse   535
I saw all claith of gold men mycht devyse,
Purpur coulour, punyk and skarlot hewis,
Velvot robbis maid with the grand assyse,
Dames, satyn, begaryit mony wyse,
Cramessy satin, velvot enbroude in divers rewis,   540
Satyn figuris champit with flouris and bewis,
Damesflure, tere pyle quhare on thair lyis
Perle orphany, quhilk every state renewis.

Thare ryche entire, maist peirles to behald,
My wyt can not discrive, howbeit I wald.   545

526. condescend *harmonised*
    ane *one*
527. juynt *point of contact*
    discord *discordant*
528. werren *were*
529. array *appearance*   gyf *if*
530. spryngaldis *young men*
531. yonglyngis *children*
533. utheris *others*   remord *criticise*
534. lakkest weid *poorest garment*
    ovirbrouderit *embroidered*
535. vesturis quent *elegant clothes*
    syndry gyse *different fashions*
536. claith *cloth*
537. purpur *purple* punyk *orange*
    skarlot *scarlet* hewis *shades*
538. robbis *gowns* assyse *design*

539. dames *damask* begaryit mony
    wyse *variagated in many colours*
540. cramessy *crimson*
    enbroude *decorated* rewis *stripes*
541. figuris *embroidery*
    champit *embellished*
    flouris *flowers* bewis *branches*
542. damesflure *flowered damask*
    tere pyle *Spanish velvet* lyis *lies*
543. perle orphany *pearl and gold
    embroidery* state *dignity*
    renewis *bestows again*
544. thare *their* entire *attire*
    peirles *peerless*
545. discrive *describe* howbeit I
    wald *no matter how much I would
    like to*

527. 'That their sound was not discordant at any point at which they
    came together'.
532. 'Older ladies who knew more about the art of desire, with various
    other people whom I do not wish to criticise in any way, whose
    poorest garment was made of embroidered silk'.

Mony entrappit stede with sylkis sere,
Mony pattrell nervyt with gold I tald,
Full mony new gylt harnasyng not ald,
On mony palfray lusum ladyis clere.
And nyxt the chare I saw formest appere,   550
Upon a bardyt cursere stout and bald,
Mars, god of stryf, enarmyt in byrnist gere:

Every invasybill wapyn on hym he bare;
His luke was grym, his body large and square,
His lymmys weil entailyeit til be strang;   555
His nek wes gret, a span lenth weil or mare,
His vissage braid with crisp broun curland hare;
Of statur, not ovyr gret nor yit ovyr lang.
Behaldand Venus, 'O ye my luif,' he sang,
And scho agane with dalyans sa fare   555   560
Hir knycht hym clepis quhare so he ryde or gang.

Thair wes Arsyte and Palemon alswa
Accumpanyit with fare Emylya,
The quene Dido with hir fals luf Enee,
Trew Troylus, unfaythfull Cressida,   565
The fair Paris and plesand Helena,
Constant Lucres and traist Penolype,

546. entrappit stede *horse in fine trappings* sylkis sere *various silks*
547. pattrell *horse's breastplate* nervyt *banded* tald *counted*
548. gylt harnasyng *golden harnesses* ald *old*
549. palfray *saddle-horse* lusum *lovely* clere *fair*
550. formest *in front*
551. bardyt *armoured* cursere *war horse* stout *strong* bald *spirited*
552. stryf *war* enarmyt *armed* byrnist gere *burnished armour*
553. invasybill wapyn *offensive weapon*
554. luke *demeanour*
555. lymmys *limbs* entailyeit *formed* strang *strong*

556. span *hand's breadth*
557. vissage *face* braid *wide* curland hare *curly hair*
558. statur *build* ovyr gret *too large* lang *tall*
559. behaldand *watching* luif *love*
560. agane *in return* dalyans *flirtatiousness*
561. clepis *calls* gang *go*
562. Arsyte *Arcite* alswa *also*
563. accumpanyit with *accompanied by* Emylya *Emily*
564. Enee *Aeneas*
565. trew Troylus *faithful Troilus*
566. plesand *pleasing*
567. constant Lucres *faithful Lucrece* traist Penolype *loyal Penelope*

556. 'His neck was thick, easily a hand's breadth or more'.
561. 'Calls him her knight, no matter where he goes'.

Kynd Pirramus and wobegone Thysbe,
Dolorus Progne, triest Philomena,
King Davidis luif thare saw I, Barsabe.   570

Thare wes Ceix with the kynd Alcyon,
And Achilles, wroth with Agamemnon
For Bryssida his lady fra hym tane,
Wofull Phillys with hir luf Demoophan,
Subtel Medea and hir knycht Jasone.   575
Of France I saw thair Paris and Veane.
Thare wes Phedra, Thesyus and Adriane,
The secrete, wyse, hardy Ipomedon,
Asswere, Hester, irraprevabill Susane.

Thare was the fals unhappy Dalida,   580
Cruel wikkyt and curst Dyonera,
Wareit Bibles and the fair Absolon,
Ysyphele, abhomynabil Sylla,
Trastram, Yside, Helcana and Anna,
Cleopatra and worthy Mark Anthon,   585
Iole, Hercules, Alcest, Ixion,
The onely pacient wyfe Gressillida,
Nersissus, that his hed brak on a ston.
Thare wes Jacob with fair Rachel his make,

568. kynd Pirramus *loving*
     Pyramus Thysbe *Thisbe*
569. dolorus Progne *sorrowful*
     Procne triest *sad*
570. Barsabe *Bathsheba*
571. Alcyon *Alcyone*
572. wroth *angry*
573. Bryssida *Briseis* tane *taken*
574. Phillys *Phyllis*
     Demoophan *Demophoon*
575. subtel *artful* Jasone *Jason*
576. Veane *Vienne*
577. Phedra *Phaedra*
     Thesyus *Theseus*
     Adriane *Ariadne*
578. secrete *disguised* hardy *brave*
579. Asswere *Ahasuerus*
     Hester *Esther* irraprevabill

Susane *blameless Susana*
580. unhappy Dalida *unfortunate*
     Delilah
581. curst *cursed*
     Dyonera *Deianira*
582. wareit Bibles *accursed Byblis*
583. Ysyphele *Hypsipyle*
     Sylla *Scylla*
584. Trastram *Tristram*
     Yside *Iseult* Helcana *Elkanah*
     Anna *Hannah*
585. Mark Anthon *Mark Anthony*
586. Alcest *Alcestis*
587. Gressillida *Griselda*
588. Nersissus *Narcissus*
     brak *broke open*
589. make *wife*

The quhilk become til Laban for hir sake   590
Fourtene yere boynd with fyrm hart immutabill –
Thair bene bot few sic now, I undertake:
Thir fair ladyis in silk and claith of lake
Thus lang sall not all foundyn be so stabyll.
This Venus court quhilk wes in luif maist abil   595
For till discrive my cunning is to wake.
A multitude thay wer, innumerabill,

Of gudly folk in every kynd and age.
With blenkis swete, fresch lusty grene curage,
And dalians they rydyng furth in fere.   600
Sum leivys in hope and sum in great thyrlage,
Sum in dispare, sum findis his panys swage.
Garlandis of flouris and rois chaplettis sere
Thay bare on hede and samyn sang so clere
Quhil that thair myrth commovit my curage   605
Till syng this lay quhilk folowand ye may here:

'Constrenyt hart, bylappit in distres,
Groundit in wo and full of hevynes
Complene thy paynfull caris infinyte,
Bewale this warldis frele unstedfastnes   610
Havand regrait sen gone is thy glaidnes

590. the quhilk *who*
591. boynd *bound*
  immutabill *unchangeable*
592. bene *are* sic *such*
  undertake *declare*
593. thir *these* lake *fine linen*
594. thus lang *for this long*
  foundyn be *be found*
  stabyll *loyal*
595. maist abil *most adept*
596. discrive *describe*
  cunning *skill* wake *weak*
599. blenkis *glances* grene
  curage *flourishing vigour*
600. dalians *flirtatiously*
  rydyng *went riding* in
  fere *together*
601. leivys *live* thyrlage *servitude*

602. dispare *despair* panys
  swage *pains grow less*
603. rois chaplettis *wreaths of
  roses* sere *many*
604. bare *wore* samyn *together*
605. quhil that *until* myrth *joy*
  commovit *stirred* curage *desire*
606. lay *song* folowand *following*
  here *hear*
607. constrenyt hart *imprisoned
  heart* bylappit *wrapped*
608. groundit *entrenched*
  hevynes *sorrow*
609. complene *bemoan* caris *cares*
610. warldis *world's* frele *frail*
611. havand regrait *having regret*
  sen *since* glaidnes *happiness*

590–1. 'Who, for her sake, became bound to Laban for fourteen years
with a firm, unchangeable heart'.

And all thy solace returnyt in dispyte.
O cative thrall involupit in syte,
Confesse thy fatale wofull wrechitnes,
Divide in twane and furth diffound all tyte,   615
Aggrevance gret in miserabill endyte.

'My crewell fait, subjectit to penance
Predestinat, sa void of all plesance,
Has every greif amyd myn hart ingrave.
The slyd inconstant destany or chance   620
Unequaly doith hyng in thair ballance
My demeritis and gret dolour I have.
This purgatory redowblys all the lave.
Ilk wycht has sum weilfare at obeysance
Save me, bysnyng, that may na grace ressave.   625
Dede, the addresse and do me to my grave.

'Wo worth sik strang mysforton anoyus
Quhilk has opprest my spretis maist joyus!
Wo worth this worldis freuch felicite!
Wo worth my fervent diseis dolorus!   630
Wo worth the wycht that is not pietuus

612. solace *pleasure* returnyt
in *turned into* dispyte *distress*
613. cative thrall *wretched slave*
involupit in *enveloped in*
syte *sorrow*
614. fatale *fated*
wrechitnes *wretchedness*
615. twane *two* furth
diffound *pour out* tyte *at once*
616. aggrevance *distress* miserabill
endyte *poetry of misery*
617. fait *fate* subjectit *subjected*
penance *suffering*
618. predestinat *predestined*
void *empty*
619. greif *grief* amyd *upon*
ingrave *engraved*
620. slyd *slippery*
621. hyng *hang* ballance *scales*

622. demeritis *worthiness to be
punished or rewarded*
623. redowblys *redoubles* lave *rest*
624. ilk wycht *every creature*
weilfare *happiness*
obeysance *[their] command*
625. save *except* bysnyng *monster*
grace *mercy* ressave *receive*
626. Dede *Death* the
addresse *prepare yourself* do
me *take me*
627. wo worth *a curse upon*
sik *such* strang *terrible*
mysforton *misfortune*
anoyus *troublesome*
628. spretis *spirit* joyus *joyful*
629. freuch felicite *frail happiness*
630. fervent *burning* diseis *distress*
631. pietuus *merciful*

617–9. 'My cruel fate, subjected to every predestined suffering, so empty
of all pleasure, has engraved every grief upon my heart'.

Quhare the trespassor penitent thay se!
Wo worth this dede that dayly dois me de!
Wo worth Cupid and wo worth fals Venus,
Wo worth thaym bayth, ay waryit mot thay be!   635
Wo worth thair court, and cursit destane!'

Loude as I mocht in dolour al distrenyeit
This lay I sayng and not a lettir fenyeit.
Tho saw I Venus on hir lyp did byte
And all the court in hast thair horsys renyeit   640
Proclamand loude, 'Quhare is yone poid that plenyeit
Quhilk deth diservis committand sik dispite?'
Fra tre to tre thay serchyng but respyte
Quhill ane me fand, quhilk said in greif disdenyeit,
'Avant, velane, thou reclus imperfyte!'   645

All in ane fevyr out of my muskan bowr
On knees I crap and law for feare did lowr.
Than all the court on me thayr hedis schuke,
Sum glowmand grym, sum grinand with vissage sowr.
Sum in the nek gave me feil dyntis dour.   650
'Pluk at the craw,' thay cryit, 'deplome the ruke!'

633. dede *death* dois me de *kills me*
635. bayth *both* ay waryit *forever accursed* mot *may*
637. mocht *could* al distrenyeit *entirely gripped*
638. fenyeit *make up*
639. tho *then* byte *bite*
640. hast *haste* renyeit *reigned in*
641. proclamand *proclaiming* quhare *where* poid *toad* plenyeit *complained*
642. quhilk *who* diservis *deserves* dispite *crime*
643. tre *tree* serchyng *went searching* but respyte *without rest*
644. quhill *until* ane *one* fand *found* greif

disdenyeit *disdainful anger*
645. avant *come out* velane *villain* reclus imperfyte *faulty recluse*
646. fevyr *sweat* muskan bowr *rotten bower*
647. crap *crept* law *low* lowr *grovel*
648. on *at* hedis *heads* schuke *shook*
649. glowmand grym *scowling grimly* grinand *snarling* vissage sowr *sour face*
650. feil *many* dyntis dour *heavy blows*
651. craw *crow* cryit *cried* deplome the ruke *pull out the rook's feathers*

632. 'Where they see that the sinner is penitent'.
638. 'I sang this song and did not make up a single letter'.
642. 'Who deserves death for committing such a crime'.

Pulland my hare, with blek my face they bruke.
Skrymmory Fery gaif me mony a clowr.
For Chyppynuty full oft my chaftis quuke.

With payne, torment thus in thayr teynfull play,   655
Till Venus, bund, they led me furth the way
Quhilk than wes set amyd a golden chare,
And so confoundit into that fell affray
As that I micht consydyr thair array.
Me thocht the feild, ovirspred with carpetis fare,   660
Quhilk wes tofore brint, barrant, vile and bare,
Wox maist plesand, bot all, the suyth to say,
Micht not amese my grevous pane full sare.

Entronit sat Mars, Cupyd and Vcnus.
Tho rais a clerk wes clepit Varius   665
Me tyl accusyng of a dedly cryme
And he begouth and red a dittay thus:
'Thou wikkyt catyve, wod and furious,
Presumptuusly now at this present tyme
My lady here blasphemed in thy ryme.   670
Hir sonne, hirself and hir court amorus
For till betrais awatit here sen prime.'

652. hare *hair*   blek *blacking*
    bruke *make dirty*
653. Skrymmory Fery *Scary*
    Fairy   clowr *bump on the head*
654. for *because of*
    Chyppynuty *Chip-Nut*
    chaftis *jaws*   quuke *rattled*
655. torment *tormented*   teynfull
    play *spiteful game*
656. till *to*   bund *tied up*
657. quhilk *who*   set *seated*
    amyd *upon*   chare *chair*
658. confoundit *confused*   fell
    affray *cruel attack*
659. array *appearance*
660. me thocht *it seemed to me*

ovirspred *covered*
661. tofore *before*   brint *scorched*
    barrant *barren*
662. wox *grew*   suyth *truth*
663. amese *lessen*   grevous *grievous*
664. entronit *enthroned*
665. rais *arose*   wes clepit *who was
    called*
667. begouth *began*   red *read*
    dittay *indictment*
668. wod *mad*   furious *demented*
671. sonne *son*   amorus *of love*
672. betrais *betray*   awatit *waited*
    prime *sunrise*

658–9. 'And so confused in that cruel attack that I could scarcely think
    about their appearance'.
670. 'Blasphemed against my lady here in your rhyme'.
671–2. 'You have lain in wait here since sunrise to betray her son, Venus
    herself and her court of love'.

Now God thow wate, me thocht my fortune fey.
Wyth quakand voce and hart cald as a key
On kneys I knelyt and mercy culd implore,   675
Submyttand me but ony langer pley
Venus mandate and plesour till obey.
Grace wes denyit and my travel forlore
For scho gaif chargis till procede as before.
Than Varius spak rycht stoutly me till fley,   680
Injonand silence tyll ask grace ony more.

He demandit myn answere, quhat I sayd,
Than as I mocht it with curage all mysmaid
Fra tyme I undirstude na mare supple,
Sore abasyt, belive I thus out braid: 685
'Set of thir pointis of cryme now on me laid
I may me quyte giltles in verite,
Yit fyrst, agane the juge quhilk here I se,
This inordenat court and proces quaid
I wyll object for causys twa or thre.'   690

673. wate *know* fey *was doomed*
674. cald *cold*
675. culd implore *implored*
676. submyttand me *submitting myself* but *without* langer pley *longer appeal*
677. mandate *command*
678. grace *mercy* denyit *denied* travel *effort* forlore *wasted*
679. scho *she* chargis *orders*
680. stoutly *firmly* me till fley *to scare me*
681. injonand *imposing*
683. mocht *could* curage *mind*

mysmaid *troubled*
684. fra tyme *once* mare *more* supple *help*
685. sore abasyt *greatly dismayed* belive *at once* braid *burst*
686. set *although* pointis *charges*
687. me quyte *acquit myself* in verite *in truth*
688. agane *against* juge *judge* quhilk *whom*
689. inordenat *irregular* proces quaid *improper proceedings*
690. causys *reasons* twa *two*

677. 'To obey the command and will of Venus'.
681. 'Imposing silence and preventing me from asking again for mercy'.
683–90. 'Then, as best I could with my mind all troubled, once I understood that there would be no further help for me, greatly dismayed, I cried out at once: 'Although I can, in truth, fully acquit myself of these criminal charges which have been laid against me, yet first, I wish to object to the judge whom I see here, and to this irregular court and these improper proceedings, on two or three counts'.

Inclynand law, quod I with pietuus face,
'I me defend, madame, plesyt your grace.'
'Say on,' quod sche, than said I thus but mare:
'Madame, ye may not syt in till this cace
For ladyis may be jugis in na place.   695
And, mare attour, I am na seculare,
A spirituall man, thocht I be void of lare,
Clepyt I am, and aucht my lyvys space
To be remyt till my juge ordinare.

'I yow beseik, madame with byssy cure,   700
Till gyf ane gracius interlocuture
On thir exceptionys now proponyt late.'
Than suddanly Venus, I yow assure,
Deliverit sone and with a voce so sture
Answeryt thus: 'Thow subtyle smy, God wait!   705
Quhat wenys thou? Till degraid myne hie estate,
Me till declyne as juge, curst creature?
It beis not so. The game gois othir gate.

'As we the fynd, thow sall thoill jugement.
Not of a clerk we se the represent   710
Save onely falsshed and dissaitfull talys.
Fyrst quhen thow come, with hart and hail entent
Thow the submyttit till my commaundement.

691. inclynand law *bowing low*
quod *said* pietuus *sorrowful*
692. I me defend *I shall defend
myself* plesyt *if it please*
693. but mare *without delay*
694. syt in till *preside over*
cacc *case*
696. mare attour *in addition*
seculare *layman*
697. thocht *although* void of
lare *without learning*
698. clepyt *called* aucht *ought*
my lyvys space *during my life*
699. remyt *handed over*
ordinare *proper*
700. beseik *beseech* byssy
cure *utmost respect*
701. gyf *give* gracius *favourable*
interlocuture *interim judgement*
702. exceptionys *defences*

proponyt late *lately put forward*
704. deliverit *delivered [her
judgement]* sone *at once*
voce *voice* sture *stern*
705. thow subtyle smy *you are a
cunning wretch* wait *knows*
706. wenys *intend*
degraid *degrade* estate *rank*
707. declyne *refuse* curst *cursed*
708. beis not *shall not be* othir
gate *another way*
709. the fynd *find you* thoill *suffer*
710. not *nothing*
711. save *except*
falsshed *falsehood* dissaitfull
talys *deceitful tales*
712. come *came* hail entent *whole
intention*
713. the submyttit *submitted
yourself*

Now, now, thairof me think to sone thow falys!
I weyn nathyng bot foly that the alys: 715
Ye clerkis bene in subtyle wordis quent
And in the deid als scharpe as ony snalys.

'Ye bene the men bewrays my commandis.
Ye bene the men distrublys my servandis.
Ye bene the men with wikkyt wordis fele   720
Quhilk blasphemys fresch, lusty, yong gallandis
That in my servyce and retenew standis.
Ye bene the men that clepys yow so lele
With fals behest quhill ye your purpose stele,
Syne ye forswere baith body, treuth and handis,   725
Ye bene sa fals. Ye can no word consele!

'Have doyn,' quod sche, 'syr Varius, alswyith
Do writ the sentence. Lat this cative kyith
Gyf our power may demyng his mysdeid.'
Than God thow wait gyf that my spreit wes
                                                blyith!   730
The feverus hew in till my face dyd myith
All my male eys for swa the horribill dreid
Hail me ovyrset I mycht not say my creid.

714. to sone *too soon* falys *give up*
715. weyn *think* the alys *ails you*
716. bene *are* quent *elaborate*
717. deid *deed* scharpe *eager*
    snalys *snails*
718. bewrays *[who] malign*
719. distrublys *[who] molest*
    servandis *servants*
720. wikkyt *wicked* fele *many*
721. lusty *handsome* gallandis *men*
722. retenew *retinue*
723. clepys yow *call yourselves*
    lele *loyal*
724. behest *promise* quhill *until*
    stele *achieve*
725. syne *then* forswere *betray*
    body *person* handis *undertakings*
726. consele *keep secret*
727. doyn *done* alswyith *at once*
728. do writ *record* lat *let*
    cative *wretch* kyith *see*
729. gyf *whether* demyng *judge*
    mysdeid *crime*
730. spreit *mind* blyith *happy*
731. feverus hew *feverish colour*
    myith *reveal*
732. male eys *discomfort* swa *in
    such way* dreid *fear*
733. hail *completely* me
    ovyrset *overcame me* creid *Creed*

715–7. 'I think there is nothing wrong with you except your own
    stupidity: you clerics are full of clever, elaborate words but are as eager
    as snails when it comes to the deed'.
729. 'Whether or not our power is great enough to pass judgement on
    his crime'.

For feir and wo within my skyn I wryith.
I mycht not pray, forsuyth, thocht I had neid.   735

Yit of my deth I set not half a fle.
For gret effere me thocht na pane to die
But sore I dred me for sum othyr jape:
That Venus suld throw hir subtillyte
In till sum bysnyng best transfigurit me   740
As in a bere, a bair, ane oule, ane ape.
I traistit so for till have bene myschaip
That oft I wald my hand behald to se
Gyf it alteryt, and oft my vissage grape.

Tho I revolvit in my mynd anone   745
Quhow that Diane transformyt Acteone
And Juno eik as for a kow gert kepe
The fare Io that lang wes wo begone:
Argos hir yymmyt that eyn had mony one
Quhom at the last Mercurius gert slepe   750
And hir delyverit of that danger depc.
I remembrit also quhow in a stone
The wyfe of Loth ichangit sore did wepe.

I umbethocht quhow Jove and ald Saturn
In tyll a wolf thay did Lycaon turn   755

734. feir *fear* wryith *squirmed*
735. forsuyth *in truth*
    thocht *although* neid *need*
736. set *cared* fle *flea*
737. gret effere *great fear* me
    thocht *it seemed to me* na
    pane *no pain*
738. dred me for *was in dread of*
    jape *trick*
739. subtillyte *devious skill*
740. bysnyng best *monstrous beast*
    transfigurit *transform*
741. as *such as* in *into* bere *bear*
    bair *boar* oule *owl*
742. traistit *expected*
    myschaip *deformed*
743. behald *examine*

744. alteryt *changed* vissage *face*
    grape *touched*
745. tho *then* revolvit *considered*
    anone *at once*
746. quhow *how*
747. eik *also* kow *cow* gert
    kepe *had guarded*
748. lang *for a long time*
749. yymmyt *guarded* eyn *eyes*
750. Mercurius *Mercury* gert
    slepe *caused to fall asleep*
751. delyverit *rescued*
753. Loth *Lot*
    ichangit *transformed* wepe *weep*
754. umbethocht *considered*
    ald *old*
755. in tyll *into*

747–8. 'And also how Juno had fair Io guarded as a cow, who was
miserable for so long'.

And quhow the mychty Nabugodonosore
In bestly forme did on the feild sudjourn
And for his gilt wes maid to wepe and murn.
Thir feirfull wondris gart me dreid ful sore
For by exemplys oft I herd tofore   760
He suld bewar that seys his fallow spurn:
Myschans of ane suld be ane otheris lore.

And rolland thus in divers fantasyis,
Terribil thochtis oft my hert did gryis
For all remeid wes alterit in dispare.   765
Thare wes na hope of mercy till devyis.
Thare wes na wycht my frend be na kyn wyis.
Alhalely the court wes me contrare.
Than wes all maist wryttyn the sentence sare.
My febyll mynd, seand this gret suppris,   770
Wes than of wit and every blys full bare.

THE SECONDE PARTE

Lo, thus amyd this hard perplexite
Awaytand ever quhat moment I suld de
Or than sum new transfiguration,
He quhilk that is eternall verite,   775
The glorious Lord ryngand in personis thre,
Providit has for my salvation

756. mychty *mighty*
Nabugodonosore
Nebuchadnezzar
757. sudjourn *dwell*
758. gilt *guilt* murn *mourn*
759. wondris *wonders* gart me
dreid *made me worry*
760. tofore *before*
761. bewar *beware* seys *sees*
fallow *companion* spurn *stumble*
762. myschans *misfortune*
ane *one* lore *instruction*
763. rolland *thinking*
divers *various* fantasyis *notions*
764. gryis *frighten*
765. remeid *help* alterit in *turned
into* dispare *despair*

766. devyis *obtain*
767. wycht *creature* na kyn
wyis *no means*
768. alhalely *entirely* me
contrare *against me*
769. all maist *almost* sare *terrible*
770. febyll *feeble* seand *expecting*
suppris *shock*
771. wit *sense* blys *joy* bare *bereft*
772. hard perplexite *intense
bewilderment*
773. awaytand *anticipating* de *die*
774. or than *or else*
775. quhilk that *who* verite *truth*
776. ryngand *reigning* personis
thre *three persons*

766–7. 'There was no hope of obtaining mercy. No creature was my
friend by any means'.

Be sum gude spretis revelation
Quhilk intercessioun maid, I traist, for me.
I foryet all imagination.   780

All hail my dreid I tho foryet in hy
And all my wo, bot yit I wyst not quhy,
Save that I had sum hope till be relevyt.
I rasyt than my vissage hastely
And with a blenk anone I did espy   785
A lusty sycht quhilk nocht my hart engrevit,
Ane hevinly rout out throw the wod eschevyt
Of quhame the bonty, gyf I not deny,
Uneth may be intill ane scripture brevit.

With lawrere crownyt in robbis syd all new,   790
Of a fassoun and all of stedfast hew,
Arrayit weil, a court I saw cum nere
Of wyse degest eloquent fathers trew
And plesand ladyis quhilkis fresch bewtie schew,
Syngand softly full swete on thair manere   795
On poete wyse all divers versis sere,

778. be *by*   spretis *spirit's*
779. quhilk intercessioun
    maid *who interceded*
    traist *believe* for me *on my
    behalf*
780. foryct *forgot*
    imagination *fanciful thoughts*
781. all hail *entirely* tho *then*
    foryet in hy *quickly forgot*
782. wyst *knew* quhy *why*
783. save *except* relevyt *rescued*
784. rasyt *lifted* vissage *face*
785. blenk *glance* anone *at once*
    espy *see*
786. lusty sycht *beautiful sight*
    nocht . . . engrevit *did not grieve*
787. rout *company* wod *wood*
    eschevyt *emerged*
788. bonty *excellence* gyf *if*

deny *contradict*
789. uneth *scarcely* scripture *text*
    brevit *recorded*
790. lawrere *laurel*
    crownyt *crowned* robbis
    syd *flowing robes*
791. a fassoun *one style* stedfast
    hew *unvarying colour*
792. arrayit weil *well dressed*
    nere *near*
793. degest *solemn*
    eloquent *honourable* fathers *old
    men*
794. quhilkis *whose* schew *could
    be seen*
795. syngand *singing* on *in*
    manere *manner*
796. on poete wyse *like a poet*
    versis *verses* sere *many*

788–9. 'Whose excellence, if it is not a contradiction to say so, can
scarcely be written down in any text'.

Historyis gret in Latyne toung and Grew
With fresche endyt and soundis gude till here.

And sum of thaym *ad lyram* playit and sang
So plesand vers quhill all the rochys rang,   800
Metyr Saphik and also elygee.
Thair instrumentis all maist wer fydlys lang
Bot with a string quhilk nevyr ane wreist yeid wrang.
Sum had ane harpe and sum a fair psaltree;
On lutis sum thair accentis subtelle   805
Devydyt weil and held the mesure lang
In soundis swete of plesand melodie.

The ladyis sang in vocis dulcorate
Facund epistillis quhilkis quhilum Ovid wrate
As Phillys Quene send till Duke Demophon   810
And of Pennolepe the gret regrate
Send till hir lord, sche dowtyng his estate,
That he at Troy suld losyt be or tone.
Quhow Acontus till Cedippa anone
Wrate his complaint thair hard I weil, God wate,   815
With othir lusty myssyvis mony one.

797. historyis gret *great narratives* Grew *Greek*
798. fresche endyt *new composition* till here *to hear*
799. thaym *them* ad lyram *on the lyre*
800. quhill *until* rochys *rocks*
801. metyr Saphik *Sapphic metre* elygee *elegiac*
802. all maist *for the most part* fydlys lang *monochords*
803. wreist *tuning peg* yeid *went*
804. psaltree *psaltery*
805. lutis *lutes* accentis *notes* subtelle *skilfully*
806. devydyt *divided* mesure lang *larger rhythm*
808. vocis dulcorate *sweet voices*

809. facund epistillis *eloquent epistles* quhilkis *which* quhilum *sometime* wrate *wrote*
810. as *such as* Phillys Quene *Queen Phyllis* send till *sent to*
811. Pennolepe *Penelope* regrate *letter of complaint*
812. dowtyng *not knowing* estate *condition*
813. losyt be *be killed* tone *captured*
814. Acontus *Acontius* Cedippa *Cydippe* anone *in haste*
815. wrate *wrote* hard *heard* wate *knows*
816. lusty *beautiful* myssyvis *letters*

803. 'With only one string which never went wrong in tuning'.

I had gret wondir of thair layis sere
Quhilkis in that arte mycht have na way compere
Of castis quent, rethorik colouris fyne
So poete-lyk in subtyle fair manere 820
And elaquent fyrme cadens regulere.
Thair vayage furth contenand rycht as lyne
With sang and play, as sayd is, so dyvine,
Thay fast approchyng to the place well nere
Quhare I wes torment in my gastly pyne. 825

And as the hevynly sort now nomynate
Removyt furth on gudly wyse the gate
Towert the court quhilk wes tofore expremit,
My curage grew, for quhat cause I not wate
Save that I held me payit of thayr estate; 830
And thay wer folk of knawlagis as it semit,
Als in til Venus court full fast thay demit,
Sayand, 'Yone lusty rout wyll stop our mate
Till justefy thys bisning quhilk blasphemit.

'Yone is,' quod they, 'the court rethoricall 835
Of polit termys, sang poeticall
And constand ground of famus historyis swete.
Yone is the facund well celestiall.

817. of *at* layis *songs*
818. na way *in no way*
    compere *an equal*
819. castis quent *eloquent turns of
    phrase* rethorik colouris
    fyne *fine rhetorical embellishments*
821. fyrme *steady* cadens *rhythm*
822. vayage *journey*
    contenand *continuing* rycht as
    lyne *straight as a line*
824. well nere *very near*
825. pyne *pain*
826. sort *company* now
    nomynate *just referred to*
827. removyt furth *proceeded*
    wyse *fashion* gate *way*
828. towert *towards*
    expremit *described*

829. I not wate *I did not know*
830. save *except* held
    me *considered myself* payit
    of *pleased by* estate *dignity*
831. knawlagis *intelligence*
    semit *seemed*
832. als *since* demit *expressed
    opinions*
833. lusty rout *fine company*
    mate *friend*
834. justefy *condemn*
    bisning *monster*
836. polit termys *elegant words*
    sang *song*
837. constand ground *constant
    source* historyis *stories*
838. facund *inspiring eloquence*

833–4. 'Saying, "This fine company will prevent our dear Venus from
condemning this monster who blasphemed." '.
838. 'Yonder is the heavenly well which inspires eloquence'.

Yone is the fontayn and origynall
Quharefra the well of Hylicon dois flete.   840
Yone ar the folkis that comfortes every sprete,
Be fyne delyte and dyte angelicall
Causand gros lede all of maist gudnes glete.

'Yone is the court of plesand stedfastnes.
Yone is the court of constant merynes.   845
Yone is the court of joyus disciplyne
Quhilk causys folk thair purpos till expres
In ornat wyse, provocand with gladnes
All gentyll hartis to thare lare inclyne.
Every famus poet men may devyne   850
Is in yone rout. Lo yondir thair Prynces
Thespis, the mothyr of the Musis nyne,

'And nixt hir syne hir douchter fyrst byget,
Lady Cleo, quhilk craftely dois set
Historiis ald lyk as thay wer present;   855
Euterpe eik, quhilk dayly dois hir det
In dulce blastis of pipis swete but let;
The thyrd systir, Thalia, diligent
In wanton wryt, and cronikillis doith imprent;

839. fontayn *fountain*
    origynall *original source*
840. quharefra *from which*
    flete *flow*
841. sprete *soul*
842. be *through* delyte *delight*
    dyte angelicall *angelic writing*
843. gros lede *barbarous language*
    glete *glitter*
844. plesand *pleasant*
845. merynes *happiness*
847. purpos *intention*
848. ornat wyse *elaborate fashion*
    provocand *inspiring*
849. gentyll *noble* lare *erudition*

inclyne *pay attention*
850. devyne *think of*
851. Prynces *Princess*
852. Musis nyne *nine Muses*
853. syne *then* douchter fyrst
    byget *her eldest daughter*
854. Cleo *Clio* craftely *skilfully*
    set *write*
855. historiis ald *ancient stories*
856. eik *also* det *duty*
857. dulce *gentle* pipis *pipes* but
    let *without cease*
859. wanton wryt *writings about
    love* cronikillis *chronicles*
    imprent *impart*

843. 'Causing our barbarous language to glitter with the greatest
    goodness'.
849. 'All noble hearts to pay attention to their erudition'.
855. 'Ancient stories as if they were in the present'.

The ferd endityth, oft with chekis wet,   860
Sare tragedyis, Melphomyne the gent;

'Tarpsychore the fyft with humyll soun
Makis on psaltreis modolatioun;
The sext, Erato, lyk thir luffirs wylde
Will syng, play, dans and leip baith up and doune;   865
Polimnya, the sevynt Muse of renoun,
Ditis thir swete rethorik cullouris mylde
Quhilkis ar so plesand baith to man and chylde;
Uranya, the aucht and sistir schene,
Wrytis the hevyn and sternys all bedene;   870

'The nynt, quham till nane othir is compere,
Caliope, that lusty lady clere,
Of quham the bewtye and the worthynes
The vertuys gret schynis baith far and nere,
For sche of nobillis fatis hes the stere   875
Till wryt thair worschyp, victory and prowes
In kyngly style, quhilk dois thair fame encres,
Clepyt in Latyne *heroicus*, but were,
Cheif of al wryt lyk as scho is maistres.

860. ferd *fourth* endityth *writes*
chekis *cheeks*
861. sare *sorrowful*
Melphomyne *Melpomene*
gent *noble*
862. Tarpsychore *Terpsichore*
fyft *fifth* humyll soun *gentle sound*
863. psaltreis *psalteries*
modolatioun *melody*
864. sext *sixth* thir *these* luffirs
wylde *insane lovers*
865. dans *danse* leip *leap*
866. Polimnya *Polyhymnia*
sevynt *seventh*
867. ditis *composes* rethorik
cullouris *devices of rhetoric*
868. chylde *child*

869. Uranya *Urania* aucht *eighth*
schene *fair*
870. sternys *stars* all bedene *all at once*
871. nynt *ninth* compere *equal*
872. clere *fair*
873. of quham the *from whose*
worthynes *excellence*
874. vertuys gret *great power*
schynis *shines* nere *near*
875. nobillis *noble people*
fatis *fates* stere *control*
876. till wryt *to write*
worschyp *honour*
877. encres *increase*
878. clepyt *called* heroicus *epic*
but were *without doubt*
879. wryt *writing* maistres *mistress*

871. 'The ninth, who has no equal'.
875. 'For she has control over the fates of noble people'.
879. 'Greatest of all writing just as she herself is mistress of the Muses'.

'Thir Musis nyne, lo yondir may ye se 880
With fresch nymphis of watir and of see,
And phanee, ladyis of thir templis ald,
Pyerides, dryades, saturee,
Neriedes, Aones, napee,
Of quham the bontyis nedis not be tald.' 885
Thus dempt the court of Venus monyfald
Quhilk speche refreschyt my perplexite,
Rejosand weil my sprete afore wes cald.

The suddand sycht of that fyrme court foresaid
Recomfort weil my hew tofore wes faid. 890
Amyd my brest the joyus heit redoundyt
Behaldand quhow the lusty Musys raid,
And al thair court quhilk wes so blyith and glaid,
Quhois merynes all hevynes confoundyt.
Thair saw I, weil in poetry ygroundyt, 895
The gret Homere, quhilk in Grew langage said
Maist eloquently, in quham all wyt aboundyt.

Thare wes the gret Latyn Virgillyus,
The famus fathir poet Ovidius,
Ditis, Daris, and eik the trew Lucane. 900
Thare wes Plautus, Pogius, Parsius.

880. se *see*
881. fresch *young*
  nymphis *nymphs*   see *sea*
882. phanee *fauns* templis
  ald *ancient temples*
883. Pyerides *Pierides*
  dryades *dryads* saturee *satyrs*
884. Neriedes *Nereids*
  Aones *Aonians* napee *napaeae*
885. bontyis *good qualities*
  nedis *need* tald *told*
886. dempt *mused*
  monyfald *diverse*
887. refreschyt *relieved*
888. sprete *spirits* afore *before*
  cald *cold*
889. sycht *sight*
  foresaid *aforementioned*
890. recomfort *restored*
  hew *colour* faid *pale*

891. heit *heat* redoundyt *flowed
  back*
892. behaldand quhow *watching
  how* raid *rode*
893. blyith *happy*
894. hevynes *sadness*
  confoundyt *overcame*
895. ygroundyt *accomplished*
896. Homere *Homer*
  Grew *Greek* said *spoke*
897. wyt *knowledge*
  aboundyt *abounded*
898. Virgillyus *Virgil*
899. Ovidius *Ovid*
900. Ditis *Dictys Cretensis*
  Daris *Dares Phrygius*
  Lucane *Lucan*
901. Pogius *Poggio Bracciolini*
  Parsius *Persius*

888. 'Making my spirits rejoice which before were cold'.

Thare wes Terens, Donat, and Servius,
Francys Petrark, Flakcus Valeriane.
Thare wes Ysop, Caton, and Alane.
Thare wes Galterus and Boetius.   905
Thare wes also the gret Quintilliane.

Thare wes the satyr poete Juvinale.
Thare wes the mixt and subtell Marciale.
Of Thebes bruyt thare wes the poete Stace.
Thare wes Faustus and Laurence of Vale,   910
Pomponeus quhais fame of late, sans fale,
Is blawin wyd throw every realme and place.
Thare wes the morale wyse poete Orace,
With mony other clerkis of gret avayle.
Thare wes Brunell, Claudyus, and Bocace.   915

So gret a pres of pepill drew us nere
The hunder part thare namys is not here.
Yit thare I saw of Brutus Albion
Goffryd Chaucere, as *A per se*, sance pere
In his vulgare, and morell John Gowere.   920
Lydgat the monk raid musand him allone.

902. Terens *Terence* Donat *Aelius Donatus*
903. Francys Petrark *Frances Petrarch* Flakcus Valeriane *Valerius Flaccus*
904. Ysop *Aesop* Caton *Dionysius Cato* Alane *Alain de Lille*
905. Galterus *Gautier de Chatillon* Boetius *Boethius*
906. Quintilliane *Quintilian*
907. satyr poete *satirist* Juvinale *Juvenal*
908. mixt *versatile* subtell *clever* Marciale *Martial*
909. Thebes bruyt *Theban fame* Stace *Statius*
910. Faustus *Fausto Andrelini* Laurence of Vale *Lorenzo Valla*
911. Pomponeus *Giulio Pomponio Leto* sans fale *without fail*
912. blawin *blown*
913. Orace *Horace*
914. avayle *repute*
915. Brunell *Leonardo Bruni* Claudyus *Claudian* Bocace *Boccaccio*
916. pres *crowd* pepill *people* us nere *near us*
917. hunder *hundredth*
918. of Brutus Albion *from Britain*
919. Goffryd Chaucere *Geoffrey Chaucer* as A per se *like the letter A* sance pere *without equal*
920. vulgare *writing in English* morell *moral* John Gowere *John Gower*
921. Lydgat *Lydgate* raid *rode* musand *thinking* him allone *by himself*

917. 'That not even a hundredth part of their names is recorded here'.

Of this natioun I knew also anone
Gret Kennedy and Dunbar, yit undede,
And Quyntyne with ane huttok on his hede.

Howbeit I couth declare and weil endyte   925
The bonteis of that court, dewlye to wryt
Wer ovir prolyxt, transcendyng myne engyne.
Twychand the proces of my panefull syte:
Belive I saw thir lusty Musys quhyte
With all thair route towart Venus declyne   930
Quhare Cupyd sat with hir in trone divyne,
I standand bundyn in a sory plyte
Byddand thair grace or than the dedly pyne.

Straucht til the quene sammyn thir Musis raid,
Maist eloquently thare salutationys maid.   935
Venus agane yald thaym thair salusyng
Rycht reverently, and on hir fete upbraid,
Besekand thaym to lycht. 'Nay, nay,' thay said,
'We may as here make na langer tariyng.'
Caliope, maist facund and bening,   940
Inquyryt Venus what wicht had hir mismaid
Or wes the cause thair of hir sudjournyng.

922. anone *at once*
923. yit undede *still alive*
924. Quyntyne *Quintin*
    huttok *little hat*
925. howbeit *even though*
    couth *could* endyte *describe*
926. bonteis *excellences*
    dewlye *properly*
927. ovir prolyxt *too lengthy*
    transcendyng *surpassing*
    engyne *powers*
928. twychand *concerning*
    syte *sorrow*
929. belive *at once* quhyte *white*
930. declyne *turn*
931. in trone divyne *on a heavenly throne*
932. standand *standing*
    bundyn *tied up* sory

933. plyte *terrible state*
933. byddand *awaiting*
    grace *mercy* or than *or else*
    pyne *torment*
934. straucht til *straight to*
    sammyn *together*
935. salutationys *greetings*
936. agane yald thaym *returned*
937. upbraid *stood up*
938. besekand *asking*
    lycht *dismount*
939. as here *in this place*
    tariyng *delay*
940. facund *eloquent*
    bening *gracious*
941. inquyryt *asked*
    wicht *creature* hir
    mismaid *upset her*
942. sudjournyng *stay*

925–7. 'Even though I could attempt to declare and describe the
excellences of that court, to write about them properly would be too
lengthy a process, requiring more than my creative powers'.

'Syster,' sayd scho, 'behald that bysnyng schrew.
A subtyle smye – considyr weil his hew –
Standis thair bond,' and bykkynit hir to me.   945
'Yone cative hes blasphemyt me of new
For tyl degraid and do my fame adew;
A laithly ryme dispitefull, subtelle
Compelit hes, rehersand loud on hie
Sclander, dispite, sorow and wallaway   950
To me, my sonne and eike my court for ay.

'He has deservit deth – he sal be dede –
And we remane forsuith in to this stede
Till justefy that rebell renygate.'
Quod Caliope, 'Sister, away all fede.   955
Quhy suld he de? Quhy suld he leis his hede?
To sla him for sa small a cryme, God wate,
Greter degradyng wer to your estate
All out than wes his sclander or sich plede.
Quhow may a fule your hie renoun chakmate?   960

'Quhat of his lak? Your fame so wyd is blaw,
Your excellens maist peirles is so knaw,

943. bysnyng schrew *monstrous rogue*
944. subtyle smye *cunning wretch* hew *colour*
945. bond *tied up* bykkynit hir to *made a sign towards*
946. blasphemyt me *blasphemed against me* of new *lately*
947. degraid *degrade* fame *good name* do . . . adew *destroy*
948. laithly *loathesome* ryme dispitefull *insulting rhyme* subtelle *cunningly*
949. compelit *composed* rehersand *reciting*
950. sclander *slander* dispite *malice* wallaway *misery*
951. sonne *son* eike *also* for ay *forever*

952. dede *dead*
953. remane *linger* forsuith *in truth* in to *in* stede *place*
954. till justefy *to condemn* renygate *renegade*
955. fede *anger*
956. de *die* leis *lose* hede *head*
957. sla *slay* wate *knows*
958. degradyng *degradation* estate *dignity*
959. all out *altogether* sich plede *any such words*
960. quhow may *how can* fule *fool* renoun *reputation* chakmate *checkmate*
961. lak *crime* blaw *blown*
962. peirles *unequalled* knaw *well-known*

947. 'To degrade me and destroy my good name'.
955. 'Calliope said, "Sister, put away your anger" '.
958. 'Would be a greater degradation of your dignity'.

Na wrichis word may depare your hie name.
Gyf me his lyfe and modefy the law
For on my hed he standis now sic aw　　　　965
That he sall eft disserve nevir mare blame.
Not of his dede ye may report but schame.
In recompence of this mysyttand saw
He sall your hest in every part proclame.'

Than Lord quhow glad becam my febil gost!　　　　970
My curage grew, the quhilk afore wes lost,
Seand I had so gret ane advocate
That expertly, but prayer, pryce or cost,
Opteynit had my frewel accion all most
Quhilk wes afore perist and desolate.　　　　975
This quhyil Venus stude, in ane study strate,
Bot fynally scho schew till all the ost
Scho wald do grace and be not obstinate.

'I wyll,' said sche, 'have mercy and pyete,
Do slake my wreth, and lat all rancour be.　　　　980
Quhare is mare vice than till be ovir cruel
And specially in wemen sic as me?
A lady – fy! – that usis tirranne
No woman is, rather a serpent fell.
A vennamus dragon or a devill of hell　　　　985

963. wrichis *wretch's* may
　　depare *can ever injure*
964. gyf *give* modefy *moderate*
965. on my hed *I swear on my life*
　　sic aw *in such fear*
966. eft *afterwards*
　　disserve *deserve*
968. recompence of *compensation
　　for* mysyttand saw *unbecoming
　　speech*
969. hest *law* proclame *proclaim*
970. gost *spirit*
971. the quhilk *which* afore *before*
972. seand *seeing*
973. but prayer *without request*
974. opteynit *won* frewel

accion *trifling legal case*
975. perist *lost* desolate *abandoned*
976. thus quhyil *meanwhile*
　　stude *stood* study strate *state of
　　concentration*
977. schew till *indicated to*
　　ost *company*
978. do grace *show mercy*
979. pyete *pity*
980. do slake *diminish*
　　wreth *anger* lat *let*
981. mare *a greater*
982. sic *such*
983. usis *exerts* tirranne *tyranny*
984. fell *cruel*
985. vennamus *venomous*

967. 'Nothing will come of his death except dishonour'.
984. 'Is not a woman but a cruel serpent?'.

Is na compare to the inequyte
Of bald wemen, as thir wyse clerkis tell.

'Gret God diffend I suld be ane of tho
Quhilk of thare fede and malyce nevir ho.
Out on sik gram! I wyll serve na repreif.   990
Caliope, sistir,' said til Venus tho,
'At your request this wreche sall frely go.
Heir I remyt his trespas, and all greif
Sal be foryet swa he wil say sum breif
Or schort ballat in contrare pane and wo   995
Tuychand my laud and his plesand releif.

'And secundly the nixt resonabil command
Quhilk I him charge: se that he not ganestand.
On thir conditions, sister, at your requeist
He sall go fre.' Quod Caliope inclynand,   1000
'Grant mercy, sister, I oblys by my hand
He sall observe in al poyntis your beheist.'
Than Venus bad do slake sone my arreist,
Belyve I wes releschit of every band,
Uprais the court and all the perlour ceist.   1005

Tho sat I doun lawly upon my kne
At command of prudent Caliope,
Yeildand Venus thankis a thousand sith

986. na *nothing* inequyte *cruelty*
987. bald *arrogant*
988. diffend *forbid* tho *those*
989. fede *hostility* ho *cease*
990. gram *anger* serve *deserve*
  repreif *reproof*
991. tho *then*
993. remyt *pardon*
  trespas *offence* greif *injury*
994. foryet *forgotten*
  swa *providing* say *recite*
995. ballat *poem* in contrare *in
  opposition to*
996. tuychand *concerning* my
  laud *praise of me*
998. him charge *give to him*

se *see* ganestand *resist*
1000. inclynand *bowing*
1001. oblys *promise*
1002. poyntis *aspects*
  beheist *command*
1003. bad *ordered* do slake *be
  loosened* sone *at once*
  arreist *bonds*
1004. belyve *immediately*
  releschit *released* band *chain*
1005. perlour ceist *discussion ceased*
1006. sat I *I set myself*
  lawly *humbly*
1007. prudent *wise*
1008. yeildand *offering* sith *times*

990. 'Away with such anger! I shall deserve no reproof'.
1003. 'Then Venus ordered that I be loosened at once from my bonds'.

For sa hie frendschip and mercyfull piete,
Excelland grace and gret humanyte   1010
The quhilk to me, trespassour, did scho kyth.
'I the forgeve,' quod sche, than wes I blyth.
Doun on a stok I set me suddanlye
At hir command and wrate this lay als swyth:

'Unwemmyt wit, deliverit of dangear,   1015
Maist happely preservit fra the snare,
Releschit fre of servyce and bondage,
Expell dolour, expell diseyses sare,
Avoyd displesour, womentyng and care,
Ressave plesans and do thy sorowe swage,   1020
Behald thy glaid fresche lusty grene curage,
Rejois amyd thir lovers lait and air,
Provyde a place till plant thy tendir age
Quhair thou in joy and plesour may repair.

'Quha is in welth, quha is weill fortunat,   1025
Quha is in peace, dissoverit from debbat,
Quha levys in hop, quha levys in esperance,
Quha standis in grace, quha standis in ferme estat,
Quha is content, rejosyt air and lat,
Or quha is he that fortune doith avance   1030
Bot thow, that is replenyst with plesance?
Thow hes comfort, all weilfare dilligat;

1009. sa *such* hie frendschip *noble
benevolence* piete *pity*
1011. the quhilk *which*
trespassour *sinner* kyth *show*
1012. blyth *happy*
1013. stok *tree-stump*
suddanlye *at once*
1014. wrate *wrote* lay *poem* als
swyth *as quickly as I could*
1015. unwemmyt *unharmed*
deliverit of *rescued from*
1016. happely *fortunately*
1017. releschit fre of *freely released
from*
1018. dolour *sorrow* diseyses
sare *bitter suffering*
1019. womentyng *lamenting*
1020. ressave *take* do *let*
swage *be lessened*

1021. grene curage *youthful vigour*
1022. lait and air *late and early;
continually*
1023. provyde *find* till *to* tendir
age *youthful years*
1024. repair *go*
1025. quha *who*
1026. dissoverit from
debbat *separated from conflict*
1027. levys *lives* hop *hope*
esperance *hopefulness*
1028. ferme estat *assured position*
1029. rejosyt *rejoices*
1030. doith avance *causes to
prosper*
1031. replenyst *filled*
1032. weilfare *well-being*
dilligat *delightful*

Thow hes gladnes; thow hes the happy chance;
Thow hes thy wyll: now be not dissolat.

'Incres in myrthfull consolatioun,   1035
In joyus swete ymaginatioun,
Habond in luif of purifyit amouris
With diligent trew deliberatioun.
Rendir lovyngis for thy salvatioun
Till Venus, and ondir hir gard all houris   1040
Rest at all ease, but sair or sytful schouris.
Abyde in quyet, maist constant weilfare.
Be glaid and lycht now in thy lusty flouris,
Unwemmyt wyt, delyverit of dangare.'

This lay wcs rcd in oppyn audience   1045
Of the Musis, and in Venus presence.
'I stand content: thow art obedient,'
Quod Caliope, my campion and defence.
Venus sayid, eik, it wes sum recompence
For my trespas I wes so penytent,   1050
And with that word all sodanly sche went.
In ane instant scho and hir court wes hence,
Yit still abayd thir Musis on the bent.

1034. dissolat *forlorn*
1035. incres *grow* myrthfull *joyful*
1036. ymaginatioun *thoughts*
1037. habond *abound* luif of *love
for* purifyit amouris *flawless
lovers*
1038. diligent *tireless*
trew *faithful*
deliberatioun *thoughts*
1039. rendir lovyngis *give praise*
1040. till *to* ondir *under*
gard *protection* all houris *at all
times*
1041. but *without* sair *painful*
sytful *sorrowful* schouris *showers*
1042. quyet *tranquil* weilfare *well-
being*

1043. lycht *light hearted* lusty
flouris *fine flower of youth*
1044. unwemmyt *unharmed*
delyverit of *rescued from*
1045. red *read out* oppyn
audience *plain hearing*
1048. quod *said*
campion *champion*
defence *protector*
1049. eik *also*
recompence *compensation*
1050. trespas *offence*
penytent *penitent*
1051. sodanly *suddenly*
1052. hence *gone away*
1053. abayd *lingered* bent *field*

1041-2. 'Rest entirely at your ease, without any painful or sorrowful
showers of grief. Live in a state of tranquil, complete well-being'.

Inclynand than, I sayd, 'Caliope
My protector, my help and my supple,   1055
My soverane lady, my redemptioun,
My mediatour quhen I wes dampnyt to de,
I sall beseik the Godly majeste
Infynyt thankis, laud and benysoun
Yow till acquyte, accordyng your renoun,   1060
It langyth not my possibillite
Till recompence ten part of this gwardoun.

'Glore, honour, laude and reverence condyng
Quha may foryeild yow of so hie a thyng?
And in that part your mercy I implore   1065
Submyttand me my lyftyme induring
Your plesour and mandate till obeysyng.'
'Silence,' said scho, 'I have eneuch heirfore.
I will thow passe and vissy wondris more.'
Than scho me hes betaucht in kepyng   1070
Of a swete nymphe, maist faythfull and decore.

Ane hors I gat, maist rychely besene,
Was harnyst all with wodbynd levis grene.

1054. inclynand *bowing*
1055. supple *support*
1056. redemptioun *saviour*
1057. dampnyt to de *condemned to die*
1058. beseik *pray*
1059. laud *honour*
    benysoun *blessing*
1060. till acquyte *to repay*
    accordyng *as befits*
1061. langyth *belongs*
    possibillite *power*
1062. ten part *a tenth part*
    gwardoun *reward*
1063. glore *glory* laude *praise*
    condyng *worthy*

1064. foryeild yow of *repay you for*
1066. my lyftyme induring *for the length of my life*
1067. mandate *command* till obeysyng *to obey*
1068. eneuch heirfore *enough of this*
1069. I will *I want* passe *proceed* vissy *see*
1070. betaucht *entrusted* kepyng *care*
1071. decore *beautiful*
1072. gat *got* rychely *splendidly* besene *arrayed*
1073. harnyst *harnessed* wodbynd levis *woodbine leaves*

1058-62. 'I shall pray to God in his majesty to repay you with infinite thanks, honour and blessings, as befits your reputation, for it is not within my own power to pay back one tenth of this reward'.
1069. 'I want you to continue on your journey and see more wonders'.
1070. 'Then she entrusted me into the care of a sweet nymph, most trustworthy and beautiful'.

On the same sute the trappuris law doun hang.
Ovir hym I straid at command of the quene,   1075
Tho sammyn furth we rydyng all bedene
Als swyft as thocht with mony a mery sang.
My nymphe alwayis convoyt me of thrang,
Amyd the Musys till se quhat thay wald mene,
Quhilkis sang and playt bot nevir a wrest yeid
                                        wrang.   1080

Throw cuntreis seir, holtis and rochys hie,
Ovir valys, planys, woddis, wally se,
Ovir fludis fare and mony strate montane
We wer caryit in twynklyng of ane e.
Our horssis flaw and raid nocht, as thocht me,   1085
Now out of France tursyt in Tuskane,
Now out of Flandris heich up in Almane,
Now in till Egypt, now in Ytalie,
Now in the realme of Trace and now in Spane.

The montayns we passit of all Garmanie,   1090
Ovir Appenynus devydand Ytalie,
Ovir Ryne, the Pow and Tiber fludis fare,
Ovir Alpheus, by Pyes the ryche citie,
Undir the erth that entres in the see,

1074. sute *colour* trappuris *horse-
cloths* law doun hang *hung down
low*
1075. ovir *upon* straid *mounted*
1076. tho sammyn *then together*
rydyng *rode* all bedene *at once*
1077. als *as* thocht *thought*
1078. convoyt *guided* of
thrang *away from the crowd*
1079. amyd *amongst* till se *to see*
wald mene *intended*
1080. quhilkis *who* wrest *tuning-
peg* yeid wrang *went wrong*
1081. cuntreis seir *many countries*
holtis *forests* rochys *cliffs*
1082. valys *valleys* planys *plains*
woddis *woods* wally se *stormy sea*
1083. fludis fare *fine rivers*

strate *steep*
1084. caryit *carried* e *eye*
1085. flaw *flew* raid nocht *did not
gallop* as thocht me *as it seemed
to me*
1086. tursyt *carried*
Tuskane *Tuscany*
1087. Flandris *Flanders* heich up
in *far up into* Almane *Southern
Germany*
1088. Ytalie *Italy*
1089. Trace *Thrace* Spane *Spain*
1090. Garmanie *Germany*
1091. Appenynus *Appenines*
devydand *dividing*
1092. Ryne *Rhine* Pow *Po*
1093. Pyes *Pisa*

1094. 'That flows underground into the sea'.

Ovir Ron, ovir Sane, ovir France and eik ovir
                                         Lare   1095
And ovir Tagus, the goldin sandyt ryvare.
In Thessaly we passit the Mont Oethe,
And Hercules in sepulture fand there.

Thare went we ovir the ryver Peneyus.
In Secil eik we passyt the Mont Tmolus,   1100
Plenyst with saphron, huny and with wyne;
The twa toppyt famus Pernasus;
In Trais we went out ovir the mont Emus
Quhare Orphius lerit his armony maist fyne,
Ovir Carmelus, quhare twa prophetis devyne   1105
Remanyt, Helyas and Heliseus,
Fra quhome the Ordur of Carmelitis come syne.

And nixt untill the land of Amyson,
In hast we past the flude Termodyon
And ovir the huge hill that hecht Mynas.   1110
We raid the hill of Bachus, Citheron,
And Olympus, the mont of Massidon,
Quhilk semys heich up in the hevyn to pas.
In that countre, we raid the flude Melas
Quhais watter makith quhite scheip blak anon.   1115
In Europe, eik, we raid the flud Thanas.

1095. Ron *Rhone*   Sane *Seine*
   Lare *Loire*
1096. goldin sandyt ryvare *river*
   with golden sands
1097. Mont Oethe *Mount Oeta*
1098. sepulture *tomb*   fand *found*
1099. Peneyus *Peneus*
1100. Secil *Cilicia*
1101. plenyst with *abounding in*
   saphron *saffron*   huny *honey*
1102. twa toppyt *twin-peaked*
   Pernasus *Parnassus*
1103. Trace *Thrace*
   Emus *Haemus*
1104. Orphius *Orpheus*
   lerit *learned*   armony *harmony*
1105. Carmelus *Mount Carmel*
   twa *two*   prophetis
   devyne *heavenly prophets*

1106. remanyt *dwelt*
   Helyas *Elijah*   Heliseus *Elisha*
1107. Ordur of
   Carmelitis *Carmelite Order*
   come syne *then came*
1108. untill *to*   Amyson *Amazonia*
1109. Termodyon *Thermodon*
1110. hecht *is called*
   Mynas *Mimas*
1111. raid *rode over*
   Bachus *Bacchus*
   Citheron *Cithaeron*
1112. Massidon *Macedonia*
1113. semys *seems*   heich *high*
   pas *stretch*
1114. raid *crossed over*
1115. quhite scheip *white sheep*
   anon *at once*
1116. flud Thanas *River Don*

We raid the swyft revere Sparthiades,
The flud of Surry, Achicorontes,
The hill so full of wellis clepit Yda,
Armany hillis and flude Eufrates, 1120
The fluid of Nyle, the pretius flude Ganges,
The hyl of Secyle, ay byrnand Ethna,
And ovir the mont of Frygy, Dindama,
Hallowit in honour of the modir goddes.
Cauld Cacasus we passit, in Sythia. 1125

We passyt the fludis of Tygris and Phison,
Of Trace the riveris Hebrun and Strymon,
The mont of Modyn and the flud Jordane,
The facund well and hill of Elicon,
The mont Erix, the well of Acheron, 1130
Baith didicat to Venus in certane.
We past the hill and desert of Lybane,
Ovir mont Cinthus, quhare god Appollo schone
Straucht to the Musis Caballyne fontane.

Besyde that cristall strand swete and degest 1135
Them till repois, thayr hors refresch and rest,
Alychtit doun thir Musis clere of hew.

1117. revere *river*
    Sparthiades *Sperchius*
1118. Surry *Syria*
    Achicorontes *Orontes*
1119. wellis *springs* clepit *called*
    Yda *Ida*
1120. Armany *Armenian*
    Eufrates *Euphrates*
1121. Nyle *Nile* pretius *precious*
1122. Secyle *Siciliy*
    ay byrnand *ever burning*
    Ethna *Etna*
1123. Frygy *Phrygia*
    Dindama *Dindymon*
1124. hallowit *consecrated*
    modir *mother*
1125. cauld *cold*
    Cacasus *Caucasus*
    Sythia *Scythia*

1126. Tygris *Tigris*
1127. Trace *Thrace*
    Hebrun *Hebrus*
    Strymon *Strimon*
1128. Modyn *Modin*
    Jordane *Jordan*
1129. facund *overflowing*
    Elicon *Helicon*
1130. Erix *Eryx*
1131. didicat *dedicated* in
    certane *indeed*
1132. Lybane *Lebanon*
1133. Cinthus *Cynthus*
1134. straucht *straight*
    Caballyne *Hippocrene*
1135. strand *river* degest *calm*
1136. repois *relax* hors *horses*
1137. alychtit doun *dismounted*
    clere of hew *of fresh complexion*

1134. 'Straight to the Hippocrene spring of the Muses'.

The cumpany all halely, lest and best,
Thrang to the well tyl drink, quhilk ran southwest
Throwout a meid quhare alkyn flouris grew. 1140
Amang the layf ful fast I did persew
Tyll drynk, bot sa the gret pres me opprest
That of the watir I micht never tast a drew.

Our hors pasturyt in a plesand plane
Law at the fute of a fare grene mountane 1145
Amyd a meid schadowed with cedir treys,
Save fra al heit thare micht we weil remane,
All kynd of herbis, flouris, frute and grane
With every growand tre thair men micht cheis.
The byrriall stremys rynnand ovyr sterny greis 1150
Maid sobir noys; the schaw dynnyt agane
For byrdys sang and soundyng of the beis.

The ladyis fare on divers instrumentys
Went playand, syngand, dansand ovir the bentis.
Ful angelyk and hevynly wes thair soun. 1155
Quhat creatour amid his hart imprentis
The fresche bewty, the gudly representis,

1138. all halely *altogether* lest and
best *lowest and highest*
1139. thrang *thronged*
1140. meid *meadow* alkyn *all
kinds of* flouris *flowers*
1141. layf *rest* persew *hurry*
1142. sa *in such a way* pres *crowd*
me opprest *crushed me*
1143. tast *taste* drew *drop*
1144. hors *horses* pasturyt *grazed*
plane *plain*
1145. law *down* fute *foot*
1146. cedir treys *cedar trees*
1147. save *safe* heit *heat*
1148. herbis *plants* grane *crop*
1149. growand *growing*
cheis *choose*

1150. byrriall stremys *crystal
streams* rynnand *running* sterny
greis *glittering steps*
1151. sobir noys *peaceful sound*
schaw *wood* dynnyt
agane *resounded*
1152. for *with* byrdys
sang *birdsong*
soundyng *humming* beis *bees*
1153. fare *beautiful*
1154. dansand *dancing*
bentis *fields*
1155. angelyk *angelic* soun *sound*
1156. quhat *whatever*
creatour *creature*
imprentis *imprints*
1157. representis *appearances*

1149. 'With every tree growing there that a man might choose to name'.
1156–9. 'Any person able to imprint in his heart their youthful beauty,
fair appearance, happy talk, good manners, and noble reputation,
would have been able to make a wise man almost faint with the beauty
of it all'.

The mery spech, fare havinges, hie renoun
Of thaym wald set a wyse man halfe in swoun.
Thair womanlynes writhyt the elementis,   1160
Stonyst the hevyn and all the erth adoun.

The warld may not consydyr nor discryve
The hevynly joy, the blys I saw belyve,
So ineffabill, abone my wyt so hie
I wyll na mare thairon my forhed ryve,   1165
But breifly furth my febill proces dryve.
Law in the meid a palyeon pycht I se,
Maist gudlyest and rychest that myght be.
My governour ofter than timys fyve
Untill that halde to pas commandit me.   1170

Swa fynally strycht to that rial steid
In fallowschip with my leder I yeid.
We entryt sone: the portar wes not thra;
Thare wes na stoppyng, lang demand nor pleid.
I knelyt law and onheldit my heid   1175
And tho I saw our Musis twa and twa
Sittand on deace, famylliaris to and fra

1158. fare havinges *fine manners*
1159. swoun *swoon*
1160. writhyt *unsettled*
1161. stonyst *stunned* adoun *below*
1162. warld *world*
   consydyr *account for*
   discryve *describe*
1163. belyve *at once*
1164. ineffabill *indescribable*
   abone *above* wyt *understanding*
   hie *far*
1165. mare *more* my forhed
   ryve *make my head split*
1166. febill proces *feeble narrative*
1167. law *down below*
   palyeon *pavilion* pycht *erected*
   se *see*
1168. maist gudlyest *the best*
1169. governour *guardian*

ofter *more often* timys fyve *five
times*
1170. untill *to* halde *shelter*
   pas *go*
1171. swa *so* strycht *directly* rial
   steid *royal place*
1172. leder *leader* yeid *went*
1173. sone *at once* portar *porter*
   thra *stubborn*
1174. lang demand *long
   interrogation* pleid *argument*
1175. knelyt *knelt*
   onheldit *uncovered* heid *head*
1176. tho *then* twa and twa *two
   by two*
1177. deace *dais*
   famylliaris *members of the
   household* to and fra *going to
   and fro*

1169. 'The Muse who had been my guardian many times'.

Servand thaym fast with epocres and meid,
Dilligate meatis, daynteis sere alswa.

Grete wes the preis, the feist ryall to sene.   1180
At ease thay eit with interludyis betwene,
Gave problemys sere and mony fare demandis,
Inquirand quha best in thair tymys had bene,
Quha traist lovers in lusty yeris grene;
Sum said this way, and sum thairto ganstandis.   1185
Than Caliope Ovid till appere commaundis:
'My Clerk,' quod scho, 'of Registere, bedene
Declare quha wer maist worthy of thair handis.'

With lawrere crownyt, at hir commaundment
Up stude this poet degest and eloquent   1190
And schew the fetis of Hercules the strang,
Quhow he the grysly hellis houndis out rent,
Slew lyonys, monstreis and mony fell serpent,
And to the deth feil mychty giantis dang.
Of Thesyus eik he tald the weris lang   1195
Agane the quene Ypollita the swete
And quhow he slew the Mynotaure in Crete;

1178. servand *serving*
  epocres *spiced wine*   meid *mead*
1179. dilligate meatis *fine food*
  daynteis sere *many delicacies*
  alswa *also*
1180. preis *crowd* feist *feast*
  ryall *splendid*   sene *behold*
1181. at ease *at their leisure*
  eit *ate*   interludyis
  betwene *interludes between courses*
1182. problemys *puzzles*
  demandis *questions*
1183. tymys *times*
1184. traist *faithful* lusty
  yeris *youthful years*   grene *green*
1185. ganstandis *disagrees*
1186. till appere *to come forward*
1187. Clerk of Registere *Official*

Keeper of the Records   bedene *at once*
1188. of thair handis *with their hands*
1189. with lawrere
  crownyt *crowned with laurel*
1190. stude *stood* degest *dignified*
1191. schew *revealed* fetis *feats*
  strang *strong*
1192. hellis houndis *hounds of hell*
  out rent *tore apart*
1193. lyonys *lions* fell *cruel*
1194. feil *many* mychty *mighty*
  dang *beat*
1195. Thesyus *Theseus* eik *also*
  tald *told* weris *wars*
1196. agane *against*
  Ypollita *Hippolyta*
1197. Mynotaure *Minotaur*

1182–4. 'They set many puzzles and many fine questions, asking who
  had been the best in their time, who had been faithful lovers in their
  youthful, vigorous years'.
1186. 'Then Calliope orders Ovid to come forward'.

Of Persyus he tald the knychtly dedis
Quhilk vincussyt (as men in Ovid redis)
Crewell tyrrantis and monsturis mony one;　　　　1200
Of Dianis bore in Callydon the dredis,
Quhow throw a ladyis schot his sydis bledis –
The bretheris deith and syne the systeris mone;
He schew quhow Kyng Priamus sonne Ysacon
Efter his dede, body and all his wedis　　　　1205
In till a skarth transformyt wes anon;

He schew at Troy quhat wyis the Grekis landis,
Quhow fers Achylles stranglyt wyth his handis
The valyeant Cignus, Neptunus sonne maist dere,
Quhilk at Grekis aryvale on the strandis　　　　1210
A thousand slew that day apon the sandis,
Faucht with Achill and blontit al his spere.
Na wapyn wes that micht him wond nor dere
Quhill Achalles bryst of his helm the bandis
And wyrryit hym be fors for all his fere.　　　　1215

He schew full mony transmutationis
And wondirfull new figurationis
Be hondris mo than I have here expremyt.
He tald of lovys meditacionis,
The craft of love and the salvationis,　　　　1220

1198. Persyus *Perseus* dedis *deeds*
1199. vincussyt *vanquished*
　redis *read*
1200. crewell *cruel*
1201. Dianis bore *Diana's boar*
　Callydon *Calydon*
　dredis *dangers*
1202. schot *shot* sydis
　bledis *flanks bleed*
1203. bretheris *brother's*
　deith *death* syne *then*
　systeris *sister's* mone *lament*
1204. Priamus *Priam's* sonne *son*
　Ysacon *Aesacus*
1205. dede *death* wedis *clothes*
1206. in till *into* skarth *cormorant*
1207. quhat wyis *how*
　Grekis *Greeks*
　landis *disembarked*
1208. fers Achylles *fierce Achilles*

stranglyt *strangled*
1209. valyeant Cignus *valiant*
　Cygnus Neptunus' *Neptune's*
1210. quhilk *who* aryvale *arrival*
　strandis *shores*
1212. faucht *fought* blontit *blunted*
1213. wapyn *weapon*
　wond *wound* dere *harm*
1214. quhill *until* bryst of *tore*
　from helm *helmet*
1215. wyrryit *strangled* be fors *by*
　strength fere *companions*
1216. transmutationis
　metamorphoses
1217. figurationis *forms*
1218. hondris mo *hundreds more*
　expremyt *described*
1219. lovys meditacionis *discourses*
　on love
1220. salvationis *deliverance*

Quhow that the furie lustis suld be flemyt.
Of divers other materis als he demyt
And be his prudent scharpe relationys
He wes expart in all thyng, as it semyt.

Up rais the gret Virgilius anone   1225
And playd the sportis of Daphnis and Coridon.
Syne Therens come, and playit the commedy
Of Permeno, Thrason and wyse Gnaton;
Juvynale, lik a mower, hym allone,
Stud skornand every man as thay yeid by;   1230
Marcyall was cuyk, till rost, seith, fars or fry;
And Pogyus stude with mony gyrn and grone
On Laurence Valla spyttand and cryand 'Fy!'

With myrthys thus and meatis diligate
Thir ladyis, festit accordyng thair estate,   1235
Uprais at last, commandand till tranoynt.
Retret wes blawyn lowd, and than God wate
Men micht have sene swyft horssys halden hate,
Schynand for swete as thay had bene anoynt.
Of all that rout wes never a pryk disjoynt   1240
For all our tary, and I, furth with my mate,
Montyt on hors, raid sammyn in gude poynt.

1221. furie lustis *fiery desires*
flemyt *banished*
1222. divers *various* demyt *gave judgement*
1223. scharpe relationys *acute statements*
1224. expart *expert* semyt *seemed*
1225. rais *rose* Virgilius *Virgil*
1226. playd *performed*
sportis *entertainment*
1227. Therens *Terence*
1228. Permeno *Parmeno*
Thrason *Thraso* Gnaton *Gnatho*
1229. Juvynale *Juvenal*
mower *jester* hym allone *by himself*
1230. skornand *mocking* yeid *went*
1231. Marcyall *Martial*
cuyk *cook* rost *roast* seith *boil*
fars *stuff*

1232. Pogyus *Poggio* gyrn *snarl*
grone *groan*
1233. spyttand *spitting*
1234. myrthys *entertainments*
meatis diligate *fine food*
1235. accordyng thair estate *as befitted their rank*
1236. tranoynt *leave swiftly*
1237. retret *signal for departure*
blawyn *blown* wate *knows*
1238. halden hate *ridden hard*
1239. schynand *glistening*
swete *sweat* as *as if*
anoynt *anointed*
1240. rout *company* pryk
disjoynt *stride out of place*
1241. tary *delay* mate *companion*
1242. sammyn *together*
poynt *order*

Ovir many gudly plane we raid bedene,
The Vail of Ebron, the Campe Damascene,
Throw Josaphat and thorow the lusty vail,   1245
Ovir watres wan, thorow worthi woddis grene,
And swa at last in lyftyng up our eyne
We se the fynall end of our travail:
Amyd ane plane a plesand roch till wail.
And every wycht fra we that sycht had sene,   1250
Thankand gret God, thare hedis law devail.

With syngyng, lauchyng, merines and play
On till that roch we rydyng furth the way.
Now mare till writ for fere trymlys my pen.
The hart may not thynk nor manis toung say,   1255
The eyr not here nor yet the e se may,
It may not be ymagyned with men
The hevynly blys, the perfyte joy to ken
Quhilk now I saw. The hundreth part all day
I micht not schaw, thocht I had tonges ten.   1260

Thocht al my membris tongis were on raw,
I wer not abill the thousandfald to schaw.
Quhairfore I fere ocht forthirmare to wryte,
For quhiddir I this in saule or body saw

1243. bedene *straightaway*
1244. Vail of Ebron *Vale of Hebron* Campe
Damascene *Field of Damascus*
1245. Josaphat *Jehoshaphat*
1246. wan *dark*
1247. eyne *eyes*
1248. travail *journey*
1249. roch *mountain* till
wail *exceptionally fine*
1250. wycht *creature* fra *once*
1251. law devail *bow down low*
1252. lauchyng *laughing*
merines *merriment*
1253. rydyng *rode*

1254. now mare *no more*
writ *write* fere *fear* trymlys my
pen *makes my pen shake*
1256. eyr *ear* here *hear* e *eye*
1257. with *by*
1258. to ken *to know*
1260. schaw *describe* thocht *even*
if tonges *tongues*
1261. thocht *even if*
membris *limbs* on raw *in a row*
1262. thousandfald *thousandth part*
1263. quhairfore *therefore* I fere *I
am afraid* ocht
forthirmare *anything more*
1264. quhiddir *whether* saule *soul*

1256. 'The ear cannot hear, nor even the eye see'.
1261-2. 'Even if all my limbs had tongues laid out in a row, I would not
be able to reveal a thousandth part of it all'.

That wait I not, bot he that all duth knaw,   1265
The gret God, wait in every thyng perfyt.
Eik gyf I wald this avyssyon endyte
Janglaris suld it bakbyt and stand nane aw
Cry out on dremes quhilkis ar not worth a myte!

Sen thys til me all verite be kend   1270
I reput bettir thus till mak ane end,
Than ocht til say that suld herars engreve.
On othir syd, thocht thay me vilepend,
I considdir prudent folk will commend
The verete, and sic janglyng rapreve.   1275
With quhais correction, support, and releve
Furth till proceid this proces I pretend,
Traistand in God my purpose till escheve.

Quhowbeit I may not every circumstance
Reduce perfytly in rememorance,   1280
Myn ignorance yit sum part sal devyse
Twychand this sycht of hevynly swete plesance.

1265. wait *know*   duth knaw *does know*
1267. gyf *if*   avyssyon *vision* endyte *write down*
1268. janglaris *detractors* bakbyt *backbite* aw *fear*
1269. on *against*   dremes *dreams* myte *mite*
1270. sen *since*   all verite be kend *is shown to be the truth*
1271. reput betir *think it is better*
1272. ocht til say *to say anything* herars *listeners* engreve *annoy*
1273. thocht *although* vilepend *abuse*
1274. considdir *think that*

1275. verete *truth*   sic *such* janglyng *idle chatter* rapreve *condemn*
1276. releve *assistance*
1277. proces *discourse* pretend *plan*
1278. traistand *trusting* escheve *achieve*
1279. quhowbeit *even though* circumstance *detail*
1280. reduce *recall* rememorance *memory*
1281. yit *nevertheless*   devyse *retell*
1282. twychand *concerning* sycht *sight*

1265–6. 'That I do not know, only He who knows everything, great God Himself, has complete knowledge'.
1268–9. 'Detractors would only speak ill of it and show no hesitation in speaking out against dreams which they would say are not worth anything at all'.
1277. 'I plan to continue with my story'.
1281–2. 'Nevertheless, even in my ignorance I shall still manage to recall something about this sight of heavenly sweet delight'.

Now empty pen, wryt furth thy lusty chance,
Schaw wondris fele, suppose thow be not wyse,
Be dilligent and rypely the avyse,   1285
Be qwyke and scharpe, voydit of variance,
Be swete and cause not jentill hartis gryse.

THE THYRD PARTE

Ye Musis nyne, be in myne adjutory
That maid me se this blys and perfyte glory,
Teche me your facund castis eloquent,   1290
Len me a recent, scharp, fresch memory,
And caus me dewly til indyt this story.
Sum gratius swetnes in my brest imprent
Till make the heraris bousum and attent,
Redand my wryt illumynyt with your lore,   1295
Infynyt thankis rendrand yow thairfore.

Now breifly to my purpose for til gone.
About the hyll lay ways mony one,
And to the hycht bot a passage ingrave,
Hewyn in the roch of slyde hard merbyll stone.   1300
Aganne the sonne lyk as the glas it schone.
Ascens wes hie and strait for till consave,
Yit than thir Musis, gudly and suave,

1283. wryt *write* lusty chance *fine opportunity*
1284. schaw *reveal* wondris fele *many wonders* suppose *even though*
1285. rypely the avyse *consider well*
1286. qwyke *mentally agile* voydit of variance *free of contradiction*
1287. swete *pleasing* jentill *noble* gryse *to shudder*
1288. be in myn adjutory *come to my assistance*
1289. maid me se *enabled me to see*
1290. teche *teach* facund castis *graceful terms of rhetoric*
1291. len *give* scharp *discerning* fresch *vivid*
1292. dewly *properly* til indyt *to write*
1293. gratius *pleasing* brest *heart*

1294. heraris *audience* bousum *receptive* attent *attentive*
1295. redand *reading* illumynyt *illuminated* lore *teaching*
1296. rendrand *offering*
1297. breifly *directly* purpose *subject* for til gone *to proceed*
1298. about *around* ways *paths* mony one *many*
1299. hycht *summit* bot a *only one* passage route *route* ingrave *carved out*
1300. hewyn *hewn* roch *rock* slyde *slippery* merbyll *marble*
1301. aganne *reflecting* sonne *sun*
1302. ascens *ascent* hie *steep* strait *difficult* consave *observe*
1303. gudly *fair* suave *gracious*

Alychtyt doun and clam the roch in hy
With all the route, outtane my nymphe and I.   1305

Styl at the hillys fute we twa abaid.
Than suddandly my keper to me said,
'Ascend, galand!' Tho for fere I quuke.
'Be not effrayit,' scho said, 'be not mismaid,'
And with that word up the strait rod abraid.   1310
I followit fast; scho be the hand me tuke,
Yit durst I nevir, for dreid, behynde me luke.
With mekill pane thus clam we nere the hycht,
Quhare suddandly I saw ane grysly sycht.

As we approchit nere the hillis heid,   1315
A terrible sewch – birnand in flawmys reid,
Abhominable and hol as heill to se,
All full of bryntstane, pyk, and bulnyng leid,
Quhair mony wrechit creatour lay deid,
And miserable catyvis yeland loude one hie   1320
I saw, quhilk den mycht wele comparit be
Till Xantus, the flud of Troy so schill,
Byrnand at Venus hest, contrar Achill.

Amyd our passage lay this ugly sicht,
Not brayd, but so horrible till eviry wicht   1325

1304. alychtyt doun *dismounted*
clam *climbed*   in hy *quickly*
1305. route *company*
outtane *except for*
1306. twa *two*   abaid *lingered*
1308. galand *man*   fere *fear*
quuke *trembled*
1309. effrayit *afraid*
mismaid *disturbed*
1310. strait rod *narrow path*
abraid *leapt*
1311. be *by*   tuke *took*
1312. durst *dared*   dreid *fear*
luke *look*
1313. mekle pane *great effort*
clam *climbed*
1314. grysly sycht *terrible sight*
1315. nere *near*   heid *top*
1316. sewch *gulf*   birnand *burning*
flawmys reid *red flames*

1317. hol *deep*   heill *hell*   se *look at*
1318. brynstane *brimstone*
pyk *pitch*   bulnyng leid *boiling lead*
1319. wrechit *wretched*   deid *dead*
1320. catyvis *wretches*
yeland *crying*   one hie *at the top of their voices*
1321. quhilk den *the ravine of which*   comparit be *be compared*
1322. till Xantus *to Xanthus*
flud *river*   schill *chilling*
1323. hest *command*   contrar Achill *against Achilles*
1324. amyd *across*
1325. brayd *broad*
horrible *horrifying*   wicht *living creature*

That all the warld to pas it suld have dreid.
Wele I considerit nene upparmar I mycht,
And to discend, sa hiddous wes the hicht
I durst not aventur for this erth on breid.
Trymland I stud, with teith chatterand gud speid. 1330
My nymphe beheld my cheir and said 'Lat be:
Thow sall not aill, and, lo, the caus,' quod sche.

'To me thow art commyt. I sall the keip.
Thir pieteous pepill amyd theis laithly deip
War wrechis quhilkis in lusty yeris fair 1335
Pretendit thaym till hie honour to creip;
Bot suddandly thay fell on sleuthfull sleip
Followand plesance, drynt in this loch of cair.'
And with that word sche hynt me by the hair,
Caryit me to the hillis hed anone 1340
As Abacuk wes brocht in Babilone.

As we bene on the hie hill sittuate,
'Luke doun,' quod scho, 'Consave in quhat estat

1326. warld *world* dreid *fear*
1327. nene *no* upparmar *further upwards*
1328. hicht *height*
1329. durst *dared* aventur *attempt* on breid *in breadth*
1330. trymland *trembling* stud *stood* teith *teeth* gud speid *rapidly*
1331. cheir *expression* lat be *be calm*
1332. aill *come to harm* lo *look* caus *reason*
1333. commyt *entrusted* the keip *protect you*
1334. thir *those* pieteous *pitiful* theis laithly deip *this loathesome pit*
1335. quhilkis *who* lusty yeris

fair *the pleasant years of their youth*
1336. pretendit thaym *aspired* creip *proceed*
1337. on sleuthfull sleip *into slothful sleep*
1338. followand *pursuing* plesance *pleasure* drynt *drowned* loch of cair *lake of sorrow*
1339. hynt *grabbed*
1340. caryit *carried* hillis hed *summit* anone *at once*
1341. Abacuk *Habakkuk* brocht in *brought into* Babilone *Babylon*
1342. as *while* bene *were* sittuate *standing*
1343. luke *look* consave *observe* estat *state*

1327. 'It seemed to me that I could go no further upwards'.
1329. 'I dared not attempt it for the whole world'.
1343–4. ' "Look down," she said. "Observe what state you can perceive your wretched world to be in now" '.

Thy wrechyt warld thow may considdir now!'
At hir command, with mekill dreid, God wate,   1345
Out ovir the hill sa hiddous hie and strate
I blent adoun, and feld my body grow:
This brukkill erth, sa littyl to allow,
Me thocht I saw byrn in a fyry rage
Of stormy see, quhilk mycht na maner swage.   1350

That terribbill tempest, hiddous wallys huge
Wer maist grysly for till behald or juge,
Quhare nothyr rest nor quyet mycht appere.
Thare wes a peralus palyce folk to luge.
Thare wes na help, support nor yet refuge.   1355
Innowmerabill folk I saw flottrand in fere
Quhilk peryst on the weltrand wallys were,
And secondly I saw a lusty barge
Ovirset with seyes and mony stormy charge.

This gudly carvel, taiklyt traist on raw,   1360
With blanschyt sail, mylk quhyte as ony snaw,
Rycht sover tycht and wondir strangly beildyt,
Wes on the boldyn wallys quyte ovirthraw.
Contrariusly the bustuus wynd did blaw
In bubbys thik, that na schip sail mycht weld it.   1365

1344. considdir *perceive*
1345. mekill dreid *great dread*
    wate *knows*
1346. hiddous *horribly*   strate *steep*
1347. blent *glanced*   feld *felt*
    grow *shiver*
1348. brukkill erth *fragile world*
    allow *praise*
1350. see *seas*   na maner *in no*
    way   swage *subside*
1351. wallys *waves*
1353. quhare *where*
    noyther *neither*   quyet *quiet*
1354. peralus palyce *dangerous*
    place   luge *house*
1356. innowmerabill *innumerable*
    flottrand *floundering*   in
    fere *together*
1357. quhilk *who*   peryst *perished*

weltrand *heaving*   were *tumult*
1358. lusty barge *fine ship*
1359. ovirset *capsized*   seyes *wild*
    waves   charge *rush of water*
1360. carvel *fast ship*   taiklyt
    traist *securely rigged*   on
    raw *everywhere*
1361. blanschyt *whitened*   mylk
    quhyte *milk white*   snaw *snow*
1362. sover tycht *safely watertight*
    beildyt *constructed*
1363. boldyn wallys *swelling*
    waves   quyte *entirely*
    ovirthraw *overturned*
1364. contrariusly *in opposition*
    bustuus *violent*
1365. bubbys thik *heavy gusts*
    weld *stand*

1354. 'That was a dangerous place in which to house people'.
1357. 'Who perished in the tumult of the heaving waves'.

Now sank scho law, now hie tyl hevyn upheldyt.
At every part the see and wyndis drave
Quhill on a sand the schip tobryst and clave.

It wes a pietuus thyng, allake, allake,
Till here the duylfull cry quhen that scho strake,   1370
Maist lamentabill the peryst folk till se
Sa famyst, drokyt, mait, forwrocht, and wake;
Sum on a plank of firre and sum of ake,
Sum hang apon takill, sum on a tre,
Sum fra thair gryp sone weschyne with the se.   1375
Part drynt, and part to the rolke flet or swam,
On rapis or burdis, syne up the hill thay clam.

Tho at my nymphe breifly I did inquere
Quhat sygnyfyit tha feirfull wondris fere.
'Yone multitude,' said scho, 'of pepill drint   1380
Ar faythles folk, quhilkis, quhyle thay ar here,
Mysknawys God, and followys thare plesere,
Quhairforc thay sall in endles fyre be brynt.
Yone lusty schip thow seyst peryst and tynt,
In quhame yone pepill maid ane parralus race,   1385
Scho heycht the Carvell of the State of Grace.

1366. law *low* hie *high*
upheldyt *raised*
1367. see *sea* drave *buffeted*
1368. quhill *until* sand *shore*
tobryst *shattered* clave *broke apart*
1369. allake *alas*
1370. here *hear*
duylfull *mournful* strake *ran aground*
1371. peryst *doomed* till se *to see*
1372. sa *so* famyst *starving*
drokyt *drenched* mait *beaten*
forworcht *exhausted* wake *weak*
1373. firre *fir* ake *oak*
1374. takill *rigging* tre *barrel*
1375. gryp *grip* sone *quickly*
weschyne *washed away*
1376. part *some* drynt *drowned*
rolke *rock* flet *floated*
1377. rapis *ropes* burdis *planks*
syne *then*
1378. tho *then* nymphe *nymph*
inquere *ask*
1379. sygnyfyit *signified*
fere *many*
1380. drint *drowned*
1381. faythles *faithless*
quhyle *while*
1382. mysknawys *refuse to acknowledge* plesere *desire*
1383. endles *eternal* brynt *burned*
1384. seyst *saw* peryst *wrecked*
tynt *lost*
1385. quhame *which* parralus
race *perilous voyage*
1386. heycht *is named*
Carvell *Ship*

1375. 'Some quickly washed away by the sea from whatever they clung to'.
1379. 'What was the meaning of those many frightening wonders'.

'Ye bene all borne the sonnys of ire I ges,
Syne throw baptyme gettis grace and faythfulnes.
Than in yone carvell suyrly ye remane,
Oft stormstad with this warldis brukkyllnes   1390
Quhill that ye fall in synne and wrachitnes.
Than, schipbrokyn, sall ye droun in endles pane,
Except bye fayth ye fynd the plank agane,
Bye Chryst, workyng gud workys, I onderstand,
Remane thairwith, thir sall you bryng to land.   1395

'This may suffice,' said scho, 'twychand this part.
Returne thy hed, behald this othir art,
Considdir wondris, and be vigilant
That thow may bettir endytyng eftirwart
Thyngis quhilkis I sall the schaw or we depart.   1400
Thow sall have fouth of sentence and not skant.
Thare is no welth nor welfare thow sall want.
The gret Palyce of Honour salt thou se.
Lift up thy hed. Behald that sicht,' quod sche.

At hir commaund I rasit hie on hycht   1405
My vissage till behald that hevenly sycht.
Bot tyl discryve this matter in effek
Impossibill wer till ony erdly wicht.

1387. bene *are* borne *born*
  sonnys *sons* ire *anger* ges *suppose*
1388. baptyme *baptism*
  gettis *obtain*
1389. suyrly *securely*
1390. stormstad *beset by storms*
  warldis *world's*
  brukkyllnes *instability*
1391. in *into*
  wrachitnes *degradation*
1392. schipbrokyn *shipwrecked*
  droun *drown* pane *pain*
1393. except *unless* bye *by*
1394. bye Chryst *with Christ's*
  help workyng *performing*
1396. twychand *concerning*
1397. returne *turn* art *region*

1398. wondris *marvels*
1399. endytyng *write down*
  eftirwart *afterwards*
1400. quhilkis *which* the
  schaw *show you* or *before*
1401. fouth *abundance*
  sentence *matter* not skant *no
  scarcity*
1402. want *lack*
1405. rasit *raised* hie *high* on
  hycht *aloft*
1406. vissage *face* till *to*
  sycht *sight*
1407. tyl discryve *to describe* in
  effek *in fact*
1408. till *for* erdly wicht *earthly
  creature*

1395. 'And remain with that plank, for this alone shall bring you to land'.
1408 'Would be impossible for any earthly creature'.

It transcendes sa far abone my micht
That I with ynk may do bot paper blek.   1410
I man draw furth, the yok lyis in my nek,
As of the place to say my lewd avyse,
Plenyst with plesance, lyke to parradyce.

I saw a plane of peirles pulcritude
Quharein abondyt everythingis gude: 1415
Spyce, wyne, corn, ule, tre, frute, flour, herbis grene,
All foulys, bestis, byrdys and alkynde fude.
All maner fyschis, bayth of see and flude,
Wer kepit in pondis of polist silver schene
With purifyit wattir as of the cristall clene.   1420
Till noy the small the grete bestis had na will
Nor ravanus fowlys the littil volatill.

Styll in the season all thyng remanyt thare
Perpetually, but othir noy or sare.
Ay rypyt were bayth herbys, frute and flouris.   1425
Of everythyng the namys till declare
Until my febill wyt impossybill ware.

1409. transcendes *surpasses* abone *above* micht *power*	1418. fyschis *fishes* see *sea* flude *river*
1410. ynk *ink* blek *blacken*	1419. polist *polished* schene *bright*
1411. man *must* furth *onwards* yok *yoke* lyis *lies* in *upon*	1420. clene *clean*
1412. lewd avyse *ignorant opinion*	1421. till noy *to attack* grete *big* will *desire*
1413. plenyst *filled* plesance *delights* parradyce *paradise*	1422. ravanus fowlys *birds of prey* volatill *birds*
1414. peirles pulcritude *unparalleled beauty*	1423. styll *always* remanyt *remained*
1415. abondyt *abounded*	1424. but *without* noy *trouble* sare *sorrow*
1416. ule *oil* tre *trees* flour *flowers* herbis grene *green plants*	1425. ay rypyt *always fully ripe* herbys *plants*
1417. foulys *fowls* bestis *beasts* byrdys *birds* alkynde fude *all kinds of food*	1426. namys *names*
	1427. until *for* impossybill ware *would be impossible*

1410–13. 'That all I would be doing is making the paper black with ink.
I must proceed, the yoke lies upon my neck, forcing me to give my
ignorant opinion about that place, full of delights, like a paradise'.
1420. 'With water so pure it seemed to be like clean crystal'.
1423–4. 'Everything there was perpetually in season, without any trouble
or conflict'.

Amyd the med replete of swete odouris,
A palyce stude with mony riall touris
Quhare kernellys quent, feil turretis men mycht
$\qquad$ fynd   1430
And goldyn fanys wavand with the wynd.

Pynnakillis, fyellis, tournpikes mony one,
Gylt byrnyst torris, quhilk lyk til Phebus schone,
Skarsement, repryse, corbell, and battelyngis,
Fulyery, borduris of mony pretius stone,   1435
Suttyl muldry wrocht mony day agone
On buttres, jalmys, pilleris and plesand spryngis,
Quyke ymagry with mony lusty syngis
Thare mycht be sene, and mony worthy wychtis
Tofore the yet, arrayit all at rychtis.   1440

Furth past my nymphe; I followyt subsequent.
Straucht throw the plane to the first ward we went
Of the palyce and entryt at that port.
Thare saw we mony statelie tornament,
Lancis brokyn, knychtis layd on the bent.   1445
Plesand pastance and mony lusty sport
Thair saw we als, and sumtyme battel mort.

1428. med *meadow* replete of *filled with*
1429. palyce *palace* riall touris *majestic towers*
1430. kernellys quent *fine battlements* feil turretis *many turrets*
1431. fanys *vanes* wavand *moving*
1432. pinnakillis *pinnacles* fyellis *finials* tournpikes *spiral staircases*
1433. gylt *gilded* byrnyst *polished* torris *ornaments* Phebus *the sun*
1434. skarsement *recesses* repryse *mouldings* corbell *buttresses* battelyngis *battlements*
1435. fulyery *carvings of foliage* borduris *borders* pretius *precious*
1436. suttyl *skilful* muldry *decoration*
1437. jalmys *doorposts* pilleris *pillars* spryngis *columns for arches*
1438. quyke ymagry *lifelike designs* lusty syngis *beautiful statues*
1439. wychtis *people*
1440. tofore *in front of* yet *gate* at rychtis *in good order*
1441. past *passed* subsequent *behind*
1442. straucht *straight* throw *across* ward *guarded entrance*
1443. port *gateway*
1444. statelie *grand*
1445. layd *knocked* bent *ground*
1446. pastance *entertainment*
1447. battel mort *deadly combat*

'All thir,' quod scho, 'on Venus service wakis
In dedis of armys for thayr ladyis sakis.'

Vissyand I stude the principal place but pere, 1450
That hevynly palyce, all of crystall clere,
Wrocht, as me thocht, of polyst beriall stone.
Bosiliall nor Oliab, but were,
Quhilk Sancta Sanctorum maid, maist ryche and dere,
Nor he that wrocht the tempill of Salomon, 1455
Nor he that beild the riall Ylyon,
Nor he that forgete Darius sepulture
Couth not performe sa craftely a cure.

Studiand here on, my nimphe on to me spak:
'Thus in a stare quhy standis thou stupefak, 1460
Gouand all day and na thyng hes vissyte!
Thow art prolixt. In haist retourn thy bak.
Go efter me, and gud attendence tak.
Quhat thow seyst, luke eftirwartis thow write.
Thow sall behald all Venus blys perfyte.' 1465
Thairwith sche till ane garth did me convoy
Quhare that I saw eneuche of perfyte joy.

1448. wakis *are engaged*
1449. dedis *deeds* sakis *sake*
1450. vissyand *gazing*
principal *sublime* but
pere *without equal*
1452. wrocht *made*
polyst *polished* beriall *beryl*
1453. Bosiliall *Bezaleel*
Oliab *Aholiab* but were *without
doubt*
1454. Sancta Sanctorum *Holy of
Holies* dere *precious*
1455. Salomon *Solomon*
1456. beild *built* riall Ylyon *royal
Ilion*
1457. forgete *forged*
sepulture *sepulchre*

1458. couth *could* craftely *skilful*
cure *task*
1459. studiand *studying*
1460. stare *trance*
stupefak *stupefied*
1461. gouand *gaping*
vissyte *visited*
1462. prolixt *tedious* retourn thy
bak *turn around*
1463. gud attendence tak *pay close
attention*
1464. seyst *see* luke *take care*
1465. perfyte *perfect*
1466. garth *garden* did me
convoy *guided me*
1467. eneuche *a great deal*

1448–9. ' "All these people," she said, "are engaged in deeds of arms for
the sake of their ladies" '.
1450. 'I stood gazing at that sublime, unparalleled place'.
1459. 'While I was studying this, my nymph spoke to me'.

Amyd a trone with stonys ryche ovirfret
And claith of gold, lady Venus wes set,
By hir, hir sonne Cupyd quhilk nathing seys.   1470
Quhare Mars entrit, na knawlege mycht I get.
Bot straucht afore Venus vissage but let
Twelf amarant stagis stude, twelf grene precius greis,
Quhareon thare grew thre curius goldyn treis,
Sustenttand weil, the goddis face aforne,   1475
A fair myrrour, be thaym quently upborn.

Quhare of it makyt wes I have na feil,
Of beriall, cristall, glas or byrnyst steil,
Of diamant or of the carbunkill jem:
Quhat thing it wes diffyne may I not weil.   1480
Bot all the bordure circulare, every deill,
Wes plate of gold – cais, stok and utter hem –
With vertuus stanis picht that blud wald stem.
For quha that wound wes in the tornament
Wox hale fra he apon the myrrour blent.   1485

1468. trone *throne* ovirfret *covered*
1469. claith *cloth* set *seated*
1470. sonne *son* quhilk nathing
seys *who sees nothing*
1471. entrit *entered*
1472. straucht *directly*
vissage *face* but let *without
obstacle*
1473. amarant *emerald*
stagis *steps* greis *stairs*
1474. grew *stood* curius *skilfully
made* treis *posts*
1475. sustenttand *holding up*
aforne *before*
1476. myrrour *mirror*
quently *ingeniously*
upborn *supported*

1477. quhare of *of what substance*
makyt wes *was made* na feil *no
knowledge*
1478. beriall *beryl* byrnyst
steil *polished steel*
1479. carbunkill jem *carbuncle gem*
1480. diffyne *define*
1481. bordure circulare *circular
border* deill *part*
1482. cais *frame* stok *stand* utter
hem *outer rim*
1483. vertuus stanis *powerful
stones* picht *inlaid* blud *blood*
1484. quha that *whoever* wound
wes *was wounded*
1485. wox hale *became whole
again* fra *after* blent *looked*

1472. 'But directly in front of Venus' face, without any obstacle in between'.
1475–6. 'Holding up a fine mirror in front of the face of the goddess, ingeniously supported by them'.
1480. 'I cannot say exactly what it was'.
1483. 'Inlaid with stones with the power to stem the flow of blood'.

This riall rillik, so ryche and radius,
Sa pollyst, plesand, purifyed, precius,
Quhoys bontyis half to wryt I not presume,
Thairon tyll se wes sa dellicius
And sa excelland schadois gratius,   1490
Surmontyng far in brichtnes, to my dome,
The costly subtil quent spectacle of Rome
Or yet the myrrour send to Canyce
Quhairin men micht ful many wondrys se.

In that myrrour I mycht se at a sycht   1495
The dedes and fetes of every erdly wycht,
All thinges gone lyk as they wer present,
All the creacion of the angeilys brycht,
Of Lucifer the fall for all his mycht,
Adam fyrst maid and in the erth ysent,   1500
And Noys flude thair saw I subsequent,
Babilon beild that toure of sic renoun,
Of Sodomus the fele subversyoun.

Abram, Ysak, Jacob, Josoph I saw,
Hornyt Moyses with his ald Ebrew law,   1505
Ten plagis in Egypt sent for thair trespas.
In the Reid See, with al hys court on raw,

1486. riall *magnificent* rillik *precious object* radius *radiant*
1487. sa *so* pollyst *polished* purifyed *flawless*
1488. quhoys *whose* bontyis *virtues*
1489. tyll se *to look upon* dellicius *delightful*
1490. sa *such* schadois *reflections*
1491. surmontyng *surpassing* to my dome *in my opinion*
1492. subtil *ingenious* quent spectacle *skilfully made mirror*
1493. send *sent* Canyce *Canacee*
1494. ful *very* se *see*
1495. mycht *could* sycht *glance*
1496. dedes *deeds* fetes *feats* erdly wycht *earthly creature*
1497. gone *gone by* lyk as *as if*
1498. angeilys *angels*
1499. for *in spite of*
1500. maid *created* in *into* ysent *sent*
1501. Noys flude *Noah's flood* subsequent *next*
1502. beild *build* toure *tower* sic renoun *such fame*
1503. Sodomus *Sodom* fele subversyoun *fierce overthrow*
1504. Abram *Abraham* Ysak *Isaac* Josoph *Joseph*
1505. hornyt Moyses *horned Moses* ald *old* Ebrew *Hebrew*
1506. plagis *plagues* trespas *sin*
1507. Reid See *Red Sea* on raw *together*

1488. 'I do not think I can write down even half of its virtues'.
1507–8. 'I saw King Pharaoh, who would never acknowledge the true God, drowned in the Red Sea together with all his court'.

Kyng Pharo drynt that God wald nevir knaw.
I saw quhat wyse the see devydyt was
And all the Ebrewes dry fut ovir it pas,   1510
Syne in desert I saw thaym fourty yeris.
Of Josuy I saw the worthy weris.

In Judicum the batellis strang anone
I saw of Jepty and of Gedione,
Of Ameleth the cruel homosyd,   1515
The wonderful werkis of douchty duke Sampsone,
Quhilk slew a thousand with ane assys bone,
Rent templis doun and yettis in his pryde,
Of quhais strenth mervalys this warld so wyde.
I saw duke Sangor there, with many a knok   1520
Sax hundreth men slew with a plewchis sok.

The praphet Samuell saw I in that glas
Anoynt Kyng Saule, quhais sonne Jonathas
I saw wyncus ane gret ost hym allane,
Yong David sla the grysly Golyas,   1525
Quhais speirheid wecht thre hundreth uncis was,
Jesbedonab, the giant mekill of mane,
Lay be the handis of douchty Davyd slane,

1508. Pharo *Pharaoh*
drynt *drowned*
knaw *acknowledge*
1509. quhat wyse *in what way*
devydyt *parted*
1510. dry fut *dry footed*
1511. syne *then*   yeris *years*
1512. Josuy *Joshua*   weris *wars*
1513. Judicum *the Book of Judges*
batellis strang *fierce battles*
anone *then*
1514. Jepty *Jephthah*
Gedione *Gideon*
1515. Ameleth *Abimelech*
homosyd *murderer*
1516. werkis *deeds*
douchty *heroic*
Sampsone *Samson*
1517. assys bone *jaw-bone of an ass*
1518. rent *tore*   templis *temples*

yettis *gates*   pryde *pride*
1519. quhais *whose*
strenth *strength*
1520. Sangor *Shamgar*   knok *blow*
1521. sax hundreth *six hundred*
plewchis sok *ploughshare*
1522. praphet Samuell *prophet
Samuel*
1523. anoynt *anoint*   Saule *Saul*
Jonathas *Jonathan*
1524. wyncus *vanquish*   ost *army*
hym allane *by himself*
1525. sla *slay*   grysly
Golyas *terrifying Goliath*
1526. speirheid *spearhead*
wecht *weight*   uncis *ounces*
1527. Jesbedonab *Ishbibenob*
mekill of mane *great in strength*
1528. be *by*

1526. 'Whose spearhead weighed three hundred ounces'.

With fyngris sax on athir hand but weir.
David I saw sla baith lyon and beir.   1530

This David, eik, at ane onset astond
Aucht hundreth men I saw hym bryng to grond.
With hym I saw Bananyas the strang
Quhilk twa lyonys of Moab did confond
And gave the stalwart Ethiop dedis wond   1535
With his awyn spere that of his hand he thrang.
Onabysytly this champion saw I gang
In a deip sistern and thare a lyon slewch
Quhilk in a storme of snaw did harm eneuch.

Of Salomon the wysdom and estate,   1540
Thare saw I, and his ryche tempill, God watc,
His sonne Roboam, quhilk throw his hely pride
Tynt all his ligis hartis be his fate:
He wes to thaym sa outragius ingrate
Of twelf tribis, ten did fra hym devyd.   1545
I saw the angell sla, be nychtis tyd,
Four score thousandis of Synachorybis ost
Quhilkis come to weir on Jowry with gret bost.

I saw the lyfe of the Kyng Esachy
Prolongit fifteen yere, and the prophet Hely   1550

1529. fyngris sax *six fingers*
athir *either* but weir *without doubt*
1530. lyon *lion* beir *bear*
1531. eik *also* at *by* onset *attack*
astound *surprised*
1532. aucht *eight* grond *ground*
1533. Banayas *Benaiah*
1534. confond *kill*
1535. Ethiop *Ethiopian* dedis
wond *a mortal wound*
1536. awyn *own* thrang *threw*
1537. onabysytly *fearlessly*
gang *walk*
1538. in *into* sistern *cistern*
slewch *slew*
1539. snaw *snow* harm eneuch *a great deal of harm*

1540. Salomon *Solomon*
estate *dignity*
1541. watc *knows*
1542. Roboam *Rehoboam*
hely *arrogant*
1543. tynt *lost* ligis *lieges'*
hartis *hearts* fate *behaviour*
1544. outragius
ingrate *outrageously ungrateful*
1545. tribis *tribes* devyd *separate*
1546. sla *kill* be nychtis
tyd *during the night*
1547. Synachorybis
ost *Sennacherib's army*
1548. weir *wage war*
Jowry *Judea* bost *boast*
1549. Esachy *Hezekiah*
1550. Hely *Elijah*

1542. 'Lost the loyalty of all his lieges through his behaviour'.

Amyd a fyry chare to paradyce went;
The stories of Esdras and of Neamy
And Danyell in the lyonys cave saw I,
For he the dragon slew, Bell brak and schent.
The chyldir thre amyd the fornace sent.   1555
I saw the transmygracion in Babillon
And baith the Bukis of Parelipomenon.

I saw the haly archangell Raphell
Mary Sara the dochter of Raguell
On Thobyas for his just fatheris sake,   1560
And bynd the crewel devyll that wes sa fel
Quhilk slew hir sevin first husbandis, as tha tel;
And quhow Judyth Olyfarnus heid of strake
Be nychtis tyd, and fred hir town fra wrake.
Jonas in the quhalys wame dais thre   1565
And schot furth syne, I saw, at Ninive.

Of Job I saw the patyence maist degest.
Of Alexander I saw the gret conquest,
Quhilk in twelf yeris wan nere the warld on breid,
And of Anthiacus the gret onrest,   1570

1551. fyry chare *fiery chariot*
1552. Esdras *Ezra*
Neamy *Nehemiah*
1553. Danyell *Daniel*
1554. Bell *Bel* brak *destroyed*
schent *disgraced*
1555. chyldir *young men*
1556. transmygracion *removal of
the Jews* in *into*
Babillon *Babylon*
1557. baith *both* Bukis of
Parelipomenon *Books of
Chronicles*
1558. haly *holy* Raphell *Raphael*
1559. mary *marry*
dochter *daughter*
1560. on Thobyas *to Tobias*
1561. crewel *cruel* fel *ferocious*

1562. as tha tel *so they say*
1563. Judyth *Judith* Olyfarnus
heid *Holofernes' head* of
strake *cut off*
1564. be nychtis tyd *during the
night* fred *freed*
wrake *persecution*
1565. Jonas *Jonah* quhalys
wame *whale's belly* dais
thre *three days*
1566. schot furth *vomited out*
syne *afterwards* Ninive *Nineveh*
1567. patyence *patience* maist
degest *most resolute*
1569. wan *conquered* nere *almost*
warld on breid *whole world*
1570. Anthiacus *Antiochus*
onrest *strife*

1554. 'For he slew the dragon, and destroyed and disgraced Baal'.
1555. 'I saw the three young men sent into the furnace'.
1563. 'And how Judith cut off Holofernes' head'.
1570. 'And the great strife caused by Antiochus'.

Quhow tyrrand lyk all Jowrye he opprest;
Of Macabeus, full mony knychtly deid,
That gart all Grece and Egypt stand in dreid,
In quyet brocht his realm throw his prowes.
I saw his brethir Symon and Jonathas,   1575

Quhilkis wer maist worthy quhil thair dayis rang.
Of Tebes, eik, I saw the weris lang
Quhare Thedeus allone slew fyfty knychtis,
Quhow fynaly of Grece the campyonys strang,
All hail the floure of knychtheid, in that thrang   1580
Wes distroyit, quhill Thesyus with his mychtis
The toun and Creon wan, for all his slychtis.
Thare saw I quhow, as Stacius dois tell,
Amphiorax the bischop sank to hel.

The faithfull ladyis of Grece I mycht considdir   1585
In clathis blak all barfute pas togyddir
Till Thebes sege fra thair lordis wer slane:
Behald, ye men that callys ladyis liddir
And lycht of latis, quhat kyndncs brocht thaym thidder,
Quhat treuth and luif did in thair brestis remane.   1590
I traist ye sall reid in na wryt agane

1571. tyrrand lyk *tyrannically*
  Jowrye *Judea* opprest *oppressed*
1572. Macabeus *Judas Maccabeus*
1573. gart *caused* dreid *fear*
1574. in quyet *into peacefulness*
  brocht *brought* prowes *skill*
1575. brethir *brothers*
  Symon *Simon*
  Jonathas *Jonathan*
1576. quhil thair dayis rang *during their lives*
1577. Tebes *Thebes* eik *also*
  weris lang *long wars*
1578. Thedeus *Tideus*
  allone *single-handedly*
  knychtis *knights*
1579. campyonys strang *mighty champions*
1580. hail *entirely* floure *flower*
  knychtheid *knighthood*
  thrang *crowd*
1581. quhill *until*

Thesyus *Theseus* mychtis *forces*
1582. toun *town* for all his
  slychtis *in spite of all his cunning*
1583. Stacius *Statius*
1584. sank to *sank down into*
  hel *hell*
1585. mycht considdir *could look upon*
1586. clathis *clothes*
  barfute *barefoot* pas *pass*
1587. Thebes sege *the siege of Thebes* fra *after*
1588. liddir *weak-natured*
1589. lycht of latis *fickle in behaviour* kyndnes *natural attributes* thidder *there*
1590. treuth *loyalty* luif *love*
  brestis *hearts* remane *reside*
1591. traist *believe* reid *read about* na wryt agane *no other book*

In a realme sa mony of sic constance.
Persave thairby wemen ar til avance.

Of duke Pyrrotheus the spousage in that tyd
Quhare the Centauris reft away the bryd　　　　　1595
Thare saw I, and thair battell huge till se;
And Hercules, quhais renoun walkis wyd,
For Exiona, law by Troyis syd,
Fecht and ovircome a monsture of the se,
For quhilk, quhen his reward denyit wes, he　　　　1600
Maid the first sege and the distructioun
Of mychty Troy, quhylum the rial town.

To wyn the fleys of gold tho saw I sent
Of Grece the nobillis with Jason consequent,
Hail that conquest and all Medeas slychtis,　　　　1605
Quhow for Jason Ysiphile wes schent,
And quhow to Troy, as thay to Colchos went,
Grekis tholyt of Kyng Lamedon gret onrychtis,
Quhairfore Troy distroyt wes be thair mychtis,
Exiona ravyst and Lamedon slane,　　　　　　　　1610
Bot Priamus restoryt the town agane.

1592. a realme *one realm*
constance *constancy*
1593. persave *deduce* til avance *to be praised*
1594. Pyrrotheus *Pirithous*
spousage *wedding* tyd *time*
1595. Centauris *Centaurs*
reft *stole* bryd *bride*
1596. till se *to see*
1597. renoun *fame* walkis wyd *is widespread*
1598. Exiona *Hesione* law *down* Troyis syd *the walls of Troy*
1599. fecht *fought* se *sea*
1600. denyit *denied*
1601. sege *siege*
1602. quhylum *formerly* rial *royal*

1603. fleys *fleece* tho *then*
1604. of *from* nobillis *noblemen* consequent *next*
1605. hail *whole* slychtis *cunning tricks*
1606. Ysiphile *Hypsipyle* schent *disgraced*
1607. Colchos *Colchis*
1608. tholyt *suffered* Lamedon *Laomedon* onrychtis *injustices*
1609. quhairfore *for which reason* distroyt wes *was destroyed* be *by* mychtis *power*
1610. ravyst *abducted*
1611. bot *but* Priamus *Priam* restoryt *built*

1605. 'That whole conquest and all Medea's cunning tricks'.
1608. 'Greeks suffered great injustices at the hands of King Laomedon'.

The Jugement of Parys saw I syne
That gave the appil, as poetis can diffyne,
Till Venus as goddes maist gudlye,
And quhow in Grece he revest quene Helyne   1615
Quharefore the Grekis with thair gret navyn,
Full mony thousand knychtis, hastely
Thaym till revenge salyt towart Troy in hye.
I saw quhow be Ulixes with gret joy
Quhat wyse Achil wes fond and brocht to Troy.   1620

The crewel battellys and the dyntis strang,
The gret debate, and eik the weris lang
At Troy sege, the myrrour to me schew,
Sustenit ten yeris, Grekis Trojanys amang,
And athir party set ful oft in thrang,   1625
Quhare that Hector did douchty dedis enew,
Quhill fears Achil baith hym and Troylus slew.
The gret hors maid I saw, and Troy syn tynt
And fair Ylion al in flambys brynt.

Syne out of Troy I saw the fugityvys,   1630
Quhow that Eneas, as Virgill weil discrivis,
In countries seir wes by the seis rage

1612. Parys *Paris* syne *then*
1613. appil *apple* can diffyne *say*
1614. till *to* gudlye *beautiful*
1615. revest *abducted*
   Helyne *Helen*
1616. navyn *navy*
1617. knychtis *knights*
   hastely *swiftly*
1618. salyt *sailed* in hye *in haste*
1619. be Ulixes *by Ulysses*
1620. quhat wyse *in what way*
   Achil *Achilles* fond *found*
1621. crewel battellys *fierce*
   battles dyntis strang *heavy blows*
1622. debate *strife* weris lang *long*
   wars

1623. sege *siege* schew *showed*
1624. sustenit *it lasted*
   yeris *years* Trojanys *Trojans*
1625. athir *either* set . . . in
   thrang *weighed into battle*
1626. douchty dedis *brave deeds*
   enew *many*
1627. quhill *until* fears *fierce*
   Troylus *Troilus*
1628. maid *made* tynt *destroyed*
1629. Ylion *Ilion, Troy*
   flambys *flames* brynt *burnt*
1630. fugityvys *fugitives*
1631. Eneas *Aeneas*
   Virgill *Virgil* discrivis *describes*
1632. in *to* seir *many* seis *sea's*

1624. 'It lasted ten years, the Greeks among the Trojans'.
1628. 'I saw the great Trojan Horse made, and then Troy destroyed'.
1632–3. 'Was often driven to many countries by the sea's rage, and how
he arrives'.

Bewavyt oft, and quhow that he arryvys
With all his flote but danger of theyr lyvys,
And quhow thay wer reset, baith man and page,   1635
Be Quene Dido, remanand in Cartage,
And quhow Eneas syne, as that they tell,
Went for to seik his father doun in hell.

Ovir Stix the flude I saw Eneas fair,
Quhare Carone wes the bustuus feryair.   1640
The fludis four of hell thair mycht I se,
The folk in pane, the wayis circulair,
The weltrand stone wirk Sisipho mych cair,
And all the plesance of the Camp Elysee
Quhare ald Anchyses did common with Enee,   1645
And schew be lyne all his successyon.
This ilk Eneas, maist famus of renoun,

I saw to goddis make the sacrifice
(Quhairof the ordour and maner to devyse
Wer ovir prolext), and quhow Eneas syne   1650
Went to the schyp, and eik I saw quhat wyse
All his navy gret hunger did suppryse,
Quhow he in Italie fynalie, with huge pyne,
Arrivit at the strandis of Lavyne,

1633. bewavyt *driven*
     arryvys *arrives*
1634. flote *fleet* but *without*
     lyvys *lives*
1635. reset *received* page *boy*
1636. remanand *staying*
     Cartage *Carthage*
1638. seik *seek*
1639. Stix the flude *the River
     Styx* fair *go*
1640. Carone *Charon* bustuus
     feryair *uncouth ferryman*
1641. fludis *rivers* mycht *could*
1642. pane *pain* wayis *paths*
1643. weltrand *rolling* wirk *cause*
     Sisipho *Sisyphus* mych
     cair *much sorrow*
1644. plesance *delight* Camp

Elysee *Elysian Fields*
1645. ald Anchyses *old Anchises*
     common *converse* Enee *Aeneas*
1646. schew *showed* be lyne *by
     lineal descent*
     successyon *progeny*
1647. ilk *same* famus *famous*
1649. quhairof *of which*
     ordour *order* devys *describe*
1650. wer *would be* ovir
     prolext *too tedious*
1651. schyp *ship* quhat wyse *the
     way in which*
1652. suppryse *overcome*
1653. pyne *suffering*
1654. strandis of Lavyne *shores of
     Lavinium*

1652. 'His entire navy was overcome by great hunger'.

And quhow he faucht weil, baith on land and
seys, 1655
And Tarnus slew, the kyng of Rutuleis.

Rome saw I beildit fyrst be Romulus,
And eik quhow lang, as wryttis Levius,
The Romane kyngis abone the pepill rang,
And how the wickit proud Terquinius, 1660
With wyfe and barnis, be Brutus Junius
Wer exilit Rome for thair insufferabil wrang.
Bot al the proces for to schaw wer lang,
Quhow chast Lucres, the gudliest and best,
Be Sextus Terquine wes cruelly opprest. 1665

The Punik batalis in that mirrour cleir
Atwene Cartage and Romanis mony yeir
I saw, becaus Eneas pietuus
Fled fra Dido be admonicionis seir
Atwene thair pepil rais ane langsum weir. 1670
I saw quhow worthy Marcus Regulus
Maist valiant, prudent and victorius
Howbeit he micht at liberty gone fre
For common profyt chesyt for till de.

Servilius, Tullus, dowchty in his daw, 1675
And Marcus Curtius eik in the myrrour I saw,
Quhilk, throw his stowtenes, in the fyry gap

1655. faucht *fought* seys *seas*
1656. Tarnus *Turnus*
   Rutuleis *Rutulians*
1657. beildit *built* be *by*
1658. lang *long* wryttis *writes*
   Levius *Livy*
1659. abone *over* pepill *people*
   rang *reigned*
1660. Terquinius *Tarquinius*
1661. barnis *children* be *by*
1662. exilit *exiled from*
   wrang *wrongdoing*
1663. schaw *show*
1664. chast Lucres *chaste*
   Lucretia gudliest *most beautiful*
1665. opprest *raped*
1666. Punik batalis *Punic Wars*

1667. atwene *between*
   Cartage *Carthage*
   Romanis *Rome* yeir *year*
1668. Eneas pietuus *pious Aeneus*
1669. be *because of* admonicionis
   seir *many warnings*
1670. rais *arose* langsum
   weir *long-lasting war*
1673. howbeit *even though* gone
   fre *have gone free*
1674. common profyt *for the
   common good* chesyt *chose*
   de *die*
1675. Servilius Tullus *Servius
   Tullius* dowchty *valiant*
   daw *day*
1677. stowtenes *courage* fyry *fiery*

For common profyt of Rome himself did thraw
Richt onabasitly, havand na dreid nor aw:
Montit on hors, onarmyt, thairin lap.   1680
And Hannyball I saw, by fatell hap
Wyn contrare Romanys mony fair victory
Quhyll Scipio eclypsyt all hys glory.

This worthy Scipio clepyt Affrycane
I saw vincus thys Hannyball in plane   1685
And Cartage bryng untyll fynall rewyn
And to Rome conquerit all the realme of Spane.
Quhow Kyng Jugurtha hes his brethir slane
Thare saw I eik, and of his were the fyne.
Rycht weil I saw the batellis intestyne   1690
Of Catulyna and of Lentulus
And atwine Pompey and Cesar Julyus,

And, breifly, every famus douchty deid
That men in story may se or cornakyll reid.
I mycht behald in that myrrour expres   1695
The miserie, the crewelte, the dreid,
Pane, sorow, wo, baith wretchitnes and neid,
The gret envy, covatus, dowbilnes
Twychand warldly onfaithful brukkylnes.

1678. himself did thraw *threw
himself*
1679. onabasitly *boldly*
havand *having* dreid *dread*
aw *fear*
1680. montit *mounted*
onarmyt *unarmed* thairin
lap *leapt inside*
1681. Hannyball *Hannibal* fatell
hap *destined occurrence*
1682. contrare *against*
1683. quhyll *until*
eclypsyt *overshadowed*
1684. clepyt *called*
Affrycane *Africanus*
1685. vincus *vanquish* in plane *on
the battlefield*
1686. untyll *to* fynall
rewyn *ultimate ruin*

1687. to *for* Spane *Spain*
1688. brethir *brothers*
1689. were *war* fyne *end*
1690. batellis intestyne *civil wars*
1691. Catulyna *Catiline*
1692. atwine *between* Cesar
Julyus *Julius Caesar*
1693. douchty deid *valiant deed*
1694. se *find* cornakyll *chronicle*
reid *read*
1695. expres *clearly*
1696. dreid *fear*
1697. pane *pain* neid *need*
1698. covatus *greed*
dowbilnes *treachery*
1699. twychand *concerning*
onfaithful *treacherous*
brukkylnes *frailty*

1694. 'Which men can find in stories or read in the chronicles'.
1699. 'All involved in the treacherous frailty of the world'.

I saw the Fend fast folk to vicis tist 1700
And al the cumming of the Antecrist.

Plesand debaitmentis, quha sa rycht reportis,
Thare mycht be sene and al maner disportys:
The falkonnis for the revere at thair gate
Newand the fowlys in periculo mortis, 1705
Layand thaym in be companeis and sortis,
And, at the plunge, part saw I handlyt hate;
The wery huntare, byssy ayr and late,
Wyth questyng hundis syrchand to and fra
To hunt the hart, the bare, the da, the ra. 1710

I saw Raf Coilyear with his thrawin brow,
Craibit Johne the Reif and auld Cowkewyis sow
And how the wran come out of Ailssay,
And Peirs Plewman that maid his workmen fow,
Gret Gowmakmorne and Fyn Makcoull, and how 1715
Thay suld be goddis in Ireland, as thay say.
Thair saw I Maitland upon auld Beird Gray,
Robene Hude and Gilbert with the quhite hand,
How Hay of Nauchtoun flew in Madin land.

1700. Fend *Devil* vicis *sin*
tist *enticing*
1701. cumming *coming*
Antecrist *Antichrist*
1702. debaitmentis *amusements*
quha sa rycht reportis *whoever recounts it all properly*
1703. sene *seen* disportys *recreations*
1704. falkonnis *falcons* for *to*
revere *river* at *in* gate *flight*
1705. newand *chasing*
fowlys *birds* in periculo mortis *in fear of death*
1706. layand *gathering* be
companeis *by groups* sortis *species*
1707. handlyt hate *fiercely handled*
1708. wery huntare *weary hunter*
byssy *busy* ayr *early*
1709. questyng hundis *baying*

hounds *syrchand searching*
1710. bare *boar* da *doe* ra *roe-deer*
1711. Raf Coilyear *Rauf Coilyear*
thrawin *frowning*
1712. craibit *bad-tempered* Johne
the Reif *John the Reeve*
auld *old* Cowkewyis *Colkelbie's*
1713. wran *wren* Ailssay *Ailsa
Crag*
1714. Peirs Plewman *Piers
Plowman* fow *full of food*
1715. Gowmakmorne *Goll Mac
Morna* Fyn Makcoull *Finn Mac
Coul*
1717. Beird Gray *Grey-Beard*
1718. Robene Hude *Robin Hood*
quhite *white*
1719. Nauchtoun *Naughton* in *to*
Madin land *Paradise*

1704–5. 'The falcons in flight chasing the birds, in fear of death, into the river'.
1707. 'And, during the plunge underwater, I saw some of them fiercely handled'.

The nigramansy thair saw I eik anone   1720
Of Bonitas, Bongo, and Frere Bacon
With mony subtell poynt of juglory:
Of Flandris peys maid mony precius stone,
A gret lade sadil of a sychyng bone,
Of a nutmog thay mayid a monk in hy,   1725
A parys kirk of a small penny py,
And Bonytas of a mussil made ane ape,
With mony othir subtell mow and jape.

And schortly, til declare the veryte,
All plesand pastance and gemmys that micht be   1730
In that myrrour wer present to my sycht.
And as I wondryt on that grete ferlye,
Venus at last, in turning of hir e,
Knew weil my face and said, 'Be Goddis micht,
Ye bene welcum, my presoner, to this hycht.   1735
Quhow passit thou,' quod scho, 'that hidduus depe?'
'Madame,' quod I, 'I not more than a schepe.'

'Na fors thairof,' said scho, 'sen thow art here.
Quhow plesys the our pastance and effere?'
'Glaidly,' quod I, 'Madame, be God of hevyn.'   1740
'Remembris thow,' said scho, 'withouten were,

1720. nigramansy *sorcery*
1721. Bonitas *Bonatti*
Bongo *Bungay* Frere *Friar*
1722. subtell poynt *clever trick*
juglory *conjuring*
1723. Flandris peys *Flanders peas*
1724. lade sadil *pack saddle*
of *from* sychyng bone *funny bone*
1725. nutmog *nutmeg*
mayid *made* in hy *quickly*
1726. parys kirk *parish church*
py *pie*
1727. mussil *mussel*
1728. subtell mow *clever trick*
jape *jest*
1729. schortly *in short* til
declare *to tell* veryte *truth*
1730. pastance *pastimes*

gemmys *games*
1731. sycht *sight*
1732. wondryt on *wondered at*
ferlye *marvel*
1733. e *eye*
1734. be Goddis micht *by God's
power*
1735. bene *are* hycht *summit*
1736. quhow passit thou *how did
you manage to pass through*
1737. I not more *I know no more*
schepe *sheep*
1738. na fors thairof *no matter*
sen *since*
1739. quhow plesys the *how do you
like* pastance *pastime*
effere *entertainment*
1741. were *doubt*

1723. 'Many a precious stone created from Flanders peas'.

On thy promyt quhen of thy gret dangere
I the deliverit as now is not to nevyn?'
Than answerit I agane with sober stevyn:
'Madame, your precept, quhat so be your wyll,　　1745
Here I remane ay reddy till fulfill.'

'Weil, weil,' said scho, 'thy wyll is suffycyent.
Of thy bousoum answere I stand content.'
Than suddandly in hand a buke scho hynt
The quhilk to me betaucht scho or I went,　　1750
Commandand me to be obedient
And put in ryme that proces than quyt tynt.
I promised hir, forsuyth, or scho wald stynt,
The buke ressavand, thairon my cure to preve.
Inclynand syne lawly, I tuke my leve.　　1755

Twychand this buke peraventur ye sall here
Sumtyme efter quhen I have mare lasere.
My nymphe in hast tho hynt me by the hand
And as we sammyn walkyt furth in fere
'I the declare,' sayd scho, 'yone myrrour clerc　　1760
The quhilk thow saw afore dame Venus stand
Signifyes nothing ellis till understand
Bot the gret bewty of thir ladyis facis
Quhairin lovers thinkis thay behald all gracis.'

1742. promyt *promise* of *from*
1743. the deliverit *rescued you*
　nevyn *mention*
1744. sober stevyn *serious voice*
1745. precept *command* quhat so
　be *whatever is*
1746. fulfill *obey*
1748. bousoum *obedient*
1749. buke *book* hynt *took*
1750. betaucht *gave*
1751. commandand *commanding*
1752. proces *narrative* than *then*
　quyt tynt *entirely forgotten*
1753. forsuyth *truly* or *before*
　stynt *cease*
1754. ressavand *receiving*
　cure *diligence* preve *test*

1755. inclynand *bowing*
　lawly *humbly* leve *leave*
1756. twychand *about*
　peraventur *perhaps* here *hear*
1757. mare lasere *more leisure*
1758. tho *then* hynt *took*
1759. sammyn *together*
　walkyt *walked* in
　fere *companionably*
1760. I the decleare *I can tell you*
1761. afore *before*
1762. ellis *else*
1763. bewty *beauty* ladyis
　facis *ladies' faces*
1764. quhairin *in which*
　gracis *graces*

1750. 'Which she gave to me before I went'.

Scho me convoyit, finally to tell,   1765
With gret plesance straucht to the ryche castell,
Quhare mony saw I pres til get ingres.
Thare saw I Synon and Achittefell
Pressand til clym the wallis and how thay fell.
Lucyus Catalyn saw I thare expres,   1770
In at a wyndow pres til have entres
Bot suddandly Tullius come with a buke,
And strake hym doun quhill all his chaftis quuke.

Fast clymmand up thay lusty wallys of stone
I saw Jugurtha and tressonabill Tryphon   1775
Bot thay na grippis thair mycht hald for slyddir.
Preissand to clym stude thousandis many one,
And into the ground thay fallen every one.
Than on the wall a garatour I considdir,
Proclamand lowd, that did thayr hartis swiddir: 1780
'Out on falshed, the mother of everye vyce!
Away invy and brynnand covetyce!'

The garatour, my nymphe tho to me tald,
Wes clepyt Lawte, kepar of the hald
Of hie honour, and thay pepyll out schete,   1785
Swa presand thaym to clym, quhilum wer bald,

1765. me convoyit *guided me*
1766. straucht *straight*
1767. pres *pushing forward* til get
   ingres *to gain entrance*
1768. Achittefell *Ahithophel*
1769. clym *climb*
1770. Lucyus Catalyn *Lucius
   Catiline* expres *clearly*
1771. entres *entry*
1773. strake *struck* quhill *until*
   chaftis *cheeks* quuke *trembled*
1774. thay *those* lusty *fine*
1775. tressonabill *treasonous*
1776. slyddir *slipperiness*
1777. preissand *pushing forward*

1779. garatour *watchman*
   considdir *beheld*
1780. lowd *loudly* did *made*
   hartis *hearts* swiddir *falter*
1781. out on *down with*
   falshed *falsehood*
1782. invy *envy* brynnand
   covetyce *burning greed*
1783. tald *explained*
1784. clepyt *called* Lawte *Loyalty*
   kepar *keeper* hald *fortress*
1785. out schete *shut out*
1786. presand thaym *pushing
   themselves* quhilum *once*
   bald *brave*

1776. 'But the slipperiness of the wall prevented them from getting a
   grip there'.
1786–8. 'Pushing themselves forward like this to climb, were once bold,
   full of virtue and young; but as soon as they grew old, they turned
   their minds from honour and set them entirely on vice'.

Rycht vertuus young; but fra tyme thay woux ald,
Fra honour hail one vice thair mindis sete.
'Now sall thow go,' quod sche, 'straucht to the yete,
Of this palyce and entre but offence,   1790
For the portar is clyped Pacience.

'The mychty prynce, the gretest empriour
Of yone palyce,' quod scho, 'hecht Hie Honour,
Quham to disservys mony traist officiare.
For Charite, of gudlynes the flour,   1795
Is Maister Houshald in yone cristall tour,
Ferme Constance is the kyngis secritare
And Liberalite heicht his thesaurar.
Innocens and Devocyon, as efferis,
Bene clerkis of closet and cubeculeris.   1800

'His Comptrowere is clepyt Discretioun.
Humanyte and Trew Relatioun
Bene yscherris of his chalmer morow and eve.
Peace, Quyet, Rest, oft wakis up and doun
In till his hall as marchellis of renoun.   1805
Temperance is cuke, his mete to tast and preve.

1787. vertuus *virtuous* woux
  ald *grew old*
1788. hail *entirely* one *on* sete *set*
1789. quod *said* straucht *straight*
  yete *gate*
1790. entre *enter* but *without*
1791. portar *doorkeeper*
1792. empriour *emperor*
1793. hecht *is called* Hic *High*
1794. disservys *serve*
  traist *trusted* officiare *officers*
1795. of gudlynes the flour *the*
  flower of goodness
1796. Maister Houshald *Master of*
  the Household yone *that*
  tour *tower*
1797. Ferme Constance *Firm*
  Constancy secritare *secretary*
1798. Liberalite *Generosity*

heicht *is the name of*
  thesaurar *treasurer*
1799. Devocyon *Devotion* as
  efferis *as is fitting*
1800. bene *are* clerkis of
  closet *private secretaries*
  cubeculeris *attendants of the*
  royal bedchamber
1801. Comptrowere *Comptroller*
1802. Humanyte *Kindness* Trew
  Relatioun *Faithful Report*
1803. yscherris *ushers*
  chalmer *chamber*
  morow *morning*
1804. wakis *walks*
1805. marchellis *marshals*
  renoun *good reputation*
1806. cuke *cook* mete *food*
  tast *taste* preve *test*

1794. 'Who is served by many trusted officers'.

Humylyte, karvar, that na wycht lyst greve.
His maister sewer hecht Vertuus Discipline.
Mercy is copper, and mixis weil his wyne.

'His chanceller is clepyt Conscyence,   1810
Quhilk for na meid will pronounce fals sentence.
With him are assessouris four of one ascent,
Science, Prudence, Justice, Sapience,
Quhilkis to na wycht lyst committing offence –
The chekker rollys and the kyngis rent   1815
As auditouris thay ovirseis quhat is spent.
Labourus Diligens, Gud Werkis, Clene Livyng
Bene out-stewartis and catouris to yone kyng.

'Gud Hope remanys ever amang yone sort,
A fyne menstral with mony mow and sport.   1820
And Piete is the kyngis almoseir.
Syne Fortitude, the rycht quha lyst report,
Is lieutenand, al wrachys to comfort.
The kyngis mynyeon, roundand in his eyr,
Heicht Verite, did nevir leyl man deir,   1825

1807. Humylyte *Humility*
karvar *carver* wycht *man* lyst
greve *wants to grieve*
1808. maister sewer *chief server*
hecht *is named* Vertuus *Virtuous*
1809. copper *cup-bearer*
wyne *wine*
1810. chanceller *chancellor*
1811. meid *bribe*
sentence *judgement*
1812. assessouris *advisers*
ascent *accord*
1813. Science *Knowledge*
Sapience *Wisdom*
1814. quhilkis *who* wycht *person*
lyst *wish*
1815. chekker rollys *exchequer*
accounts rent *income*
1816. auditouris *auditors*
ovirseis *oversee*

1817. Labourus Diligens *Diligent*
Labour Gud Werkis *Good*
Works
1818. out-stewartis *land stewards*
catouris *caterers*
1819. remanys *remains*
sort *company*
1820. menstral *minstrel* mow *jest*
sport *entertainment*
1821. Piete *Pity* almoseir *almoner*
1822. syne *then* the rycht quha
lyst report *whoever wishes to*
report it correctly
1823. lieutenand *king's deputy*
wrachys *wretches*
1824. mynyeon *favourite servant*
roundand *whispering* eyr *ear*
1825. heicht *is named*
Verite *Truth* leyl *loyal*
deir *harm*

1807. 'Humility, the carver, who wishes to grieve no one'.
1814. 'Who wish to offend no one'.
1825. 'Is named Truth, who never harmed a loyal man'.

And, schortly, every vertew and plesance
Is subject to yone kyngis obbeysance.

'Come on,' sayd sche, 'this ordenance to vysyte.'
Than past we to that cristall palyce quhyte
Quhare I abayd the entre til behald.   1830
I bad na mare of plesance nor delyte,
Of lusty sycht, of joy and blys perfyte,
Nor mare weilfare til have abone the mold,
Than for til se that yet of byrnyst gold,
Quhare on thair was maist curiusly ingrave   1835
All naturall thyng men may in erd consave.

Thare wes the erth enveronyt wyth the see
Quhare on the schyppes saland mycht I sc,
The ayr, the fyre – all the four elymentis –
The speris sevyn and primum mobile,   1840
The sygnis twelf, perfytly every gre,
The zodiak, hale as bukis represents,
The Poil Antertik that ever himselfe absentis,
The Poil Artik, and eik the Ursis twane,
The Sevyn Sterris, Pheton and the Charle Wane.   1845

Thare wes ingraf quhow that Ganamedis
Wes reft till hevyn (as men in Ovyd redis),

1826. schortly *in short*
vertew *virtue* plesance *pleasure*
1827. obbeysance *command*
1828. ordenance *establishment*
vysyte *visit*
1829. past *passed* quhyte *white*
1830. abayd *lingered*
entre *entrance*
1831. bad *expected*
1833. weilfare *good fortune* abone
the mold *upon the earth*
1834. yet *gate* byrnyst *polished*
1835. quhare on *upon which*
curiusly *skilfully*
ingrave *engraved*
1836. in erd *in the world*
consave *imagine*
1837. enveronyt wyth *surrounded by*
1838. schyppes *ships*

saland *sailing* se *see*
1839. ayr *air* elymentis *elements*
1840. speris sevyn *seven planets*
primum mobile *outermost sphere*
1841. sygnis twelf *twelve*
astrological signs gre *degree*
1842. hale *exactly* bukis *books*
1843. Poil Antertik *Antarctic Pole
Star* himselfe absentis *absents
himself*
1844. Poil Artik *Artic Pole Star*
eik *also* Ursis twane *two Ursas*
1845. Sterris *Stars*
Pheton *Phaethon* Charle
Wane *Charlemagne's Wain*
1846. ingraf *inscribed*
Ganamedis *Ganymede*
1847. reft *carried off* till hevyn *to
heaven* Ovyd *Ovid* redis *read*

And on till Jupiter made his cheif butlare;
The douchters, fare in to thayr lusty wedis,
Of Dorida, amyd the see but dredis   1850
Swymmand, and part wer figurit thare
Apon a crag dryand thair yalow hare,
With facis not onlyk, for quha thaym seyng
Mycht weil consyddir that thay al sisteris beyng.

Of the planetis all the conjunctionys,   1855
Thare episciclis and opposionis
Wer porturyt thair, and quhow thair coursis swagis,
Thare naturale and dayly motionis,
Eclipse, aspectis and degressyonys.
Thare saw I mony gudly personagis   1860
Quhilkis semyt all lusty quyk ymagis,
The werkmanschip excedyng mony fold
The precyus mater, thocht it wes fynest gold.

Wondrand here on, agane my wyll but lete
My nymphe in grif schot me in at the yet.   1865
'Quhat devyl,' said scho, 'hes thou not ellis ado
Bot all thy wyt and fantasy to set
On sic dotyng?' and tho for fere I swet

1848. butlare *cup-bearer*
1849. douchters *daughters*
  fare *beautiful*   lusty wedis *fine clothes*
1850. Dorida *Driada*   but dredis *without doubt*
1851. swymmand *swimming*
  part *some*   figurit *depicted*
1852. crag *rock*   dryand *drying*
  hare *hair*
1853. onlyk *unalike*   for *so that*
  quha *whoever*   seyng *saw*
1854. consyddir *think*   beyng *were*
1855. conjunctionys *conjunctions*
1856. thare *their*
  episciclis *epicycles*
  opposionis *oppositions*
1857. porturyt *depicted*   coursis
  swagis *courses decrease*
1858. dayly *daily*
1859. aspectis *aspects*

degressyonys *deviations*
1860. personagis *portraits*
1861. quhilkis semyt *which seemed*
  lusty *fine*   quyk ymagis *lifelike images*
1862. werkmanschip *workmanship*
  mony fold *many times*
1863. mater *material*   thocht *even though*
1864. wondrand *wondering*
  agane *against*   but lete *without delay*
1865. grif *annoyance*
  schot *pushed*   yet *gate*
1866. not ellis ado *nothing else to do*
1867. bot *except*   wyt *intelligence*
  fantasy *thought*
1868. sic dotyng *such folly*
  tho *then*   fere *fear*   swet *broke into a sweat*

Of her langage, bot than anone said scho,
'List thou se farlyes, behald thaym yondir, lo;   1870
Yit study not ovir mekil a dreid thow vary,
For I persave the halflyngis in a fary.'

Within that palyce sone I gat a sycht
Quhare walkand went ful mony worthy wicht
Amyd the close, with all myrthys to wale;   1875
For lyk Phebus with fyry bemys brycht
The wallys schane, castand sa gret a lycht,
It semyt lyk the hevyn imperiall.
And as the cedir surmontyth the rammale
In perfyt hycht, sa of that court a glance   1880
Excedis far all erdly vane plesance.

For lois of sycht considdir micht I nocht
Quhow perfytly the ryche wallys wer wrocht.
Swa the reflex of cristall stanys schone
For brychtnes skarsly blenk thairon I mocht.   1885
The purifyit silver, soithly as me thocht,
Insteid of syment wes ovir all that wone,

1869. of *at*   langage *words*
1870. list thou se *if you want to*
   see farlyes *wonders* lo *look*
1871. ovir mekil *too closely* a
   dreid *for fear that* vary *go mad*
1872. persave *see* halflyngis *half*
   fary *trance*
1873. sone *soon* sycht *glimpse*
1874. walkand *walking*
   wicht *creature*
1875. close *courtyard*
   myrthys *pleasures* to wale *to*
   choose from
1876. Phebus *Phoebus*
   bemys *beams*
1877. schane *shone* lycht *light*
1878. semyt lyk *seemed like* hevyn

imperiall *empyrean heaven*
1879. cedir *cedar*
   surmontyth *surpasses*
   rammale *brushwood*
1880. hycht *height*
1881. erdly *earthly* vane *vain*
1882. lois *loss*
1883. wrocht *built*
1884. swa *in such a way* reflex
   of *reflection from* stanys *stones*
1885. brychtnes *brightness*
   skarsly *scarcely* blenk *glance*
1886. purifyit *refined*
   soithly *truly* as me thocht *it*
   seemed to me
1887. syment *mortar*
   wone *dwelling*

1871–2. 'But do not look at them too closely in case you go insane, for I can see that you are already half in a trance.'
1882–5. 'Loss of my sight meant that I could not appreciate how perfectly the fine walls were built. The reflection from the crystal stones shone in such a way that I could scarcely glance at them on account of their brightness'.

Yet round about ful mony a beriall stone,
And thaym conjunctly jonyt fast and quemyt.
The close wes paithit with silver, as it semyt.   1890

The durris and the wyndois all wer breddyt
With massy gold, quhareof the fynes scheddit.
With byrnyst evyr baith palyce and touris
Wer thekyt weil, maist craftely that cled it:
For so the quhitly blanchit bone ovirspred it,   1895
Mydlyt with gold, anamalyt all colouris,
Inporturat of byrdis and swete flouris,
Curius knottis and mony sle devyse,
Quhilkis to behald wes perfyt paradice.

And, to proceid, my nympe and I furth went   1900
Straucht to the hall, throwout the palyce jent,
And ten stagis of thopas did ascend.
Schit wes the dure. In at a boir I blent,
Quhare I beheld the gladdest represent
That evir in erth a wrachit catyve kend.   1905
Breifly theis proces til conclude and end:
Me thocht the flure wes al of amatist,
Bot quhareof war the wallis I ne wist.

1888. yet *scattered* beriall *beryl*
1889. conjunctly *together*
  jonyt *joined* quemyt *closely fitted*
1890. paithit *paved*
1891. durris *doors*
  wyndois *windows*
  breddyt *covered*
1892. massy *solid* quhareof *from which* fynes *purity*
  scheddit *radiated*
1893. byrnyst evyr *polished ivory*
  touris *towers*
1894. thekyt *roofed* cled *covered*
1895. quhitly blanchit *bleached white* ovirspred *spread over*
1896. mydlyt *mingled*
  anamalyt *enamelled in*

1897. inporturat of *decorated with*
  byrdis *birds* flouris *flowers*
1898. curius *intricate* sle
  devyse *skilful design*
1900. proceid *continue*
1901. straucht *straight*
  throwout *right through* jent *noble*
1902. stagis *steps* thopas *topaz*
1903. schit *closed* dure *door*
  boir *chink* blent *peeped*
1904. gladdest represent *most wonderful sight*
1905. wrachit catyve *worthless wretch* kend *saw*
1906. theis proces *this narrative*
1907. flure *floor* amatist *amethyst*
1908. quhareof *of what* ne wist *do not know*

1894. 'Were well roofed, most skilfully by those who covered it'.
1908. 'But of what substance the walls were made I do not know'.

The multitud of prectius stonis sere
Thairon swa schane, my febill sycht, but were,   1910
Mycht not behald thair vertuus gudlynes.
For all the ruf, as did to me appere,
Hang full of plesand lowpyt saphyrs clere.
Of dyamantis and rubys, as I ges,
Wer all the burdis maid, of mast riches.   1915
Of sardanus, of jaspe and smaragdane
Trestis, formys and benkis wer, pollist plane.

Baith to and fro amyd the hall they went,
Rial princis in plate and armouris quent
Of byrnist gold cuchit with precyus stonys.   1920
Intronyt sat a god armypotent,
On quhais gloryus vissage as I blent,
In extasy, be his brychtnes, atonys
He smate me doun and byrsyt all my bonys.
Thare lay I still in swoun, with cullour blaucht, 1925
Quhil at the last my nymphe up hes me kaucht.

Syne wyth gret pane, with womentyng and care,
In hir armys scho bare me doun the stare
And in the clois full softly laid me doun,

1909. prectius *precious* sere *many*
1910. schane *shone* sycht *vision*
but were *without doubt*
1911. vertuus gudlynes *powerful
excellence*
1912. ruf *ceiling*
1913. lowpyt *looped*
saphyrs *sapphires*
1914. dyamantis *diamonds*
1915. burdis *tables* mast *greatest*
1916. sardanus *sardonyx*
jaspe *jasper*
smaragdane *smaragd*
1917. trestis *trestles*
formys *chairs* benkis *benches*
pollist plane *polished smooth*
1919. rial *regal* plate *plate*
armour quent *skilfully made*

1920. byrnist *polished*
cuchit *inlaid*
1921. intronyt *enthroned*
armypotent *mighty in arms*
1922. vissage *face* blent *looked*
1923. in extasy *in a trance*
atonys *suddenly*
1924. smate *knocked*
byrsyt *bruised* bonys *bones*
1925. swoun *faint* with cullour
blaucht *pale in colour*
1926. quhil *until* up hes me
kaucht *picked me up*
1927. pane *pain*
womentyng *lamenting*
care *sorrow*
1928. bare *carried* stare *stairs*
1929. clois *courtyard*

1912–13. 'For, it seemed to me, that the whole ceiling consisted of clear
sapphires arranged in spiral patterns'.

Held up my hede to tak the hailsum ayre   1930
For of my lyfe scho stude in gret dispare.
Me till awalk ay wes that lady boun,
Quhill, finally, out of my dedly swoun
I swyth ovircome and up my eyne did cast.
'Be myrry, man,' quod scho, 'the werst is past.   1935

'Get up,' scho said, 'for schame, be na cowart.
My hede in wed, thow hes a wyfis hart
That for a plesand sycht is so mysmaid!'
Than, all in anger, apon my fete I start;
And for hir wordis wer so apyrsmart,   1940
On to the nymphe I maid a bustuus braid.
'Carlyng,' quod I, 'quhat wes yone at thow said?'
'Soft yow,' said sche, 'thay ar not wyse that stryvys,
For kyrkmen wer ay jentill to ther wyvys.

'I am rycht glaid thou art wordyn so wycht.   1945
Lang ere, me thocht, thow had nothir fors ne mycht,
Curage nor wyll for till have grevyt a fla.
Quhat alyt the to fall?' Quod I, 'The sycht
Of yone goddes grym fyry vissage brycht
Ovirset my wyt and all my spretis swa   1950
I mycht not stand.' 'Bot wes that suyth?' 'Ya, ya!'

1930. hede *head*   hailsum
     ayre *health-giving air*
1931. stude *stood*   dispare *despair*
1932. awalk *revive*   boun *intent*
1933. quhill *until*
1934. swyth ovircome *suddenly
     came round*   eyne *eyes*
1935. myrry *happy*   werst *worst*
1936. cowart *coward*
1937. hede *head*   wed *pledge*
     wyfis *woman's*
1938. mysmaid *troubled*
1939. fete *feet*   start *jumped*
1940. for *because*   apyrsmart *sharp*
1941. bustuus braid *rough gesture*
1942. carlyng *old woman*   quhat
     wes yone at *what was it that*

1943. soft yow *calm down*
     wyse *wise*   stryvys *quarrel*
1944. kyrkmen *men of the church*
     jentill *courteous*   wyvys *wives*
1945. rycht glaid *very happy*
     wordyn so wycht *become so
     strong*
1946. lang ere *a while ago*
     nothir *neither*   fors *power*
     mycht *strength*
1947. grevyt *hurt*   fla *fly*
1948. alyt the *caused you*
1949. goddes *god's*
1950. ovirset *disturbed*   wyt *mind*
     spretis *faculties*   swa *so that*
1951. suyth *true*   ya *yes*

1932. 'That lady was intent on reviving me'.
1937. 'I'm willing to bet my life that you have a woman's heart'.

Than said the nymphe rycht merylie and leuch,
'Now I considdir thy malt hart weil eneuch.

'I wyl,'quod scho, 'na mare the thus assay
With sic plesance, quhilk may thy sprete effray.   1955
Yit sall thow se suythly, sen thou art here,
My lydyis court in thair gudly array.
For till behald thair myrth cum on thy way.'
Than hand in hand suyth went we furth in fere
At a postrum towart the fair herbere.   1960
In that passage full fast at hir I franyt
Quhat folk thay wer within the hall remanyt.

'Yone wer,' said scho, 'quha sa the richt discrivys,
Maist vailyeand folk and vertuus in thair lyvys.
Now in the court of Honour thay remane   1965
Victoriusly, and in all plesance thryvys,
For thay with spere, with swerdys and wyth knyvys
In just battell wer fundyn maist of mane.
In thair promyttis thay stude evir fyrm and plane.
In thaym aboundit worschyp and lawte   1970
Illumynyt with liberalite.

'Honour,' quod scho 'to this hevinly ryng
Differris richt far from warldly honoring,
Quhilk is but pompe of erdly dignyte

1952. leuch *laughed*
1953. considdir *understand*
   malt *confused* eneuch *enough*
1954. mare *more* assay *test*
1955. sprete *senses* effray *frighten*
1956. suythly *truly* sen *since*
1957. lydyis *lady's*
1958. myrth *joy*
1959. suyth *quickly* in
   fere *together*
1960. postrum *side gate*
   towart *towards* herbere *garden*
1961. franyt *asked*
1962. remanyt *remained*
1963. quha sa *whoever* the
   richt *correctly* discrivys *describes*

1964. vailyeand *valiant* lyvys *lives*
1966. plesance *pleasure*
   thryvys *thrive*
1967. swerdys *swords*
1968. fundyn *found to be* maist of
   mane *greatest in strength*
1969. promyttis *promises*
   stude *remained* plane *honest*
1970. aboundit *abounded*
   worschyp *honour* lawte *loyalty*
1971. illumynyt *made bright*
   liberalite *generosity*
1972. to *in* ryng *kingdom*
1973. differris *differs*
1974. but *nothing but*
   pompe *pomp* erdly *earthly*

1962. 'What kind of people they were who remained within the hall'.

Gyvyn for estate or blude, micht, or sic thyng.   1975
And in this countre, prynce, prelate or kyng
Alanerly sall for vertu honoryt be;
For erdly glore is not bot vanyte
That, as we se, sa suddandly will wend;
Bot vertuus honour nevir mare sall end.   1980

'Behald,' said scho 'and se this warldly glore:
Maist inconstant, maist slyd and transitore.
Prosperite in erd is bot a dreme,
Or lyk as man wer steppand ovir a score:
Now is he law that wes so hie tofore,   1985
And he quhilum wes borne pure of his deme,
Now his estate schynys lyke the sonne beme.
Baith up and doun, baith to and fro we se
This warld weltrys as dois the wally see.

'To papis, bischoppis, prelatis and primatis,   1990
Empriouris, kinges, princes, potestatis,
Deth settis the terme and end of all thair hycht.
Fra thay be gan, late se quha on thaym watys.
Na thyng remanis bot fame of thair estatis,
And not ellis bot vertuus werkis richt   1995
Sall with thaym wend, nother thair pompe nor mycht.
Ay vertu ryngis in lestand honour clere;
Remembir than that vertu hes no pere.

1975. estate *rank*   blude *family*   beme *sunbeam*
  micht *power*   sic *such*   1989. weltrys *welters; plunges*
1976. prelate *church official*   wally see *stormy sea*
1977. alanerly *alone*   1990. papis *popes*
1978. glore *glory*   not bot *nothing*   primatis *archbishops*
  but   vanyte *vanity*   1991. empriouris *emperors*
1979. se *see*   wend *go*   potestatis *potentates*
1980. vertuus *virtuous*   1992. terme *limit*   hycht *glory*
1982. slyd *slippery*   1993. fra *once*   gan *gone*   late se *let*
  transitore *transitory*   *us see*   watys *waits*
1983. in erd *on earth*   dreme *dream*   1994. remanis *remains*
1984. steppand *stepping*   estatis *positions*
  score *precipice*   1995. not ellis *nothing else*   werkis
1985. law *low*   hie *high*   richt *good deeds*
  tofore *before*   1996. wend *go*   nother *neither*
1986. quhilum *once*   pure *poor*   1997. ay *eternally*   ryngis *reigns*
  deme *mother*   lestand *lasting*
1987. schynys *shines*   sonne   1998. pere *equal*

1977. 'Shall be honoured for their virtue alone'.

'For vertu is a thing sa precyous,
Quhareof the end is sa delycious   2000
The warld ma not consyddir quhat it is.
It makis folk perfyte and glorious.
It makis sanctis of pepill vicious.
It causis folk ay leve in lestand blys.
It is the way til hie honour iwys.   2005
It dantis deth and every vice thorow mycht.
Without vertu, fy on all erdly wycht!

'Vertu is eik the perfyte sikkyr way,
And not ellis, til honour lestand ay.
For mony hes sene vitious pepil upheit   2010
And eftir sone thair glory vanys away,
Quharof exemplis we se this every day.
His erdly pompe is gone quhen that he deyt.
Than is he with no erdly frend suppleit
Savand vertu – weill is him hes sic a fere.   2015
Now wil I schaw,'quod sche, 'quhat folk bene here.

'The strangest Sampson is in to yone hald,
The forsy, pyssand Hercules so bald,
The feirs Achill and all the Nobillis Nyne,
Scipio Affricane, Pompeyus the ald,   2020

2000. delycious *pleasing*
2001. ma not *cannot*
  consyddir *understand*
2002. perfyte *perfect*
2003. sanctis *saints* of *out of*
  pepill vicious *wicked people*
2004. ay leve *to live always*
  lestand blys *enduring happiness*
2005. til *to* iwys *indeed*
2006. dantis *conquers*
  thorow *through* mycht *power*
2007. fy *a curse* all erdly
  wycht *every earthly creature*
2008. eik *also* sikkyr *secure*
2009. not ellis *no other* lestand
  ay *everlasting*
2010. sene *seen* vitious

pepil *wicked people*
upheit *exalted*
2011. sone *soon* vanys *vanish*
2012. quharof exemplis *examples of this*
2013. erdly *earthly* deyt *died*
2014. suppleit *provided*
2015. savand *except* fere *friend*
2016. schaw *reveal*
2017. hald *fortress*
2018. forsy *mighty*
  pyssand *powerful* bald *bold*
2019. feirs Achill *fierce Achilles*
  Nobillis Nyne *Nine Worthies*
2020. Scipio Affricane *Scipio Africanus* Pompeyus *Pompeius*
  ald *old*

2006. 'It conquers death and every vice through its power'.
2015. 'Except virtue – it is well for him who has such a friend'.
2017. 'Samson, the strongest man, is in that fortress'.

Uthir mony quhais namys afore are tald
With thousandis ma than I may here diffine,
And lusty ladyis amyd thay lordis syne:
Semiramis, Thamar, Ypolytha,
Pantyssale, Medea, Cenobia.   2025

'Of thy regyon yondir bene honorit part,
The kyngis Gregor, Kened and Kyng Robert,
With otheris mo that beis not here rehersyt.
Waryit,' quod scho, 'ay be thy megyr hart.
Thow suld have sene, had thou biddin in yon art,   2030
Quhat wyse yone hevynly company conversyt.
Wa worth thy febyll brane, sa sone wes persit.
Thow mycht have sene, remanand quhare thow was,
A huge pepyl punyst for thair trespas

'Quhilkis be wilfull, manyfest arrogance,   2035
Invyus pryd, pretendit ignorance,
Fowle dowbilnes and dissate unamendit,
Enforcis thaym thair selvyn til avance,
Be sle falsheid, but lawte or constance,
Wyth subtelnes and slychtys now commendit,   2040

2021. uthir *others*   afore *before*
2022. ma *more*   diffine *describe*
2023. lusty *beautiful*
  amyd *mingling with*   syne *then*
2024. Thamar *Tomyris*
  Ypolytha *Hippolyta*
2025. Pantyssale *Penthesilea*
  Cenobia *Zenobia*
2026. regyon *land*   bene *have
  been*   part *some*
2027. Gregor *Grig*
  Kened *Kenneth*
2028. mo *more*   beis *are*
  rehersyt *named*
2029. waryit *accursed*   megyr *feeble*
2030. suld *should*   sene *seen*
  biddin *stayed*   art *place*
2031. quhat wyse *in what way*
  conversyt *conversed*
2032. wa worth *woe betide*
  brane *brain*   persit *wounded*

2033. remanand *remaining*
2034. huge pepyl *huge number of
  people*   punyst *punished*
  trespas *wrongdoing*
2035. quhilkis *who*   be *through*
  manyfest *flagrant*
2036. invyus *envious*
2037. fowle dowbilnes *foul
  duplicity*   dissate
  unamendit *unmitigated deceit*
2038. enforcis thaym *exert
  themselves*   selvyn *selves*
  avance *advance*
2039. sle falsheid *sly falsehood*
  but *without*   lawte *loyalty*
  constance *constancy*
2040. wyth *through*
  subtelnes *cunning*
  slychtys *trickery*
  commendit *commended*

2021. 'With many others whose names were mentioned earlier'.
2026. 'Some from your land have been honoured'.

Betraisand folk that nevir to them offendit,
And upheis thaimself throw frawdful lippis,
Thocht God cause oft thare erdly glore eclippis.

'And nobillis cumyn of honorabill ancestry
Thair vertuus nobilite settis nocht by,   2045
For dishonest, unlefull, warldly ways
And throw corruppit, covatus invy.
Bot he that can be dowbill, nane is set by.
Dissate is wisdum; lawte, honour away is.
Rycht few or nane takis tent thairto thir days.   2050
And thair gret wrangis till reforme but let
In judgement yone god wes yondir set.

'Remanand yondir thow mycht have herd belyve
Pronouncit the gret sentence diffinytive
Twichand this actioun, and the dreidful pane   2055
Execute on trespassouris yit on lyve,
Swa that thair malyce sall na mare prescryve.'
'Madame,' quod I, 'for Goddis saik, turn agane.
My spreit desyris to se thair torment fane.'

2041. betraisand *betraying*
2042. upheis *exalt*
  frawdful *deceitful*
2043. thocht *although*   glore *glory*
  eclippis *to be eclipsed*
2044. nobillis *noble people*   cumyn
  of *descended from*
2045. settis nocht by *value at
  nothing*
2046. for *because of*
  unlefull *unlawful*
2047. corruppit *corrupt*
  covatus *covetous*
2048. bot *except for*
  dowbill *duplicitous*   set by *valued*
2049. dissate *deceit*   lawte *loyalty*
2050. takis tent *pays attention*

2051. wrangis *wrongdoing*   but
  let *without hindrance*
2053. remanand *remaining*
  herd *heard*   belyve *swiftly*
2054. pronouncit *pronounced*
  sentence diffinytive *final
  judgement*
2055. twichand this actioun *upon
  this case*   pane *punishment*
2056. execute *executed*
  trespassouris *sinners*   yit on
  lyve *still alive*
2057. swa *so*   malyce *malice*   na
  mare *no longer*   prescryve *prevail*
2059. spreit *soul*   se *see*
  fane *eagerly*

2042–3. 'And exalt themselves by means of their deceitful lips, even
  though God often causes their earthly glory to be eclipsed'.
2048–9. 'No one is valued except for the man who can be duplicitous.
  Deceit is the new wisdom; loyalty and honour have gone away'.
2051–2. 'And that god was placed there in judgement to reform their
  great wrongdoing without hindrance'.

Quod scho, 'Richt now thare sall thow be rejosyt   2060
Quhen thow hes tane the ayr and bettir apposyt.

'Bot first thow sal considdir commoditeis
Of our gardyng, lo, full of lusty trees,
All hie cypres, of flewer maist fragrant.
Our ladyis yonder, bissy as the beis,   2065
The swete florist colouris of rethoreis
Gaddris full fast, mony grene tendir plant;
For with all plesance plenist is yone hant,
Quhare precious stanys on treis doyth abound
In sted of frute, chargyt with peirlis round.'   2070

On till that gudly garth thus we proceid
Quhilk with a large fowsy, fare on breid,
Inveronyt wes, quhare fysches wer enew.
All wattir foulis wer swomand thair gud speid;
Als out of growand treis thair saw I breid   2075
Foulys that hyngand by thair nebbis grew.
Out ovir the stank of mony divers hew
Wes laid a tre, ovir quhilk behovyt we pas,
Bot I can not declare quhareof it wes.

My nymphe went ovir, chargeand me felow fast.   2080
Hir till obbey my spretis woux agast,

2060. richt now *straight away*
rejosyt *gratified*
2061. tane the ayr *had some fresh air* bettir apposyt *in better condition*
2062. commoditeis *benefits*
2063. gardyng *garden* lo *look* lusty *beautiful*
2064. hie cypres *lofty cypresses* flewer *scent*
2065. bissy *busy* beis *bees*
2066. florist colouris *blossoming terms* rethoreis *rhetoricians*
2067. gaddris *collect*
2068. all plesance *every delight* plenist is *is filled* hant *place*
2069. stanys *stones* treis *trees*
2070. chargyt *laden* peirlis *pearls*

2071. on till *into* garth *garden*
2072. fowsy *ditch* fare on breid *very broad*
2073. inveronyt *surrounded* fysches *fish* enew *in plenty*
2074. foulis *birds* swomand *swimming*
2075. als *also* growand *growing* breid *breed*
2076. hyngand *hung* nebbis *beaks*
2077. stank *moat* divers *different* hew *colours*
2078. behovyt we pas *we had to pass*
2079. quhare of *of what substance*
2080. chargeand me *telling me* felow *follow*
2081. woux agast *became terrified*

2076. 'Birds that grew hanging by their beaks'.

Swa peralus wes the passagis till aspy.
Away sche went, and fra tyme sche wes past,
Apon the bryg I entrit at the last.
Bot swa my harnys trymlyt bissyly,   2085
Quhyl I fell ovir and baith my fete slaid by,
Out ovir the hede, into the stank adoun,
Quhare, as me thocht, I wes in point to droun.

Quhat throw the byrdis sang and this affray,
Out of my swoun I wallkynnyt quhare I lay   2090
In the gardyn quhare I fyrst doun fell.
About I blent, for richt clere was the day,
Bot all thys lusty plesance wes away.
Me thocht that fare herbere maist lyk to hel
In till compare of this ye herd me tell.   2095
Allace, allace, I thocht me than in pane,
And langyt sare for till have swounyt agane.

The byrdis sang nor yit the mery flouris
Mycht not ameys my grevows gret dolouris.
All erdly thyng me thocht barrant and vyle.   2100

2082. peralous *dangerous*
    passagis *path* till aspy *to look at*
2083. fra tyme *once* past *across*
2084. bryg *bridge*
2085. harnys *brains*
    trymlyt *trembled*
    bissyly *incessantly*
2086. quhyl *that* fete *feet* slaid
    by *slipped past*
2087. out ovir the hede *head over
    heels*
2088. in point to droun *about to
    drown*
2089. quhat throw *what with*
    byrdis sang *birdsong*
    affray *fright*
2090. swoun *swoon*
    wallkynnyt *awakened*
    quhare *where*

2091. doun fell *fell down*
2092. blent *blinked*
2094. fare herbere *fair garden*
    maist lyk to *most like*
2095. in till compare *in comparison
    with* tell *describe*
2096. allace *alas* I thocht me
    than *I thought I was then*
    pane *pain*
2097. langyt sare *sorely longed*
    swounyt *swooned*
2098. yit *even* mery flouris *pretty
    flowers*
2099. ameys *alleviate*
    grevows *terrible*
    dolouris *sorrows*
2100. erdly *earthly*
    barrant *barren* vyle *vile*

2081–2. 'My soul became terrified at the thought of having to obey her,
the path looked so dangerous'.
2085. 'But so incessantly did my brains tremble'.
2095. 'In comparison with the one you have heard me describe'.

Thus I remanyt into the garth twa houris
Cursand the feildis with all the fare coullouris,
That I awolk oft wariand the quhyle.
Always my mynd wes on the lusty yle,
In purpose evir till have dwelt in that art,   2105
Of rethorik cullouris til have fund sum parte.

And maist of all my curage wes aggrevit
Becaus sa sone I of my dreme eschevyt,
Nocht seand quhow thay wrechis wer torment
That honour mankyt and honeste myschevyt.   2110
Glaidly I wald amyd thys wryt have brevyt,
Had I it sene, quhow thay were slane or schent.
Bot fra I saw all thys weilfare wes went,
Till mak ane end, sittand under a tre,
In laude of honour I wrait thir versis thre: 2115

'O hie honour, swete hevynly flour degest,
Gem vertuus, maist precius, gudlyest
For hie renoun, thow art guerdoun condyng,
Of worschyp kend the glorius end and rest,
But quham, in rycht, na worthy wicht may lest;   2120

2101. remanyt into *remained within* garth *garden* twa houris *two hours*
2102. cursand *cursing* coullouris *devices*
2103. awolk *awoke* wariand *cursing* quhyle *time*
2104. lusty yle *beautiful isle*
2105. in purpose *intending* art *region*
2106. rethorik cullouris *devices of rhetoric* fund *found*
2107. curage *mind* aggrevit *distressed*
2108. eschevyt *came out*
2109. nocht seand *not seeing* wrechis *wretches* torment *tormented*
2110. mankyt *mutilated* myschevyt *injured*

2111. amyd *in* wryt *narrative* brevyt *recorded*
2112. sene *seen* schent *disgraced*
2113. fra *once* weilfare *happiness* went *gone*
2114. till mak an end *to conclude* sittand *sitting*
2115. laude *praise* wrait *wrote* versis thre *three verses*
2116. flour degest *dignified flower*
2117. gudlyest *worthiest*
2118. for *of* renoun *fame* guerdoun condyng *suitable reward*
2119. worschyp *noble deeds* kend *known as* rest *abode*
2120. but quham *without which* in rycht *as is proper* wicht *person* lest *prevail*

2108. 'Because I awoke from my dream so soon'.
2119–20. 'Known as the glorious end and abode of noble deeds, without which, as is proper, no worthy person can prevail'.

Thy gret puissance may maist avance all thyng,
And poverale to myche avale sone bryng.
I the requere, sen thow, but pere, art best,
That eftir this in thy hie blys we ryng.

'Of grace thy face in every place so schynys,　　2125
That, swete, all spreit baith heid and feit inclynis
Thy glore afore, for til implore remeid.
He docht rycht nocht quhilk out of thocht the tynis.
Thy name but blame, and riall fame, dyvine is,
Thow port, at schort, of our comfort and reid　　2130
Tyll bryng all thyng tyll gladyng eftir deid.
All wycht but sycht of thy gret mycht ay crinis.
O schene, I mene, nane may sustene thy feid.

'Hail rois, maist chois til clois thy foys gret mycht.
Hail stone quhilk schone apon the trone of lycht.　　2135
Vertew, quhais trew swet dew overthrew all vyce,
Was ay, ilk day, gar say, the way of lycht.
Amend offend, and send our end ay richt.
Thow stant ordant as sant, of grant maist wyse,

2121. puissance *power* maist
　avance *bring the greatest
　advancement to*
2122. poverale *poor people* myche
　avale *great repute* sone *soon*
2123. the requere *ask you*
　sen *since* but pere *without equal*
2124. ryng *reign*
2125. of *with* schynys *shines*
2126. swete *sweetly* spreit *soul*
　heid and feit *head and feet*
　inclynis *inclines*
2127. glore *glory* afore *before*
　remeid *help*
2128. docht *achieves* the
　tynis *loses you*
2129. but *without* dyvine *divine*
2130. port *gateway* at schort *in
　short* reid *guidance*
2131. tyll *to* gladyng *joy*

deid *death*
2132. all wycht *every person* but
　sycht *without sight*
　mycht *power* ay crinis *grows
　forever smaller*
2133. schene *bright one*
　sustene *endure* fcid *hostility*
2134. rois *rose* chois *choice*
　clois *overcome* foys *foe's*
　mycht *power*
2135. trone *throne* lycht *light*
2136. quhais *whose* swet *sweet*
　overthrew *overcame*
2137. ay *always* ilk day *every
　day* gar say *I dare say*
2138. offend *offence* ay
　richt *always right*
2139. stant *stand* ordant *of
　grant *in bestowing favours*
　wyse *wise*

2126–8. 'That, sweetly, every person bows and kneels before your glory,
in order to beg for help. He who lets you slip from his mind achieves
nothing at all'.

Til be supple and the hie gre of pryce.   2140
Delyte the tite me quyte of syte to dycht
For I apply, schortly, to thy devyse.'

The auctor direkit his buke to the rycht
nobill Prynce James the Ferd, Kyng
of Scottis.

Tryumphus laud with palm of victory,
The laurere crown of infynyte glory,
Maist gracius prince, our soverane James the
Ferd,   2145
Thy Majesty mot have eternally
Suppreme honour, renoun of chevalry,
Felycite perdurand in this erd,
With etern blys in the hevyn by fatal werd.
Resave this rusty, rurall rebaldry,   2150
Lakand cunnyng, fra thye puyr lege onlerd,

Quhilk, in the sycht of thy magnificence,
Confydand in so gret benevolence,
Proponis thus my vulgare ignorance,
Maist humely, wyth dew obedyence,   2155
Besekand oft thy mychty excellence
Be grace til pardon all sic variance

2140. til *to*   supple *support*
gre *prize*
2141. delyte the *may it please you*
tite *quickly*   quyte *destitute*
syte *sorrow*   dycht *release*
2142. apply *submit*   schortly *in
short*   devyse *plan*
auctor *author*   direkit *dedicates*
Ferd *fourth*
2143. tryumphus *triumphant*
laud *praise*
2144. laurere *laurel*
2146. mot *shall*
2147. chevalry *chivalry*
2148. felycite *joy*
perdurand *perpetual*   in *on*

erd *earth*
2149. etern blys *eternal bliss* fatal
werd *decree of destiny*
2150. resave *receive*   rusty *rustic*
rurall *boorish*
rebaldry *uncultured verse*
2151. lakand *lacking in*
cunnyng *wisdom*   puyr lege
onlerd *poor unlearned servant*
2152. quhilk *who*   sycht *sight*
2153. confydand *trusting*
2154. proponis *offers*
2155. humely *humbly*   dew *due*
2156. besekand *beseeching*
2157. be *by*   sic variance *such
rambling*

2140. 'To be the support and the lofty prize of great value'.
2141. 'May it please you swiftly to release my destitute person from
sorrow'.

With sum benyng respect of ferme constance,
Remyttand my pretendit negligence
Thow quhais mycht may humyll thyng avance. 2160

Breif burall quair, of eloquence all quyte,
With russet weid and sentence imperfyte,
Til cum in plane, se that thow not pretend tha.
Thy barrant termis and thy vyle endyte
Sall not be min; I wyll not have the wyte. 2165
For, as for me, I quytcleme that I kend tha.
Thow art bot stouth. Thyft lovys lycht but lyte.
Not worth a myte, pray ilk man till amend tha.
Fare on with syte, and on this wyse I end tha.

Finis.

2158. benyng *gracious* of *for*
ferme constance *loyal constancy*
2159. remyttand *forgiving*
pretendit *acknowledged*
2160. quhais *whose* mycht *power*
humyll *humble* avance *prosper*
2161. burall quair *unlearned book*
all quyte *devoid*
2162. russet weid *homespun dress*
sentence imperfyte *imperfect meaning*
2163. in plane *into plain view*
pretend tha *put yourself forward*

2164. barrant termis *barren terms*
vyle endyte *ugly style*
2165. min *mine* wyte *blame*
2166. quytcleme *give up any claim* kend tha *have known you*
2167. bot *nothing but* stouth *robbery* Thyft *theft* lycht *light* lyte *little*
2168. myte *penny* pray *ask* ilk man *everyone* tha *you*
2169. fare *go* syte *sorrow* wyse *way*

2162–3. 'Dressed up in homespun terms and with imperfect meaning, see that you don't push yourself forward to come into plain view'.

Notes

Robert Henryson

The Fables
The fable was a very popular medieval genre, though its tradition is an ancient one. It relied on simple stories, often humorous, and yet it was a favourite form amongst preachers and moralists who used the tales of beasts to hold a mirror up to mankind. The animals speak, argue and act in many ways like human beings, but retain their animal characteristics, so that the boundary between the two is uncertain and shifting. In this way, the fabulist underlines human vice and folly, showing how close man comes to the beasts and the petty nature of many earthly concerns. The genre is heavily dependent on irony and the satire extends from contemporary institutions such as the law, to a condemnation of human nature itself. A formal *moralitas* is given at the end of each fable to explain the moral of the tale, but it is usually only one of several possible interpretations and Henryson is always careful to point out that this is the case, occasionally providing a shockingly unexpected moral or even two possible interpretations.

Prologue
The Prologue offers a defence of poetry which was sometimes viewed with suspicion in the Middle Ages, fiction being viewed as dangerously close to deceit. Henryson is concerned with showing how truth can be contained in fictitious stories in a way that can instruct men and improve their lives. But his concern is not only with the moral, for he is anxious that poetry should also entertain, the wisest of scholars having already noted that it is best amongst 'ernist' matters to mingle some 'merie sport' (I.20).

22–3. Henryson probably has in mind the legend of St Anthony in which the saint's tutor is annoyed to find that the boy has left his studies in order to play. St Anthony then fetches a bow and demonstrates to his tutor that if it is constantly held taut and never allowed to relax, it will eventually become slack and useless. In the same way, says Henryson, authors must mix serious matters with entertainment.
27. There are many legends surrounding the life of the ancient

Greek writer Aesop but he was probably a slave on the island
of Samos and composed his collection of fables in the early
sixth century BC.
34. Henryson may or may not have composed the *Fables* for a
noble patron, but it is traditional to claim to have done so
regardless.
59–60. The idea here is that by using the fable form the author is
able to educate the *hie*, learned people who can see the deeper
meaning, while still entertaining those of *low estate*.

The Cock and the Jasp

Jasper is the medieval name for some of the varieties of quartz. It
was prized in the Middle Ages as the stone of the heavenly city:
'the holy city of Jerusalem coming down out of heaven from
God, . . . its radiance like a most rare jewel, like a jasper, clear as
crystal' (Revelation 21:10–11). However, while Henryson's
Cock acknowledges the beauty of the stone, he also insists that
it is of no use to him and wanders away leaving the jewel on the
ground (I.113). Modern readers are often inclined to praise the
Cock for this and are surprised by the *moralitas* which condemns
him. However, surprise may have been Henryson's intention,
forcing the complacent reader to realise that he can no more
recognise wisdom when he sees it than the bird-brained Cock.

86. In the Middle Ages, precious stones were regarded as
having certain properties or powers. Specific stones were
thought to be effective in curing diseases and were also
thought to protect the wearer from certain dangers. Jasper
was worn to cure many ailments and was held to be very
powerful as a protective charm, as Henryson points out at
II.123–6.

The Two Mice

The tale of the town mouse and the country mouse would have
been familiar to Henryson from a number of different sources,
but his version is set firmly in medieval Scotland with the town
mouse described as a citizen of the burgh and a member of the
guild (I.172) and the country mouse living on *nuttis and peis*
(I.206) which her gentrified sister claims would break her teeth
(I.223). The fable depends on the comic opposition of the two
mice: the proud older sister, used to the dangerous delicacies of
the town; and the timid younger mouse, trying to cope with it all
and eventually surrendering to a dead faint (I.301). However,

this is as close as the mice come to death. The steward may chase them round the pantry and the cat dangle them from paw to paw but they live to hear the moral of the tale: 'blessed be the simple life, lived without fear' (I.373).

164. A *borous toun* was a town possessing a charter which granted it the rights of a burgh. This meant that it had its own courts and laws to protect its traders. The term survives as a place-name in various parts of Scotland, for example, Bo'ness (a contraction of Borrowstounness).

172. Medieval merchants and craftsmen formed themselves into groups according to their profession. These groups were known as guilds and were intended to protect the professional rights of the members or 'brothers'. In the later Middle Ages the Scottish merchant guilds became increasingly powerful, taking over many of the duties that would have been performed originally by the burgh council (cf. Dunbar, 'Quhy will ye, merchantis of renoun').

173. Medieval traders were subject to two kinds of customs duty, the greater being *magna custuma* which was levied on imports and exports, while the lesser *parva custuma* was applied to goods sent to market.

198. Critics are divided on the translation of *misterlyk*: Fox translates it as poorly, Smith interprets it as masterfully.

232–5. Henryson is here referring to one of the biblical proverbs of Solomon: 'Better a dinner of herbs where love is, than a stalled ox and hatred therewith' (Proverbs 15:17).

248. Good Friday, the day of Christ's crucifixion, was the most solemn day in the calendar of the medieval Church. People were expected to fast and to abstain from eating meat. Easter Sunday, the day of Christ's resurrection, was a day of celebration and feasting after the forty days of denial required by Lent.

251. A distinction is being made between various kinds of trap: those with doors that fall shut behind the creature and those like the more traditional mouse-trap.

285. White bread was regarded as a great delicacy in the Middle Ages.

289. The mice are in festive mood but Henryson is also referring to a medieval proverb: 'It is easy to cry "Merry Christmas" at another man's expense', i.e. it is easy to celebrate freely when someone else is paying the bill.

326. *Gib* is a shortened form of the name Gilbert, but this was

such a common cat's name in the Middle Ages that it often simply meant cat. The modern equivalent would be Tom.

329. *Bawdronis* is another name for a cat, though this one was confined to use in Scotland.

The Cock and the Fox

This fable is ostensibly a warning against pride, though many human weaknesses are exposed in the course of events that find a cock tricked by a fox. Henryson plays throughout with the notion of the 'noble' cock and parodies tales of chivalric romance. Thus, the customary list of knightly chargers is replaced with the names of a pack of dogs (II.546–7), and the lament for the dead hero is given by a hysterical chicken (II.495–508).

410. *Chantecleir*, meaning 'clear song', is a traditional name for the cock.

416. The word *curageous* can mean either brave or lustful. Henryson is exploiting the ambiguity (cf. Dunbar 'Apon the midsummer evin, mirriest of nichtis', II. 188 and 215.)

417. Cocks were commonly believed to crow on the hour and to have an innate sense of time and astrological movement.

429. *Lowrence* is a traditional name for the fox. Smith suggests that it derives from the Scots word *lour* meaning to skulk or lurk.

449. The dirge forms part of the mass for the dead.

455. The *blissit sacrament* is the eucharist, the body and blood of Christ.

483. The names of the hens are again traditional. *Sprutok* probably derives from *sprutlit*, meaning 'speckled'. *Toppok* has connotations of top or tuft, a reference to the comb on a chicken's head.

    Pertok is the most literary of the three, her name being derived ultimately from the medieval French *perte* meaning 'one who confuses'.

500. *Aurora*, goddess of the dawn.

519. The amount of heat and moisture in a body was believed to have an effect both physically and psychologically. An excess of coldness and dryness was thought to cause impotence.

546–7. The names of the dogs rely as much on sound as sense but the lines can be roughly translated as follows: 'Barker, Shaggy, Belle, Brownie, search the thicket, run well, Curtes and Brown Clyde'. Some translators choose to make *Rype-*

Schaw (Search-Thicket) and *Rin-Weil* (Run-Well) dogs' names too.

The Fox and the Wolf

Crucial to this fable is an understanding of the sacrament of confession. Confession of one's sins to a priest was a fundamental requirement of the medieval church (cf. Dunbar, 'O synfull man, thir ar the fourty dayis'), and in a sudden fit of religious fervour, the Fox goes in search of a suitable confessor. The characterisation of the Wolf as naturally a 'Grey' Friar (Franciscan) enables Henryson to satirise the Church and the lax attitude of some of the orders towards the sacraments. Accordingly, not only is confession abused but the Fox goes on to parody baptism as he attempts to keep to his penitential diet of fish by plunging a young goat into the river declaring 'Go down, sir Kid, come up again, sir Salmon' (I.751). The *moralitas* stresses the need for true repentance and the idea that death can strike at any time (cf. Dunbar, 'O wreche, be war, this warld will wend the fro').

661. There were two methods of hanging in medieval Scotland. The term *withy-neck* refers to the practice of hanging criminals from a withy, a noose or halter of twisted willow twigs. The other method was by a normal rope. The term *crack-rope* would seem to apply to the cracking of the neck upon hanging.

671. The Fox uncovers his head as a gesture of humility.

693. *Benedictie* is the prayer that begins the act of confession.

712–5. The Wolf is referring to the fact that medieval confession was comprised of three parts: repentance (*contritio*), confession (*confessio*), and submission to penitential discipline (*satisfactio*). The Fox's repentance consists only of him being sorry that he has not killed many more lambs and chickens, and he cannot see how he can change his ways without starving to death. Neither sorry nor desiring to change, he fails to fulfil the two main criteria of repentance. The Wolf then moves on to the final stage of confession, the matter of a suitable penance for the sins. This was frequently a combination of prayer and fasting.

760. The Fox thinks that his big round stomach looks like a target.

The Trial of the Fox

The atmosphere in this fable is one of dread as all the animals are called before the *wild* lion (I.878), king of the beasts, for a meeting of the parliament. Henryson draws upon mythology and heraldry as well as more humble nature to provide a catalogue of creatures who answer the summons, and lurking at the back is Lowrence the Fox, *perplexit . . . in his hart* (I.964). He has good cause to fear, as he will be sentenced to death in the end, but not before Henryson has provided us with a satire on the Scottish legal system as the Fox and the Wolf go in search of the Mare to demand her presence at court. The *moralitas* is surprising in that the Mare is *men of contemplatioun* (I.1111) who overcome sensuality and temptation (the Wolf and Fox). In other versions of the story the moral is almost the reverse: the Wolf is strength, the Fox prudence, and it is the kicking Ass which is the uncontrollable flesh.

827. The sense of the proverb seems to be that a villain cannot be easily stopped (cf. Dunbar, 'In vice most vicius he excellis', II.47–8).

828. The Fox buries his father in a hole left over from the cutting of peat for the fires.

835–7. It was believed that the soul went to purgatory after death where it suffered until atonement was made for its sins. Once in purgatory, no one could do anything to save themselves or lessen their time there. However, they could be helped by the prayers and masses of those still alive. Many people tried to ensure their eternal salvation by bequeathing sums of money for masses to be said for their souls.

857. The Middle Ages derived from the ancient world the belief that there were three stages in the development of life: vegetative, animal and rational. Only human beings could achieve the third stage and thus animals were, by their very nature, irrational.

866. *Phoebus* is the sun.

875–6. Jasper is a variety of quartz, prized in the Middle Ages (cf. Henryson, *The Cock and the Jasp*, I.69).

887. Due to the trickery of the gods, Pasiphae, wife of King Minos of Crete, fell in love with a bull. Her son was the Minotaur, a creature with the body of a man and the head of a bull.

888. Henryson is in fact referring to the Chimaera which was killed by the hero Bellerophon. In Greek myth, the Chimaera

is a fire-breathing monster with the head of a lion, body of a goat, and tail of a snake.

889. Pegasus is the winged horse of ancient mythology. One version of his legend tells how he was ridden by Bellerophon who was then able to kill the dreaded Chimaera.

895. *Sparth* has not been identified. Denton Fox suggests that it is a misreading of *pard*, a large cat like a leopard. This would fit with the swiftness attributed to the creature. Other suggestions include Dickins' proposal that it should be emended to swan. Elliott draws attention to the word's connection to a term for battle-axe and suggests that Henryson is referring to some kind of horned deer.

898. A *jennet* is a small Spanish horse.

902. The *wodwo* is a wild man of the woods, often found elsewhere in lists of animals and regarded as more beast than human in spite of his form.

907. *Fiber* is the Latin word for beaver, which is acceptable in this context. However, as the beaver has only just been mentioned on the preceding line, it is possible that Henryson was thinking of some other aquatic mammal, perhaps an otter.

912. *Feitho* appears to mean polecat, but the polecat has already been mentioned at line 907 in its more usual Scots form, *fowmart*. Henryson may have had some other furred animal in mind. *Fents* are decorative slits on a garment which allow another colour to show through from underneath. They were fashionable at the end of the Middle Ages.

914. *Bowranbane* and *lerion* have both posed problems for translators. Suggestions for *bowranbane* range from werewolf to badger while *lerion* has been translated as many things, from young rabbit and little greyhound, to the *alerion*, a heraldic eagle with neither beak nor feet.

975–7. The art of physiognomy involved judging someone's character by their appearance. According to this method, ugliness was regarded as a likely sign of inner sinfulness (cf. Henryson, *The Paddock and the Mouse*, II.2819–32).

1053. Those who possessed a doctoral degree were permitted to wear a *pillion*, a close-fitting cap. This was not necessarily red, but the choice of colour here reflects not just the Wolf's injury but also associates him with the Church, and the red caps of cardinals.

1130–1. The biblical king Solomon was famed for his wisdom. However, this appears to be a reference not to Solomon, but to Ecclesiasticus 7:40.

1139–41. Mary was appealed to frequently as a mediator. She was viewed as merciful towards mankind and it was hoped that any requests made to her for intercession would be successful as Christ would surely not refuse his mother.

The Sheep and the Dog

What begins in this fable as a satire on the Church courts becomes an attack on the whole Scottish justice system as a poor sheep (I.1147) is brought before the courts by *Perrie* Dog (I.1166) to account for a loaf of bread. The officers of the law read like members of the rogues' gallery – the Wolf, the Raven, the Fox, the Vulture – all creatures normally found lying, cheating and lurking in the darkness. Here, however, they reign supreme and the Sheep is forced to sell his fleece in order to meet their demands. The final image of the fable is of suffering innocence as the Sheep trembles with cold and asks: 'O Lord, why do you sleep so long?' (I.1295). Cf. Dunbar, 'Ane murlandis man of uplandis mak'.

1147. The *he* in this line refers to the sheep.

1148. By the late Middle Ages the ecclesiastical consistory courts dealt mainly with cases which had no direct relevance to the Church or issues of morality. Most of its cases were disputes over property.

1153. Henryson is here parodying legal language.

1156–7. The Wolf is referring to the three levels of punishment which could be imposed by the Church. *Suspensioun* is the lowest of the three and would have involved the suspension of the cleric's rights. *Interdictioun* is more serious, requiring that the person be excluded from participation in the mass and sacraments. The third level, *Grit cursing*, is outright excommunication: the permanent expulsion of a person from the Church and the most serious penalty which could be imposed.

1160. *Corbie* was a traditional name for the raven and is frequently used as another word for raven in medieval Scots. It would appear to be derived from the cawing sound made by the bird.

1164. A peremptory summons was a final warning and anyone failing to appear would be held in contempt of court. Its issue is, therefore, a sign of the Wolf's severe attitude towards the Sheep.

1166. *Perrie* is a traditional name for the Dog. It is a variant on the Scots *berrie* or *burry*, meaning 'shaggy'.

1172–3. According to ancient mythology, Hesperus climbed Mount Atlas to look at the stars but was swept away by a whirlwind and disappeared. People supposed that he had been turned into the evening star which was thereafter called Hesperus.

1200–1. It was against canon law to hold court sessions after dark.

1265–6. The sheriff would have presided over local courts and is being accused here of buying bad debts from the king which he will then pursue.

1269. Coroner is used here in the wider sense of an officer of the court.

1310. Simony is the sin of bestowing church positions for money or for political reasons instead of allocating them to truly religious men.

The Lion and the Mouse

This fable begins with a prologue in which Aesop appears and is implored to tell a story. He tells the fable of the noble lion, encountered one day as he lay sleeping by a troop of little mice. Thinking that the lion is dead, the mice scamper over his body, twirling on his whiskers and dancing round the 'corpse'. However, the lion awakes and seizes the leader of the mice who gives an impassioned speech on the necessity of justice being tempered with mercy (II.1461–1509). This, indeed, would appear to be the crux of the fable, which is concerned with the concept of kingship and the actions of a good ruler. However, true nobility is not simply a matter of birth, and the mice have their role to play too as they come to the rescue of the king of the beasts. The ideal of this mutually supportive society is summed up by the mouse: 'one good turn deserves another' (I.1557).

1352. Aesop is being presented as wearing the headdress of an old fashioned poet, wrapped or folded under the chin like a cock's hackle (cf. Henryson, The Testament of Cresseid, II.244–5).

1375. The ancient Greek writer Aesop is the source for many of Henryson's fables (cf. Henryson, Prologue, I.27).

1601–7. Fortune was frequently portrayed as a woman holding a wheel in the Middle Ages. One turn of her wheel could raise people to great heights but she could easily turn it again and reduce them to poverty. She was often thought of as blind or

blindfolded to indicate that the movements of her wheel were
not due to the merit of individuals but were in fact entirely
arbitrary.

The Preaching of the Swallow

Nature plays a key role in this fable in which we see the passing
of the seasons and the workers in the fields. The result is both an
understanding of the order of God's universe and a realisation
that all things must pass away (cf. Dunbar, 'I seik aboute this
warld onstable'). The tone is less political than some of the other
fables, and the *moralitas* makes it clear that what we are dealing
with here is the Devil himself laying traps for the unsuspecting
and unprepared. The birds who will not listen to the advice of
the Swallow are foolish but the carnage at the end is complete
and horrific and recounted not without pity by the narrator.
Foresight is advisable but the souls of men are as blind as bats
(II.1636–42).

1629–32. The body was frequently viewed as the prison of the
    soul. It was thought that it weighed down the soul with
    earthly concerns and desires, preventing it from making its
    way to God (cf. Henryson, *The Paddock and the Mouse*,
    II.2936–61).

1636–7. The ancient Greek philosopher Aristotle viewed the
    human mind as weak and unable to grasp what ought to be
    obvious.

1657–60. The Middle Ages believed that the universe was
    enclosed by a solid sphere known as the firmament. Within
    this, all the planets circled around the earth, their motion
    creating beautiful music (cf. Henryson, *Orpheus and Eury-
    dice*, II.186–225).

1661. The entire universe was believed to consist of four ele-
    ments: fire, earth, water and air.

1680. *Flora* is the Roman goddess of flowers and plants.

1685–90. *Ceres* is the ancient goddess of the harvest, whom
    Henryson depicts here with her traditional horn of plenty. He
    also gives her responsibility for the vintage with the help of
    Bacchus, Roman god of wine.

1707. Spring is viewed as summer's secretary, coming before
    him to arrange everything and bearing his seal as a sign that
    summer himself will follow.

1763. The Swallow is being accused of thinking too far ahead.
    A modern equivalent would be 'counting her chickens

before they are hatched'. The proverb at I.1764 has a similar sense.

1765. The Lark is claiming that there is no point in worrying about things that have not happened yet, and that things will turn out as they must anyway.

1935. Lucifer is another name for the Devil.

The Fox, the Wolf and the Cadger
This fable relies upon word-play and the Wolf's misunderstanding of *nekhering* (I.2089) which he takes to be a gigantic herring, not realising that the cadger has in fact offered him a swift blow to the neck. The cadger is Death which the Wolf ignores in his greedy attempts to reach the fish. His companion the Fox is to be interpreted as the 'world which tempts man with false delights' (II.2219–20) only to abandon him to the clutches of death in the end.

1962. *Russell* is a traditional name for the fox, derived from the medieval French for reddish.

2000–4. Lent, the forty days before Easter, was a time of penitence and fasting. People were supposed to refrain from eating meat and eat fish instead.

2009–10. Henryson is referring to popular sayings: 'you can't fool an old dog' and the similar 'an old cat will not jump at a straw'.

2026. In Roman mythology, Jupiter was the king of the gods.

2035. The steward would have been in charge of the larder.

2036. *Silver-seik*, literally silver-sick, would appear to mean without money, with a poorly purse (cf. Dunbar, *Sanct salvatour, send silver sorrow*).

2074. Scotland had a flourishing trade in furs with merchants in Flanders.

2083. This is a reference to a very old song that traditionally roused hunters in the morning.

2089. *Nekhering* is a very unusual word in Scots, meaning a blow to the neck. The Wolf obviously does not understand it, thinking that a neck-herring sounds appetising.

2154. *In principio* (In the beginning) are the first words of the Book of Genesis and of the Gospel of St John. The first fourteen verses of St John's gospel were thought to be effective in warding off evil, but the mere repetition of *in principio* would clearly be seen as mere nonsense.

The Fox, the Wolf and the Husbandman
Several well-known medieval stories find their way into this comic fable. The idea of the Devil listening in corners and taking oaths literally (cf. Dunbar, 'This nycht in my sleip I wes agast') appears in the form of the Fox and Wolf attempting to claim the Husbandman's oxen which he has unwisely cursed as fit only for the wolves (I.2244). The Fox then negotiates a settlement and sets about trying to convince the Wolf that the moon he sees reflected in a well is in fact a large cheese. The fable combines social, legal and moral satire within the framework of a humorous tale of foxes and wolves whizzing up and down wells in buckets in search of the largest *caboik* (I.2398) in existence.

2231. Aesop, the author of an ancient collection of fables, is thought to have lived in the early sixth century BC.

2236. It took two people to work the plough: a goadsman to urge the animals on and keep them straight, and a ploughman to hold the plough itself.

2242. The hare is traditionally associated with madness, a belief derived from the wild behaviour of the male during the breeding season. The idea survives in modern times in phrases such as 'hare-brained' and in characters such as Lewis Carroll's mad March Hare.

2243. The *patill* or plough-staff was shaped like a paddle and was used to scrape away any earth that stuck to the plough.

2251. The Wolf is referring to the medieval proverb that 'a king's word must be upheld'.

2270-1. A *plank* or *plack* was a small copper coin worth four Scots pennies. In Henryson's time it was a byword for something worthless.

2282. The sense here is that a gentleman need give no more guarantee than his word.

2353-5. A *cabok* is a large round cheese. The implication appears to be that cheese made in the summer is the best.

2389. A *draw well* had two buckets, one of which would go down into the water as the other was pulled up on a winch.

2418-9. This is a reference to the wheel held by the goddess Fortune, which could elevate a man to riches one minute only to turn again and leave him in poverty at the bottom the next.

The Wolf and the Wether
This is a simple story of a self-deluded *wether*, or ram, falling victim to a wolf who seizes him by the *crag-bane* (I.2586) and

shakes him to death. In spite of the sympathy the reader feels for the unfortunate wether who bravely attempts to *counterfait* (I.2497) the dead dog in all things and thus protect the flock, the *moralitas* deals harshly with him. Pride leads to delusion which is a dangerous state in life and in fables, for the moral of all fables is ultimately 'know thyself'.

2550. The Carmelite order were commonly known as White Friars on account of the white cloaks they wore.

2608. The seating in any medieval banqueting hall was allocated according to strict hierarchy, with the wealthy and powerful placed at the high or top table. The reference to slippery benches, however, indicates that fortune can change quickly and those in power now may not be so tomorrow.

The Wolf and the Lamb

The unjust oppression of the poor and weak is once again Henryson's theme in this fable. An innocent lamb, whose *lippis* never touched anything *contagious* (I.2652), is accused by the Wolf of contaminating the stream. The *moralitas* is an expansive account of the problems of contemporary society, particularly the legal system, which advantages the cleverest rather than the innocent (II.2715–20); the system of farming which allows wealthy landowners to force tenant-farmers off the land (II.2728–41); and unjust and corrupt landlords who exploit their tenants to the point of starvation (II.2742–62). The final prayer is that God should grant the king the will and power to deal with the 'wolves' who ravage the land.

2634. At this point in history, 'drawing' is likely to mean dragging behind a horse rather than the stretching and disembowelling which became a form of execution later.

2663–75. The Wolf and Lamb are exchanging quotes from the Bible. The Lamb's words are based upon Ezekiel 18, while the Wolf's are from Exodus 20:5.

2683–5. The Lamb is frantically using all the legal jargon he knows in order to stall the Wolf.

2708. *Maill men* are tenant farmers. The system of tenant-farming was widespread in Scotland but, as Henryson points out, it could be abused by landlords who lived upon the labour of others and could legally evict families who had farmed the land for generations.

The Paddock and the Mouse

The moral of this fable is usually that evil redounds on itself, and although this is implicit here, Henryson has a number of other interpretations in mind. A mouse is trying to cross a river, jumping up and down on the bank with the pitiful cry of *Help over! Help over!* (I.2784), when she receives an offer of assistance from a frog. According to the *moralitas*, the mouse is the soul and the ugly frog is the body. The two are attached to one another on the river of life until death, in the form of a ravenous kite, intervenes. It is a brooding and sinister fable which takes as its theme the soul's precarious journey through life. However, there are touches of humour still and a more homely moral too, that one should take care who one's friends are (II.2924–5).

2824–5. Physiognomy is the medieval 'science' of judging someone's character by their appearance. Hair colour, warts, and the spacing of the teeth were, for example, all significant in establishing a person's temperament. In general, beauty was equated with goodness while an ugly appearance was believed to indicate an evil nature.

2842. The biblical Absolon was renowned for his beauty, and particularly for his long golden hair. This, however, was his downfall as his luxuriant hair became tangled in a tree, enabling his enemies to kill him while he hung from its branches. His story was often told by medieval moralists as a warning against pride.

2869. Jupiter was the ancient king of the gods, sometimes equated with God by medieval poets.

2901. *Pew* is intended to imitate the cry of the kite.

2944. The biblical Job had a prosperous life until God decided to test him and deprived him of his family, his wealth and possessions (Job 1–2).

2947. The fortunes of men were often thought of as turning on a large wheel which could raise them to success one minute, only to reduce them to poverty the next as the wheel lowered them to the ground once more.

Orpheus and Eurydice

The ancient story of Orpheus, who so loved Eurydice that he attempted to bring her back from the dead, is found in a number of medieval versions. In some of these the story ends happily and the couple are reunited in the world; others are more faithful to the original and Orpheus loses Eurydice once again because he cannot resist turning to look at her as they travel back, thus breaking the promise he made in the underworld. Henryson draws upon several traditions and presents us not only with the lover Orpheus but also the musician, famed for the harmonies of his harp. Indeed, harmony is one of the central themes of the poem. In his search for Eurydice, Orpheus travels through the spheres and hears the perfect music they make (II.219–39), a perfection that is mirrored in his own music which can restore harmony to the world for a time and relieve souls in torment (II.261–73). The world is not, however, a harmonious place and order and goodness cannot last for long. The love which ennobles Orpheus and inspires his heroism, is also the cause of Eurydice being lost a second time. The plan of the universe may be good but on earth all is contradiction.

All is neatly explained in the *moralitas* at the end of the poem but its very neatness has caused some critics concern. Aristaeus, the lustful herdsman whose pursuit of Eurydice ultimately causes her death, is presented as *gud vertew* (I.436). Eurydice herself is *oure affection* (I.431), the appetite, while Orpheus is the intellectual part of the soul (II.428–9). The moral is that our desire, our appetite, is unstable and seeks various amusements, fleeing from what is good and falling instead into a state of sin. Reason, the intellectual part, can see the perfection of heaven but turns away and follows its appetite into the regions far below. The moral is fully developed but that it is found so unsatisfying by so many may be part of Henryson's message: reason tells us one thing but desire demands something else.

29–63. According to ancient legend, the king of the gods lay with Memoria (Mnemosyne in Greek) for nine nights. Their union resulted in the nine goddesses known as the Muses, each of whom was associated with a different intellectual pursuit. The Middle Ages viewed them as the movers of the spheres who produced heavenly music, conducted by the god Apollo. Thus, Apollo and the Muse Calliope produced a musically gifted son, Orpheus. The names ascribed to the Muses here are traditional but the explanations for their names are derived from medieval commentaries and are, strictly speaking, more creative than correct. The home of the Muses was traditionally Mount Helicon, a mountain in Greece, not Arabia as Henryson has it here.

164. *Phebus*, meaning 'bright one', is another name for Apollo, god of the sun.

174–5. *Jupiter* is the king of the gods and father of Apollo. he is, therefore, the grandfather of Orpheus.

186–217. Orpheus travels through the spheres. In the Middle Ages it was believed that the earth was the centre of the universe and that the sun and all the planets travelled around it. As the moon was the closest heavenly body to the earth, it was believed to have the smallest distance to circle, and thus the smallest sphere. Mercury, the next closest planet to the earth, had to circle both the earth and the moon, and so on with all seven of the known planets, culminating in the stars, which formed the outermost sphere. Orpheus starts with this outer sphere and works down through all the planets in order.

188. *Wedlingis streit* is the old name for the Roman road which connected London to Wroxeter and Chester. The name is being used here merely as that of a great road, one grand enough to describe the Milky Way. Its use is not unique to Henryson.

189. The god Saturn was one of the most ancient of the Italian gods. He was believed to have been overthrown by his own son, Jupiter, and is usually portrayed as the old man of the gods (cf. Henryson, *The Testament of Cresseid*, 1.151).

213. Mercury, known in ancient mythology as the messenger of the gods, was sometimes regarded as the god of rhetoric and of eloquence in general.

223–5. It was believed that each of the heavenly spheres produced a musical note as it revolved and that these formed the basis for all earthly music.

226–9. Henryson is drawing here on Pythagoras' theory of music: a string when plucked will produce a note of a certain pitch. If only half the string is allowed to vibrate then the note will be higher (duplar) and if only a third then the note will be higher still (triplar) and so on. Henryson's vocabulary becomes very difficult at this point, the intention being to show the impressive nature of the music by use of highly technical terminology.

233–6. Line 235 has caused critics some concern. It does not make sense as it stands and it has, therefore, been suggested by Fox that the word *dyapenty* should be repeated: *dyapenty, and dyapenty componyt with a dys* (a fifth and double fifth). This would produce the five required by 1.236: 'First comes the interval of a fourth, very sweet indeed, and then the octave and double octave; the fifth, and double fifth; these make five augmented from three'.

252. Cerberus is the three-headed dog of the underworld whose task it was to prevent the living from entering the realm of the dead and to prevent the dead from leaving.

261. Henryson does not name the river but such rivers were commonly used in medieval literature to indicate the boundary with another world. Hades, the Greek underworld, was said to be surrounded by the River Styx, sometimes the River Acheron, but souls were ferried across by boat and there is no mention of a bridge, nor were the Furies traditionally associated with any kind of bridge.

264. The three Furies traditionally inhabited the darkest pit of the underworld and tortured those who had offended the gods, especially those who had upset the social order by committing crimes against the family. They were usually depicted as hideous winged spirits with serpents for hair.

266. According to ancient Greek legend, Ixion was the first to murder one of his own kin. He also attempted to have intercourse with Hera, queen of the gods, but was tricked into copulating with a cloud in the form of the goddess, thus creating the centaurs, half man and half horse. He was condemned for his crimes to spend eternity attached to a constantly revolving wheel.

277. Tantalus killed his son and offered him up as a meal for the gods. His punishment was to spend eternity in a state of hunger and thirst: he stood in water up to his neck but the water withdrew from him whenever he tried to drink. Similarly, branches laden with fruit hung constantly just out of his reach.

295. Tityus was condemned by the gods to have his liver forever torn apart by vultures. There are numerous versions of his story, most usually that he was punished for attacking Leto as she gave birth to Apollo and Artemis, but his crime here appears to have been attempting to steal the power of divination from Apollo, sometimes viewed as the god of prophecy.

308–9. Rhadamanthys was one of the judges of Elysium, the ancient Greek abode of the blessed after death. He is here being equated with Pluto, lord of the underworld, who stole Proserpina away from her mother, the goddess of the harvest. She was to be returned to earth for half of the year when her mother would celebrate with summer, and then return to the underworld as its queen for the other six months when the earth would become barren as a sign of her mother's mourning.

321. Priam was the last king of the ancient city of Troy which finally fell to the Greeks after a ten year siege. His eldest son, Hector, led the Trojan army but was killed in battle and his body dragged behind the Greek chariots and then left for the wild animals and birds of prey.

322. This is a reference to Alexander the Great (356–323 B C), king of Macedonia in northern Greece, whose conquests took him as far as India. To medieval scholars he often symbolised overweening pride.

323. Historically, Antiochus (324–261 B C) married his father's young wife but in medieval literature he was said to have committed incest with his daughter.

324. Julius Caesar, emperor of Rome and a medieval type of the cruel ruler.

325. Herod Antipas, son of the biblical Herod the Great, was said to have married his brother's wife.

326. The Roman emperor Nero was renowned for the violence and terror of his rule. The Middle Ages focused particularly on his murder of his own mother.

327. Pontius Pilate, governor of Judaea, under whose jurisdiction the crucifixion of Christ took place, was regarded in the Middle Ages as a corrupt judge.

329–30. Henryson is here conflating the lives of the Roman leader Marcus Licinius Crassus, and King Croesus. Croesus was the last king of Lydia, famous for his wealth, but it was Crassus who was said to have died by being forced to drink molten gold.

331–2. The Bible (Exodus 1–12) recounts how God sent plagues to Egypt because Pharaoh refused to give the Israelites their freedom.

333. The Bible describes many injustices perpetrated by Saul, the first king of Israel, many of them prompted by his hatred for David (I Samuel 13–28).

335–7. When her husband Ahab was disappointed at not obtaining the vineyard of Naboth, Jezebel arranged to have the man killed. Both Ahab and Jezebel worshipped pagan gods and refused to believe in the true prophets (I Kings 18–21).

338–44. The religious figures are being accused of concerning themselves with worldly matters. They abuse their positions and indulge in the sin of simony, where church positions are bestowed for political reasons or money instead of being allocated to truly religious men.

362. This time Henryson is referring to Herod the Great. Herod

was a popular figure in medieval drama where he ranted and raved, wore a golden crown and was surrounded by all the trappings of worldly wealth.

369–70. It is not clear what Henryson means here, and *yporler-ica* is probably his invention. However, the sense appears to be that Orpheus is singing in harmony with his harp.

386. Henryson seems to be viewing the underworld as a medieval castle.

415–7. Boethius (AD 480–524) had a very successful early career, being made consul in 510. However, he was later accused of treason, was imprisoned and finally put to death. It was while in prison that he wrote his great work, *The Consolation of Philosophy*, a dialogue between himself and Philosophy in a part of which the story of Orpheus is told.

421. This is a reference to Dr Nicholas Trivet, an English Dominican who wrote a commentary on Boethius' *Consolation* at the beginning of the fourteenth century. Henryson draws on this in his *moralitas*.

522. According to classical mythology, the *god of riches* is Plutus. He is traditionally a blind god as wealth is given to the wicked and the good indiscriminately, but Henryson makes no mention of this detail here. Indeed, the inclusion of Plutus as a rich guest staying at the inn of Tantalus would appear to be original to Henryson. In most other versions Tantalus himself is a wealthy man.

528. According to ancient Greek legend, the Acheron is one of the names for the river which the dead must cross to reach the underworld. It was believed to be almost stagnant, its banks choked with mud and weeds.

571–99. Henryson is here differentiating between what he calls *trew astronomy*, the study of the stars and the movements of the planets and their influences, and superstitious attempts to predict the future.

614. Proserpina is the *quene of hellis fyre*.

The Testament of Cresseid

A medieval audience would already have known the story of Troilus and Criseyde. It would have been familiar to them and to Henryson from the work of the English poet Chaucer and from many other sources. Each version differs in detail but in one respect all are the same: Criseyde in the end betrays her lover Troilus. Chaucer's story is set in Troy in the final stages of the ten-year war against Greece. Troilus is a valiant prince, much loved by the people, and Criseyde is a beautiful widow. Her father, the seer Calchas, has defected to the Greek camp leaving Criseyde in Troy. Troilus, who had previously been scornful of love, is captivated by her beauty and the two eventually become lovers. However, having predicted the fall of Troy, Calchas wants to rescue his daughter and convinces the Greeks to exchange her for one of their Trojan prisoners. The lovers are grief-stricken, but Criseyde promises that she will make her way back to Troy as soon as possible. In the meantime, she goes along with her father's plan and rides to the Greek camp with her escort, Diomedes. Troilus waits night after night on the city walls for her return but Criseyde does not come back to him. He continues to do battle until one day he sees a brooch, a love token he had given Criseyde, on Diomedes' coat. At the sight of this he assumes that Criseyde must have transferred her affections to the Greek warrior, and in a rage he renounces love and eventually dies alone in battle.

Henryson takes up the story at the point where Criseyde has been abandoned by Diomedes. It is therefore not a sequel to Chaucer's poem but instead tells the part of the story which Chaucer does not tell. Like the English poet, Henryson handles Criseyde's character carefully. While to other writers there is a simple opposition between 'true Troilus' and 'false Criseyde', Henryson's tale is not so straightforward. His Cresseid is a sinner and the leprosy with which she is afflicted may be Henryson's own addition to the sources, but nevertheless she is not dismissed and classified as the whore she is in so many other versions of the legend. While her death is a horrible one, and the disease was often thought to be the result of sexual promiscuity, leprosy has a biblical history in which the leper's suffering leads to true understanding and eternal bliss. Critics are divided as to whether or not such self-knowledge is finally achieved by Cresseid, but there are certainly some developments in the course of the tale. The mirror into which she looks at the beginning of the poem confirms her vanity and inward-looking nature (II.347–55). By the end of the poem, however, her self-pity has gone and the only mirror in which she is interested is the one she will be to others, warning them of the dangers of self-indulgence and pride (I.457). Cresseid cannot change what she has done, but it is interesting to note that her last thoughts are of Troilus and her final words 'true love' (I.591).

1–2. It was a favourite device of medieval authors to begin a work with a short piece of wisdom, known as a *sententia*.

4. *Tragedie* is used here in the medieval sense of a reversal of fortune. Critics are divided on Henryson's use of the word *fervent*. The astrological sign of Aries was traditionally associated with the properties of heat and dryness and April is frequently referred to as hot in medieval literature. The move from spring heat to hailstorms might then be in keeping with the extreme change from good to ill-fortune bound up in the medieval notion of tragedy. However, the hot and dry qualities of Aries were believed to make those born under this sign quick-tempered and passionate like their ruling planet, Mars, god of war. Henryson's intention might then have been to describe severe or stormy weather in which the showers of hail would not be out of place.

5. The forty days before Easter are referred to as Lent and were a traditional time of fasting and penance in the Middle Ages. With Lent, however, also came spring with its connotations of rebirth and love.

8. The narrator's *oratur* is a small chapel or, possibly, a private study.

9. According to Greek myth, the marriage of Heaven and Earth produced twelve giant children known as the Titans. In turn, they produced many offspring including Helios, the sun.

11. Venus, the brightest of the planets, sometimes called the day star, and also the ancient goddess of beauty and love. Henryson later claims that her light is bright enough to see by (II.15–16) but this is not, in fact, possible.

13. In order for planets to be in opposition they must face one another at an angle of 180 degrees. This is not possible with Venus which is never further than 48 degrees from the sun. In terms of astrology, therefore, there is an impossible evil in the alignment of the planets here.

14. Phoebus Apollo, an ancient god often identified, as here, with the sun. The classical gods had many different names and Henryson was learned in many different mythologies. It is not, therefore, inconsistent that the sun should be the Titan at I.9 and Phoebus at I.14.

41–2. Henryson is referring to Geoffrey Chaucer's *Troilus and Criseyde*. The next few stanzas give a faithful account of Chaucer's poem in which Criseyde is sent to the Greek camp in exchange for a Trojan warrior. She promises to return to her Trojan lover, Troilus, but never does. Instead, she accepts the attentions of Diomedes, the Greek warrior sent to fetch her from Troy.

61. The other book referred to here is probably imaginary. It was common for medieval poets to refer to an ancient author even when none existed.

74. *Lybell of repudie* is the term found in the Latin Bible for a bill of divorce.

77. Cresseid, no longer the mistress of the powerful Diomedes, becomes available to the common court. Her status has been reduced to that of mere courtesan.

78. Cresseid is ranked first among women, like the letter A in the alphabet.

89. Fortune was often depicted as a blind or blindfolded woman turning a great wheel. As the wheel turned, so the fate of people changed for good or bad, regardless of their merit (cf. Dunbar, 'Full Oft I Muse and Hes in Thocht').

97. According to medieval tradition, Calchas was a Trojan with the ability to see into the future. When he foresaw that the Greeks would win the war and destroy Troy he fled to their camp, later asking that his daughter Cresseid should be brought to him. His reputation as a prophet explains his role as a priest here.

108. Calchas is more usually a priest of Apollo, god of prophecy among other things. Henryson's decision to make him a priest of Venus, goddess of love, and her son Cupid, emphasises love as one of the poem's themes.

119. Diomedes was not a king but he was of royal blood.

135. Venus is almost never represented as blind, unlike her son Cupid who frequently fires the dart of love at unlikely subjects on account of his inability to see. In this poem, however, neither is blind and Cresseid is making a mistake for which she will later be reprimanded (II.282–3). As Denton Fox points out, she has confused blind lust with love. Images of blindness recur throughout the poem.

147. In the Middle Ages there were believed to be seven planets in addition to the earth: Saturn, Jupiter, Mars, the sun, Venus, Mercury, and the moon. Each of these was thought to travel in a circle round the earth, with each one enclosing its inferior spherically. Thus, Saturn, being furthest from the earth, makes the widest circle; while the moon, the planet closest to the earth, has the smallest sphere (cf. Henryson, *Orpheus and Eurydice*, II.186–217).

151. Saturn is represented as the old man of the gods. Perhaps originally a blight god in the ancient world, associated with the failure of crops, his astrological influence is malign. In the

Middle Ages he is associated with the old and the poor, and is often depicted as a peasant with a sickle (cf. Henryson, *Orpheus and Eurydice*, I.189).

155. The medieval west believed that there were four basic properties in the universe: cold, heat, dryness and moisture. Any imbalance of these in the body could lead to illness. Leprosy was believed to be the result of an excess of cold and dryness, both of which are elements intrinsic to Saturn. Most medieval authors explain the leprosy of Robert Bruce in this way, his exposure to the chilling wind on the Scottish hillsides causing an imbalance in his body which resulted in the disease.

169. Jupiter is the king of the gods. In the Middle Ages he was viewed as the son of Saturn who had rebelled against his father and vanquished him (cf.I.182). He was regarded as Saturn's opposite: warm and moist where Saturn is cold and dry; and a bringer of life as opposed to Saturn's death and destruction. Jupiter can be equated with Christ though this is not obviously Henryson's intention here.

170. It was believed that the universe was surrounded by a solid sphere, known as the firmament, in which the stars were set.

173. A large, smooth forehead was regarded as a sign of beauty in the Middle Ages.

178. The colour green was deeply ambiguous in the Middle Ages. It can be a positive and life affirming colour, associated with springtime, youth and rebirth. However, its association with envy is an ancient one, as is the superstition that it is an unlucky colour. The devil was often portrayed as green in the Middle Ages, while Scottish folk tales regard green as a fairy colour and anyone wearing it is in danger of falling into their power.

179. Gores are triangular pieces of cloth let into a garment to widen it. They were very fashionable in the later Middle Ages and were often made a feature of the garment. In this case they have been trimmed with gold.

183. Mars is the ancient god of war and was, like Saturn, regarded as a malign planet.

186. A *habergeon* is a sleeveless coat of chainmail. Mars was usually depicted as heavily armed.

187. A *falchion* is a large sword with a curved blade. Some critics suggests that *roustie* should be translated as bronze. Mars is, however, more frequently associated with iron (each planet being allocated their own metals). According to Fox, there

may be a reference here to the ancient Germanic belief that the blood of enemies strengthened the blade and was consequently allowed to dry on the sword. In either case, the overall effect is to contrast Mars with the gleaming gold of Jupiter.

197. As nothing can grow without the sun, Phoebus Apollo is regarded as a bringer of life, like Jupiter. For this reason, he too can sometimes be viewed as a Christ figure.

204–5. Ancient Greek mythology explained the passing of the day in terms of the Sun's chariot being driven through the sky. Phaethon, his son, asked to drive the chariot one day but lost control of the horses and came too close to the earth. In order to save the world from destruction, the king of the gods hurled a thunderbolt at Phaethon who fell to the earth and died. In the Middle Ages, Phaethon was often used to symbolise pride and was equated with the angel Lucifer whose pride caused him to rebel against God.

209–16. The chariot of the sun was traditionally drawn by four horses, each of which represents a different part of the day. The first horse, *Eoye* (Eous), is a reddish colour like the dawn. The second, *Ethios* (Aethon), is white like the bright morning sun. *Peros* (Pyrois), the third, is fiery like the sun in the afternoon. And the fourth horse, *Philogie*, is black like the night.

221. The idea of a two-coloured Venus is a very ancient one. The black symbolises the despair which is often inherent in love, while the green represents the hopeful and joyous side, though even this could be ambiguous (cf. I.178). Henryson uses the image here to stress the fickleness of Venus and her similarities to the goddess Fortune. Fortune, according to medieval lore, can 'both smile and frown' and is unstable in her affections like Venus here who weeps with one eye and laughs with the other.

239. Mercury had many attributes. He was the god of merchants, medicine and rhetoric and symbolised the constant activity of the human intellect. His quickness, however, could have a negative side and he was also the god of thieves and liars, a fact which is likely to make I.252 ironic.

244–5. Mercury was usually depicted wearing a winged cap. In some medieval pictures this became an elaborate headdress and Henryson makes the connection between this and Mercury's role as god of poets and intellectuals by giving him the hood of an old fashioned poet.

250–1. Medieval Scots doctors wore red gowns with the more successful also wearing furs.

253–5. Lady Cynthia is the moon, last and swiftest of the planets because she is closest to the earth and therefore revolves around it in the shortest time. She was often depicted as having a crescent moon on her head which was interpreted as a fashionable horned headdress in some medieval works.

261–3. The spots on the moon were thought to represent an old man carrying a bundle of thorns for firewood. Some versions of the story identify him with the man executed by Moses for gathering wood on the Sabbath; some say that he is Judas, banished to the moon for his betrayal of Christ; and according to others he is Cain, who committed the first murder when he became jealous of the burnt offering his brother made to God. For his crime he was then condemned to carry his own bundle of thorns on the moon forever. It is a sinister image no matter which version of the legend Henryson had in mind.

287. The object of Cupid's favour here is Cresseid.

302. *Proceidit* is a Scots legal term, as is *modifie* (I.299). Cresseid's trial by the gods is being conducted using the language of the medieval Scottish law courts.

334–43. All of these afflictions are consistent with leprosy. Its causes were believed to be various in the Middle Ages and Henryson exploits them all. Excessive coldness and dryness, or the conjunction of Saturn and the moon were two, often related, possibilities. But leprosy was also frequently viewed as a venereal disease, the disintegration of the flesh being seen as an outward manifestation of the moral disintegration which preceded it. The disease was associated with sin and came to be a symbol of sin in general.

376. Leprosy was believed to be generally incurable though some outlandish recipes survive in medieval medical texts and literature. These include the earth from an anthill, the gold from an alchemist, and the bath water of the Christ child. As leprosy was often thought to be caused by moral degeneracy, the blood of innocent children was believed to be able to reverse the process. Legend has it that the emperor Constantine was advised to bathe in the blood of three thousand children in order to cure his leprosy. However, when he caught sight of them with their weeping mothers he took pity on them and prevented the massacre.

382–4. Leper hospitals were situated beyond the town boundaries and large cities would have had more than one. Food and alms were brought to the hospitals as an act of charity but also to discourage lepers from entering the towns. In Edinburgh in the sixteenth century, lepers were forbidden to leave the hospital 'under the payne of hanging' and a gallows was erected for the purpose in the grounds. Glasgow lepers had slightly more freedom, being allowed to leave the hospital under stringent conditions. St Ninian's, Glasgow's main leper hospital, was founded around 1350 at the south end of Glasgow Bridge in the Gorbals. Another existed on the north boundary of the city until the eighteenth century when it became the site for the Saracen's Head Inn. Leprosy had died out in Scotland by the eighteenth century with only a few new cases in the Shetland Islands.

407. A *sop* is a piece of bread soaked in liquid, and a metaphor for worthlessness. Cresseid is therefore saying that she is worthless, soaked in her sorrow.

416–7. Cresseid begins a catalogue on the theme *ubi sunt* (where are they?). This device is used to emphasise the transitory nature of the world and the ultimate futility of all earthly desires as the speaker asks where all the glories and beautiful things of the past are now. Inevitably they have passed away or decayed and the realisation of this brings the speaker to wisdom and the understanding that only the divine is ultimately important.

418. *Collatioun* is a late supper, usually with connotations of intimacy and even sexual impropriety. Cf. Dunbar, 'Thir ladeis fair that maks repair', I.14, where women use such intimate settings to influence powerful men.

421. Orange-red in colour, saffron was regarded as a medieval delicacy. According to popular belief, it took over four thousand crocus flowers to yield one ounce of saffron. It was prized for its flavour, colour and medicinal qualities.

423. Lawn is a type of fine linen which first appeared in Britain at the end of the fourteenth century. It was used in only the most expensive garments.

426. Flora, the Roman goddess of flowers.

429. It was an ancient custom for girls to wash their faces in May morning dew in order to enhance their beauty (cf. Henryson, *Orpheus and Eurydice*, I.95).

436. Cresseid is referring to the wheel of fortune which has revolved and cast her from her exalted place at the top of the wheel.

440-1. Perry is fermented pear juice, an inferior form of cider. A surviving fragment of an old Scottish law shows that lepers could be presented with far worse than this. It declares that any rotten pork or salmon brought to market would be confiscated and sent as an act of charity to the lepers, or else destroyed if there were no lepers to eat it.

464. Henryson deals with this subject at greater length in 'The Thrie Deid Pollis', where the skulls themselves address the living.

482. According to Scottish law, lepers were only free to beg in certain places which included the city gates but excluded the church and all the food markets. They were prohibited from entering any private home and the punishment for disobedience was banishment for the leper and a fine for the citizen concerned.

531. Lepers were frequently referred to as lazars due to their association with the biblical Lazarus, the poor man at the rich man's table in Luke (16:19–26). The Bible describes him as 'full of sores', an affliction which the Middle Ages associated with leprosy. When Lazarus died his soul was received into heaven while the rich man's soul suffered torment. The poor man's leprosy was therefore to be seen as a gift from God which allowed him to suffer for a short time on earth and so enjoy eternal bliss in heaven. In the midst of general condemnation for lepers, therefore, there was one tradition which viewed them as specially chosen by God for salvation. It is perhaps significant that Henryson chooses to call Cresseid a *lazar* rather than a leper at this point in the poem.

541. *Ochane* is Gaelic *ochoin*, a cry of grief or lamentation.

567. A weathervane turns to show the direction of the wind. It is, therefore, a metaphor for changeable or fickle people.

587. The Roman goddess Diana had many functions but most relevant here are her roles as goddess of chastity and protector of women.

589. The brooch is mentioned in Chaucer's *Troilus and Criseyde*. Troilus finally realises that he has lost Criseyde when he sees the brooch which he had given her as a love token on the coat of Diomedes.

Robene and Makyne

This poem is sometimes called a *pastourelle*, though it does not have all the characteristics of the genre. The French poems have a country setting in which a couple debate about love, but the protagonists are more usually a knight and a shepherdess. Here, the couple are social equals, a shepherd named Robin and a wench named Marion. Their conversation, however, contains many of the traditional elements of courtly love such as the demand for pity (I.4), the need for secrecy (I.7), and the complaint that otherwise the lover will die (I.8). The tradition of suppliant knight and disdainful lady is, however, reversed and these words are placed in the mouth of Makyne as she attempts to woo the reluctant Robene. A similarly incongruous pairing of rustic lovers and courtly love is found in Dunbar's 'In secreit place this hyndir nycht', but Henryson's poem is less satirically obscene and more playful.

37–40. The sense of these lines would appear to be that God will always bring comfort to the afflicted, even if that can only be achieved by death. Makyne says, therefore, that she is certain to die if Robene refuses to sleep with her.

The Garmont of Gud Ladeis
There is a long tradition of describing moral qualities in terms of armour or clothing. St Paul urged the Ephesians to put on the 'whole armour of God' including the 'breastplate of righteousness', the 'shield of faith' and the 'helmet of salvation' (Ephesians 6:13–16), and the *topos* was popular in literature throughout the Middle Ages. Henryson's poem is unusual in that it describes women and women's clothing and the moral qualities desired are those suitable to a lady.

26. A *tepat* is a long, thin strip of cloth which either hung down from the hood or else was worn around the shoulders.
27. A *patelet* is a kind of large collar which some editors have chosen to translate as ruff. However, Fox suggests that it is too early for the fashion to be for ruffs.

The Bludy Serk
The theme of Christ as a lover-knight and the soul as his lady was a popular one in medieval literature. Usually the disdainful lady is besieged by enemies to represent the reluctant soul besieged by sin, and the knight must rescue her even if this means his own death (just as Christ died on the cross to redeem the souls of mankind). Henryson's damsel in distress is more appealing than many and the story is more than mere allegory.

However, the poem ends with a *moralitas* which makes the religious meaning clear.

28. This appears to be one ell and a quarter long, which is a little over a metre in modern terms.
100. Lucifer is another name for the Devil.

The Annunciation

This poem in honour of the Virgin focuses on the angel Gabriel's annunciation that Mary would conceive and bear Christ. The poet employs all the imagery traditionally associated with the Virgin Birth, including the burning bush of Moses, rod of Aaron, and Gideon's fleece (II.37–46). The paradox of virgin motherhood is echoed in paradox and oxymoron throughout, from the commonplace of bitter-sweet love (II.1–2) to the unexpected *chaist with child* (I.23). The poem culminates in a prayer to Mary to protect the poet from evil and bring him to the bliss of heaven (cf. Dunbar, 'Hale, sterne superne, hale, in eterne').

11. Mary was believed to have conceived Christ without sin when she agreed to become the Mother of God at the Annunciation.
17–18. The idea of the 'unwounded' and sinless womb refers once again to Mary's immaculate conception. Penetration is thought of as 'piercing' the womb but as the Virgin conceived without sexual intercourse the womb remained intact and her body remained sinless.
31. Not only was Mary believed to have conceived Christ without violation to her virginity, she was also thought to have remained intact both during and after the birth. A popular way of explaining the mystery of perpetual virginity was to say that Christ entered and left Mary's womb like sunshine through glass. She could thus be both virgin and mother.
39–40. The burning bush of Moses (Exodus 3:2) which was in flames and yet not consumed by the fire was regarded as a symbol of the Virgin Birth, for Mary conceived and gave birth without being consumed by sin.
43–4. The Book of Numbers tells how each of the twelve tribes of Israel brought a wooden rod to Moses and how Aaron's flowered to show that he had been chosen by God (Numbers 17:1–8). This blossoming of dead wood through the power of God was interpreted as a symbol of Mary's immaculate conception of Christ.

45–6. Gideon's fleece which was moist with dew even though all the ground around it was dry (Judges 6:37) was yet another symbol of Mary's intact virginity as she remained inviolate and yet Christ entered her womb.

68. *Termigant* is used here as another name for the Devil.

The Praise of Age
Ancient literature from Plato to Cicero praises old age, finding in it a release from the unwanted desires of youth, and the Middle Ages sympathised with the sentiment. Henryson's poem adds to this criticism of youthful passions (II.17–24), a lament for the sad state of the world (II.9–16) and a general complaint against fickle fortune and transitory joys (II.25–8). The refrain makes it clear that the only true bliss is that of heaven, which each passing day of old age brings closer.

The Ressoning betwix Aige and Yowth
Debate poems in which opposing sides alternately present their arguments were popular in the Middle Ages. The combatants could be anything from a carpenter's tools to the body and soul (cf. Dunbar, 'In May as that Aurora did up spring' in which the contest is between a merle and a nightingale) but the contest of old age and youth was a favourite theme. The descriptions of the protagonists in this poem are traditional, and although the majority of debate poems declare a winner, the unresolved ending is not uncommon.

14. Henryson envisages both characters as having a scroll in front of them on which is written their refrain. In the case of Age, *O yowth, thy flouris fedis ferly sone!* (cf. I.55 and I.69).

37. Both *mell* and *mowis* are words associated with copulation and it is likely that some sense of double entendre is intended here.

46. The moon does not remain constant but waxes and wanes in the course of the month. It was also regarded as a cold and sterile planet (cf. Henryson, *The Testament of Cresseid*, II.258–9).

The Ressoning betwix Deth and Man
The presentation of Man in this poem has similarities with Youth in 'The Ressoning betwix Aige and Youth'. Both take pride in their strength and vigour and believe that they should fear no one. However, Man's adversary here is Death himself, and even youthful power must bow before him. The confronta-

tion of Death and Man was popular in both medieval art and literature. Medieval churches frequently contained images of skeletal figures leading popes, emperors and ploughmen, amongst others, in a Dance of Death to indicate that no rank of society could escape him (cf.II.3–6). Occasionally, Death encounters just one figure, in which case it is likely to be a young man whose strength, youth and beauty make him think that he will live forever. The poem is, therefore, a warning and a reminder that death conquers all.

2. The idea that the living should look upon death as a mirror of their future selves was a popular one. It functioned not just as a warning of what they would become but also as a reflection of their true selves.

6. In medieval art, Death was frequently represented as carrying not a scythe, but a spear.

32. Pride was considered to be the deadliest of the seven deadly sins.

43. It has been suggested that this line refers to *cape of lede*, a lead coffin.

The Thre Deid Pollis

Medieval encounters between the living and the dead, as opposed to those between Death and Man (cf. Henryson, 'The Ressoning betwix Deth and Man'), traditionally involve three corpses. These usually represent the three ages of man – youth, middle age and old age – and stress the idea that death can come at any time, not just to the old. Accordingly, this poem has the skulls appeal first of all to reckless youth and beautiful ladies (II.17–32), then to those with power (II.33–40), and finally to the aged (II.49–56). The poem is both a warning in the *memento mori* tradition, and a request for prayer.

18. A white and red complexion was a sign of youthful beauty (cf. Dunbar, 'Sweit rois of vertew and of Gentilnes').

29. *Quhailis bane* is ivory, but literally whale's bone. In fact, the early Middle Ages obtained their ivory from the tusks of the walrus before elephant tusks became widely known.

33. Pride was commonly believed to be the deadliest of the seven deadly sins as it was considered to be the root cause of all the others.

37–40. The image of the emperor, king and queen being no more able to escape death than the poor would have been familiar from the medieval *Dance Macabre* tradition. Here, Death leads all ranks of society in its dance, from the pope and emperor to the ploughman and little child. It was a popular image in churches and churchyards. One of the few surviving examples can be seen at Rosslyn Abbey near Edinburgh.

42. The art of physiognomy, or judging someone's character by their appearance, was very popular in the Middle Ages. For example, someone with red hair was believed to be easily angered, someone with a gap in their teeth was thought to have a lecherous nature (cf. Henryson, *The Paddock and the Mouse*, II.2826–32).

41–8. Medieval corpses were left in the ground only long enough for the flesh to decompose. They were then exhumed and the bones stored in a charnel house. Here the skeleton would be divided up and the corpse would lose its identity: its skull would merely be placed with other skulls, the hands with other hands. The bones of rich and poor were placed side by side and were indistinguishable from one another. The image of skulls in the charnel house therefore shows death as the great leveller and stresses the ultimate vanity of earthly things.

55–6. This is a reference to the second coming of Christ when, according to the Bible, bodies will rise from the dead in order to take part in the final judgement. This was considered such a literal reality in the Middle Ages that it was the custom for bodies to be buried with feet pointing east so that the corpse would be facing the direction of Christ's coming.

Ane Prayer for the Pest

It is not clear which pestilence is being referred to in this poem but it is most likely to be the Black Death, bubonic plague, which first arrived in Scotland in 1349 and broke out intermittently throughout the fifteenth and sixteenth centuries. It has been estimated that up to a third of the population of Europe may have died of plague in the Middle Ages.

21. It was regarded as very important in the Middle Ages that the dying person should receive the last rites, which would have included the confession of sins, from a priest. However, so many are dying from the plague that the priests cannot attend to them all, and the clergy too are dying.

75–6. These lines are difficult, but the sense appears to be that death is claiming everyone and those left alive may not be so for long.

The Abbey Walk

The moral of this poem is patience in adversity and the setting is an abbey in which the speaker catches sight of a poem on the wall. Given Henryson's connections with Dunfermline, critics have often wanted to link the poem to Dunfermline Abbey which would have been an impressive building in the fifteenth century. No such poem now survives in the abbey but verses of this kind were often painted on the walls and were thus very easily destroyed in the course of the centuries. Whether or not such a wall-painting was ever viewed by Henryson, the theme of the poem was a well-known one: fortune is fickle and the joys of this world can easily pass away, thus one can only accept what happens and thank God for what one is given (cf. Dunbar, 'Of Lentren in the first mornyng').

17. In the biblical story of Job, God decides to test the loyalty of Job by causing him to suffer. All his good fortune disappears, his children are killed, his cattle and servants die and he is stricken with a plague of boils. The people conclude that he must be being punished for his sins but Job maintains that he has led a righteous life (Job 1–2). The point of the book of Job was not to explain the mystery of suffering but to extol the virtue of patience and the importance of faith in spite of suffering.

18. Tobit was, like Job, a righteous man and was performing an act of charity when sparrows' droppings fell into his eyes and blinded him. However, he did not curse his fate but instead accepted the will of God (Tobit 2:10).

Against Hasty Credence

The picture here of a lying, grasping society in which lords neglect the innocent and pay heed only to dissemblers and flatterers is familiar from a number of Henryson's fables (cf. *The Paddock and the Mouse*, ll.2910–25). It is also a favourite theme of Dunbar's poetry (cf. Dunbar, 'This waverand warldis wretchidnes'), usually in the form, as here, of a plea to the lord to realise the error of his ways and learn to distinguish the false from the true, for everyone's sake.

2. The metaphor here refers to the grafting of a branch onto the trunk of another tree.

Sum Practysis of Medecyne

This poem appears to be a parody of medieval medicinal recipes which often contained surprising or even dangerous ingredients. The speaker seems to have been slandered as a quack doctor and is describing some of his prescriptions in answer to his critic. The first is a cure for the colic, the second an aphrodisiac, the third a medicine to cure the folly of a fool, and the last a remedy for hoarseness, coughing or heartburn. Some of the ingredients are disgusting, others impossible to acquire, and the whole poem is a humorous look at a dubious profession and perhaps the stupidity of the patients.

1. The first line has caused controversy amongst critics. Most take *guk guk* as the call of the cuckoo, associated in the Middle Ages, as now, with craziness. The speaker is therefore calling his adversary a fool. As for the call to *gaip quhill ye get it*, this seems to be related to a proverb: 'if you stand open-mouthed until you get it, you will be wide-mouthed', i.e. whatever you want is going to take a long time coming. *Gaip* may also be associated with medicine in the sense of the call to open wide. The listener appears to be a gaping fool to whom the speaker will administer his tender mercies.

27. It is not clear what Henryson means by *cukmaid*. *Cuk* appears to be related to *cack*, meaning to void excrement, but the compound with *maid* is not found elsewhere. It is perhaps a common name for a plant chosen for its offensive connotations, as is the case with *colleraige* on the same line, a variety of water pepper commonly known as arsesmart.

29. Both sorrel and sage were used in many medieval prescriptions.

31. Laurel, linseed and lovage are all commonly found in medicinal recipes and were used for a variety of purposes. All could, however, be used as purgatives.

    Dia longum – the reference to *longum* is obscure. However, the less outlandish ingredients in the recipe which follows are traditionally associated with medieval aphrodisiacs, making *longum* a likely reference to the penis.

40–1. The first few ingredients are all impossible to acquire. The first is a reference to the tugging of a rook at carrion, as intangible as the yawn of a mare and the cry of a goose which follow. Also, no species of rook has red feathers.

42. *Dram* is open to interpretation but most likely refers to the eighth of an ounce measurement employed by apothecaries.

46. It was a common belief that the crescent moon denoted an ill-omened time.

48. Red nettle seeds are found in a number of aphrodisiac recipes. *Strang wesche* is stale urine which Fox points out was used both in medieval pharmacy and for washing clothes.

61. *Lundin* may here refer to London but it is also possible that the poet is referring to Lundin in Fife. The idea would then be that no other such medicine would be found in Scotland, from Lothian in the south to Lundin in the north. A claim, given the ingredients, which would be undeniably true.

69. According to Fox, *gowpene* is 'the fill of two hands held out together in the form of a bowl'.

86. The meaning here seems to be either that the medicine will shake the patients out of their illusions, or else that it will remove them from this 'illusory world' altogether and in fact kill them.

90–1. This is a parody of the proverb: 'Another man's mind is a dark mirror'. There is probably a reference to the fact that medieval medicine advised examining the patient's urine and excrement for purposes of diagnosis.

William Dunbar

My heid did yak yester nicht

This poem is both a vivid description of a headache and also an apology for the poet's illness and apparent writer's block. It is perhaps one of the most personal pieces of verse produced by Dunbar, though it has been interpreted by some critics as calculated criticism of royal neglect.

9. The memory was believed to be situated at the back of the head.

Sir Jhon Sinclair begowthe to dance

This poem satirises the members of the queen's court and may have been written for her amusement. Uncharacteristically, however, Dunbar turns the satire on himself and we are presented with one of the few descriptions of the poet (II.22–8), although the context means that it cannot be taken at face value. His love for *Mussgraeffe* may, for example, be genuine but could equally be an ironic reference to a woman he loathed. Still, there is something poignant about his desire to be, for her sake, the *grytast erle or duk in France*.

1. Sir John Sinclair of Dryden was part of a delegation sent to England in 1501 when the marriage of James IV and Margaret Tudor was being negotiated, and he was still in the queen's service in 1513. His friendly relations with the king are illustrated by various entries in court records which show them to have played bowls and cards together.
2. France was regarded throughout the Middle Ages as a place of high fashion.
8. Robert Shaw appears in the records as a court physician, assisting the queen on one occasion with a nose bleed. Kinsley suggests that he may be the same Robert Shaw who became a priest and said his first mass in the presence of James IV in 1508.
13. Strathnaver is in Sutherland, in the far north of Scotland.
15. The giving of alms to the poor was regarded as one's Christian duty in the Middle Ages, and monarchs employed almoners to perform this function for them. Bawcutt points

out that the term *maister almaser* was usually applied to the king's chief almoner, and that Sir Andrew McBeck held this post throughout the reign of James IV.

19. John Bute the court fool and his attendant *Spark* appear in court records from 1506. His name may suggest that he came from the Isle of Bute.

24. The *dirrye dantoun* appears to be a lively dance but it may also have a sexual implication (cf. Dunbar, 'In secreit place this hyndir nycht', I.60).

26. Musgrave is probably Agnes Musgrave, wife of Sir John Musgrave, who is mentioned as one of the queen's attendants from 1511 until 1513.

36. *Dounteboir* is almost certainly an insulting nickname and not a real name. Kinsley draws attention to John Knox's contemptuous reference to 'old downtybowris . . . that long had served in the court'.

44. This is a reference to James Dog, the queen's wardrobe master (cf. Dunbar, 'The wardraipper of Venus boure' and 'O gracious princes guid and fair').

Now fayre, fayrest of every fayre

This poem was intended to be set to music and is thought to have been part of the marriage celebrations of Margaret Tudor and James IV (cf. Dunbar, 'Quhen Merche wes with variand windis past'). The marriage was negotiated when Margaret was nine years old but did not take place until 1503, when she was thirteen. It is a simple piece in which the new queen is praised for two things: her beauty and her royal lineage. The imagery is conventional, with some of it being familiar from poems to the Virgin Mary.

5. The new queen was only thirteen years old when she arrived in Scotland.

10–11. Margaret was the daughter of Henry VII and Elizabeth of York.

13. The parti-coloured rose became the symbol of the Tudors in 1486 when Elizabeth of York married the Lancastrian Henry VII, thus uniting the red rose of York and the white rose of Lancaster. It was also an image of beauty in courtly literature, the white and red complexion of the woman frequently being compared to the rose. The metaphor is, therefore, doubly appropriate (cf. Dunbar, 'Gladethe, thoue queyne of Scottis regioun', I.25).

Quhen Merche wes with variand windis past
(The Thrissill and the Rois)

This poem has long been associated with the marriage of James IV to Margaret Tudor, the poem's Scottish thistle and English rose, possibly being intended for recitation during the five days of celebrations which followed the ceremony on 8 August 1503 in Holyrood Abbey. The entwined thistle and rose appear on many documents associated with the marriage, and on some of the stained-glass windows of Holyrood Palace at which the wedding festivities were held. The Rose is presented as the most beautiful, perfect, delightful and pleasing of all flowers (II.144–6) which the Thistle is instructed to honour above all others (II.134–43), a reference perhaps to the notorious womanising of James (cf. Dunbar, 'This hindir nycht in Dumfermeling'). Elsewhere in the poem, the king is the mighty lion, called upon to exercise both justice and mercy, and protect his people from oppressors (II.92–119); and the noble eagle, encouraged to be just in his laws (II.120–6). The poem is set within the framework of the dream vision and has all the traditional elements of the genre including the May morning setting, the beautiful garden and the wondering narrator.

5. Hours are church services, sung at various times throughout the day and night.

9. Aurora was the Roman goddess of the dawn.

20. Phoebus, meaning bright, was one of the names of the ancient Greek god of the sun.

33. Aeolus was the ancient Greek god of the winds.

62. The Roman deity Flora was responsible for everything which blooms.

65. Neptune was the Roman god of the sea.

83. Both the roe and swallow have been chosen for their swiftness. Milfoil, or yarrow, also has associations with speed, witches being traditionally thought to fly on yarrow stalks.

96–8. Dunbar's description of the lion closely resembles that on the royal arms of Scotland which shows a red lion against a gold background with a border of fleur-de-lys.

109. The unicorn was a symbol of purity and chastity while the ape was associated with lust and sin (cf. Dunbar, 'Lang heff I maed of ladyes quhytt', I.6).

119. This is a reference to a popular Latin maxim: *Parcere prostratis scit nobilis ira leonis; Tu quoque fac simile, quisquis dominaris orbe* ('The noble wrath of the lion refrains from

injuring those who are prostrate before him; You also, who
will rule the world, should act in the same way'). It was often
used to remind those with power that they ought to be
merciful (cf. Henryson, *The Trial of the Fox*, II.929–30).

120. The eagle was traditionally the king of birds.

122. The finch does not usually have any bad connotations in
medieval literature, unlike the nocturnal owl, but probably
appears in this line as a small and therefore slightly insignif-
icant bird, very different from the showy peacocks, parrots
and cranes of the next line.

150. The Lily (fleur-de-lys) can simply be an image of purity
and perfection as it is at II.138–40, but the reference here
appears to be more specifically to the royal arms of France.

171–2. The parti-coloured rose became the symbol of the
Tudors when the Lancastrian Henry VII married Elizabeth
of York (cf. Dunbar, 'Now fayre, fayrest of every fayre',
I.13).

Gladethe, thoue queyne of Scottis regioun

This poem praising the young queen takes her name as its
inspiration. *Margarita* is Latin for pearl and Dunbar plays with
the image of the lady as a precious jewel. The Middle Ages had a
tradition of lapidaries, catalogues of gem-stones which praised
not just their beauty but also explained their various virtues and
properties. Jewels could protect, bring light in darkness, signify
all virtues and heal all wounds and Dunbar draws on this
tradition as he frames his poem with lapidary imagery intended
to compliment the queen. It is a highly rhetorical poem which
depends on repetition and hyperbole, citing the names of clas-
sical beauties and goddesses (II.11–12) and praising Nature
which could produce such a work of art (II.17–23).

2. Margaret's marriage to James IV took place when she was
thirteen.

4. *Margarita* is Latin for pearl, regarded in the Middle Ages as a
symbol of perfection. There is also a reference here to the
biblical 'pearl of great price' for which the merchant gave up
all other possessions (Matthew 13:45–6). It is certainly a
compliment to Margaret's great worth but may also refer
to the many love affairs of James IV.

5. The carbuncle, or ruby, was a symbol of excellence. It was
though to radiate light in darkness.

6. The rose was a conventional symbol of beauty but here also

refers to the heraldic image of the Tudors, the parti-coloured rose, cf. I.25.

10. The lodestar is a guiding star, a 'shining example'.

11. Polyxena was a Trojan princess with whom the hero Achilles fell so deeply in love that he was willing to betray his country. She was famed in the Middle Ages for her beauty.

12. Pallas Athena was the Greek goddess of wisdom.

30–1. The country's stability depended on the queen producing an heir and James's reluctance to marry had caused considerable concern.

34. The beryl is a pale-coloured stone much prized in the Middle Ages.

38. Dunbar may have had in mind the virtuous woman of Proverbs 31:10 who is valued above rubies.

This hindir nycht in Dumfermeling

This beast-fable is clearly intended to allude to some court scandal and has traditionally been thought to refer to the womanising of James IV. The king had many mistresses and a number of illegitimate children and the poem may be referring to one of his exploits. However, it is the nature of fables that they are open to many interpretations. In medieval literature, the fox is a type of cunning and treachery, the wolf is always a violent bully, and the lamb symbolises innocence (cf. Henryson, *The Fox, the Wolf, and the Husbandman* and *The Wolf and the Lamb*). Dunbar takes these traditional figures and produces a disturbing picture of force and exploitation in which nothing is really certain, not even the virtue of our 'lamb'.

1. Dunfermline in Fife was an important burgh in the Middle Ages. Several Scottish kings were buried in its great abbey and James IV had a palace there, a crucial point for those who want to relate this fable to the king's amorous exploits. However, the reference to Dunfermline could also be a tribute to Robert Henryson, its famous denizen and master of the beast-fable.

3. Bawcutt opposes the identification of the fox with James on the grounds that Dunbar usually represents him as a lion or eagle and that foxes in medieval literature usually signify unprincipled churchmen. However, someone who is a lion when ruling well can easily become a fox when things go badly, and in any case the 'cunning' fox has never been

limited to satires against the church (cf. Henryson, *The Fox, the Wolf, and the Husbandman*).

12. The mercy the fox is looking for is of a sexual nature but the word is ambiguous (cf. I.47).

13. The *lady* is Our Lady, an appropriate appeal in this context to the eternal Virgin.

16. The reference to red hair has led some critics to discount the possibility that the fox is James, but there is little evidence other than the Mytens portrait for the king's colouring. In any case, the reference need not be so specific.

19. The musical pun here is sexual, the bass being the lower position with the treble 'on top'.

39. *Prenecod* is a metaphor for the female genitalia.

59–60. It is not clear what happens to the lamb. It could be that the fox is metaphorically 'covered' by her skin as she distracts the wolf, but it could also be the case that she has been slaughtered by the fox.

Schir, for your grace, bayth nicht and day

This poem is ostensibly addressed to the king but its irreverent tone suggests that it may have been meant for the queen's amusement, to convince her to intercede on Dunbar's behalf. It appears that Dunbar is out of favour with the king (I.23) and he wishes that James would allow himself to be ruled by the *fair and gude* Margaret (I.14). The poem, however, humorously mixes heraldic imagery and courtly language with a refrain about a henpecked husband, John Thomson's man.

4. It is not clear what the origin of the phrase *Johne Thomsounis man* is, though it clearly means a husband who is under the control of his wife, 'like John Thomson'. Bawcutt suggests that it may be related to a surviving English tale, a *mery jest of John Tomson and Jakaman his wife* in which the wife is a shrew who constantly nags her husband. The phrase was still current in the time of Sir Walter Scott: 'D'ye think I am to be John Tamson's man, and maistered by women a' the days o' my life?' (*Old Mortality*, chap. 38).

6. A benefice is a position in the church, most of which were within the gift of the king.

19. It became fashionable in the later Middle Ages to make vows before birds of symbolic or heraldic significance such as the swan or the eagle. It was largely the practice of chivalric romance but there are recorded instances of such vows being

taken in real courts. At a great feast in 1306, Edward I and his
son swore upon two swans that they would punish Robert
Bruce for the murder of John Comyn. But the white swan is
also an image of female beauty and Dunbar may also be
referring to the queen.

21–2. According to heraldry, Margaret is the rose of England,
while James is the thistle of Scotland (cf. Dunbar, 'Quhen
Merche wes with variand windis past', II.129–161).

31. St Anne, mother of the Virgin Mary, was extremely popular
throughout the Middle Ages. Legend had it that she was
conceived when her mother breathed in the scent of a rose,
which may be the reason for her presence in this petition to
the rose of England.

O lusty flour of yowth, benyng and bricht

It is not clear who is being addressed in this poem, and
Dunbar's authorship has also been called into question. How-
ever, it has traditionally been thought of as a poem of consola-
tion to Queen Margaret. James IV was killed at Flodden in
1513 when Margaret was still only twenty-four years old, and
the poem makes much of the lady's youth and noble blood. Her
beauty and virtue are also praised in traditional, if extravagant,
terms: she is the pure lily (I.5), the morning star (I.9), the
embodiment of all womanly virtues (II.17–21); while the poet is
her faithful servant (II.25–32), urging her to be comforted and
to *leif in lustines*.

12. *Sable* is a reference to mourning clothes.

Thir ladyis fair

This is a satire on the behaviour of both men and women in the
court, characterised by ambiguity and sexual innuendo. It mock-
ingly 'praises' the wives who exert themselves to advance the
careers of their husbands, trading sexual favours for the favour
of the court. Women are regarded as sexually predatory and
calculating, but the men fare no better and may in fact fare
worse, caring more for their position than for honour. Dunbar's
tone is ironically sympathetic throughout.

3. *Kend* is ambiguous, known but also 'known' in the biblical
sense, sexually.

21. *Collatioun* is a late supper, taken in the intimacy of one's
chamber. For medieval authors it signified decadence and

luxury (cf. Henryson, *The Testament of Cresseid*, I.418) with the added possibility of amorous intrigue.

48. *Geir* can mean either property or sexual equipment. As the latter, it is more usually applied to men but the women in this poem have already taken on many of their husbands' roles.

54. The *compositouris* were in charge of legal fines. They attended the circuit courts and negotiated payments with those convicted. The 'payments' here are obviously of a sexual variety.

72. *Honestie* had several possible meanings: honesty, honour, chastity.

To dwell in court, my freind, gife that thow list

Poems on good conduct were a popular genre in the Middle Ages. This one purports to be addressed to a 'freind' (I.1) but then uses the word *son* several times. This is, no doubt, the result of the genre itself as most of these poems were written in the form of a father's advice to his son, or occasionally as a mother's advice to her daughter. Very few, however, were genuinely meant for use by the poet's children but were instead intended to instruct young people in what was regarded as acceptable behaviour. The advice tended to be of both a social and moral nature. Thus, the poet advises against trusting other courtiers too readily (II.9–10), associating with flatterers (I.26), and whispering in corners (II.33–4), all issues which arise elsewhere in his poems on court life. The final stanza, however, gives more general moral advice: to work hard, trust in God, care for the poor, and do no one any harm.

How sowld I rewill me or quhat wyis

Like 'To dwell in court, my freind, gife that thow list', this poem is concerned with behaviour, especially one's behaviour at court. However, the certainties of that poem are replaced by doubts as the poet realises that he will be slandered no matter what he does. The refrain is an appeal to God to provide an answer, and this comes in the final stanza with the realisation that God himself is the answer: 'merciful God must guide me' (I.45).

9. The word *confort* implies gratification of the senses and is often used by Dunbar in a sexual context.

Musing allone this hinder nicht

The theme of this poem is similar to that found in 'How sowld I rewill me or quhat wyis': the world criticises everyone, even the good, and the only safe course is to trust in God (II.51–4). This time, however, there is greater focus upon the slanderers – the thieves, pick-pockets, gossips and *Towsies* (I.32) – who see fit to judge their fellow creatures. No one escapes their envy and back-biting but the poem is a warning to them too, for there will be a judgement of a more final kind which they will not be able to escape.

24. A *withy* was a Scottish alternative to the hangman's noose, made with willow twigs instead of rope.
32. *Towsy* is a common woman's name.
49–50. The reference is to Matthew 7:1–2: 'Judge not, that you be not judged. For with the judgement you pronounce you will be judged, and the measure you give will be the measure you get'.

Madam, your men said thai wald ryd

This poem is usually thought to be addressed to the queen, though an account of men going in search of prostitutes to 'cure' their syphilis does not seem to be an appropriate topic. Poems about the disease were, however, popular and this one uses word-play to present the courtiers on the 'battlefield' (I.8) of love, full of ambiguous *curage* (I.11), and valiantly breaking down doors and through locks in order to reach – a *pamphelet* (whore). Syphilis was widespread in Scotland at the end of the fifteenth century. In 1497, Edinburgh even implemented the Grandgore Act, ordering all those infected with the disease to assemble on Leith Sands for transportation to the island of Inchkeith, in an effort to contain the sickness.

1. There is clearly meant to be a sexual pun on 'ride'.
2. Fastern's Eve, now called Shrove Tuesday, was the last day before the beginning of Lent. It was therefore a time of games and celebration before the fasting, penance and prayer which would last for the next forty days (cf. Dunbar, 'Of Februar the fyiftene nycht').
7. Venus, the goddess of love.
11. *Curage* is ambiguous, meaning both courage and sexual desire.
15. The sense here appears to be that having sex will cure the syphilis. Kinsley suggests that it is a joke along the lines of 'the hair of the dog that bit me', and that this 'cure' is being used as an excuse by the men for having sex with prostitutes.

21–4. Syphilis is a wasting disease which attacks the bones, muscles, and eventually the brain.

30. Syphilis was thought to have originated in various countries, including France and Italy, but Dunbar usually refers to it as Spanish (cf. Dunbar, 'He that hes gold and grit riches', I.14).

Of Februar the fyiftene nycht

Like 'Madam, your men said thai wald ryd' this poem is linked to the carnival atmosphere of Fastern's Eve or Shrove Tuesday in which sin is seen as running rampant before Lent begins. The first half of the poem is a vivid description of the Seven Deadly Sins, a popular subject in medieval art and literature, though the details are all Dunbar's own: an over-dressed Pride leads his followers through fire (II.16–30); Anger with his homicidal band (II.31–42); back-biting Envy (II.43–54); Avarice (*Cuvatyce*) whose followers are forced to swallow molten gold (II.55–66); sleepy Sloth (II.67–78); Lechery, whose devotees are led by the testicles (II.79–90); and the monstrous Gluttony (II.91–102).

The poem then becomes an account of a mock tournament. Medieval festivities often involve reversal of some kind, such as the Lord of Misrule celebrations in which a mock-king has control of the town for the day. The account of a duel between a tailor and a soutar is in keeping with this spirit of comic reversal. Both occupations were regarded as lowly, tailors being as likely to mend old clothes as make new ones while soutars mended shoes. Neither is a likely candidate for the role of knight errant. Dunbar exploits the conventions of medieval chivalric romance: heraldic banners are replaced by rags (II.133–6) and tanned hides (I.163), while the thunder of battle is replaced by the thunderous farting of the tailor (II.155–6).

6. *Mahoun* is literally the prophet Muhammad, viewed by medieval Christians as a false god. The name is, however, frequently used simply as another name for the Devil.

7. *Schrevin* specifically refers to the sacrament of confession, which was regarded as necessary to cleanse the soul of sin. The reference is particularly appropriate here as the Church obliged people to attend confession at least once a year, during Lent (cf. 'O synfull man, thir ar the fourty dayis').

8. Fastern's Eve, or Shrove Tuesday, was the last day of carnival before the solemnity of Lent (cf. 'Madam, your men said thai wald ryd'). The practice survives in modern Mardi Gras celebrations.

12. France was regarded as the home of fashion.

16. The sins do not tend to appear in any strict order, but it is the nature of Pride that it should come first in any procession.

19–21. Fashions of the period could be elaborate and required what many moralists regarded as excessive amounts of cloth. The idea here is that the great cost of such garments is likely to bankrupt the wearer and lead to *waistie wanis* as their homes fall into ruin.

30. These would appear to be the names of demons.

37. Bawcutt suggests that *stryppis* are strips or splints of overlapping metal used particularly to protect the elbows.

48. 'White words' are insincere.

56. This is a reference to 1 Timothy 6:10: 'The love of money is the root of all evil'.

74. Belial, 'iniquity', is another name for the Devil.

80. Various animals are associated with lechery in the Middle Ages, but the horse or stallion has been a symbol of lust since Plato's *Phaedrus*.

83–4. The corpse-like appearance of Lechery's followers may be intended to link them to leprosy, a disease which was believed to be sexually transmitted in the Middle Ages. Lepers were, in fact, the living dead, as anyone contracting the disease was immediately declared legally dead and their property distributed accordingly.

95. It is not clear what *collep* means but the context suggests that some vessel associated with drinking is intended. The sin of gluttony was associated not just with large amounts of food but also with excessive drinking.

103–5. According to medieval treatises, there was no music in hell. Heaven, the fount of all order and harmony, possessed the sweetest music imaginable, but hell was silent except for the screams of the tormented.

106–8. Dunbar is playing with the legal phrase *breve de recto* (*breif of richt*) which referred to one's right to inherit property. In extreme cases disputes could be settled by armed combat, however the minstrel here is clearly just a murderer and has only managed to lay claim to a place in hell for himself.

110. *Makfadyane* is likely to be simply a name for a Highlander, but it is also the name of the fictional traitor in Blind Hary's *Wallace* against whom William Wallace was said to have fought.

130. *Seme byttaris* ('seam-biters') refers to the practice of press-

ing seams together with the teeth in order to make them smooth while *beist knapparis* appears to refer to biting the basting-thread used to tack cloth loosely together. Bawcutt suggests that *beist knapparis* are those 'who crack vermin between their teeth or with the shears' but mere 'thread-snappers' seems more likely in this context.

131. Both men and women wore stomachers, ornamental coverings for the chest, often jewelled or highly decorated. Kinsley's suggestion that Dunbar is referring to 'those who work protective steel into horses' pectoral covers' seems too specific.

137. The Mediterranean, or 'Greek Sea', has no tide.

158. In medieval tournaments the challenger traditionally comes from the east while the defender comes from the west.

164. *Sanct Girnega* is not a medieval saint but rather the name of a demon.

167–8. Cobbler's oil or blacking bursts from the armour instead of the blood normally found in tales of knightly combat.

Betwix twell houris and ellevin

This poem survives in two manuscripts, one of which places it immediately after 'Of Februar the fyiftene nycht' as an apology to the two crafts maligned in Dunbar's mock tournament. It is, of course, a highly ambiguous panegyric, with every term of praise also having a far less flattering meaning. Hyperbole is present in almost all such poems, but the praise here becomes dangerously outlandish as the skill of tailors and cobblers is said to put God's slipshod handiwork to rights (II.25–7) as they perform their 'miracles' on earth (I.37).

4. *Blist* is ambiguous. The most obvious translation is blessed but it can also mean cursed.

17. This line appears to suggest that the setting for this poem is a fair, a common event in sixteenth-century Scotland. One of the manuscripts, however, states that the poem was to be read at a craftsmen's feast.

31. *Craftis slie* is another ambiguous phrase which can either mean expert skill or cunning deception.

39. The word *knavis* originally referred to ordinary workers but the pejorative sense rogue was better known at this point.

Lang hef I maed of ladyes quhytt

Court records show that a royal tournament was held in 1507

(and repeated in 1508) at which a black woman was the 'prize', a travesty of the medieval joust for the hand of the 'fair' lady. James IV took part and, according to some sources, won the tournament, holding a celebration banquet at Holyrood Palace for three days afterwards. The Black Lady was not the only African at the court. Records mention several, mostly as entertainers, and it is clear that they were paid members of the household and not slaves. Black slavery, however, became more widespread in the later sixteenth century.

1. Poets traditionally praised the whiteness of their lady's skin.
3. It is not clear what ships are being referred to here but Bawcutt infers a link to the 'piratical Barton brothers'. Trade with Africa was dominated by the Portuguese and Portuguese ships were in turn plundered by the Bartons. Armed with a letter of marque from James IV, they were authorised to attack any Portuguese vessel they encountered and confiscate both the ship and the cargo. Officially, this was intended to be a reprisal for a Portuguese crime committed in the 1470s.
6. The Barbary ape would have been the one most familiar to medieval writers but the ape generally was regarded as a lecherous and evil beast.
7. The toad was not only thought of as ugly but also as a creature of darkness and evil (cf. Henryson, *The Paddock and the Mouse*).
9. Medieval soap was black and usually in liquid form.
11. The treasurer's accounts reveal that for the tournament the Black Lady wore a gown of golden damask, trimmed with green and yellow taffeta, with black sleeves and gloves.
12. The blackness of tar was a commonplace but the barrel may also be a reference to the woman's shape.
13. The Black Lady's birth itself was in darkness, during a solar eclipse. Eclipses were believed to portend evil events and disaster.

Now lythis of ane gentill knycht
In this poem, Dunbar parodies the medieval genre of romance in a mock-eulogy for a man named Thomas Norny. Norny's status in the court has been much debated but it is likely that he was a court fool. Dunbar here dubs him 'Schir Thomas' and presents him as a medieval knight, performing deeds of valour in the wastelands (II.11–12), battling against heathens and monsters (II.13–17), and jousting in tournaments (II.31–3). Royal ac-

counts show that payments were made to a number of 'fools' and the idea of mock-chivalry appears to have been popular, reaching its apotheosis in the court in 1507–8 with the tournaments for the hand of the Black Lady (cf. 'Lang heff I maed of ladyes quhytt').

4–6. Heroes of medieval romance were often conceived by magic or else had supernatural origins. Giants, however, were regarded as the evil progeny of Cain and *sossery* is demonic rather than simply magical.

9. A buckler is a small round shield.

12. Ross and Moray are in the far north of Scotland, and Kinsley points out that Norny was in the north with the king in 1505. Romance heroes often had to battle their way through wild or barren landscapes.

14. Medieval romances are full of monsters and supernatural creatures but the *Helland gaist* here is a starving Highlander.

16. The members of the Chattan clan, among whom were the Macintoshes, were regarded as the fiercest in the Highlands. They were present at the battle of the clans at Perth in 1396, and were still threatening the king's lands in Moray in 1502.

25–30. *Wyld Robein* is the outlaw hero Robin Hood, who was popular in Scotland as well as England (cf. Douglas, *The Palis of Honoure*, I.1718). The people of Aberdeen performed a Robin Hood pageant in 1508, with a fine of forty shillings to be imposed on any member of the burgh who did not participate. *Roger of Cleakniskleuch* has not been identified. Guy of Gisburne, an ally of the evil Sheriff of Nottingham, was killed by Robin Hood. *Allan Bell* is likely to be Adam Bell, another popular outlaw from medieval ballad. 'The sons of Simon of Whinfell' is the title of a dance mentioned elsewhere in medieval literature but it is not clear who they were. It was traditional in medieval romance to compare the hero with the heroes of the past, but all the names here are, or would seem to be, the names of popular 'wild men' or outlaws rather than 'knights'. They are also the sort of characters who belonged to the Lord of Misrule celebrations, when a mock king would rampage through the streets of Scottish towns.

35. *Sir Bevis of Hampton* was a popular medieval romance.

37. It is not clear who *Quenetyne* is, though it is tempting to equate him with the cousin of Walter Kennedy, mentioned elsewhere by Dunbar (cf. 'Schir Johine the Ros, ane thing thair is compild, I.34).

43. Curry was a court fool, married to 'Daft Anne' of Linlith-
gow. It seems that he was not just a wit like some of the other
fools, but that he in fact needed an attendant, or *knef*, to look
after him.

49. Special entertainment was organised at the court at Easter
and at Christmas.

In vice most vicius he excellis

There has been some debate about the identity of Donald Owyr
but most critics identify him with Donald Dubh, the son of Angus
Og and Mary of Argyll, and claimant to the Lordship of the Isles.
The Lords of the Isles were Norwegian in origin and had virtual
independence from the rest of Scotland until the reign of James IV
when John, eleventh Earl of Ross and Lord of the Isles, was
charged with treasonable communications with England. After
John died in a state of obscure semi-imprisonment at the Scottish
court, there was widespread movement to revive the Lordship of
the Isles on behalf of his grandson, Donald Dubh. Donald had
been held at court in the service of James IV but escaped and in
1503 was part of a rebellion against the crown which lasted until
1506. Many trials and accusations resulted from this insurrection
but the king reacted with clemency, giving many conditional
pardons and refusing even to execute the ringleaders. Donald
Dubh himself was imprisoned in Stirling Castle but survived to
lead another rebellion in 1545.

7. In spite of its classical associations with wisdom, the owl is
usually regarded as an evil bird in the Middle Ages. It was
often used in churches to symbolise the sinner, and in
literature it was sometimes portrayed as challenging the
authority of the noble eagle.

12. A cowl is the hooded robe worn by a monk.

19. The name Dubh means dark and its equivalent in Gaelic is
odhar, brown, thus Donald Owyr.

31. The fox always symbolised craftiness and deceitfulness (cf.
Henryson, *The Cock and the Fox*).

47–8. This appears to have been a Scottish proverb (cf. Hen-
ryson, *The Trial of the Fox*, I.827).

Renownit, ryall, right reverend and serene
(The Ballade of Barnard Stewart)

This poem can be dated to May 1508 when Bernard Stewart,
third Seigneur d'Aubigny and captain of the French Scots

Guard, visited Scotland. The Stewarts entered the service of the French early in the fifteenth century, when Sir John Stewart of Darnley, lord of Castlemilk, fought on their behalf. Bernard (or Berault) was his grandson, famed for his skills as both a soldier and diplomat. He fought in support of Henry VII at Bosworth in 1485, and in many battles in Italy on the French side. He had been France's ambassador to Rome and to Scotland, and was visiting Scotland in 1508 to confirm the alliance between Louis XII of France and James IV. The poem is typical of Dunbar's panegyric style: there is much use of hyperbole and repetition with references to ancient heroes. It is made personal, however, by the references to specific events in Bernard Stewart's life and by the final acrostic-style game with the letters in 'Barnardus' (II.89–93).

ii. Beaumont-le-Roger is in Normandy. *Bonaffre* is Venafro, near Capua in Italy, the earldom of which Stewart was awarded in 1501.

4. A crown of laurel was the ancient sign of the victor.

12. Mars was the god of war. James is alleged to have honoured Stewart with the title 'father of war'.

17. Julius Caesar, the great Roman military leader, strategist and statesman. He was so highly regarded in the Middle Ages that he was named as one of the Nine Worthies.

57. The Greek warrior Achilles was renowned for his fierceness and courage.

58. The Trojan prince Hector was another of the Nine Worthies. For ten years he led the Trojans in battle against the Greeks but eventually died at the hands of Achilles.

59. King Arthur, the legendary king of Britain, was also one of the Nine Worthies. Medieval literature presented his court as the supreme example of knightly conduct.

60. Agamemnon led the triumphant Greek side in the Trojan War.

61. Hannibal (247–183 B C), the great Carthaginian general who marched across the Alps to invade Italy. A particularly appropriate comparison as Hannibal was besieged in Capua by the Romans.

68. The olive branch has been a symbol of peace since biblical times (Genesis 8:11).

73–9. Dunbar invents a horoscope for Stewart which gives him more than just the martial prowess of the god of war. He is given the deadliness of Saturn, a cold, malign planet but he is also handsome, the gift of Venus, goddess of beauty and love. While Mercury, the swift messenger of the gods, makes him eloquent. *Fortuna major* is an astrological name for Jupiter, the king of the gods (cf. Henryson, *The Testament of Cresseid*, II.151–96, 218–52).

85. *Bertan*, 'Britain', is a reference to Bosworth, at which Stewart led the French army in support of Henry VII.

93. The letters 'v' and 'u' were largely interchangeable in the Middle Ages.

Illuster Lodovick, of France most cristen king

This is an elegy for Bernard Stewart, third Seigneur d'Aubigny, who arrived in Scotland in May 1508 on a diplomatic mission for the king of France (cf. 'Renownit, ryall, right reverend and Serene'). He became ill while travelling from Edinburgh to Stirling and died on 11 June, asking before he died that he be buried Blackfriars church in Edinburgh. The praise which Dunbar had heaped upon him in his poem of welcome is here repeated in his funeral lament, only now he is the 'flower of chivalry' devoured by death, the dragon (II.17–18). The poem ends with a prayer for his soul.

1. Lodovick is Louis XII of France (1462–1515) on whose business Stewart was in Scotland.

13. The *Turk sey* is the Black Sea. The Ottoman Turks were notoriously fierce and it is, therefore, a compliment to Aubigny to say that even they feared him.

24. The carbuncle, or ruby, was a medieval symbol of excellence.

I maister Andro Kennedy

This is a parody of the last will and testament form, satirising someone named Andrew Kennedy. It is not clear who Andrew Kennedy was, though suggestions range from a court physician to a name simply invented by Dunbar. Some of the references in the poem appear, however, to be topical and specific (e.g. II.60–1, 81–8) and it seems more likely that he is yet another member of the court to feel the sting of Dunbar's mockery. The poem humorously follows the form of genuine medieval wills: it establishes the testator's identity (II.1–8); commends the soul to the Lord and makes provision for the disposal of the body (II.17–48); makes bequests of property (II.49–92); and gives directions for the funeral (II.94–116).

1. The title *maister* was applied to university graduates. Dunbar may, however, be using it ironically.

3. An incubus was the male demon of medieval myth which was thought to rape sleeping women.

4. Womanising friars were the object of much medieval satire.

12. *Blind Allane* appears to have been the subject of a medieval tale but the source has not been identified. It is clear, however, that his inability to see and comprehend is the point of the analogy.

17–20. It was common for the soul to be commended to the Lord, not to the wine-cellar of the lord.

24. Cuthbert has not been identified.

35–7. People frequently stated in their wills where they wanted to be buried, as Bernard Stewart did before he died (cf. 'Illuster Lodovick, of France most cristen king'). However, Dunbar satirises Kennedy as a great drinker as he asks to be buried in the 'malt midden' with all the dregs left over from making whisky. The reference to Ayr may imply that this was Kennedy's birthplace.

41–4. It was a medieval custom for the remains of the good and the great to be distributed to various religious houses or for the heart in particular to be retained by a loved one. Devorguilla, widow of the Scottish king John de Balliol, was said to have carried his heart around with her after he died, finally having it buried with her in Sweetheart Abbey. Such hearts, however, would have been expected to be 'true', unlike the one Kennedy leaves to Jacoba, presumably his wife or mistress.

45. The 'withy', an alternative to the hangman's noose, was made with willow twigs.

49–52. It was part of ancient feudal custom that the landlord could claim the dead man's most valuable possession, which Kennedy explains here as *caupe*, a Gaelic word for the tribute paid to the head of one's family or clan. Dunbar is, therefore, insulting him in two ways, firstly as a peasant and secondly as an ignorant Highlander. The insult is finished off with an accusation of bastardy as Kennedy confesses that he does not know who the head of his family would be.

55–6. This is a medieval proverb, though Dunbar appears to want it to sound like an empty boast.

60–1. St Anthony's, which cared for the poor and sick, was situated at the bottom of St Anthony's Wynd in Leith.

William Gray was presumably an Augustinian canon there but has not been identified.

73. *Jok Fule* may simply be a general reference but a real Jock the Fool is mentioned in court records from 1503 until 1505.

81–8. John Clerk has not been identified but seems unlikely to be the poet mentioned elsewhere by Dunbar (cf. 'I that in heill wes and gladnes', I.58). On the evidence of I.88, Kinsley suggests that he is an incompetent doctor who made a mistake in a medical context: 'for writing *dentes* (teeth) without a *d*'. Certainly, omission of the letter 'd' from *dentes* would give a word dangerously close to *enteron*, the Greek for intestine, confusion which could prove fatal.

Schir Johine the Ros, ane thing thair is complid
(*The Flyting of Dumbar and Kennedie*)

Flyting has a long tradition in Scots poetry but Dunbar is undoubtedly one of the masters of the genre. Basically, it is an exchange of insults in which the combatants compete for imaginative and linguistic supremacy. Insults range from the topical and personal to the more broadly cultural. Here, therefore, the antagonism of Lowlander and Highlander is a recurring theme together with many more specific abuses. A large amount of poetic licence is permitted, otherwise some of the claims here would be very serious indeed (e.g. II.77–9) and it would not be correct to assume that Kennedy is truly a dirty, lying, poverty-stricken cattle-rustler. The portrait is a comic travesty and it is likely that the two poets collaborated to some extent, the manuscripts perhaps being circulated in the court before a verbal 'duel' in the presence of the king.

1. Critics are divided on the identity of Sir John Ross. He is mentioned in another of Dunbar's poems, in the list of makars claimed by Death: 'I that in heill wes and gladnes' (I.83). As the list is roughly chronological and Ross appears immediately before John Reid ('Stobo'), who died in 1505, a guess can be made at the date of his death. The two most likely candidates are Sir John Ross of Montgrenan in Ayrshire and Sir John Ross of Halkhead, near Renfrew. The former was a king's advocate in the reign of James III, dying in 1494; while the latter was a member of James IV's court who was dead by 1502. No poems survive to aid identification but critics have found marginally in favour of Sir John Ross of Halkhead.

2. Walter Kennedy was a great-grandson of Robert III, son of

Gilbert, first Lord Kennedy of Dunure, and nephew of James, Bishop of Dunkeld and St Andrews and founder of St Salvator's, St Andrews. He himself graduated from the University of Glasgow in 1478. In all, the family was characterised by wealth, power and education. Some of Kennedy's poetry has survived and he is called *Greit Kennedie* by Douglas in his *Palis of Honoure* (I.923) where he is placed next to Dunbar in the honour list. Dunbar himself laments Kennedy's imminent death in 'I that in heill wes and gladnes' (II.89–92), though he seems not to have died until around 1518. Less is known about Quintin. He is said to be a relative of Kennedy's but the exact relationship is unclear. It is likely, however, that he is the Quintin who appears in Douglas' *Palis of Honoure* beside Kennedy and Dunbar (I.924). He may also be the Quintin who appears briefly in Dunbar's 'Now lythis of a gentill knycht' (I.37).

7. Lucifer was the original name of Satan, whose pride lead him to rebel against God.

9. The firmament was the name of the solid sphere which was believed to encircle the universe and in which the stars were set.

16. Most towns had a warning bell which was meant to be rung in times of disaster or invasion.

27. The expression *att the roist* literally means at the roast meat, the idea being that this is a verbal feast at which Dunbar will not hold sway.

29. The Middle Ages had many strange stories about the mandrake plant, so called because it was meant to have the form of a man. The insult here, of course, is that Dunbar is not a man but only resembles one. Dunbar is thought to have received his masters degree from St Andrews University in 1479.

30. *Thrys scheild* is a miller's term meaning that the crop has been put through the mill three times.

37. The *skaitbird* has never been positively identified. Kinsley's suggestion of the skua or Scots 'skatie-goo', a large predatory gull, seems likely but the overall sense is merely of an unpleasant scavenger, hence vulture.

43. Critics are divided on the exact meaning of this particular insult. Kinsley translates *verlot of the cairtis* as the knave in a deck of cards, and refers to the popularity of card games at court. The knave is not, however, traditionally low in value in these games. Bawcutt prefers to translate *cairtis* as carts, thus

translating the phrase as 'a menial servant who loads carts'. She observes that this is regarded as an insult elsewhere in Dunbar's poetry when he complains that those being given preference in court are descended from 'cart-fillers': 'Complane I wald, wist I quhome till' (I.25).

51. The *ratt* was a particularly horrific form of medieval execution in which the victim was placed on a large wheel which broke the bones as it turned. Thirty-six Danish pirates were executed in this way in Edinburgh in 1489.

53. The ancient world believed that the waxing and waning of the moon was responsible for intermittent madness in susceptible people. Thus, 'lunacy' is derived from the Latin *luna* (moon).

66. Dagon was a fertility deity of the Philistines whose idol, according to the Bible, fell before God (1 Samuel 5). The insult is vague but Dunbar is evidently equating Kennedy with false gods and idols.

77–8. The threat of poisoning was a real one for early monarchs who went to great lengths to protect themselves. Elaborately carved 'unicorn's horns' (in fact, the tusk of the narwhal) fetched a great price as the only thing believed to be able to detect all poisons. There were many rumoured attempts to poison the Scottish kings and their families, though the reference here is not clear. The mention of Paisley leads Kinsley to suggest it is an allusion to the rebellion of the Earl of Lennox and Lord Lyle when James IV besieged their Renfrewshire castles in 1489. At any rate, it may be only a reference to 'poisonous' behaviour.

81–2. The art of physiognomy, or assessing someone's personality by their appearance, was a popular one in the Middle Ages. According to its principles, an ugly appearance was a sign of an ugly and malicious soul. Cf. Henryson, *The Paddock and the Mouse* (II.2830–2).

83. Ganelon betrayed his kinsman, Roland, at the battle of Roncesvalles. His name was a byword for treachery in the Middle Ages.

91. Aeolus, ancient Greek god of the winds, and Neptune, the Roman god of the sea. Together they signified bad weather (cf. Dunbar, 'Quhen Merche wes with variant windis past', I.65).

94. Kinsley and others prefer to read *Yetland* as Jutland and maintain that Dunbar's intended destination was Denmark, with a stop at Norway on the return voyage. He sees the

description as that of a rough, dark voyage but maintains that Dunbar's ship was not blown off course. However, the poet's account of near starvation on an empty sea would appear to refute this.

99. Dunbar appears to be mocking Kennedy's highland dress.

102. The phrase 'not worth a leek' was a common one in the Middle Ages.

110–12. Carrick in Ayrshire, where Kennedy owned lands, remained largely Gaelic-speaking throughout the Middle Ages.

123–6. Dunbar continues with the theme of physiognomy here, alleging that the ugly, evil persecutors of the saints all looked like Kennedy. The saints appear to have been selected for their grisly deaths: St Lawrence was a third-century martyr who was roasted alive on a gridiron; St John the Baptist's head was cut off and presented to Pharaoh's daughter; St Augustine of Canterbury was lacerated with the razor-sharp tails of fish when he came to convert the English to Christianity; and St Bartholomew the apostle was believed to have been crucified upside down, flayed alive and finally beheaded.

145. *Rilling* are rough shoes made of hide often associated with Highlanders.

149. *Heggirbald* is an obscure term, though obviously intended to be abusive. The imagery in these lines is of predatory animals and *heggirbald* may be a reference to a creature 'boldly' waiting in the hedges and undergrowth like a fox.

160. The sacring bell was rung at the most solemn part of the mass, when the bread and wine of the eucharist became the body and blood of Christ (cf. Dunbar, 'As young Aurora with cristall haile', I.50).

161. Lazarus lay for four days in the tomb before Christ raised him from the dead (John 11: 1–44).

164–7. Dunbar is here humorously using the *memento mori* tradition in which the sight of a corpse or a skull reminds the author that he too must die and that he should take care to lead a sinless life in the meantime. The subject is treated seriously in Henryson's 'The Thre Deid Pollis'.

171. Kennedy is being accused here of having dry, yellow skin. Bags of saffron were worn to ward off various ailments in the Middle Ages.

172. This is a reference to the popular medieval tale of Guy of Cordo. After his death, he returned to haunt his wife, telling

her of all the torments of purgatory. Kennedy is, therefore, being compared to a tormented ghost.

199. This line is acknowledged as difficult by all translators of the poem. Kinsley feels that the 'metaphor of a jaundiced face bound to Kennedy's back . . . [is] a grotesque way of saying that his jaundice has run into a flux' (p.291). Bawcutt translates the line as: 'You cannot rid yourself of it because of your past jaundice' (p.416). It may be best to view the line as an explanation as to why all the filth will redound upon Kennedy. His jaundiced face will make people more eager to apply filthy insults to him than to Dunbar: 'Your ugly jaundiced face makes the filth stick to your own back'.

200. Dunbar would appear to have returned to the topic of diarrhoea.

205. The idea here is that Kennedy is so poor he is living only on handfuls of wheat which he rubs with his hands to extract the very last grains.

209. Court records show that a payment was made in 1503 to someone named Strait Gibbon. He was likely to have been a jester or entertainer of some kind.

211. Dunbar is here referring to Edinburgh's Mercat Cross, the true centre of the old city, on the east side of Parliament Square. As the name suggests, this was the main marketplace. It was also the site of proclamations and public punishments. The present cross is nineteenth-century but incorporates part of its medieval predecessor (cf. Dunbar, 'Quhy will ye, merchantis of renoun', I.22).

213. *Wattis* or 'welts' are strips of leather used to stitch the upper to the sole of the shoe. Dunbar accuses Kennedy of stuffing his old, worn shoes with straw to keep out the cold.

219. The owl is usually a symbol of something sinister in the Middle Ages. The image of it being attacked by other birds was popular in medieval church carvings and represented the sinner being assailed by the righteous.

221–4. Dunbar seems to be accusing Kennedy of stealing clothes from the washing-lines of Edinburgh. The more usual reading of *gallowis* is 'hangman's gallows', but the word can mean any contrivance with posts from which things can be suspended, thus, a washing-line. This wider definition is the only one which seems to make sense here.

241. Hillhouse, near Edinburgh, was the home of Sir John Sandilands. The reference is obscure but is evidently not complimentary.

242. Oysters were regarded as food for ordinary people in the Middle Ages.

247. The most obvious translation of *carlingis pet* is 'old woman's favourite' which is certainly possible but may be a little mild for this context. Bawcutt has, therefore, suggested a variation on the less common *pett* meaning fart.

Schir, I complance of injuris

Dunbar is here complaining that his verse has been imitated by an inferior poet and has been presented to the court in a mangled and bastardised form. It is not clear who the culprit is, the reference to 'thieving Mure' (I.2) being too vague, but the poem is ostensibly an appeal to the king for justice. Critics are divided as to Dunbar's seriousness, but if it were indeed a genuine complaint then the poem itself would publicly humiliate the offending poet without any further action by the king.

9. Saltpetre was regarded as poisonous, with an unpleasant taste and smell.

18. The court had a constant stream of fools and entertainers but their games and nonsense were really 'in season' at the great festivals of Christmas and Easter.

19. Medieval fools are often depicted with close-cropped hair.

24. A fool named Cuddy Rug entertained the king when he visited Dumfries in 1504.

26. Records show that many of the court fools were provided with yellow and red garments.

Quhy will ye, merchantis of renoun

This poem is addressed to the merchants of Edinburgh, berating them for the state of their *nobill toun* (I.2). The squalor in the streets is vividly described as Dunbar complains that the merchants have chosen personal gain over *common* profit (I.73). This notion of the community was very important, with all merchants being required to be official members of the burgh. Such burgesses had rights and privileges but they also had duties to the community, amongst which was the protection of its good name. Dunbar appeals to this throughout but, with characteristic shrewdness, also adds that the merchants themselves will suffer if disgruntled customers go elsewhere (II.62–3).

8. The main streets to which Dunbar refers would have been the area to the east of Edinburgh Castle, principally Lawnmarket

leading onto High Street. The streets would have been
crammed with a mixture of permanent shops and temporary
booths. Most Scottish burghs had one main street with
narrower streets running off from it at right angles. The
function of the burgh was originally to supply the castle and
consequently this main trading street traditionally ran
straight to the castle gate, as is the case in Edinburgh and
also, for example, in Elgin and Forres.

9. Middens, or large rubbish tips, were piled up on either side of
the street. Butchers and fishmongers added their waste to
these middens just like everyone else, resulting in an unbear-
able stench. Many statutes were drawn up in an attempt to
prevent this practice but they were ignored by the traders.
The fishmongers appear to have been a particular target of
the authorities and are singled out in a statute from 1511
which decrees that the bailies should take officers with them
to the fishmarket in order to enforce the rules.

11. Dunbar himself was no stranger to *flyting* (cf.'Schir Johine
the Ros, ane thing thair is compild') but there is nothing
poetic about these *feusum flyttingis of defame* which are in fact
mere street brawls. It appears that the problem was regarded
as so serious that countless acts were passed to prevent
flyting, slander and backbiting amongst the citizens. Punish-
ments for these crimes were far from lenient, the culprit being
sentenced to a period in the stocks, the pillory or even a
whipping. Women could also be charged and faced the extra
prospect of the 'branks', or 'scold's bridle', an iron framework
which enclosed the head, with a metal gag or bit placed in the
woman's mouth to restrain her tongue. Stirling and Ayr also
offered the possibility of 'creeling' in which the guilty party
was suspended in a cage from the top of the tolbooth.

15. Bawcutt identifies this with a large tenement building which
was erected on the north side of St Giles in the middle of the
fifteenth century. The Stinking Style was the name of the
passage which led to the north door of the church, but the
whole church was in the shadow of the surrounding tene-
ments and the area was generally overcrowded.

16. The *parroche kirk* is the church of St Giles on High Street.

22. Edinburgh's *Mercat Cross*, or market cross, is still to be seen
in the north-east of Parliament Square. It was intended to be
a place of solemn proclamation and justice but had clearly
been devalued in Dunbar's eyes. Most towns would have had
such a cross which marked the central point in the main

market-place. Culross in Fife provides another good example.

24. The *trone* was the public weighing-house in Edinburgh. Such a place was obviously necessary to any trading community and most Scottish towns had one near the market cross.

25. *Pudingis* are entrails stuffed with meat and oatmeal. Dunbar regards such food as fit only for the 'Jocks and Jamies', i.e. people of the lower class. Henryson's rascally fox has a liking for both *pansches* and *pudingis*: Henryson, *The Fox and the Wolf* (II.727–8).

29–30. Every town had its minstrels who would perform on holidays and special occasions. Records show that the Edinburgh minstrels were paid fourteen shillings by James IV for playing in front of the cannon Mons Meg as it was drawn down High Street on the way to the Raid of Norham. Dunbar can be complimentary towards minstrels as he is in 'Blyth Aberdeane', but his complaint here is that the Edinburgh players knew only two tunes.

31. It is not clear who St Cloun is. Kingsley suggests St Claunus, a sixth-century Irish abbot apparently associated with eating and drinking, but the reference is not obvious. The overall sense seems to be that better musicians are kept busy and are not allowed to play while the public minstrels drone on.

39. The busy merchants, trading in narrow passageways and generally overcrowded conditions, are compared to bees in a hive.

53. The crippled or blind begging for alms would have been a very common sight in any medieval street, but in Edinburgh perhaps particularly so around St Giles. Not only was the area the centre of trade and commerce, but St Giles was traditionally the patron saint of cripples and beggars. His legend has it that one day he sheltered a deer from the king's hunt but was himself shot in the leg by an arrow. His life is depicted throughout the cathedral.

65–8. Measures are recorded in most burghs to ensure that trade was fair and customers were not cheated. Dundee, for example, decreed that fish were not to be sold in bundles which allowed little or rotten fish to be placed unseen in the middle. As for Edinburgh, when one woman had a complaint about the meat she had bought and was 'misused' by the butchers concerned, they were sentenced to sit at the market cross with a paper on their heads declaring their offence.

77. There is a word missing in this line and various suggestions
     have been put forward to fill it, all however have the general
     sense of Small's 'win back to'.

This nycht in my sleip I wes agast

Blasphemy and violent oaths are Dunbar's subject in this poem.
The Devil prowls around the marketplace listening to the people
cursing God, swearing that they are true and offering their souls
to Satan if they are not – and thanks them for their generosity.
He begins with the priest who swears by the very body and blood
he consecrates on the altar (II.6–8), and moves down the social
scale through the *courtier, merchant,* craftsmen and tradesmen
who lie and curse and offer themselves to the Devil. Next, he
moves to the fringes of the marketplace and encounters the
minstrel, gambler, thief and the notorious fishwives, all eager
to add their souls to the list. The motif of the Devil taking a
violent oath literally and holding the speaker to the promise is an
ancient one (cf. Henryson, *The Fox, the Wolf, and the Husband-
man*) but Dunbar combines this idea with social satire of a
broader kind.

46. A maltster prepared the barley or grain for brewing by
     steeping it first and then drying it in a kiln.
54. It was expected that a *boll* would produce twelve gallons of
     ale.

Ane murlandis man of uplandis mak

The Edinburgh legal establishment and those foolish, desperate,
or wicked enough to become involved with it, are satirised in this
poem. It takes the form of a scandalised report from a country
man, recently returned from the Court of Session where he has
seen sin, injustice, and a good deal of subterfuge. His rural
innocence throws the normally corrupt behaviour of the courts
into stark relief (cf. Henryson, *The Two Mice*) as first the law and
then the Church is criticised.

7. The Court of Session was the highest court of justice in
    Scotland. It was made up of the king's representatives and
    had sittings, or sessions, three times a year at the Tollbooth in
    Edinburgh.
18. *Patteris* is derived from *pater noster,* the Lord's Prayer in
     Latin. It is used to denote rapid muttering rather than true
     prayer.

45. The Carmelites, sometimes called White Friars, were a contemplative order dedicated to Our Lady of Carmel. They were founded in Palestine in the twelfth century and arrived in Scotland in the middle of the thirteenth century, establishing their first house at Tullilum, near Perth in 1262. The Franciscan order, dedicated to a life of poverty, wore a plain grey habit belted with knotted cord, thus their common name *Cordilleris*. Their order was established in 1209 by St Francis of Assisi, and by 1231 they had arrived in Scotland and established a house at Berwick.

50. It was believed throughout the Middle Ages that the human body was made up of four essential fluids known as 'humours'. These were blood, phlegm, yellow bile and black bile and the proportions in which they were possessed by the body largely determined a person's physical and mental qualities. *He complexioun* indicates hot-bloodedness and therefore a dominance of blood, which would suggest a sexually voracious nature (cf. Henryson, *The Testament of Cresseid*, II.29–31).

Blyth Aberdeane, thow beriall of all tounis

This poem was written to celebrate the visit of Queen Margaret to Aberdeen in 1511 as she made a pilgrimage to Tain. Poems addressed to cities are not uncommon in the Middle Ages. Dunbar himself composed more than one but his address to the merchants of Edinburgh ('Quhy will ye, merchantis of renoun'), criticising the squalor in their city, is in stark contrast to this eulogy to Aberdeen. Indeed, the burgh records show that great care was taken to make the city presentable for the queen's visit, the citizens being charged to remove any middens from their doors and decorate their houses with flowers and tapestries. Dunbar appears to have been part of the queen's retinue and his poem records the day's events and may have been intended for performance at a banquet in the city. The poem's refrain urges the thriving port to be thankful for all its gifts; while the final stanza urges Margaret to give thanks to her loyal subjects in Aberdeen.

1. Beryl was much prized in the Middle Ages as a precious stone with almost magical properties. It came in various colours including pale blue and yellow but pale green was the most usual.

3. There is a gap in this line in the manuscript which editors have traditionally filled with the word *ascendit*. Bawcutt

suggests *upheyt* (raised, exalted). The general sense is certainly that the reputation of Aberdeen is so high that heaven itself knows of it.

9. A medieval burgess was a fully paid up member of the community. Men (and only men) were not simply burgesses by virtue of living in the burgh. They had to be admitted into the community, swearing an oath of loyalty to the king and to the burgh, and paying dues known as burgess silver which went to fund common projects. Privileges came with the title, especially of trade, but in return the burgess had to take care to act as a good neighbour. The duties were taken seriously, the new burgess having a year and a day to build himself a house within the confines of the burgh so that he could be relied upon to play his part in the community. Nor would that community hesitate to demolish the house of a burgess who failed to act properly, thus depriving him of his place in the town.

17. Medieval cities traditionally had walls to protect them from attack and to control movement within the town. Access could only be gained through the city gates.

21-2. This is a reference to a play of the Annunciation in which the Angel Gabriel declares to Mary that she has been chosen as the Mother of God (Luke 1:26-33). This is only the first of three plays which the citizens of Aberdeen perform for the Queen's visit based on episodes from the Bible. Such drama was very popular and productions tended to be community events performed by the local people in the streets of their own town. Each burgh had its own collection of props for the purpose. Dundee, for example, was particularly well-equipped, possessing sixty crowns, six pairs of angel's wings, Abraham's hat, and twenty-three wigs. As for Aberdeen, it was renowned for its pageants and in 1496 even went so far as to authorise the town council to look into performances in Edinburgh so that they would not be outdone. Certainly, no one could have surpassed Aberdeen in 1508 when all the burgesses were ordered to be ready with green and yellow costumes and bows and arrows, so that they could be 'foresters' in a production of Robin Hood.

25-8. The next play is a performance of the Nativity, complete with three kings and the traditional gifts of gold, frankincense and myrrh.

29-31. The third religious play tells of the expulsion of Adam and Eve from Paradise (Genesis 3:24). This should come before the Annunciation and Nativity so either the plays were performed out of sequence or Dunbar has switched their order.

33. *The Bruce* is Robert Bruce, king of Scotland (1306–29). The pageants have now switched from the religious to the patriotic.

37. There is another gap in the manuscript here. Laing supplied the words *nobill Stewartis* while Kinsley prefers *royal Stewartis*, both of which make sense. The *stok ryell* is Bawcutt's suggestion and fits very well within the context. The pageant here is of a tree of the kings of Scotland similar to that performed in Edinburgh in 1590 for James VI where the kings from Robert Bruce to James himself appeared in a *tableau vivant*.

42. Green clothing was particularly associated with May festivities (cf. Dunbar, 'Ryght as the stern of day begouth to schyne', I.127).

58. The *croce* is a reference to the town's mercat cross, the public centre of the city (cf. Dunbar, 'Quhy will ye, merchantis of renoun', I.22). The accounts of several Scottish towns mention the provision of wine 'at the cross' during times of great public celebration. In 1566, for example, Edinburgh provided wine to celebrate the birth of James VI and Aberdeen celebrated the birth of his son in the same way. However, to say that the cross *aboundantlie rane wyne* may be an exaggeration. While Edinburgh produced 'a puncheon' (anything from seventy-two to one hundred and twenty gallons) for James VI, Aberdeen contributed only five gallons of wine for its celebration.

61–3. The *propyne* was a lavish gift given to important visitors to the burgh. It could be gold or some other kind of luxury. James II, for example, was presented with two tuns (almost two hundred and fifty gallons) of Gascony wine when he visited Aberdeen in 1448. However, by 1526 the town was appealing for suggestions as to how to raise money for the next *propyne*, as they were *superexpendit*.

We that are heir in hevynnis glorie

The medieval Christian dead could go to one of three places: the virtuous went straight to heaven; the damned went straight to hell; while those who had sinned but not too much could atone for their misdeeds in purgatory where their time of torment could only be shortened by the prayers of those still living. This poem is thus a parody of the Office of the Dead which was said at burials and memorial services, praying that God would release the dead from purgatory and allow them to enter heaven. Dunbar plays here with the notion that the town of Stirling is a purgatory where the inhabitants must suffer helplessly. He 'prays' that one day they will be released from their torment and be admitted to the bliss of 'heavenly' Edinburgh.

There was certainly rivalry between the two towns, both of which were royal burghs. James IV had both a castle and a mistress in Stirling; while, in more penitent mood, he made visits to a Franciscan friary which he had founded there in 1494. It has sometimes been thought that this poem is a reference to one such Lenten visit by the court. However, it need not be anything so specific. It is clear that Dunbar did not enjoy Stirling but this may have been more to do with personal animosities than conditions at Stirling Castle. The great hall of the castle, for example, was the first large-scale building in Britain to show the influences of the Renaissance. It was also a centre for invention with figures such as John Damian de Falcusis conducting experiments for the king. Dunbar's dislike of this man is well-known from his poetry (cf. 'As yung Awrora with cristall haile') and he may have had similar reasons for composing this poem.

2. The town of Stirling is being compared to purgatory, the place where souls had to suffer after death until God, in his mercy, would allow them into paradise.

9. Anchorites (*ankirsadillis*) and anchoresses were religious men and women who chose a life of isolation and asceticism. Traditionally, they lived alone in a small room 'anchored' to the side of a church, the door of which was sealed up in a ceremony at which the mass for the dead was said to indicate their withdrawal from the world.

10. Hermits and anchorites had strict rules about what they were allowed to eat, so strict that pleas from their spiritual advisers survive, urging them to eat a little more for the sake of their health.

31. There were traditionally nine orders of angels.

47. The patriarchs are the 'fathers' of the Old Testament: Abraham, Isaac, Jacob and his twelve sons who founded the twelve tribes of Israel.

48. *Confessouris* are those saints who 'confessed' their faith to the world but were not called upon to die for it like the martyrs.

57. Wine was an important commodity in Scotland, the finer vintages being a gift fit for a king (cf. 'Blyth Aberdeane, thow beriall of all tounis', II.61–3), with claret being the most highly valued.

62. St Giles is invoked because of his connection with Edinburgh, the burgh's main church being dedicated to him (cf. Dunbar, 'Quhy will ye, merchantis of renoun', II.16 and 53).

69–70. The Middle Ages believed that there were seven planets (*sternis*) orbiting the earth, with the whole universe being enclosed in a solid sphere known as the firmament. Heaven was on the other side of the firmament, with the stars, according to some, being merely holes through which the light of heaven could be seen on earth.

78. The archangel Gabriel was sent to announce the birth of Christ to those suffering in purgatory, and thus bring them comfort.

100. *Spyrling* are smelt, very small green and silver fish.

103–4. A medieval audience would have clearly seen the reference to the Paternoster ('Our Father') in these words.

112–13. This is from Psalm 102 which would have been familiar from the Office of the Dead.

As yung Awrora with cristall haile
(*A Ballat of the Abbot of Tungland*)

The subject of this poem is a man named John Damian, a French or Italian favourite of James IV whom he made abbot of Tongland in Galloway in 1504. He was best known as an alchemist whom the king funded in his useless attempts to turn base metal into gold, but the subject of this poem is his attempt to fly using a pair of feather wings. Having strapped the wings to his arms, he leapt from the battlements of Stirling Castle before the assembled crowd – and broke his leg. Unabashed, he claimed that the 'scientific' reason for his failure was that there had been some chicken feathers in his wings, and of course, chickens do not fly very well. Damian is the object of Dunbar's mockery in more than one poem (cf. 'Lucina schyning in silence of the nycht') and the first half of this one is a diabolic biography, accusing him of theft, murder and a complete lack of the scientific knowledge he claimed. The poem then humorously presents him in the heroic tradition, but all the classical names only show him to be a hideous monster guilty of overweening pride (II.65–8), and the catalogue of birds, familiar from ancient poetry, is not a decorous list of names but a comic account of a winged attack on the unfortunate Damian.

1. Aurora was the Roman goddess of the dawn.
5. The area of central Asia known as Tartary was believed to have derived its name from Latin *Tartarus*, the deepest region of the underworld, so horrible that even the gods were afraid of it. Thus, Dunbar draws upon its hellish connotations to present Damian as diabolic.
6. *Barbary* refers to the land of the Saracens, regarded in the Middle Ages as the enemies of God. The term *barbarian* implies one unable to speak properly, capable only of making 'barbar' sounds. Damian is, therefore, being presented as both pagan and stupid.
7. The reference to Lombardy in northern Italy may be a true detail in Damian's history but it may also be an attempt by Dunbar to link him with the University of Bologna, a well-known producer of poisons in the Middle Ages.
11–12. The accusation here is that Damian's ability to read and write, skills which ordinary people did not possess at this time, enabled him to pose as a friar.
31. Anti-semitism was common in medieval England and *Jow* here is simply a form of abuse.
32. The taunt that Damian was descended from giants is another reference to his 'diabolic' origins. According to the Bible, the giants were the horrible offspring of the fallen angels and the 'daughters of men' (Genesis 6:1–4).
34–5. Medieval doctors were frequently satirised for their greed and incompetence.
38. Bloodletting was very popular in the Middle Ages as a cure-all remedy. The blood was believed to become stale and bad occasionally and it was thought that causing the patient to bleed encouraged the production of fresh, healthy blood.
50. The moment of consecration of the eucharist was the most solemn point of the mass and was indicated by the ringing of a bell known as the sacring bell. It would have been a terrible thing for a true priest to ignore this.
51–2. Damian may have used a furnace in his alchemical experiments. The treasurer's accounts show that the king paid for large quantities of coal, among other things, to be sent to him.
54. Matins was the church service conducted every morning. Dunbar is accusing Damian of ignoring the rules of the church with regard to its services.

55. The stole and fanon, or maniple, are both priests' vestments. They are both long strips of cloth, the stole being worn draped around the shoulders while the fanon is wrapped around the left arm. Dunbar's point is that even though Damian was made abbot of Tongland by James IV, he has not attended at all to his priestly duties, spending the time instead on his alchemical experiments.

58. The world was believed to consist of four elements: earth, water, fire and air. However, alchemists believed in the existence of the *quintessance* or 'fifth element', the element of the stars, sometimes confused with the philosopher's stone which was believed to be able to turn base metal into gold. James IV was very interested in alchemy and funded Damian's experiments, even giving him five years' study leave to pursue the subject. He was in Scotland, however, in 1513 when the king attempted to mine for gold at Crawford in Lanarkshire.

65. Daedalus was a legendary Athenian inventor who was held captive by King Minos on the island of Crete. In order to escape, he made wings from wax and feathers for himself and his son, Icarus. Icarus, however, flew too close to the sun, melting his wings and causing him to fall from the sky and drown. He was viewed as a symbol of pride in the Middle Ages.

66. King Minos of Crete refused to sacrifice a favourite bull to the god of the sea. The god became angry and made Minos' wife fall in love with the animal and give birth to the Minotaur, half-man and half-bull. Minos had Daedalus construct a labyrinth in order to try and hide the creature from the world. It is the Minotaur's hybrid existence which Dunbar is evoking here.

67. Vulcan was the deformed god of fire. He was frequently portrayed as the blacksmith of the warrior god Mars. According to some versions of his legend he became lame when he fell from Mount Olympus.

68. Saturn was regarded as a malign planet, whose influence was evil. Damian is being referred to as his 'cook' because of his potions and alchemical brews.

73. It is not clear what birds Dunbar is referring to in this line. For *Sanct Martynis fowle*, Kinsley suggests the hen-harrier, a bird of prey known as the 'oiseau de Saint-Martin' in France. Diving birds are mentioned in the legend of the fourth-century saint, Martin of Tours.

74. The term *hornit* probably refers to the long-eared owl which has tufts of feathers like horns on its head. In medieval art and literature the owl often represents the sinner and this is reinforced here by the use of the diabolic 'horned' imagery.

Lucina schyning in silence of the nycht

The subject of this poem is once again the alchemist John Damian, whose attempt to fly from Stirling Castle is ridiculed in 'As yung Awrora with cristall haile'. Many of Dunbar's poems speak of his own loyal service to the king and contain pleas for preferment, particularly asking for a benefice in the church (cf. 'Of benefice, sir, at everie feist'). It no doubt galled him, therefore, to see Damian being patronised by the king, receiving gifts and large grants for his useless alchemical experiments and also being given the church position which Dunbar craved. This poem therefore serves a twofold purpose: it mocks Damian and draws attention to Dunbar's own plight, for he is told by lady Fortune that he will not receive a benefice until an abbot flies to the moon. It is, of course, clear that Dunbar feels he has as much chance of receiving preferment as Damian does of flying anywhere, but the attempt provides him with the opportunity to ridicule. The poem takes the form of a mock-apocalyptic prophecy from Fortune. The Book of the Apocalypse or Revelation which ends the Bible refers to strange events and creatures which will signal the end of the world and the coming of the Antichrist. Dunbar uses these images to present Damian himself as an antichrist figure, dabbling in the black arts and in league with the Devil.

1–6. Lucina is one of the ancient names for the moon. She is often paired with the 'goddess' Fortune in the sense that both were regarded as unstable (cf. Dunbar, 'Ryght as the stern of day begouth to schyne', I.79); the waxing and waning of the lunar sphere was believed to be the cause of lunacy. Fortune was regarded as equally inconstant. She was thought of as carrying a wheel on which she raised people to great success one minute, only to turn them to the bottom again the next.

22. A benefice is a Church office which provides a living. Dunbar's desire for such a position is the subject of many of his poems.

26. The griffin was a mythological beast with the head and wings of an eagle and the body of a lion. It was regarded as an evil creature and was characterised by a desire for gold.

Dunbar is, therefore, satirising both Damian's greed and his half-man, half-bird attempt to fly from Stirling Castle.

27–9. The Devil appears as a dragon in Revelation 12:3–17, waiting to devour Christ as he is born. This was probably Dunbar's inspiration as he describes the conception of the Antichrist, the dragon now female in order to accommodate John Damian as literally the father of Satan. There were many different accounts of the birth and conception of the Antichrist in the Middle Ages, most of them reversing the account of the Annunciation and Nativity to describe a monstrous conception in obscene lust and a birth in squalor and agony.

31. Saturn was regarded as the most distant of all the planets and was thus usually thought to be cold (cf. Henryson, *The Testament of Cresseid*, II.149–68). However, he was regarded as a malign planet and worldly calamities, death and disaster were often ascribed to his influence, all things which could also be identified as the work of the Devil. Dunbar therefore seems to be conflating Saturn and Satan, giving him a fiery domain like hell.

32. According to medieval legend, Simon Magus was a magician in Jerusalem who styled himself the 'ultimate truth' and promised immortality to those who believed in him. In order to impress the emperor Nero, he attempted to fly to heaven with the help of demons. However, St Peter saw him and instructed the demons to let him fall to the earth. The brief mention of him in the Bible is not so spectacular but he is still regarded as a sorcerer (Acts 8:9–24). Muhammad, the prophet of Islam, was also believed to have had magical powers including the ability to fly. Both figures were regarded by the medieval Christian church as demonic.

33. Merlin, the wizard in King Arthur's court, was believed to have been conceived through sorcery and in some versions of the legend was the son of the Devil himself. The moon was thought to be the natural home of witches and sorcerers.

34. *Jonet* or Janet riding on a broomstick is obviously a reference to witchcraft. It is unlikely to be a specific reference but witch trials were common in the period and it has been estimated that 4,400 women and men were executed for witchcraft in Scotland between 1510 and 1727.

This nycht befoir the dawing cleir

Critics have traditionally dwelt on what they view to be the autobiographical details in this poem and have concluded that

Dunbar was at one time a Franciscan friar, or had at least been a Franciscan novice. However, recent scholarship has found this more dubious and has focused more on the poem as anti-mendicant satire. There was a long tradition of medieval writing which criticised the church and found fault with lazy and greedy friars in particular. The Franciscans were no worse than any other order in this respect but their vow of poverty and the harsh living conditions set out in their rule meant that there was an even greater disparity when its members became avaricious or self-serving. The key symbol here is the friar's habit which is used to disguise many crimes (II.36–45) but the cynical voice does not in the end belong to the true St Francis but to a fiend.

2. The Franciscan Order was founded by St Francis of Assisi in 1209. Its rule emphasised poverty and austerity.
18. The medieval life of St Francis explains how he was the son of a rich cloth-merchant who sold some of his father's cloth in order to repair the local church. When his family objected he renounced them, refusing even to keep the clothes he stood up in.
20. The term *confessor* was applied to saints who suffered for confessing their faith but who did not become martyrs.
34. The French town of Calais belonged to England until 1558.
38. *Derntoun* is Darlington, County Durham, a popular place for pilgrims to stop on the route south to the great shrine of Canterbury.

Of benefice, sir, at everie feist

A benefice was an ecclesiastical office which provided the holder with revenues in return for performing certain duties. In medieval Scotland, this often meant the control of a parish and it was not uncommon for prominent churchmen to possess many such benefices. This unequal distribution led Dunbar and others to protest against the practice, claiming that those with too many parishes would not in the end be able to do justice to any of them (II.21–5). Dunbar, on the other hand, has received no benefice and the poem centres on the metaphor of the feast, where the poet sees wealthy churchmen helping themselves to yet more while he looks on poor and hungry. It is a personal complaint but Dunbar manages to transcend this in the later stanzas as he criticises a system which leads to the neglect of parishes and parishioners.

1. A benefice was a living from a church office which provided the recipient with regular income.
6. Recipes for both swan and duck appear in medieval cookery books. Swan was, however, a dish for special occasions and here signifies the most profitable benefices, while those with a 'duck' benefice would still be very comfortable.
12. Many saints had their own feast days and were commemorated in the service known as *proprium sanctorum*. Those who had no specific feast were celebrated altogether in the *commune sanctorum*. Dunbar makes the distinction here between *propir* and *commoun* office, claiming to have sung in honour of all the saints in the hope that a lord of one of their churches will grant him a benefice.

Schir, at this feist of benefice

As in 'Of benefice, sir, at everie feist', Dunbar's theme here is ecclesiastical preferment. He wants to see church positions given out to all deserving applicants (including himself) instead of being hoarded by a few greedy churchmen. Once again, he uses the metaphor of the feast, showing how equal distribution and reasonable portions for all create happiness all round.

1. A benefice is a church office.
11. Dunbar is here punning on the two senses of *collatioun*: a meal; and the bestowal of a benefice.

Complane I wald, wist I quhome till

Dunbar here complains about the people gaining preferment at court whom he sees as ignorant (I.49), ungrateful (II.35–6) and, above all, socially unacceptable. The end of the Middle Ages saw a breakdown in the social barriers which had been staunchly maintained in the early medieval period. People were no longer confined to the social class into which they were born, and the sons of merchants and even craftsmen were gaining royal favour. However, such social changes were not welcomed by all. There were even those who believed that James III's downfall had been caused by his low-born favourites and that James IV's patronage was equally indiscriminate. Dunbar appears to subscribe to this view, though the king is not criticised directly. He complains that noblemen are kept down (II.64–6) by those who have newly acquired power, and that those who should 'naturally' rule are the victims of social and intellectual humiliation (II.41–51). However, the greater part of this poem is a catalogue of abuse in the flyting style (cf.'Schir Johine the Ros, ane thing thair is compild').

5. According to the Bible, there were seven days of creation: six in which God made the world and all its creatures and a seventh on which he rested (Genesis 1–2).
6. The Virgin Mary is traditionally referred to as the Queen of Heaven.
18. This is a difficult line to translate as all three terms are obscure. *Haschbaldis* and *haggarbaldis* appear to be similar, both having the suffix-*bald* meaning bold or fierce. *Hasch* and *hag* are associated with striking or cutting. Thus, both terms seem to denote untamed and violent behaviour and can best be translated as ruffians or vandals. *Hummellis* is recorded in later Scots as a word for polled cattle. The sense here, therefore, seems to be of hornless or ineffectual beasts.
21. The mandrake root was thought to resemble a human being and to shriek when plucked. Dunbar is implying that these people are not real men.
26. Both *glaschewe* and *gorge-millaris* are difficult terms to translate. *Glaschewe* is not recorded elsewhere but is similar to *glaschane* in I.59, which, as Bawcutt points out, appears to have some connection to the Scottish word for coalfish, *glashan*. Both words might, therefore, be translated as something akin to fish. As for *gorge-millaris*, this seems to mean throat-miller, perhaps an elaborate term for a glutton.
28–38. The theme here is that those being advanced in the Church are not truly religious figures, but are instead interested in acquiring power and wealth. Such 'men of religion' were the object of much medieval satire, being criticised for their worldliness, lordly airs and obvious liking for the finer things in life.
33–4. It is not clear what Dunbar means by line 34. Kinsley suggests that the word *sa* should be added: 'One gets a bishop's rochet out of the king by clamour and so – by disguise – puts an end to a stupid sot'. A more direct translation of these lines might be: 'One pesters the king for a bishop's vestment and manages to hide the fact that he is a coward'.
49. *His odius ignorance* is a parody of the usual respectful form of address such as 'his high reverence'.
51. People did not simply choose where they sat in hall. There was a strict hierarchy and people were placed according to their social position.

55. The hopper was a wide container like a funnel into which grain was poured for milling. Its jerky movements gave rise to its name.

60. The mortar stone was a hollowed stone used for grinding barley. The insult is, therefore, double-edged: a head like a rock with nothing in the middle.

Schir, yit remember as befoir

In this poem Dunbar complains that his loyalty (II.2–3), nobility (I.11) and literary merit (I.17) all go unrewarded in the court while the newly-arrived, foreign, low-born and untalented are all promoted by the king. The claims of those of noble birth are particularly emphasised in a manner reminiscent of 'Complane I wald, wist I quhome till', though this is a poem more of complaint than attack. The first half uses bird imagery to describe the situation under James IV but this is not sustained in the latter section which simply focuses on Dunbar's desire to live *as utheris dois* (I.39).

8. The lure is a feathered apparatus used to recall a hawk, within which the hawk finds food. Dunbar is complaining that even though he is hungry and old, his master is not calling him in to the comfort of his service.

11. Falcons were esteemed as noble birds.

12. It is not clear what bird Dunbar specifically has in mind here but the *myttell* would seem to be some inferior bird of prey.

13–14. The kite (*gled*) preys on rodents, frogs, and carrion. It was therefore viewed as a greedy and cowardly bird and was not highly regarded in medieval literature. The 'noble' goshawk, on the other hand, preys on smaller birds like partridges and was consequently regarded as more valiant and high-minded. However, when the king feeds partridges to the greedy kites there is nothing left for the goshawks.

18. The point of this musical analogy is that the 'magpies' who come to the court and try to pass themselves off as poets cannot match the poetic virtuosity of the 'nightingale' Dunbar.

21–4. James IV had a strong interest in foreign affairs. He was said to be able to speak Latin, French, German, Flemish and Spanish and was anxious to emulate other European rulers in whatever brought renown and prestige. His court was consequently filled with Italian musicians, Moorish dancers, Flemish metal-workers and many more. It is this interest in the continent which Dunbar criticises here, accusing the king of neglecting the offspring of noble Scottish families (cf. Dunbar's vitriol against the king's French favourite: 'As yung Awrora with cristall haile'). The owl was regarded generally as an ugly and loathsome bird.

26. The eagle as the king of birds is a suitable symbol for James IV (cf. 'Quhen Merche wes with variand windis past', II.120–6).

33. This is a reference to two popular medieval tales. In the first, a charcoal burner named Ralph unwittingly entertains Charlemagne and is knighted by him; in the second, John, the village overseer, performs a similar service for Edward I and is also knighted as a reward. Dunbar is complaining that men of low rank are being favoured by the king while noblemen are passed over (cf. 'Complane I wald, wist I quhome till').

49. Dunbar is claiming to be an innocent in the court, unable to flatter and deceive his way into the king's favour.

58. A benefice is a church office. Such positions were valuable and were allocated by the king (cf. 'Of benefice, sir, at everie feist').

62. This seems to be a reference to a nursery rhyme or song in which the child is dandled on its nurse's knee and called a bishop, perhaps a play on the bishop riding his mule (cf. 'Schir lat it never in toune be tald', I.74).

64. Vicars were not themselves in receipt of benefices, rather they looked after the parish when the benefice holder was not resident. They were notoriously poor and exploited.

72. Papal dispensations gave the recipient permission to carry out an act which would otherwise have been against Church law. In this context it is likely that 'country Michael' is being permitted to hold several church offices simultaneously.

74. This is a reference to a medieval game played with a four-sided spinning top, each side of which had a word denoting a different fortune. Dunbar feels that for others the spin lands at *totum* (everything) while he always spins *nychell* (nothing).

Schir, ye have mony servitouris

Unlike 'Complane I wald, wist I quhome till', this poem contains a great deal of praise for James IV's court and presents an impressive picture of the intellectual activity, skilled craftsmen, and loyal soldiers who surrounded the king. However, this catalogue of worthy servants (II.1–24) is matched by an equally long list of fakers, rogues and hangers-on (II.35–60) and Dunbar soon reverts to his personal claim for preferment. The poem is almost perfectly balanced between praise and disparagement but ends with a warning that the poet will return to his vitriolic 'flyting' style unless his feelings of resentment are assuaged by some token from the king.

4. The *doctouris in jure* are specifically doctors of canon law, the law of the Catholic Church. St Andrews University and the University of Glasgow both had faculties of canon law which could have supplied James IV with advisers, but some of those in the court undoubtedly came from outside Scotland.

6. It was common for medieval courts to have their own astrologers.

10. This line divides the critics into two basic groups: those who think that Dunbar is discussing court entertainers and those who think that he is referring to military men. According to the first group, *chevalouris* are unlicensed minstrels, while *flingaris* are dancers (who 'fling' their legs around). The alternative to this is that *chevalouris* are mounted soldiers, while *flingaris* are soldiers involved in throwing missiles of some kind. If this were the case, then the notoriously obscure *cawandaris* may be connected to modern Scots *caw*, meaning to turn, indicating that the missile is hurled around the head, as could have been the case with a mace or a war-hammer.

13. James implemented an impressive building programme during his reign, including the northern tower of Holyrood Palace, as well as a chapel, gallery, and great hall; the great hall of Stirling Castle, together with a 'king's house' and gardens; a chapel, hall, and galleries at Linlithgow; halls at Methven and Dingwall; and new buildings or significant changes at Dunbar, Tarbert and Inverness.

16. *Pryntouris* may be a reference to those who worked in the royal mint, but it seems more likely to be an early reference to Scottish book printing. James IV issued a licence to the printers Chepman and Myllar in 1507 and the first Scottish printed book appeared in 1508. The same printers would later go on to produce editions of some of Dunbar's poetry.

41. *Groukaris* is an obscure word but the context indicates that they are scroungers of some sort; while *gledaris* are likely to be linked to the *gled* or kite in the sense of scavengers. As for *gunnaris*, the artillery men, they were a notorious expense and may also have been objected to by Dunbar as foreigners, many of them having come from Germany and France.

55–8. James IV had a strong interest in science, experimenta-
tion, and in alchemy where he funded many attempts to
discover the *quintiscence* or 'fifth element' which would turn
base metal into gold (cf. 'As yung Awrora with cristall haile',
I.58). It is not clear what other *fantastik fulis* Dunbar had in
mind but the king was connected, at least in popular myth,
with many strange experiments, including the tale that he had
two infants placed on Inchkeith in the charge of a woman who
could not speak in order to discover what language would
come to them naturally.

60. The tolbooth was important to any Scottish town as both
court and prison.

66. Dunbar is referring to *Colkelbie's Sow*, a humorous tale in
which a collection of fools are invited to feast on a *gryce*, or
little pig.

73. The manuscript here reads *panance* (penance) but this
makes little sense in this context. Bawcutt suggests that it
should be amended to *pacience*.

79. Flyting is a genre of abuse and insult in which Dunbar was
particularly skilled (cf. 'Schir Johine the Ros, ane thing thair
is compild').

Be divers wyis and operatiounes

Dunbar once again criticises the members of the king's court,
not this time for their lack of nobility, laziness, or foreign origins
(cf. 'Schir, yit remember as befoir') but for the degrading
attempts they make to win the king's favour. He produces a
catalogue of fawning courtiers, singing, dancing and whispering
in corners; flattering, deceiving and almost going mad with
greed. He 'confesses', however, that he cannot act like this,
but claims that the 'gracious face' of the king is enough reward
for his services. His modesty is clearly a boast and the poem itself
a claim for preferment.

8. Although strongly associated with England, the morris dance
is in fact derived from 'Moorish dance' and was popular
throughout Europe in the later Middle Ages. Records show
that several such performances took place in the court of
James IV but Dunbar may be thinking in particular of one
organised by his old adversary John Damian (cf. 'As yung
Awrora with cristall haile') for a Twelfth Night celebration in
1504.

Of every asking followis nocht

This poem and the two which follow are linked together in the manuscripts. All are concerned with service and payment, the first with a matter close to Dunbar's own heart – the thorny issue of asking for reward. The poet sees nothing wrong in asking for what is due but urges discretion on two issues: merit and opportunity. The first half of the poem advises clear-headed reflection on the matter of what one truly deserves (II.1–20); the second half advises biding one's time and waiting for an opportune moment (II.21–40). In the end, however, the matter is in the hands of those with power and it is the next poem, 'To speik of gift or almous deidis', which deals with the issue of giving.

To speik of gift or almous deidis

This poem contains many of the complaints found elsewhere in Dunbar's poetry: the rich are always made richer (II.31–2); Scots are neglected in favour of foreign favourites (II.36–9); liars and flatterers succeed (II.41–2); and benefices are given to the undeserving (II.56–9). The politics of 'giving' are shrewdly explained in the first half of the poem and it emerges that the court is rarely motivated by honest generosity. The call is instead for the same discretion requested in the first poem, and a reminder that with power comes responsibility.

36–7. These lines have often been interpreted as a reference to the foreign alchemist, John Damian, a favourite of James IV and the object of much of Dunbar's scorn (cf. 'As yung Awrora with cristall haile').

57. St Bernard's and St Bride's were common names for churches and it is unlikely that Dunbar intends any specific reference here.

Eftir geving I speik of taking

The final instalment in Dunbar's treatise on service and reward considers those who take. Once again he appeals for discretion, urging people to take neither too little nor too much as both are injurious in their own way (II.3–4). The poem has a wider social framework than the previous two poems. Church benefices are again an issue (II.6–9) but Dunbar also turns his attention to the plight of tenant farmers (II.11–14), the terrible predicament of those being evicted from their land (II.16–19), and the unequal treatment of rich and poor in the law courts (II.36–9). The topic is found in a large number of Dunbar's poems but nowhere with more concern for social injustice.

6–9. Dunbar frequently complains that clerks greedily collect the income from their many parishes without caring about the parishioners they neglect by having so many churches (cf. 'Of benefice, sir, at everie feist').

13. A *gersome* was rent paid in advance.

37. The Court of Session was the highest court of justice in Scotland, with sittings three times a year in Edinburgh.

This waverand warldis wretchidnes

In spite of the initial reference to the *waverand* world, this poem is not so much concerned with painful mutability as with the painful state of Dunbar's purse. It begins with a sorry picture of the sixteenth century in which workers, church and family, the great pillars of medieval society, are seen to be failing in their duty: labourers are neglecting the fields (II.32–5); sons are turning against their fathers (II.37–9); while the church promotes sinful and unworthy men to benefices (II.41–52). This last observation leads Dunbar to his own complaint and the poem becomes a more witty account of his long wait for preferment. He develops the analogy of a merchant waiting for his ship to come in (II.61–84), both worried and expectant, as Dunbar is before the king. The king is, however, his 'greatest hope' (I.97) as the refrain of worldly pain explicitly becomes *my pane* in the final line.

29. The border between Scotland and England was regarded as a particularly dangerous and lawless place. A medieval Latin schoolbook survives from Eton College, in which the pupils were asked to translate the line: 'he was robbed as he entered Scotland'.

34. It is a sign of social stability to Dunbar that the earth should be fruitful, farms be worked, and labourers be present in the fields (cf. 'Fredome, honour and noblines', II.17–24).

42–3. The accusation here is that churchmen have a great capacity for sin, with large consciences capable of accommodating any number of misdemeanours.

46. The fair distribution of benefices, or church positions, is a favourite theme of Dunbar's poetry (cf. 'Of benefice, sir, at everie feist').

55. Bawcutt points out the references to gambling in this line:

'*Thraif*, an agricultural term, signified two stooks of corn, usually containing twelve sheaves; the word figuratively meant "a large number, a lot". . . . *Passage* was the name given to a game of dice, corresponding to French *passe-dix* and Italian *passa-dieci*. . . . Dunbar imagines a churchman openly (*plane*) playing dice with a large number (of *kirks*); the sense is either that he wins them by gambling, . . . or squanders their revenues on trivial pursuits'. The latter seems more likely to be the case.

62. Calicut (Kozhikode), on the Malabar coast of south-west India, was a main supplier of cloth (calico) to Europe, together with gold, jewels and spices. The *new fund yle* cannot be identified so specifically. It could be a reference to Newfoundland, discovered by John Cabot in 1497, but could also refer to the discoveries of Columbus in the Caribbean. Either would have entailed a long and arduous sea journey.

63. In the sixteenth century, the meridian in the Atlantic was regarded as the great dividing line which separated the Old World from the New. However, the phrase is very technical, and Dunbar is equally likely to be using it to refer to the lands south of the equator.

67. The *grit se occeane* is a translation of Latin *mare oceanum*, the great expanse of water believed to surround the world's central land-mass, as opposed to the Mediterranean, the inland sea.

71. The Canary Islands and the island of Madeira both appear in maps of the African coast from the mid-fifteenth century.

78. *Unicornis*, gold coins named after the image of the unicorn they bore on one side, were first issued by James III.

86. Heather was commonly used for thatching in villages and in poorer dwellings in the towns. It would not, however, have been used to roof any of the wealthier churches.

89–91. It was against church law for anyone to hold more than one benefice. Anyone wishing to do so had to receive special dispensation from the pope (cf. 'Schir, yit remember as befoir', l.72). Dunbar is clearly being ironic in thanking the king for preventing him from sinfully holding several offices since he does not even have one.

This hinder nycht, half sleiping as I lay

This plea for preferment takes the form of an allegory in which the poet lies despondent in bed, surrounded by Grief, Misery and Wretchedness (ll.16–25). He dreams that a fine company led by Nobility come dancing and singing towards him. They want to help and Reason points out that the poet has been neglected even though he has served the king honestly and patiently (II.66–70). However, he is overlooked in favour of those who make constant demands (II.76–85) and characters such as Sir John Churchacquirer who have more churches than they can possibly serve, while men such as Dunbar have none (II.86–95). Patience urges the poet to trust in the king, but his justification for this may be ironic. The dreamer is awakened by the firing of a gun on Leith Sands, perhaps a reference to James IV's military interests and the focus of his concern in place of his loyal subjects.

5. According to the Bible, God created Adam from clay (Genesis 2:7).

58. Blind affection, or partiality, was regarded as a particularly undesirable attribute in a king.

92–5. Some clerics employed agents to inform them of church vacancies as soon as they became available in order that they might quickly put forward a petition for the office.

109–10. While a bishopric was vacant, all its revenues went to the crown. It was, therefore, in the king's financial interest to delay the process of appointing new bishops, a practice which would in its turn mean that vacancies amongst the lower orders would also be slow in emerging.

114. Leith was a thriving port during James IV's reign and a centre for much of his military and shipbuilding activity, including the manufacture of guns and cannons.

My prince in God, gif the guid grace

Gifts were traditionally given in Scotland at New Year as a token of good luck, and the court would have eagerly awaited the distribution of the king's gifts on Handsel Monday. In return, Dunbar has composed a poem which wishes the king every joy, every virtue, and all good fortune. The call to God to help in governing the country (II.13–15) is sobering but the poem ends in festive spirit with a playful nudge towards 'generosity'.

18. French gold crowns, so-called because of the crowned fleur-de-lys imprinted on them, were common currency in Scotland. They were, in fact, regarded as finer than Scottish gold coins.

Schir, lat it never in toune be tald

This is a Christmas carol in which Dunbar simultaneously tugs on the heart strings and makes the reader laugh. This was undoubtedly the effect he wished it to have on James IV as, once again, it is an appeal to his purse. However, this is one of the wittier poems on this theme, as Dunbar compares himself to an old, neglected horse, put out of his nice court stable by a 'big horse' and without even his expected Christmas horse-blanket to console him. Clearly, the poet is metaphorically out in the cold for some reason and wants to be readmitted to the king's favour, and the arrival of his new clothes would not go amiss either. The poem ends with a reply from the king, telling his treasurer to fit out 'old Dunbar' with all the finery he desires.

1–2. It was customary for courtiers to be granted an allowance for clothing twice a year: at Christmas and in the summer. It seems that Dunbar may have been passed over in this regard and is comparing himself to an old horse, neglected and out in the cold.

5. Strathnaver lies at the very top of mainland Scotland, in the district of Sutherland, and thus a very long way from the comforts of the royal court.

11–12. The sense here is that a 'big court horse' (presumably some courtier) has pushed him out of his warm stable where he was fed good straw and out into the fields where he is forced to live on *fog*, old grass more suitable for thatching houses. The poor country mouse in Henryson's fable has a house thatched with *fog* (Henryson, *The Two Mice*, I.198).

18. This is a difficult line, with *spruning* usually translated as sticking out. However, it is not clear what this would mean in an old horse or, for that matter, an old man. It is perhaps better translated as falling out. 'My big, fierce teeth are falling out'.

36. Animal hides were chewed first by the craftsman to make them supple enough to work with.

46–8. *Gillettis* can mean both mares and young women and Dunbar obviously intends a *double-entendre* here. He sees himself as the honest riding-horse who deserves to be looked after if even the mares in the stable are going to be well turned out.

69–76. This may or may not be a genuine reply from James IV. However, an entry in *The Lord High Treasurer's Accounts* shows that Dunbar was paid £5 in January 1506, *be the kingis command, for caus he wantit* [lacked] *his goun at Yule.*

74. The clergy in this period traditionally rode upon mules. However, this Christ-like practice was undermined by the very rich and elaborate trappings the animals frequently wore, a fact which did not go unnoticed by moralists.

The wardraipper of Venus boure

This poem is addressed to the queen, Margaret Tudor (flattered here as Venus, I.1), whose wardrobe master was a man named James Dog (Doig). The poem forms a pair with *O gracious Princes, guid and fair* and concerns Dunbar's battle to obtain a new set of clothes. Courtiers traditionally received new clothes at Christmas and in the summer but Dunbar's poetry suggests that this may sometimes have been the theory rather than the practice (cf. 'Schir, lat it never in toune be tald'). He plays here with the wardrobe master's name, claiming that the queen has a 'dangerous dog' who barks (I.6) and snarls (I.10) at the poet, and the canine imagery is consistently witty throughout.

1. The *wardraipper* or Keeper of the Wardrobe was responsible for all of the cloth ordered for the court, from tapestries and furnishings to uniforms and the general clothing of the royal servants.

3. A *frog* was a large, floor-length cloak usually worn over armour.

4. Dunbar is exploiting the various meanings of the word *dangerous*: stingy, reluctant, disdainful, and, of course, dangerous in the modern sense.

5. All important people in the Middle Ages possessed a personal seal to authenticate documents. Margaret Tudor's seal, interestingly in this context, depicts her as seated and crowned with a hound leaping up.

14. Dunbar complains elsewhere about the open rubbish-heaps known as middens (cf. 'Quhy will ye, merchantis of renoun', II.8–9). As they were filled with the scraps and waste from the butchers and fishmongers there was inevitably a problem with stray dogs.

19. It is not clear who or what Dunbar is referring to here. Gog and Magog are biblical names associated with the apocalypse. Kinsley and Bawcutt both suggest that the reference may be to Goemagot, legendary leader of the giants of Albion, who had to be defeated in order that Britain might be created.

However, the general sense is merely that Dog could frighten the most frightening monster.

O gracious princes, guid and fair

The Maitland Folio copy of this text bears the colophon: *Quod Dunbar of the said James quhen he had plesett* [pleased] *him*, which sums up the poem. After his acrimonious dealings with James Dog, the queen's wardrobe master (cf. 'The wardraipper of Venus boure'), he and Dunbar appear to have been reconciled. Dunbar declares that James is no longer a dog but a lamb, a slightly dubious compliment which sets the tone for what follows. It professes to be a poem of reconciliation, but as one of its early editors said, 'If so, whether was it most dangerous to displease, or to please Dunbar?' (John Pinkerton).

4. The lamb was a positive symbol of goodness and innocence, with Christ himself being the Lamb of God. The comparison is, however, more ambiguous when applied to a sixteenth-century wardrobe master. Lambs in the medieval fables, while still undeniably innocent, tend to be the helpless victims of cleverer animals and this may be the implication here (cf. Henryson, *The Wolf and the Lamb*).

23. *Dram* can mean dejected but there is also the implication of drooping with its sexual connotations.

Sanct salvatour, send silver sorrow

This is another appeal to the king, who is mentioned in the final lines as the only 'doctor' who can heal Dunbar's 'sick' purse. Poems on empty purses are common in medieval literature, as poets appeal to their wealthy patrons to end their poverty, but Dunbar's is particularly witty, employing the imagery of illness throughout.

3. Charity is used here in its wider sense, not just the giving of alms to the needy, but that of general benevolence and good humour.

5. Dunbar's claim is that his purse is 'sick' and 'in pain', not healthily plump and full of money.

22. A *cors* was a coin with the St Andrew's cross stamped on one side. Dunbar is playing with the name, implying that he must have a 'devilish' purse because no 'cross' will stay within it. It was a medieval saying that 'the devil dances in an empty purse'.

My lordis of chalker, pleis yow to heir
This comic poem is addressed to the Lords of Exchequer, a small group of officials who were required to hold an audit once a year into the expenditure of royal revenues. Dunbar's financial state was not strictly their concern, and he certainly would not have been called upon to account for his spending. However, he uses the occasion of the audit to talk about money anyway, complaining about the emptiness of his purse in the hope that someone might be listening (cf. 'Sanct salvatour, send silver sorrow').

4. A *corce* (cross) is technically a coin with a cross on it, but the sense here is obviously any coin of low value.
11. Dunbar received his allowances from the Lord High Treasurer, who may have been present as one of the lord auditors of the Exchequer (cf. 'I thocht lang quhill sum lord come hame').

I thocht lang quhill sum lord come hame
This is a jubilant poem addressed to the Lord High Treasurer, who at this point was probably Andrew Stewart, Bishop of Caithness. It is thought to date from around 1510 when Dunbar's pension was dramatically increased to £80 a year, a sum which the poet declares to be 'splendid' (I.27). The treasurer was responsible for paying allowances, and the poem makes it clear that Dunbar has been eagerly, not to say anxiously, awaiting his return from the circuit courts. He has returned safely, however, and it is a joyful piece, full of delight and gratitude.

19. The justice ayres, or circuit courts, were held twice a year, north and south of the Forth. These courts generated a good deal of revenue for the king in terms of fines and payments and the treasurer often attended.
21–2. Allowances were paid twice a year, in the spring and in November. The court accounts show that Dunbar usually received his pension promptly, although in 1512 he did have to wait until Christmas Eve for his November payment.

To speik of science, craft or sapience
Dunbar's subject here is the value of learning. The Maitland Folio has the colophon *Quod Dumbar at Oxinfurde* and much of the critical attention the poem has received has been a debate as to whether or not Dunbar ever visited or studied at Oxford. However, the subjects mentioned would have been central to any

university and the poem is clearly addressed to scholars in general. Dunbar modestly places himself amongst the unlearned (II.19–20) as he appeals to learned men to set an example for all others. However, it is not their scholarship but their behaviour which is truly important, for without moral virtue learning is nothing.

7. The call to 'remember the end' was common in medieval moral poetry.

9–13. Logic, rhetoric, natural philosophy, astronomy and theology formed the core university subjects.

He that hes gold and grit riches

This poem is a call to be happy with one's lot, a common enough subject in medieval poetry though not treated entirely conventionally here. The man who has riches and is not happy; the man who has a pleasant life but decides to marry anyway; the man who commits adultery; and the faithful servant who stays with an ungrateful master, are all regarded as the authors of their own misfortune. The final call is to drink and be merry, not a common sentiment in Dunbar's poetry but not entirely unknown.

11–13. There is an obviously phallic meaning behind *genyie* (arrow-shaft), while *butt* (shooting-butt) and *schell* (target) also have sexual connotations. The metaphor of the man not content to shoot his arrows at his own perfectly adequate target is clearly meant to criticise infidelity in marriage.

14. The *fleis of Spenyie* can be translated as Spanish fly, a poisonous concoction made from crushed beetles which was widely used as an aphrodisiac. Bawcutt, however, suggests that it is more likely to be a reference to syphilis, sometimes called the Spanish fleas in Scotland because of the similarity between its small red spots and flea bites. The disease was erroneously believed to have originated in Spain.

Man, sen thy lyfe is ay in weir

Dunbar here parodies the moral poems which urge people to realise that wealth is transitory and cannot be taken with you after death. He grants the truth of this, and urges the reader to spend it all while they have time. Ingenious arguments are put forward to justify this: if you leave it behind someone may be murdered for it (II.13–15); if you leave it to your heirs they will only gamble it away (II.25–7); and, of course, the best argument of all, the fact that it is simply more fun to spend it (II.17–19). It may be a serious poem on the *carpe diem* theme, encouraging the audience to enjoy themselves, but the clear parody of moral poetry appears to indicate an ironic view of the world in which the audience are intended to see everyone, including themselves, as greedy, grasping and intent on their own pleasure.

1–4. The idea that time passes quickly and death is approaching is common in medieval moral poems. However, the usual call is to repent rather than spend money, while there is still time.

22. This may be a reference to a relative who was never concerned about the dead man but it could also be a more specific reference to the idea of prayers being said for the souls of the dead. As only the prayers of the living could ease the suffering of souls in purgatory, it was common for people to arrange for prayers and masses to be said for them, often leaving money in their wills for this purpose. There was, however, no guarantee that relatives would spend the money in this way, or that any clerics paid would do their duty by these dead strangers.

29. Dunbar appears to be playing with the idea found in moral poems that the only wealth which is credited to you after death is that which you have given away in charity during your life. *Spend* can mean either spend or give away (cf. 'Be mery, man, and tak nocht fer in mynd', II.10–11).

37. Medieval religious literature often urges people to be 'like little children' in their innocence and lack of worldly concerns. However, Dunbar appears to be drawing on another tradition, prevalent at least since St Augustine, in which the child is seen as selfish and obsessed only with its own desires.

Quhom to sall I compleine my wo

This poem begins, like many of Dunbar's poems to the king, with a complaint that he is being neglected (II.1–4), that his faithful service goes unnoticed (I.7), and that noblemen in the court are suffering injustice (II.21–4). A picture is presented of liars and flatterers wearing furred gowns while the truthful and faithful suffer. However, the appearance of beckoning Death in the middle of the poem changes its tone. Wealth seems like a liability at the Last Judgement (II.61–4), merely useless in the face of heaven and hell (II.66–9), and like dross in the fires and floods of the Second Coming (II.76–9). What seemed at first to be a petition for advancement has become far more. The plea to the lord is still there at the end, but it is a plea to the heavenly Lord that the poet should be spared the burden of earthly office and received instead into the kingdom of heaven (II.81–3).

11–12. Falsehood gets to ride around with a group of attendants, enjoying the fruits of his lies. Truth, on the other hand, has not been received so favourably in the court and must travel by foot.

24. Benefices, well-paid positions in the church, are the subject of several of Dunbar's poems (cf. 'Of benefice, sir, at everie feist').

26–7. The idea that noble candidates are passed over is another of Dunbar's favourite themes (cf. 'Complane I wald, wist I quhome till').

28. Dunbar is here employing legal terminology: Generosity has had his own lands taken away by Forfeiture.

36. Flattery has also done very well in the court and wears a gown lined and trimmed with fur, a sign of considerable wealth.

46. *Quhall bone*, medieval ivory, in fact came from the tusks of the walrus. It is being evoked here for its hardness and coldness.

48. *Asure* is lapis lazuli, a semi-precious blue stone much prized in the Middle Ages. Once again, it is beautiful but hard.

51–3. The reference here is to the resurrection of the body when the dead as well as the living must appear before Christ at the Last Judgement.

57–9. That Lady Fortune was untrustworthy was a commonplace but Dunbar goes further than most in calling her a whore.

63. According to St Paul, the Last Judgement will be signalled by an angel blowing a trumpet (I Corinthians 15:52).

64. Unless the stolen property was returned to its owner, absolution could not be granted for the theft in confession.

71–2. These words are similar to those found in the Office of the Dead.

73–4. Cf. Job 3:3–4: 'Let the day perish wherein I was born, and the night in which it was said, there is a man child conceived. Let that day be darkness'.

76–9. According to the Bible, the end of the world and Day of Judgement will be preceded by fire, flood and natural disaster.

Foure maner of men ar evill to pleis

This poem purports to criticise the four kinds of men who are hard to please but in fact it has one central theme: greed. The discontented rich man (II.2–4), the powerful man who wants still more (II.5–8), the man who has plenty to drink and yet continues (II.9–11), and the man with a beautiful and virtuous wife who lusts after other women (II.13–15) are all criticised for wanting more and not being content with what they have. The poem finishes with a personal appeal as the poet declares that he himself has nothing, a victim of the greed of others.

Fredome, honour and nobilnes

This poem reveals the harm done when people are not content with what they possess (cf. 'Quho thinkis that he hes sufference'). Its theme is covetousness, not just in the sense of greed but also the self-obsession which causes that greed. The whole of society, which should have flourished as a community, is seen to be poorer both spiritually and financially as everyone thinks only of themselves. Towns which had prospered are now destitute (II.17–20); farms are empty of everything except cats and mice (II.21–4); and tenants are left to starve so that the lord can wear silk (II.29–31). In the midst of this, anyone who thinks of others is regarded as a fool (II.33–5). There is no apparent hope for the world and the reader is merely exhorted to prepare for the one to come.

Quho thinkis that he hes sufficence

This poem on the subject of worldly wealth presents a very different view of the world from that of 'Man, sen thy lyfe is ay in weir'. It is a more conventional exhortation to be content, urging the reader to be happy with the adequate means he has been given. It conveys the traditional Christian message that true poverty is spiritual poverty, and that only the person who is never content can truly be called 'poor'.

6. India was regarded as a place of fabulous wealth, particularly precious stones.
11. *Brother* is used here in the sense of fellow human being.
19. It is not clear what is meant by *subchettis*. Most editors believe it is a misreading of *subcharges*, extra courses served at dinner. Henryson's two mice indulge in *subcharges* during their decadent feast in the pantry, and the country mouse finds their 'sauce' to be very 'sour' when the cat has her by the tail (Henryson, *The Two Mice*, II.281–2; 345–6).

Full oft I mus and hes in thocht

In this poem, Dunbar reflects on the mutability and transitory nature of the world. References to instability and change abound, and the Wheel of Fortune is a pervasive image, granting people prosperity one minute only to take it away the next. Neither Fortune nor any other aspect of earthly life is to be relied upon, for the world is merely a *fraudfull farie*, an 'illusory dream' (I.39) which will pass away in the twinkling of an eye (I.29). In spite of this, the poet calls not for contempt for the world but for contentment with what one has until that too is taken away by death (cf. 'Quho thinkis that he hes sufficence').

7. The idea of the Wheel of Fortune was a very popular one in the Middle Ages. Fortune was personified as a woman turning a wheel on which people sometimes rose, enjoying prosperity and good fortune, only for the wheel to turn and bring them down into bad luck and poverty again. She was notoriously changeable and fickle.

27. The vanity of the world was a common theme (cf. 'O wreche, be war, this warld will wend the fro').

29. The reference to earthly life as merely the *twynkling of ane e* would have reminded a medieval audience of I Corinthians 15:52, used as part of the service for the burial of the dead: 'We shall not all sleep, but we shall all be changed, in a moment, in the twinkling of an eye, at the last trump; for the trumpet shall sound and the dead shall be raised'.

Be mery, man, and tak nocht fer in mynd

This poem is similar in theme to 'Quho thinkis that he hes sufficence': happiness is far more important than wealth. However, it deals more with the transitory nature of the world and the idea that everything must pass away. This, of course, includes money, for all the gifts and honours of the world last only as long as a brief cry (I.20). It encourages generosity, for someone's misfortune tonight *may be thine tomorow* (I.5), and anyway, wealth is only a burden one can better do without. The final image takes domestic accounts into the heavenly sphere as the reader is reminded of the dangers of having had worldly wealth when it comes to the Last Judgement: complicated accounts may be a sign of prosperity on earth, but in heaven 'a short account leads to a correct bill' (I.37).

25–31. The folly of wasting one's life miserably acquiring wealth which one's heirs will only squander is a theme elsewhere in Dunbar's poetry (cf. 'Man, sen thy lyfe is ay in weir'). However, the moral here is not to spend recklessly but to dispose of wealth responsibly, generously and charitably.

36. This is a reference to the Final Judgement when all will be held to account for their actions during their lifetime.

In to thir dirk and drublie dayis

This poem employs the familiar medieval association of mortality and winter. The life of man was frequently likened to the passing of the seasons in which a joyful and springlike youth eventually gives way to a wintry old age. Here the mournful season prompts thoughts of death (II.36–40), of the transience of earthly joys (II.26–30), and the necessity of preparing for the world to come (II.16–20). The poem's imagery is of death and mutability but the final image is not of submissive old age but the cyclical nature of the seasons and an appeal to summer to come again.

2. The word *sabill* (black) implies mourning dress.

25. The *glas* is an hourglass in which time is measured by sand running from the top container to the bottom.

37–9. The grave is sometimes described as a poor dwelling with a low roof, earthen walls and no windows which the dead man must stoop to enter.

I seik aboute this warld onstable

This brief poem uses the changeable nature of Scottish weather to discuss the mutability of the world. One minute the flowers are blooming, the next they are battered by rain (II.11–12); and the birds which sang in the sunshine yesterday are chilled in their nests today (II.13–15). The untrustworthy nature of the world is made clear without direct reference to any of the traditional images of death and fickle fortune usually found in these poems (cf. 'Full oft I muse and hes in thocht').

8–9. 'When March comes in with an adder's head, it goes out with a peacock's tail' was a medieval Scots saying.

10. *Concluding* means both ending and also overcoming in debate. The weather defeats Dunbar's argument.

Of Lentren in the first mornyng

This poem is similar to 'I seik aboute this warld onstable' in its theme of worldly mutability and its use of antithesis and repetition. Its scope is wider, however, if more predictable in its imagery. It is set on Ash Wednesday, the first day of Lent and a time when the Catholic Church calls on its members to contemplate their mortality. It is, therefore, not merely a poem about mutability but explicitly a poem about the earthly mutability which must lead to death: 'all earthly joy turns into pain'. The speaker is a bird, a not uncommon device in medieval Scots poetry, though Dunbar does not develop the image and it remains a mere voice.

1. Lent, the forty day period before Easter, was a traditional time of penance and prayer in the medieval church.
6–7. The words 'Remember man that thou art ash, and to ash thou wilt return' were repeated over every penitent at the services on Ash Wednesday, the first day of Lent (cf. 'Memento, homo, quod cinis es').

Memento, homo, quod cinis es

This meditation on death takes its refrain from the mass for Ash Wednesday: 'Remember, man, that thou art ash' (cf. 'Of Lentren in the first mornyng'). It gathers together many of the best known images of death and mutability from medieval poetry: the passing shadow (II.5–6), the fading flower (I.26), the jaws of death (II.27–8). The names of the greatest men in history are placed alongside the corpse, the *ugsum, uglye tramort* (I.20) and the reader is reminded that all must pass away. Hope is given, however, in the final image of the ship tossed at sea, the ship of the soul which can still be saved if Christ is the anchor and rudder.

7. Brass was often used as a metaphor for hardness and permanence in the Middle Ages.
9–13. All these ancient figures were great in their time but were eventually claimed by death: Hector was a prince of Troy and the city's main defender; Hercules was renowned for his strength and heroism; Achilles was the greatest of the ancient Greek warriors; the biblical Samson had the strength of many men; Alexander the Great conquered most of the known world; King David was both great and humble; his son, Absolon, was famed for his beauty.

37. Confession of sins was crucial to the Lenten process of repentance (cf. 'O synfull man, thir ar the fourty dayis').

41–4. The image of the soul as a ship on stormy seas, battling against the temptations of the world, was a popular one in the Middle Ages (cf. Douglas, *The Palis of Honoure*, II.1351–95).

45. Devotion to the five wounds of Christ (hands, feet and side) was widespread from the fifteenth century. It is appropriate that the sinner should contemplate Christ in this way as the wounds were venerated as a symbol of Christ's own humanity and his compassion for sinners (cf. 'To the, O marcifull salviour myn, Jesus', I.23).

O wreche, be war, this warld will wend the fro

The refrain of this poem reflects on the vanities of the world. It is structured around antitheses: day becomes night, sorrow follows joy, and repentance should be now and not later; all will pass away and even the greatest will be no more than dust in the end. Death broods over the poem, as night creeping up on the traveller (II.11–12), as the swift ship on the sea (I.14), and implicitly throughout. It is a straightforward piece in which the message is simply conveyed in the opening line: *be war*.

3. The *freynd* is God while the *fo* is the devil.

5. The call to repent *in tyme* is a preoccupation of most penitential literature (cf. 'To the, O marcifull salviour myn, Jesus').

8. 'Vanity of vanities, all is vanity' (Ecclesiastes 1:2).

9–12. Life was often viewed as a pilgrimage or journey, with death as the fast approaching night.

13. For the image of life as a sea voyage cf. 'Memento, homo, quod cinis es' (II.41–4). The 'port of grace' is heaven.

14. The reference here is to dying while in a state of sin (cf. I.5).

Quhat is this lyfe bot ane straucht way to deid

Brevity and simplicity are the keys to this poem, in terms both of form and theme. Life is short and death will come soon so the choice is simple: heaven or hell; a brief life of torment and eternal happiness, or transitory happiness and eternal sorrow.

1. The image of life as a road or journey was a popular one in the Middle Ages (cf. 'O wreche, be war, this warld will wend the fro', II.9–10).

3. Life was often viewed as a circle or wheel, with infancy starting at the bottom and ascending until middle age was

reached at the top. Then, however, the wheel turns again and life gradually declines until old age is reached, once more at the bottom of the wheel.

4. The medieval church based its teachings on the principle that all human beings have free will, sufficient to withstand the temptations of sin but free to choose sin if desired.

5. Death was frequently viewed as a devouring beast with terrifying jaws.

I that in heill wes and gladnes
(*The Lament for the Makars*)

Dunbar draws here on the medieval *Danse Macabre* tradition in which the figure of Death takes each individual by the hand and drags, leads or whisks them away in his 'dance'. It was a popular image in medieval churches and in literature. Usually Death is portrayed as approaching each rank of society (the king, the bishop, the ploughman, etc.) in order to show that no one can escape death, with a little child being tenderly led at the rear to show that death is not just for the aged either. This is what we find at the beginning of this poem (II.17–35) but what follows is a far more personal account of the deaths of Dunbar's fellow 'makars'. He moves through the names of poets, becoming more personal as he reaches the names of his friends and contemporaries until at last he can only conclude that he will be next (II.93–5).

4. The refrain of this poem is taken from the Office of the Dead.

6–7. The world, the flesh and the devil were traditionally regarded as the three enemies of man's soul.

17. Death was frequently thought of as the Great Leveller, as the rich man had no more hope than the poor man of escaping him. This was part of the message of the *Danse Macabre* tradition in which all ages and all ranks of society were compelled to join the dance of death. A small carved example of the Dance survives in Rosslyn Abbey, near Edinburgh. However, it tended to be one of the images destroyed during the Reformation.

50. Geoffrey Chaucer, author of the *Canterbury Tales*, died in 1400. He was followed eight years later by John Gower and in 1449 by John Lydgate, member of the Benedictine order in Bury St Edmunds. They were regarded as the great figures of Middle English poetry and were frequently named as a trio (cf. 'Ryght as the stern of day begouth to schyne', II.253–70).

53. Sir Hugh Eglinton, not otherwise known as a poet, was the brother-in-law of Robert II of Scotland. He died in 1377.

54. *Heryot* has never been identified but *Wyntoun* is almost certainly Andrew Wyntoun, author of one of the early chronicles of Scotland (d.1425).

57. Death was sometimes viewed as a scorpion, the sting of which was always thought to be mortal.

58. There are a number of possible poets named John Clerk. The Bannatyne Manuscript, which contains many of Dunbar's own poems, also contains several by someone named 'Clerk', though Bawcutt argues that these are likely to date from a later period. Another suggestion is the English author of the alliterative *Destruction of Troy*. This, however, would interrupt the catalogue of what would otherwise appear to be Scottish poets. *Afflek* or 'Auchinlek' has not been firmly identified, though James Auchinleck, the eldest son of Sir John of that Ilk, who died at the end of the fifteenth century, has been suggested.

61. Richard Holland, author of the *Buke of the Howlat*, was secretary to Archibald Douglas, the Earl of Moray, and canon of Moray Cathedral. John Barbour was archdeacon of Aberdeen and the author of *The Bruce*, an account of the life of Robert Bruce. Both poets died at the end of the fifteenth century.

63. Not much is known about this Sir Mungo but Bawcutt points out that there were Lockharts of the Lee in Lanarkshire, among whom was a *Sir Mongo Lokart knycht* who was dead by 1489. No evidence of any poetry survives.

65–6. Neither the poet nor the poem has been identified, but Tranent is not far from Edinburgh. The Arthurian hero, Sir Gawain, was very popular in medieval literature.

67. Sir Gilbert Hay was a graduate of St Andrews and the author of *The Buik of King Alexander the Conqueror*. He was also famed as a translator of French works into Scots, having spent many years in France as the chamberlain of Charles VII.

69. Blind Hary was the author of a life of William Wallace. *Sandy Traill* has not been identified.

71. Patrick Johnston was an employee of the king in West Lothian, also producing several plays and entertainments for the royal court. Henryson's poem, *The Thre Deid Pollis*, is also attributed to him in one of the manuscripts.

73. Several love poems in the Bannatyne Manuscript are attrib-

uted to a 'Mersar' but nothing more specific is known about him.

77–8. Neither of these poets has been identified.

81–2. Robert Henryson, one of the great makars whose work is contained in this volume.

83. Sir John Ross has not been identified with complete certainty, though he is likely to be Sir John Ross of Halkhead, near Renfrew. He is mentioned elsewhere by Dunbar (cf. 'Schir Johine the Ros, ane thing thair is compild', I.1).

86. John Reid, known as Stobo, had a long history in the court, having been secretary to three successive kings. He was also rector of Kirkcrist in Kirkcudbright. None of his poetry survives. Quintin Shaw was his contemporary, possibly dying only a year before Stobo, in 1504. One brief satire on court life is all that survives of his work but it is likely that he is the Quintin who appears in Douglas' *Palis of Honoure* next to Dunbar himself (II.924).

89. Walter Kennedy, great-grandson of Robert III, was Dunbar's sparring partner in 'Schir Johine the Ros, ane thing thair is compild', and the author of several other surviving poems, most notably *The Passioun of Crist*. He is called *Gret Kennedy* by Douglas in his *Palis of Honoure* (II.923).

Hale, sterne superne, hale, in eterne

A poem in honour of the Virgin Mary, this is the finest example of Dunbar's aureate diction. The extravagant praise is matched by the extravagance of the language as the Virgin is celebrated in a poem full of rhetorical devices and intricate rhyme schemes. All the traditional images of the Virgin are drawn upon: she is the star (I.1), the rose (I.40), the precious spice (I.71) and also queen (I.6), mother (I.22) and virgin (I.32). Indeed, the poem makes much of the paradoxes inherent in Mary's life: she is virgin and mother, the light in darkness, the rose without thorns. Poems to the Virgin were extremely popular throughout the Middle Ages, and there is almost no end to the virtues attributed to her. Nevertheless, Dunbar rivals any poem of the age with his almost exhaustive list of Marian attributes and imagery.

1. In medieval art, a single star worn on the shoulder or breast is the symbol of the Virgin. Mary was also known as *stella maris* or 'star of the sea'.

6. Mary was frequently given the title 'Queen of Heaven' and

the 'Coronation of the Virgin' was a popular subject in medieval art and literature.

9. According to the gospel of Luke 1:26, *Ave, Maria, gracia plena* (Hail, Mary, full of grace) were the first words spoken by the angel Gabriel at the Annunciation. They formed the first line of the most popular prayer to the Virgin.

11. The paradox of the virgin mother was central to the doctrine of Christ's Incarnation. Mary was believed to have conceived Christ and also to have given birth to him without loss of her virginity.

13. Mary's youth is frequently stressed by medieval writers, many of whom present her as fourteen years old at the time of the Annunciation.

14. *Alphais habitakle* is a reference to Revelation 1:8: ' "I am the Alpha and the Omega, the beginning and the end" says the Lord'.

16. The Virgin was frequently viewed as God's tabernacle.

26. 'Day star' was more frequently used as a term for Christ, whose second coming was believed to be from the east.

34. The nightingale had positive connotations on account of the beauty of its song and is used elsewhere as a symbol of the Virgin. It appears in another of Dunbar's poems as the representative of divine love (cf. 'In May as that Aurora did up spring').

40. It was popularly believed that the rose in paradise before the fall of man would not have had thorns and would never have faded. The Virgin is not just a rose, therefore, but a flower of the utmost perfection.

42. The lily was associated with chastity and was often used in depictions of the Annunciation to symbolise Mary's complete purity and perpetual virginity.

43. The Anglo-Saxons named the daisy after the 'eye of the day' due to its imagined resemblance to the sun. It was, therefore, an appropriate flower for the Virgin, associated as she was with images of light (cf. II.1–3, 25–8). The expression *fro the splene* is a reference to the belief that love originated in the body's spleen.

47–8. Mary was frequently prayed to in order that she might intercede on the sinner's behalf.

51. This is a reference to the glory of paradise which was lost by Eve when she ate the apple. Mary was regarded as the 'new Eve' who would restore what had been lost by giving birth to Christ who would redeem mankind. Thus, a woman would repair the damage done by a woman.

56. Dunbar appears to be referring here to the weighing of good deeds against bad. The Virgin was frequently depicted in medieval art as being present at the Last Judgement, tipping the scales in favour of those being judged.

58. The number eleven does not appear to be significant in this context and may be better translated simply as 'many'. Bawcutt suggests that it may be a misreading of *all evyn* meaning in truth or indeed.

71. Spices were very valuable in the Middle Ages and once again Mary is being compared to an item of great worth. The comparison was further strengthened by a verse from Ecclesiasticus 24:15: 'I gave a sweet smell like cinnamon and aromatic balm'.

72. The image of Mary as a flower and Christ as her *grayne* or 'seed' which was reaped on Calvary and became the Bread of Life was a popular one.

73. Mary can be seen as the defender of sinners, like the great walls of medieval towns and fortresses, protecting those within. The words of the Song of Songs 8:9 were frequently applied to her: 'If she be a wall, we will build upon her a palace of silver'.

78. The idea of Mary's womb as an enclosed room or *closet* was derived from the *porta clausa* of Ezekiel (44:1–3). Here, Christ was seen as entering the Virgin's womb through a closed door, a reference to her perpetual virginity. Medieval artists were fond of depicting the Virgin at the Annunciation in an enclosed room or in front of a closed door in order to emphasise her inviolate purity.

79. Crystal was associated with purity and is used here to refer to Mary's virginity and the purity of Christ's birth which, because of the sinlessness of his conception, was believed to have been painless and as clean as crystal.

80. Dunbar is playing here with the two definitions of *fude*: food and child. Psalm 78 refers to *panis angelorum*, 'the bread of angels' and this was widely interpreted as a reference to Christ who would become bread in the eucharist. But Mary was also filled with *angell fude* in the form of the heavenly infant Christ.

83. It was believed that there would have been no death in paradise and that mankind only became prey to death on account of the actions of Adam and Eve. Thus, the fall is described here as *mortall*.

Rorate, celi, desuper

This is a nativity hymn, celebrating the triumphant incarnation
of Christ. It does not, however, use the expected imagery of
mother and child. Christ is referred to throughout almost
entirely in images of light: he is the day star (I.3), the true
sun (II.5–6) and the new dawn (II.38–9), while Mary is a rose,
the 'flower of flowers' (I.4). All of these terms are traditional but
they are used here with unusual consistency. In his use of natural
imagery, Dunbar appears to be drawing on the idea that all of
creation was in harmony at the nativity. Medieval tales of the ox
and ass kneeling down in the stable and warming the Christ child
with their breath were popular and the general principle of
harmonious nature is seen here. The birds and flowers are called
upon to worship, together with the earth itself. The whole of
creation from the angels in the highest heaven to the lowliest
sinner are assembled by the poet for this jubilant hymn.

2. The purity of the conception of Christ was frequently com-
   pared to Gideon's fleece which became moist with dew
   without the ground around it becoming wet (Judges 6:37).
3. Christ was often referred to as the day star from a reference in
   Revelation 22:16: 'the bright and morning star'.
5–6. Phoebus, the sun, powerful as it is, is nothing compared to
   the son of God, the light of the world. According to medieval
   literature, great light accompanied the birth of Christ and
   medieval paintings often show Joseph holding a candle which
   has been made unnecessary by the light radiating from the
   child.
9–10. There were traditionally nine orders of angels which were
   in turn divided into three hierarchies: seraphim, cherubim
   and thrones; dominations, virtues and powers; principalities,
   archangels and angels. Seraphim stand immediately around
   the throne of God and are absorbed in divine love; cherubim
   know God and worship him and are the representatives
   of divine wisdom; thrones sustain the seat of God. Domina-
   tions, virtues and powers govern the stars and the elements.
   Principalities, or princedoms, dispense the fate of nations;
   archangels are the warriors of heaven; angels guard the
   innocent and the just. All, however, act as the choristers of
   heaven.
12. The firmament was believed to be the solid sphere which
   enclosed the universe and in which the stars were set.
13. Fire, earth, air and water were regarded as the four basic

elements of the universe, from which all matter was composed.

38. Aurora is a classical name for the dawn, here used as another name for Christ as light of the world. In medieval art, Christ is occasionally depicted in a rosy coloured garment to indicate his status as the one who brought light once more to mankind.

49. Heaven was not regarded as a place of uniform happiness but was believed to have various regions and hierarchies. Dunbar's *hevin imperiall* equates with the *coelum empyreum*, the highest heaven in which God dwelt and which was characterised by perfect light (cf. Douglas, *the Palis of Honoure*, I.1878).

Amang thir freiris, within ane cloister

The later Middle Ages showed an increased interest in the physical horrors of the crucifixion. Theologians debated the way in which Christ's feet would have been pierced with nails; artists increasingly portrayed instruments of torture in scenes of the Passion; and poets focused in detail on the torments of Christ's death. Dunbar's poem belongs to this tradition and describes the Passion of Christ in vivid detail. The material is faithfully taken from the various gospel accounts of the crucifixion but the language used is homely and intimate with the emphasis on Christ's suffering humanity as he is *hurlit . . . heir and thair* (I.20), the crown of thorns cruelly pressed onto his head (I.46), and his feet cut by stones (I.55). The purpose of these medieval images was to move the audience to compassion and from compassion to sorrow for their sins, and this is what happens in the latter part of the poem as the description of the crucifixion gives way to allegory. The dreamer is assailed by various personified emotions, the first of which is Compassion (I.97) but others include Pity, Remembrance and Contrition, until the dreamer is finally overcome by Repentance (I.125).

2. An oratory is a small private chapel.

3. *Pater noster* are the first words of the Lord's Prayer in Latin.

7. *Gaude flore virginali* (Rejoice, flower of virginity) are the first words of a popular medieval hymn to the Virgin Mary.

9. It was Judas, one of the apostles, who betrayed Christ, bringing an armed mob to arrest him (Matthew 26:47).

26. An account of Pilate's soldiers robing Christ in scarlet or purple and mocking him as King of the Jews is found in three of the gospels and was a popular subject in medieval literature

(cf. I.41). Luke (23:11), however, has Christ dressed up like a fool in Herod's palace and Dunbar clearly treats the two accounts as separate events.

39. In early Christian art and literature Christ was frequently portrayed as a warrior, with the crucifixion as his battlefield. The image persisted throughout the Middle Ages, though the necessity of Christ willingly accepting his death meant that his heroism was increasingly viewed as passive.

105–8. Representations of the implements of Christ's torture were popular in the later Middle Ages. Nails, whips and lances were depicted surrounding the figure of the bleeding Christ or, increasingly, could surround the image of a heart encircled by thorns. The Aisle of the Holy Blood in St Giles' Cathedral in Edinburgh possesses an example of the latter sort on a tomb recess.

115–20. Christ's resurrection took place three days after the crucifixion but these lines also refer to receiving Christ in the eucharist which the members of the Church would also do at Easter. The image of the body as the 'house' of the soul is an ancient one.

135. The *hous within* is a metaphor for the soul.

143. The Church remembers the crucifixion and death of Christ on Good Friday.

Done is a battell on the dragon blak

According to medieval theology, all souls had to wait in hell until Christ redeemed mankind by dying on the cross. During the three days which Christ spent in the tomb, it was believed that he descended into hell where he vanquished death and the Devil. Thereafter, he was able to lead the souls of the righteous into bliss. This event, known as the 'Harrowing of Hell', was a popular theme in medieval literature, particularly medieval drama. The subject was less popular in medieval poetry which tended to focus more on the crucifixion itself. Here, however, we are presented with the triumphant Christ, presented like a medieval warrior, raising his battle-standard (I.4) and facing the forces of the Devil. The souls in hell are presented as prisoners held in the enemy dungeons, rescued from their chains by their lord (II.34–7).

1. The Devil is frequently described as a dragon in the Bible (cf. Revelations 12:9).

6. No one, not even the great figures of the Old Testament,

could enter heaven until Christ conquered death and the
Devil by dying on the cross himself. Only then could they
be redeemed and led into the bliss of heaven.

7. The image here is of a document of redemption which is
written in Christ's blood.

9. Lucifer is another name for the Devil. Meaning light, it was
his name before he led the rebel angels against God and was
banished to hell where he became Satan, the adversary.

11. The Devil is occasionally portrayed as a tiger in medieval
literature.

19. According to medieval lore, lion cubs were stillborn until
the third day when they were brought to life by the breath of
their father. The lion was therefore a particularly apt symbol
of the resurrected Christ.

21–2. Aurora is the goddess of the dawn, Apollo is the god of the
sun. The image is of the coming of light which is appropriate
to Christ as 'light of the world'.

27. This is a reference to Christ as the sun and also to the
darkening of the sun when he was crucified (Luke 23:45).

29. All church bells were silenced from Good Friday until
Easter Sunday when they were rung triumphantly to cele-
brate the Resurrection of Christ.

To the, O marcifull salviour myn, Jesus
(*The Tabill of Confessioun*)

The sacrament of confession was fundamental to the medieval
church. Repentance alone was not sufficient for the forgiveness of
sins, which had instead to be formally confessed to a priest; only
then could absolution be granted. The process of confession began
with the penitent examining their conscience in order to establish
what sins they had committed (cf. 'O synfull man, thir ar the fourty
dayis', II.10–14). In order to aid this process, penitential manuals
were common, listing various sins as an aid to the memory. This
poem should be viewed in the same way, and not as a catalogue of
Dunbar's own sins. It is intended to prompt the reader or listener
to consider his sinfulness and reflect on God's mercy. It begins
with an examination of various formal categories such as the ten
commandments, the seven acts of corporal mercy and the seven
deadly sins, questioning whether or not the laws have been kept
and sin avoided (II.9–104). It then moves to a consideration of
more specific sins: of speech, thought, greed, lust, anger and envy
in their various manifestations (II.105–44). The final stanzas
contemplate the suffering Christ endured on the cross for the sake

of sinners and also the life of Mary Magdalene, sometimes called Mary the Sinner, who repented and was forgiven.

3. The speaker is praying in front of a crucifix, on which the image of Christ's *bludy figour dolorus* helps prompt feelings of penitence.

18–20. References to the seven deadly sins are frequent in the Middle Ages. They appear in typical order here with Pride, often regarded as the cause of all the others, first in the list (cf. Dunbar, 'Of Februar the fyiftene nycht').

23. The five wounds of Christ refer to those on his hands and feet and to the opening in his side (cf. John 20:24). They were regarded as a sign of his humanity and compassion and were the subject of much late medieval literature and art.

27–30. This stanza refers to the seven deeds of corporal mercy: feeding the hungry, giving drink to the thirsty, visiting the sick, attending to prisoners, sheltering strangers, clothing the naked, and burying the dead (Matthew 25:35–6). They are often presented in juxtaposition to the seven deadly sins. One of the architraves in Rosslyn Chapel, near Edinburgh, depicts the seven deadly sins on one side and the seven acts of corporal mercy on the other.

33–9. The seven acts of spiritual mercy are traditionally: teaching the ignorant, converting the sinner, counselling those who doubt their faith, bringing comfort to the sorrowful, praying for the living and the dead, bearing the wrongdoing of others patiently, and forgiving injuries.

42–5. This is a reference to the seven sacraments of the Catholic Church: eucharist (receiving the body and blood of Christ); baptism; penance (the forgiveness of sins); confirmation (being confirmed as an adult member of the Church); marriage; ordination into the religious life; and extreme unction (the anointing of the dying).

49–54. According to the Bible, the ten commandments were given by God to Moses on tablets of stone (Exodus 20:1–17).

57–69. The Creed summarises in prayer the beliefs of the Catholic Church. Its twelve articles were thought to have been composed by the twelve apostles.

74. Faith, hope and charity were known as the theological virtues (I Corinthians 13:13)

75–8. The cardinal virtues, which were thought to form the basis for a moral life, were courage, prudence, temperance and justice.

81–8. The commandments of the church vary in number according to the authority followed but the seven given by Dunbar are the most popular: to pay tithes (a proportion of your income) to the church; to avoid excommunication from the church; to observe holy days and keep the fasts imposed by the church; to go to mass every Sunday; to confess sins to a priest; and to receive the eucharist every Easter.

89. Despair, the feeling that one's sins were too great to be forgiven, was commonly regarded as a sin against the Holy Ghost.

90. Postponing confession placed the soul in a state of mortal danger, for the greatest fear of a medieval Christian was that death would come before confession could be made. Thus, the refrain of this poem is a plea for the time to repent.

91. A proper confession required true penitence from the sinner and also judgement on the part of the priest, who was required to differentiate between sins and degrees of sins in order to give absolution and a proper penance.

92. It was a sin to receive the body and blood of Christ in the eucharist without having first attended confession.

93. After listening to the sinner in confession, the priest imposed a penance of prayers or good works which had to be carried out in order for the act of confession to be complete and satisfaction achieved.

94. The seven gifts of the Holy Spirit were derived from Isaiah (11:2).

95. The *Pater Noster* or Lord's Prayer was divided into seven clauses (cf. Matthew 6:9–13).

133. Anyone of importance had their own seal which was imprinted in wax on documents. The reference here is to counterfeit sealing.

134. *Sessioun* refers to the law courts which held several sessions a year in Edinburgh. Dunbar regards them elsewhere as sinful places, cf. 'Ane murlandis man of uplandis mak'.

145–50. St Mary Magdalene was the great example of the penitent sinner, absolved from sin through faith in Christ. She was usually identified with the woman who washed the feet of Christ with her tears and dried them with her hair (Luke 7:37–8).

O synfull man, thir ar the fourty dayis
(*The Maner of Passyng to Confessioun*)

In its exhortation to make a proper confession of one's sins, this poem is similar to 'To the, O marcifull salviour myn, Jesus'.

Confession was required by the church every Easter and the poem is designed to be read in the forty days of Lenten preparation for this event. Like the previous poem, it asks the reader to call to mind his sins, but it then goes beyond this to consider the act of confessing itself. The importance of not omitting any sins (II.15–28) and of revealing them in appropriate detail (II.40–2), carefully and without undue haste, are part of the poem's message, together with the warning that an ignorant priest is of no use to the sinner (II.29–38). It is a poem of careful instruction but with homely references to shoes which pinch and wounds requiring a *leiche* (I.17).

1–4. The forty days of Lent mirror the forty days which Christ spent fasting in the wilderness (Matthew 4:1–2). They were supposed to be spent in a similar fashion, praying, fasting and contemplating his death on the cross in preparation for Easter.

11–12. Confession had to be complete. No sins could be withheld from the priest and it was important that the penitent person made every effort to call to mind all their sins. There were even penitential manuals for this purpose which listed possible sins (cf. 'To the, O marcifull salviour myn, Jesus').

28. Confession had to be detailed. Sins had to be described in sufficient detail to allow the priest to assess the gravity of the offence and decide on an appropriate penance. This is a particular concern of this poem (cf. II.40–1).

29–35. It was a concern of all penitential literature that confession should not merely take place but that the confessor should be an ordained priest, properly trained to administer the sacrament.

48. A state of contrition, or repentance for sin, was the first stage in a proper confession. This should then be followed by actual confession to a priest which will then allow one to reach the final stage which is reparation for sin.

62–3. It was required by the church that a full confession should be made each year at Easter, but many members of the church felt that this was not frequent enough and encouraged more regular attendance.

Salviour, suppois my sensualite

This short poem is similar in theme to some of Dunbar's longer penitential pieces (cf. 'To the, O marcifull salviour myn, Jesus'): the body has led the soul into error but the speaker now begs

God for mercy and the time to repent. It is unusual, however, in that the final lines are still concerned with the things of this world and that the desire for an honourable life does not preclude the desire for a comfortable one.

1. *Sensualite* is indulgence in the pleasures of the flesh, literally of the senses. The Middle Ages viewed the body as constantly undermining the soul, dragging it down to base pleasures rather than allowing it to seek God.
4. *Witt* is the human capacity for understanding while *ressoun* is the power to make moral decisions based on that understanding.
6. It was common in penitential literature to ask not just for mercy but for the time to make amends (cf. 'To the, O marcifull salviour myn, Jesus', I.8).

In may as that Aurora did up spring

The genre of debate poetry was popular in the Middle Ages. Such poems normally involve two protagonists arguing over their relative merits or way of life. Thus, debates existed such as that between the soul and the body, spring and winter, and the sheep and the flax plant. Debate poems involving birds were particularly popular and the nightingale features in many of these, usually as a defendant of romantic love. Here, however, Dunbar draws upon a different tradition and the nightingale advocates love of God, leaving the merle to defend human love.

The birds voice their arguments in alternate stanzas, each of which has a refrain which summarises their contrasting viewpoints. The merle claims that life in the service of love is a pleasant one while the nightingale argues that all love is wasted except love of God alone. The debate suddenly comes to an end when the merle confesses her error (I.97) and the birds sing together an antiphon in praise of God.

1. Aurora was the Roman goddess of the dawn, used here simply as a poetic term for sunrise.
3. The *merle*, or blackbird, is traditionally associated with springtime (cf. Henryson, *The Testament of Cresseid*, II.425–30) and consequently with romantic love.
13. Like the blackbird, the nightingale is associated with springtime and romantic love. Indeed, in many debate poems it is the nightingale who defends erotic love, acting as the confidante of lovers and carrying messages between them. Here,

however, the nightingale is seen as transcending earthly affection, focusing instead on love of God. 'Gentle nightingale' is a term used elsewhere in Dunbar's poetry for the Virgin Mary (cf. 'Hale, sterne superne, hale, in eterne', l.34).

21. Flora is the goddess of flowers and assistant to the goddess Natura or Nature.

35. A medieval proverb: 'young saint, old devil', i.e. there is a natural time for everything and those who are virtuous when young are going against the established order and will only become sinners when they are older and ought to know better.

47. The image seems very striking in modern terms but Christ was frequently described as the lover of the soul in the Middle Ages.

65–6. The distinction is being made between two kinds of love: *eros* (erotic love) and *caritas* (spiritual love).

70–1. The merle is twisting the second commandment: 'Love thy neighbour as thy self' (Matthew 22:39).

78. Apollo is the god of the sun.

101–2. The image of the Devil catching sinners in a net was a popular one (cf. Henryson, *The Preaching of the Swallow*, ll.1911–36).

Ryght as the stern of day begouth to schyne
(*The Goldyn Targe*)

The Goldyn Targe is an allegory: a poem in which the meaning is presented symbolically. The narrator is a dreamer who thinks that he sees a fine ship arrive, full of gods and goddesses. He is spotted by Venus, goddess of love, who sends women to assail him (ll.136–8). The first to do so have names like Beauty (l.146), Fine Manners (l.149) and Lovely Expression (l.150) but Reason steps in to save the dreamer, protecting him with the golden shield of the poem's title. The battle continues, with Venus ranging many more female warriors against them, among whom are Deceit (l.182). Intimacy (l.190) and, deadliest of them all, Presence, the personification of the power of the lady's presence. It is she who finally manages to blind Reason and the dreamer is taken prisoner, at which point all the fair ladies abandon him and he is handed over to Misery (l.227). Thus, Dunbar presents a picture of a man assailed by womanly wiles, protected only by his own sense of reason, which ultimately cannot withstand the full barrage of female charms. When he succumbs, however, he learns of the inconstancy and pain of love. As a poem, it displays great technical virtuosity and this, together with the final tribute to the great medieval poets (II.253–70) has led critics to suggest that poetry itself is as much its theme as love.

1. The planet Venus was commonly known as the day star but Dunbar is using the term here to refer to the sun.

2. Vesper is the evening star while Lucina is one of the names for the moon.

7. Phoebus is the ancient Greek god of the sun, about to be clothed in the scarlet cloak of dawn.

10. The medieval church had seven fixed points in the day when prayers were sung or said. These services, known as hours, each had a specific name. Dunbar's birds are singing lauds, the office sung at daybreak.

16. Aurora was the Roman goddess of the dawn. Classical legend presents her as a very amorous goddess, though Phoebus is not traditionally one of her lovers. The morning dew was traditionally viewed as her tears, shed over the death of her son Memnon. Dunbar represents them here as tears of sorrow at parting from the sun god, Phoebus.

37. It was believed that the universe was surrounded by a solid sphere known as the firmament.

42. Flora is the goddess of all plants and flowers; the grass is presented here as her cloak (I.48).

52. The *merse*, or ship's top-castle, was a platform at the top of the mast.

67. Homer was an ancient Greek writer, famous for his epic poems, the *Iliad* and the *Odyssey*.

69–70. The Roman author, Marcus Tullius Cicero was particularly popular in the Middle Ages for his treatises on rhetoric.

75. Juno is queen of the gods and goddess of the sky; Proserpina is goddess of the spring. The appearance of the name Apollo in this line has, however, concerned editors. It does not seem likely that Dunbar would have purposefully placed the name of a god in the midst of a catalogue of goddesses. Bawcutt suggests that Dunbar had in mind a goddess named Apolleine who appears once or twice in medieval literature. Kinsley believes that Dunbar intended to call Juno, Juno Apollo in her role as goddess of the sky.

76. Diana was the goddess of the hunt and thus often associated with woods and forests. Being a virgin goddess and warrior,

independent of men, she was also often appealed to as the goddess of chastity.

77. Clio is one of the nine heavenly Muses, each of which is associated with some intellectual pursuit. Strictly speaking, she is the Muse of history but she is frequently mentioned by poets too, the distinction between genres not being absolute.

78. Thetis was a divinity of the sea. Pallas Athena was the ancient Greek goddess of wisdom, often identified with the Roman goddess Minerva. In spite of this, Dunbar refers to them both here separately.

79. Fortune, personified as a woman, was frequently referred to as a goddess in the Middle Ages. Her notorious changeability is a likely reason for her being placed here with Lucina, the moon-goddess, also regarded as changeable on account of the waxing and waning of the moon.

81. Lucifera is one of the names of Venus. Meaning light-bearing, it was applied to Venus as the brightest of the planets.

110–11. Cupid is the son of Venus, seen here with the bow and arrows he used to make people fall in love.

112. Mars was the Roman god of war.

114. Saturn, father of the king of the gods, was usually portrayed as an old man (cf. Henryson, *The Testament of Cresseid*, II.151–68).

116–7. Mercury, the messenger god, was a suitable divinity of rhetoric and eloquence (cf. Henryson, *The Testament of Cresseid*, II.239–52).

118–9. Priapus and Faunus were both fertility deities associated with fields and general growth. Dunbar gives Priapus jurisdiction over gardens while Faunus is allocated the open countryside.

120. Janus was the god of two faces, one looking forwards and the other backwards. For this reason, he was the Roman god of doors and gateways, watching those who came and went.

121. Neptune was the Roman god of the sea.

122. Aeolus, Lord of the Winds, was the son of the sea god. As the wind changes, so Aeolus was himself thought to be changeable and untrustworthy.

124. Bacchus was the ancient god of wine and festivity.

125–7. Pluto, god of the underworld, snatched Proserpina from her mother and carried her off to be his queen. For this reason, Dunbar calls him an *incubus*: one of the demon lovers of medieval legend. The realm of the dead and the realm of fairies are often equated in medieval literature (cf. Henryson, *Orpheus and Eurydice*) and Pluto consequently wears green, the fairy colour, instead of black.

187. The *plicht anker* was the principal anchor on a ship; it is used here as a metaphor for the most trustworthy person.

223. Medieval lovers frequently complained of the *dangere* of their ladies. It is a combination of coldness, disdain and an unwillingness to yield.

253. The English poet Geoffrey Chaucer (c.1343–1400), author of the *Canterbury Tales*, was frequently praised by medieval Scots poets.

262. John Gower was the author of the *Confessio amantis*, a collection of tales of vice and virtue in love, structured around the seven deadly sins, hence *morall Gower*. The poet Lydgate is being praised as worthy of the laurel crown.

Sen that I am a presoneir

Like 'Ryght as the stern of day begouth to schyne', this poem is an allcgory of love. It symbolically represents the relationship between the lover and his lady as he attempts to woo her. As is traditional in the medieval literature of courtly love, the lover is first captivated by the lady's charms; thus the allegory here represents him as being taken prisoner by Beauty (I.15) and locked in the prison of his love by her disdain and indifference (*Strangenes* and *Comparesone*, II.17–28). He manages a counter-attack, however, and his own forces of ingenuity (*Thocht* I.58), strong desire (*Lust* I.59), and diligence (*Bissines* I.60) lead the way. The castle is stormed, and he wins the lady's love. Slander and Envy pose a final threat to the couple (II.89–96) but they are disposed of by the arrival of Matrimony.

6. It was believed that love began in the eyes. Ancient Greek and Arabic medicine propounded the theory that beams of light were transmitted from the eye to the viewed object. Thus in love, beams from the eyes strike through the eyes of the beloved into the heart, causing a physical reaction.

24. The unworthiness of the lover to be loved was a common theme in medieval courtly literature.

27. *Comparesone* is a personification of how far the lover falls short of what the lady really wants.

36. Medieval jesters carried a mock sceptre as a symbol of their privileged status in the court.

55. *Thocht* is the ingenuity which the lover displays as he tries to win his lady. It should not be confused with Reason which tries to prevent people falling in love (cf. 'Ryght as the stern of day begouth to schyne', II.199–207).

My hartis tresure and swete assured fo

The relationship of lady and lover in this poem is similar to that in 'Sen that I am a presoneir'. This time, however, the man is not just a captive but is being killed by her lack of *mercy*, a traditional complaint in the literature of courtly love. He appeals to all her womanly virtues, her humility, pity and compassion (II.36–42), all of which are familiar medieval lovers' complaints (cf. 'Sweit rois of vertew and of gentilnes'), but his prayers go unanswered. The final stanzas reveal instead an increasingly intense emotion as the lover claims that he will continue to beg for her mercy until his tongue fails him, his eyes close with pain, and death itself breaks his heart in two (II.43–8). These final stanzas have led some critics to suggest that the poem is not a true expression of love but a parody of the courtly love relationship. However, other critics point out that the poem is no more excessive than other serious courtly literature and thus state that the extravagant language should not be taken as conclusive proof of parody.

6. The lover is the lady's vassal, her humble and loyal servant.
24. Murder *undir traist* is a Scots legal term. It is applied to homicides where the victim had every reason to expect protection from their murderer, for example in the relationship of ward and guardian, or in periods of official truce. Such crimes were considered to be particularly heinous and were regarded not just as murder but as treason. As the lady's *vassal*, the lover feels that she is killing him *undir traist*.
37. The dove was a symbol of meekness in the Middle Ages, while the turtle-dove was used to represent fidelity in love. Both qualities were essential to the medieval ideal of woman.

Sweit rois of vertew and of gentilnes

The protagonists in this poem occupy traditional roles in the literature of medieval courtly love. The lady is beautiful and virtuous but denies the man her love. He complains that she is merciless and appeals to her for pity. Dunbar cleverly uses the image of the garden of love, popular in medieval poetry as a setting for amorous intrigue, and develops the idea of the flower of love being killed by coldness, with a pun on the word *rew*.

1–2. Beautiful women in medieval poetry were frequently compared to flowers, particularly roses and lilies. The combination of red and white was an ideal of female beauty, where red lips and very pale skin were prized.

8–9. The garden contains great beauty but is also *halsum*, a garden of virtue.

10. Dunbar is here punning on the two senses of *rew*: the herb and pity. Pity was regarded as a great feminine virtue and is constantly appealed to by the lover in order to prevent him dying of unconsummated love (cf. 'Sen that I am a presoneir', I.49). The medicinal uses of the herb rue are also interesting in this context, as the leaves of the plant were believed to increase sexual desire in women.

Be ye ane luvar, think ye nocht ye suld

The first line of this poem indicates that it is addressed to a lover but it is not a poem of instruction in love but one of general moral and social instruction. Such pieces were popular in the Middle Ages, sometimes written in the form of a father's advice to his son, sometimes addressed to those in love, as here, and often simply as general poems of moral advice with no particular audience in mind. The link to love is, however, not entirely tenuous for it was believed that the good lover had also to be a good man, not just for the sake of his own honour but for that of his lady, and that love in turn had an ennobling effect on the lover, leading him to behave well and excel in honourable deeds.

8. The code of courtly love required that the lover always be *secreit* and guard his lady's reputation, never naming her in public (cf. 'Sen that I am a presoneir', ll.87–100, where Slander attacks the lovers once Good Reputation has been drowned and it takes Matrimony to save them). However, the reference here is to more than this, urging general discretion and good judgement.

Quha will behald of luve the chance

This poem is a rejection of love, which is regarded as chaotic, upsetting and unstable. It does not directly criticise women, though love itself is personified as female and the poem draws upon all the fickle and untrustworthy characteristics usually

attributed to Venus by medieval Scots poets (cf. Henryson, *The
Testament of Cresseid*, II.218–38). Dunbar does not here offer
the alternative of divine love as he does elsewhere (cf.
'Now cumis aige quhair yewth hes bene' and 'In May as that Aurora
did up spring') but the final image of the man being asked to
dance in his tomb together with the warning about misspent time
(II.19–20) does raise the question of the next life, though in a
disconcerting, rather than comforting, way.

11–12. Earthly love was often regarded by moralists as only a
  fleeting pleasure.
13. 'New Acquaintance' is one of the ladies who spurns the lover
  in 'Ryght as the stern of day begouth to schyne' (II.220–2),
  giving him her favour at first but quickly moving on to
  someone new once she has captured his heart.

Apon the midsummer evin, mirriest of nichtis
(*The Tretis of the Twa Mariit Wemen and the Wedo*)

This poem plays with the conventions and stereotypes of wo-
men, men, love and marriage. It begins with three beautiful
women in a garden, with the male narrator listening from his
hiding place to what promises to be a conversation about courtly
love. The medieval literature of courtly love describes unattain-
able ladies being tirelessly served by devoted men who hope only
to receive the lady's 'mercy'. By line 49, however, it is clear that
our ladies are far from unattainable and that the men who 'serve'
them will be begging for a different kind of mercy. The first
Wife is married to an impotent old man (II.49–145); the second
Wife to an impotent young one (II.158–239); while the Widow
tells of her economic and sexual triumphs over men.

Dunbar exploits many of the medieval stereotypes about
women. There was a strong anti-feminist literary tradition in
which women were seen as ignorant, cunning, lecherous, and
selfish creatures who were of no use to men. Dunbar takes this
material but presents the story from the point of view of the
women themselves. For this reason, his poem has often been
compared to Chaucer's *Wife of Bath*'s *Prologue* which is also,
unusually for the Middle Ages, told from the female point of
view. Chaucer, however, cannot prepare us for the venom we
find in Dunbar's work. The coarse humour of the descriptions is
unrivalled as Dunbar presents a picture of marital suffering, for
both the women and the men. This has led to a great divergence
of critical opinion. Some critics believe that Dunbar himself is

writing in the anti-feminist tradition and is revealing the true feminine horror which belies the golden hair and beautiful faces. Others, however, point out that men are reduced to the level of beasts in the poem and argue that Dunbar may in fact be revealing the horror of a world in which marriages are dictated by financial considerations and love is confined to a literary genre which allows women no feelings and men no ultimate success.

1. Midsummer Eve was celebrated on 23 June with bonfires and revelry. It was the eve of the nativity of John the Baptist but the feast was pagan in origin and came to be condemned by medieval preachers.

19–25. Hair glittering like gold was the archetype of medieval beauty and these women with their carefully parted golden hair are reminiscent of Henryson's Venus (*The Testament of Cresseid*, II.218–24). Like Venus too, they wear green, a deeply ambiguous colour denoting life but also inconstancy and fairy magic. They are, however, well dressed with their heads decorously covered.

37. The word *wantoun* is ambiguous. It could mean playful but could just as easily mean lascivious.

39. *Wauchtit* is not usually found in the context of ladies drinking. It implies drinking hard and fast, as in Robert Burns' *a right gude-willie-waught* (Auld Lang Syne, I.23).

60–3. It was a popular medieval belief that birds chose their mate every year on St Valentine's Day (cf. I.206).

92. *Skarth* has caused debate amongst translators. Bawcutt suggests 'cormorant' while Kinsley favours the more obviously insulting 'hermaphrodite monster'.

100–4. The old husband is being described as an incubus, the demon lover of medieval fairy stories who had intercourse with sleeping women.

101. While *Mahowne* literally means Muhammad, the name was often simply used by medieval authors as a name for the Devil.

112. In the Bible, Beelzebub is 'Lord of the Flies' and 'prince of demons' (Matthew 12:24), thus his name too is used simply to refer to the Devil.

114. *Farcy* is a horse disease involving swellings below the jaw and a heavy mucus discharge from the nostrils.

201. Jet beads were not highly regarded. While jet can be highly polished it is not a precious stone and was used only as costume jewellery in the Middle Ages.

214. By no means all medieval marriages were arranged by the woman's family, but the practice was more favoured amongst those with money or power.

262. The turtle-dove was believed to mate for life and was a symbol of fidelity throughout the Middle Ages.

263–4. This is a reference to Christ's words to the Apostles: 'Be you therefore as wise as serpents and as gentle as doves' (Matthew 10:16).

293. The husband was impotent long before the child was conceived but he blindly assumes that it is his own and treats it as his heir.

338. This is a reference to land in the burgh on which tenements have been built.

379. The peacock was a symbol of pride.

382. The parrot was associated with lechery and illicit love while the *plukit herle* is the husband, 'plucked' in all senses of the word, and roasted and served with ginger.

384. This is similar to the modern saying: 'He made a rod for his own back'.

424–5. Illuminated manuscripts were very costly and a sign of their owner's wealth and status. They were so precious that they tended to be specifically mentioned in wills.

426. White skin was viewed as extremely beautiful throughout the Middle Ages and beyond, when women even resorted to powdered lead to whiten their complexions.

432. The moon was regarded as changeable because of its waxing and waning. It was thus a favourite metaphor for the 'inconstancy' of women.

474–5. Pilgrimage was a sign of the devotion of a true Christian but medieval moralists increasingly criticised those going on pilgrimage. They felt that there was more of a holiday than a religious atmosphere, a fact to which the Widow testifies here.

502. *Sabot* appears to be a form of *Dominus sabaoth* (Lord God of Hosts), and should, therefore, be translated as 'God'.

In secreit place this hyndir nycht

This comic poem parodies the courtly love tradition of medieval poetry in which a valiant lover pleads with his disdainful lady to look kindly upon him. The first stanza is full of the vocabulary normally found in medieval love poetry, as the lady is accused of refusing to give *confort* (I.5) to her 'faithful' lover (I.4). However, we discover in the next stanza that the beard of our hero is spattered with broth and that he is in fact inexperienced and awkward, while the lady is far from the demure and disdainful ideal usually found in literature. Instead of the soaring vocabulary of love poetry, we hear a torrent of pet-names, crude endearments and complete nonsense as their wooing descends into baby-talk. The lofty ideals of love are satirised as they babble their way to the inevitable physical conclusion, a conclusion never mentioned by the courtly poets, and the 'lady' decides that she had better love her *sweit cowhubye* (I.58) after all.

2. *Beyrne* is an ancient word for a warrior, used here as a very poetic term for 'man'. *Bricht* (bright one) also belongs to the genre of courtly poetry as an expression for a woman.

6. *Danger* was an attribute of the courtly lady who was expected to treat her lover with cold disdain, refusing to grant him her love (cf. 'Ryght as the stern of day begouth to schyne', I.223).

23. A *tuchan* or *tulchan* is a calf-skin stuffed with straw which was placed beside the cow to induce it to give milk: hence, 'dummy'. All the images in II.23–4 are associated with the breast.

29. *Curldodie* (round-headed) is the common medieval name for ribwort plantain, a weed characterised by its short brown head.

30. Editors are divided on the meaning of *possodie*. Bawcutt takes it to be a variant of *posset*, a drink made with hot milk, wine and spices. However, Kinsley's suggestion that it is connected to *powsosdy*, a type of sheep's head broth, remains the more attractive possibility. In either case, some sort of warm refreshment seems to be indicated.

33. Technically speaking, *quhalis bane* (whale's bone) is ivory from walrus tusks, regarded as a paradigm of whiteness in the Middle Ages. It is usually used in poetry to refer to the white hands or white breasts of courtly ladies, not to the heels of a barefoot wench.

38. *Hurle bawsy* has caused critics some difficulty. Bawcutt suggests that it is related to Hurlbasie, the name of a Scottish demon. However, literally *hurle* means a violent rush while *bawsy* means big or clumsy. The phrase could, therefore, simply mean clumsy-clot.

39. *Slawsy gawsy* is again obscure. *Gawsy* is recorded in later Scots as a word for someone plump and fresh-complexioned.

Slawsy is found only in this poem but seems most likely, given the context, to be related to *slaw* (slow), hence sluggard.

44. The meaning of *brylyoun* is debated. Bawcutt suggests that it is a scribal misreading of *rylyoun*, the shoes made of rough animal hide worn by Scots peasants which Dunbar ridicules elsewhere (cf. 'Schir Johine the Ros, ane thing thair is compild', I.243). Medieval ladies were often praised for their dainty feet so it may again be a parody of courtly poetry. Kinsley, however, thinks that the word is likely to be obscene and suggests that it is a reference to the female genitalia.

46. Both *tyrlie myrlie* and *crowdie mowdie* are obscure terms. *Crowdie mowdie* can be taken literally as 'mouldy porridge' but it is possible that some sexual meaning was intended. *Tyrlie myrlie* is more difficult and the sound may in fact be more important than a precise definition, with most editors again suspecting a sexual meaning.

51. *Marie land* seems most likely to be a reference to fairyland. Kinsley cites the tale of Mayok, the *golk of Maryland* who was the daughter of the king of the fairies.

60. It is clear that copulation is what is meant here but the reference to *dery dan* is more obscure. It may have been the name of a popular song or may be related to a dance named the dirre dantoun (cf. 'Sir Jhon Sinclair begowthe to dance', I.24).

Now cumis aige quhair yewth hes bene

Like 'In May as that Aurora did up spring', this poem contrasts earthly and divine love. This time, however, there is only one speaker: a man who finds that wisdom and contentment come with old age (cf. Henryson, 'The Praise of Age'). In his youth, his passion left him miserable and jealous (II.39–45), too ashamed to name his lady (II.51–2). Now, in old age, love of women has been replaced by love of God, and for the first time he feels true love in his heart: a love which makes him so joyful that he would like everyone to share in it, and about which he would happily tell the world. The world, of course, is still full of young men in the grip of earthly desires but the poem's refrain reminds us that for everyone, 'old age comes where youth has been'.

2. It was thought that the spleen was the source of various emotions, including love.

3. The connection between love and fire is an ancient one and classical literature frequently depicts Venus with a flaming torch or firebrand.

24. This line has been variously interpreted but the sense would appear to be that he is a very commendable man who is able to turn his mind to the love of God even though he is still young and thus still susceptible to the temptations of earthly love.

59. A bean was a symbol of worthlessness.

Richt arely on Ask Weddinsday

Dunbar is the author of several serious Ash Wednesday poems (cf. 'Of Lentren in the first mornyng' and 'Memento, homo, quod cinis es') in which the reader is urged to prepare themselves for Easter by fasting and penance. Here, however, two women discuss how the *lang Lentrin* is making them skinny, even though Lent in fact only began a few hours earlier. They sit drinking, gossiping and abusing their husbands in a style reminiscent of *The Twa Mariit Wemen and the Wedo*, but this time the object of the satire is not just women but those who go to great lengths to avoid the obligations imposed on them by the Church.

1. Ash Wednesday is the first day of Lent, the forty days of fasting and penance before Easter. It was a particularly solemn day in the calendar of the medieval Church. People were expected to contemplate their mortality, abstain from eating meat and generally restrict what they ate and drank.

14. Malmsey was a particularly fine sweet wine from Monemvasia (Malvasia) in Greece.

Now of wemen this I say, for me

Anti-feminist satire was very popular in the Middle Ages and Dunbar himself could claim to be a master of the genre (cf. 'Apon the midsummer evin, mirriest of nichtis'). In this poem, however, he claims that he has an alternative viewpoint to put forward. He points out that without women there could be no men (I.7); the great pain which women have in bearing children (II.13–16); and the fact that no child can survive without its mother (II.17–21). Finally, he turns to the Virgin Mary and the argument that without a woman, God could not have been born as a man. And without Christ, fully God and fully man, there could have been no redemption for mankind.

7–8. Dunbar is punning in these lines on *wemen* and *we men*.

13. Pain in childbirth was the punishment God inflicted upon Eve for her disobedience in paradise (Genesis 4:16). The whole process from conception to lactation was consequently referred to as 'pain' in some medieval literature.

27–8. It was the supreme defence of womankind that God chose to have his only son born of a woman, the Virgin Mary. A woman was, therefore, the human being who had come closest to God.

31. The *scho* in this line is the Virgin Mary.

Gavin Douglas

The Palis of Honoure

The Palis of Honoure is an allegorical dream-poem, a popular medieval genre, which generally shows a reluctant and slow-witted dreamer engaged in a process of gradual discovery and dawning awareness. Such poems frequently begin with a description of a May morning in which the narrator enjoys the beauty of nature before falling asleep, or into a swoon, and finding himself in a wondrous new landscape. It is typical of these dreamer–narrators that they are entirely uncomprehending of their new environment and they blunder around causing offence and questioning everyone they meet. After this initial stage, they usually encounter someone far more wise than they are who becomes their guide and (frequently impatient) teacher. The learning process continues until the dreamer has achieved wisdom and awakens from his dream in a state of comprehension.

The lesson which the dreamer–narrator must learn can be of a secular or religious nature and Douglas fuses both in his poem. It is an examination of the nature of true honour, not the honour which accompanies power and wealth, but the honour which comes from living a good life. The poem offers, in fact, a model for how one must live. There are strong Christian elements in the poem, but figures from the Bible take their places next to characters from pagan mythology and Honour himself is a mixture of Christian God and pagan deity. In short, it is not a model for the religious life but a model for how the Christian nobleman should live. The apparent digressions on music, myth and history serve in fact to promote the appropriate pastimes for a nobleman, the sentiments which should occupy a noble mind, and the sense of worth and history which should inspire a lord. It is not surprising, therefore, that the poem should have been dedicated to King James IV, nor that it appears to have found favour with him.

Prologue

The poem opens with a traditional description of a May morning. The sun is just rising, the birds are singing and the flowers are unfolding their petals. The narrator roams through the garden enjoying the beauty of it all when suddenly he has a *vision or fanton* (I.60) in which he hears a voice singing in praise of May. The voice claims that May gladdens the beasts and the birds (II.73–81), prompts valour in young men and encourages lovers (II.82–8). The narrator becomes uneasy. He claims that he serves May, Nature and Venus but his sense of panic increases until a sudden meteoric flash causes him to faint in terror (II.105–8). When he regains consciousness he finds himself in a forest, with a hideous river and *grysly fysche* (I.124) nearby.

1–2. Aurora is the Roman goddess of the dawn, seen here as wearing a red cloak on the fringes of which is still the blackness of night. Legend had it that her son, Memnon, was slain in battle by the warrior Achilles and that the goddess constantly lamented his death, the morning dew being thought of as her tears.

4–5. Flora is the goddess of flowers. Douglas is presenting her as lying in a four-poster bed with tapestry hangings.

6. Britain has a long tradition of May rituals which are frequently mentioned in medieval literature. They often involve rising at dawn, making garlands and performing ceremonies in honour of the month of growth and fertility, and hence love.

30. In classical mythology the god of the sun rides in a chariot pulled by four horses, each of which represents a certain part of the day. Thus, the reddish-brown horse, Eous, is associated with the dawn (cf. Henryson, *The Testament of Cresseid*, II.209–17).

32. The axletree is the part of the chariot to which the wheels are attached.

33. In some legends, the sun was thought of as the offspring of the Titan Hyperion and the Titaness Theia, two of the race of giants from which the Olympian gods were descended.

36. Phoebus, meaning shining, is another name for the sun.

42. The sun was frequently celebrated as the giver of life (cf. Henryson, *The Testament of Cresseid*, II.197–203).

49. Aeolus was the ancient Greek Lord of the Winds.

50–1. Saturn was regarded as a malign planet, often depicted as an old man, though here his spear is also reminiscent of the medieval figure of death. He was frequently associated with coldness (cf. Henryson, *The Testament of Cresseid*, II.155–68).

52. Neptune is the Roman god of the sea, capable of provoking storms and creating landslides, particularly when found in conjunction with Aeolus (cf. Dunbar, 'Quhen Merche wes with variand windis past', II.64–8).

60. The medieval world clearly differentiated between types of dream. The essential difference between *vision* and *fanton* is that the former was thought to exhibit truth while the latter was held to be delusory.

83. Mars, the Roman god of war, associated here with acts of bravery.

105. The *impressioun* is some sort of shooting star or meteoric flash.

The First Parte

The landscape in which the narrator now finds himself is one of stagnation and decay. The fish scream in the blood-red river (I.140) and all the plants are withered and rotten. He rails against fickle Fortune who has brought him to this place (II.165–92), criticising her 'contrary wheel' and the 'inconstant world' (I.192). The sound of an approaching herd of beasts, however, rouses him and he hides inside a hollow tree. The 'beasts' are in fact well-dressed people on horseback, with a golden chariot in their midst pulled by four milk-white horses (II.211–14). In the chariot sits a fair 'queen' accompanied by twelve damsels. Two further figures lag behind the company and the narrator accosts them to demand some explanation. They tell him that the beautiful woman is Minerva, the Queen of Wisdom, and that her attendants are the wisest people who have ever lived. Their own names are Ahithophel and Sinon and they were granted great wisdom and skill in their lives but abused their powers. They now struggle behind the company as it makes its way towards the *Palis of Honoure* (I.264).

Diana, the goddess of chastity, then appears riding upon an elephant and accompanied by the noble virgins of history (II.328–45). This is closely followed by the sound of sweet music, so pleasing that it should have had the power to make anyone joyful. However, it only makes the narrator more miserable (II.398–9) and it is in this sorrowful state that he sees another chariot approach. This one is jewelled and pulled by twelve war-horses and inside is a woman so beautiful that he can scarcely look at her. With her is a fine young man, blind but carrying a bow and arrows. This is Cupid and the lady, he now realises, must be Venus. She too is accompanied by a large group of people, this time the famous lovers of legend. The music which surrounds them is the most beautiful he has ever heard and even Mars, god of war, sings to his love, Venus (II.550–61).

Moved by the music and the sight of them all, the narrator decides to sing a song of his own, lamenting his cruel fate and cursing everything, including Cupid and his mother (I.634). Venus hears him and bites her lip in anger, and the whole company goes in search of the foul 'toad' (I.641) who could sing such a song. They tie him up and take him to Venus and her clerk, Varius, and he is formally charged with blasphemy (II.665–72). His feeble attempts to defend himself are angrily dismissed by the goddess and he awaits a fate worse than death.

138. Cocytus or the 'River of Groans' was one of the rivers in the ancient Greek underworld which had to be crossed by the souls of the dead.

146. A popular medieval account of the signs of Doomsday attributed to St Jerome lists screaming fish as one of the phenomena which will signal the end of the world. As for elves, they are not traditionally thought of as yelling but this may be a reference to the banshee, an elvish or fairy woman, whose wailing was thought to be heard in a house when someone was about to die.

166–72. Fortune was most frequently portrayed as a goddess turning a large wheel upon which the fortunes of men rose or fell. She was sometimes presented as blind or blindfolded to indicate that she does not reward merit or punish the wicked but instead grants her favours at random. At other times she is shown as alternately laughing and weeping, a sign of her fickle nature.

214. The lily-white throat was a conventional image of female beauty.

215. It was the fashion at the end of the Middle Ages for garments to have *gores*: pieces of cloth, often of a contrasting colour, which were let into the garment to widen it (cf. Henryson, *The Testament of Cresseid*, I.179).

220. *Granyt* in fact means dyed in grain. It was an expensive way of dyeing cloth and was reserved for costly garments. An Act of 1455, for instance, decreed that all Scottish earls should officially wear furred cloaks of 'brown granyt'.

236. Ahithophel plotted against King David and hanged himself when the plan failed (2 Samuel 17:1–23). Sinon was the Greek who persuaded the Trojans to take the Wooden Horse into

their city, and released the Greek soldiers within it so that they could massacre the sleeping citizens. Both men were regarded as types of cunning and treachery in the Middle Ages.

242. Minerva was the ancient goddess of wisdom.

243. Sibyl is an ancient name for a prophetess.

244. Cassandra was a Trojan princess who predicted the fall of Troy; Deborah is a prophetess of the Old Testament, and the only woman judge of Israel (Judges 4 and 5); and Circe is the sorceress of ancient Greek legend who changed the companions of Odysseus into beasts.

245. The three sisters of ancient mythology who controlled the lives of men were known as the Fates. They were imagined as old women who spun a man's destiny around him like a thread.

246. The biblical heroine Judith was a beautiful widow whose town was beseiged by the Assyrians. She beguiled their leader, Holofernes, into entertaining her in his tent, where she decapitated him (Judith, 8–14). Jael received Sisera, the captain of the Canaanite army, into her home when he fled from the Israelite forces led by Deborah. She then took a tent peg and drove it through his skull while he slept (Judges, 4:17–22).

250. Solomon, the third king of Israel, was famed for his wisdom (1 Kings, 3:3–14).

251. The ancient Greek thinker Aristotle was the author of many influential works on philosophy, science, politics and literature.

252. Sallust (86–35 B C) acted against Cicero and was expelled from the Senate but formed an alliance with Caesar. He spent his latter years writing about his political life. The Middle Ages did not differentiate between Seneca the writer on rhetoric and his son Seneca the philosopher. The ancient historian Livy was the author of a history of Rome.

253. Pythagoras, philosopher and mathematician of the sixth-century B C. Porphyry (third-century A D) scholar, philosopher and student of religions. Parmenides of Elea, ancient Greek philosopher thought to have given his city laws.

254. Melissus of Samos, philosopher and follower of Parmenides.

255. Shadrach (Daniel 1:3–7) was famed for his knowledge and was the reputed author of a medieval encyclopaedia; Secundus is believed to have been a philosopher at the court of the

Emperor Hadrian; Solinus was a Roman whose work on natural history appears to have been influential in the Middle Ages.

256. Ptolemy, astronomer, geographer and mathematician; Hippocrates, medical writer of the fifth century B C; Socrates (469–399 B C), the great Athenian philosopher.

257. Empedocles (c.493–c.433 B C) was famed as a philosopher, scientist, poet, statesman, and even miracle-worker and healer. According to medieval legend, Nectanabus was an Egyptian magician and the real father of Alexander the Great. Hermes Trismegistus, the Greek version of Thoth, the Egyptian god of letters. He was the reputed author of various philosophical and religious works and some dealing with astrology, magic and alchemy.

258. The philosopher and court-physician Galen was the author of many texts, particularly of a medical nature. Averroes (1126–98) was an extremely influential Arabic medical writer. The philosopher Plato (c.429–347 B C).

259. The Old Testament patriarch Enoch (Genesis 5:18–21) was regarded as a skilled astrologer in the Middle Ages; Lamech is another Old Testament patriarch, and the father of Noah (Genesis 5:25–31); the biblical Job was renowned for his patience in adversity as God sent him afflictions in order to test him (Job 1–2); Diogenes was a Greek philosopher of the fifth century B C.

260. In Greek myth, Odysseus (Ulysses) quarrels with Ajax over the armour of the dead Achilles and manages to convince the assembled army through his great powers of persuasion and rhetorical skill that the prize should fall to him. Homer presents him as equally good in counsel and in battle.

261. Flavius Josephus (A D 37–c.100) Jewish statesman and historian of the Jewish revolt against Rome; Cicero (106–43 B C), great Roman orator and statesman.

262. Melchizedek (Genesis 14:18–20) was both priest and king of Jerusalem.

282–6. The Greek Sinon gave himself up to the Trojan camp, pretending that he was an enemy of the Greeks and wanted to join the Trojans. That night, however, he sneaked out to the great Wooden Horse which had been brought into the city and released the Greek soldiers who were hiding within it. It was thus Sinon's treachery which brought about the fall of Troy.

321. Actaeon was transformed into a hart by Diana and devoured by his own hounds when he was caught watching the goddess bathing.

330. The elephant was symbolic of chastity in the Middle Ages due to the belief that it only ever copulated in order to reproduce.

338. The Israelite Jephthah prayed to God for victory against the Ammonites and vowed that he would sacrifice the first thing which came to meet him on his return home. He was met by his only daughter but fulfilled his promise (Judges 11:29–40).

340. The Trojan princess, Polyxena, was sacrificed on the tomb of the warrior Achilles in order to ensure a safe voyage for the Achean ships.

341. Penthesilea was queen of the Amazons, the race of warrior women who fought on the Trojan side during the ten-year war with Greece. She was killed by Achilles who fell in love with her as she died.

342. Iphigenia was sacrificed by her father, Agamemnon, when the wrath of the goddess Artemis meant that his ships were becalmed; Virginia, daughter of the Roman Virginius, was killed by her father in order to prevent her rape.

359. The planet Venus can be seen very early on spring and summer mornings.

360–1. Line 361 precedes line 360 in the manuscripts but it is strange to talk of 'hearing' a light and thus Bawcutt suggests that their order should be reversed.

444. It was a widely held belief that there were nine ranks, or orders, of angels.

492–6. Douglas appears to know a great deal about music in spite of his disclaimer (II.517–9) (cf. Henryson, *Orpheus and Eurydice*, II.226–42).

500. *Faburdoun* is 'the system of harmonizing a plainsong melody by sight, so that the harmonic intervals never vary and the result is a series of parallel sixths' (Bawcutt, p.260). In contrast to this extemporising harmony, *priksang* deals with vocal music which has been written ('pricked') down. *Discant* and *conturyng* both involve singing accompaniments, with *discant* meaning singing above the main melody.

501. *Cant organe* is the earliest form of polyphony: 'the simultaneous combination of a number of parts, each forming an individual melody, and harmonizing with each other' (OED). *Figuration* involves variation on this simple form of poly-

phony. *Gemmell* is a two-part harmony with the melody being carried by the higher voice.

504–5. The citole and psaltery are both stringed instruments, the former played like a modern guitar and the latter similar to a hand-held harp.

507. This line is widely regarded as puzzling. However, Bawcutt provides a likely translation: '[I heard] short notes divided by intervals of silence or sung rapidly in close succession' (p.181).

508. Pan, the ancient god of shepherds, had the upper body of a man and the lower body of a goat. He was traditionally depicted as playing his pipes in the paradisal realm of Arcadia.

509–10. King Saul was tormented by an evil spirit which could only be controlled by the music produced by David on his lyre (I Samuel 16: 14–23).

511–12. Amphion, son of the king of the gods, was famed for his playing on the lyre. Legend has it that he built the walls around the city of Thebes by charming the stones into place with his music.

513. There was great debate in the Middle Ages about who the creator of music actually was. Candidates included Pythagoras and Orpheus.

523. It was widely believed that the revolving of the planets created perfect music (cf. Henryson, *Orpheus and Eurydice*, II.219–25).

524. Orpheus was famed in classical myth for his musical ability which was said to be so great that he could tame wild beasts and make the trees themselves bow down before him. He used his music to charm the king of the underworld into restoring his dead wife to him, but could not resist looking behind him on the journey back to earth, thus breaking his promise to the gods and losing his wife once more.

525. Glasgerion was a Welsh bard of the tenth century.

562–3. The story of Arcite, Palamon and Emily is recounted by several medieval authors. Both young men fell in love with Emily and were willing to compete in a tournament to win her love. Each prayed to the gods to aid them: Arcite to Mars, god of war, that he should win the competition; and Palamon to Venus, goddess of love, that he should win Emily. The gods responded to the letter of their requests, Arcite winning the tournament but meeting with a fatal accident as he went to claim Emily's hand, leaving Palamon free to marry her.

564. Dido, queen and founder of Carthage, became the lover of the Trojan hero, Aeneas, when he was driven by storms onto her shores. However, the gods had decreed that it was his destiny to found the Roman empire and he left Dido, whereupon she built her own funeral pyre and threw herself upon Aeneas' sword. Medieval authors tended to take a harsher attitude to Aeneas than classical authors.

565. The Trojan prince, Troilus, fell in love with the beautiful Cressida during the Trojan War. She, however, was sent to the Greek camp in exchange for a Trojan warrior and, in spite of her promises, she never returned to Troilus. He was regarded as the most faithful of lovers while Cressida's name became a byword for deceit and infidelity (cf. Henryson, *The Testament of Cresseid*).

566. It was the love of Paris for Helen which started the Trojan War. Paris was a Trojan prince while Helen was the wife of the Greek general Menelaus. She fell in love with Paris and eloped with him, but was pursued by her husband and thus became 'the face which launched a thousand ships' as the two great civilisations went to war.

567. Ancient history tells the story of Lucrece, or Lucretia, who was raped by a member of the royal family of Rome. She committed suicide after telling her husband what she had suffered. Penelope, wife of Odysseus, remained faithful to her husband during his twenty-year absence, steadfastly resisting the advances of her one hundred and eight suitors.

568. According to Ovid, Pyramus and Thisbe were neighbours in Babylon who were forbidden by their parents to marry. They arranged to meet but Thisbe was frightened away by a lion and Pyramus assumed that the beast had killed her. He therefore killed himself and when Thisbe returned and discovered what he had done, she too committed suicide.

569. Philomela was raped by Tereus, the husband of her sister, Procne. He then cut out her tongue so that she could not reveal what had happened but she made a tapestry so that her fate should be known to her sister. To protect them from Tereus, the gods eventually changed Procne into a swallow and Philomela into a nightingale.

570. King David fell in love with Bathsheba and arranged the death of her husband in order that he could marry her (2 Samuel 11:3–27).

571. When Ceyx was drowned at sea, the grief of his wife,

Alcyone, was so great that the gods reunited them, changing them both into birds.

572–3. Briseis was the favourite concubine of the Greek warrior, Achilles. When Agamemnon was told that he must return his own concubine to her family he demanded Briseis as compensation and the two warriors became enemies.

574. Phyllis, princess of Thrace, fell in love with Demophoon who said that he must temporarily return to Greece. He did not come back to her, however, and Phyllis hanged herself.

575. The sorceress Medea betrayed her father and murdered her brother in order to help Jason obtain the Golden Fleece, and so secure his love. However, he then grew tired of her and wanted to take a new bride. Medea took her revenge by killing the children she had borne with Jason.

576. *Paris and Vienne* was a popular medieval romance.

577. Ariadne fell in love with Theseus and helped him to defeat the monstrous Minotaur. However, he then abandoned her and married her sister, Phaedra. She, in her turn, fell in love with her stepson but hanged herself when he rejected her advances.

578. Ipomedon, hero of medieval romance, pretends to prefer hunting to jousting and is mocked by the ladies. Meanwhile, he disguises himself and excels in the tournament, winning the hand of the princess.

579. The Persian king Ahasuerus was so much in love with Esther that he removed her from his harem and made her his queen (Esther, 2:12–18); Susanna was falsely accused of adultery by the elders appointed as judges of the people (Daniel 13).

580. Delilah betrayed her husband Samson when she discovered that the source of his great strength was in his hair (Judges 16:4–18).

581. Deianira, wife of Hercules, attempted to secure the love of her husband by dressing him in a magic shirt. However, the shirt was in fact poisoned and Hercules burned to death.

582. In ancient legend, Byblis fell in love with her twin brother and went mad with grief. The biblical Absolon was famed for his great beauty (2 Samuel 14:25).

583. Jason stayed with Hypsipyle for two years and then abandoned her in order to search for the Golden Fleece; Scylla betrayed her own father out of love for Minos but he despised her action and attached her to the prow of his boat so that she drowned.

584. Tristram, one of the knights of the Round Table, fell in love with Iseult, the wife of King Mark; Elkanah and Hannah were the parents of the prophet Samuel (1 Samuel 1–2).

586. Iole was abducted by Hercules, in some legends trying to commit suicide by throwing herself from the city walls rather than yield to him; the marriage of Alcestis and Admetus was so perfect that Alcestis wanted to die in place of her husband. Hercules retrieved her from the underworld and brought her back younger and more beautiful than ever; Hesione was rescued from a sea-monster by Hercules. However, her father was not grateful enough and Hercules then offered her as a prize to the first man to scale the walls of Troy.

587. Griselda was renowned in the Middle Ages for her loving patience. Chaucer tells how her husband took away her children and informed her that he was taking a new bride, all in order to test her devotion to him.

588. In the medieval version of the legend, Narcissus falls in love with the reflection of a woman he has seen in the water and dies when he dashes his head against a stone.

589–90. Jacob worked for seven years in order to marry Rachel. However, he was tricked at the wedding and married her older sister instead. He then worked for another seven years until he was allowed to marry his original choice of bride (Genesis 29).

615. This appears to be an early reference to the idea that a trouble shared is a trouble halved.

620–2. Douglas is here conflating two images. Fortune is usually depicted with a wheel which turns and changes the lives of those on it unpredictably for good or bad. A balance or set of scales is more usually associated with judgement and one's fate here depends on merit. The effect is two-fold sorrow for the narrator: the unpredictability of fortune coupled with unfair judgement.

639–42. Similar anger greets Cresseid's attack on Venus and Cupid in Henryson's *The Testament of Cresseid* (II.124–343).

645. The narrator has hidden himself away like a religious recluse but is full of impure and angry thoughts which make him *imperfyte*.

651. This is a reference to a medieval game which appears to have involved a person being roughly handled.

653–4. These names are not found elsewhere but Bawcutt suggests that they are names for goblin-like creatures, which is supported by the word *fery* (I.653). The Old Norse word *skrimsl* means a horrifying apparition and this may be the root for *Skrymmorie*. There may also be some association with the Scots word *skrym* which suggests an attack (cf. Dunbar, 'As yung Awrora with cristall haile', I.123). As for *Chyppynutie*, it would literally seem to mean nut-breaker. Small raises the possibility that it is a reference to the mischievous Celtic spirit which fatally wounded the cattle but there is no more evidence for this. Parkinson suggests that the names may have been familiar from the Lord of Misrule festivities which took place in Scotland. These involved the election of a mock-king who went through the town with a number of unruly attendants. Records show that the antics of *Skrymmorie* and *Chyppynutie* would not have been out of place during these celebrations. Amongst many similar incidents in the accounts of the Lord High Treasurer we find that one man in Stirling had to be paid compensation in 1496 after the 'Abbot of Unreason' 'spoiled' his house. And in 1504 the accounts record a payment to a barber-surgeon for attending to 'Paules hed when he wes hurt with the Abbot of Unresoun'.

665. The name *Varius* for the clerk of Venus would appear to be an allusion to the goddess's fickleness and instability.

696–9. It was an old Scottish law that anyone in holy orders had the right to be tried by an ecclesiastical court instead of a lay court.

747–51. Jupiter transformed his lover, Io, into a white heifer in order to conceal her from his wife, Juno. Juno, however, was suspicious and demanded that the animal be given to her. She then had her guarded by the hundred-eyed Argus until she was eventually rescued by Jupiter's messanger, Mercury.

752–3. Lot's wife was turned into a pillar of salt when she turned back to look at the destruction of Sodom and Go-morrah (Genesis 19:26). The story is here being conflated with that of the classical Niobe who wept for her dead children even after the gods had turned her to stone.

754–5. Lycaon was turned into a wolf by the gods who were furious that he had tried to test them by serving them the flesh of a child.

756–8. King Nebuchadnezzar was brought down at the height of his pride and became like a beast in his madness (Daniel 4:28–33).

The Seconde Parte

Another group approaches as the narrator awaits his punishment and he feels an inexplicable surge of hope. The court of Venus

informs him that the new group consists of poets and intellec-
tuals. He sees the Muses, the great writers of ancient Greece and
Rome, the famous poets of the Middle Ages, and even Willam
Dunbar *yit undede* (I.923). The Muse Calliope draws near and
pleads for the narrator, urging Venus to realise that killing him
would bring her no honour (I.967). The goddess relents on two
conditions: firstly, that he should write a poem about the joy of
love (II.994–6); and secondly, that he should obey the next
command that she gives him (II.997–8). The narrator is released
and immediately writes his new poem (II.1015–44) to the
approval of Venus and the Muses. He is then entrusted to the
care of a nymph and travels across the globe with the Muses.
They finally stop near a pavilion and the narrator approaches it
with his guide, the nymph. Inside he observes the Muses
feasting with the poets and calling upon Ovid, and then Virgil
and the others to tell their tales. A trumpet blast signals that their
journey must begin once more and the narrator travels onwards
with them.

801. Sapphic and elegiac are metres used in classical verse. The
former is traditionally found in lyric poetry while the latter is
more common in epigrams or inscriptions.
802–3. A monochord was originally a musical instrument with a
single string.
804. The psaltery is another stringed instrument, similar to the
lyre.
809. This is a reference to the *Heroides*, 'letters of heroines', of
the Roman writer Ovid. The poems are written in the form of
letters from various women of legend to their husbands or
lovers.
810. Phyllis was abandoned by her lover Demophoon (cf.I.574)
811–13. Penelope was left alone by Odysseus for twenty years
while he fought in the Trojan War and travelled throughout
the ancient world (cf.I.567).
814–5. Acontius caught sight of Cydippe in a temple and fell in
love with her. He scratched the words 'I promise to marry
Acontius' on a pomegranate and rolled it towards her. The
girl picked it up and read it aloud and was thus bound to him
by an oath before the gods. She had been betrothed to another
man but became violently ill each time the wedding was about
to take place. Her father eventually relented and permitted
the marriage to Acontius.
833. *Mate* seems like a very familiar way to refer to Venus but

the word had considerably more dignity in the Middle Ages. It could also refer to Varius, who would pronounce Venus' judgement.

840. Mount Helicon was believed to be the home of the Muses and its sacred spring, Hippocrene, was believed to bring poetic inspiration.

852. There are various classical legends concerning the parentage of the Muses, but Thespis is not normally associated with them (cf. Henryson, *Orpheus and Eurydice*, II.31–5).

853–79. Each of the nine goddesses known as the Muses was associated with a different intellectual pursuit.

881. Nymphs are minor female deities, spirits of the fields and of nature in general.

882. Fauns were Roman country deities; 'ladies of the ancient temples' is a vague reference but may perhaps refer to the Vestal Virgins who were consecrated to the goddess of fire in their youth and who lived their lives in her temple.

883. The Pyerides, the nine daughters of Pierus, challenged the Muses to a singing contest and were changed into magpies when they lost; dryads are tree-nymphs while satyrs are woodland gods, usually thought of as lecherous and having the lower body of a goat.

884. The Nereids are beautiful sea-deities; Aonians are the inhabitants of the area around Helicon, and are thus the neighbours of the Muses; napaeae are forest nymphs.

896. The ancient Greek poet Homer is the author of two great epic works, the *Iliad* and the *Odyssey*.

898. The Roman poet Virgil (70–19 BC) is the author of numerous poems, including the epic *Aeneid*.

899. Ovid (43 BC–AD 17) is best known for his *Metamorphoses*, a collection of tales of miraculous transformations.

900. Dictys of Crete was said to have been part of the Greek army during the Trojan War and his diary of the event was supposedly translated into Latin in the fourth century AD; Dares Phrygius is also the alleged author of an account of the fall of Troy; *trew* Lucan (AD 39–65) is another epic poet, who was first supported by Nero and who later incurred his wrath. When his part in a conspiracy against the emperor was revealed he was forced to commit suicide.

901. The Roman playwright Plautus (c.250–184 BC) was the author of popular comedies; Poggio Bracciolini (1380–1459), an Italian writer, associated with the classics because of his discovery of ancient manuscripts in French and German

monasteries; his own works include a history of Florence. The Latin satirical poet Persius (AD 34–62) was known for the moral nature of his poetry.

902. Terence (d.159 BC) was the author of a number of Roman comedies which were widely known and studied in the Middle Ages; Aelius Donatus (fourth century AD), teacher of St Jerome, wrote two books on Latin grammar which were used throughout the Middle Ages; Servius was a fourth-century grammarian whose commentary on Virgil was used by Douglas in his *Eneados*.

903. The Italian poet Petrarch, known for his sonnets to Laura but also the author of an unfinished epic; Valerius Flaccus was one of the writers rediscovered by Poggio Bracciolini. He too was the author of an unfinished epic poem.

904. The Greek writer Aesop probably lived in the early sixth century BC. He was the author of the fables, moral tales with animals as the protagonists. The form was popular in the Middle Ages, an example being the *Fables* of Robert Henryson; Dionysius Cato was the author of a popular collection of Latin maxims, used throughout the Middle Ages as a text in schools; Alain of Lille (c.1127–1203) is the author of several allegorical works. Like Aesop, he believed that nature could be held up as an educating mirror to mankind.

905. The twelfth-century author, Gautier de Chatillon, was the author of a version of Aesop's fables which was used as a source by Henryson; the work of the philosopher Boethius (c.480–524) was widely disseminated in the Middle Ages, being translated by Chaucer, among others.

906. The first-century rhetorician, Quintillian, was one of the classical authors rediscovered by Poggio Bracciolini.

907. Juvenal, who lived in the early second century AD, is widely regarded as the greatest of the Roman satirical poets.

908. Martial (c. AD 40–104) is the author of numerous poems in Latin, including over 1500 shorter poems known as the *Epigrams*. These range from a description of the hot-sausage seller in the market to poems in praise of faithful friends.

909. Statius was born in Naples in the first century AD. His best known poem is the *Thebaid*, an epic account of the quarrel between the sons of Oedipus in Thebes. His work was very popular in the Middle Ages.

910. Fausto Andrelini (1462–1518) was an Italian poet and lecturer at the University of Paris; Lorenzo Valla (1407–1457) was a professor of rhetoric at Rome and a papal

scriptor. He was known as a great classical scholar, the author of a treatise on the Latin language and the author of several Greek translations.

911. Giulio Pomponio Leto (1425–1498) was a pupil of Lorenzo Valla and the editor of several Latin authors. Bawcutt points out that 'his recent fame' may refer to his spectacular funeral, where his corpse was crowned with a laurel wreath while dignitaries, including foreign ambassadors and forty bishops, looked on.

913. Horace (65–8 BC) is the author of numerous poems in Latin. His philosophy was generally that of moderation in all things.

915. Leonardo Bruni (1369–1444), a chancellor of Florence and Latin scholar. The fourth-century author Claudian was considered to be the last great poet in the classical Latin tradition. The Italian Giovanni Boccaccio (1313–1375) wrote many popular poems which were widely imitated by other medieval poets.

918. The name 'Britain' was thought to derive from that of Brutus, who was believed to have conquered Albion, renaming it Brutain after himself.

919. The English poet Geoffrey Chaucer (c.1343–1400) was frequently hailed as the greatest of medieval poets by writers in the fifteenth century.

920. Gower's name often accompanies that of his near contemporary, Chaucer, in lists of great English poets. His *Confessio Amantis* (The Lover's Confession) describes some of the sins of love and it was Chaucer who first gave him the epithet 'moral'.

921. Lydgate is traditionally the third name in the triumvirate of famous English poets. He was a monk at the Benedictine monastery in Bury St Edmunds in the fifteenth century and was the author of numerous celebrated poems including a version of Baccaccio's *De casibus* (*Fall of Princes*).

923. The Scottish poets Walter Kennedy and William Dunbar. The two were frequently connected and are artistically united in the great poem of insult and vitriole known as *The Flyting of Dumbar and Kennedie* (cf. Dunbar, 'Schir Johine the Ros, ane thing thair is compild').

924. Quintin is an obscure figure but is likely to have been Kennedy's kinsman and collaborator (cf. Dunbar, 'Schir Johine the Ros, ane thing thair is compild', I.2).

1073. The woodbine or honeysuckle was thought of as one of the flowers of Venus.

1093–4. This is a reference to the Greek city of Pisa, situated in the western Peloponnese. The river Alpheus flows in the same region, according to Ovid, underground and into the sea.

1096. The Spanish river Tagus was famed from ancient times for its golden sand.

1097–8. The poisoned shirt given to him by his wife caused Hercules so much pain that he built his own funeral pyre on Mount Oeta and begged his servants to see that he was consumed in the flames.

1100. Tmolus is a mountain in Lydia, not Cilicia, which is further to the south.

1103–4. According to classical legend, Orpheus managed to bring back his wife from the underworld. However, when he lost her for a second time, he was believed to have gone to Mount Haemus (cf. Henryson, *Orpheus and Eurydice*).

1105–7. It was popularly believed that the Carmelite order was established on Mount Carmel by the prophet Elijah. In fact, the order originated in the twelfth century when Berthold, a crusader from Calabria, founded a community of hermits on the mountain.

1108–10. The race of warrior women, the Amazons, were believed to have lived on the banks of the river Thermodon, on the southeastern shore of the Black Sea. Mimas is a mountain range in Asia Minor.

1111. Cithaeron is a mountain range in Greece, part of which was sacred to Bacchus (Dionysus).

1112–3. Mount Olympus, in northern Greece, is so high that it was believed to be the home of the gods.

1114–5. The name of the River Melas was believed to be derived from the ancient Greek word for black.

1116. The Tanais, or River Don, marked the boundary between Europe and Asia.

1117. Sperchius is a river in Thessaly.

1118. Orontes is the principal river in Syria.

1119. Mount Ida, on the northwest shore of modern Turkey. Zeus was believed to have watched the Trojan War from its summit.

1120. Noah's ark was believed to have come to rest on the hills of Armenia (Genesis 8:4). As for the Euphrates, it is one of the rivers of Mesopotamia and is mentioned in the Bible as the fourth river of Eden (Genesis 2:14).

1123. Mount Dindymon in Phrygia was the centre of the cult of

Cybele, the great mother-goddess, whose stone image was believed to have fallen there from heaven.

1125. Scythia is the ancient name of the land north and east of the Caspian Sea.

1126. The Tigris and Phison are mentioned in the Bible, as the third and first rivers of Eden respectively (Genesis 2:11–14).

1128. Modin, in Judaea, was the fortified mountain town of the Maccabees (1 Maccabees 2:23).

1129. Mount Helicon, in Greece, was regarded as the home of the Muses. The winged horse, Pegasus, was said to have struck the mountain with its hoof, and from this came the Hippocrene Spring. Anyone drinking its waters was granted great eloquence, thus Douglas calls it the *facund well*.

1130. Eryx is a mountain in Sicily, believed to have been a centre for the cult of Venus. There is a River Acheron in western Greece and also a mythical Acheron which flowed in the underworld, but neither of these is traditionally associated with Venus.

1133. Mount Cynthus, on the Greek Island of Delos, was believed to have been the birthplace of the sun god Apollo.

1178. Hippocras is a mixture of red wine, spices and sugar.

1191–4. The ancient hero Hercules was renowned for his strength. Douglas is here referring to the Twelve Labours which Hercules had to perform in order to satisfy the gods. One of these required him to overcome Cerberus, the three-headed dog which guarded the underworld; in another, he had to defeat the Nemean lion, a monstrous animal whose skin was impervious to steel and fire. In both instances he could only succeed by using his bare hands.

1195–7. Theseus, ruler of Athens, married Hippolyta, queen of the Amazons, after the two encountered one another in battle. His legend tells how he had earlier defeated the Minotaur, the monster with the body of a man and the head of a bull, on the island of Crete.

1198–1200. The hero Perseus, son of Zeus and the mortal Danae, protected his mother from the advances of the tyrant Polydectes. He was the slayer of the Gorgon, Medusa, the snake-haired female monster capable of turning a man to stone with a look.

1201–3. Angry that she had been neglected by the people, Diana sent a monstrous boar to terrify the people of Calydon. A hunt was arranged and the huntress Atalanta was the first to wound the animal. Meleager, who was in love with her, awarded her the spoils once the beast was killed. His uncles objected that they, as his nearest relatives, should have been awarded the prize and Meleager slew them in anger. When his mother heard this, she was distraught at the loss of her brothers and in her rage allowed Meleager to die by magic.

1204–6. Aesacus son of Priam, the last king of Troy, threw himself into the sea in despair when his wife died. The gods took pity on him and transformed him into a cormorant.

1208–15. Cygnus, the son of the god of the sea, took the side of the Trojans in their war with Greece. He could not be harmed by human weapons but died when the warrior Achilles strangled him with his bare hands.

1225–6. Daphnis and Corydon are shepherds in Virgil's *Eclogues* (cf. I.898).

1227–8. This is a reference to *Eunuchus*, a comedy of the Roman dramatist Terence (cf. I.902) in which Phaedria, a young Athenian, and the boastful soldier Thraso (always attended by the parasite Gnatho) are in love with the same woman. The play was imitated in *Ralph Roister Doister* (c.1554), the earliest known English comedy.

1229–30. As a satirist, the description of Juvenal's behaviour here is appropriate (cf. Dunbar, 'Of benefice, sir, at everie feist' and 'Schir, yit remember as befoir').

1231. In the Middle Ages, Martial was referred to as 'the cook'. This may simply have been the result of a misreading of the Latin word *coce* (*quoque*), meaning also, as *coci*, meaning cook. However, Douglas here plays on the name, depicting Martial as 'roasting' the people he satirises, amongst other things.

1232–3. Poggio Bracciolini and Lorenzo Valla were rivals. Poggio accused Valla of everything from bad Latin to heresy while Valla replied in kind.

The Thyrd Parte

The learned company approaches a hill, slippery and shining like glass and with only one pathway carved out to the top. The narrator hangs back in fear but his nymph urges him on until their way is blocked by a fiery gulf full of tormented bodies. The narrator's teeth chatter in terror (I.1330) but the nymph explains that these are the people who put themselves forward for high honours in their youth only then to become slothful and neglectful (II.1334–8). She then seizes him by the hair and forces him to look down at the world. He sees a ship in trouble on a stormy sea and people drowning in the waves. This ship, the nymph tells him, is named the 'State of Grace' (I.1386) and the people are invited aboard through baptism. Sin, however, leads them into trouble and they can be tossed from the ship and drown. Only faith and good works, she tells him, will bring them safely to land (II.1393–5).

The nymph then shows him the *Palyce of Honour* (I.1403), a paradise of beauty and plenty. Here they encounter Venus once more and see in her magical mirror the history of the world and all its people. The goddess then reminds the narrator of his promise to grant her next request and gives him a book to translate. He is then led out of her presence and sees many people, including Synon and Ahithophel, struggling to climb up the slippery slope.

He is then taken to a palace where Honour is emperor and is served by all manner of virtues. Patience is his gate-keeper (I.1791), Charity is the Master of the Household (I.1795), and Loyal Constancy is his secretary (I.1797), with a whole host of other virtues in attendance. The narrator is awe-struck by the splendour of it all and falls into a dead faint when he sees Honour himself (II.1920–6), leaving the nymph to carry him outside. She explains that all the people he sees have lived an honourable life in the proper sense, not measured by worldly success but full of the true honour of virtue. It is with this disquisition on virtue that she and the narrator part company. Attempting to follow her across a bridge, he falls head-over-heels into the moat and awakens from his dream (II.2084–91). The beautiful garden of the poem's opening no longer fills him with joy and he turns his attention instead to the writing of a poem in praise of honour.

1322–3. According to Homer, the river god became angry with Achilles, whose bloodshed was polluting his waters, and overflowed his banks to pursue the hero. Hera intervened to help him, commanding that the river be set on fire. Douglas has slightly confused the story.

1341. The prophet Habakkuk was carried by the hair to Babylon by the Angel of the Lord in order to bring food to Daniel in the lions' den. The story is told in the apocryphal book of the Bible, Bel and the Dragon 33–9).

1431. The reference here is to the triangular metal pointers, often looking like little golden flags, which were placed on top of towers and revolved in the wind.

1453–4. Bezaleel and Aholiab were the craftsmen who made the ark of the covenant, the chest containing God's commandments, and the great tabernacle which housed it (Exodus 35–8).

1455. The Bible does not name Solomon's builder but the temple he created was vast and ornate, overlaid entirely with gold (1 Kings 6).

1456. Ilion is another name for the ancient city of Troy, the walls of which were said to have been built by the gods Apollo and Poseidon.

1457. Legend had it that Darius, warrior king of the Persians, had a wonderfully and elaborately carved tomb.

1483. Precious stones were valued in the Middle Ages not just for their appearance but for the magical or medicinal properties which each was thought to possess. A number of them were believed to be able to staunch the flow of blood, including the sapphire, topaz and red jasper.

1492. According to medieval legend, the Romans possessed a magic mirror which showed the image of approaching enemies, no matter how distant they were.

1493. In Chaucer's *Squire's Tale*, the princess Canacee, daughter of Genghis Khan, is given a mirror which allows her to foretell disaster, distinguish friends from enemies, and discover whether or not a lover is faithful.

1499. Lucifer, the brightest and most powerful of all the angels, rebelled against God and was cast out of heaven as Satan.

1502. The similarity in sound between Babel and Babylon led many early authors to equate the two names. However, Douglas is clearly referring to the Tower of Babel (Genesis 11:1–9).

1503. The city of Sodom was destroyed by the Lord because of the wickedness of its inhabitants (Genesis 13:11–13).

1504. The Old Testament tells how Abraham was willing to sacrifice his only son, Isaac, if that was what God demanded (Genesis 21–2). Isaac lived and in turn became the father of Jacob who loved his own son, Joseph, so much that he gave him a coat of many colours (Genesis 30–7).

1505. Moses is said in the Bible to have a 'shining' face (Exodus 34:29) but early mistranslation of the Hebrew led to the medieval belief that he had horns.

1506–11. The London manuscript here tells of *twelf* plagues while the Edinburgh text reads *ten*. In fact, the Bible recounts how ten plagues were visited upon the people of Egypt because Pharaoh would not release the Israelites. Moses led them to freedom by parting the Red Sea until they had crossed but when Pharaoh and his army attempted to follow they were drowned. The Israelites then spent the next forty years in the wilderness (Exodus 5–15).

1512. Joshua led the Israelites in battle against the cities and tribes of Palestine and divided the land amongst them (Joshua 6–14).

1513–14. The Book of Judges recounts the exploits of the Israelite warrior Jephthah (cf. I.338) and of Gideon who, heavily outnumbered, carried out a daring midnight attack against the Midianites (Judges 7 and 11).

1515. Abimelech, the son of Gideon and one of his concubines, murdered seventy of his brothers in order to become king (Judges 9:1–5).

1516–19. Samson slew a thousand Philistines using the jawbone of an ass and finally died when he pulled down their palace, killing himself and three thousand of his enemies (Judges 15–16).

1520–1. Shamgar, a judge of Israel, killed six hundred Philistines with an ox-goad or ploughshare (Judges 3:31).

1522–4. The prophet Samuel anointed Saul to indicate that he would become the first king of Israel (1 Samuel 10:1). His son Jonathan attacked the Philistine camp, taking with him only his armour-bearer and brought about the deliverance of the Israelites (1 Samuel 14).

1525–6. The story of David who slew the mighty Goliath with only a slingshot is found in 1 Samuel 17. The Bible states that Goliath's spearhead weighed six hundred shekels, Douglas converts this into ounces.

1527–9. Goliath had three sons, amongst whom were Ishbibenob and an unnamed son who had six fingers on each hand and six toes on each foot. They were killed by King David's followers in the final years of the king's reign. Douglas has conflated the two and attributed the act to David himself (2 Samuel 21:16–20).

1530–2. Both incidents are found in the Bible but the slaying of the eight hundred is usually attributed to Adino, one of David's captains (1 Samuel 17:34–7; 2 Samuel 23:8).

1533–9. Benaiah was one of David's champions. His exploits are recounted in 2 Samuel 23:20–3.

1540–45. While Solomon was acclaimed as a wise king, his son Rehoboam was cruel towards his people, causing ten of the twelve tribes of Israel to revolt against him (1 Kings 12:1–21).

1546–8. Sennacherib, king of Assyria, was threatening the city of Jerusalem. God sent his angel to the soldiers' camp and in the morning the king awoke to find his entire army dead (2 Kings 19:35–6).

1549–50. The dying King Hezekiah, ruler of Judaea, prayed to God that he should not die and was granted fifteen more years of life (2 Kings 20:6–7).

1550–1. The prophet Elijah was carried to heaven upon a chariot of fire (2 Kings 2:11).

1552. Ezra was welcomed into Jerusalem as a true priest of the Lord and the keeper of his laws (Ezra 7–10); Nehemiah repaired the walls of Jerusalem and was overseer in the proper settlement of the city (Nehemiah 1–13).

1553–5. Daniel famously remained unharmed when he was cast into the lion's den, and rescued three young men who were consigned to a fiery furnace by Nebuchadnezzar for refusing to worship an idol (Daniel 6 and 3). The Apocrypha also tells how Daniel proved to the king that Bel, whom he worshipped, was nothing more than a brass idol, and slew the dragon worshipped by the Babylonians (Bel and the Dragon, 1–27) .

1556. The removal of the Jews into captivity in Babylon (2 Kings 24:14).

1558–62. The demon Asmodaeus had killed each of Sara's previous seven husbands on their wedding night. In order to avoid the same fate, Tobias was advised by the angel Raphael to burn the heart and liver of a fish, the smell of which would drive the devil out (Book of Tobit 6:10–18).

1563–4. The beautiful Judith gained access to the Assyrian general Holofernes and beheaded him in order to rescue her people (Book of Judith 8–14).

1565–6. Jonah spent three days in the belly of the whale, coming to terms with the mysterious workings of God (Jonah 1–2).

1567. Job was legendary for his patience as he endured all the torments God sent to test him (cf. 1.259).

1568–9. Alexander the Great (356–323 BC), known as 'the Conqueror'. His empire stretched from Greece to India.

1570–1. The persecution of the Jews by Antiochus Epiphanes is recounted in 1 Maccabees 1:21–67.

1572–6. Judas, one of the sons of Mattathias, who led the revolt against Antiochus Epiphanes with his brothers Jonathan and Simon, was known as Maccabeus ,'the Hammer' (1 Maccabees 2–9).

1577–82. Tideus was sent on a mission to Thebes but was

ambushed by fifty men of whom he killed all but one. After much bloodshed, the Athenian leader Theseus attacked Thebes and defeated the tyrant, Creon.

1583–4. The history of Thebes was recounted by Statius in his Thebaid, including the legend of the seer Amphiorax who was swallowed up by the earth after a bolt of lightning hit the ground.

1585–93. It was the widows of those who died at Thebes who implored Theseus to attack the city and avenge their husbands' deaths.

1594–6. The Centaurs, half-man and half-horse, interrupted the wedding feast of Pirithous, dragging the bride away by the hair and attempting to abduct many of the women present. The marriage festivities became a battleground as the men defended their women.

1597–1602. Hercules rescued Hesione, daughter of the king of Troy, from a sea monster. However, when her father refused to hand over the reward Hercules had been promised, he sacked the city and gave Hesione as a prize to the first man to scale the walls.

1603–11. For Medea, Jason and Hypsipyle cf. 1.575 and 1.583.

1612–18. The Trojan prince Paris, renowned as the most handsome man on earth, was chosen by the goddesses to decide which of them was the most beautiful. He awarded the prize, a golden apple, to Venus, and she in turn helped him to steal away Helen, wife of one of the Greek generals and the most beautiful woman on earth. The Greeks then besieged Troy in a war that lasted ten years.

1619–20. The mother of Achilles was warned that her son would die at Troy and therefore disguised him as a girl in order that he would not be called upon to fight in the war; the deception was discovered by Ulysses.

1626–7. Once he arrived at Troy, Achilles proved himself to be a valiant warrior, killing both Hector and Troilus, the Trojan princes.

1628. The Wooden Horse was the means by which the Greeks finally gained access to the city of Troy. The Trojans found it outside their gates and brought it into their city but it was full of Greek soldiers who proceeded to massacre the citizens.

1631–40. The Latin author Virgil describes in his Aeneid how Aeneas escaped the burning of Troy and sought refuge with his men in Carthage. There he had an affair with Queen Dido but he abandoned her at the urging of the gods, his destiny

being to found the Roman empire. He entered the under-
world in order to speak to his father, crossing the River Styx,
which separates the underworld from the mortal realm, on the
boat of the ferryman Charon.

1641. There were traditionally five rivers associated with the
underworld but as Douglas has just mentioned the Styx he
may now be referring only to the four within the domain of
the dead: Acheron, Cocytus, Lethe and Phlegethon.

1643. Sisyphus was condemned by the gods to push a rock up a
great hill from the top of which it would always roll down
again.

1644. Within the underworld, the souls of the blessed were said
to reside in the Elysian Fields.

1645. Anchises is the father of Aeneas, whom he went to the
underworld to seek.

1656. Turnus, king of the Rutulians, was the rival of Aeneas for
the hand of Lavinia. He attacked Aeneas and his army but was
killed, leaving Aeneas to marry Lavinia and become ruler of
the Latins.

1657. Romulus, mythical founder of Rome, believed to have
been suckled by a she-wolf when abandoned as a child with
his brother Remus.

1658–9. According to Livy's History of Rome, the Roman kings
ruled for two hundred and forty four years.

1660–5. The last king of Rome, Tarquinius Superbus, gained
the throne by plotting with his wife to murder her father.
Their son, Sextus Tarquinius, famously raped Lucretia, wife
of one of the Roman consuls. Their exploits resulted in the
abolition of the monarchy and the family was exiled during
the revolt led by Lucius Junius Brutus.

1666–70. Ancient literature records that Acneas' abandonment
of Queen Dido led to long term hostilities between Rome and
Carthage.

1671–4. During the wars between Rome and Carthage, the
Roman general Marcus Regulus was taken prisoner. He
was sent back to his people in order to present the terms
for peace offered by the Carthaginians but he persuaded the
Romans not to accept the terms. He then returned to Carth-
age knowing that he must face certain death.

1675. Servius Tullius was widely held to have been a good king.
He was murdered by Tarquinius Superbus, his own son-in-
law.

1676–80. When a great chasm suddenly appeared in the Roman

Forum, an oracle stated that it would only close after the greatest strength of Rome was sacrificed. Hearing this, Marcus Curtius leapt fully armed and on horseback into the gulf.

1681–7. During the second Punic War, the great Carthaginian general, Hannibal was defeated by the Roman commander Scipio Africanus. He was also responsible for conquering large parts of Spain.

1688–9. Jugurtha was another victim of Rome's plans for northern Africa. He had seized control of Numidia by murdering his cousins but he in turn was put to death after the Romans waged war.

1690–1. Catiline was defeated by Cicero in his attempt to become a Roman consul. Together with Lentulus, he attempted a rebellion; both were killed for their trouble.

1692. Julius Caesar and Pompey, at one point his son-in-law, were involved in a civil war.

1701. It was widely believed that the expected Second Coming of Christ would be preceded by the coming of the Antichrist.

1711. Rauf Coilyear is the tale of Ralph, a charcoal burner, who unwittingly entertains Charlemagne and is knighted by him.

1712. The popular medieval tale of John the Reeve describes the meeting between Edward I and a village overseer. Colkelbie's Sow is another medieval tale in which a host of comic characters gather together for a feast.

1713. Ailsa Crag in the Firth of Clyde was populated by large numbers of birds but it is not clear what the legend is here. The wren is associated with a number of folktales, usually as a clever and lucky bird.

1714. William Langland's Piers Plowman tells how Piers becomes irate when he sees the people idling and appeals to Hunger to spur them on.

1715–16. Gaelic legend tells how Goll Mac Morna, bodyguard of the High King of Ireland, slew Cumhal. Cumhal's son, Finn (Fingal), then became leader of the king's bodyguard and became one of the greatest Irish heroes.

1717. Bawcutt refers to a poem in the Maitland Quarto that celebrates Sir Richard Maitland and 'his auld baird gray'. Critics are divided but 'auld Beird Gray' would appear to be the name of a horse.

1718. Robin Hood was a popular legend in medieval Scotland, many towns and cities performing their own Robin Hood pageants. Aberdeen, for example, required all its burgesses to supply their own costumes for a Robin Hood pageant in 1508.

Gilbert of the White Hand was one of Robin Hood's companions, famed for his skills at archery.

1719. 'Madin land' is evidently a land of maidens and such realms of women were popular in legend from the Celts to the ancient Greeks. The Hays of Naughton were a noble family but it is not clear what the connection is here.

1721. Bonatti, or Guido Bonatus de Forlivio, was a thirteenth-century astrologer. Roger Bacon and Thomas Bungay were both Franciscan friars, also living in the thirteenth century. Although Bacon is better known, both were learned men, Bungay holding posts at the universities of Oxford and Cambridge. The nature of their work lead to all three being popularly linked to magic.

1749. The book given to the dreamer by Venus is probably Virgil's Aeneid, a work that Douglas would later translate into Scots.

1770–4. Cf. l.1691. Marcus Tullius Cicero wrote four speeches against Catiline who competed against him for the position of consul and consequently attempted a rebellion. The book here is probably a reference to these speeches.

1775. Jugurtha cf. ll.1688–9. Like Jugurtha, Tryphon was known for his treachery. He pretended to support the claims of Antiochus Epiphanes to the throne of Syria but in fact had designs on the throne himself and later murdered the rightful king (1 Maccabees 13:31–2).

1784–1825. It was a popular medieval device to personify vices and virtues. Cf. Dunbar, 'This hinder nycht, half sleiping as I lay'.

1845. Charlemagne's Wain is another name for the constellation known as the Plough (Ursa Major).

1846–8. Jupiter, the king of the gods, fell in love with the boy Ganymede and carried him off to Mount Olympus to be his cup bearer.

1878. The heavens were believed to be divided into various regions: each planet had its sphere and enclosing all of these was the solid sphere of the firmament in which the stars were set. Beyond these was empyrean heaven, the blissful home of God and the angels.

1921. This line has led to a great deal of debate. Only two editions of the poem survive and each offers a different reading here. The London edition reads armypotent at this point while the Edinburgh edition reads omnipotent. The latter makes the poem explicitly Christian and has been favoured by many critics for this reason. However, Douglas has maintained a delicate balance throughout the poem between the religious and secular and it is likely that he is continuing to do so here. His armypotent God of Honour has elements of Mars, Apollo, even Cupid, together with aspects of the Christian God.

1957. The Muse Calliope's court.

1995. The idea that earthly glory passes away and only good works remain was a common one in medieval poetry. Cf. Dunbar, 'Of Lentren in the first mornyng'.

2017. Samson, cf. ll.1516–19.

2018. Hercules, cf. ll.1191–4.

2019. The Greek warrior Achilles, cf. ll.1619–27. The Nine Worthies were traditionally Joshua, David, Judas Maccabeus, Hector, Alexander, Julius Caesar, King Arthur, Charlemagne, and the knight Godfrey of Boulogne.

2020. Scipio Africanus, the Roman commander who defeated Hannibal; Pompey strove against Julius Caesar for control of Rome.

2024. Semiramis, queen of Assyria, was regarded as a great conqueror and was held to be responsible for the building of walls around Babylon. Another medieval tradition, however, viewed her as lustful and sexually aggressive and this is how she is portrayed in Dante's Inferno. Queen Tomyris of Scythia was another warrior queen, famous for defeating Cyrus the Great of Persia. Hippolyta was queen of the Amazons.

2025. Penthesilea, cf. l.341; Medea, cf. 1603f; Zenobia succeeded her husband, Odaenathus, as ruler of Palmyra and conquered Syria, Egypt and most of Asia Minor. She was praised for her beauty, intelligence and virtue but in some accounts was reported to have been a ruthless woman and possibly responsible for her husband's death.

2027. Grig ruled Scotland from 878 until 889. He was reputed to have been a valiant king, the equal of Arthur in England, and was also attributed with having first permitted Christianity into Scotland. Kenneth MacAlpin, king of Scotland in the middle of the ninth century, united the Picts and the Scots and was thus hailed as the founder of modern Scotland. Robert Bruce was King of Scotland from 1306 until 1329.

2035–46. Condemnation of those who push themselves forward by lying and cheating is a favourite theme of Dunbar's poetry too. Cf. 'Be divers wyis and operatiounes'.

2075–6. Tales of trees upon which miraculous things grow are popular in folklore but the legend of the barnacle goose was particularly popular in Scotland. Originally, these geese were believed to grow from the barnacles upon driftwood but gradually they became associated with a magical tree upon which they were said to grow until fully formed when they would fly away.

2150f. Such apparently modest disclaimers were conventional in medieval literature.

FURTHER READING

The following is a brief list of suggestions for further reading. It is confined to book-length studies which in turn contain fuller bibliographies.

Robert Henryson

EDITIONS

Fox, Denton (ed.), *The Poems of Robert Henryson* (OUP, 1987).

Smith, G. Gregory (ed.), *The Poems of Robert Henryson* (Edinburgh, 1906–14).

SECONDARY READING

Gray, Douglas, *Robert Henryson* (Brill, 1979).

Gray, Douglas, *Robert Henryson* (Aldershot, 1996). Variorum, 1995

MacQueen, John, *Robert Henryson: A Study of the Major Narrative Poems* (Clarendon, 1967).

McDiarmid, Matthew P., *Robert Henryson* (Scottish Academic Press, 1981).

Powell, Marianne, *Fabula Docet* (Odense University Press, 1983).

William Dunbar

EDITIONS

Bawcutt, Priscilla (ed.), *William Dunbar Selected Poems* (Longman, 1996).

Kinsley, James (ed.), *The Poems of William Dunbar* (OUP, 1979)

SECONDARY READING

Bawcutt, Priscilla, *Dunbar the Makar* (OUP, 1992).

Baxter, J.W., *William Dunbar: A Biographical Study* (Edinburgh, Oliver & Boyd, 1952).

Gray, Douglas, *William Dunbar* (Aldershot, 1996). Variorum, 1995

Reiss, Edmund, *William Dunbar* (Twayne Publishers, Boston, Mass., 1979).

Ross, Ian, *William Dunbar* (Brill, 1981).

Gavin Douglas

EDITIONS

Bawcutt, Priscilla (ed.), *The Shorter Poems of Gavin Douglas* (Scottish Text Society, W. Blackwood 1967).

Parkinson, David (ed.), *Gavin Douglas: The Palis of Honoure* (Western Michigan University, 1992).

SECONDARY READING

Bawcutt, Priscilla, *Gavin Douglas: A Critical Study* (Edinburgh University Press 1976).

Scottish History

Macdougall, Norman, *James III: A Political Study* (Edinburgh John Donald 1982).

Macdougall, Norman, *James IV* (Edinburgh, John Donald 1989).

Mackie, R. L., *King James IV of Scotland* (Edinburgh, Oliver & Boyd 1958).

Wormald, Jenny, *Court, Kirk and Community: Scotland 1470–1625* (EUP, 1991).